Lincoln's Assassins

Lincoln's Assassins

A Complete Account of
Their Capture, Trial, and Punishment

by

Roy Z. Chamlee, Jr.

McFarland & Company, Inc., Publishers
Jefferson, North Carolina, and London

British Library Cataloguing-in-Publication data are available

Library of Congress Cataloguing-in-Publication Data

Chamlee, Roy Z., 1924–
    Lincoln's assassins : a complete account of their capture, trial,
and punishment / by Roy Z. Chamlee, Jr.
        p. cm.
    [Includes index.]
    Includes bibliographical references.
    ISBN 0-89950-420-5 (lib. bdg. : 50# alk. paper) ∞
    1. Lincoln, Abraham, 1809–1865 – Assassination. 2. Trials
(Assassination) – United States – History – 19th century.
3. Assassins – United States – History – 19th century. I. Title.
E457.5.C47   1990
973.7′092′2 – dc20   89-42708
                                                                 CIP

Manufactured in the United States of America

McFarland & Company, Inc., Publishers
  Box 611, Jefferson, North Carolina 28640

To my wife Martha

Contents

Preface

The assassination of Abraham Lincoln set off one of the most extensive and emotional investigations in American history. Solving the crime involved thousands of detectives, soldiers, witnesses, and the most renowned personalities in the United States. The crime and subsequent investigation involved not only President Lincoln, but two future presidents—Andrew Johnson and Ulysses Grant. Popular generals, senators, authors, cabinet members, newspaper editors and national leaders played a part.

The Lincoln conspiracy first attracted my attention in 1966. While passing by an old, run-down house in Prince Georges County, Maryland, some friends observed that John Wilkes Booth had stopped there after shooting President Lincoln. (The house has since been restored and is open to the public.) They remarked that the owner, a widow, was accused unjustly of involvement in the crime. The ensuing casual discussion about Mary Surratt's innocence increased my interest in the conspiracy and created a desire to know more.

A decade later, during a sabbatical leave from Belmont College, I had an opportunity to investigate the Lincoln assassination in detail. *Lincoln's Assassins* is the result of that effort. It demanded extensive research of War Department files, trial testimony, newspaper accounts and personal manuscript collections.

Although I began this research with a preconceived notion of Mary Surratt's innocence, I have allowed the records to guide my conclusions. I have not tried to prove any particular thesis, rather I have endeavored to examine thoroughly all pertinent documents related to the crime and accept the results.

There are two keys to unraveling the crime. One is the investigation of documents held for many years in the War Department files, now on microfilm in the National Archives. These files contain revealing pretrial interrogations. The second key is the conspiracy trial, which was thorough and was recorded in detail by several eyewitnesses. This work concentrates on the investigation and trial as revealed by War Department files and the trial evidence.

The narrative is taken primarily from recorded statements. I have emphasized the actual words given in sworn testimony in pretrial interrogations and on the witness stand. This included harmonizing five separate accounts (four of the conspiracy trial and one of the John Surratt trial). I have included references to all major witnesses in each court session, but long examinations are often summarized. The more crucial testimonies are included verbatim.

Contemporary news reports add glimpses of the prisoners' attitudes, the emotions of witnesses and the courtroom atmosphere.

The trial records used in this study have been available since 1865. It was not until after 1886, however, that Government records of the investigation became more accessible. In that year Robert Scott, in charge of War Department records, asked that copies be made. Even so, these records were not available to the public until the 1930s.

The four versions of the trial, each published in book form in 1865, preserve essentially the same impression of the proceedings but vary greatly in style. By far the best-known version is the so-called "official" record compiled and edited by Benn Pitman. This record, though widely criticized, has value when balanced with the other accounts. Its chief drawback is the editing arrangement. Pitman arranged the trial according to subject rather than chronology. Thus the progressive unfolding of the evidence is lost.

Pitman's account is practically worthless in revealing any idea of the interrogation process. Not only did he leave out questions put to the witnesses, but frequently he rearranged the responses. Pitman mutilated the trial proceedings. He edited testimony, added words, left out sentences, filled in names for clarity and often distorted court actions. He made these changes, he said, to make a more readable narrative rather than present an exact, verbatim record. In spite of these shortcomings, Pitman presented a more accurate account of dates, numbers and names than other versions.

The best overall account is the so-called Peterson version, named for its Philadelphia publisher. This account is complete, accurate and unaltered. It presents the word-by-word exchange between the interrogators and witnesses as published daily in the *Philadelphia Inquirer*. Occasionally there are errors in proper names due to faulty recording. Thus "Lloyd" was consistently called "Floyd."

Another shorter account published in Philadelphia is the Barclay version. It is based on the Associated Press report and is helpful when compared with the other trial records. It does not include the first few days of proceedings before newsmen were allowed in the courtroom. The reporter gives a condensed summary of each day's testimony. The essence of only the most valuable testimony is preserved. This shorter form occasionally misses some of the drama of the sharp verbal battles.

The version that apparently was considered most accurate by contemporaries was that prepared by Ben Perley Poore and published in Boston. Poore was a gifted Washington newspaper correspondent. His record was used at the trial of John Surratt by the defense counsel as a guide to what had actually been said in the previous trial. The Ben Poore version presents a daily, accurate, verbatim account.

Other versions of the proceedings include the *Washington National Intelligencer* account made from Pitman's transcript. This record was used by the defense counsel, as well as the Military Commission, as a daily guide to what had transpired in the courtroom the previous day. In addition to these, there is available today, on microfilm, the original longhand version of the trial. The differences in the words in these various accounts is remarkably slight.

These four or five accounts of the trial, when considered together, give a reasonably accurate presentation of the words spoken. They cannot, however, convey the tone of voice in which they were spoken—the pauses, the timidity or audacity of the witness, or the harshness of the interrogator. They do not picture the condition of the witnesses or the courtroom. These important details can be gleaned from numerous daily newspaper reports.

The accounts, while essentially the same, vary in hundreds of details, not counting spelling. For instance, Barclay's version has Atzerodt asking "Booth" (which makes no sense in the context) for a horse, while the Peterson account has Atzerodt asking "Brook," the owner of a stable, for the horse. Pitman, in his more carefully edited version, also correctly identified the person in question as Brooke of Howard's Stables. But Pitman has Booth telling Weichmann that he "might" hire a horse to make the trip to Surrattsville, while the Peterson version used the more emphatic word "should." As a rule, the wording was changed more in Pitman's version because of his editing. Peterson maintained the actual interrogation process used in court. Pitman would often correct grammar. According to the Barclay version, Lloyd testified that Mrs. Surratt asked him to "have them shooting irons ready." Pitman recorded it, "have those shooting irons ready."

Dates could usually be determined exactly only when they were crucial enough for the witness to be asked about the same event on several occasions. The Pitman and Peterson versions had Weichmann moving to Mrs. Surratt's house on November 1, 1864. Barclay said it was the 18th. Barclay had Mary Surratt going to the Herndon house on March 12, 1865. Peterson and Pitman both said it was the 19th.

In some cases, the differences were more significant. For instance, when Payne showed up at the Surratt house claiming he was a Baptist minister, the Peterson account has Miss Surratt saying he was a queer-looking Baptist preacher. Pitman had Mrs. Surratt remarking that he was a good-looking Baptist preacher. Barclay's version said it was Mrs. Surratt who said he was a meek-looking Baptist preacher. The important point was not so much in *how* the individuals described Payne, but *who* said it. In this case, it seems that it was Mrs. Surratt rather than Anna. Similar differences are found throughout the accounts. In only a few cases are they very significant and, in those cases, comparisons with other testimony usually clarify the problem.

Most errors were caught in court during the reading of the previous day's record, but some were not recognized and continued to cloud the issue.

When John Surratt was put on trial two years later, the record of the military trial was constantly referred to. Slight mistakes in the first trial were used to discredit witnesses. Louis Weichmann, who gave lengthy testimonies at both trials, was particularly vulnerable. In one case, the record showed that Weichmann had testified that Payne had asked Mrs. Surratt to play the piano and lifted the cover for her. Weichmann had actually said "Miss," not "Mrs." Records of the military trial had Weichmann saying that Atzerodt had been going to get a horse and send *for* Payne. What Weichmann had actually said was that Atzerodt had been going to get a horse and send *off* Payne.

It was evident, even as the conspiracy trial was in progress, that neither the newspaper accounts nor the records of daily sessions gave a complete picture of what went on in the courtroom. A reporter for the *Boston Advertiser* said that reading his reports was not like actually hearing the testimony, and "when one loses the hesitations, the emphasis, the gestures of the witness and has to judge his credibility by what he says without the aid of knowing how he says it, the process of following the course of the trial becomes much like groping in the dark." I have tried to overcome this problem by comparing many eyewitness accounts.

The conspiracy investigation was not an isolated event and cannot be comprehended apart from the turbulent atmosphere at the close of the bitter Civil War. It was a chaotic period unequaled in this country. Political, religious and personal rivalries affected the investigation and trial. To understand the tensions influencing the crime and its punishment, I have probed the character of the participants and set the events in their political context. Through hundreds of personal documents, letters and diaries, I have tried to recreate the environment surrounding the investigation.

I am grateful to Mon Suey Lee, present owner of the Surratt house on H Street, who graciously took me through the house. In addition to the assistance of my wife, Martha, I am particularly indebted to the helpful staffs of the Library of Congress and the National Archives and to Sandy Roussell, who typed the final manuscript.

I
"Blood, Blood, All Around"

Shortly after ten o'clock Good Friday evening, 1865, a massive figure on horseback rode down the dimly lit street in front of the Executive Mansion and stopped before a fashionable three-story brick house facing Lafayette Park on 15½ Street. In a second floor bedroom 63-year-old Secretary of State William H. Seward had just dropped off to sleep. He was recuperating from serious injuries received earlier when thrown from his carriage.

The horseman dismounted and approached the entrance with a small package. A young black servant, responding to the bell, opened the door only to be pushed rudely aside by the caller, who forced his way in, explaining that he had some medicine prescribed by Seward's physician, Dr. F. S. Verdi. The deliveryman claimed the doctor had given special instructions concerning the medicine and, therefore, he had to see the Secretary personally. Resisting, the servant apologetically declared that Mr. Seward had retired for the night and could see no one. The determined stranger, however, continued to bully his way into the hallway, insisting, "I must go up—must see him, must see him!"[1]

The perplexed servant, seeking politely to block the way, repeated his orders not to allow anyone to see the Secretary of State, but promised to convey the doctor's special instructions. Ignoring the houseboy, the muscular man forced his way up the steps. The confused youth, sensing trouble, ran frantically ahead of him. Still trying to be polite, he asked the stranger to excuse him for getting in the way. The enigmatic intruder said he understood, even as he continued to push up the stairs. Evidently he knew the location of Seward's bedroom.

On reaching the top of the staircase, near the Secretary's door, he was confronted by Frederick Seward, who informed him emphatically that his father was asleep and that he would take the medicine in to him later. But the stranger responded intently, "I must see him, must see him."[2] When Frederick forcefully blocked his advance, the intruder meekly turned around and started back down the steps. The black youth, relieved, hurried along in front, pleading that he not walk so heavily. At that moment the stranger whirled around and struck Frederick to the floor with his pistol. Terrified, the servant fled down the stairs and out the front door, screaming, "Murder, murder!"[3]

Sgt. George F. Robinson, the male nurse attending the Secretary of State, heard scuffling in the hall and opened the bedroom door to investigate. As he

1

Secretary of State William Seward's residence. Seward and his sons were savagely attacked here at approximately the time Booth assassinated Lincoln. (From a sketch by Albert Berghaus, Library of Congress.)

peered out, the stranger knocked him down, rushed to the bed and slashed Secretary Seward repeatedly about the head and neck with a knife. Robinson struggled to his feet trying desperately to pull the assailant away, but the gaslights had been turned down making it difficult to see.

Seward's fragile young daughter, Fanny, sitting in the shadows at her father's bedside, was terrified and began to scream, waking her older brother, Maj. Augustus H. Seward. He dashed into the room in his nightclothes and, dimly making out two figures struggling over the bed, thought his father was delirious and that the nurse was trying to control him. Augustus grabbed the man he assumed was his father, only to be confronted with the muscular intruder. Robinson striking wildly in the darkness, and with the help of Major Seward, succeeded in subduing the trespasser for a moment. The attacker broke loose, however, hit the sergeant and bolted down the stairs screaming, "I'm mad, I'm mad!"[4] In the tumult, Secretary Seward was thrown from the bed, bleeding profusely.

Meanwhile, the servant, William Bell, had raced to Gen. Christopher C. Augur's headquarters, only a few yards from the house, but found no guard on duty. As he turned helplessly back, three loitering soldiers, hearing his screams, followed him. About forty feet from the Seward residence, they saw a large man casually mounting a horse. On recognizing the attacker, Bell yelled,

Graphic contemporary depiction of the attack on Seward as his daughter reacts in horror.

"There he is—getting on his horse!"[5] The assailant rode slowly north on 15½ Street. Bell chased after him as far as the corner of I Street where the felon broke into a gallop toward the northeast.

At that moment Federal leaders were conducting a victory celebration in Charleston, South Carolina. Although some Confederate forces were still holding out, Pres. Abraham Lincoln had deemed it fitting to commemorate the Union victory by hoisting the Stars and Stripes again over Fort Sumter. There the first shots of the devastating Civil War had been fired exactly four years earlier. Union Gen. Robert Anderson, in command of the fort when it surrendered, was on hand to unfurl the Old Flag. The symbolic occasion was of great significance to the country. Secretary of War Edwin M. Stanton had been invited but declined the honor and sent Judge Adv. Gen. Joseph Holt in his place.

Climaxing the festivities, Holt delivered a stirring speech at the Charleston House, where nullification and secession were first proposed. His words lacked the generosity in victory that marked the President's public utterances. He pointedly referred to the "insolent and treacherous foe" that had torn down the flag. Even the title of his remarks, "Treason and Its Treatment," indicated Holt's unrelenting character. He branded Confederate leader John B. Floyd, former United States Secretary of War, a traitor and a conspirator.

The Judge Advocate General made a passing reference to President Lincoln's order initiating the victory celebration but reserved his most energetic praise for Stanton. He regretted the absence of the one "to whom the nation is grateful for the masterly ability and lion-like courage with which he has fought this rebellion in all the vicissitudes of its career—your Secretary of War...."[6] Before Holt could finish, the audience rose spontaneously, cheering Stanton. Holt's remarks were not intended to slight the President; they were, rather, an appeal to the militant spirit among the radicals—an element better typified by Stanton than by Lincoln.

In his rousing conclusion, Holt spoke of the endurance of the Republic which, he declared, was born for immortality and which, though besieged by conspirators, had proved invincible. He proclaimed prophetically, "Neither the swords nor bayonets of traitors can ever reach the seat of its great and exhaustless life."[7] Holt was unaware that even as he spoke, traitors were attacking that very seat of government.

Simultaneous with the ceremonies in Charleston, the Nation's capital pulsated with victory celebrations. April 14, 1865, was a day of rejoicing. The festive atmosphere had gained momentum daily since the fall of Richmond eleven days before. Flags waved over public buildings, candles blazed in the Presidential Mansion, and most business activity was suspended. Candles illuminated private houses, and bonfires lighted streets. Around the city "the watch-fires of a hundred circling camps" which had stirred Julia Ward Howe to write "The Battle Hymn of the Republic" four years earlier now lit the sky in recognition of peace.

Nearly a thousand celebrating Arsenal employees marched down Pennsylvania Avenue carrying torches and waving banners in cadence with blaring bands. They stopped before the Secretary of War's three-story brick residence on K Street. Responding to the serenading throng, the usually austere Stanton appeared on his front steps to make a short speech. An unaccustomed exhilaration distinguished his manner, and a note of satisfaction filled his voice.

After Stanton withdrew, the boisterous crowd swept along Washington's unpaved streets to the home of Gen. A. B. Dyer, chief of ordnance. No serenade was arranged for Lincoln that night, as he planned to attend a play at Ford's Theatre.

Earlier that day the *Washington Star* printed a brief announcement under the heading "City News":

> "Honor to our Soldiers," a new and patriotic song and chorus, has been written by Mr. H. B. Phillips and will be sung this evening by the entire company to do honor to Lieutenant General Grant and President Lincoln and Lady, who visit the theatre in compliment to Miss Laura Keene whose benefit and last appearance is announced in the bills of the day.

Grant had given the President a half-hearted promise to attend the performance, but Mrs. Grant refused to go. The First Lady had earlier thrown one of her temper tantrums in front of the General's wife and had further alienated Mrs. Grant by excluding her in an invitation to the General for a drive around the city the preceding day. Thus, she was in no mood to attend the popular play. In addition, Mrs. Grant was anxious to leave on the 4:00 P.M. train to join her children in Burlington, New Jersey.

About two o'clock, Good Friday afternoon, Grant informed the President that yielding to his wife's wishes, they would be unable to see the play. Later Mrs. Lincoln invited Miss Clara Harris, daughter of Sen. Ira Harris of New York, and her fiancé, Maj. Henry R. Rathbone, to accompany them.

As Mrs. Grant was packing for the trip, she mentioned to her husband that at lunch a strange man had followed her into the hotel dining room and seemed to be watching her. The General dismissed her apprehensions, explaining that all members of his family were objects of curiosity. At half past three, as the Grants and General and Mrs. Daniel H. Rucker drove up Pennsylvania Avenue to the railway station, a horseman rode alongside their carriage staring intently at them. Mrs. Grant noticed that he was the same person she had seen earlier in the dining room. The horseman turned and passed the carriage again, scrutinizing the occupants. This time, he attracted the attention of the General, but Grant remarked that it was not important. Before the train reached Baltimore, however, an unidentified man attempted unsuccessfully to enter the General's private car.[8]

That evening, as the Grants traveled toward New Jersey, George Atzerodt, a stooped, misshapen little man, was conversing in his heavy German accent with John Fletcher, the hostler at Naylor's stable. Fletcher asked the whereabouts of Atzerodt's friend, David Herold, who had not returned a rented horse. Atzerodt promised that Herold would be back soon and calmly rode away on a big, dark bay mare, blind in one eye. But Fletcher, growing apprehensive about the horse rented to Herold, followed Atzerodt to the Kirkwood House—the hotel where Vice-President Andrew Johnson was lodging. Atzerodt entered the hotel, on the corner of 12th Street and Pennsylvania Avenue, where he remained about five minutes. When he came out, Fletcher was waiting. After a brief conversation, the hostler left in disgust, continuing his search for Herold and the missing horse.[9]

Two blocks northeast, at Ford's Theatre on 10th Street, Henry Clay Ford, treasurer of the theater and brother of its owner, was in the office when he noticed his friend, John Wilkes Booth, the well-known actor, arrive after the play had started. Passing by the office window, Booth stopped and placed a partly smoked cigar on the ledge, remarking jokingly, "Whoe'er this cigar dares displace must meet Wilkes Booth face to face."[10] He never returned.

Mrs. Lila Edmonston was also in the packed theater. John Dyatt, one of the leading actors, had invited her to see *Our American Cousin*. She was aware of President Lincoln's late arrival, because the performance was stopped in the second act as the band struck up "Hail to the Chief."[11]

The President, in an unaccustomed gesture, stepped to the front of the box and bowed. Spectators responded with a courteous but not wildly enthusiastic applause. Lincoln then sat down behind curtains, which hid him from view, to enjoy the relaxing comedy.[12]

Booth, wearing seemingly inappropriate high riding boots and spurs, moved through the elegantly dressed patrons, up the staircase to the balcony, then down the sloping aisle adjacent to the right wall of the theater. Arriving at the door to a narrow hallway leading to the President's box, he presented a random

Ford's Theatre. The muddy street in front made it difficult for finely dressed ladies to keep their long skirts clean (Library of Congress—B8171-7765).

letter (some said card) to Officer John Parker, who allowed him to pass without question. Once inside the hallway, Booth closed the door behind him and braced it shut with a wooden bar. Peering through a small hole in the door leading directly into Lincoln's box, he could see the back left side of the President. Opening the door, which had loose hinges, he slipped quietly into the box holding a 44-caliber, single-shot, muzzleloading derringer.

Down on the stage, Mrs. Mountchessington, the English society lady (played by Mrs. H. Muzzy), had just said to the American cousin, "I am sure, Mr. Trenchard, you are not used to the manners of good society, and that alone will excuse the impertinence of which you have been guilty." This snub left Mr. Trenchard (portrayed by Harry Hawk) alone on the stage. With his thumbs in his galluses he soliloquized, "Don't know the manners of good society, eh? Well, I guess I know enough to turn you inside out, old gal—you sockdologizing old man-trap."[13]

At this moment (10:15 P.M.) Booth shouted, "*Sic semper tyrannis,*" the motto of Virginia and the cry of Brutus to Caesar, and fired point-blank into the head of the unsuspecting President. (Some spectators swore they heard these words after the shot.) Alarmed, Major Rathbone jumped up to grapple with the intruder. Booth slashed him with a knife and vaulted onto the stage twelve feet below. The audience, laughing at the play, was unaware that Booth's leap was not part of the act until someone yelled to stop the man.

Henry Ford was still in his office when he heard the shot. He, too, thought it was part of the performance. Looking through his office window, he saw a man who looked like Booth, crouching on the stage, knife in hand. Several moments passed before Ford could comprehend what was happening.

As Booth escaped across the stage, Major Rathbone, bleeding profusely from a deep gash on his arm, hurried to find aid for the wounded President. Reaching the door to the hallway, he found it barred by the brace. Excited people were beating against the door, trying to get in. With difficulty, the Major removed the bar and rushed out.

Albert Daggett, William Seward's private secretary, attended the play, having been attracted by a placard announcing that General Grant would be there. He heard the pistol shot just as he was being seated. In the confusion that followed, he saw a spectator, later identified as Joseph B. Stewart, jump quickly onto the stage in pursuit of a man. Unfortunately, Stewart stumbled over stage scenery and ropes, allowing the culprit to escape through the back stage door.

Daggett then hastened to the President's box, where Dr. Charles A. Leale was cutting away Lincoln's clothing in an attempt to locate the wound. Leale, a young army surgeon, had climbed to the box from the stage and was the first to reach the wounded President.[14]

Mrs. Edmonston heard one of the doctors remark, "Nothing can be done."[15] A few moments later, Lincoln was carried out past where she was sitting. She left the theater with her party, being careful not to stain her long skirts in the blood which had gushed from Rathbone's wound.

Daggett helped carry his stricken leader across the street to the Petersen house, which had been made available for the President's use, and remained in the house to help gather witnesses.[16]

Meanwhile, as the victory celebrants surged through the Washington streets, Joseph A. Sterling left the procession to return to his room in the Falstaff House across from Ford's Theatre. By chance, this young man had just arrived in the capital from Secretary Stanton's hometown, Steubenville, Ohio. The Sterlings and the Stantons were friends, and it was through the Secretary that the youth had secured employment in the War Department.

Standing at the door of his rooming house, Sterling heard someone shout that there was a fight in the theater. Dashing across the street, he had no trouble entering the building because the doorkeeper had left his post. Inside he saw everyone standing—many on chairs—looking excitedly toward the stage. He then heard that the President had been shot. Sterling's immediate reaction was to get word to Stanton. He and his roommate J. C. Johnson hastened to the Secretary's house. On the way they heard of the attack on Secretary Seward.

The door of the Stanton residence was answered by Sterling's close friend, the Secretary's son. Exhausted and gasping for breath, Sterling and Johnson blurted out the terrible news. Although Stanton had retired for the night, he was out of bed and downstairs in a moment, agitatedly demanding, "What news is this you bring?"[17]

As the youth recounted what he knew, including a rumor that the culprit was named Booth, Stanton paced the floor nervously. While Sterling was still talking, reports arrived confirming the attack on Seward. Stanton, not knowing the condition of either man, impulsively asked his wife to call for his carriage, explaining that he must go to Seward. Mrs. Stanton sought in vain to dissuade her husband. Before he left, confirmation of the shooting at Ford's Theatre was brought from the Provost Marshal's office. Stanton then decided he should go to the President's side.

Former governor Leonard J. Farwell of Wisconsin, who had been in the theater, was immediately concerned for the safety of Vice-President Andrew Johnson. He hurried to Johnson's room at the Kirkwood House and banged on the door repeatedly before arousing the Vice-President. Inside, he related the frightening news, then locked and bolted the door. Several persons came by the room, but Farwell and Johnson were careful to admit only those they knew personally.[18]

Johnson's behavior contrasted with Stanton's. In spite of possible danger, the Secretary of War attended the dying President. The Vice-President, however, waited several hours before making a brief visit to Lincoln's bedside.

From a nightmare of destruction, the Seward family rallied and sent for Dr. Verdi, who arrived shortly before 11:00 P.M. The doctor was horrified at the mayhem and the sight of the Secretary, "covered with blood, blood all around him and blood in the bed."[19] He had three severe wounds—one large gash across his right cheek, running down to his jaw; a stab wound on the right side of his neck and another deep one on the left. Ironically, the previous accident, in which his right arm had been broken and his jaw fractured, may have saved his life. Wires applied to his jaw may have protected his throat from being slit.[20]

Frederick Seward was insensible, his cranium fractured in two places. He was bleeding excessively, could not speak, and had very little pulse. In addition, a messenger from the State Department, named Hansell, who happened to be in the house, had been slashed in the side leaving a gash about 2½ inches deep. Sergeant Robinson miraculously escaped injury.

Augustus Seward's injuries did not require doctor's care. His sister, Fanny, was hysterical and never fully recovered. Mrs. Seward was also badly shaken. The mysterious brute left behind a broken revolver and a slouch hat; he also left the Seward household practically destroyed.

Surgeon General Joseph K. Barnes did not arrive until after eleven. He, too, was overwhelmed at the scene of utter devastation.

After 10:00 P.M. Fletcher found David Herold near the Willard Hotel on the horse he had rented. Fletcher ordered the immediate return of his mount. The youth responded by digging in his spurs and galloping away. The determined Fletcher gave chase.[21]

City detective James McDevitt was busy at his desk at police headquarters on 10th Street, about one hundred yards from Ford's Theatre, when Captain A. C. Richards rushed past him toward the telegraph transmitter. Richards called over his shoulder that the President had been shot and told McDevitt to sound the general alarm on the other telegraph line. They immediately contacted Metro police precincts and put the entire force on duty. Richards dispatched every available detective to gather information.

William Seward and his family never fully recovered from the events of April 14, 1865 (Briggs collection. Library of Congress—USZ62-22180).

Richards, 37-year-old superintendent of the Washington Metro Police Department, was born Almarin Nehemiah Richards in Cummington, Massachusetts. He had changed his name to Almarin Cooley Richards but was generally known by the initials A. C. After graduation from Western Reserve he moved to Washington in 1851. Lincoln appointed him to head the city police force on December 1, 1864. Thus, he was new at the job, having been in the position less than five months.

When police found anyone suspicious, they hauled him or her to head-quarters for questioning. Soon an angry crowd descended on the police station thirsting for revenge. The mob fiercely denounced all suspects brought in, threatening to storm the building and hang them.

A rabble gathered around the theater and the police station, but gradually soldiers pushed the rowdy crowd back, temporarily clearing the area on 10th Street between E and F streets. The mounting hysteria became so intense that Richards and his detectives had difficulty getting into the station with their witnesses. When police escorted men from the theater who were known friends of John Wilkes Booth, it further aggravated the problem. At such times the uncontrollable crowd swarmed menacingly around the station.

Frederick W. Seward, son of the Secretary of State, was severely wounded defending his father (Library of Congress – BH824-5347).

Danger was growing that the mob might break into the building. McDevitt, recognizing the threat, stepped into the street and begged to be heard. He explained briefly that some brought in were not suspects, but rather individuals who had volunteered their services, and that the crowd was hindering the investigation. The rabble reluctantly accepted this explanation, but some vengeful citizens lingered around the building late into the night.[22]

Shortly before eleven, violent knocking at his door awakened Maj. D. H. L. Gleason. He jumped out of bed, turned up the gaslight and opened the door. His roommate, Lt. Joshua Sharp, and several companions entered frantically to recount the awful events. The Lieutenant, an assistant Provost Marshal on General Augur's staff, asked Gleason to go with him to Augur's office. When they reached Pennsylvania Avenue, the frenzied mob would scarcely let them pass. Pushing into Augur's headquarters, they found the usually calm officers bewildered. No one seemed to know what to do.

According to an account given by Gleason years later, he told the officers of a conversation he had had with a suspicious fellow clerk, Louis Weichmann, and advised the arrest of everyone in the house where Weichmann boarded. All available evidence, however, indicates that Gleason waited several days before he mentioned Weichmann. In any case, Augur's forces did not act on Gleason's advice.[23]

The President's eldest son, Robert, was in the Executive Mansion, talking with Maj. John Hay, Lincoln's private secretary, when he heard of the shooting. When the two arrived at 10th Street, inflamed crowds blocked the area. After forcing his way through to the Petersen house, Robert spent the night comforting his mother as she sat, disconsolate, on a sofa in the front parlor. The President lay surrounded by friends and dignitaries in a little back room at the end of a dark, narrow hallway.[24]

In a room between that of the dying President and that occupied by his weeping wife, Stanton was seated at a little table intently writing dispatches with a pencil. Even as the unconscious President lay moaning softly, Stanton was informing the Nation and gathering information.

At approximately 11:00 P.M. an officer recorded on the police blotter:

> At this hour the melancholy intelligence of the assassination of Mr. Lincoln, President of the U.S., at Ford's Theatre was brought to this office, and the information obtained from the following persons goes to show that the assassin is a man named J. Wilks [sic] Booth. Secretary Seward and both his sons and servant were attacked at the same hour by a man supposed to be John Serrett [sic].[25]

This first notice, recorded within 45 minutes of the crime, mentioned two men, albeit inaccurately, connected to the conspiracy. Why John Surratt's name was associated with the attack on Seward so early has never been fully explained. The thin-framed mustachioed Surratt did not resemble the husky assailant. Among the witnesses police had rounded up was James L. Maddox, a property man at Ford's Theatre. Maddox, a friend of John Wilkes Booth, very likely knew of the plot against the Government and may have mentioned Surratt.

When Richards was asked later how he associated Surratt with the Seward attack, he said that he thought a man named Matthews yelled out the name in a crowd. John Matthews, an actor and one of Booth's boyhood friends, knew of the plot and was another who might have made the identification.

The Metro Police Department had a file on John Surratt before April 14, as did the Provost Marshal's office.[26] Surratt was known to have been Booth's close associate. The two had made no effort to disguise their intimacy in the months before the assassination. While this relationship was not obvious to the casual observer, it was apparent to anyone who knew either man. It might have been natural, therefore, when Booth was identified as the assassin to suspect his crony as Seward's attacker.

Although Secretary of War Stanton began to mobilize his far-flung army resources, Superintendent Richards continued his own independent investigation. Among the first suspects he interrogated was James C. Ferguson, whose bar next door to Ford's Theatre was frequented by Booth. The barkeeper revealed that Booth often drank there with friends, among them Louis Payne, David Herold and George Atzerodt. Stanton's officers questioned Ferguson later that same night in the Petersen house, but he revealed practically nothing. Early in the investigation, many suspects were interrogated by both the city police and the War Department.[27]

Although the assassin was tentatively identified as the handsome actor John Wilkes Booth, an ardent Southern sympathizer, the fact was not absolutely certain. Even Richards, who by coincidence had been in the theater when the President was shot, had not recognized Booth.

It was known that Booth kept a private stable in the alley behind Ford's Theatre, but military authorities failed to search it. However, Sergeant Johnson, a city policeman from the 2nd Precinct, did check it out but found nothing more than three fishing lines, a halter, and a saddle cloth, which he took to police headquarters soon after dawn.[29]

Detective McDevitt brought in Laura Keene, star of the play. That night was to have been the highlight of her professional career in a widely acclaimed benefit performance. Miss Keene was an unusually versatile woman who not only acted but also produced her plays. At times she even painted the scenery and made her own costumes in addition to managing business affairs.

Laura Keene was born in England of a family said to have been highly respected. Her first success came in her native country and later in Australia as "Pauline" in *Lady of Lyons*. She moved to America in 1852 as manager of a theater in New York City. Miss Keene was an aggressive businesswoman when such conduct was considered unbecoming for women. In 1857 she married her second husband, John S. Lutz. They lived in the Georgetown section of the District of Columbia and sent the two daughters from her first marriage to a Georgetown convent for schooling. At about this time Laura Keene began production of Tom Taylor's play, *Our American Cousin*.[29]

The actress told Superintendent Richards that the man who jumped from the President's box was Booth. Although police identified him as the culprit within the hour, the Secretary of War, who was busily contacting military leaders throughout the country, still refrained from making a positive identification.

Before midnight Richards was making headway tracking the culprits. In addition to interrogating suspects, he and his men were the first to search the theater. In the vicinity of the President's box, they found a derringer, a slouch hat, an opera-glass case, one spur, two buttons and Lincoln's beaver hat. Richards turned the articles over to the officer in charge, except for Lincoln's hat which he kept.[30]

Throughout the night, suspicious persons were apprehended. Most were examined and dismissed. The first witnesses questioned by police were E. D. Wray of the surgeon general's office, Joseph B. Stewart, who chased Booth across the stage, actor Harry Hawk, soldiers Andrew C. Manwoning, and William Brown. Most of these people have been lost to history, and no record of what they said has been found.[31]

II
Two Horsemen Riding Very Fast

John Fletcher pursued Herold up Pennsylvania Avenue and around the south side of the Capitol, but then lost track of him. Desperate, he asked a passerby if he had seen anyone go by on horseback recently. The man replied that he had seen two horsemen riding very fast toward Navy Bridge. Fletcher hurried to the bridge where the guard stopped him. The stableman described Herold and the horse and asked if anyone of that description had crossed the river. The guard replied that such a person had waited at the bridge a short time for an acquaintance but then crossed over alone. Soon after, another man riding a bay horse crossed the bridge. Fletcher asked permission to go over after them. The guard gave permission but warned he would not be allowed to return. As it was nearly midnight, Fletcher turned dejectedly back to the city, still unaware of the assassination.

By this time, Chief Justice David Cartter of the District of Columbia supreme court had arrived at the Petersen house to help Stanton interrogate witnesses. Stanton had been laboriously recording evidence in longhand. About midnight Gen. C. C. Augur searched for someone who could use shorthand. He called to the crowds in front of the Petersen house for such a person. Albert Daggett, who had been gathering witnesses, lived in the house next door. Hearing the request, he thought of his fellow boarder, Corp. James Tanner, and pushed through the throng to inform the corporal that he could help.

The 20-year-old Tanner had lost both legs in the war and had since studied shorthand at Ames Business College in Syracuse, New York, in an effort to rebuild his life. Having arrived in the Nation's capital a few months earlier, he found work in the Ordnance Bureau and rented a modest room on 10th Street, close to Ford's Theatre. Tanner had been in Grover's Theatre when news of the tragedy was announced. The play was immediately stopped and the theater vacated. He had just returned to his dwelling. After being escorted to Stanton, the handicapped corporal took over the work.

His first witness was Alfred Cloughly, who had seen Seward's attacker. B. A. Hill interrogated him for Cartter, and Tanner took down the statements while Stanton listened intently. Among the witnesses who followed were several who had been in Ford's Theatre; they hesitatingly identified Booth as the criminal. Others, however, were not certain. Harry Hawk, who had already been questioned by Richards, was interrogated again. Laura Keene

13

had also been questioned by police but voluntarily gave her statement again. Her testimony, however, was later missing from the files and has never been found. Tanner declared that within fifteen minutes, he "had testimony enough down to hang Booth."[1]

Stanton constantly interrupted the interrogations to receive reports and to dispatch orders, but by 1:30 A.M. the questioning in the Petersen house was over (although Stanton worked on). The young stenographer, fearful he might have trouble transcribing his rough shorthand copy when it got cold, began the task immediately.

The man accused of shooting President Lincoln was born May 10, 1838, in Maryland. Booth was named for John Wilkes, the famous British maverick politician and longtime mayor of London, to whom he was distantly related. His father, Junius Brutus Booth, Sr., a well-known actor, had left his wife, Adelaide Delannoy, in England and run off to America with a flower girl, Mary Ann Holmes. They settled in a wooded area north of Baltimore in 1824. Booth's American family grew to include four boys and two girls. John Wilkes was next to the youngest. His grandfather, Richard Booth, an English lawyer, came to live with the family in Maryland. His great-grandfather was John Booth, a Jewish silversmith, whose ancestors had been driven out of Portugal.

Junius became one of the most celebrated actors in America. But his family continued to live in primitive isolation. Their home was a cabin filled with crude, rough furniture. Junius made several trips back to England to visit his first family. For years Adelaide was not aware of his common-law wife in America.

Excessive drinking and the death of three children began to affect the actor's mind. He became completely deranged for long periods, a condition the family spoke of as "father's calamity." On one occasion in Natchez, Mississippi, he perched himself on top of a ladder and began to crow like a rooster. The theater manager pleaded with him to come down, but the actor said he would stay there until Andrew Jackson was reelected president.[2] His friends could not always determine whether he was drunk or mentally unbalanced. The elder Booth's health gradually deteriorated as a result of abuses, fights and fits of madness. Although his common-law wife tried to shield the children from the scandal, it could not be kept secret. Their father came to be known as "Crazy Booth, the mad tragedian."

In November 1846, Adelaide learned of Booth's second family. She packed her bags and sailed to the United States where she visited him in Baltimore. Adelaide tried unsuccessfully for years to break up his other family. Finally in 1851, she divorced Booth and he married Mary Ann. A year later, Junius Brutus took a steamboat from New Orleans to Cincinnati and became sick after drinking impure river water. There was no physician on board, and after five days of fever, vomiting and diarrhea, he died near Louisville, Kentucky.[3]

John Wilkes, his mother's favorite, was 13 years old at the time. Johnny, as he was known in the family, was placed in a Quaker boarding school. Later he studied at St. Timothy's Hall in Baltimore County, Maryland. John Wilkes' classmates remembered him as cheerful, kind and generous. But even then he was fond of guns and developed into a good marksman.

Among his friends was a boy named Sam Arnold, on whom Booth was to call in later years. Sam's father, a well-known confectioner in Baltimore, was genuinely interested in his son's welfare. During a disagreement between students and St. Timothy's administration, Booth, Arnold and other students stole guns from the school offices and set up a camp on the grounds, daring the faculty to come and get them. Among the parents who tried to reason with the boys was Sam's father.[4] Twelve years later, he counseled his son concerning a more serious offense.

Johnny's two older brothers, Junius, Jr., and Edwin, thespians like their father, were often away from home but sent money to help their mother. Mrs. Booth warned the older brothers not to scold or even hint at correcting Johnny. When Johnny realized that Edwin, who had become a great Shakespearian dramatist, could make lots of money acting, he decided to give it a try.

John Wilkes was fiercely competitive and wanted to be the best of the three acting brothers. Occasionally the three worked together, as they did in *Julius Caesar*. Junius played Cassius, Edwin was Brutus and John Wilkes took the part of Marc Antony. Such joint ventures did not lessen John's jealousy of his older brother Edwin. John wanted to be *the* Booth. His posters proudly proclaimed, "I AM MYSELF ALONE!"[5]

Although John Wilkes inherited some of the brilliant qualities of his father, he developed what seemed incurable bronchial troubles. Critics commented increasingly on his "hoarseness," and some friends thought his acting days might be over. Early in 1864, when he played the St. Charles Theatre in New Orleans, the engagement had to be cut short because of problems with his voice.

During the Civil War, Booth became almost pathologically defensive of the South. He was never actually in uniform, except when he borrowed one in December 1859, to stand guard at the foot of the scaffold as John Brown was hanged. John Wilkes' Southern sympathies were so outspoken that Edwin refused to discuss war-related subjects with him.

John Wilkes also acquired a taste for the theatrical in real life and began to see himself as destined for some great moment. Early in 1863, while acting at the McVickers Theatre in Chicago, he remarked, "What a glorious opportunity there is for a man to immortalize himself by killing Lincoln!" A friend asked him what good it would do. Waxing dramatic, Booth quoted some lines from antiquity, "The ambitious youth who fired the Ephesian dome outlives in fame the pious fool who reared it." When asked the name of the ambitious youth, Booth admitted he had forgotten it. "Then where's the fame you speak of?" he was asked.[6] The confused Booth did not seem to fathom the contradiction.

After Booth became a prime suspect, the Provost Marshal's office assigned William Eaton to search his room at the National Hotel. He gathered up articles in Booth's trunk and turned them over to Lt. W. H. Terry. Among Booth's papers, authorities found a letter dated March 21, 1865, addressed to "J. Wilkes Booth, Esq." The return address was "Hookstown, Baltimore, Co." It read:

Dear John:

Was business so important that you could not remain in Baltimore till I saw you? I came in as soon as I could, and found you had gone to Washington. I called, also, to see Mike, but learned from his mother he had gone out with you and not returned. I concluded, therefore, he had gone with you. How inconsiderate you have been. When I left you, you stated we would not meet for a month or so; therefore I made application for employment, an answer to which I shall receive during the week. I told my parents I had ceased with you. Can I then, under existing circumstances, come as you request? You know full well the Government suspicions [sic] something is going on there; therefore the undertaking is becoming more complicated. Why not, for the present, desist, for various reasons, which if you look into you can readily see, without my making any mention thereof. You nor any one can censure me for my present course. You have been its cause, for how can I come after telling them I had left you? Suspicion rests upon me now from my whole family, and even parties in the country. I will be compelled to leave home anyhow, and how soon I care not. No one was more in for the enterprise than myself, and today would be there, had you not done as you have; by this I mean the manner of proceeding. I am, as you well know, in need; I am, you may say, in rags; whereas, today I ought to be well clothed. I do not feel right, stalking about without means, and from appearances a beggar. I feel my dependence, but even this was forgotten, for I was one with you. Times more propitious will arrive; you do not act rashly or in haste. I would prefer your first way. Go and see how it will be taken in R_____d, and ere long I shall be better prepared to again assist you....[7]

It was signed "Sam." Military authorities quickly traced the letter to Booth's old friend, Samuel Arnold, whose parents lived in Hookstown. The letter revealed more than Arnold's complicity in the original plot; it associated authorities in Richmond with Booth. It also indicated that a change in plans was contemplated before March 21.

Authorities also found in Booth's trunk a secret cipher. Maj. Thomas Eckert, in charge of Federal ciphers, had for several years deciphered Confederate messages and recognized the code as identical to one found in the office of the Confederate Secretary of State, Judah Benjamin. Eckert had used the same code to translate captured Confederate dispatches sent from Canada to Richmond.[8]

About 1:00 in the morning when Fletcher arrived back at his stable, he learned that Lincoln had been shot. Sitting wearily outside on the step, he heard someone say the culprit had escaped on horseback. Fletcher, fighting fatigue, decided to walk to the Provost Marshal's office on 14th Street to inquire about his horse. Officers there informed him a horse had been found, and that he could check on it at police headquarters. Lt. John J. Poffey had picked up a stray one-eyed horse, saddled and bridled, about midnight near Camp Barry, a mile from the Capitol.

It was not Fletcher's horse, but he wanted to follow this lead. Police told him the horse had been taken to General Augur's headquarters. Officer

Charley Stone agreed to accompany him there. Fletcher told the General of his pursuit of Herold to the Navy Bridge and the word he received there about two suspicious men crossing the bridge shortly before he arrived. As he was talking, his eyes fell on the saddle and bridle which he recognized as having been on Atzerodt's mount. He described Atzerodt's horse to officers as brown and blind in one eye but said he could not remember the name of the man riding it, although he knew him to be a friend of the one who had absconded with his horse. After 2:00 A.M., Stone accompanied Fletcher back to the stable to get Atzerodt's name. Apparently the officer was not interested in Fletcher's lost horse or the rider who had taken it across the river, but only in the one-eyed stray.[9]

In the meantime, Police Officer McDevitt was trying to determine Booth's escape route. He traced his probable progress from the back stage door through the alley behind the theater, then east (some witnesses said Booth turned west) along F Street and past the Capitol to the Navy Bridge which crossed the East Branch (now the Anacostia River). The guard he questioned described a man on horseback who had crossed at about the time detectives estimated Booth could have reached that point. With this information, McDevitt and his men rushed back to the city to get horses to follow the suspects. McDevitt's clues were substantiated when Fletcher related his experiences to police.

Superintendent Richards was on a similar trail. When he learned that two mounted men had passed the guard at the Navy Bridge, he directed Detective John Clarvoe to take twelve policemen and follow the suspects. The police department did not have horses, but military forces had hundreds available. Richards sent an urgent request for a loan of military horses. After a long delay, a police officer reported that he had been sent from one army official to another without results. He said that finally one officer promised to send the horses.[10] At that moment, the suspects were traveling an isolated road in Maryland headed for the home of a country doctor named Samuel Mudd.

Clarvoe and his men were anxious to give chase, but the horses did not arrive. At 11:00 the next morning the army provided them; more than ten crucial hours had been lost. During the morning hours while police waited, military detectives hurried south across Navy Bridge into Maryland. Presumably they did not want to share their expected reward with the city police. (By that time Augur had offered a reward.)

Augur's failure to act quickly on Fletcher's information was indefensible, even considering the confusion and scores of conflicting rumors. Fletcher's account was by far the most concrete lead. If anyone was at fault on the night of the murder, it was not the oft-criticized Stanton, but rather General Augur, who had the information, as well as the authority and manpower, to pursue the assassins that night; yet he failed to act. However, to his credit and on his own initiative, the General offered a $10,000 reward for the capture of the criminals. A few days later, Stanton increased the rewards. Counting what other authorities and individual states offered, the total eventually came to nearly $200,000.

Before daylight military officers had dispatched mounted patrols throughout the city. Both they and Metro police searched houses occupied by known Southern sympathizers during the night. Soldiers from nearby Camp Baker were sent to a poor section of the city, which included the home of a hardworking plasterer named Kraft. The family was roused from sleep by heavy pounding on the door as soldiers surrounded the house. Mrs. Kraft instinctively grabbed up two stolen army blankets and threw them out back onto the roof of a shed before opening the door. The late-night intrusion caused Kraft's elderly mother to break down in tears. Still, it did not awaken the baby sleeping in a nearby crib. After searching upstairs and down, the soldiers left abruptly and moved on to the next house.[11]

III
While the President Still Breathes

Washington inhabitants had gradually settled down to an uneasy sleep, as police officers approached a narrow, three-story house at 541 H Street, just six blocks northeast of Ford's Theatre. At about 2:30 in the morning of April 15, detectives John Clarvoe and James McDevitt arrived at the modest boarding-house.[1] Mary Surratt, a 42-year-old widow, lived there with her daughter, Anna, and son, John. Their boarders included Louis Weichmann, Honora Fitzpatrick, and the John Holohan family. Occasionally Mrs. Surratt's niece, Olivia Jenkins, also stayed with her.

Although John Surratt's name had come up repeatedly, the first hint of suspicious events occurring at the boardinghouse came from an anonymous individual who advised McDevitt to investigate the boardinghouse. This tip came within a few hours of the shooting.

Stationing subordinates at strategic points in back and in the alley to the east, detectives climbed the front stairs and knocked on the door. After getting Mrs. Surratt's permission to search the premises, they encountered Weich-mann and the other occupants. They failed, however, to find John Surratt and left without arresting anyone.

While city police were searching the boardinghouse, the President was lying unconscious in a small back room of a plain three-story brick house on 10th Street, the home of William Petersen, a German tailor. The small room was sparsely decorated with a popular lithograph by Rosa Bonheur, titled "Horse Fair." The President's pulse had dropped to 54. Several cabinet members stood around his bed in stunned silence. An eyewitness of the somber scene described Government leaders as equally paralyzed as the dying President. In the front parlor Mrs. Lincoln, moaning periodically, sat with her son, Robert.

In another room, Stanton, aided by Assistant Secretary of War Charles Dana, continued to dictate dispatches which helped maintain order in the Government. Stanton, remembering some deciphered Confederate messages regarding the burning of New York City and Rebel plans to spread terror in Chicago, was convinced the conspiracy was part of a nationwide plot. He advised military commanders across the country to take extra precautions, informed leaders, strengthened the defenses of Washington and initiated a widespread search for the fugitives.

Stanton ordered Gen. Thomas M. Vincent to take charge of activities around the Petersen house, telegraphed Grant to return to Washington with caution and ordered the military alerted for any emergency. He called Col. LaFayette C. Baker to Washington, suggested that Supreme Court Justice Salmon Chase be ready to administer the oath of office to Andrew Johnson, contacted Vice-President Johnson and continued to issue bulletins informing military authorities of Lincoln's failing condition.[2] His dispatches were precise and lucid. Dana later wrote that no clearer, brief account of the events existed than Stanton's telegrams written during the turmoil and confusion of that un-paralleled night.

At 3:00 A.M. Stanton telegraphed Gen. John A. Dix in New York:

> The President still breathes, but is quite insensible, as he has been ever since he was shot. He evidently did not see the person who shot him, but was look-ing on the stage as he was approached from behind.
> Mr. Seward has rallied, and it is hoped he may live.
> Frederick Seward's condition is very critical.
> The attendant who was present was shot through his lungs, and is not ex-pected to live.
> The wounds of Major Seward are not serious.
> Investigation strongly indicates J. Wilkes Booth as the assassin of the Presi-dent. Whether it was the same or a different person that attempted to murder Mr. Seward remains in doubt.
> The Chief Justice is engaged in taking the evidence.
> Every exertion has been made to prevent the escape of the murderer. His horse has been found on the road near Washington.[3]

Throughout the ordeal Stanton made a special effort to comfort Mrs. Lin-coln. Previously his relationship with the First Lady had been strained. Among other things, he was annoyed by her friendship with Congressman and Mrs. Fernando Wood. The Congressman was a strong and vocal supporter of the South. Stanton strenuously objected to Mrs. Lincoln's sending flowers to the Wood family from the Government greenhouse. But in spite of their differences, Stanton was especially considerate during this night of overwhelming grief. Early in the morning he dismissed his assistant, Charles Dana. Yet Stanton remained by the side of the unconscious President.

Superintendent Richards also worked through the night. But his concern was more localized. He ordered the closing of all places where liquor was sold. (The order, however, was generally ignored.)

Early that morning Stanton ordered a Union officer, James O' Beirne, to bring Vice-President Johnson from the Kirkwood House to Lincoln's bedside. Major O'Beirne, a Civil War hero, had been shot through the lungs and legs in the Battle of Chancellorsville, forcing him to retire from active field duty. On the way to the President's side, the wary Vice-President told the major that he had listened for hours to footsteps in the room above his. O'Beirne went back later that morning to investigate. In the room, which had been rented to George Atzerodt, he found a large bowie knife, a Colt revolver, a handker-chief with the initial "H" and a few other items which he turned over to Stanton.

Atzerodt had checked out several hours before the attacks. About 11:30 that night he boarded a horse-car at 6th Street and rode toward the Navy Yard,

One of the last photographs of President Lincoln (Photo by Alexander Gardner, Library of Congress – VSZ62-11896).

a little more than a mile south of the Capitol. In the car he encountered an old friend, Washington Briscoe. Briscoe asked if he had heard the news. George, happy to see a friendly face, casually exchanged a few words about the tragedy and then asked if he could sleep in Briscoe's store that night. His friend, an unsavory character with strong Southern leanings, said no. George begged, but Briscoe remained firm. Arriving at the Navy Yard, Atzerodt made another urgent plea for a place to stay. Briscoe, perhaps suspicious of his friend, insisted he had no room.

Dejected, George Atzerodt wandered about aimlessly, finally ending up at the Pennsylvania House, where he had occasionally lodged, and asked for his old room, Number 51. By that time, after 2:00 A.M., Atzerodt had a man named Thomas with him. When asked to sign the register, Thomas hesitated. John Greenawalt, manager of the seedy little hotel, informed Atzerodt that his old room was occupied and that he would have to take another.

Atzerodt and Thomas were put in quarters rented earlier by Lt. W. R. Keen. Because of the search for the assassins, it was 4:00 A.M. before the officer returned. The Lieutenant, like Atzerodt, had been an occasional guest at the

Mary Todd Lincoln. The assassination involved two Marys—one left a widow; the other accused of conspiracy (Library of Congress).

hotel, and the two had a speaking acquaintance. It was no surprise for Keen to find other guests in his rented space—as filling every bed, even with strangers, was a common practice in the less-fashionable lodging places. As the army officer was preparing for bed, he asked George if he had heard of the shooting. Atzerodt responded that he had and commented on what an awful thing it was. When the lieutenant awoke the next morning, Atzerodt and Thomas were gone.[4]

Although Booth was widely thought to be the gunman, the identification was still not absolutely certain. "No one said positively that the assassin was John Wilkes Booth," Corporal Tanner recalled later, "although everyone thought that it was he."[5] The corporal believed that the awfulness of the crime kept other actors from actually accusing Booth. It was difficult for the performers to believe that an amiable fellow actor could be guilty.

Of course, Stanton had heard many accounts, but several witnesses had been hesitant in their identification. An important early statement was given by Harry Hawk, the only actor on the stage at the time. But even Hawk was less than certain, as Tanner's notes indicate. Hawk testified that, to the best of his knowledge, it was John Wilkes Booth who leaped onto the stage, but he added that he was not positive. By 6:45 A.M. Tanner had transcribed all the testimony. Stanton, busy with other matters, did not see the completed notes until that afternoon.

The Secretary of War was not alone in his hesitation to name the felon. L. A. Gobright, a diligent reporter for the Associated Press, worked through the night, but could not find positive identification of the fugitive before he dispatched his story early the next morning.

Washington papers published several extra editions to keep their demanding readers informed. In its 5:00 A.M. edition, the *Washington National Intelligencer* had not yet identified any suspect, not even Booth. Later editions quoted Stanton as saying there were strong indications that J. Wilkes Booth was the assassin. Surprisingly, there was no description whatever of Seward's attacker.

Thoroughness and caution were the marks of Stanton's character, traits which had helped bring the war to a successful conclusion. Identifying the wrong man was risky and hampered the early search for Seward's attacker. Stanton wanted the identity firmly established. It was not as vital that Booth's name be circulated before 3:00 A.M. on April 15 as it was to get the facts established.

The picture of Stanton under these tense circumstances was that of an austere, autocratic, yet remarkable man. Those who worked with him that night and in the weeks that followed testified to his extraordinary efforts. Tanner described him as a man of steel. The stern Secretary barked out a steady stream of orders and took command of the chaotic situation which he did not relinquish for several months.

Stanton had previously pondered the possibility of a last-ditch Confederate effort to destroy the Government. After the attacks, he became more convinced of a widespread plot to disrupt the Nation. As a result he placed guards around his house and around the homes of other Cabinet members.

Stanton's investigation, although extensive, was not as productive as that of city police. He had discovered nothing about the house on H Street or about the Surratts. However, he did know about the collaboration between Confederate President Jefferson Davis and his so-called Canadian Cabinet and thus pushed his investigation far beyond the boundaries of the District of Columbia.

At 5:30 A.M. Saturday, police booked Nellie Starr, a 20-year-old prostitute, on suspicion of complicity in the crime. Nellie, whose real name was Ella Turner, was also known as Fannie Harrison and Ella Starr. She was a small, pretty, light-haired girl who lived on the south side of Pennsylvania Avenue in the infamous "Hooker's Division" section. Nellie was Booth's most frequent female companion. She had known the actor for three years and had evidently followed him to Washington during the Christmas season. When questioned, Nellie claimed that Booth was a good man who had never spoken against the President. This pretense of innocence satisfied Metro police and she was released by Officer Miller.[6]

At the time, Booth was engaged to marry Bessie Hale, daughter of former Republican senator from New Hampshire John P. Hale. Senator Hale, a strong antislavery advocate, was the Free-Soil party's unsuccessful choice for president in 1852. It is doubtful that his daughter knew much, if anything, of Booth's plans, but it is possible that she could have provided some background information. No evidence exists that Bessie was ever questioned.

Louis Weichmann could not get back to sleep after police searched the Surratt boardinghouse. He arose before dawn, dressed and walked aimlessly around the neighborhood. About six o'clock he encountered liveryman Brooke Stabler standing in front of Howard's Stable. Stabler knew him by sight, because Weichmann had occasionally procured a horse and buggy from him for his landlady. The hostler also knew the Surratts. Howard's Stable was located on G Street, directly behind their house.

The frightened boarder, anxious to talk to somebody, gave a highly agitated account of the police raid. He seemed eager to explain that John Surratt was in Canada. Asking for a drink, Weichmann continued his animated and often incoherent account of the events.

Soon after this conversation, Weichmann consulted with his fellow-boarder, John Holohan, about the police search. The two decided that their only recourse was to go directly to the police. Holohan was an unsavory character who had left his work as a stone cutter in Baltimore for a more profitable but less reputable position as a bounty broker. A bounty broker negotiated in human lives, serving clients who could buy their way out of military service by paying someone to take their place. The business was despised by both Confederate and Union officials. The bounty broker operated like a loan shark, taking advantage of the distress of others. Most authorities considered bounty brokers loathesome opportunists who should be put out of business.

After eating an early breakfast at the boardinghouse, Weichmann and Holohan excused themselves about 7:30 and walked to the Metro police station.[7] Both were anxious to find the culprits and, at the same time, to exonerate themselves. The landlady, however, and the other boarders felt no need to contact police.

When Weichmann and Holohan arrived at headquarters, Captain Richards, who had been up most of the night, had not yet returned, so they talked to Detectives Clarvoe and McDevitt. Both Weichmann and Holohan told of unusual visitors to the boardinghouse. It was later claimed incorrectly that Weichmann was put under arrest at this time.[8] The voluntary disclosure of his suspicions made him a valuable source, however, and he was kept under supervision. McDevitt thought Weichmann so important that he hardly let him out of sight, even taking him home with him for meals.

Although Weichmann had wanted Brooke Stabler to keep their conversation confidential, within thirty minutes Stabler wrote it down and sent it to a detective named Fry. Later that day Stabler was called in for questioning. In addition to describing his meeting with Weichmann, he gave some interesting details about other suspicious clients, namely: David Herold, George Atzerodt, John Surratt and Mrs. Mary Surratt.

Stabler informed police that, about April 1, Mrs. Surratt had rented a carriage and had taken a young black boy down to her country house. According to Stabler, the purpose of the trip was to get her son John. A few days earlier, on March 26, John had written Stabler advising him that he was sending back a team of horses because he would be busy for a week or so with "women on the brain."[9] Weichmann later indicated that this phrase was John's ruse for avoiding suspicion about his real activities.

In the short time that Superintendent Richards had been away from his office, new developments occurred. In the first fearful hours, Metro police arrested everyone associated with Ford's Theatre. Edward Spangler, a stagehand and a friend of Booth, had been brought to headquarters about 6:00 A.M. by Sergeant Skipper of the 6th Precinct. Spangler had been backstage when Booth made his escape. He confessed that he had known Booth for eleven years and that Booth had left a horse for him to hold in readiness behind the theater a few hours before the shooting. Skipper also arrested a man named Joseph Boser. After being locked up for a short time, they were both dismissed by order of Officer Miller.[10] Nothing more is known of Boser, but this was the first of many encounters with Spangler.

Also during the night, Officer John Parker, who had been assigned to guard Lincoln and who had allowed Booth to approach the President's box, apparently tried to atone for his error by arresting a prostitute named Lizzie Williams. She was quietly dismissed.[11] Much was later made of Parker's negligence in protecting the President, but his mistake seems to have been due to human error rather than to disloyalty. He was not punished, but on May 1, 1865, Richards reprimanded him for neglect of duty.

Soon after dawn a vague picture of the assassination plot was emerging. Authorities had uncovered at least three strong suspects: John Wilkes Booth, John Surratt and Samuel Arnold. They had already searched the house on H Street and Booth's hotel room. Furthermore, they had information that two suspicious men had crossed the Navy Bridge, and police had found a fully saddled horse wandering in the woods east of the Capitol. They also had Weichmann.

IV
Someone to Fill the Vacuum

Daylight revealed a poignant scene in the Petersen house, as Stanton and about nineteen other Government leaders continued their vigil. At 7:22 A.M. Surgeon General Joseph Barnes, chief medical officer of the army, placed Lincoln's limp hands across his dead body. The silence was only "interrupted by the sobs of Stanton," Tanner observed.[1] The Secretary of War stood by the death bed, his pale cheeks glistening with tears.

Within minutes Stanton regained his composure and began to direct the affairs of state which could not be postponed. The Vice-President was fearful for his life and the Secretary of State lay gravely wounded. Someone had to fill the vacuum. The Secretary of War had directed important affairs through the war years. Immediately he began to make funeral arrangements and called a Cabinet meeting. No one objected as the energetic Secretary took over the Government.

Soon after the President died, his body was carried from the little room to the White House. A melancholy group of bareheaded army officers led the procession, followed by solemn-faced soldiers, carrying his remains. A Union flag covered the casket. As the procession moved forward, the stillness was broken only by the measured beat of soldiers' feet and the occasional sobs of mourners who reverently lined the streets. The corpse was placed in a room on the north side of the Presidential Mansion, opposite Mrs. Lincoln's second-story chamber.[2]

Surgeon General Barnes and Dr. Robert K. Stone cut the skull open to remove the flattened bullet which had lodged in Lincoln's brain. The nature of the wound had discolored the protruding eyes of the cadaver. Mrs. Lincoln remained in her bedroom as the morticians prepared the body. She had not attended her son Willie's funeral and would not attend services for her husband.

The dull, overcast sky reflected the sentiments of the Nation. As news of the President's death spread, grieving multitudes thronged the streets. Flags were lowered to half-mast throughout the city, and church bells tolled mournfully. The city's attitude had changed abruptly from the jubilant celebration of the day before. Houses previously decorated with victory flags were now draped in black. Stores and Government offices closed. Soldiers stood guard at every corner.

Lincoln died just as he reached the pinnacle of popularity. Throughout the war years, he had been ridiculed and criticized, but early in April the country sensed that the war was nearly over. Lincoln was gradually recognized for the effective and gentle leader he was. L. E. Chittenden noted, "We were beginning to know how great and good a man our President was, and to reproach ourselves because we had not long before made the discovery."[3]

Friends recalled incidents reflecting the humble, gentle spirit of the departed leader. Chittenden remembered that a few days earlier, Lincoln had visited the captured Confederate capital with his young son, Tad. As the President approached Richmond on a warship, he asked the admiral if he would permit the sailors to pick some flowers which his son had seen on the river banks, "for the boy loves flowers," explained the President quietly.[4]

Gideon Welles remembered Lincoln's last Cabinet meeting less than twenty-four hours earlier. The President told his Cabinet that he was certain something big was about to happen because of a dream he had the night before. He explained that he had dreamed the same thing before the battles of Bull Run, Antietam, Stones River, Gettysburg and Vicksburg. In his dream, the President saw a large indescribable boat which seemed to be "moving with great rapidity toward a dark and indefinite shore." He felt certain the dream "signaled some good news." General Grant, who was present with the Cabinet, remarked that the Battle of Stones River had not been a Union victory, but the President remained optimistic.[5]

Many recalled his remarks three nights before the murder. An elated crowd had gathered around the White House to praise the victorious Commander-in-Chief. Lincoln had jotted down a few words for the occasion. The tall, lanky leader stepped out on the front porch with his beloved Tad at his side. Lincoln delivered a short but masterful address. After thanking the country for victories won on the battlefields, he dealt with the dispute over whether the South had been in or out of the Union during the war.

> We all agree that the seceded states, so-called are out of their proper practical relation with the Union, and that the sole object of the Government, civil and military, in regard to those states, is to again get them into that proper practical relation. I believe it is not only possible, but in fact easier, to do this without deciding, or even considering, whether these states have ever been out of the Union than with it. Finding themselves safely at home, it would be utterly immaterial whether they had ever been abroad.[6]

As the President finished reading each page, he let it fall on the porch. Tad playfully picked them up anxiously waiting for another one to fall.

With a few remarks about his plan for Reconstruction in Louisiana, Lincoln concluded his last public speech. The crowds had come expecting a rousing celebration; what they got was a low-keyed discourse on reconciliation.

Still fresh in the minds of many was Lincoln's reaction to similar throngs on April 10. In response to demands for a speech the charitable President called upon the band to play a song which he said Southerners had tried to appropriate. Then he added, in his own humorous fashion, that the Attorney General had given his legal opinion that the North had fairly captured the tune and it was now their property. So he asked the band to play "Dixie."

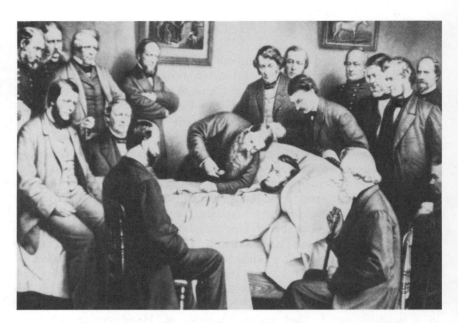

Several hours before the assassination, the War Department received a telegram from the Provost Marshal in Portland, Maine, advising that he had positive information that Jacob Thompson, chief Confederate agent in Canada, was traveling to Portland to embark for England. Assistant Secretary of War Charles Dana took the telegram to Stanton who promptly ordered Thompson's arrest. Then, reflecting a moment, he decided that Dana had better check with the President first. Dana found Lincoln in his office late that afternoon and asked him what to do about the telegram. After being told of Stanton's desire to arrest Thompson, the President responded slowly, "No, I rather think not. When you have got an elephant by the hind leg, and he's trying to run away, it's best to let him run."

Dana hurried back across the White House lawn to the War Department to report the President's witticism.

"Oh, stuff!" responded Stanton in disgust.[7]

After the President's death, one of Stanton's first orders was for Dana to arrest Thompson, but it was too late. He had escaped to Halifax, Nova Scotia. Stanton was convinced that Thompson knew about the plot against Lincoln.

An hour before Lincoln died, Atzerodt, desperate for money, cautiously approached the Matthews and Company grocery in Georgetown and tried to sell his watch to the manager, John L. Caldwell. The merchant declined, saying he did not need a watch. Atzerodt then displayed his revolver and asked for a loan of ten dollars with the gun as security. Caldwell thought that a better bargain and gave him the money.[8]

Even though every road out of Washington was supposedly patrolled at this time, Atzerodt had no trouble escaping to Montgomery County, Maryland. Perhaps it was because he did not fit the description of any prime suspect.

News of the tragedy spread rapidly. Bold headlines proclaimed the heinous act in morning newspapers across the Nation. Early editions sold out in New York and it was impossible to buy a paper by 8:00 A.M. *The Detroit Free Press*, a pro–Southern paper strongly opposed to Lincoln's policies, bordered the notice of the President's death in black but, nevertheless, expressed belief that Confederate General Joseph E. Johnston would make a stand against Union forces in Augusta, Georgia. Another Copperhead paper, the *Constitutional Advocate*, published in Schuykill County, Pennsylvania, printed a poorly timed tirade against Lincoln in its April 14 issue:

> When the bloody hours of Lincoln's life is [sic] over, we think we see a funeral procession, at the head of which marches a man bearing a negro's skull, and the impaled body of a white man, exclaiming, "Behold the emblem of all he accomplished by the slaughter of two millions of people and the crushing of unborn generations beneath the mountain of his debts."[9]

Opposite, top: Each picture of Lincoln's death included different personalities. Actually as the President lingered, various friends visited briefly and left the room. Only a few individuals, like Stanton, shown standing in the background, stayed close by all night (Library of Congress – USZ62-2074). Bottom: Funeral of President Lincoln at Washington, D.C. (Library of Congress – USZ62-6935).

In the next issue the editor abruptly changed his opinion. Commenting on the President's death, he wrote "Men truly felt as if the first born of all the households of the land had died; felt as men feel when they have lost their best earthly friend."[10] The writer admitted that he had been extreme in his previous denunciations.

A story circulated at the time, and frequently repeated, was that all but one of the telegraph lines from Washington had been cut. Actually, none of the lines was cut or put out of service. Stanton's dispatches were not interrupted and reporters had no trouble getting the story out.

In Boston, Edwin Booth, hearing the bells tolling Lincoln's death, sent a telegram to his mother urging her to be strong. He said it was not yet certain that Johnny had done it. Later, Edwin received a message from Henry Jarrett, manager of the Boston Theater, stating that as suspicion pointed to Edwin's brother, he had decided to close the theater where Edwin was performing.

Junius Brutus, Jr., acting in Cincinnati, was nearly lynched. He stayed in his hotel room as a maddened throng tore down his playbills all over town. The house Edwin had bought for his mother in New York City became an object of curiosity. Mrs. Booth grieved inside with her daughter, Rosalie, lamenting, "If it is true, let him shoot himself. Let him not live to be hanged."[11]

In Philadelphia, John Clark, Booth's brother-in-law, was trying to calm his distraught wife, Asia, when a guard was placed around their house. Both John Clark and Junius Booth were eventually arrested and transported to Old Capitol Prison. Edwin was closely watched but not arrested. John and Junius resented Edwin's relative freedom. Joseph, the younger brother of John Wilkes, was arrested as he arrived from Australia and placed in a New York jail.[12]

The investigation had brought in an assortment of seamy characters, each of whom had aroused the suspicions of some diligent officer. The police blotter for the night of the 14th indicated something of the scramble for clues immediately following the crime. Police arrested a shady individual named Luther Emerson Davis. On searching him, they found $115 in his money belt, a knife and two Colt revolvers. Leda Young, a prostitute, and Annie Clark were charged with using treasonable language; Mary Jane Windell's charge was malicious mischief and disloyalty; two restaurateurs, Adolph Myers and William Wiggars, whose establishments were frequented by Booth were brought in; Louis J. Carland, a costumer at Ford's Theatre, was suspected of conspiracy, and Maurice Duvalt was faulted for threats of violence. Most were interrogated, released and forgotten.[13]

One man on his way to work saw a small group gathered near the intersection of 9th and D streets. Drawing near, he heard someone exclaim, "I wouldn't pick it up." On investigation, he saw a dagger lying in the street, which he picked up without hesitation. His daring cost him two nights in prison as a suspect. The dagger was later thought to have been used by Seward's attacker.[14] Finding the knife at that location would have indicated an irregular route taken by the would-be murderer. After heading northeast from Seward's house, he would have doubled back south, passing close to Ford's Theatre. He would then have headed due east past the Capitol into the wooded area east of the city.

Soon after Lincoln was pronounced dead, Secretary of the Treasury Hugh McCulloch and Attorney General James Speed asked the Chief Justice of the United States Supreme Court to administer the oath of office to Vice-President Andrew Johnson. Leaders agreed that the Vice-President should be sworn in at 10:00 that morning in the lobby of the Kirkwood House. Chief Justice Salmon P. Chase hurried to the Attorney General's office to examine the constitutional provisions and to examine previous examples of vice-presidents John Tyler and Millard Filmore who had ascended to the presidency on the death of their predecessors. When he returned to the hotel, twelve or so Government leaders had assembled. Chase administered the oath of office in the lobby making Andrew Johnson the 17th President of the United States.[15]

The new President was born on December 29, 1808, in Raleigh, North Carolina. His background was similar to that of Abraham Lincoln. Born into a poor Southern family, he was forced to make his way with few material goods and scanty education. As a child, Johnson lost his father and became an apprentice in a tailor's shop. After moving to South Carolina, he worked at this trade for several years, later moving to Greenville, a nonslaveholding area of Tennessee. After his wife taught him to write, he became active in politics. Johnson advanced from the Tennessee State Legislature to the United States Congress and then became governor of Tennessee before being elected to the United States Senate in 1857. In 1862 he was appointed military governor of Tennessee by President Lincoln. His denunciation of secession and his support of emancipation brought him to the attention of the Republican Convention of 1864. Some Republican leaders, particularly Secretary of State Seward, felt that Johnson would be more acceptable to a ticket stressing "Union" than Vice-President Hannibal Hamlin. Although Johnson had always been a Democrat, he was the only Southern Senator in the Thirty-Sixth Congress to remain faithful to the Federal Government.

Both Johnson and Lincoln had known hardship and poverty; both were self-educated and ambitious; both lived close to the people and knew the rigors of frontier life. But there were significant differences. Lincoln was a sensitive man of strong moral courage. He was pliable and accommodating on insignificant matters but resolutely firm on questions he considered vital. Johnson, on the other hand, lacked a strong moral sense. His stubbornness was sometimes seen as courage, and he could be very determined when he thought he was right. But he was often petty and quibbling on unimportant issues. Furthermore, while Lincoln was sure of his position and magnanimous to his enemies, Johnson was insecure and vindictive. Lincoln was easygoing and pleasant. Johnson was uptight and defensive. Lincoln's speech was wonderfully reasonable. Johnson's was frequently intemperate and bombastic. To some extent, these differences in character were due to their individual natures, but circumstances also molded them. Johnson was reared in slave states and opposed slavery because of its association with the envied planter aristocracy. Lincoln was reared in free states and was opposed to slavery on moral principles.

Lincoln was elected to office and enjoyed the security of majority support.

Johnson became President under suspicious circumstances which robbed him of this confidence.

When he had become Vice-President at Lincoln's second inauguration, Johnson appeared to have been inebriated. He was undoubtedly under the influence of alcohol, and his slurred, incoherent speech was unfortunate, but circumstances may have been partly to blame; his health and the crowded Senate chamber made his condition worse. Six weeks later, he was propelled into the presidency—ready or not.

As he stood in the Kirkwood House that April morning, President Johnson received the usual round of congratulations and offers of assistance. He then asked the Chief Justice if he should make a speech. Chase suggested that it would be better to make a brief announcement to be printed in the newspapers. In agreement, the new President asked the Chief Justice to prepare a statement. While Chase was busy in another room composing the announcement, Johnson took the opportunity to make a short speech on his own.

His extemporaneous remarks were scrutinized by politicians to gain insight into the President's future course. But he frustrated their hopes, announcing that the direction of his administration "must be made by the acts as they transpire." The overall effect was not good. Not only was he evasive about his aims, but he was also noticeably lacking in respectful reverence to the late President. At a time when the Nation was in deep mourning, Johnson's only reference to his great predecessor was a declaration that he was "almost overwhelmed by . . . the sad event. . . ."

Johnson, however, found time to make considerable mention of his own accomplishments. "My past public life which has been long and laborious has been founded . . . upon a great principle of right. . . ." The new President dwelt on his toil for the "great principles of free Government," his labor to "ameliorate and alleviate the condition of the great mass of the American people." As if exhilarated by his new-found importance, Johnson grandly declared to the few dignitaries surrounding him that, "The duties have been mine, and the consequences God's." This last pompous statement inspired one Senator to observe that "Johnson seemed willing to share the glory of his achievements with his Creator, but utterly forgot that Mr. Lincoln had any share of credit in the suppression of the rebellion."[16]

A few days later when visited by a delegation from Illinois, Johnson was able to correct his oversight. "The beloved of all hearts has been assassinated," he stated with genuine emotion. The Nation's new leader also indicated his feelings towards the assassins. He promised to impose the extreme penalty, asserting that no one would "say that mercy should interpose." Then he launched into a larger topic:

> When the question of exercising mercy comes before me it will be considered calmly, judicially—remembering that I am the Executive of the Nation. I know men love to have their names spoken of in connection with acts of mercy, and how easy it is to yield to that impulse. But we must never forget that what may be mercy to the individual is cruelty to the State.[17]

The passion for relics connected with the calamity was excessive. The mania

After aiding the dying President, Laura Keene was interrogated, but her statement was later missing from Government files and has never been found (Library of Congress—USZ62-55263).

may have been prompted by a sense of the historical. Both the famous and the unknown were eager to save some memento. Relic fanatics gathered in the morning near the house where Lincoln had died and began chipping away the blood-spattered pavement and steps, thinking it was the President's blood. According to Albert Daggett, however, little blood fell from the President's wound. It was actually that of Major Rathbone, whose slashed arm bled profusely as he followed the President across the street.[18]

When Laura Keene heard the call for water, she rushed to the box with water from her dressing room. She remained with the President, holding his head as blood stained the cuffs of her gown. Following her interrogations, Miss Keene went to the Metropolitan Hotel on the north side of Pennsylvania Avenue rather than return to her Georgetown home. The next morning she was visited by M. J. Adler, a merchant in Georgetown, and nephew of her husband, to whom she gave the blood-stained cuffs. Adler regarded the relics as his most treasured possession.

The rage for Lincoln relics became a national phenomenon. In Springfield, Illinois, a respectably dressed man was noticed pocketing a brick from the wall in front of Mr. Lincoln's home. One newspaper reported that entire stairways had been pulled down by souvenir hunters. A writer in the *Cincinnati Commercial* complained that an elm, planted by Lincoln in front of his house, would be destroyed by relic hunters in veneration for Lincoln.

Tanner finished transcribing his shorthand notes shortly before the President died. He took them to his room where he made a more legible copy for the Secretary of War. Before noon the stenographer delivered his work to Stanton's residence, but even the Secretary had limits; he had retired, exhausted. While he slept, the War Department continued its efforts to identify and apprehend the assassins. By Saturday morning soldiers were swarming over the countryside around Washington, although police still had no horses.

Stanton was back in his office soon after noon and began to consolidate the investigation. Joseph Barrett, a farmer, was arrested on suspicion and sent to police headquarters on his order. Barrett was examined and released on bail. Apparently Stanton did not like his prisoners released, even on bail, because he never sent any more to the police. Richards and his police department were gradually being pushed out of the investigation, particularly after large rewards became widely known.[19]

V
The Man Called Mars

Edwin McMasters Stanton, the most powerful man in the Nation at this time, was born December 19, 1814, in Steubenville, Ohio. His father, David Stanton, a respected physician, died when Edwin was a boy. The father was from Rhode Island, of Quaker background, the son of Benjamin Stanton, who had been a Virginia slaveholder. Edwin's grandmother on his father's side was a descendant of Thomas Macy, one of the persecuted Quakers of New England's colonial history. Friends of the family said that Dr. Stanton left his widow and four young children in strained circumstances because he was too generous to be rich.

Stanton derived his middle name from his mother's godfather, the Reverend David McMasters. Stanton possessed a strong, genuinely religious quality. At twelve years of age he confessed Christ publicly and joined the Methodist church. Edwin never sought great wealth, although he was a hard worker. As a boy he worked as a salesman in a bookstore, earning six dollars a month, which he faithfully turned over to his mother.

Young Stanton played with snakes and talked to a human skeleton; this, understandably, caused some to think him odd. Actually his natural curiosity motivated him to organize his own natural history museum for which he collected snakes, along with other specimens. His talking to a skeleton was partially explained as the result of his father's desire for his first son to become a physician. To excite the young boy's interest, the elder Stanton hung a skeleton behind the barn for Edwin to study. One of Stanton's boyhood friends remembered Edwin putting "a lighted candle inside the skull."[1] This was surely just a youthful prank. The story that young Stanton invariably carried "a fine dagger seven inches in length" inside his vest, complicates the evaluation of his youth.

Later in life, Stanton smoked occasionally but did not drink. He was careful with money and did not indulge in hobbies or amusements. He was never heard to sing a note or known for frivolity.

Stanton entered Kenyon College in 1831 but left after two years to study law. He practiced law for twenty-four years neither desiring nor holding any position outside his practice except when he became a reporter to the Supreme Court of Ohio. Stanton was not a climber, but he performed his duties with energy.

When his infant daughter, Lucy, died, Stanton was inconsolable. A year after her death, he had her body exhumed and cremated. He placed the ashes in a metal box which he kept in his room. On August 11, 1842, his first son, Edwin Lamson Stanton was born, which restored some joy.

His greatest sorrow was the death in 1844 of his first wife, Mary, during childbirth. Overcome with grief, Stanton seemed unbalanced for days. He insisted that his wife be buried in her wedding dress and then threw all her jewels and rings into her coffin. He buried her and their daughter's ashes in the same grave. The anguished husband could not be comforted. He placed Mary's nightcap and gown on her bed and wept for her night after night. This tragedy changed his personality—while he had never been frivolous, he became even more withdrawn and stoic.[2] The suicide of Darwin, Stanton's younger brother, a year later understandably deepened his depression. These incidents have occasionally been alluded to, in an effort to picture him as unstable. Circumstances had turned the Secretary of War into an austere leader, but old friends knew another side. Secretary of State Jeremiah Black, his fellow Cabinet member under Buchanan, remembered when Stanton first came to Washington: "His language was habitually deferential, his whole bearing decent, and his behavior at the council board was entirely free from insolence...."[3]

Stanton was a short, stocky, broad-shouldered man whose noticeably large head was covered with black hair. His heavy black beard was streaked with white. Stanton's small gray eyes peered out intensely at the world through wire-rimmed spectacles, giving him the appearance of a stern schoolmaster. William Doster thought Stanton looked perpetually as if he had not slept well and acted as though it would not cause him much pain to refuse the most urgent request. He seemed to have a special contempt for army officers. Praise of the masses did not interest him. In many ways, he was a misfit in the Washington political environment. President Buchanan remarked that he knew the character and personality of everyone in his Cabinet except for Stanton's.[4] He was, indeed, a complex man, understood by few.

As attorney for Simon Cameron, his predecessor in the War Department, Stanton advised that he include in his annual report a recommendation that the Government arm slaves and train them as soldiers. This suggestion, coming at a sensitive time, apparently increased Cameron's already strained relations with Lincoln. The President reacted by appointing Cameron minister to Russia and replacing him with Stanton.

When he became Secretary of War, Stanton took immediate control of the telegraph lines. Within a few days, he had all the equipment moved from the telegraph office and placed in a room next to his office. This action exasperated some military leaders, particularly Gen. George McClellan. The patient President, however, obligingly adapted his schedule to visit the War Department daily to review messages personally.

By that time, Union leaders realized the need for sending messages in code. The first simple cipher was worked out by Gen. Anson Stager and gradually refined. Stanton, zealous to keep control of the secret code, would not allow even President Lincoln to use it.

Though domineering, Stanton was careful not to accept plaudits that belonged to others, or grasp for honors that might be misunderstood. At one particularly encouraging moment in the war, Horace Greeley used his *New York Tribune* to praise Stanton. Recognizing that field generals might take offense at the excessive adulation, Stanton wrote the editor that glory belonged to God and the soldiers. His expressions of gratitude to God were genuine and consistent throughout his life.

Even though occasionally lauded, no man was more hated than Edwin Stanton. To this day, the overbearing Secretary is most often pictured as a selfish autocrat. Autocrat he was; selfish he was not. He was both cruel and tender, both extremely courageous and yet, occasionally, cowardly. He deserved his reputation for unbending incorruptibility, yet there were times when he appeared to be inconsistent. He was, like most men, complex and contradictory.

Stanton's enemies claimed he was a coward who bowed to generals and yelled at corporals. This was not entirely true. He yelled at everybody, most of all at generals, and occasionally even at presidents. He was constantly at odds with General McClellan and was accused of undercutting McClellan's position and spreading doubts about the General's loyalty. Stanton may have used poor judgment, but he undoubtedly felt he was doing his duty.

When Gen. J. M. Schofield commandeered a hospital ship for his personal use, Stanton did not hesitate to take it away and later oppose his promotion on the basis of Schofield's "irregularity." Gen. Lucius Fairchild, who became governor of Wisconsin, told of an occasion at Fredricksburg, Virginia, when he felt it necessary to return to his home state for a few days. Stanton briskly refused his request. The General, although provoked, remarked later that Stanton was a man with "a big heart, bent on doing his duty thoroughly, no matter who suffered; but it seemed to me his head was harder than his heart."[5]

Stanton was one in authority who made no financial gain from the war. He was also among the few who seldom allowed his heart to influence his decisions. Although not always successful, Stanton tried to be impartial. When his sister, Oella, sought a favored position for her son, Benjamin Tappan, Jr., he surprised his nephew by casually turning down the request.

The burden carried by the Secretary of War during the critical days of the rebellion was heavier than many realized. Politicians, even of his own party, complained of his conduct; generals grumbled and his few friends often failed to understand him; he did not seem to care. No man, not even Lincoln, labored harder. Those close to Stanton knew that he often slept overnight in his office, frequently working until two or three in the morning and taking only a brief rest before starting again. He was seldom seen outside the drab War Department building, seeming to spend both day and night attending to duties. His office, unlike the polished elegant suites of later Cabinet members, was simple and unadorned.

While receiving visitors, he usually stood behind a long, high desk, facing the entrance to his office. There was no pretense of privacy—anyone could approach him, but he did not hesitate to dismiss an unworthy request with a simple "no." Stanton performed the almost inhuman task of hearing hundreds of petitions and making as many crucial judgments every day. "He was opinionated, almost immovable in his judgments; yet absolutely just," according to Noah Brooks, a Washington reporter familiar with political life in the capital.[6]

A flaw often mentioned was Stanton's admiration of power. He used his power to control those under him, and he respected those he felt could exercise power over him. Edward Bates, who served as Attorney General in Lincoln's Cabinet, wrote that the Secretary of War "believes in mere force, so long as he wields it, but cowers before it, when wielded by any other hand."[7] His indifference to both President Lincoln and President Johnson was likely due to Stanton's feeling that they were not really powerful men. If Stanton was free from greed of money, he was not entirely free from greed of power, a trait that made him resentful of the increasing importance of others. His attitude toward General Sherman was dictated in part by this trait. General Grant, on the other hand, was too strong for the Secretary to handle. He was one of few men Stanton refrained from challenging, and even in Grant's case, the War Secretary did not always back down. It was only after Grant had risen to General-in-Chief of the Armies that Stanton fully acknowledged him.

When Grant was a relatively insignificant commander fighting in Tennessee, he needed the key to the secret cipher. The telegraph operator refused to turn it over, saying that Secretary Stanton had ordered him to give it to no one—not even to generals. With his customary stubbornness, Grant threatened to discipline him if he did not hand over the key immediately. The operator reluctantly submitted. When Stanton heard of the incident, he severely reprimanded the operator and dismissed him from his position. However, General Grant intervened on behalf of the hapless man, who he said was only following his orders.[8] This ended the affair, and, with a few minor exceptions, the stern Secretary never tangled with General Grant again.

Gideon Welles, Lincoln's Secretary of the Navy, expressed concern at Stanton's apparent effort to usurp President Lincoln's authority. In a Cabinet meeting only a few hours before the President's assassination, Stanton proposed, that as Secretary of War, he would issue an order reopening trade with the South, and that he would also issue orders concerning which ships were to be permitted to reenter Southern ports. Secretary Welles, recognizing that Stanton was pushing his authority over that of the President, objected, explaining that any orders to be issued should be made by the President of the United States.

After four years of devastating war, in which constitutional guarantees had given way to military rule, any Secretary of War would have acquired enormous authority. But Stanton's personality made his position stronger than even these wartime emergencies would demand, and he required absolute obedience. Grant, in comparing Lincoln to Stanton, noted that the two were opposites. Lincoln gained influence over men by "making them feel that it was a pleasure to serve him. . . . He hated to disappoint people." Grant described Stanton as caring nothing for the feelings of others. In fact, it seemed to be pleasanter to him to disappoint than to gratify.[9]

The first Cabinet meeting of Johnson's administration. This meeting, held the day following Lincoln's death, was clearly dominated by Stanton. The Secretary of War is shown standing—apparently instructing the sitting President. (Drawn by Albert Berghaus, Library of Congress—USZ62-4597.)

Grant corroborated the opinion of others that Stanton often assumed the authority of President Lincoln without advising him. This remained his attitude toward President Johnson. The only effective way to deal with Stanton was to stand up to him, as both General Sherman and President Johnson belatedly learned.

At no other time in American history has the military had the power and the excuse to take over the Government as it did on April 15, 1865. One part of the Nation had been subdued militarily by the other, and the most powerful leaders in the country were military officers. Stanton was in absolute control for at least three weeks following the assassination. President Johnson remained, discreetly, in the background. Stanton controlled all official communications; even confidential messages to other Cabinet members were passed through his hands. He was the most persuasive and powerful member of the Cabinet. Gideon Welles noted that during those calamitous days Stanton took charge, directing even the most insignificant affairs of state, frequently without consulting other members of the Cabinet, Congress or even the President.

In the Cabinet meeting Sunday morning after Lincoln's death, Stanton was already armed with papers and suggestions on how to deal with the Rebels. That same evening the Secretary of the Navy, while visiting the War Department, accidentally stumbled into a meeting Stanton had arranged with leading members of the Senate in which the Secretary of War was setting forth his Reconstruction plans.[10]

Horatio King, Postmaster General when Lincoln became President, knew Stanton well. King admitted that Stanton "did not hesitate to speak contemptuously of Mr. Lincoln and that, not infrequently, while a member of his Cabinet, his bearing toward the President was highly disrespectful...."[11] But King added that this was Stanton's attitude toward others. Stanton was known as the "Great War Secretary"; King wrote that he would not detract from that title.

The relationship between Lincoln and Stanton was remarkable. The men were almost totally different in temperament but surprisingly similar in their dedication to the war effort. Evan Jones, biographer of Stanton and Lincoln, wrote that "if there lived a man whom Lincoln loved, it was Stanton."[12] Because of their respective positions, the interchange was greater between the two than between the President and any other Cabinet member. Lincoln seemed to see beyond Stanton's sternness and appreciated his attention to duty. Lincoln's respect for Stanton's abilities, which complemented his own, developed into admiration if not intimate friendship.

On the eve of his second inauguration, Lincoln reviewed a dispatch from General Grant indicating that Lee was willing to consider a peace proposal. The President was in favor of letting Grant begin negotiations favorable to the South. Stanton opposed the meeting on the grounds that the war was practically over, and the only treaty acceptable was absolute surrender. In addition, Stanton strongly opposed allowing generals on the field to negotiate peace terms, which he believed was strictly the prerogative of the President. He admonished Lincoln flatly that, the next day being inauguration day, it would be better for him not to be inaugurated unless he intended to be President.

Lincoln agreed. He advised Grant not to meet with Lee unless the latter was prepared for complete surrender. This same attitude later brought Stanton into conflict with General Sherman. Although the Secretary of War was zealous in defending the President against ambitious generals, he had no qualms against assuming Lincoln's authority for himself.

President Lincoln had the wondrous ability to work in harmony with men totally different from himself. There was never any real conflict between the Secretary of War and the President according to David Bates. As manager of the War Deparment telegraph office located next to Stanton's office, Bates saw President Lincoln once or twice a day throughout the war. "It suited both to treat the public, each in his own characteristic way," Bates noted. "And when in case the pinch came, each knew how far to yield to the other without sacrifice of prerogative."[13] He illustrated this harmony by recounting their reactions to a cotton speculator who wanted to overrule Stanton's orders prohibiting the purchase of Confederate cotton. In May 1864, the merchant, a prominent man, told the President that the cotton had already been paid for, and he only wanted permission to get it through Union lines. After a long discussion, Lincoln gave the entrepreneur a note introducing him to Stanton and suggested that he see the Secretary of War about the problem. Stanton indignantly tore up the note, threw it in the wastebasket and curtly informed the merchant that War Department orders would not be abrogated. The speculator rushed back to the Presidential Mansion and reported Stanton's disrespect for the President's note.

"Did he do that?" responded Lincoln. "Well, that's just like Stanton."[14]

The President usually accepted Stanton's advice in issuing pardons, raises and promotions. On one occasion, the son of a longtime Lincoln friend sought a favored army position. Congressmen George W. Julian of Indiana and Owen Lovejoy of Illinois got the President to endorse the application and took it to Stanton, who refused it. The Congressmen insisted that Lincoln wanted the man to have the position, to which Stanton replied that he did not care what the President wanted, adding, "The country wants the very best it can get, I am serving the country." The Congressmen returned to the President with their complaints. Lincoln replied without hesitation, "Gentlemen, it is my duty to submit. I cannot add to Mr. Stanton's troubles. His position is one of the most difficult in the world."[15]

Lincoln not only respected his Secretary of War, but hesitated to thwart him. Noah Brooks noted that the President disliked to contradict or interfere with Stanton if he could avoid it. Mrs. Winfield Hancock, wife of the General, told of special passes signed by Lincoln, permitting individuals to cross into enemy territory, that were ignored by Stanton. In talking to a guard in Alexandria, Virginia, she was told that it was not unusual for Stanton to invalidate the President's passes. When Lincoln signed a pass that the Secretary disapproved of, Stanton would simply telegraph the guard to destroy it. When Mrs. Hancock complained to Stanton about his arbitrary actions, he answered casually that she should have told President Lincoln.[16]

His practice of signing an order with one hand and countermanding it with the other was considered by his critics as worse than hypocrisy. Not only did he order guards to ignore President Lincoln's passes, he occasionally instructed them to reverse his own orders.

The Secretary of War used his power widely against political offenders. The War Department arrested more than 13,000 persons for political reasons. Many were held arbitrarily without knowing the charges against them.[17]

The brusque Secretary did not have many genuine friends. Even though the President trusted and admired him, Lincoln hardly considered him an intimate friend. Certainly, Stanton did not consider Lincoln so. Charles Dana came as close to being a friend as Stanton had in Government circles. Dana was not blind to his superior's weaknesses, but he recognized Stanton's outstanding qualities. Dana had opportunity to observe Stanton's intense nature, his energy and his almost superhuman attention to duty. He understood that Stanton's efforts made the War Department relatively free of corruption and that he infused the armies with greater determination.

Dana was impressed by Stanton's deep religious nature, his knowledge of the Bible and his conviction that the Lord was directing his armies. Whatever may be said of his faults, he genuinely felt that he was an instrument of God.

Edwin M. Stanton. The powerful, incorruptible Secretary of War performed efficiently and honestly in time of National crisis. After a lifetime in high Government positions, he died in debt. (Photo by Brady, Library of Congress — USZ62-40603.)

Stanton's religion was as "real to him as the principles of his business," according to Dana.[18]

James Blaine, a longtime political leader and frequent Republican presidential aspirant, recognized Stanton's weaknesses but also found something to praise. He acknowledged that Stanton was "at all times and under all circumstances absolutely free from corruption and was savagely hostile to every man in the military service who was even suspected of irregularity or wrong."[19] Apparently Stanton wanted to project this image. Some acquaintances, however, hinted this was not entirely true.

Lincoln's friend, Orville Browning, was often in conflict with Stanton. Browning told of an incident in which he tried repeatedly to get a man named Maddox out of a Baltimore prison and was unsuccessful until "Mrs. Maddox paid somebody $1,600.00 and Maddox went home." Browning naturally suspected "foul play and corruption." Three days before Lincoln's assassination he told Stanton about the payoff, thinking the incorruptible Secretary would be interested. Instead, Stanton seemed unimpressed and even "a little crusty in his manner."[20] This inference that the War Secretary might have condoned a bribe contradicts all that is known of his character.

More typical of Stanton's nature was a confrontation he had with civic leaders from Baltimore in 1864. The War Department had allowed a double agent to operate as a blockade-runner between Baltimore and Richmond. The agent would stop in Washington and allow the War Department to inspect material he carried to Virginia. On one trip authorities noticed the spy was also carrying prohibited military goods. The War Department had bills showing where these contraband articles had been purchased. Valued at about $25,000, they were confiscated, and the double agent put in prison. Stanton then ordered the arrest of all merchants involved. Officers were apprehensive because the arrests might involve more than a hundred of Baltimore's most distinguished citizens. Nevertheless, the undaunted Secretary of War insisted. The next day nearly one hundred leading citizens were arrested, brought to Washington and placed in solitary cells in Old Capitol Prison. It caused the expected uproar. Union citizens in Baltimore applauded the arrests, but Southern sympathizers denounced them and sent a delegation to President Lincoln demanding that the merchants be released immediately and damages paid them. Lincoln sent the delegation to the Secretary of War.

The men, including bank presidents, wealthy merchants, the powerful and the rich, marched over to the War Department. Stanton was ready. He cordially invited the group to sit down around the fire in his office and gave each an opportunity to speak. After listening patiently, Stanton delivered an eloquent denunciation. Describing the election of Lincoln, the war, the suffering and loss of half a million soldiers, he went on to condemn the merchants' greed in sending illegal contraband to the enemy. He added that if anyone wanted to see the bills, he had them on the table before him. When he finished, the delegation got up without a word and left the office. They never complained again.[21]

Lincoln sometimes alleviated the pressures of office by telling little stories or jokes. Stanton had no such relief mechanism. He could not joke or even respond to the President's small talk. Lincoln was the only person who dared speak lightly to the gloomy Secretary. The President, knowing Stanton's dedication to the war effort, sometimes called him "Mars." While Stanton did not object, he never responded happily to the playful sobriquet.

Stanton grieved genuinely at Lincoln's death. The man he had once called a gorilla, he had come to regard as the most perfect ruler of men.

One longtime friend of Stanton, Alexander Johnson, a member of the District of Columbia Supreme Court, observed that no man so widely known as Stanton was actually so little known. Another friend predicted that "some day it will become history, that a leading characteristic of Edwin M. Stanton was charity . . . ." Admitting that Stanton was brusque in both his personal and professional contacts, he believed that "no man was ever possessed of more of human sympathy or had more of the milk of human kindness."[22]

In spite of this prediction, Stanton is not remembered for his charity, but rather for arbitrariness and rudeness.

VI
"... Find the Murderer"

After Charles Dana recovered from the shock of Lincoln's death, he remembered a letter from Gen. John A. Dix. The General, Commander of the Department of the East, had written from New York City about a lady named Hudspeth. The woman had reported overhearing a suspicious conversation between two men on the Third Avenue car. When the horse-drawn car jolted to a stop, she noticed false whiskers on one man and a pistol tucked in his belt. She heard the other say he was going to Washington the next day. When they left, her daughter picked up two letters they had apparently dropped. After reading the letters, Mrs. Hudspeth took them to Gen. Winfield Scott, who, impressed, sent her to General Dix.

Dix concluded that one was fake, but the other, written in delicate penmanship, appeared to be genuine. He turned them over to Dana. After first reading them, Dana took them to President Lincoln. The President examined both letters, but made no comment. He gave the impression that he did not consider them important.

On the day Lincoln died, these curious epistles took on new significance. When Stanton was reminded of the circumstances surrounding the letters, he dispatched Dana to the White House to look for them. As Lincoln had received many communications, including numerous threats, there seemed little chance of retrieving the five-month-old documents. Nevertheless, Dana searched the late President's office and private desk. Apparently Lincoln had considered the letters more serious than he pretended, because Dana found them in an envelope labeled, in Lincoln's penmanship, "assassination."[1]

The contents of one letter, addressed to "Dear Louis," deserved scrutiny.

> The time has at last come that we have all so wished for, and upon you everything depends. As it was decided before you left, we were to cast lots. Accordingly we did so, and you are to be the Charlotte Corday of the nineteenth century. When you remember the fearful, solemn vow that was taken by us, you will feel there is no drawback—Abe must die, and now. You can choose your weapons. The cup, the knife, the bullet. The cup failed us once, and might again. Johnson, who will give [you] this, has been like an enraged demon since the meeting, because it has not fallen upon him to rid the world of the monster.
>
> . . . .
>
> Your disguises are so perfect and complete that without one knew your face no police telegraphic dispatch would catch you. The English gentleman

45

"Harcourt" must not act hastily. Remember he has ten days. Strike for your home, strike for your country; bide your time, but strike sure. Get introduced, congratulate him, listen to his stories—not many more will the brute tell to earthly friends. Do anything but fail, and meet us at the appointed place within a fortnight. Enclose this note, together with one of poor Leenea. I will give reason for this when we meet. Return by Johnson. I wish I could go to you, but duty calls me to the West; you will probably hear from me in Washington. Sanders is doing us no good in Canada.

Believe me, your brother in love,
Charles Selby[2]

General Dix thought this letter was "a manufacture." The other, in a woman's handwriting, seemed genuine:

St. Louis, October 21, 1864

Dearest Husband: Why do you not come home? You left me for ten days only, and you now have been from home more than two weeks. In that long time you only sent me one short note—a few cold words—and a check for money, which I did not require. . . .

. . . .

As a last resource, yesterday I wrote to Charlie, begging him to see you and tell you to come home. I am so ill, not able to leave my room; if I was, I would go to you wherever you were, if in this world. Mama says I must not write any more, as I am too weak. Louis, darling, do not stay away any longer from your heart-broken wife.

Leenea[3]

Dana, not certain that the letters were particularly revealing, kept them a few days, then gave them to John Bingham, who was working on the case. Bingham thought them extremely important and requested Dix to locate Mrs. Hudspeth and send her to Washington.

The General found the lady keeping a small store in New York City. As a widow with several young children she had no convenient way to make the trip to Washington. Nevertheless, after a few days, she arrived in the capital. On being shown a photograph of Booth, she identified him as one of the men she had seen. Additional checking of dates also showed that Booth had been in New York on November 11 (the day Gen. Benjamin Butler left the city, which was the time Mrs. Hudspeth remembered finding the letters). Hotel records revealed that Booth left New York for Washington the next day, as the lady had reported five months earlier. News reporters generally ridiculed the epistles as frauds; their genuineness remains uncertain.

As soon as they obtained horses, Holohan, Weichmann and police detectives McDevitt, Bigley and Clarvoe set out to search for Booth. They stopped briefly at Mrs. Surratt's boardinghouse for Weichmann to change clothes. He then led detectives to Naylor's Livery Stable, which he knew Booth had used frequently. They found that on the night of the murder a young man named David Herold had rented a horse there. Weichmann then escorted police to the studio where John Surratt had photographs made and obtained a picture of him.

Weichmann knew David Herold and suggested that they go to Herold's house, but he first had to get directions from Dr. Walsh, a druggist for whom Herold had worked. Arriving at the house near the Navy Yard, they asked Mrs. Herold if her son was in. The woman, a widow, had known that her only son had been running around with unwholesome friends, among them, John Wilkes Booth. She admitted sadly that David had failed to return home the night before. Mrs. Herold revealed that she had not seen her son since Friday and gave detectives a picture of him from the family album.[4]

David E. Herold was born in Washington, D.C., the son of George Herold, who, for more than twenty years, was the chief clerk at the Navy Store at the Washington Navy Yard. David's father died less than a year before the assassination. David was described by many as "trifling"; perhaps "spoiled" would have been more accurate. He loved horses and hunting, accompanying his father on frequent hunting trips into Virginia.

Herold finished his public schooling in Washington then attended Georgetown College, after which he was employed by a druggist. After his father's death, he quit work and spent most of his time in the country. His mother and several sisters were members of Christ Episcopal Church at the Navy Yard. David seldom, if ever, took any interest in religious matters. He did not drink, however, until a few months before the murder.

Major Gleason had been detained at General Augur's headquarters most of the night. Towards morning he was allowed to go back to his room but got little sleep. He was anxious to get down to his office at the Commissary General of Prisoners, where he had a desk next to Weichmann's. At the office he found more excitement and confusion. The major was disappointed that Weichmann had not yet come to work. Finally about ten o'cock, Weichmann arrived, accompanied by a cavalry officer, to borrow a pair of riding boots.

At midday the police, guided by Weichmann, galloped off across Navy Bridge. They were headed for Surrattsville, a little crossroads village composed of three or four modest houses including the country home of Mrs. Mary Surratt which she rented to John Lloyd. The men had been delayed because of difficulty getting horses. By the time they reached Surrattsville, soldiers under the direction of the War Department had already searched the area and had questioned Lloyd. He had denied vehemently that Booth or anyone else had stopped at the house. Soldiers were already questioning other inhabitants beyond Surrattsville and making a routine check of every house on roads leading from Washington.[5]

The alarmed Lloyd, having already been interrogated, had his answers ready for police. He swore to McDevitt that he knew nothing about the assassination and that no one had come by the house. Police officers then proceeded down the road toward Piscataway, passing close by the house of a doctor named Samuel Mudd.

At this time Herold and Booth were sleeping in a second-story bedchamber in Dr. Mudd's house. Seward's attacker was hiding in a cedar tree on the outskirts of Washington, afraid to move. Atzerodt was making his way to his brother-in-law's house in Maryland, and John Surratt was in upper New York on his way to Canada.

Friends often described David Herold as "trifling"; this picture reenforces that impression (Library of Congress).

That afternoon when police, led by Weichmann, reached Charles County, Maryland, the entire area was swarming with soldiers and detectives. After several hours of searching, having found no evidence that Booth had passed that way, the discouraged police returned to Washington. Weichmann then suggested that they check the Pennsylvania House where Atzerodt had occasionally lodged.[6]

The War Department concentrated its search south of Washington. An important center in the area was Bryantown, Maryland, about 30 miles south of the capital. Dr. Mudd's house stood only a few miles away. What little evidence officers had, led them to believe the fugitives must be in the area of Bryantown. They rode up and down the country lanes but did not search Mudd's place that first crucial day.

About 3:00 that afternoon Mudd left his house headed toward Bryantown. The doctor was looking for a wagon to help his two night visitors on their way. He paused briefly at his father's house and then proceeded on to the small village which was buzzing with soldiers and locals speculating about the terrible events. Mudd stopped at Bean's store and bought a piece of calico.[7] Bean was not certain that Booth was the President's assassin, but his name was frequently mentioned by excited crowds. The merchant naturally discussed the assassination with the doctor. Exactly what was said is not known, but by that hour it was generally acknowledged in Bryantown that the assassin had been traced to the surrounding area and that one of the suspects was John Wilkes Booth.

Booth and Herold had arrived at Mudd's farmhouse at 4:00 in the morning, heavily armed. They carried a rifle, ammunition, several pistols, knives, a compass and field glasses. Obviously they were not innocent wayfarers.

During his stay at Mudd's, Booth began to write an explanation of his actions in an outdated diary he used as a notebook. He dated the entry April 14, Friday (although it was Saturday morning – the 15th), and penciled several pages of emotional self-justification:

> Until today nothing was ever *thought* of sacrificing to our country's wrongs. For six months we had worked to capture. But, our cause being almost lost, something decisive and great must be done. But its failure was owing to others, who did not strike for their country with a heart.[8]

These first few lines indicated Booth's understanding of his crime. He had planned to capture the enemy leader in time of war. Exactly what failure he alluded to was never determined. At this time he could not have known that Secretary of State Seward was alive. Very likely he was aware that no one had attacked General Grant, or Vice-President Johnson. Evidently sometime on Saturday he saw a newspaper. Booth later continued his self-justification, although inaccurately.

> I struck boldly and not as the papers say. I walked with a firm step through a thousand of his friends, was stopped, but pushed on. A colonel was at his side. I shouted *sic semper before* I fired. In jumping broke my leg. I passed all his pickets, rode 60 miles that night with the bone of my leg tearing the flesh at every jump. I can never repent it. Though we hated to kill, our country owed all her troubles to him, and God simply made me the instrument of his punishment. The country is not what it was. This forced Union is not what I have loved.[9]

Booth then referred to a "long article" he had left to be published in a Washington paper. This document, explaining his actions, was never printed. For days Booth searched newspapers for it in vain.

Booth and Herold left Mudd's house soon after the doctor returned from Bryantown. In the midst of hundreds of searching soldiers, the two men found a hiding place in a nearby swamp.

Louis Weichmann, Surratt's schoolmate and boarder in the Surratt house. He became both a suspect and the chief witness against the conspirators. (Sketch from a contemporary photograph.)

Booth's diary did not explain how he assured the President's attendance at the theater, but his presence was not accidental. Booth had schemed for days to get Lincoln to the play. No one could have known for certain on April 13 that Abraham Lincoln would attend Ford's Theatre the next night. Yet, plans for the murder were taking definite shape on the 13th with Booth making several deliberate decisions. He sent George Atzerodt to lodge at the Kirkwood House. Significantly, Atzerodt did not have reservations for the night of the 14th because he was to flee after completing his assignment to kill Vice-President Johnson.

"Satan Tempting Booth to Murder the President." This imaginary scene involved an important issue — just when did Booth alter the plot from capture to murder, if ever (Library of Congress — USZ62-8933).

In addition, on April 13, he addressed a letter to the *Washington Intelligencer* explaining his planned crime. Although this letter was not given to his friend, John Matthews, until Booth was sure of the President's intentions to see the play, it was written the night before. Late on the night of the 13th, Booth also wrote to his mother accounting for his intentions. Thus, the assassin made several moves in anticipation of his crime some eight to twelve hours before Lincoln himself had decided to attend the theater.

Other preparations had gone into setting up the murder at Ford's Theatre. Booth had arranged for his friends to occupy the President's box on two previous occasions. He also had a horse stabled behind the theater. Booth seemed determined to commit the deed at Ford's.

In case the President did not attend the play, *Our American Cousin*, Booth had suggested to the management of Grover's Theatre that they put on "some exciting play and invite the President on Friday evening."[10] In fact, the President's young son, Tad, did see the presentation at Grover's.

Just how much pressure was put on the President will probably never be known. Obviously Booth urged the management of Ford's to have the President there, although they denied they ever invited Lincoln.

The stage was definitely set for murder at Ford's Theatre. Someone had

bored a hole in the door of Lincoln's box and had carved a niche in the wall to secure the brace and had carefully covered his handiwork. The brace, a yard-long wooden bar, had been conveniently placed in the hallway before the play started. Booth also knew how to jump from the box. He prided himself on his gymnastic abilities and had introduced a similar jump onto the stage when doing the witch's scene in *Macbeth*.[11] He had previously examined both boxes 7 and 8, which were joined into one when used by the President. The hinges on the door to the box had also been loosened so that it would not stay locked.

Usually the presidential box was decorated with two American flags, but on this night, the theater management made a slight change. When it was thought that General Grant would accompany the President, Henry Clay Ford, decorating the area (the workman usually in charge was sick), thought of adding a picture of George Washington under the box and placing another flag around the picture. Ford sent to the Treasury Department for a third flag. The additional treasury flag proved Booth's downfall; as he jumped, he caught his spur in it, causing him to break his leg (more accurately a small bone in his foot).

Gradually, bits and pieces of the plot came to light. Metro police were told by a black man, John Miles, that he had seen Booth enter the back of Ford's Theatre before the shooting and had heard him call for Edward Spangler. Police then questioned Spangler again. The interrogation, as most conducted by the police, was held in the presence of Justice Abram B. Olin of the Supreme Court of the District of Columbia.

Spangler was a vulgar sort, not very bright, but generally considered harmless. Questioning revealed that he had known the actor and had worked for the Booth family. Four hours before the murder, Booth left his horse, ready to mount in Spangler's care. On searching Spangler's modest room in the theater, police found a long, suspicious-looking rope in his trunk, which he could not satisfactorily explain.[12]

Superintendent Richards and Justice Olin continued their investigation independently of the War Department. Richards had been given the spur which Booth caught in the flag. In his effort to identify the spur, Richards questioned James Pumphrey, owner of a livery stable sometimes used by the assassin. Pumphrey identified the spur as belonging to Booth. He added that the actor often came to the stable with a man named Surratt, whose mother kept a boardinghouse. Although Richards' men had already searched the house, Pumphrey's statement further confirmed their suspicions.[13]

Through intensive interrogation of known Southern sympathizers, detectives linked John Surratt with James Judson Jarboe (alias Smith), who was known to have been a courier in the Rebel mail service. Investigation showed

Opposite, top: This steep stairway led from the Ford's Theatre lobby to the dress circle. Several witnesses noticed Booth going up the stairs to the dress circle. Bottom: As Booth moved along the back wall toward the President's box, several spectators had to adjust their chairs in order for him to pass.

Top: The assassination as seen through the eyes of a Currier and Ives artist (Library of Congress—USZ62-2073). Bottom: The assassin jumping to the stage and catching his spur in a flag. (Drawing by A. Berghaus, "Frank Leslie's Illustrated Newspaper," May 6, 1865. Library of Congress—USZ62-6934.)

Jarboe had been in Washington the week of the assassination. He boarded in the house of Sallie Tretter, also a Rebel supporter, who housed Confederate sympathizers. He and the other boarders were arrested and interrogated, but nothing was proved against them.[14]

During the agitation and growing confusion in Washington, James and Henry Clay Ford took time to telegraph Joseph H. Simonds in Franklin, Pennsylvania, informing him of the assassination. There was no apparent reason for the Ford brothers to have known about Simonds and no urgent reason for them to have informed him of the President's death.

One cover used by the conspirators was "oil business." Booth had actually been engaged in business with Joseph H. Simonds and Company, a real estate firm that dealt in oil property around Franklin. During the winter of 1864–65, Booth abandoned the business to give full attention to the conspiracy. Simonds wrote Booth on February 21, 1865, that he did not understand why the actor was "so different from your usual self. Have you lost all your ambition or what is the matter?" Simonds claimed that Booth could have made money in oil, adding "that staying around Washington, doing nothing, must be expensive."[15]

Booth, however, was doing *something,* and it was expensive. For most of the winter months, with little personal income, Booth managed to live handsomely and support five or six others. Someone or some group must have been backing him financially at this time. His few appearances on the stage provided little income.

Col. H. H. Wells' examination of John Greenawalt, owner of the Pennsylvania House, provided more clues. He readily admitted that a man named Atzerodt had stayed at the hotel. Atzerodt's name had not yet been widely associated with the murder, but Greenawalt's statements brought him under suspicion. Although Atzerodt had no employment, he kept two horses at Naylor's Livery Stable. Greenawalt bought one for $140. Atzerodt kept the other horse, which was blind in one eye. This one-eyed horse continued to weave a thread through the fabric of the conspiracy. Greenawalt revealed that Booth had visited Atzerodt ten or twelve times at the hotel. He also mentioned another young man living near the Navy Yard who had visited Atzerodt. Detectives soon identified this individual as David Herold. Greenawalt stated that Atzerodt, under the influence of alcohol, had bragged that he was going to make lots of money—enough to last the rest of his life.[16]

Evidence accumulated that Booth planned to implicate both Atzerodt and Sam Arnold in the crime. Not only did he plant Arnold's incriminating letter in his trunk, but he apparently rigged Atzerodt's room at the Kirkwood House. Atzerodt carried his own knife and pistol with him when he left, but detectives found another bowie knife and a pistol, loaded and capped, hidden in the bed. Why would Atzerodt have left these suspicious articles? Police also found a map of Virginia and Herold's coat hanging in the room with a checkbook in the pocket. In the checkbook was written, "Mr. J. Wilkes Booth, in account with the Ontario Bank, Canada, 1864, October 27—By deposit credited $455." These incriminating articles obviously did not belong to Atzerodt. He seemed to realize later that he had been set up by Booth and Herold.

The *Washington Star*'s Saturday evening edition printed more details of the crime. Booth's activities and his talk about "oil business," as well as the recent sale of his horses and buggy, were reported to an anxious public. The paper published some of Arnold's letter in conjunction with comments which seemed to link the conspiracy to Confederate leaders: "[it] appears from a letter found in Booth's trunk that the murder was planned before the 4th of March but fell through because the accomplice backed out until Richmond could be heard from." The *Star* noted that authorities had arrested Spangler and that John Surratt was suspected of the attack on Seward. It reported that Surratt was from Prince Georges County and that the conspiracy probably originated in Maryland. For years police had branded Surratt "a desperado of the worst character," and a suit had been brought against him by a young lady for seduction, according to the reporter.

While news of the tragedy was known immediately in cities throughout the North, it took several days to reach many isolated areas of the South. The morning after the assassination, Robert E. Lee rode through the rubble of Richmond toward his old residence. The Confederate hero tried to be unobtrusive, but citizens recognized him, and a large crowd gathered. Lee passed quickly through the throng, pausing briefly to shake outstretched hands as he entered his house. Apparently, word of Lincoln's death had not yet reached the ravaged capital of the Old Confederacy. John Ford, who was visiting Richmond at the time of the murder, said that he did not hear the news until Sunday.

The previous day LaFayette Baker heard of the assassination while in his room at the Astor House. He had gone to New York to investigate frauds in the recruiting service. At noon, April 15, he received a telegram from Stanton: "Come here immediately and see if you can find the murderer of the President."[17]

Baker, an adventurous 38-year-old detective, was a slender, agile man of average height. A heavy brown beard and mustache accented his face. Unusually deep-set, piercing gray eyes gave him what he imagined to be a cold, terrifying expression which intimidated witnesses. Actually, while many people hated Baker for his arrogant deceptiveness, few really feared him. Yet he possessed some qualities that made him a good detective—he was an excellent marksman, a good horseman and sure of himself. He did not drink, and avoided profanity. But Baker was egotistical, ambitious, and not entirely trustworthy. His aggressive concern for his own advantage kept him from being really likable.

After an amazing cloak-and-dagger episode in Richmond during which he succeeded in interviewing Jefferson Davis and collecting valuable information for the Union, Baker was named the first head of the Bureau of Secret Service under the direction of the War Department. This man was to play a major role in the investigation.

VII
Easter Sunday, 1865

Strong Rebel sympathies in Washington hampered the investigation and occasionally fomented violence. Before the Civil War, both Baltimore and Washington were essentially Southern cities, their customs and social life derived from leading Maryland and Virginia families, related through decades of intermarriage. Their semifeudal civilization was based on slavery. The established Washington families were generally secessionists and prone to aid the Southern cause. Rarely, however, were these sentiments made public. Only among trusted associates were such feelings voiced. Yet after four years of war the persuasions of most citizens were generally known.

Southern sympathizers in Washington had at least three secret meeting places where letters could be delivered and information exchanged. One rendezvous was the home of Mrs. Philip Phillips, another on 7th near E Street and a third at the Georgetown home of Miss Annie Matthews. Washington police knew of these places and could easily have broken up the meetings, but it was deemed more profitable to infiltrate the groups. Although not all efforts were successful, some were. As a result, several Rebel mail carriers were captured, including Miss D. M. Dietz of Alexandria, Virginia.[1] Washington authorities knew well the ability of Southern women to serve the Rebel cause.

In the first years of the war, Federal Government employees and Union soldiers were required to take an oath of allegiance to the Constitution. But President Lincoln continued to be troubled by the many Southern sympathizers living in the Nation's capital and working in all departments of Government.

On August 6, 1861, the Federal Government created a Metropolitan police force in Washington to help deal with security as well as to keep order. Growing concern about Confederate agents in Government positions caused Congress to pass a more explicit oath of allegiance. The oath was required of the mayors of Georgetown and Washington. Georgetown's mayor willingly took the oath, but Mayor Berret of Washington refused. He was arrested and imprisoned until he was willing to swear allegiance. In the meantime, a new mayor, Richard Wallach, was selected. He was a brother of the owner and editor of the influential *Washington Evening Star*. Wallach continued as mayor throughout the difficult war period.

In May 1862, the Government required citizens in the District of Columbia to take the loyalty oath as a prerequisite for voting. As the war progressed, many suspected Southern sympathizers either were jailed or had fled the city, yet thousands remained, often engaging in direct aid to the Rebels whenever possible. Lincoln's subsequent suspension of the writ of habeas corpus and the continuing arrests of suspected subversives created further strain among citizens.[2]

When Gen. Jubal Early made his daring raid in 1864, reaching the outskirts of the capital, many residents hoped for a Confederate victory. The Senate reacted by proposing, in December 1864, the requirement of the "iron-clad" loyalty oath for every citizen of the city. These already strong antagonisms became more intense as a result of Lincoln's assassination.

On Easter Sunday, April 16, the awful significance of the President's death seized the Nation. A sense of frustration, coupled with wild threats of vengeance, permeated loyal citizens. One Union officer stated that the South would have to be depopulated and "replaced with another race." Southern sympathizers in Washington were overcome with a palpable fear of retaliatory mob action. The Reverend Mr. Chester preached an inflammatory sermon stating that the President had been killed because he was too lenient on the South. He added happily that the country now had "an avenger who would execute wrath." Crowds continued to gather ominously around Ford's Theatre, gaping at the site of the crime.[3]

When rumors spread that a conspirator had been captured, mobs converged on the scene. A rumor circulated that two of the assassins were being conducted to Provost Marshal Timothy Ingraham's headquarters, nearly causing a riot. A large and excited throng gathered at his door, and officers were barely able to restrain the mob from battering it down. A military guard was promptly ordered to surround the building, and the prisoners were whisked away to Old Capitol Prison in an army ambulance.

Adolphe de Chambrun, a French diplomat living in Washington, wrote to his wife that immediately following the murder, the spirit of vengeance spread like a fire. There were so many shouts and passionate exhortations that de Chambrun feared the Nation would again erupt into violence. "Nothing we have witnessed in Europe can give an idea of what today can be seen and heard in the United States." De Chambrun, who had apparently forgotten the Bastille, mentioned a Rebel general who was almost lynched by the enraged populace as he was brought through the Washington streets. The Frenchman could see that the city was divided in sentiment with so many Copperheads that he feared "blood will flow." He told his wife not to worry about him because he was going to hide in the Prussian Legation in case of an outbreak of violence.[4]

One openly defiant citizen, Lizzie Brow, was arrested for tearing the mourning decorations from her window at a boardinghouse on 12th Street. Brow said she tore down the crepe and flags and threw them out of the window because she did not want her Southern friends to be insulted by such symbols. These demonstrations of disloyalty were quickly dealt with, either by the police or by an aroused public.

Near the Navy Yard a woman named Edwards caused a commotion on Easter Sunday when she made disloyal remarks and decorated her house with a Rebel flag. Police ripped the flag down, and the house was besieged by a frenzied mob. Angry citizens advised the woman that if she made any more demonstrations, they would hang her son, who had just been arrested by military authorities on his return from the Confederate army. She made no further commotion.

A visiting minister, preaching at a mission church near Camp Fry, proclaimed that if President Lincoln's successor should follow in Lincoln's footsteps in his treatment of the South, he, too, would share the same fate. Several members of the Veterans' Reserve Corps spontaneously rushed to the pulpit and thrust the speaker from the church. He was rescued by a Lieutenant Dempsey, who turned the cleric over to Colonel Ingraham. The minister explained that what he really meant to say was that Johnson should not deal as leniently with traitors as Lincoln had.[5]

Although lamentation throughout the North was usually genuine, even there, not everyone grieved. Most who rejoiced over the President's death had the good judgment to remain inconspicuous, but a few could not contain their satisfaction. One man in New York City nearly started a riot when he asked, "Did you hear Abe's last joke?"[6] Another in the same city had to be rescued from a mob by police after expressing a desire to see Lincoln buried. Authorities arrested several men for cursing the late President or expressing joy that he was dead.

New York City was the most violent place, but similar incidents occurred throughout the Nation. A young lady in Saratoga, New York, was expelled from school for saying that the day Lincoln died was the happiest time of her life. In Poughkeepsie, New York, a mob forced a known Southern sympathizer to give three cheers for an American flag. In Cleveland a well-known architect, rejoicing over the assassination, said it had been a good day for him when Lincoln died. A mob chased him from his office, and, when finally caught, he was kicked and beaten until rescued by friends. His name was then chipped from a stone on the courthouse honoring him as its architect.[7]

Fewer Rebels advertised their sympathies as a result of the tensions. Immediately after the shooting, no one wore gray uniforms in public. Many families known to have favored the Confederacy tried to conform—at least outwardly—by draping their houses with mourning black. Most private residences displayed some emblem of sorrow, and places of amusement were closed. Commercial activities and private parties were voluntarily postponed. The Government closed Ford's Theatre until further notice. W. B. Lewis postponed his auction scheduled for the day of the funeral, but it was business as usual for a few merchants. H. A. Hall, for one, continued his closeout sale of "India Rubber Goods."[8]

The city of Richmond was quiet. Shortly before his assassination, Lincoln had discussed the problem involving Richmond's Episcopalian churches, where prayer for the Confederate Government was part of the official ritual. Authorities made an effort to solve the difficulty by issuing General Order Number 29, which required all churches where prayers had previously been offered for the President of the Confederate States to change the words so that the prayers would be offered for the President of the United States. Since many

Hole cut in door to President Lincoln's box.

clergymen would not accept this order, the Episcopalian bishop suggested that it would be acceptable to omit the words "Confederate States," but that the churches need not substitute the words "United States." Feelings were so strong that the military thought it best to close the churches. Thus, on Easter Sunday, 1865, there were no Episcopal services in Richmond.[9]

Judge Olin, who had spent Saturday taking depositions, visited Ford's Theatre on Sunday to examine the scene of the murder thoroughly. He noticed the notch in the wall where the brace had been placed. The Judge looked around for bits of plaster that would have fallen, but they had been cleaned up. Examining the dark hallway from the dress circle to the President's box, Olin found the little hole cut through the door, which seemed to have been carved with a small penknife. Anxious to make certain of the exact location of the chairs in the box, Olin sent for Miss Harris who, escorted by Major Rathbone, had accompanied the President and Mrs. Lincoln. She positioned the chairs as they were at the time of the crime. Olin closed the door and looked through the hole. He could easily see the back of the President's chair. His attention was next attracted by the loose hinges on the door. He discovered that, with his fingers, he could open the door, even when it was locked.

However, the Judge could not find the bar that had braced the outside door shut. Isaac Jaquett had taken it. After helping carry the President from the theater, Jaquett returned to the box and found the blood-spattered wooden bar on the floor. The desire for souvenirs overcame him, and he took the piece home. There he sawed off part of it and gave it to a friend.[10]

While Olin was searching the theater, LaFayette Baker reported to Stanton, who briefed him on the known facts. A year later, when Baker tried to collect the reward money, he insinuated that practically nothing had been accomplished before his arrival, and that it was not until Sunday afternoon that John Surratt became a suspect.[11] Actually Weichmann and the Metro police were preparing for a trip to Canada in pursuit of Surratt before Baker arrived.

Baker did add a professional quality to the investigation and undoubtedly aided in capturing the culprits, although he claimed much more than he actually accomplished. He took credit for suggesting that photographs of the three prime suspects be circulated throughout the country. Records in Government archives indicate that it was Col. Henry Burnett who asked Baker to prepare 50 reward posters with the likenesses of Booth, Surratt and Herold.

It took time to find photographs and to print posters. In the haste, some placards seem to have had the wrong picture for John Surratt. The descriptions of the supposed conspirators were also faulty. The sandy-haired Surratt was described as having dark hair, and David Herold's description was not particularly useful. Among other things, he was described as having small feet with a high instep.

The reward for Booth, identified as the murderer of the President, was approximately $100,000, including $50,000 from the War Department ($75,000 was actually paid); $25,000 was offered for apprehension of John Surratt and $25,000 for David Herold. The notices warned that anyone harboring or aiding the suspects could be tried "before a Military Commission and the punishment of DEATH."

When Baker began his investigation, detectives and soldiers under the direction of General Augur already crowded Washington, and the police department was still conducting its separate operation. In addition, the detective forces of New York, Philadelphia, Boston, Baltimore and other cities were congregating in Washington to aid in the manhunt.

The Government sent for John S. Young, head of the New York detective force, and assigned him to Maj. James O'Beirne's large company of military detectives. Detectives from the Philadelphia police force were assigned to work with Colonel Baker in the area north of Washington. Provost Marshal McPhail, who was well acquainted with citizens of Lower Maryland, joined one of O'Beirne's men named Lloyd, a native of the area, and the two conducted their own intensive search of the region.[12] Approximately 500 independent detectives and private citizens searched for Booth – all, apparently, hoping for reward money. Added to this large number was another military force commanded by Col. H. H. Wells with the assistance of Col. David R. Clendenin.

Baker developed his own leads independently. Soon after arriving in Washington, he received a revealing telegram:

> The following information has just been received from Polk Gardiner, a lad who left Upper Marlborough, Prince Georges County, on Friday night, to come here to see his father, who is dying. On the road, about four miles from Washington, he met a man on a roan horse, who inquired the way to Upper Marlborough, and whether he had seen a man riding rapidly in that direction. About two miles from Washington he met another man, on a bay horse, who also inquired the road to Upper Marlborough, and asked him if he had seen a man riding in that direction. The last named then rode on rapidly. This occurred at eleven o'clock, or a little later.[13]

Baker immediately sent for Gardiner, whose description of the horses corresponded with information previously given by Fletcher. This convinced Baker that Booth was somewhere in Lower Maryland. But by that time, thousands of searchers were already combing the area. A military force, consisting of over a thousand cavalrymen plus the aforementioned detectives and private citizens, had converged on the region. Nevertheless, Baker sent a small group of his own men to investigate and to distribute pictures of the suspects, but after days of futile efforts, they returned empty-handed.

The citizens living south of Washington, where the search was centered, were mostly all Southern sympathizers. Many knew of a plot against Lincoln but refused to reveal anything. Although Baker's detectives were unsuccessful, the army was making progress.

Detectives Daniel Bigley, John Clarvoe and James McDevitt did not report for the eight o'clock roll call at police headquarters on Sunday morning. Instead, accompanied by Holohan and Weichmann (who had stayed at McDevitt's house all night), they traveled to Baltimore in search of Atzerodt or any sign of the conspirators. Baltimore, just 50 miles northeast of the capital, had been a hotbed of Rebel activity. When Lincoln came to Washington for his first inauguration, he passed through Baltimore without fanfare to avoid antagonizing its pro–Southern sentiments. Constant communication and contraband passed between Richmond and Baltimore. In addition to the possibility of finding Atzerodt, the police were closing in on Sam Arnold, whose letter to Booth implicated him. Weichmann also helped McDevitt locate the house of Michael O'Laughlin, who associated with Booth; but O'Laughlin, himself, was not found.

After the search, Weichmann remained in Baltimore Sunday night and returned to Washington early Monday morning. McDevitt reported back to the police station Sunday afternoon. John Holohan also returned Sunday and quickly moved his family out of the Surratt house.[14]

In keeping with Sabbath blue laws, the *Washington Star* and the *Intelligencer*

This photograph of John Surratt replaced a picture of his brother, Isaac, which mistakenly appeared on early reward posters (Library of Congress – BH826-476).

did not publish Sunday editions. By press time Monday morning, a general outline of the crime came into clearer focus. Booth was definitely identified as the assassin, and the *Star* stated positively that the conspirators had escaped across Navy Bridge.

Newspapers throughout the North began to editorialize on the meaning of the President's assassination. James Gordon Bennett's *New York Herald*, as usual, vacillated. Saturday, April 15, the paper printed an editorial opposing the death sentence for Jefferson Davis; then Sunday it strongly recommended severe punishment for the assassins. In an effort to place the blame for the crime, the *Herald* claimed that the culpability lay with publications which had fed the minds of citizens with hatred and ridicule of the President. Although this condemnation was directed primarily against Copperhead newspapers, it applied to all irresponsible reporting:

> . . . that press has, in the most devilish manner, urged men to the commission of this very deed. They who jeered at the first attempt to assassinate Mr. Lincoln, in 1861, and said that it was gotten up to bring odium upon the South; they who coolly advertised that for one hundred thousand dollars Mr.

Lincoln and Mr. Seward could both be killed before the 4th of March; they who thought the attempt to burn this city a very good joke—excellent food for laughter—and they who specifically incited to this murder by their invocation to the dagger of Brutus—they are indeed the real authors of this horrible crime.[15]

At the time pro–Southern papers were being soundly denounced, one of the most notorious offenders, the *Chicago Times*, strongly condemned the murder and expressed hope that Confederate leaders had not been involved. The *Times*, one of Booth's favorite newspapers, would have been no comfort to him. The April 19 edition stated:

At the moment he struck down Mr. Lincoln he also struck himself from existence. There can be no more a J. Wilkes Booth in any country. If caught he will be hanged. If he escapes he must dwell in a solitude. He has the brand of Cain upon his brow . . . an outcast.[16]

Southern newspapers said little about the assassination until several days after the event, partly because Stanton had ordered information of the crime withheld. Even when the Southern press was permitted to print accounts of the murder, it did so timidly.

Metro police still took part in the investigation, although with less support from the military each day. In this period of overlapping responsibilities, Stanton resented any interference. Richards and the Metro Police Department were gradually being pushed aside.

The War Department investigation extended beyond the United States to Canada and even Europe. There was no possibility in a search this extensive and widespread for a cover-up as some supposed. There were human errors, false leads, wrong premises, considerable tensions and many jealousies, but no cover-up. There was no reason for one.

Why the Secretary of War, rather than the new President, some Congressional committee, or the Metro Police Department, should have directed the investigation was mostly a matter of Stanton's assuming leadership. No Government agency such as the Federal Bureau of Investigation existed to take charge. The Washington Police Department was relatively new, understaffed, and in no position to carry out a sweeping nationwide search. The Secretary of War's takeover was natural. The Nation was still technically at war.

Tracking down the conspirators, possibly more than fifty, demanded enormous efforts. The Government used every new device available, the most important of which was the telegraph. The newly developed science of photography was also useful, and a type of truth serum was even suggested for use in interrogations.

In addition to managing the investigation, Stanton was occupied with arrangements for Lincoln's funeral. Lincoln's longtime friend, Orville Browning, and Richard Oglesby, newly elected governor of Illinois, assisted him. Mrs. Lincoln's wish that her husband not be buried at Springfield had to be ignored. Robert Lincoln, supported by several leading citizens from Illinois, went ahead with plans for the eventual transfer of the President's remains to the Illinois capital where he began his political career.

VIII
First Confessions

Secretary of State William Seward was prominent in national politics long before Lincoln's name became widely known. He won the governorship of New York in 1839 and was elected United States Senator in 1849. Seward, a longtime opponent of slavery, supported unsuccessful legislation to give blacks the right to vote. As an early leader in the newly formed Republican party he became the most conspicuous candidate for president in 1860. On the first ballot, Seward received 172½ votes to Lincoln's 102. When Lincoln eventually won the party's nomination, however, Seward worked earnestly for his election. On becoming President, Lincoln appointed him Secretary of State. Seward urged moderation in an unsuccessful attempt to preserve the Union.

Several days after the attacks, Secretary Seward remained uninformed of the President's death or of his son's precarious condition, and he began to wonder why Lincoln did not visit him. Unable to speak, he motioned for pen and paper and wrote, "Why doesn't the President come to see me?"[1] Feeling that it would be worse for him not to know the truth, Seward was told of the assassination and of the attack on his son.

Both the police and the War Department made notable progress on Monday. Superintendent Richards was aware of Stanton's determination to control the investigation, yet he felt a responsibility to check every lead. At this point, Metro police continued to be closer to the facts than the War Department. They were still working with Weichmann, and he could supply more information than all the witnesses gathered by Stanton's forces. Weichmann correctly surmised that John Surratt was in Canada and convinced Richards that he could lead officers to him.

Stanton's soldiers were also following significant leads. On Monday morning Dr. George Mudd reported to the military commander in the Bryantown area that two suspicious persons had visited the residence of his third cousin, Dr. Samuel Mudd. He revealed that his cousin told him at church on Sunday morning about the strange characters. The next day, Tuesday, April 18, authorities sent for George Mudd and interrogated him. Detectives accompanied him to Samuel Mudd's house.[2]

Metro police continued to arrest citizens for disloyalty and on suspicion. Det. John F. Kelly and several patrolmen of the 2nd Ward, following orders of Judge Olin, investigated a house of prostitution run by Mollie Turner, sister

As first head of the Metropolitan Police Department, Almarin C. Richards was directly involved in the assassination investigation. Richards had practically nothing to do with the trial, however, because the military had completely taken over the operation. (Sketch from a contemporary photograph.)

of Booth's girl friend, Ella Turner (also known as Nellie Starr). They arrested all eight of the young women, including Miss Starr. This house, in which Booth had spent many hours, was raided the night of the shooting, and Miss Starr had already been interrogated and released. Soon after her release she attempted suicide. On being arrested the second time, she was questioned briefly and again set free.[3]

Police had particular trouble with the women of the area known as "Hooker's Division." Several were arrested for expressing joy at the President's death and for decorating their houses with Rebel emblems.

The cast of *Our American Cousin* had been kept in custody since the assassination. On Monday, authorities reassembled the group behind closed doors at the theater to duplicate the scene onstage at the time Booth fired. Photographs were made of the positions of the actors and stagehands in order to determine how Booth managed to escape across the stage and who might have helped him. These photographs were not used in the trial and have never been found. Probably as a result of this study Henry Clay Ford was arrested, as was James Maddox, an employee of the theater and close friend of Booth. The theater itself remained closed and under military guard.[4]

At this time, Stanton sent an urgent telegram to Col. H. L. Burnett in Cincinnati, directing him to report to the War Department immediately. Burnett had just conducted a long treason trial in Indianapolis. He was assigned a room in the War Department close to Stanton and given responsibility for cataloging the mass of evidence in preparation for a trial.

Detectives located Samuel Arnold's address in Hookstown, Baltimore County, Maryland, and rushed there to arrest him. They were told that he had taken a job a few weeks earlier at Fortress Monroe, a Federal installation in Virginia. On Monday morning, he was arrested on the job by orders of Gen. Lew Wallace.[5]

Arnold was instructed to divulge all he knew about Booth and the suspicious letter. At first he denied any knowledge of the correspondence, swearing that he was not connected with Booth or any conspiracy. When excerpts of this letter were read and his signature was described, Arnold admitted that he knew Booth and something of a plot to abduct Lincoln. Aware that Booth had been careful to destroy other evidence, Arnold suspected that Booth had purposely betrayed him by leaving the inculpatory item in his trunk. The document, while exonerating Arnold of complicity in the actual murder, clearly pictured his part in the plot to kidnap.

On several occasions Booth had reminded would-be deserters that they were already involved deeply enough to be hanged, if caught. Even those included in the plot to kidnap the President realized that they were subject to capital punishment. But during his interrogation, Arnold sought to pass off the abduction plot as a foolish adventure of little consequence.

After he acknowledged the letter, detectives took Arnold back to his place of work, confiscated his few possessions and turned him over to military authorities. On Monday afternoon soldiers took him to the Provost Marshal's office at Fortress Monroe and again questioned him before putting him on a steamboat to Baltimore. On Tuesday morning Provost Marshal James McPhail questioned him. Arnold then sent for his father, who came immediately and convinced his son to confess. Arnold then revealed his part in the plot.

Police already had Weichmann's statement of suspicious activities at the boardinghouse, but Arnold was the first person closely associated with Booth to talk openly of the conspiracy. Sitting at a desk in McPhail's office, and without any interrogation, he wrote a long confession—a revealing document. Practically all the facts of this first admission were later substantiated, although hardly any of the details were known to authorities at the time.[6]

Arnold told of being contacted by Booth late in August 1864. As the two drank wine, smoked fine cigars and reminisced about their school days at St. Timothy's, Booth mentioned the possibility of seizing President Lincoln. During the conversation, Michael O'Laughlin, another former schoolmate, entered. O'Laughlin, born in 1840, did ornamental plaster work and engraving; he had also served in the Confederate Army. Booth had not seen his boyhood friends for years, but he knew of their strong Rebel sympathies. He revealed details of his scheme to capture Lincoln and exchange him for all Southern prisoners in Federal hands.

According to Arnold, Booth's plan was to kidnap the President as he rode, unprotected, to the Soldiers' Home. The intrigue, as Booth set it forth, seemed plausible. O'Laughlin and Arnold consented to join the daring scheme and promised not to reveal it. Booth informed Arnold that he was also making contact with a Confederate courier named John Surratt, who carried Rebel dispatches to Confederate agents in Canada. Booth also had contacts in Canada.

This project, as first presented to Arnold and O'Laughlin, was almost certainly known to Confederate leaders. In its original form, the scheme was altogether in keeping with Confederate aims. Many in the vicinity of Lower Maryland knew that Rebel agents kept a boat (large enough to transport 15 men and a carriage) hidden on the Potomac River for several months. Another group of Confederate sympathizers in close contact with authorities in Richmond had procured this boat, although it seemed that Booth paid for it.

Several months passed while Booth and his cohorts laid their plans. Then in January 1865, according to Arnold, Booth again contacted him and O'Laughlin. Booth had acquired a trunk full of Spencer rifles, revolvers, knives, belts, handcuffs, canteens, boxes of cartridges and cartridge caps, all ready for use. The original conspiracy was obviously a large, and possibly bloody, operation. The trunk was too heavy to carry, so Booth entrusted some of the pistols, knives and handcuffs to Arnold and O'Laughlin to transport to Washington. (Within a few hours of Arnold's confession, one of these Spencer rifles was found.) Booth also bought a horse and buggy.

In the January meeting the actor first suggested the possibility of abducting the President from a theater if the Soldiers' Home attempt should fail. He rented a stable at the rear of Ford's Theatre and showed Arnold a back entrance to the theater through which he could escape. Arnold divulged that Booth was spending a lot of time with John Surratt, who was known to Arnold only by name.

Several groups working with Booth on the kidnap plot were unknown to each other. For instance, those in charge of the boat were not acquainted with the group active in Baltimore, and most of the conspirators in Baltimore were unknown to those in Washington and New York.

Arnold revealed that "dealing in oil stock" was a cover for the operation and named seven of the nine persons whom the Government eventually put on trial. But in this confession, he said nothing about Weichmann or Spangler. Authorities already knew several mentioned by Arnold. Only the night before, officers had arrested a young man whom Arnold knew as "Mosby." As yet detectives were unaware of his role.

According to Arnold, in Booth's revised plans to abduct the President at the theater, "Mosby" and Booth were to have grabbed Lincoln and lowered him from the presidential box, escaping through the back of the theater while an actor turned off the gaslights. When Arnold and O'Laughlin later informed Booth that the theater plan would not work, he reminded them of their oath and threatened to shoot them. Arnold confessed that when the plot to capture the President on the way to the Soldiers' Home failed, the group broke up temporarily, and he eventually found work at Fortress Monroe. He revealed that the buggy Booth bought was to carry Lincoln through Maryland to the Potomac, and that the guns had been transported to a small Maryland town known by the curious name T. B.

In addition to Arnold's written statement, he spoke of Booth's contact with Dr. Samuel Mudd, Dr. William Queen, and a Dr. Garland. Detectives immediately relayed these facts to Secretary Stanton.[7]

The plan to capture Lincoln as he rode to the Soldiers' Home seemed plausible. It was well known that the President made frequent trips to this retreat which was his equivalent of Camp David. Lincoln rested in Anderson Cottage on the Soldiers' Home grounds, a United States military establishment three miles north of the city. The cottage was later used by Presidents Grant, Hayes and Arthur. It was built in 1842 for George W. Riggs, the well-known Washington banker. The Riggs farm was later purchased by the Government for the Soldiers' Home. The Anderson Cottage served as a place of seclusion and quiet for Lincoln, particularly in the hot, humid summer months. There he wrote the final draft of the Emancipation Proclamation in 1862, while waiting for an appropriate victory at which to announce his decision.[8] The President rode out on summer evenings without a guard until, at the prompting of Stanton, he reluctantly accepted a military escort. He usually rode back to the White House about 8:30 A.M., accompanied by 25 or 30 cavalry with drawn sabers.

Walt Whitman, who lived close to the route Lincoln followed, described the procession:

> The party makes no great show in uniform or horses. Mr. Lincoln on the saddle generally rides a good-sized, easy-going, gray horse; is dressed in plain black, somewhat rusty and dusty; wears a stiff black hat; and looks about as ordinary in attire, etc. as the commonest man.[9]

Although Whitman wrote of the President's having ridden a horse to the home, he frequently rode in a carriage. Occasionally when the President returned, he would alter his route and ride over to Stanton's handsome house on K Street for a conference with the Secretary of War. The President was not too proud to call on Stanton and other officials. On such occasions, he would halt his coach in front of Stanton's residence and the Secretary of War would come out to consult with him.

After pawning his pistol and leaving Washington by public transportation, George Atzerodt spent Sunday north of the city, in the house of Hezekiah Metz.

That evening he found a hiding place with Hartman Richter, his cousin's husband. Officers arrested him there on April 19, a day after Arnold made his statement. Atzerodt also confessed freely.

These two confessions were made independently, early in the investigation, without any chance of corroboration, and both were confirmed by subsequent findings. Neither of the statements was proved to be false in any major point. Arnold, representative of the Baltimore conspirators, was a longtime personal friend of Booth and an early recruit, who left before final plans were made. Atzerodt, however, was recruited later by Surratt and remained active through the last stages of the conspiracy. Arnold and Atzerodt had little personal contact, yet their statements were consistent.

Atzerodt stressed his disagreements with Booth and his refusal to obey the order to kill Vice-President Johnson. He confessed that "Booth appointed me and Herold to kill Johnson." This bit of information was not made public until January 1869. Radical Republicans had insinuated that Andrew Johnson was in some way involved in the conspiracy. Apparently they did not want to destroy the myth by revealing Atzerodt's confession until it was too late to matter.

In Atzerodt's statement he clearly placed John Surratt in Washington, lodged at the Herndon boardinghouse, on the night of the murder. He told how Booth visited the Herndon house a few hours before the crime to see Surratt. Other conspirators later stated that they had not seen Surratt for at least a week before the assassination. Yet curiously, Booth made a special point to inform Atzerodt shortly before the murder that he had just seen John.

The two confessions named almost the same participants, although Atzerodt was the first to include Mrs. Surratt (albeit indirectly). He said he thought Spangler was innocent of any involvement, but he substantiated Arnold's statement that "an actor" was to have turned off the gaslights. He revealed that the boat which was to carry Lincoln across the Potomac had been purchased from one James Brawner. The lead-colored, flat-bottomed boat was kept hidden at the head of Goose Creek and later moved to Nanjemoy Creek.

Both men thought themselves innocent—Arnold, because he had left Booth—Atzerodt, because he had refused Booth's order to kill Andrew Johnson. The latter vowed that Booth first mentioned the idea of killing only a few hours before the assassination. Some evidence confirms his assertion, although there are strong indications that Booth decided on murder a few days earlier.

Atzerodt mentioned several previously unsuspected persons. One was Kate Thompson, alias Brown, who traveled from Richmond with John Surratt. Others included a Major Banon of the Confederate Army and a man he called Harborn who had been with Surratt in the early stages of the scheme. The individual Atzerodt mentioned as Harborn was surely Thomas Harbin, a signal officer and Confederate spy who was introduced to Booth by Dr. Samuel Mudd in Bryantown. Harbin and his brother-in-law Thomas Jones were both involved in Booth's escape.[10]

Atzerodt was the first to mention the elusive Mrs. Slater and to divulge her

In spite of his imprisonment with prime suspects, the Government did not seriously consider trying Hartman Richter (Library of Congress).

connections with Booth and Mrs. Surratt. He spoke of the trip made by Mrs. Slater, Major Banon, Mrs. Surratt and John from Washington to Surrattsville and John's subsequent journey with Mrs. Slater on to Richmond. He also told authorities about Kate Thompson's frequent clandestine trips between New York and Richmond, adding that she stopped over at Mrs. Surratt's house in Washington. In some ways this otherwise unknown woman resembled Mrs. Slater, but Atzerodt clearly identified them as two separate individuals. He revealed John Surratt's connection with known Confederate blockade-runner Augustus Howell. These facts were later substantiated, but at the time of Atzerodt's confession they were unknown to detectives.

Arnold was confined in a dark, filthy dungeon at Fort McHenry, the same fort over which the American flag had waved defiantly during the War of 1812, inspiring Francis Scott Key to write "The Star-Spangled Banner." The dungeon probably dated back to that war. Arnold claimed he had to cover himself with a blanket for protection from rats, bugs and snakes. He did not remain there long, however. During the night soldiers roused him, placed him

Samuel Arnold. As officials photographed most prime suspects aboard ironclad prison ships, the iron walls were clear in the background. However, neither Mary Surratt nor Samuel Mudd was held on the ships (Library of Conress-B817-7778).

in chains and transported him to Washington. They confined him on one of the ships anchored in the Potomac which Stanton had prepared to serve as prisons. On board, Arnold complained that irons on his wrists were so tight blood could not circulate. Captain Monroe, who was in charge, obligingly provided a larger pair. While the prisoner's arms felt better, living conditions were dismal on the suffocatingly hot ship.

Michael O'Laughlin, Arnold's close friend, had lived near John Wilkes Booth and had known him for 12 years. They had studied together as boys under tutor J. M. Smith. Within 24 hours of the murder, O'Laughlin's name was vaguely associated with the crime.

After spending that deadly Friday night in Washington drinking and carousing with his friends, O'Laughlin returned to Baltimore the following evening. Even before he arrived home, officers had visited the house where he was staying with his brother-in-law, P. H. Maulsby. When O'Laughlin entered, he was told that the police were looking for him. On Sunday morning Gen. Lew Wallace and his officers again searched the house without success. On Monday morning, O'Laughlin contacted his brother-in-law, who was also being questioned. Maulsby eventually located O'Laughlin at Mrs. Bailey's boardinghouse and talked him into surrendering.[11]

Michael O'Laughlin. (Sketch from a contemporary photograph.)

While Stanton's soldiers tirelessly searched Lower Maryland, police took another trail leading to Canada. On one pretext or another, Richards had kept Weichmann in custody. On the day of the murder, Weichmann had seen letters from John Surratt postmarked Montreal, although he was not allowed to read them. He still thought Surratt innocent of the attack on Seward and suggested that he could lead police to him. The police captain decided to take a chance on Weichmann's offer.

Richards assigned his best detective, James McDevitt, to accompany

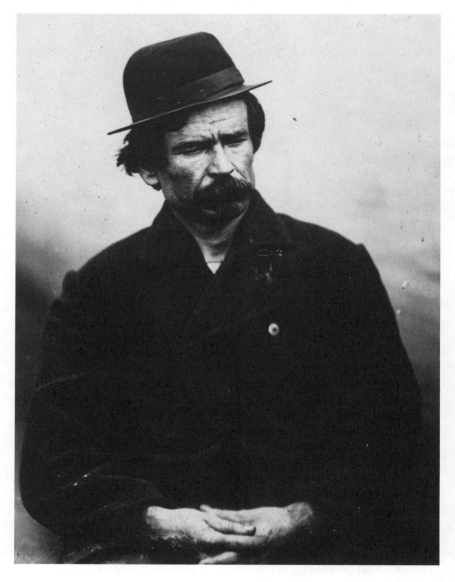

Joao Celestino. Of this mysterious Portuguese Rebel agent little is known. For a while officials treated him as a prime suspect but did not put him on trial. He is often incorrectly identified as Thomas Jones (Library of Congress).

Weichmann and fellow-boarder John Holohan to Canada. The police applied to General Augur for necessary clearance and transportation, stating only that the men were being sent on "important government business." For some reason, Stanton, whose War Department controlled passes in and out of Washington, was not made aware of this request. Augur provided transportation through the Quartermaster Department. He requested only that at the conclusion of the mission, the men report to his headquarters. However, before they departed, they had to consult with LaFayette Baker who had arrived the day before.[12]

Arrangements were made for Detectives Bigley and Clarvoe to accompany McDevitt and his charges. The group left Washington on Monday afternoon shortly before three o'clock and arrived in Philadelphia that night. There Clarvoe arrested a strange individual named Joao Celestino whom he took back to Washington. This shadowy Rebel blockade-runner, one of the chief suspects, was kept under heavy guard on one of the prison boats. The others continued on to New York City, then up the Hudson River to Canada. McDevitt carried with him a letter that had been mailed from Montreal, hoping it might provide a clue to Surratt's whereabouts.

Arriving at Montreal on the night of April 19, they barely missed their prey. By chance, Surratt caught sight of Weichmann and hurriedly left his hotel in a carriage with several friends. McDevitt conferred with the United States consul, who helped him examine the hotel register. There they found the name John Harrison, the alias used by Surratt. The Government was clearly on his trail in Canada, even as it closed in on Booth and Herold in Lower Maryland. The search for Surratt, however, was hampered by New York newspapers, available in Canada, which reported the Government's activities. McDevitt complained to authorities for allowing the reports to be published.

McDevitt also reported that George Sanders, one of the Confederate agents in Montreal, had received a telegram from Washington on the night of the assassination. This information, if true, was significant. A telegraph message from the Federal capital to the notorious Sanders should have been known immediately. Weichmann and Bigley hurried on to Quebec while Holohan and McDevitt gathered evidence in Montreal.

Soon after the group left on their Canadian trip, Joseph Clark informed the War Department that "Louis Weichmann, a clerk in the Commissary General of Prisoners Office is in all probability an accomplice of Booth."[13] This was the first clear allegation against Weichmann. However, the War Department received hundreds of accusations, some anonymous, some signed, many by cranks, but some obviously valuable. Clark's statement was both signed and valuable.

A few days later when Stanton heard that Weichmann had been sent out of the country, he was furious and ordered him returned under guard immediately. Convinced that Weichmann was in on the conspiracy, Stanton was particularly irate with Richards for having allowed him to go to Canada, where he was free of United States jurisdiction.

Stanton called the Superintendent to his office for a severe reprimand. Richards was protected, however, because he had secured permission from both General Augur and Colonel Baker before launching the expedition. This did not satisfy Stanton, who ordered Richards to catch the six o'clock train that evening and bring Weichmann and the detectives back. Stanton also instructed Col. J. A. Foster to send a telegram to Canada ordering the men back. The Secretary of War was so fearful that Weichmann might escape that he sent

Foster to question suspects imprisoned on the ironclads, hoping to get a clue as to Weichmann's involvement.

Richards, in an effort to please the dictatorial Secretary, obediently left his duties at a crucial time to search for Weichmann. He met the group in New York City and accompanied them back to the capital, arriving at noon on April 29.[14]

Weichmann, of course, could have escaped while in Canada. Most of the time only Bigley accompanied him, and, on some occasions, he was alone. While he had not been under guard in Canada, on his return to Washington he was watched closely.

Safely back, Weichmann first reported to Gen. Henry Burnett at the War Department. After giving the General an account of the trip, the officer allowed him to leave. When Stanton realized that Weichmann had been permitted to go free again, he flew into another rage. Burnett tried to explain, but Stanton would not listen. He bellowed at the General that if Weichmann were not apprehended by morning, Burnett would be discharged from the army. Burnett, disgusted, had no choice but to put out an alarm for Weichmann's arrest. The young clerk was soon apprehended and taken to Stanton's office where he was subjected to stern interrogation.

Burnett had done his job, but he was deeply hurt by the domineering and unreasonable attitude of the Secretary and tendered his resignation as Judge Advocate. This threat changed Stanton's attitude drastically. He needed Burnett and begged him to reconsider. Stanton seldom revealed his softer side to generals, but, in this case, he broke down. Almost tearfully he pictured the pressures and responsibilities weighing on him. Burnett withdrew his resignation.

The Secretary was not so tender with Weichmann. He demanded to know what the clerk was doing associating with the disloyal Surratt family. Weichmann explained that it was simply a matter of friendship with his former college schoolmate. Stanton asked if he knew John Wilkes Booth and, if so, how he met him. Weichmann replied casually that he had been introduced to Booth by Dr. Samuel Mudd. At this disclosure, the Secretary rose from his chair, hammered his fist on the desk and barked at Burnett, "Put that down."[15] Weichmann was unaware that Booth's second stopping place after the murder had been Mudd's house. After the interrogation, Weichmann was confined in Old Capitol Prison.

Louis J. Weichmann was the 22-year-old son of John C. and Mary Weichmann. His parents, of German descent, lived in Baltimore, where Louis was born September 29, 1842. A few years later the family moved to Washington, where his father was employed as a tailor. Louis attended school at Washington Seminary. They moved to Philadelphia in 1855, where Louis entered public schools. He grew to be a tall, broad shouldered, handsome young man and a serious student. After graduation from Central High School in 1859, he enrolled in college to prepare for the Roman Catholic priesthood.

Actually Weichmann had wanted to go into the pharmaceutical business, but his mother, a devout Catholic, was anxious that he become a priest. His

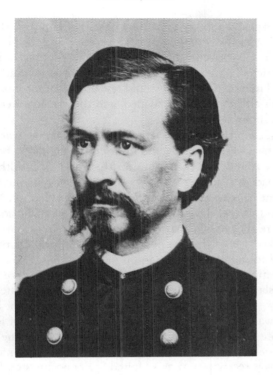

Col. H. L. Burnett had responsibility for gathering evidence and was then appointed Assistant Judge Advocate for the trial (Library of Congress – BH831-1267).

father was a Lutheran at the time, although later, grief stricken over a death in the family, he converted to Catholicism. Weichmann, a sensitive and obedient son, reluctantly followed his mother's wishes. Through the efforts of a local priest, he was put in contact with the Right Reverend John McGill, Bishop of the Diocese of Richmond. John McGill, who had been a successful lawyer before turning to a church vocation, backed the Confederate cause. He had known the Weichmann family as a patron of the elder Weichmann's tailor shop and later sponsored Weichmann in his study for the priesthood.[16]

On February 27, 1859, Weichmann bid his mother good-bye and, accompanied by his father and an uncle, made his way to St. Charles College in Howard County, Maryland, about 20 miles from Baltimore. The school had prepared many outstanding Catholic leaders, including Cardinal James Gibbons, several archbishops and numerous bishops. Years later Weichmann wrote that if he could have "foreseen how much of suffering, of trial and of persecution" would grow out of his college experience, he would have altered his course.[17]

John Surratt arrived in September 1859, seven months after Weichmann had begun his studies. He was sponsored to study for the priesthood by the Right Reverend Augustine Verot of the Diocese of St. Augustine, Florida. Surratt was a slender young man with a high forehead, stringy, sandy-colored hair, deep-set eyes and a sharp, prominent nose. The lanky youth was, in many ways, a model student, conscientious, cooperative and likable. Studies were strenuous at St. Charles and the discipline severe. Contact with the outside world was restricted, although students had a two-month vacation during July and August. While the Civil War would not break out for more than a year, the Nation was already seriously divided, and the students were conscious of the discord even among themselves.

In July 1862, shortly before his father died, and after the war had been raging for more than a year, Surratt and his friend Weichmann both left school and apparently abandoned their plans for the priesthood. Although the two young men headed in the same direction, they took separate paths. Surratt eventually went back to his home in Prince Georges County, Maryland. His mother still had several slaves working around the place, although some had fled even before they were emancipated in Maryland.

John worked for a while as postmaster of the little country post office located in one corner of the tavern in his mother's house. Mrs. Surratt maintained something of an inn which served as a gathering place for Southern-sympathizing slaveholders in the area. The Surratt house, located on the main road used by spies and blockade-runners traveling from Richmond to Washington, was a known hangout for a wide assortment of Rebels.

Even before he became postmaster, John Surratt had gone to Richmond to join the Rebel secret service. Thus, he was serving the Confederacy at the same time he was receiving pay as a United States postmaster. Part of his service for the Rebels involved the risky transportation of contraband through the Federal blockade. His older brother, Isaac, had previously left home to join Confederate forces in Texas.

Weichmann's path led to Washington where he became an instructor at St. Matthews Institute on 19th between G and H streets. For a while he slept at the Institute and took his meals in a nearby boardinghouse, but within a few months he was visited by his friend, Surratt.[18] Exactly why John sought to renew this friendship is not known. At the time, he was a Confederate agent, and it seems unlikely that he would have sought out Weichmann if he had not been confident of his former schoolmate's sympathies.

During the visit, Weichmann carefully skirted the issue of his own persuasions, at least according to the account he later gave. Weichmann's parents had switched from the Democratic party to support Lincoln in the 1864 election, and while Louis was born in the South, his formative years were divided between North and South. Later he constantly asserted his loyalty to the Federal Government, but he never denied the accusation that he had earlier supported the Confederacy. Apparently John Surratt felt that Weichmann would not disapprove of his Rebel activities, and there is little doubt that Weichmann soon learned something of John's secret involvement.

IX
The Honor of a Lady

Detectives first took serious notice of Mary Surratt when J. H. Kimball reported to authorities that a Mrs. Griffin had been informed by a black girl, Susan Mahoney, that three suspicious men had come to Mrs. Surratt's house after the murder. Miss Mahoney, a servant in the house, had pretended to be asleep on the floor. She said she overheard a conversation between the men and Mrs. Surratt. One of the visitors said that John Surratt was in the theater with Booth. Another called for a change of clothes. They left after a short time, in a buggy, the same way they had arrived.[1] Officers verified the story with the girl, and, fortified with this information, Col. H. H. Wells decided to arrest Mrs. Surratt. Upon further consideration, he concluded it best to apprehend everyone in the house. This, per se, was not an indictment of the matronly boardinghouse keeper. Scores of innocent people had been seized on flimsy evidence.

At 10:30 P.M., April 17, on Wells's instruction, Col. H. S. Olcott ordered officers working out of General Augur's headquarters to proceed to 541 H Street and arrest the occupants. Officer Charles W. Rosch and a detail of men were first stationed around the house to prevent any escape. At 11:14 P.M., Eli Devore, accompanied by several officers, walked up the steps to the main entrance on the second floor and knocked on the door. A window was opened, but the curtains remained closed. A low womanly voice asked, "Is that you, Mr. Kirby?"[2]

Devoe replied, "No, Madam, I want this door opened." He advised the major by his side to note the name "Kirby."

As the officers entered the house, Major H. W. Smith asked the woman if she was Mrs. Surratt.

"I am the widow of John H. Surratt."

"And the mother of John H. Surratt, Jr.?"

"I am."

After rounding up the boarders, Smith announced the purpose of his visit to the ladies, who seemed surprised, especially Anna Surratt. Her mother, however, took it all calmly, "as though she had been expecting it." The soldiers going through the house found it very disorderly, with clothing piled on chairs and in general confusion. They gathered up what evidence they could, however, as the girls sat quietly in the parlor, saying not a word. But as the search dragged on, Anna, obviously upset, broke down in tears. Her mother chided her.[3]

Home of Mary Surratt on H Street between 6th and 7th streets. The conspirators plotted attacks against leaders of the Government here (Library of Congress — USZ62-22438).

In their search, Major Smith and Officer Simpson found evidence that the house might have been used as a meeting place for the assassins. In Anna's portfolio they discovered an envelope addressed to J. Wilkes Booth at the National Hotel. Other officers went downstairs to question the servants. In addition to Mrs. Surratt, her daughter and the boarders, the officers arrested two black servants — a man and a girl.

Smith was surprised that Mrs. Surratt never asked him why she was being arrested. As she, Anna, Honora Fitzpatrick and Olivia Jenkins were assembled in the parlor, waiting for a carriage to transport them to General Augur's headquarters, one of the officers, Richard Morgan, heard the doorbell. The soldiers instinctively reached for their pistols and, opening the door, were confronted by a huge, dirty individual with a heavy pickax on his shoulder. The man was wearing a gray coat, black pants and a cap made from the sleeve of a shirt. Mud covered his boots up to his knees. Surprised at seeing the officers, he blurted out nervously, "I guess I am mistaken."

"Who did you want to see?" asked Morgan.

"Mrs. Surratt."

"You are right, walk in."

The wild-looking stranger then took a seat as officers began to question him.

"What did you come here for at this time of night?"

He replied that he had come to dig a gutter. After a few questions about his business, he was asked why he had come so late. The visitor answered that he wanted to start work early in the morning and needed to know where to dig.

Asked where he had lived prior to coming to Washington, he replied, Fauquier County, Virginia. He gave the officer a copy of his oath of allegiance, saying that the document would show who he was. The oath was signed "Lewis Payne." From that point on, the man who was occasionally called Wood or Mosby has been known as Lewis Payne. He took this assumed name from the real Lewis Payne of Fauquier, Virginia, a former United States attorney for the Wyoming territory.

The oath of allegiance Payne handed the detective had been sworn on March 14, 1865, in Baltimore. He listed himself as a "refugee" and solemnly swore to oppose secession and "abjure all faith . . . or sympathy with the so-called Confederate States." Added with pen and ink to the printed oath was the statement, "I . . . will proceed to remain north of Philadelphia during the war."[4]

Payne told the officers he could not read, had no money and could barely write his name. Officer Morgan then informed the rough-looking fellow that he would have to go to the Provost Marshal's office. At that Payne showed a flicker of emotion but said nothing. Mrs. Surratt, who had gone to get the bonnets and shawls of the others, returned to the front parlor. Major Smith asked her to step into the hall for a moment. "Do you know this man?" the officer queried.

Mrs. Surratt, who later impressed interrogators with her emotional control, lost her usually stoic composure. She threw up her right hand and exclaimed frantically, "Before God, I do not know this man, and have never seen him." Her protest, like that of Shakespeare's Queen Gertrude, was almost too much.

An army ambulance arrived, and as Major Smith was leading the women from the house, Mrs. Surratt asked him to wait a minute. She then knelt down and prayed aloud while the officers respectfully removed their hats. The ladies were taken to General Augur's office. Payne was also held for identification. Officers Smith, Wermerskirch and Morgan remained behind to further search the house.

The group, including the brutish-looking Payne, were kept together in Augur's office for several hours, during which time Anna became hysterical. Even though her mother tried repeatedly to calm her, nothing could be done.

Anna Surratt suffered greatly as a result of the assassination. Although 22 years old at the time of the crime, her immature mannerisms made her seem younger.

Mary Surratt was seriously interrogated for the first time late that night at Augur's headquarters. The first questions concerned John Wilkes Booth and her son, John, since she was not suspected of conspiracy. Authorities still thought, however, that John was Seward's attacker.

It soon became obvious that the motherly landlady was not just another bystander, innocently entangled in the conspiracy. When asked if Booth had ever visited her boardinghouse when her son was not there, she replied almost boastfully, "He called frequently when my son was not there."[5] She further admitted that Booth often visited once or twice a day. This same surprising fact was eventually repeated by other members of the household—there was no convincing way to deny it.

Mary Surratt. This is one of many copies based on the only genuine likeness of the suspect. The Government did not photograph her, and she studiously hid her face during the trial (Lincoln Memorial University Museum).

This admission changed the course of the investigation. If Booth, the accused mastermind of the plot, had visited the insignificant boardinghouse several times a day immediately preceding the crime, even when John was not at home, whom did he visit and why? Mrs. Surratt never provided an answer. She also had trouble accounting for the rather unnatural friendship between her son and Booth—unnatural in that they seemed to have no area of common interest, other than support of the Confederacy. When asked why Booth associated with John, she responded flippantly, "I don't know."

"Has not this question occurred to you since the murder?"

"Yes, sir, but I could not account for it."

Mary Surratt eventually told her interrogator that she was not surprised that John should have established a friendship with Booth because her son was "a country-bred young gentleman." She added, with a touch of arrogance, "I never thought a great deal of his forming Mr. Booth's acquaintance."

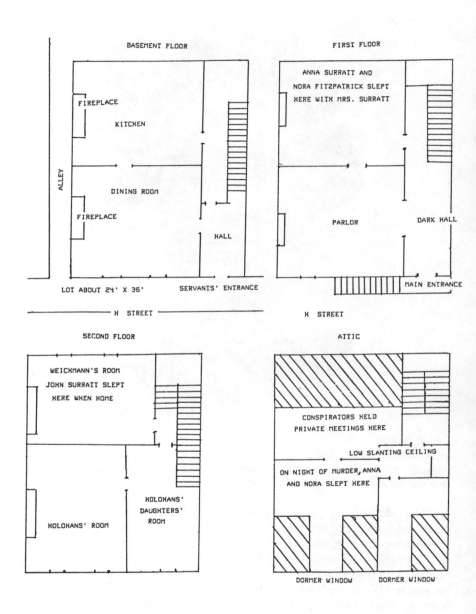

Floor plan of the Surratt house. 1)Basement floor. The servants slept here, and the family and boarders dined in the front room. 2)First floor. Booth often met here with Mrs. Surratt. Officers arrested Payne in the hall and detectives found incriminating evidence in the back bedroom. 3)Second floor. Officers found suspicious articles in Weichmann's bedroom. 4)Attic. The conspirators met in these rooms for long uninterrupted conversations.

It seemed important to Mrs. Surratt to establish John's presence in Canada at the time of the murder. She appeared anxious to mention a letter from him, apparently posted at Springfield, Massachusetts, before the murder. She explained that this indicated he was leaving the country on his way to Canada. This vital letter was not sent directly to her, but by way of Miss Anna Ward, a longtime friend of the family. Miss Ward taught at the Female School, a Catholic institution on 10th Street. Mrs. Surratt had told Weichmann about the letter, but strangely she could not find it when detectives asked to see it. "I have hunted my house over, but cannot find the letter," she lamented.[6]

In the first search of the house, a few hours after the crime, detectives found no correspondence from John Surratt, but admittedly the search had not been thorough. They looked quickly through the rooms but did not open drawers or closets. Three nights later, when Mrs. Surratt was arrested, a complete search was made. Detectives found letters to Weichmann, papers belonging to Anna and those of other boarders, but none belonging to Mrs. Surratt.

A story told by a Mrs. Safford to Mrs. George Porter may account for the failure to find the letter, or several other missing documents. A few years after the assassination, Mrs. Safford's parents moved to Washington and rented the Surratt house. Her aunt, ill with tuberculosis, was annoyed by a squeaking board in the closet of her upstairs sick room. The carpenter called to fix the squeak found a package of papers under the board. According to Mrs. Safford, her mother burned all the papers, saying there had already been too much trouble in that house. The story may not be reliable, but the letters were lost somewhere, and a good place to hide them would have been under the closet floor.[7]

Continuing Mrs. Surratt's interrogation, the officer, exasperated at her insistence that John was in Canada, exploded, "No man on the round earth believes he went to Canada."

The landlady answered firmly, "I believe it."[8]

After the long emotional night, the self-possessed woman held her ground against her inquisitor, but just as she was feeling secure, she became guilty of an obvious misrepresentation. Concerning John's travels, the officer stated that it was well known that her son had been back and forth to the South. Mrs. Surratt, apparently satisfied that the detective was not well informed, told him that her son "had never been away long enough to go South and back." This was an unfortunate statement if she expected to maintain her innocence, and the interrogator picked it up.

"How long does it take to go across the river?" he asked.

Instead of assuming the attitude of an injured woman, eager to tell the truth, she became sarcastic: "I don't know the width of the river."[9] For a woman who had never lived more than 20 miles from the Potomac and had crossed it frequently, the answer was ridiculous. The detective explained that a person could go to Fredericksburg, Virginia, and back in four days, and that her son had been away longer than that.

"I don't think he has," was her surprising response. Even before the interrogation, authorities knew of her son's long and frequent absences from home. It was not necessary for John's mother to deny that he had been absent from home long periods in order to protect him or herself. After all, she had just admitted that he had been in Canada for nearly a week.

Sensing the landlady's deception, the detective lashed out, "Oh yes he has. Have I made any error in my record so far as his movements are concerned?"

"No, sir, that is all correct."

Mrs. Surratt began to back down a little, but the damage had been done. The investigator surmised that he was questioning a woman who knew more than she revealed. When asked about Atzerodt, she admitted he had been in her house but said she asked him to leave because she had found liquor in his room. Later she contradicted herself, declaring that she never went into her boarders' rooms. When shown a photograph of David Herold, she swore, on her "honor as a lady," that she did not know him.

On being handed a photograph of John Wilkes Booth, she responded, "That's a photograph of Mr. Booth, ain't it?"[10] During the entire interview, Mary Surratt spoke defiantly; her answers were generally evasive, occasionally belligerent and sometimes false. But these were preliminary questions leading to the major issue. The detective, who had been told that three mysterious men had visited her house after the murder, wanted to know more about these unidentified visitors.

It was now several hours past midnight and the interrogator was anxious to finish. While he tried to be polite, he was tired and his impatience showed. "Speaking of visiting at your house, I will bring the thing down a little nearer. I will be happy to have you give me the names of three men who came to you on Saturday and had a private conversation with you."

"Last Saturday?"

"Yes, madam."

"No three gentlemen came to my house, I assure you."

"How many did come?"

"You mean the gentlemen who came to search the house?"

"No; you know who I mean. . . ."

Mrs. Surratt stated that to the best of her knowledge only Mr. Kirby and a priest came by her house that day. This was the only mention that a clergyman had visited her on the day after the atrocities. He was never identified, and the subject was never brought up again.[12]

The Government's persistent interest in the three men was ironic. Detectives made a strenuous effort to force her to reveal the identities of the "three men," yet the "three men" were undoubtedly McDevitt, Holohan and Weichmann. The latter had returned to the boardinghouse Saturday morning to get a few things and change clothes.

The interrogator was bluffing. He knew the servant girl had spoken of three men coming to the house while she pretended to be asleep, but with her eyes closed, she obviously had not seen the visitors. The girl undoubtedly had heard the commotion and caught a few words of conversation, but she did not claim to have seen the men. Only later would authorities realize the identities of these "mysterious" men.

On the night of Mrs. Surratt's arrest, detectives were sure that these unexplained visitors had something to do with the assassination; they were also certain that Mrs. Surratt knew who they were. She, however, was completely puzzled. When covering for John, she was cool and confident, but she did not know what the officer was after when he asked about the three men. Mary Surratt was innocent of the very accusation that led to her arrest.

Weichmann and Holohan were working with police detective McDevitt at the time the War Department was interrogating Mrs. Surratt. The two operations were being conducted separately, which made it impossible for the War Department to realize that the three men who had visited the Surratt house were working with the Metro Police Department.

Determined to finish the tiring interrogation, the officer stated forcefully that he could not waste any more time, and that he wanted the names of the men immediately. Mrs. Surratt persisted, "Upon my word, I do not know; upon the honor of a lady, I do not remember anybody except Mr. Wicket [Weichmann]."

"I can tell you what you said."

"Perhaps I can remember, then."

"I can tell you what they wanted at your house, too."

"Well, sir; if you will please to tell me, if I remember it I will tell you."

The detective realizing that he couldn't bluff the landlady, eased up a bit, "You cannot remember anything about it?"

"I don't remember indeed."

"There were three men though," the officer insisted.

"No," replied Mrs. Surratt, she didn't think so. To the best of her knowledge if it was the last word she had to say, nobody came by her house "except Mr. Wicket [Weichmann], unless Mr. Wallace Kirby was there."

"Do you make a distinction between day and evening?"

"No, sir; it is all the same to me."

"Or the night?"

"I call it all one."

In the original transcript of the interrogation, "Weichmann" was written "Wicket," an understandable mistake by the stenographer late at night. This error, however, made it less likely that military detectives would associate the men with Weichmann.

At few times in the investigation were detectives so completely baffled. They had arrested the subject on the basis of a misunderstanding. The questions became almost comical. The officer, making sure that Mrs. Surratt was allowed no loophole, covered all possible evasions as to the number of men, the time of day and days of the month. The interrogator stated that maybe he misunderstood her. "Do you say to me that no two or three or four men ever came to your house the last three or four days—on Friday, or Saturday or Sunday?"

She thought that three or four men may have come to her house on Sunday while she was at church. But, she added, "I assure you, on the honor of a lady, that I would not tell an untruth."

"The honor of a lady" was a favorite pledge of the landlady and it was getting monotonous to the investigator, who snapped back, "I assure you, on the honor of a gentleman, I shall get this information from you."

"Whatever it is, I shall tell you."

"Now, I know they were there."

"Well, sir; if you do, I do not."

"I mean the men who called at your house and wanted to change their clothes."

Mrs. Surratt really tried to understand what the detective was looking for and the last statement gave it away. She should have realized what the interrogator was talking about; unfortunately, for her, she did not.

The detective tried again, "Will you tell me, in the presence of Almighty God, who first mentioned the name of Mr. Booth in that party?"

"I don't remember."

"Indeed you do; I pledge you my word you do. And you will admit it, and I should be very glad if you would do it at once."

"If I could, I would do so."

"Reflect a moment, and I will send for a glass of water for you."[13]

Government detectives prided themselves on their ability to handle witnesses. The water routine was supposed to be a friendly gesture to soften up the obstinate. Water was brought, and the farce continued, "Now, will you be kind enough to state who first made the remark in relation to Booth."

"I don't remember that his name was mentioned."

"Do you believe what he said?"

"What who said?"

Following this clumsy trick and a few questions about her son, Mrs. Surratt was shown a letter signed, "Katie." She swore she knew nothing about it, adding, "My eyesight is not very good." This comment was surely deliberate, as it was to be used as a major defense. The letter was never brought up again and "Katie" was not identified or questioned, although Atzerodt had mentioned a Rebel spy named Katie Thompson who had stayed at the Surratt house.

Mrs. Surratt had won the first round. She realized that the officer knew very little and was bluffing. This may have led her into a false security, because she responded unconvincingly when questioned about the stranger arrested at her front door.

Asked if she had met the man before, she answered emphatically, "No, sir; the ruffian that was in my door when I came away? He was a tremendous hard fellow with a skull-cap on, and my daughter commenced crying, and said those gentlemen came to save our lives." She added, "I hope they arrested him."

Mrs. Surratt and the girls had been held in the same room with Payne at

Augur's headquarters before this interview took place—long enough for the initial shock to have worn off and long enough to have recognized him. Inadvertently, Mrs. Surratt indicated by her description of Payne and his skullcap that she had seen him clearly.

The officer continued, "When did you see him first?"

"Just as the carriage drove up, he rang the doorbell and my daughter said, 'Oh! there is a murderer.'"[14]

Anna, who had visited with Payne on several recent occasions and had accompanied him to a play at Ford's Theatre, surely recognized him. More likely she cried, "Oh! there is *the* murderer," believing that it was Payne and not her brother who had attacked Seward. But this would have revealed that she recognized Payne. Later when Anna was questioned about the incident, she gave an evasive answer.

Mrs. Surratt's first interrogation was over. When police arrived at her door a few hours earlier, she was only one of many persons to be routinely questioned. Now she was a definite suspect.

X
A View of Swampoodle

William Bell, who had not had a full night's sleep since the attack, was aggravated at being called from bed at 2:30 in the morning, until informed that he was required at Augur's headquarters. There detectives asked Bell if there had been light enough to get a good look at Seward's assailant. He admitted that it was rather dark in the hall. After discussing the attack, detectives exhibited several men for identification. When Payne was brought in and gaslights turned up, Seward's servant immediately recognized him. This identification of a man he had seen only briefly in the poorly lighted hallway contrasted with Mrs. Surratt's failure to recognize the same man although he had been a guest in her home on several occasions.

Officers who searched Payne found a pocket comb, a needle, two toothbrushes and a hairbrush. These articles revealed more about the warrior than a diary. Payne was inordinately concerned about his appearance and was proud of his physique. Although he had thrown his gun away, he was careful not to lose his toothbrushes or hairbrush.

Convinced of Payne's guilt, investigators moved him from Augur's office to the ironclad *Montauk*, anchored in the Potomac. There he was searched again by Col. H. H. Wells on April 19. Since the attack, the prisoner had not changed clothes. Aboard the *Montauk*, Wells had him take off his outer garments, exposing his undershirt minus one sleeve. On examining the undershirt, Wells discovered blood stains and demanded an explanation. The muscular Payne leaned arrogantly against the iron wall of the ship and said nothing.[1]

The women were held at the Provost Marshal's office most of the night. As the hours passed Anna became more unnerved and hysterical. Her mother tried patiently to calm her wild crying, but even she could not pacify the convulsed girl. At dawn authorities transferred the weary women to Old Capitol Prison in army carriages and confined them in the Carroll Prison Annex. The guard on duty announcing their arrival called for the corporal of the guard, who took them inside to the anteroom. Guards held them until they could be brought before one of the prison administrators. The official informed the women of the charges against them and briefly questioned them before they were escorted to their assigned rooms on the second floor.

Old Capitol and Carroll Prison Annex occupied adjoining buildings east of the recently domed Capitol. The prisons covered a city block with wings

Lewis Payne leaning back arrogantly on the iron hull of the "prison ship." Soldiers punished the Rebel for moving his head to avoid being photographed (Library of Congress).

extending back on each side. Old Capitol was generally used to confine Confederate sympathizers or prisoners of war, while the main section of Carroll Prison usually housed female inmates. This arrangement varied with the demands, and, during the assassination investigation, some male prisoners were also kept in Carroll Annex.

This collection of dilapidated buildings was located on the corner of A and First streets (later occupied by the Library of Congress). The main three-story structure which faced First Street was built to house the United States Congress after the British burned the Capitol in the War of 1812. The cornerstone of the Nation's temporary Capitol was laid on July 4, 1815.[2] The once handsome First Street entrance under which James Monroe took the oath of office was now a weather-beaten doorway with dirty, broken windowpanes.

The Senate and House of Representatives met here until the Capitol was rebuilt. Its faded walls had echoed many eloquent debates that molded the early

Republic. After the legislature moved back into the renovated Capitol, Old Capitol became a boardinghouse, its location making it convenient for members of Congress. One of its boarders, John C. Calhoun, died there. As a young Congressman, Abraham Lincoln once occupied a room in the old building. Now surrounded by woods and muddy streets, it was converted into a prison. Thus, what had been the United States Congressional chamber became a jail for Confederate spies, Union Army deserters and suspected Southern sympathizers.

Among the better-known individuals who had spent time in Old Capitol prison were George Armstrong Custer; Frank Blair, Jr., brother of Postmaster General Montgomery Blair and George Scott, nephew of General of the Armies Winfield Scott. The prison also housed famous women, including the infamous Belle Boyd. Most women were arrested as Confederate spies. The war years were plagued by women agents. For some unaccountable reason, many were Marylanders. One such prisoner, a Mrs. Baxley, took special pride in that fact. Conversing with her notorious colleague, Mrs. Rose Greenhow, she gloated that nearly every lady under arrest was a Marylander.

Mrs. Rose O'Neal Greenhow was the terror of the place. She was so belligerent that Provost Marshal Porter said he "would rather resign than continue to guard Mrs. Greenhow." Porter's replacement, a 25-year-old colonel named William E. Doster, was later counselor for the defense of several suspects. As Provost Marshal his chief concern was getting along with "Rebel Rose," as Mrs. Greenhow was not-so-affectionately known. On one of Doster's first visits to her cell he was accompanied by Dr. Seward. As the men entered her room, Mrs. Greenhow asked defiantly what their intrusion meant. The gentlemanly physician, who had endured Rebel insults for months, replied that when "a Union man called on a Secessionist it was not an intrusion but a favor."[3]

One woman held in Old Capitol was Mrs. William Henry Norris, a refined lady from Baltimore. Mrs. Norris was later released through the efforts of United States Senator Reverdy Johnson, who early in the war had established a reputation for getting Rebels out of jail—for a price. He later defended one of the accused conspirators.

Another notorious Confederate spy was the wife of Philip Phillips, a former United States Congressman from Alabama. Eugenia Phillips, mother of nine children, found time to transmit secret information to General Beauregard. She, like Mrs. Greenhow, was a prominent Washington socialite whose husband was a well-known lawyer. Like other privileged Southern women living in the capital, she strongly supported the Confederacy. In August 1861 investigators searched her house, and she was charged with spying. Yet the Government treated her very leniently. Then, without explanation, officers allowed her to go south after she promised that she would not engage in espionage. This generous handling of the known Confederate agent was difficult to explain apart from the intervention of the incorruptible Stanton.

One of Stanton's closest acquaintances was Philip Phillips. When some

William E. Doster. As a young army major, Doster was Provost Marshal of Washington. He served admirably as defense lawyer for several conspirators. (Courtesy of Mr. Wadsworth Doster.)

Southerners began stalking away from Washington at the start of the war, Stanton continued his close friendship with Phillps, even asking him to fill speaking engagements in his stead. There was talk, before fighting broke out, that Stanton and Phillips were planning to become law partners. Even though their relationship changed with the outbreak of war, and Phillips went south, the two continued to correspond.[4]

Senator Reverdy Johnson and Edwin Stanton, two future antagonists, were chiefly responsible for getting Mrs. Phillips released. She later wrote of Stanton as "our noble friend." He worked harder than Johnson on her behalf and even shed tears when she was freed, although Eugenia suspected that they might have been "crocodile tears."[5]

The grateful husband was not so cynical. After he and his family found refuge in New Orleans, he wrote Stanton, thanking him for his help. He even asked him to check the dead letter file, and to attend to any letters he thought urgent.

These events took place during the first year of fighting, however, before Stanton was appointed Secretary of War. After four years of death and destruction, Stanton was a different man. Women spies had played a large part in the bloodshed, thoroughly hardening the Secretary.[6]

On entering Old Capitol, the prisoner faced a large room used as a lounge for military guards. On the right were several small offices, where the suspect was searched and questioned. Soldiers then led the prisoner upstairs to the main area (where the United States Congress once convened), which had been divided into five large rooms. Guards confined the suspect in one of these rooms. Each contained bunks stacked three high. Inmates constantly complained that the old straw mattresses were alive with bedbugs and vermin.

Prisoners usually kept their few personal possessions on the iron bunks — boxes, bags, pans, newspapers, empty bottles, cards and clothing all thrown together in general confusion. Those with enough money to purchase meals ate in the room, adding crumbs and scraps of food to the cobwebs, dust and dirt.

Each of the areas housed between 18 and 25 prisoners in an accumulation of filth and overcrowded conditions. All rooms opened into a hallway constantly guarded by armed soldiers. Sentries policed each floor. Shouts of sentries throughout the night, the introduction of new prisoners and the general commotion associated with changing the guard made the prison a noisy place both day and night, to the discomfort of inmates.

Room 19, dubbed the "inquisitorial chamber" was the private office of Superintendent William Wood; there he and Detective LaFayette Baker interrogated suspects. Here they questioned Mrs. Surratt. No one had pleasant memories of the experience, yet none accused the detectives of physical abuse. The interrogations were severe and the sessions aptly described as mental battles. But even in the darkest hours of the war, physical brutality was avoided. However, inquisitors used intimidation, as well as promises of early release, to influence otherwise uncooperative suspects. The third floor was reserved for solitary confinement.

Carroll Prison or Annex, where Mrs. Surratt and her female boarders were held, was a long row of buildings facing A Street. The women could see the Washington countryside from their barred windows, but they were warned not to stick their heads through the bars. From the north window they had a view of the railway depot and a dirty little village called Swampoodle, the dwelling place of many former slaves.

Inmates passed the time crowded around the windows to get a glimpse of the newest arrivals. Arrests occurred daily, often hourly. The arrival of a new prisoner was simple during the day, but at night, it became an ordeal. One small candle provided the only light. Upon entering the sleeping area, the new inmate and the guard usually stumbled over prisoners sleeping on the floor. Although bunk-style cots lined the walls, the inmates usually preferred the floor or the tables to the vermin-infested beds. Nearly all of the floor space was occupied. After stumbling around with a candle, the guard would find space for the newcomer. Those awakened by the noise would subject the new arrival to a friendly cross-examination, asking his name, where he was from and what he was in for. If he had not eaten, they would search around to find food. If he had cheated the Government, or was a blockade-runner, they believed he would be held only a short period. Prisoners assumed that anyone who defrauded the Government could use the money gained to pay his way out. If, however, he had spoken disloyally, the suspect would be in for two or three months without a trial and then be released unceremoniously.

All inmates were permitted thirty minutes to eat and exercise in the prison yard. Those who could afford to buy food ate early in order to leave more time for recreation outside. In the summertime prisoners crowded the exercise yard. In the hottest months, tents were placed outside to house some inmates, relieving the overcrowding. There was hardly room to walk, much less to exercise.

As bad as the yard was, at least it afforded prisoners an opportunity to converse with each other. But conversation was closely monitored by Government spies. Authorities placed informers in all rooms and scattered them around the prison. Some were easily identifiable, but others often went undetected. These paid spies sent daily reports to Baker. In this way, authorities were generally well-informed, and the prisoners kept on their guard.

For some reason, the mess hall stood near the hospital facilities. The combination of putrid food and foul hospital odors made it almost impossible to eat. Prisoners generally grabbed a piece of bread and a hunk of fat meat and hurried into the open air. The mess hall was a long room furnished with crude pine tables on which food was heaped. The meal usually consisted of poorly cooked beans, rice and a portion of fat meat. One exception to the unappetizing menu was the bread, which was good. Superintendent Wood insisted on giving prisoners the best bread.

Victuals at Old Capitol may have been bad because the Superintendent's nephew, Corporal Brown, operated a lucrative business selling edibles. He not only sold food, but also tobacco, cigars and stationery. His big money, however, was selling liquor.

The liquor business was a little complicated. First the prisoner had to get a whiskey pass from Superintendent Wood. This he obtained by getting permission from the prison physician to keep liquor in the hospital for daily medicinal purposes. The pass, signed by Wood and the physician, permitted the bearer to purchase whiskey, from which a liberal sample had usually been taken by prison guards "for examination as to its quality."[7]

Little attention was given to the spiritual needs of prisoners by the cynical Superintendent. However, on one pleasant Sunday morning they were surprised by the announcement that "All ye who want to hear the Lord God preached according to Jeff Davis, go down to the yard; and all ye who want

to hear the Lord God preached according to Abe Lincoln, go down to Room
No. 16." When some of the inmates asked Superintendent Wood what would
happen to those who did not want to hear any preaching, he replied they could
stay in their rooms. The Superintendent scorned all religion and boasted of
being an infidel. To him, all preachers were useless and contradictory. The very
idea of men appealing to the same God as they killed one another seemed
incongruous.

Even so, most prisoners took the opportunity to get out of their rooms, if
not to hear sermons. The Gospel according to Jeff Davis was preached on this
occasion by a hard-shell Baptist whose discourse was convincing, at least to
Southerners. His text was "Glory to God in the highest and peace on earth to
men of good will." The preacher blamed the present troubles on the "bigotry of
New England," temperance leaders, tract distributors, and missionary and abolition societies. There was very little Gospel in the message, but it satisfied his
audience.

Superintendent Wood, being contemptuous of the whole service, saw an
opportunity to make the preacher look ridiculous. Commenting on the text
about "peace on earth," Wood imagined he saw a contradiction in the Scriptures. What about the verse that says, "I did not come to present you with
peace, but with a sword," he scoffed. The hard-shell Baptist, in spite of his
mixed-up loyalties, was prepared in biblical argument. The sword in this verse,
he quickly responded, referred to the Word of God, adding pointedly that God
would use it against such infidels as the Superintendent. One of few men willing to stand up to Edwin Stanton limped away from any further confrontation.
The congregation was so pleased, it could hardly refrain from applause.

Naturally the Gospel according to Abe Lincoln was not so pleasing to
Southerners. The few who heard parts of both discourses had little praise for
the abolitionist preacher or his wife who accompanied him. In the first place,
the woman spoke through her nose and what made it worse, they said, she
pressed her finger against her nose "as if to make her nasal twang more perfect
in her estimation and more disagreeable to her hearers." The congregation
almost laughed at the imprudence of "her address." Her husband was no better,
for he "made up in presumption what he lacked in ability."[8] An abolitionist
preacher could hardly have expected a joyous reception among inmates confined for their proslavery activities.

Prisoners had scratched expressions of resentment against the Government and President Lincoln on the prison walls for years. Even though the
walls were occasionally whitewashed, graffiti was quickly replaced. Anathemas
against those who had placed them behind bars filled every available space.

Occasionally some enterprising individuals decorated the walls with drawings, usually of Confederate or state flags, some with artistic merit. A life-size
drawing of Stonewall Jackson on his horse covered one wall. A Rebel poet confined in Room 10 left his sentiments on the wall to encourage future inmates:

> In fancy free my mind doth roam
> From prison walls to distant home;
> No prison walls my thoughts can bound,

> No tyrant's power can make me fear;
> Though hireling bayonets me surround,
> What I was free, I still am here.[9]

Some expressions were strangely contradictory. Confined Rebels were painfully conscious of their own lack of freedom yet failed to see any similarity between freedom denied slaves and their own temporary loss of it. One inmate wrote:

> Freeman, ye sleep while the Nation is dying;
> Arouse from your stupor, ye sons of the brave;
> See, in the Bastiles [sic] your comrades are
>   lying;
> Shall tyranny trample them down to the grave?
>   No! you reply,
>   Freemen will die,
> Rather than one shall live as a slave.

The slavery against which he objected was not, of course, the enslavement of the black man.

The atmosphere at Old Capitol Prison generally softened after Lincoln's death. Antagonism toward the dead President still persisted, however. Even his untimely death could not change those who blamed him for their ills.

Carroll Prison was a filthy place, but, in general, women prisoners were treated better than the men. Spider webs hung from the ceilings and vermin scampered across floors. But women's cells were less crowded and somewhat better equipped than those for men. Women were provided with straw mattresses on heavy iron bedsteads. One rough-textured brown blanket was provided for each inmate. In one corner of the room a stoneware jug and a tin cup stood on a small table. One wooden chair completed the sparse furnishings; a single sparingly used candle provided light. The women's food was plain and unappetizing but usually better than either Union or Confederate soldiers were used to. Each female prisoner was allotted a small coffee pot. Coarse brown sugar, savoring of molasses and crawling with ants, provided sweetening. One half cup of milk, two slices of wheat bread and a pat of butter supplied supper. Prisoners always complained of dirty plates.[10]

Guards allowed the ladies from the Surratt house considerable freedom during their first days. They were allowed to walk about freely and were not even locked up at night. Mrs. Surratt's treatment contrasted with that of Arnold, Payne, Atzerodt and O'Laughlin who were roughly handled aboard the ironclads.

Officials confined Honora Fitzpatrick with one of the most infamous Southern spies, Virginia Lomax. Honora and Olivia Jenkins were questioned intensively but were released after only a few days.

Convinced that Confederates would try to set the conspirators free, the Federal Govenment kept the prime suspects under heavy guard. Mrs. Surratt was not at this time a major suspect.

XI
"Communication with Jeff Davis"

Mrs. Surratt was born Mary Elizabeth Jenkins in 1823 in southern Prince Georges County, Maryland, and reared in Waterloo on Calvert's Manor. Her father died when she was very young. She never ventured more than 50 miles from her birthplace. Her parents and grandparents lived in the area which is today occupied by Andrews Air Force Base. Several older gentlemen observed that their parents forbade them, when boys, to call on the Jenkins girl. However, this comment may have resulted from later notoriety. Some neighbors remembered Mary Jenkins as a belle in her youth, which did not last long because of her early marriage. In 1840, when she was 17, she married John Harrison Surratt, Sr., a much older man. The young bride and her husband spent their first years together at Condin's Mill (near what later became Oxon Hill), on property which Surratt had inherited from his uncle. Here their three children were born. Unconfirmed rumors hinted that the house was later set on fire by their slaves.

In 1852 Surratt bought a 287-acre farm from Charles B. Calvert, located on the peninsula that extended southeast of Washington. Fine homes of the tobacco aristocracy once dotted the area, but it had been left behind culturally. By the 1860s there was hardly a town in the region with more than a few hundred inhabitants.

Here Surratt built a modest house. An enterprising man, he opened a tavern in a corner as soon as it was finished. The residence was ideally located at the crossroads of the main route from Washington to Port Tobacco and the Marlboro to Piscataway road. It became a favorite stopping place for local farmers and travelers from Port Tobacco. The lone abode at the crossroads became known as Surratt's villa or Surrattsville.

Leading families in Charles and Prince Georges counties, the Berrys, the Hills, and the Wests, were planters on a large scale. The Surratts were not among the elite, as they had "never been land owners to any extent, nor produced any public men, nor done anything higher than keep a roadside tavern."[2]

In 1845 the Maryland General Assembly named Prince Georges County an electoral district. Some years later, authorities designated the Surratts' house a polling place. The United States Post Office Department also granted permission to use the house as the local post office. The elder Surratt did a little blacksmithing as well as farming. His wife managed the post office and took care of the housework with the help of slaves.

The two-story Surratt house, which cost $600, was a plain white-clapboard dwelling. One visitor in 1867 described it as "disappointing."[3] The roads, dusty or muddy by turn, and the numerous sheds and outbuildings deprived the place of the simple elegance it might have possessed. Little grass or shrubs enhanced the surroundings, which were littered with broken wagon wheels and boards. A few peach trees grew behind the dwelling, and hitching rails stood near the tavern entrance. A high wooden fence encircled the family entrance. The fence provided at least some privacy from the daily gathering of patrons of the bar who tied their horses on the north side.

The post office, consisting of a few wooden pigeonholes, stood in a small area behind the bar. A second doorway in the barroom led to a room furnished with a table used by daily guests to play cards and by overnight guests as a dining table.[4]

The front—or main—entrance which faced the road to Washington opened into a hallway, to the right of which was the parlor. The family dining room extended behind the parlor. Several bedrooms on the second floor and a cellar completed the dwelling. Toward the back of the south side was a one-story attached shed used as a storage room. Scattered around the dwelling, at a distance, were several wooden sheds—the chicken house, privy and tool shed—typical of rural homes at that time.

The Surratts, like most families in the area, were slaveholders with strong Southern sympathies. Approximately 90 percent of their neighbors favored the Confederacy. Slaves still worked the Surratt farm in 1863. Lincoln's Emancipation Proclamation had only freed slaves in the states in rebellion; it had not affected those in Maryland, which remained in the Union. They had to wait until the state took action to free them in 1864. Most families in the vicinity had sons serving in the Confederate army. Maryland Rebels had easy access to the southern side of the Potomac, Richmond being less than 100 miles from the Surratts' home.

The 42-year-old, dark-haired, heavyset widow carried her neat but ample figure with pride. She was by disposition friendly and self-confident. Mary Surratt's exact age was not generally known, and most judged her to be much older. Her family, including her mother, who seems to have had little contact with her only daughter, and brothers J. Zadoc and John Jenkins, lived in the same general area.

The Surratt household had been disrupted by the slavery controversy and the ensuing war. Mrs. Surratt supported the Confederacy with all her considerable strength. By all accounts she was a "good" woman, devoted to her church, her family (especially her younger son) and the Old South. To Mary Surratt, as to multitudes of Southerners, there was no inconsistency in this devotion.

In the uneasy environment of prewar years when the slavery question split the Nation and families, the Surratts reared two sons and a daughter. John Surratt, Sr., though a proslavery man, was not an open secessionist. Immediately after Lincoln's inauguration, the elder son, Isaac, joined the Rebel army. Isaac, unlike his lanky, blond younger brother, was a powerfully built man of

Isaac Surratt. This photograph was incorrectly identified as of his brother John in the first reward posters (Library of Congress – BH821-6733).

dark complexion. Anna, the middle child, about 22, was tall and slim. She had fair skin, a large forehead and sharp features, somewhat resembling her brother John. Anna had been sent to boarding school in Bryantown and was therefore away from home most of the time.

John, at 21, the baby of the family, was his mother's pride. When about 10, he was enrolled at Father Wiget's school on 10th Street in Washington. Later he attended St. Mary's Preparatory School near Baltimore before becoming a ministerial student at St. Charles College near Elliott Mills, Maryland.[5]

The campus of St. Charles, facing the beautiful Carroll estate, was within sight of a little county road down which students watched Rebel soldiers marching to battle. John later remembered himself at that time as a red-hot rebel who dearly loved his native state. College rules prohibited discussion of the tense political and social issues dividing the Nation. Louis Weichmann confided

LaFayette C. Baker, chief of the War Department secret service. He was one of several claimants to a major share of the reward money (Library of Congress— USZ62-49959).

later, however, that the school had been favorable to the success of the rebellion and that students were kept ignorant of Union victories. Surratt became convinced that his place was "in the ranks of the Southern Confederacy."[6] An obedient student, he was well-liked by his professors. Surratt joined a school organization called the "Society of the Angels," an especially pious group. Yet feeling that the priesthood was not for him, he decided to leave school. Parting was not easy for the young man, who wept openly. The president had high praise for Surratt when he left in July of 1862.[7]

Surratt's father died suddenly only a few weeks after his son returned home. The elder Surratt bequeathed to his widow the farm and house at Surrattsville and a house he had bought in Washington.

The family lived like most middle-class citizens in the border states, but life was not easy for anyone in 1863. Mrs. Surratt supplemented her meager income by selling fruits and vegetables at the market in Washington. While John was in the capital with his mother's produce, he visited Weichmann and invited him to the farm twelve miles south of the city. Louis gladly accepted, thus initiating a friendship with the rest of the Surratt family.

The area of Maryland south of Washington served as a route for Confederate couriers traveling between the Union capital and Richmond. Early in the fighting, results of Federal Cabinet meetings were known in Richmond within 24 hours. The Confederate capital had New York newspapers almost as soon as they were available in Washington. The War Department discovered that Rebels had a regular mail route from the north, through Washington, then south through Lower Maryland, where it crossed the Potomac in the vicinity of Port Tobacco. Couriers then carried mail to Fredericksburg, Virginia, where the more urgent news was telegraphed to Richmond.

Late in 1861, LaFayette Baker attempted to break up these underground communications. He took 300 men to search Lower Maryland, with orders to occupy the region, if necessary. Detectives soon found only a few inhabitants loyal to the Union, and they were intimidated by the overwhelming majority of Southern sympathizers. Baker and his men systematically visited each hamlet and village, giving special attention to post offices. He found only two Union men in the town of Allen's Fresh, and in the post office, he discovered five letters addressed to fictitious names. On opening the envelopes, Baker observed they contained sealed letters addressed to well-known Southerners. Similar trickery existed in Newport. In the town of Chaplico, only four persons out of a population of 200–300 professed to be loyal to the Union. Upon investigation, Baker discovered that the Rebel majority had threatened to hang anyone who dared to express loyalty to the Union. The postmaster in Chaplico openly declared his support of the Confederacy. At Leonardtown, one of the largest villages in Lower Maryland, Baker found similar conditions. Most citizens declared that they were "State's Rights Men" rather than call themselves Confederates.[8]

Baker eventually visited the crossroads village of Surrattsville. In addition to the Surratt house, the hamlet included a few scattered cabins. Baker realized that Surrattsville, like other towns in the area, was strongly pro–Southern. He discovered that Confederate mail was passed from Mathias Creek, Virginia, to Port Tobacco, on to Surrattsville and from there to Washington and points north.

Baker reported the condition of each post office to both the Postmaster General and the War Department. In 1862, he investigated the area again and dismissed disloyal postmasters.[9]

Mrs. Surratt's son lost his job as postmaster after Baker's second sweep. However, while Surratt was serving as a Confederate spy, he convinced postal authorities that he was a loyal citizen. On December 16, 1863, he wrote his Yankee cousin, Belle Seaman, who had criticized him for holding an office as postmaster in a Government he pretended to despise. John bragged that although he had lost his job in "this *E poor busted up Union* . . . I have *proved my loyalty*, so that it cannot be doubted, and will regain my office as P. M. Joy is mine."[10] Most of his actions were just part of an adventurous game, but not all.

With the establishment of Confederate agents in Canada in 1864, Rebels expanded the underground mail. Confederates organized the "Canadian Cabinet," as the agents were often called, to disrupt Northern cities and hamper the United States Government. They began work in Montreal shortly before Booth opened a bank account in the same city.

The Federal Government determined to break up Rebel mail service but had difficulty capturing the couriers. On January 3, 1865, a "Report on the Secret Mail Route from Canada through Washington to Port Tobacco to Richmond" was prepared at the United States Consulate in Toronto and sent to Secretary of State Seward. The report revealed that Rebels in Canada "have a quick and successful communication with Jeff Davis. . . ." Rebels used strikingly modern methods according to the consul. Photographed letters were hidden in metal buttons and later read with a magnifying glass. As an additional precaution, the letters were written in cipher.

The secret route had been traced from Canada to Baltimore where blockade-runners received additional dispatches before proceeding to Washington. Confederate agents in the capital examined the papers and then sent them on to Port Tobacco where couriers were concealed in private homes. At Port Tobacco, the dispatch boxes were marked "mineral specimens," and passports of the blockade-runners were checked before the final leg of the journey. The couriers crossed the Potomac at night on their way to Richmond through Bowling Green, Virginia. After a short stay in the Confederate capital, they started back to Canada. The round trip took about two weeks.[11]

XII
Unanswered Questions

The *Washington National Intelligencer* headline of April 18 announced "IM-PORTANT ARRESTS," but the article did not mention the names of those apprehended. It simply alluded to arrests made the previous night at a boarding-house on H Street. The *Washington Star* also carried the news in large letters. Still, Mrs. Surratt was not the one who attracted attention, but rather the man known as Louis Payne. The evening paper told of his asking to see Mrs. Surratt, but it reported nothing of her response. Up to this point, the name Mary Surratt was unknown to the public, although it was increasingly well known to investigators.

The shadow of the gallows started to fall on Payne, however. On the day of his arrest, searchers found, near the Capitol, a light-colored sack coat, spattered with blood and fitting the description of the one worn by Seward's attacker. The pocket contained a false mustache.

Detectives quickly followed up on the arrests. In a few hours they identified Kirby, mentioned by Mrs. Surratt, as William Wallace Kirby, an officer in the criminal court of Washington and a brother-in-law of John Holohan. Kirby was called in for interrogation immediately. He admitted he had visited the Surratt house twice on the day Lincoln died and had talked to Mrs. Surratt concerning the whereabouts of her son John. She told Kirby that he was the first person to whom she had mentioned John's trip to Canada. This last part was incorrect. She impressed the fact on Weichmann and other boarders. It seemed to comfort the landlady that John was safe. The rest of her life was lived with that satisfaction.

Other members of the Surratt household never mentioned Kirby's two visits. In her first interrogation, Mrs. Surratt barely remembered one visit.[1]

Besides his calls on Saturday, Kirby talked with Mrs. Surratt again on Monday. This time he urged her to tell authorities all she knew about John. The parallels between the concerns of Weichmann and Kirby are clear; both seemed to feel that John might have been indirectly involved, and both, think-ing Mrs. Surratt innocent, expected her to cooperate with the investigation.

Not knowing she had been arrested, Kirby went to the boardinghouse again Tuesday morning. It is hard to believe that anyone actually involved in the plot would have risked so many visits to the suspect's family. Kirby's statements revealed very little to detectives, although they reaffirmed belief that Mrs. Surratt's reactions were unnatural under the circumstances.

In addition to major arrests and disclosures, bits of information drifted in which helped solve the crime. John Morris, a black man employed to raise the curtain at Ford's Theatre, said he saw Booth there several times on April 14 between 10:00 and 11:00 a.m. His testimony coincided with other statements placing Booth at the theater when it was first known that the President would attend the play that night. Morris added, almost incidentally, that while there, Booth called for Edward Spangler. This second mention of Spangler placed him more clearly among the prime suspects.[2]

Mr. and Mrs. Thomas Green, arrested on April 18, were well-known Southern sympathizers who had two sons in the Confederate army. On searching their house, detectives found a large parcel of letters ready to be sent south. Among the papers detectives discovered a letter addressed to John Surratt, signed by a man named Parker. There were also letters to Green from a Mrs. Parr who owned a china shop in Baltimore. When Payne first arrived at the Surratts' boardinghouse he identified himself by stating that he worked in Parr's china shop. Questioned about the letters, Green denied knowing anything about them. When asked if he knew Surratt, he said no. Officers sought to jar his memory, "You have a letter to him."

"I may have a letter to him," he replied caustically, "but I don't know him."

Concerning Mrs. Parr, he was asked, "Why did she write to you?"

"I don't know," answered Green.

Authorities asked Green what the lady meant when she wrote, "You got me out of an unpleasant position one time and I appeal to you again."

He replied haughtily, "I will not become the informer of anyone."[3]

Detectives observed that the letter had been delivered by hand and had not gone through the regular mails. When questioned about this, Green acknowledged that it had been brought to him personally, but declined to divulge the messenger's name. Unaccountably, the Government did not push him further, and after a brief confinement, the Greens were released.

Well-intentioned advice deluged investigators. Several suggested that detectives thoroughly search Ford's Theatre. One person wrote that Booth had dropped down through a trap door in the theater. A lady clairvoyant said that Booth was concealed at 11-J Street. Several wrote that he had escaped in women's clothing. One thought Booth was hiding in a house of ill repute. Colonel Burnett catalogued hundreds of these tips, and detectives checked the most promising leads. Most, however, were a waste of time.

Although detectives performed well, they failed to follow several critical leads. A letter from R. W. Walker revealed that John Matthews of Ford's Theatre knew something about the affair. Matthews, in fact, knew too much. Judge Joseph Holt received a clue from William Rainnie, indicating that John McCullough, who had been a close associate of Booth, had used strong language against the Union.[4] McCullough, however, took refuge in Canada before he could be questioned. McCullough and Matthews were important suspects from whom the Government learned little. Both men knew enough to have saved the President's life had they been so inclined. And both would probably have been given prison sentences had they been thoroughly investigated.

Before the murder, Booth wrote a letter justifying the impending crime. The afternoon of the attacks, he met Matthews on the corner of Pennsylvania Avenue and 13th Street. According to Matthews' later account, the meeting was accidental. Booth asked him to give the document to John F. Coyle, one of the editors of the *National Intelligencer*, "tonight by eleven o'clock, unless I see you before that." Booth added, "If I do, I can attend to it myself."[5]

The next time Matthews saw his friend, Booth was dashing past him toward the back door of the theater. In the commotion, Matthews rushed to his dressing room, got his wardrobe, passed under the stage, and left the theater through the orchestra. He walked quickly to his lodging, only a few yards from the theater, locked the door and, in changing his clothes, found Booth's letter. He opened it and read Booth's justification. Matthews, convinced there was no way he could explain his possession of the document without implicating himself, burned it and stirred the ashes. For a man who had just glanced at its contents in a moment of nervous excitement, Matthews later recalled its contents amazingly well, at least what he said were the contents.

After Matthews burned the manuscript, according to Coyle, who later learned of the incident, he went to see Father Boyle, his former classmate at St. Mary's College. He told of Booth's letter and repeated its words as he remembered them. The priest assured him that he had done right and advised Matthews to flee to Canada and remain there until the affair was over. Before Matthews escaped, however, detectives apprehended him. He was among the first suspects police questioned. Matthews revealed nothing about Booth's letter and was released. Immediately afterward he fled to Canada.[6]

His flight indicated how easy it was to escape from Washington. Where Matthews stayed in Canada, and precisely why Father Boyle advised him to go, were never determined.

Matthews returned too soon. Detectives arrested him again and Colonel Foster interrogated him on April 30. Matthews admitted he knew Booth slightly, and that on the afternoon of the murder he had accidentally met him. Booth offered him his wardrobe box, saying that he would not need it anymore. Again, Matthews made no mention of the letter.[7]

Among a few good leads which authorities failed to pursue were scores of false ones. Police received information that one Arthur Judd had disappeared mysteriously on the night of the murder. A Mrs. Anderson said the son of a radical secessionist, named Rosin, had been in Washington on the night of the crime and ought to be investigated. Receiving an anonymous letter, after the assassination, threatening Lincoln's life, H. S. Olcott hurried off on what proved to be an unsuccessful search for the writer. Another anonymous writer reported to Stanton that Mr. Grover of Grover's Theatre was disloyal.

Officials found several seemingly fake letters signed with Booth's name, and others addressed to him or to Surratt. Benjamin Booth Cook, a 22-year-old mental patient, told authorities he had heard that the President was to have been assassinated at the Soldiers' Home.[8] Detectives knew that the Soldiers' Home figured in the original plot but were not sure about the rest of Cook's testimony.

John Matthews, a trusted friend of Booth who had a minor part in the play. Booth gave him a document to be published, which Matthews destroyed.

In addition to mail received by the War Department, detectives collected a mass of documents and suspicious articles. They accumulated two packages of Weichmann's letters, a package of suspicious letters from the Washington Post Office, a bundle of evidence from the Surratt house, a stack of papers found in Arnold's quarters and a trunkful of material from Booth's room. Very little of this material was presented in court, although it contained incriminating papers.

Investigators inspected all suspicious mail. They opened hundreds of letters mailed to and from Canada, and mail to the suspects, such as the Fords or the Booth brothers. Detectives scrutinized telegrams sent both before and after the assassination. Investigators found an unusually large correspondence between John Wilkes and his brother Junius Brutus, some suspicious. When evidence indicated that Booth's sister, Blanch Booth DeBar, knew of the plot, she was called in for questioning.[9] They discovered several peculiar letters from Booth's girl friends. Government archives contain numerous papers, such as the note sent by Burnett to the post office, "Herewith I have the honor to return for mail one hundred and sixty-six letters opened by the direction of the Secretary of War."[10]

The War Department received communications from citizens stating they

Left: John Wilkes Booth in his usual dapper attire. Perhaps the actor's reputation as a fashionable dresser led witnesses to imagine that he wore a stylish flat hat rather than a crude slouch hat to the theater (Library of Congress— USZ62-25166). Top, right: Edwin Booth as Hamlet. Edwin, the most talented and successful of the Booth brothers, opposed his brother's politics but requested John's body for burial in the family plot (Library of Congress—USZ62-40342). Bottom, right: Junius Brutus Booth, Jr., as Brutus. Detectives arrested him after finding several suspicious references in his letters to John Wilkes. (Engraving by G. E. Ellis from a painting by John Neagle, in the collection of the Museum of the City of New York, Theatre and Music Collection. Library of Congress— USZ62-44491.)

had seen John Surratt on the day of the murder. Most were investigated. D. C. Reed, who lived a block from the Surratts in Washington and who had known the family for years, swore that on April 14, he had seen John, alone, on Pennsylvania Avenue between 4½ and 6th streets. Reed said he had noticed that Surratt was wearing a set of new brass spurs.[11] Evidence of Surratt's presence in Washington on the day of the murder was not strong, but those who claimed to have seen him were positive about it. Reed stuck to his story when questioned by Colonel Foster—leaving contemporaries, as well as later historians, divided on the question.

Detectives, accumulating material for the trial, reexamined Booth's possessions carefully and discovered a little note signed "J. Harrison Surratt." The notation said, "I tried to get leave but could ... [illegible]."[12] Another letter written by Surratt was addressed to "Miss Bell Seaman, in care of Thomas Seaman, Washington."

> Montreal, April 10, 1865
>
> Have been in Montreal for a week. Great many pretty girls here. Enjoying myself—nothing to do but visit the ladies and go to church.
>
> I always knew the Old Confederacy would go up the spout and that the flag Washington left us would wave again over North and South. For special reasons you can direct your letters as below.
>
> Your cousin,
> John Harrison
> St. Laurence Hall
> Montreal[13]

This notice contrasted with others he had written. It seemed designed to prove he had been in Canada several days before the murder and that he was loyal to the Union. Significantly, it was postmarked a day after Lee's surrender.

In spite of strenuous efforts, LaFayette Baker's investigation lagged behind others. General Augur directed the overall military investigation. Under his immediate command were Colonels Foster, Wells and Olcott. Baker visited Augur's headquarters to determine what progress had been made and to ferret out information. But Augur's staff let the Secret Service chief know that his services were not needed. They advised him that they had enough facts to solve the crime and knew where most conspirators were. Whenever Baker pressed the military for information, their response was either evasive or insulting. The detective, therefore, determined to carry out his own independent search and accordingly set up headquarters at 217 Pennsylvania Avenue, across from the Willard Hotel.[14]

The huge rewards chiefly motivated this reluctance to share information. Although it is impossible to equate the reward money in terms of current dollars, even a small portion of the payment for Booth's capture was enough to purchase a house and large farm. In 1865 it meant financial security.

On April 18, Baker sent six men to search Lower Maryland again. After several weary days of tracking through the countryside, they had uncovered nothing.

Maj. James O'Beirne commissioned a more successful search party under the command of Lt. Alexander Lovett. Lovett's force of 25 cavalrymen and several of O'Beirne's detectives again questioned citizens south of Washington. This group eventually secured valuable information from John Lloyd and Dr. Samuel Mudd.

Interrogating inhabitants along the way, Lovett's men continued south toward Bryantown. On learning that Dr. Mudd had received visitors on the night of the murder, they visited his house and asked if he had any information on the criminals. Mudd said no. Although the doctor had been expecting the soldiers, he seemed excited and evasive. Asked if he had seen any suspicious

Christopher C. Augur, head of the Washington Department. As commander of 31,000 troops, he played an important role in the investigation—although not always competently (Library of Congress—BH831-280).

persons around his farm, he denied this also. After the officers pressed their investigation, he finally told of two "strangers" who had come to his house at daybreak Saturday. He reluctantly mentioned that he set a broken leg for one of the "strangers." Up to that time authorities had no idea that the assassin was maimed. They were sure, however, that the man referred to was Booth. Mudd misleadingly asserted that the men remained only a short time, but his wife admitted that they stayed most of the day. The country doctor and gentleman farmer added that one of the men borrowed a razor to shave off his mustache. He also told of making a pair of crutches for the injured man and of showing the "strangers" the way across the swamp to Allen's Fresh.[15] He failed to mention that both men were heavily armed with pistols, a carbine, knives, field glasses and a supply of ammunition.

Dr. Mudd claimed that he did not know the visitors. Asked when he had first learned of the assassination, he replied Sunday, April 16. Lovett did not arrest the doctor, although he was aware that most neighbors knew on Saturday and that loyal citizens reported suspicious activities immediately.

In the meantime, O'Beirne personally escorted another team by steam tug down the Potomac to Chappell's Point. The military had established a station there to prevent blockade-running. Soon after O'Beirne's arrival at nightfall on the 18th, he set up a telegraph station, keeping in direct communication with Washington. The next day O'Beirne's men began to search the area in the direction of Port Tobacco.[16]

This little backwater town had grown up on the site of an Indian village called Potomac and had been visited by John Smith as early as 1608. The town sat in the midst of gently rolling hills, covered with sycamores, cedars, pines and oaks, overlooking the Port Tobacco Creek. The creek, more aptly described as a marshy little stream, flowed into the Potomac. Port Tobacco had been the county seat of Charles County from 1658 to 1895 and was one of the places George Washington visited frequently. Some of Maryland's earliest settlers located in the vicinity. In the colonial period, two-story clapboard farmhouses, along with a few elegant homes, covered this area.

The town figured prominently in the plot against Lincoln. In this isolated spot John Surratt enlisted the services of George Atzerodt, whom the Surratt household gave the sobriquet "Port Tobacco." Its isolation and strategic location across the Potomac from Virginia made it a natural haven for blockade-runners. The once picturesque village had changed since the days when it was a center of tobacco-rich plantations; to Federal authorities it seemed to be the most utterly depraved place in the world. One writer of the period unleashed his contempt for the village:

> The Court House of Port Tobacco is the most superfluous house in the place, except the church. It stands in the center of town in a square, and the dwellings lie about it closely, as if to throttle justice. Five hundred people exist in Port Tobacco; life there reminds me, in connection with the slimy river and the adjacent swamps, of the great reptile period of the world, when iguanodons and pterodactyls pleasauri ate each other.[17]

Most families had been slaveholders with decidedly Southern sympathies. It was, therefore, a convenient place for Rebel spies to find lodging and aid. Several inhabitants actively engaged in ferrying Confederates across the river. Signals passed messages from the bluffs overlooking the river to Confederates on the Virginia side. Fights, shootings and violence occurred frequently, and, only a week before Lincoln's assassination, a United States Provost Marshal had been killed there. The Brawner House, a dilapidated residence with a sleazy bar in the basement, provided the best lodging place.

O'Beirne's men pretended to be looking for friends, which deceived no one. Atzerodt was known to have lived there with a widow named Wheeler. O'Beirne visited the woman and vaguely hinted that Atzerodt was in trouble, hoping she might reveal something, but the widow said nothing. On searching the house, detectives found Atzerodt's trunk in her attic, and in it, the key to his carriage shop, but discovered nothing important. They arrested Mr. Crangle, who had recently been living with the widow, but he furnished no useful information.

Near Port Tobacco detectives questioned a woman who told them she had been hearing someone enter her cellar at night and leave about dawn. This excited O'Beirne. He asked her to place a lamp in the window as a signal if she heard anyone entering the cellar again. At midnight, when detectives saw the lamp, they rushed to the house and searched it, but found nothing. The lady

insisted she had distinctly heard someone enter the cellar. The disappointed soldiers later learned that the woman was mentally deranged.[18]

Although Major D. H. L. Gleason visited police headquarters on the morning of April 15, and may have mentioned his suspicions of Louis Weichmann, he waited several days before providing convincing details. Gleason, a 24-year-old officer in the Union army, had suffered battle wounds before his appointment to the Commissary General of Prisoners in January 1865. He occupied a desk next to Weichmann. The two got along reasonably well. The major found Weichmann well educated and intelligent but thought him vacillating and uncertain of himself, if not cowardly.

Weichmann occasionally spoke of mysterious affairs in the house where he boarded. He mentioned that the place seemed to be a rendezvous for Rebel sympathizers who came and went at all hours. Weichmann surmised that only disloyal people were welcome there and that consequently, even he might be suspect.

Nearly two months before the assassination, Weichmann arrived at the office extremely agitated and asked Gleason if he could talk to him privately. The two went into a little supply room where Weichmann, perspiring and trembling, told the major he had been living with a terrible secret which he must reveal, but only on condition that Gleason not repeat it. The major, hesitating at first, would not promise, but finally agreed to keep the confidence if it could be done safely. Thereupon Weichmann blurted out what he knew about activities in the boardinghouse. He told of a plan to kidnap Lincoln and of constant threats against the President. Weichmann's suspicions might have been just another hoax. But he was so convincing that Gleason listened to his tale of pistols, daggers, false mustaches, suspicious people and frequent visits by the actor John Wilkes Booth.

Weichmann said he had questioned his friend John Surratt about Booth's calls and that John had made him swear not to reveal anything he knew or might find out. Surratt told him they were smuggling cotton across the lines as a blind for their real purpose—to capture President Lincoln and his Cabinet. The group planned to take their captives to Richmond and thus force the North to end the struggle. If that did not work, they expected to hold Lincoln for ransom; in any case, there was money in it, according to Weichmann's secondhand account. He said the date was set for March 4—Inauguration Day. Everything was ready; a boat had been prepared and horses were waiting on the other side of the Potomac.[19]

Weichmann begged Gleason not to even speak to him in public, as he was being watched. He seemed genuinely frightened and the major felt sorry for him, but did not entirely believe the story. Weichmann, however, assured Gleason that he was telling the truth, even though he did not know all the details. Gleason agreed to think it over and provide what protection he could for the frightened clerk.

Opposite: Dr. Mudd's house near Bryantown, Maryland. Booth and Herold had to travel off the main road in the dark to find it.

That evening the major reflected on Weichmann's tale, and, even though it seemed absurd, he came to the conclusion that he must tell the Secretary of War. However, it was more difficult to get an audience with Stanton than with the President.

The next day the two talked again. Gleason advised Weichmann to tell Stanton. Nothing came of his conversation. They discussed the apparent conspiracy several times, but neither told authorities.

Gleason eventually related Weichmann's account to his roommate, Lt. Joshua Sharp. The lieutenant, a quiet, reasonable young man, had a better opportunity to inform the War Department because he was working on General Augur's staff. Sharp, however, thought the whole thing nonsense. No one, he said, would be foolish enough to try to kidnap the President. Gleason, nevertheless, persisted, reasoning that, absurd as it seemed, it might be true. At length, Sharp agreed to inform authorities. The next morning at work Gleason told Weichmann that Sharp was going to notify the War Department.

Weichmann became completely unnerved, complaining that his life would not be safe if the conspirators suspected him; he begged Gleason to reveal nothing. In disgust, Gleason snapped that Weichmann could take care of it himself, but if not, Sharp would do it.[20] The latter eventually informed the War Department, but it is not certain how much information Sharp passed on. Years later, Gleason recalled that Stanton had only been advised of some vague plot. Even after the assassination, Sharp refused to say anything on the subject.

Kidnapping the President at the inauguration proved too risky. Booth and his associates decided on the more practical plan of capturing Lincoln on his way to the Soldiers' Home. When Inauguration Day passed without tragic consequences, Gleason and Sharp began to think that Weichmann had been deceived. Busy with the cumbersome details of concluding the war, they forgot about Weichmann's tale until April 14.

The Secretary of War ordered two companies of cavalry to follow the President's carriage after Sharp's report. Noticing the guards, Lincoln queried the soldier in charge about his assignment. The officer replied that Stanton had ordered him to provide an escort for the Commander-in-Chief. Lincoln dismissed the danger, adding that the guard was unnecessary and that he would ask Stanton to rescind it. It is not known what Lincoln said to Stanton, if anything, but the guard continued. Weichmann's apprehensions may have saved the President from earlier capture, but they merely postponed his assassination.

Soon after Sharp's revelation, Weichmann himself revealed his concerns to police officer McDevitt. The officer, who seems to have been an acquaintance, notified local authorities. It is doubtful that McDevitt passed this information on to the War Department, but it explains why he searched the Surratt house soon after the shooting.[21]

No one to whom Weichmann revealed his suspicions was called to testify during the trial. The War Department may have concealed the fact that it had been warned, albeit vaguely. Stanton had, however, done all in his power to protect the President, occasionally against Lincoln's will. Nearly fifty years later, after Weichmann's death, Gleason told of Weichmann's first fearful conversation about his suspicions. Perhaps Gleason exaggerated his role in revealing the plot. Weichmann asserted on one occasion that neither he nor Gleason had ever spoken of their suspicions to authorities until after the assassination. The truth may never be known.

It is certain, however, that on Tuesday, April 18, Gleason told the War Department what he knew. War Department files indicate this was his first definite statement. He spoke of a French woman who carried money to the St. Albans raiders in Canada. According to Gleason, she was arrested in New York and later released. This statement confirmed an almost identical account given by Atzerodt and later by Weichmann.[22]

At the time of the assassination, only Southern blockade-runners knew of the French lady. She had been seen at Mrs. Surratt's boardinghouse, and one of her close associates was held at that moment in Old Capitol Prison. The French lady, later identified as Mrs. Sara Antoinette Slater, worked with John Surratt and his mother. Authorities never seriously investigated her, and she has remained a nebulous figure, hovering somewhere on the periphery of the assassination plot.

During his interrogation, Gleason hedged a little. At first, he intimated he had not known of any attempt to kidnap the President. Weichmann, he said, had told him only that about $100–150 had been spent on some vague scheme. Weichmann had also noted that he was not asked to join in the plot, although he thought that he could have.

According to Gleason, Weichmann bragged to other clerks that he could become rich through the intrigue. The major revealed that he advised Weichmann to join the conspirators to learn more of their plans.

Inadvertently he had confessed more than he intended. Passions were so intense that witnesses avoided acknowledging that they had any idea of a plot against the Government. Gleason, seeking to put himself in the best light, quickly added that he had advised Weichmann to get the Provost Marshal's permission to join the group in order to expose the conspirators. Weichmann, however, thought it too risky, and Gleason did not believe the fearful clerk could inspire confidence. Gleason further protected himself by claiming that he had not really believed much of the story anyway.

The major stated that Weichmann did not know details but suggested that by administering chloroform to one of the participants, he might discover some secrets. The only names Gleason remembered were Booth and Surratt, both of whom were already the main suspects. He added significantly that after the assassination, he told authorities of his suspicions.

Following the interview, a strange and never-fully-explained incident occurred. Detectives showed Gleason a pair of boots which had been taken off Louis Payne a few hours before. The witness identified them as boots that a Mr. Wright had lent to Weichmann prior to the crime. Furthermore, Gleason asserted that Wright had lent Weichmann a pistol as well.[23] Possibly Gleason was mistaken about the time, or perhaps Weichmann had a satisfactory explanation, but there is no indication that Weichmann was ever interrogated about the boots or the pistol. Officers found another pair of boots in Weichmann's room, which indicated Gleason was probably mistaken. Obviously attorneys for the conspirators never knew about Gleason's statement, which remained locked in Government archives. Stanton, who must have known these facts, talked harshly to Weichmann about his part in the plot but later seemed convinced of his innocence.

Stanton realized that recording countless interrogations was beyond the capabilities of Government stenographers. Therefore he sent to Cincinnati for Benn Pitman, founder of the Phonographic Institute and brother of Sir Isaac Pitman who invented a popular shorthand method. Pitman came to the United States from England in 1852 to disseminate his brother's system. Having written several books on the subject, he was a world-acknowledged expert on shorthand.

A day after the assassination, Pitman received a telegram requesting him to report at once to the Attorney General's office. Packing hurriedly, he left late that same night for Washington where he spent the next three months recording hundreds of statements.

After the first hectic days, Col. H. L. Burnett usually interrogated suspects, but sometimes detectives or police and occasionally Pitman himself would ask questions. As Stanton admonished him to avoid irrelevant matters, he did not record every word. Even so, he left an accurate account of the interrogation process. The original statements were then condensed and given to Secretary Stanton and the Judges Advocate in preparation for the trial.

The work was exhausting as the investigation was pushed nonstop by Stanton. Time-consuming questioning kept Pitman busy from 9:00 A.M. until ten or eleven in the evening. His desk was in the War Department next to Burnett's office. The building was guarded with more care than the White House. A heavy guard around the White House was unnecessary since President Johnson had not yet moved in (although Mrs. Lincoln continued to reside there). Everybody had to sign in and out of the War Department, indicating the time.[24] Although Pitman served as chief stenographer, other stenographers worked with detectives on the field.

Sixteen hours after Mrs. Surratt settled into Carroll Prison, guards led John T. Ford, owner of Ford's Theatre, up the steps to his room. He had always been a prime suspect. His long friendship with Booth and his questionable presence in Richmond at the time of the murder drew the Government's attention. After Lincoln's death, officers dispatched a telegram to Richmond for his arrest. By the time it arrived, he had left for his home in Baltimore. The telegram finally caught up with him, and he was arrested at his home on April 18.[25]

Ford, who had just celebrated his 36th birthday, began his career in his early twenties directing a minstrel show. He managed theaters in Richmond and Baltimore in addition to owning Ford's Theatre in Washington. A young man of growing influence, he had been elected president of Washington's city council and for two years was acting mayor of the city.

John Ford, proprietor of Ford's Theatre. Stanton incarcerated him and closed his theater. Ford never forgave the Government, which he criticized for decades.

The impresario found himself confined to a bare, dirty cell which offered no other comfort than a straw mattress on a crude bedstead. Indignant, he asked for paper and pencil and, stretching himself out on the floor, composed a letter to Secretary Stanton requesting release. He suggested that Stanton set bond at whatever amount. Seeking to sway the Secretary's decision, he stated that, if free, he might be able to help solve the crime. Stanton never answered.

Undaunted, Ford sent Stanton other appeals stressing the needs of his wife and six children. Stanton also ignored these requests. The hapless prisoner then sought the aid of two influential friends from Maryland, United States Senator John A. J. Creswell and Representative Henry Winter Davis. Both were loyal Unionists, apparently respected by Stanton. Republicans had offered Davis the vice-presidential nomination with Lincoln in 1860, but he refused. In addition to these efforts, Ford's wife made ceaseless efforts in her husband's behalf. Stanton, however, was highly distrustful of Ford and kept him in Old Capitol for more than a month.

His brothers, Harry and James Ford, who had been arrested on the night of the murder were already confined. When Harry saw his brother brought in, he tried to speak to him, but guards intervened. John Ford later wrote of his first days of incarceration as an indescribable horror. However, while in prison, he wrote friends that he was being "considerately treated" and had "no fault to find with those here in authority."[26] His treatment was neither as considerate as pictured in his prison letters nor as horrible as he later claimed.

Few prisons were pleasant places, particularly in wartimes. He had no table, chair or other conveniences except a slop bucket, a stoneware pitcher and a tin cup. This, however, was more than most prisoners had. Ironically, it was in the yard of Carroll Prison that Captain Henry Wirz, head of the infamous Confederate prison at Andersonville, Georgia, was hanged for mistreatment of Union prisoners.

Ford soon made himself more comfortable. Within a week, he was given a table and chair and was able to buy a wash basin. Considering that John Ford was a major suspect, he seems to have been treated well. He was, nevertheless, a civilian imprisoned without regard for normal legal procedure. The dead President, however, had left the area under martial law, and authorities carried out the investigation under these conditions.

Increasingly aggravated at his treatment, Ford wrote to Superintendent Wood requesting an interview. As a result, officials granted him exercise privileges in the yard twice a day and provided him an iron bedstead. Later he purchased more palatable food. In spite of efforts by prison authorities to ameliorate his condition, Ford complained about his treatment for the rest of his life. He nursed a special grudge against Secretary Stanton for holding him in prison without regard to his rights and for refusing to allow Mrs. Ford to visit him.

The distraught inmate spent hours writing to everyone he knew in authority. He wrote Assistant Secretary of War Charles A. Dana and to General Joseph Holt; he contacted Senator Reverdy Johnson, as well as the governor of Maryland. His wife tried repeatedly to see Secretary Stanton but was "brutally repulsed" according to Ford's account.

Ford later criticized the "torture" used to obtain information from fellow inmates. But he never claimed to have been abused personally. Torture, according to Ford, consisted of poor prison diet, handcuffs and solitary confinement, which he lamented "still do as much as inquisitorial torture could ever accomplish."[27] Zealous detectives, seeking desperately to solve the Nation's most heinous crime, undoubtedly used every legitimate persuasion to get the truth. No evidence indicates they used harsh "third degreee" methods, however.

Detectives repeatedly interrogated John's brother, Harry, and he confessed to several conversations with Booth on the day of the murder. He remembered that on the morning of the crime, Booth met his fiancée, Bessie Hale, who was living with her parents at the National Hotel. After a short conversation, the actor ate breakfast and then proceeded to the Surratt house—at least Harry Ford assumed this. Ford was standing outside the theater when Booth came down 10th Street from the north. Mrs. Surratt's house was north of the theater; the National Hotel was located south. The well-known actor arrived in his usual elegant fashion, complete with kid gloves, tall silk hat and walking cane. He entered the theater, picked up his mail, sat down on the front steps to read his correspondence and then casually asked Ford, "What's on tonight?" Harry

Henry Clay (Harry) Ford was a brother of the theater's owner and a friend of Booth. Officials jailed him, but he was not considered a prime suspect.

replied that President Lincoln and General Grant were to attend the theater and that he had just received a note from the President's staff reserving a box. Booth thought a moment, then walked away toward Pennsylvania Avenue.

Unlike John, Harry Ford did not deplore prison conditions. He ate the regular prison food: soup, beans and dry bread, and after the first week declared that he had a "very jolly time."[28]

Prison administration was notoriously irregular at Old Capitol. Occasionally a prisoner would get stuck there without any record of his presence. Partiality was shown to certain inmates, while others were severely treated. General Augur, for instance, ordered that Junius Brutus Booth not be put in irons. Most of the important suspects were more concerned about mob violence than about prison conditions, at least during the first week after the assassination. Some had been stoned and menaced by mobs when arrested. The fear of violence intensified as the hour of Lincoln's funeral approached.

XIII

Lamentations for a Modern Moses

During the postmortem in the Presidential Mansion, Mrs. Lincoln sent a messenger to request a lock of her husband's hair. After Dr. Stone cut hair from the back of Lincoln's head near the wound, Dr. Charles Taft also asked for a lock. He and other surgeons present each carried away a small bit of blood-stained hair.[1]

Doctors Brown and Alexander, who three years earlier had made Willie Lincoln's body appear so lifelike that the President had it disinterred to view again, prepared Lincoln's body. The cranium was little more than a shell, as it had been cut open and the brain removed, yet the cadaver preserved the appearance of the beloved leader.

On Monday evening, Lincoln's body was ready for viewing in the large East Room of the White House where the President and Mrs. Lincoln had enjoyed many festive occasions and where they had laid the body of their son Willie. The room soon filled with the Nation's leaders—congressmen, governors and generals. Mrs. Lincoln, however, never entered. An honor guard stood at attention constantly for the three days that the body lay in state. Flags remained at half-mast throughout the Nation during the period of mourning.[2]

April 19 dawned with the mournful tolling of church bells and the periodic booming of cannons from fortifications around the city. Fresh green leaves faintly colored the otherwise barren trees giving a hint of the coming spring; yet it was one of the most solemn days in the capital's history. The natural sorrow at the sudden loss of the Nation's leader was deepened by the emotion of genuine love for the kindly hero. Business in Washington stopped. An unnatural calm pervaded the city. Muffled dirges of military bands could be heard as the procession began to form.

Delegates quietly took their places in the cortege. A group of firemen from Philadelphia, immaculately uniformed, came to pay their respects. Representatives of other cities and organizations crowded the area around City Hall. Sorrowful and respectfully silent spectators thronged the streets. Mourners lined Pennsylvania Avenue from 15th Street to the Capitol. Only dignitaries with tickets were permitted to enter the White House.

Assistant Secretary of the Treasury Harrington, who handled the funeral details, issued passes to attend White House ceremonies. Ministers from every

Left: Tad Lincoln, the President's youngest living son, was in Grover's Theatre when the management announced the shooting. Right: Robert Lincoln about the time of his father's death. Robert stayed at his mother's side, comforting her through the tragic night (Kurtz and Allison – Art Studio, Lincoln Memorial University Museum).

denomination attended the funeral, including some who earlier had bitterly debated the theological implications of slavery.

Invited guests began to arrive at 11:00 A.M. They passed through the East Room, in the center of which the body lay in state as had the bodies of Presidents William Henry Harrison and Zachary Taylor.

The ceremonies were carefully organized; no confusion marred the dignity of the occasion. Officers took their respective places; heads of Government and bureaus, governors, as well as ambassadors from foreign countries, were all assigned a place. The East Room, crowded by the great of many nations, presented an impressive and solemn scene. At noon, emotion was heightened by the entrance of President Johnson with his Cabinet. Gen. Ulysses S. Grant sat apart from the others at the head of the catafalque. President Andrew Johnson stood opposite the main entrance. The only dignitaries absent were Secretary of State Seward, still confined to his bed, and Mrs. Lincoln, who remained upstairs with her son Tad. Members of her family were present, however, including several of her brothers and cousins and the Lincolns' son Robert. None of the President's family attended because the delegation from Springfield, with which they were traveling, did not arrive in time.[3]

After the Reverend Dr. C. H. Hall, rector of the Episcopal Church of the Epiphany, spoke a few appropriate words, Bishop Matthew Simpson, representing the Methodist Episcopal Church, led in a prayer which seemed more propaganda than supplication: "We bless Thee that no tumult has arisen, and in peace and harmony our Government moves onward; and that Thou hast shown that our Republican Government is the strongest on the face of the earth...."

The Bishop then rallied the mourners to give themselves to the "country's service until every vestige of this rebellion shall have been wiped out, and until slavery, its cause, shall be forever eradicated."[4]

A sermon followed by Lincoln's pastor, the Reverend Dr. Phineas D. Gurley of the New York Avenue Presbyterian Church. Lincoln had not been a formal member of that church, or any church, but it was the one he attended most regularly. Gurley's message was eloquent and moving but much too long.

The minister recalled Lincoln's words when he left Springfield: "I leave you with this request: pray for me."[5]

The participation of leaders of various denominations in a funeral service was a new experience for one of the spectators, Adolphe de Chambrun. He was not impressed. "We had to submit to an hour's discourse by Dr. Gurley," he wrote. He described Gurley's message as "the sort of eloquence belonging to this denomination; that is, not high-sounding phrases but a stock of dry commonplaces marshaled in good order."[6]

The Reverend Dr. E. H. Gray, pastor of the E Street Baptist Church and chaplain of the United States Senate, closed in prayer. He voiced the mood of the Nation: "God of justice, and avenger of the Nation's wrong, let the work of treason cease, and let the guilty author of this horrible crime be arrested and brought to justice."[7]

After the service, President Johnson approached the catafalque, looked briefly at the body of his predecessor and took his place in the procession.

Expressions of sorrow outside the White House, while less formal, were no less heartfelt. Thousands of recently freed slaves, who regarded Lincoln as a modern Moses, sincerely lamented their benefactor's death. They were the most grief-stricken group in Washington as they gathered around the Presidential Mansion in sorrow and despair.

Officials closed the coffin and conveyed it to the funeral carriage at the main entrance of the White House. The procession started at precisely one o'clock as church bells tolled and cannons, brought into the city for the funeral, boomed their salute. The cortege moved somberly up Pennsylvania Avenue to the Capitol. The pallbearers were Government leaders, including General Grant, Vice-Admiral David Farragut and Senator Reverdy Johnson, who later defended one of the accused conspirators.

The funeral car was drawn by six fine grey horses, each led by a soldier wearing a white sash. The President's own horse, saddled and bearing the boots of the slain leader, was led up the Avenue. President Johnson, Government leaders and pastors of both Protestant and Catholic churches followed.

Long before the cortege reached the Capitol, the area around it had filled with spectators. At three o'clock the first troops marched around the Capitol and entered the grounds at A and First streets in front of Old Capitol Prison and the adjoining Carroll Annex.

President Andrew Johnson. He supported the findings of the trial but later alienated Radical Republicans (Library of Congress—BH826-1516).

The conspiracy suspects were frightfully aware that the sound of drums and constantly firing cannons throughout the day expressed deep sorrow as well as restrained rage. Guards did not allow prisoners to see the procession, but the sound of shuffling feet and bands approaching caused uneasiness. Harry Ford said that the prisoners' persistent fear of mob violence was intensified by the funeral. He recalled, "we did not know but the people in their excitement would mob the prison and lynch us."[8] But most thoughts on this day were concentrated on the dead President, not on the living assassins. The soldiers and throngs passed by the prison without demonstration.

The scene in the Capitol rotunda was appropriately somber. The gigantic paintings by John Trumbull and Emanuel Leutz had been covered with black cloth and all of the statues were completely draped, except for that of George Washington, around which a black sash had been tied.[9] Soldiers placed the corpse on the catafalque at precisely 3:30. After Dr. Gurley read the burial service, the assembly filed out in silence.

The *Washington Star* did not publish an edition on April 19 in respect for Lincoln's funeral. Father Bernadin F. Wigget, a Jesuit priest, president of Gonzaga College and friend of the Surratts, had previously announced that a fair which had been planned at the college would be postponed.

The next day, the former President's body lay in state in the Capitol rotunda. Thousands passed respectfully by to get one last glimpse of the fallen giant. Not everyone mourned Lincoln's death however. Henson Kraft and his younger brother were taken by their father, a poor laboring man, to view Lincoln's body. He attended out of curiosity rather than respect. The boys could not fully understand the significance of recent events. They played along the way to the Capitol and stopped at every corner to pump a drink and soak their heads. Dressed in crude hickory shirts, Kentuckian jeans, woolen stockings and horsehide boots, they joined elegantly dressed men with top hats and ladies in hoop skirts.[10]

The funeral was impressive, but not without problems. A rumor circulated that someone had appointed known secessionists to act as marshals. Extreme Union men placed ads in several Washington newspapers on April 20 calling for a public demonstration against Marshal Lamon, who was thought to have been responsible. Orville Browning intervened in order to keep the dispute from getting out of hand and it soon died down.

The day that the President's body was to be moved from the rotunda, Stanton had arranged to pick up Secretary of the Navy Gideon Welles at 6:00 A.M. They would then escort the body to the railway station some two blocks away. The early hour was decided upon so that fewer spectators would be present when the funeral train started the long journey back to Springfield. Welles, however, ordered his own carriage because he thought Stanton might be late. Stanton was late.

Early on the morning of April 21, the President's remains were taken from the Capitol and placed on a funeral car. The casket of his son Willie was also on the train. His body had been disinterred so that it might be carried back to Illinois with that of his father.

XIV
"... To Get Him Across"

While the Nation mourned, the interrogations continued. Obscure witnesses testified that they knew Booth had planned to kill the President. Robert Fleming stated that Booth had taken a solemn oath to kill Lincoln. Fleming also told of a secret society in Washington known as the "G.D.'s." He was not sure what the initials stood for but thought it was something like "Government Demoralized," or "Great Demonstration."[1] No other witness corroborated this testimony. William Norton, a barkeeper in the little town of T. B., south of Surrattsville, told police that he was acquainted with Surratt, Herold and Atzerodt and knew of guns deposited by them in the Surratt house.[2]

The day before the assassination, John Lloyd sent his wife to the nearby village of Allen's Fresh. Soon after detectives interrogated him the second time, he drove to Allen's Fresh to bring her back. As they were returning through Bryantown, soldiers arrested him. Terrified, Mrs. Lloyd admitted that her husband's actions had been unusual in recent days. This increased distrust of Lloyd, in spite of his staunch denials.

Unionists in the area had long been intimidated by Secessionists and were reluctant to help the investigation. Among the first to come forward was a fat, elderly man named Roby. He told of questionable secret meetings held in the house John Lloyd rented from Mrs. Surratt. Partly as a result of Roby's statement, officers arrested Lloyd and turned him over to Capt. George Cottingham in Robytown, where they had set up a temporary jail. (Robytown was the short-lived name given by loyal Union men to Surrattsville, now Clinton.)

As detectives questioned Mrs. Surratt in Washington and while soldiers searched Dr. Mudd's house, detectives pressured Lloyd to confess. Cottingham insisted that Lloyd knew about the plot and should get rid of the "heavy load on his mind."[3]

After two days of vigorous interrogation, he finally broke down and admitted he had given liquor and guns to two men who claimed they had killed the President. Realizing this statement implicated him, he later denied that the men said they had "killed the President."[4]

He told of two rifles that had been hidden in the house and how the men had taken only one. Cottingham asked where the other gun was. Lloyd acknowledged casually that it was upstairs. After a thorough search failed to uncover the gun, Cottingham warned Lloyd that he would burn the house down before he would leave without it. Lloyd then sent a hired hand to get an ax and cut through the wall of one of the upstairs bedrooms. There the officer discovered the rifle. It had been suspended between the walls by a rope.

This revelation was one of the most important keys in solving the conspiracy. Arnold had already mentioned these particular guns. They were not common rifles, but a special type of breech-loading repeating carbine. Developed by Christopher Spencer shortly before the war, they were known as Spencer rifles. As yet, however, investigators had not made the connection between the carbine found in Mrs. Surratt's country house and members of her household arrested in Washington.

Evidence that Lloyd had sent his wife away a day before the assassination indicated to detectives he probably knew about the plot. Mrs. Lloyd did not know why she had been sent to Allen's Fresh and seemed to be ignorant of the conspiracy. In her absence, her sister, Mrs. Emma Offutt, helped with household duties. Mrs. Offutt did not appear quite so innocent.

Lloyd tried to shield the Surratts to avoid implicating himself. He lied repeatedly for several days about the guns and Booth's midnight visit, thus enabling Booth and Herold to escape. By this time, so many others had testified of suspicious activities around his place, he could not easily avoid confessing. Lloyd, of course, did not want to involve himself in the assassins' escape. Stanton's widely published threat was the death penalty for anyone who aided the murderers or failed to reveal vital information. This order clearly applied to Lloyd. It also touched others, including Dr. Samuel Mudd.

The 40-year-old Lloyd previously worked as a police officer in Washington. Three years before the assassination, he moved to Prince Georges County, close to the Surratts. He became acquainted with Mrs. Surratt in November or December of 1864, after she had decided to move to Washington. As Lloyd had experience keeping taverns, he inquired about the possibility of renting the Surratt property and operating the saloon.

After Lloyd rented the house, John Surratt continued to hang around. Lloyd claimed he was innocently entangled in Booth's escape because of circumstances. Other witnesses supported his story.

By this time Booth and Herold were hiding under thick bushes and pine trees about twenty-five miles south. After their midnight stop at Lloyd's place to obtain guns, field glasses and whiskey, Booth and his companion galloped southward into Charles County, Maryland. They turned off on a little country road, in the dark, and rode about one-quarter mile to Dr. Samuel Mudd's house. Booth knew beforehand the location of the isolated house. At about 4:00 A.M. the doctor opened the door to the heavily armed men. In the early morning hours, Mudd set a small bone in Booth's foot and made crude crutches for him. As Union soldiers swarmed the area, the fugitives hid in Mudd's home. That afternoon the doctor went to Bryantown to get a wagon for them. After he returned, one of Mudd's black servants guided them through the back roads to the house of Samuel Cox, a wealthy former slaveholder. Cox's property, appropriately named Rich Hill, was approximately fifteen miles south of Dr. Mudd's farm. They arrived shortly before midnight on Saturday.[5]

Herold worked his way to the front porch of the large two-story house. The imposing dwelling had large porches, front and back, double chimneys at each end and was surrounded by two fences. Booth, in great pain, remained mounted at the outer gate. Cox, knowing of their crime, would not allow them to enter the house but was willing to hide them on his farm. Booth sent the servant back to Mudd and the two hid in a secluded spot covered with low pines.

Three miles south of Cox's house lived Thomas A. Jones, a Confederate signal agent. At nine o'clock, Sunday morning, a messenger arrived at Jones' unpretentious one-story dwelling to ask a favor. The young man said that Cox needed to see Jones immediately and intimated it was urgent. Cox, Jones' foster brother, exercised considerable influence over his less-affluent kinsman. Jones obediently answered the summons. By this time, any unusual movement was dangerous. Soldiers patrolled all roads and were in the process of searching every house in the area. If Cox's messenger had been stopped, he was instructed to tell the soldiers that he had gone to see Jones to get some seed corn. Jones planned to use the same ruse. The area between the Jones and Cox houses was an isolated region covered by short pines, swampy land, deep gullies and heavy woods. Thus, he could avoid the main roads and travel without being detected.

On reaching the house, Cox told Jones that the assassin had come to his house and wanted help in getting across the Potomac. Cox, accustomed to dominating Jones, stated flatly, "You will have to get him across."[6]

Getting people across was Jones' specialty. He waited for a convenient time to contact the men, being careful not to give away their hiding place. After tying up their horses, he gave a prearranged signal to which Booth's companion responded. He found Herold armed with a carbine and Booth lying on the ground in agony. The assassin was wrapped in blankets given to him by either Mudd or Cox. His foot was bandaged and a crutch lay by his side. The usually dapper actor's clothes were rumpled and dirty, his face haggard and pale. The broken bone in his foot had not been allowed to set and the constant moving irritated the edges of the fracture. Booth's pain was continuous and unrelenting. He could hardly move.

Even in his agony, Booth first inquired about public reaction to his deed. Jones reported that some people supported him while others did not. Jones indicated that he personally was grateful. Booth, anxious to see for himself, searched the newspapers which Jones had brought. His second concern was to get to Virginia where he thought he could obtain medical help.

The next few days, Jones made daily trips to the hiding place, always going alone about ten o'clock each morning. He supplied the men with bread, meat and whiskey. Jones traveled mostly through the gullies and woods but had to use the public road part of the way.

During this time, Jones visited the bar of Brawner's Hotel in Port Tobacco. Capt. William Williams, standing next to him, offered a $300,000 reward for anyone who had information on Booth's whereabouts. Surrounded by Southern sympathizers, Williams thought that someone might reveal Booth's

Henry Woodland. This former slave probably did more, albeit unwittingly, to aid Booth's escape attempt than anyone, other than Thomas Jones or Dr. Mudd.

hiding place. The Union captain supposed that Jones knew something, but he "could not detect the least movement or change in his face."[7]

The biggest problem for Booth was getting rid of the horses he and Herold had rented. The animals were easy to identify and were very visible. Every day the United States cavalry passed close to where the horses were hidden. Jones suggested that Cox shoot the steeds. Cox then told Herold to take the animals to nearby Zekiah Swamp and shoot them. Apparently they were allowed to sink into the swamp and were never found.

In order to save the only boat Jones had left, he sent his former slave and now hired hand, Henry Woodland, out fishing every day in the little rowboat. This way Federal detectives did not confiscate it, and Woodland was kept ignorant of Jones' aid to the assassins. It is likely, however, that Woodland knew what was going on.

From late Saturday night until Thursday, Booth and Herold remained precariously hidden, but more soldiers and detectives were pouring into the region. Investigators were certain that Booth was in the area and began to search the swamp. Soldiers demolished several buildings looking for the assassins and came ever closer to their hiding place. Finally on Friday, April 21, a week after the murder, Jones went to Allen's Fresh, three miles southeast of his farm, to gather news. There he learned that soldiers planned to search nearby St. Mary's County. Thinking this might be the best time for Booth to escape, he hurried back to the hiding place and advised Booth that he must leave that night.

Herold and Jones lifted Booth, in pain, onto Jones' horse late that night. Jones led the two fugitives to his house, going before them at a safe distance and giving them signals to indicate when it was safe. He stopped short of inviting them into his house, however, asking that they wait outside while he got them something to eat. The once-proud actor begged pitifully to go inside for some hot coffee. Jones warned that it was too risky. "This is your last chance to get away," he said apologetically, adding, "I have Negroes at the house; and if they see you, you are lost and so am I."

Inside, a quiet Henry Woodland and Jones sat down to supper. Jones inquired if the servant had returned the boat to its usual place.

"Yes, Master," replied the black stoically.

Trying to appear casual, Jones feigned interest in how many shad had been caught that day.

"I caught about seventy, Master."

"And you brought all of them here to the house, Henry?"

"Yes, Master."[8]

When the two finished eating, Jones managed to scrape together some food for the anxious outlaws. After eating, they worked their way slowly through the darkness toward the river, about three-quarters of a mile away. A fence blocked the way, presenting a real obstacle for the injured Booth. His two companions had to lift him over it carefully and practically carry him the rest of the way.

They sloshed into the water and out to the boat, struggling as they aided Booth, while encumbered with the rifle, pistols, knives, Booth's crutch and other miscellaneous items. Jones lighted a piece of candle and placed it on a compass Booth carried, then gave them directions on crossing to the Virginia side. He advised them to go to Mrs. Quesenberry's house, about a mile up Machodoc Creek. Jones assured the assassins that she would take care of them if they mentioned his name.[9]

About twenty minutes later, with everything safely stowed away, Booth and Herold gratefully bid farewell to their benefactor and paddled out into the dark waters. Before leaving, Booth gave Jones $17 for his help (it did not quite pay for the boat, which Jones never recovered).

The tidewater caught the little boat, preventing the criminals from getting to Virginia that night. Being inexperienced in navigation, they missed Mathias Point and were carried west by the current, to Nanjemoy shores, still in Maryland. Herold caught sight of a house and pulled ashore to beg for food.

The two then found a concealed place where they passed the rest of that Saturday, anxiously awaiting nightfall. They pushed off again in the darkness for
Virginia but again failed to find Machodoc Creek and mistakenly entered
nearby Gambo Creek. In the meantime, the man from whom Herold begged
food became suspicious and notified his lawyer at Port Tobacco, who alerted
Federal authorities.

Finally, on Sunday morning, April 23, Herold found Mrs. Quesenberry's
house and told her that the man who had killed Lincoln was hiding nearby.
Thomas Harbin, the brother-in-law of Jones (also a Rebel spy to whom Mudd
had introduced Booth), happened to be staying with Mrs. Quesenberry. He
accompanied Herold back to where Booth lay waiting. Booth, still in great
pain, was relieved in the belief that he had found safety in Virginia. The two
carried Booth to the house for a meal. After eating his first hot food in days,
Booth asked to be taken to a physician. Dr. Richard Stewart lived only eight
miles away, and they made arrangements to take him there the next day.

First they visited the farm of a Mr. Bryan who was prevailed upon to take
the men to the summer home of Dr. Stewart. The doctor, one of the richest
men in that county, was annoyed by the intrusion and refused to permit the
men in his house, although he did allow them to rest in the slave quarters.

The reception Booth got in Virginia was not what he expected. The flam-
boyant actor had anticipated a hero's welcome, and now he was being forced
to sleep in former slave quarters! He tore a page from his outdated diary and,
writing indignantly that he would not accept hospitality without paying for it,
rolled $2.50 in the page and gave it to a servant to deliver to Dr. Stewart.

It was Monday, April 24. Everything had gone wrong, which Booth, at
last, must have realized. His next move was to cross the Rappahannock. Dr.
Stewart provided a wagon and a driver named Lucas to take the assassins to
the river. Arriving at Port Conway, Lucas stopped the wagon and refused to
go farther.

At this moment, three young Confederate soldiers on their way home rode
up. Herold got out of the wagon and asked them for aid. Maj. M. B. Ruggles,
Lt. A. B. Bainbridge and Capt. William Jett agreed to help. The group crossed
the river by ferry to Port Royal and approached the first house they saw but
were refused assistance. Guided by Jett, they proceeded three miles down the
road to the Richard Garrett home. Here Booth, now using the name Boyd,
was allowed to stay. The other men, including Herold, continued down the
road to Bowling Green, Virginia, where they had dinner. They stayed in Bowling Green that night, and the next day Herold returned to the Garrett farm.[10]

XV
The Conspiracy Puzzle

After John Lloyd's first emotional confession he subsequently added astounding details. According to Lloyd, John Surratt, Herold and Atzerodt had brought the two rifles and a few tools to him about a month before the assassination. They asked him to hide them, saying they would be called for later. The guns indicated that, from the beginning, killing was a possibility – if not of the President, perhaps of others.

Lloyd, a weak individual by all accounts, had little choice but to follow the instruction of his landlady's son. He told detectives of carrying the guns upstairs and suspending them between the walls. They were accessible only from an attic area opening off of Lloyd's bedroom.

Union soldiers periodically searched the area for blockade-runners and other pro–Southern activities. Lloyd, aware of this, hid the carbines well. Becoming concerned about the carbines being found in his rented house, he begged Surratt to take them away, but to no avail.

Up to this point, Lloyd's account was revealing, although not surprising. Then he casually mentioned that a few days before the murder "Mrs. Surratt, mother of John, met me at Uniontown and asked about the shooting irons and if I could get them out."[1] She added that they would soon be needed. Lloyd apparently avoided mentioning the incident earlier because it associated him more closely with the conspiracy.

More damaging was Lloyd's testimony about the next visit. "On the afternoon of the murder, about 5:00, Mrs. Surratt came to my place – said get those shooting irons and two bottles of whiskey ready."[2] Mary Surratt never denied the meeting at Uniontown or the even more critical one at Surrattsville.

Questioned further about the incident, Lloyd said Mrs. Surratt remained at his house only a few minutes after she gave him these instructions. "This matter seemed her whole business with me," he declared.

Lloyd also revealed that she arrived in a buggy driven by a young man whose name he did not know at the time, but later learned to be Weichmann. Weichmann had not mentioned this to the Government, and it was the first time authorities learned of that fateful trip. The young clerk now seemed definitely implicated in the plot.

Continuing his testimony, Lloyd confessed that after Mrs. Surratt left, he retrieved the guns from the hiding place and put them in his room. About 15 minutes after midnight, two men came by his house asking for the things.

Howard's stables on G Street behind Mrs. Surratt's boardinghouse. On the afternoon of the murder, Weichmann hired a horse and buggy here for Mrs. Surratt (Library of Congress).

Lloyd went upstairs and brought down one carbine and a box of cartridges. (The Spencer rifle used special cartridges not available in the South.) Trembling with fear, Lloyd explained that he had been drinking that night. He intended to intimate that circumstances—which might have made him suspicious if sober—had not seemed serious as he was "in liquor."[3] It was his only plausible excuse, and he stressed it repeatedly. However, when he described the horses pulling Mrs. Surratt's buggy he pictured them in clearer detail than most sober men could have.

Lloyd did not mention the long rope or the large monkey wrench which the conspirators left behind. These items were not hidden with the guns but were left in the storage shed. Investigators never found them, and Lloyd left them in the house when he moved out. The rope was to have been stretched across the road to throw pursuing horses. The monkey wrench was to have been used to take wheels off the carriage when the President was transported by boat across the Potomac. The conspirators needed these articles in the plot to kidnap, but they were of no value in the assassination.

Detectives took Lloyd to Bryantown and questioned him again three days later. He repeated the same narrative in a written statement. On Sunday, April 23, Colonel Wells forwarded Lloyd's confession to Washington noting that the statement indicated Booth had broken his leg at the theater or soon after and that Mrs. Surratt knew all about the plot. Lloyd's testimony helped change the thrust of the investigation. It was not the widow's son, but the widow herself, who seemed to have been directing much of the conspiracy.

So many investigations were going on at the same time, it was difficult for one group to know what others uncovered. Weichmann, in Canada, was not aware of Lloyd's confession. Lloyd did not know what others had revealed or what Mrs. Surratt might have confessed. The evidence of several independent inquiries gradually implicated her.

Two days after their first interrogation of Dr. Mudd, Lovett and his men returned. This time, they stated they would have to search his house. When the doctor heard this, he spoke a few words to his wife; she went upstairs and brought down a large boot. On examining the boot, Lovett noticed the name "J. Wilkes" printed on the inside and called it to Mudd's attention.[4] He insisted he had not seen the name before and maintained his assertion that he did not know the men. Until this time, detectives were unaware the assassin had worn boots to the theater. Numerous witnesses described Booth at the play, but none observed that he wore riding boots and spurs. The large boots went almost to his hips and flared out at the top so they could not be covered by trousers. Yet riding boots and spurs were inappropriate among elegantly dressed theatergoers. If his foot had not been broken, the only explanation for the failure of hundreds of spectators to notice this unusual attire would be that Booth put on his hip-boots after the assassination. The pain was so intense, however, that the boot had to be cut to get it off; under no circumstance would he have put the boot on over a broken bone.

When officers showed Mudd a photograph of Booth, he reluctantly admitted this was the man who had come to his house. Lovett, convinced that Mudd knew more than he was telling, arrested him. He then confessed that he had met Booth before the assassination. Mudd was subsequently taken to the temporary jail at Bryantown. Colonel Wells noted in his report that Booth and Herold had been traced to Dr. Mudd's house.

Soldiers transported Lloyd to Old Capitol Prison where Superintendent W. P. Wood questioned him again. Thus, by April 23, three more names appeared prominently in the complicated conspiracy puzzle—John Lloyd, Mary Surratt and Samuel Mudd.

Superintendent Wood had developed a special relationship with Stanton which began during a famous dispute over a patent for the McCormick reaper. Cyrus H. McCormick had built and demonstrated a successful reaper in 1831. About 20 years later John H. Manny of Wisconsin obtained patents for a similar machine. In November 1854 McCormick filed suit against Manny for patent infringement.

The trial took place in Cincinnati in 1855, with more than a dozen lawyers involved. Stanton was one attorney defending Manny while Reverdy Johnson worked with those representing McCormick. Eventually Manny also retained Abraham Lincoln. Stanton, who had spent more time on the case, spoke for

Old Capitol Prison, which held many conspiracy suspects, got its name because it had served as the Nation's Capitol until the damaged Capitol could be restored after the War of 1812 (Library of Congress—B8184-4159).

their client. Stanton's defense was extraordinary and so impressed Lincoln that he determined to go home and do further study. Stanton won the case, but McCormick took the issue to the United States Supreme Court. The legal battle raged for several years during which time Stanton came in contact with Col. William P. Wood.

The principal issue in the case centered on the invention of a special curved divider at the end of the cutter bar. Wood, having purchased an old McCormick reaper, removed and straightened the curved divider rod. The Manny patent, Wood figured, would not be an infringement on what now appeared to be a straight divider rod on the early McCormick reaper. Wood doctored the altered rod to look old and rusty and sent it to Washington where it was exhibited in court. As a result Stanton won the case.[5] Wood admitted that Stanton never knew that the reaper had been tampered with, but Stanton was impressed with the colonel's ability. Thereafter, Stanton placed great confidence in William Wood and used him for his most confidential assignments.

Several Union leaders had suggested that if Jefferson Davis were captured, the rebellion would collapse, and the Government even briefly considered the possibility of such a project. Stanton assigned William Wood to investigate the advisability of the scheme. Wood, dressed as a Rebel, infiltrated Confederate lines with the help of the unsuspecting "Rebel Rose" Greenhow and gathered the desired information. After returning from Richmond, he advised Stanton that the plan would not work, and it was forgotten.

Stanton appointed William Wood superintendent of Old Capitol Prison in 1862 and gave him absolute authority. As a soldier of fortune he had taken part in William Walker's quixotic expedition into Nicaragua. He was a short man, sloppy in dress, who pretended a rustic humility but was in fact a crafty operator. It was said that Stanton was the head of the War Department and Wood, the head of Stanton. Just what gave Wood this power, few seemed to know—they did know it was dangerous to cross him. A general once complained to Stanton of Wood's insubordination and constant insults. The officer demanded that Wood be discharged as prison superintendent. Stanton listened quietly to the complaints, then coldly informed the general that he would have to accept the superintendent's insults or resign.

Wood got along reasonably well with Rebel prisoners—in some ways, it seemed, too well. As a longtime friend of Zad Jenkins, his natural inclination was to support Jenkins' sister, Mary Surratt, but Wood saw a good chance to claim the reward money.

Wood examined Lloyd more intensely than previous interrogators. Under his probing, Lloyd mentioned frequent visits by John Surratt, Atzerodt and Herold. He repeated his account of meeting Mrs. Surratt at Uniontown and claimed that Weichmann had heard the conversation about "shooting irons."[6] This significant assertion further implicated Weichmann. The interrogation occurred about the time Weichmann was brought back from Canada and placed in Old Capitol Prison. The two inmates soon quarreled over Lloyd's accusation.

Lloyd repeated his account of Mrs. Surratt's visit to her country house and revealed for the first time that she gave him field glasses wrapped in paper. She requested that he have them ready when called for (the binoculars were later found and exhibited at the trial). This disclosure convinced Wood of her guilt.

The superintendent asked if Weichmann had overheard the conversation at Surrattsville. Lloyd replied that he had not because the communication took place privately. Throughout the interrogation, Wood showed particular interest in Weichmann's possible involvement. He then wrote the War Department, falsely claiming that he and Colonel Wells were instrumental in getting Lloyd's first confession.[7] The scramble for the reward money was heating up.

Toward the end of April the Government received several valuable tips concerning the Surratts. William Lewis reported that John Surratt had a special commission in the Confederate Government and that he held secret meetings at his mother's Surrattsville property. Lewis' information came from a Mr. Hutton, who had spent three or four weeks there. Not only were there suspicious meetings, he declared, but the house was also used as a Confederate mail station. According to Lewis, Surratt acknowledged he was a Confederate spy.[8]

A revealing letter from Henry Hanover stated that Surratt had expected to get a position in the United States Post Office with the help of Senator Reverdy Johnson. Authorities called Hanover in for questioning, and he repeated his story to Colonel Foster.[9] His account had a touch of authenticity, especially when, within two weeks, this same Senator—who had been a pallbearer at Lincoln's funeral—was requested as a defense lawyer by one of the accused.

Addison Brown, who was being held prisoner at Fort Delaware for disloyal conduct, wrote that "Young Surratt and his mother kept the post office after his father died. He had lots of friends in the area of his home who sympathize with the rebellion."[10] These statements merely confirmed what the Government already knew.

Investigators found an account book, used by Mrs. Surratt's husband, which showed that the family did indeed have numerous friends in the area, many of whom were arrested during the war for subversive activities. The little book listed bills owed to the Surratts. Samuel Cox, later arrested for helping Booth escape, had a long-standing unpaid bar bill. John Gwynn, member of a notorious Rebel family, at one time owed the Surratts $41.98 for drinks and blacksmith work.[11] Charles Calvert, from whom the Surratts had bought their farm and who later provided an alibi for Mrs. Surratt, was a frequent visitor to the tavern. John Nothey, also involved in the investigation, had an account there. Most bills were for liquor or occasional blacksmith work.

Gradually detectives put pieces of the puzzle together. In an interview with prisoner Oscar Swan, they discovered that Herold and Booth wanted to be taken to the house of Sam Cox. Swan stated that he heard one of the men say, "I thought Cox was a man of Southern feeling."[12]

Dr. R. H. Stewart volunteered information that two men had come by his house wanting help. He averred that he gave them little assistance but that one man told him Dr. Mudd had set his foot. Stewart recounted how the man left him some money rolled up in a page of a diary. The doctor left the page with Colonel Baker.[13] Samuel Sheet revealed that, about eight years before the assassination, O'Laughlin had joined the Knights of the Golden Circle, a secret order of Southern sympathizers in the North.[14]

Detectives again questioned Preston Parr of Baltimore about telegrams he sent to John Surratt. He continued to claim ignorance of the telegrams, adding that he suffered a bad stomach condition which had affected his memory.[15] Parr's china shop was undoubtedly a rendezvous for Confederate agents.

One of the most baffling suspects was Ben F. Ficklin. Born in Charlotte, Virginia, he served as quartermaster in the Confederate army. Ficklin, about six feet tall with dark hair cut short, had a long, thin nose and small black eyes. One day after Lincoln's assassination, Stanton received a letter exposing Ficklin as a Confederate agent. The writer stated that Ficklin was guilty of "making much money for himself and helping Jeff Davis."[16] Ficklin had become wealthy running the blockade from Charleston, South Carolina, to Wilmington, Delaware.

Authorities arrested and questioned him on Stanton's orders. He admitted working as a blockade-runner but declined to answer questions about his cotton business and denied that he held any position in the Confederate army, although he was called Major. Detectives interrogated him again in May; this time he admitted being a cotton speculator. Although he continually refused to answer some questions, he acknowledged that he had worked with Gen. George Washington Singleton and had shipped contraband cotton for Mrs. Lincoln's half sister, Mrs. Benjamin H. Helm.[17] Her husband, a general in the Confederate army, had been killed in the battle of Chickamauga.

Several witnesses implicated James Jarboe, alias Smith, a Rebel mail carrier and friend of both John Surratt and George Atzerodt. It was Jarboe who had refused Atzerodt's request for lodging. Jarboe's associate, Annie Mitchell, also served the Confederate cause.[18]

After Atzerodt's arrest, authorities requested that the United States consulate general in Frankfort, Germany, investigate his background. The consulate discovered that Atzerodt's full name was George Andrew Atzerodt and that he had been born in the little Prussian village of Doerna. He was the second son of good, hardworking parents who had emigrated from Germany in 1844 seeking more profitable employment in America. George never became a United States citizen and never attempted to vote. Nicholas B. Crangle confirmed reports that Atzerodt had lived with Mrs. Wheeler with whom he had a child, but he refused to marry her.[19]

George Wren, an actor at Ford's Theatre, declared that among Booth's closest friends were Henry Clay Ford and Billy Barron. The Fords had already been interrogated in prison, but Barron remains a mystery. No evidence indicates he was questioned. Many suspects were interrogated and released without a record being kept, however. One such individual was Thomas Chissen, who boarded at the house owned by David Herold's mother, and Barron may have fallen in the same category.

Wren corroborated previous testimony about Booth's having visited Grover's Theatre the day before the assassination inquiring about the planned illumination and asking if the President had been invited. In the course of conversation, Booth was asked if he was going to visit Richmond again. According to Wren, Booth responded emphatically, "I shall never go to Richmond again."[20]

While Booth and Herold were still hiding in Lower Maryland, detectives questioned John Henry Nothey, a man Mrs. Surratt claimed she had gone to see about an old debt. Nothey revealed he had seen Mrs. Surratt on the Monday before the murder. This presented a problem that the Government never bothered to solve. Nearly every witness from Lower Maryland maintained that Mrs. Surratt had visited Surrattsville on Monday, while every witness from Washington reported a trip had been made on Tuesday. Nothey signed his statement with an "X."[21]

Bennett Gwynn, a longtime friend and neighbor of the Surratts, and known in the area for his dedication to the Confederacy, told detectives that Mrs. Surratt had come to his house on the Monday before the murder and stayed about an hour. He also admitted that he saw her on the day of the assassination. Mrs. Surratt explained to interrogators that she needed to visit Gwynn because he was her agent in land dealing, although she never showed that he ever did anything other than take a letter to the illiterate Nothey.

When questioned further, Gwynn got mixed up on his story. Mrs. Surratt had affirmed that Nothey owed her money for land he had bought thirteen years earlier, but Gwynn swore that Mrs. Surratt had wanted to lease some land from Nothey.

As a result of intensive interrogations, detectives were able to follow Booth's trail from Ford's Theatre south to the Surratt tavern then to Mudd's farm and on to the house of Samuel Cox. Authorities arrested Cox and subjected him to severe questioning.

Samuel Cox was born about 1820 near Port Tobacco. His mother died while he was still a child and he was reared by a woman named Jones (probably the wife of the overseer on the Cox plantation). Her son, Thomas, was about the same age as Samuel and the two boys grew up together, attending the same rural school. Cox became wealthy and developed a strong, assertive will. When the war started, he owned a large plantation and about 35 slaves. In his zeal to support the Confederacy, he became captain of a volunteer company of Southern sympathizers that drilled at Bryantown. This group, composed mostly of slaveholders, included members of the Surratt and Mudd families.

Early in the war, slave owners in this area were not ardent secessionists, but definitely sought to protect their interests and property. Many of their sons served in the Confederate ranks as did the Surratt boys. Gradually some of their slaves found refuge among Union troops. Actual fighting hardly touched this isolated section, although occasionally Union troops passed through. When they did, they were cordially, if not enthusiastically, received. As Lower Maryland developed into a route for illegal travel between North and South, Surratt, Cox and Jones were caught up in the clandestine traffic.

Jones, a slim man of about medium height, owned a few slaves and supported the Southern cause in his characteristic low-keyed manner. He possessed a haggard, melancholy look which gave him the air of a man resigned to insignificance and misunderstood innocence—hardly the countenance of a daring Rebel. It was this deceptive appearance that got him out of prison more than once and confused soldiers investigating the assassination. His slow, mournful manner of speech matched his appearance. In personal habits, he was the opposite of George Atzerodt and most other suspects. He did not use profanity or smoke and seldom drank. (When crossing the river in the winter months, he sometimes took a little spirits to drive away the cold.) Jones was basically a quiet, simple man with plain tastes, not greedy for glory or wealth. He obeyed instructions and kept silent, yet he was the only man in Maryland with whom the Confederate government had an *official* relationship.[22]

Jones' farm on Pope's Creek was the most strategic spot on the route of illicit traffic between the North and the South. From his house, conveniently situated on a bluff nearly 100 feet high, he could view the Potomac eight or ten miles in both directions.

Maj. Roderick G. Watson, Jones' nearest neighbor, had a son in the Confederate army. The Watson house, a large two-story, wood-frame building, served the Rebels as a signal station. One of Watson's daughters would hang a

Thomas A. Jones. As a Confederate agent working in Maryland, he helped Booth escape to Virginia. Although jailed on suspicion, his woebegone look and simple manners may have saved him from the gallows.

black shawl in an upper dormer window when it was not safe to send a boat across from Virginia. A Mr. Grimes, on the Virginia side about two and a half miles distant, kept this window in view through binoculars.

Throughout the war, scores of people came to Jones and Watson seeking help in crossing the Potomac. Many were spies and blockade-runners, but they also accommodated lawyers, businessmen, adventurers and agents of foreign banks.

The Union army, vaguely aware of this activity, kept the area under surveillance. In June 1861, Gen. Daniel E. Sickles began to search the region. He found Grimes on the Maryland side and sent him to prison. Jones was caught returning from Richmond and was also incarcerated. In March 1862, the Government released him from Old Capitol through an act sponsored by United States Congressmen who were convinced that Federal prisons were full of innocent men. Jones had to take an oath that he would never again communicate with the enemy. While he was in prison, both his wife and his friend Major Watson died, and a heavy mortgage was causing him to lose his farm.

Thomas Jones knew the severe penalties for breaking his oath, and in addition, armed Union patrols kept a close watch on the area, so he obeyed the oath. It was said that the Federals had a spy on every large farm. But by this time, Grimes had also been freed and again wanted his help. At first, Jones refused, but later when Maj. William Norris, a Confederate signal officer, begged him to take charge of Rebel communications, he acquiesced and from that time until the war's conclusion, he was responsible for getting mail from Richmond on its way north.[23] In this effort, he undoubtedly worked closely with John Surratt. Yet neither Surratt nor Jones gave any indication they were acquainted.

Some of Jones' best agents were women and a few were slaves. Surprisingly, one of his own slaves, Henry Woodland, helped pass hundreds of letters along the route. Some of his slaves, however, were not so faithful; one deserted and, in all likelihood, reported Jones' activities to Union authorities.

Jones' foster brother, Cox, worked with him in setting up the Rebel mail service, which included a series of "stump post offices" where letters were hidden in old tree stumps. As the system improved, Jones made more use of unassuming Southern sympathizers in the area to gather and deliver the mail. During this time, John Surratt was dismissed as a United States postmaster and began his responsibilities as a full-time Confederate spy.

The Jones farm was a few miles from Port Tobacco. In the 1700s, when Annapolis was a major city and the Patuxent River valley a populous area, the main road to Virginia passed through this section to the crossing at Pope's Creek not far from the birthplace of George Washington.

As the war continued, Jones spent more time crossing the river with various interlopers, eventually making the trip nearly every night. Although the round trip took nearly two hours, Jones made the trip two or three times a night in the busy season. He collected little money for his efforts, being paid no more than a dollar or two per trip. He understood that the Rebel Government would eventually reimburse him, but he was never fully paid.

Even though Jones had major responsibility for relaying Confederate mail north, he was not directly involved in the plot against Lincoln. But he knew of it. About the third year of the war, he heard that a momentous intrigue had been decided upon. He heard later that it involved the capture of the President. Although Federal agents uncovered no conclusive proof in Rebel archives that Southern leaders were involved, other evidence indicates that the plot originated in Richmond.

The original conspiracy was in keeping with Confederate military tactics which included various desperate acts of sabotage. Similarly, Union forces had briefly considered the possibility of capturing Jefferson Davis. The Confederate plan, as Jones understood it, involved the capture of the President at the Navy Yard rather than at the Soldiers' Home. Lincoln was to be transported in relays to the Potomac and ferried across. Jones also knew of the boat kept in readiness for this purpose. The intrigue involved several families in Port Tobacco in addition to Atzerodt.

About December 1864, Jones heard that a "big actor" named Booth was also in on the plot.[24] Jones considered the scheme for abducting Lincoln a proper and legitimate undertaking in time of war. Yet when Booth changed the plan from capture to murder, those involved became accessories to assassination rather than participants in, as they thought, a heroic endeavor that would gain military bargaining power for the Confederacy. Thus, zealous defenders of the Old South whose values were distorted by years of hatred and war were transformed overnight into accomplices in homicide.

Widespread knowledge of the conspiracy made it imperative that none involved confess anything lest they endanger scores of others. Years after the assassination, discussion of the events remained guarded. Almost twenty years later, George Alfred Townsend visited the area to uncover more about those involved. Most participants in the kidnapping scheme discussed their involvement reluctantly and asked the reporter not to print their names for fear of reprisals.

Soldiers arrested Jones and Cox along with Samuel Mudd and held them in the makeshift jail in Bryantown. There, Colonel Wells energetically interrogated them without results. Officials placed posters in the temporary prison offering rewards for the assassins and also promising death to anyone who either aided them or withheld information. Jones felt shaky, but said nothing. Detectives thought Jones knew something, but his "sanctimonious look" saved him. While waiting in prison, he heard wild stories told by soldiers searching for Booth. He knew many of the tales were pure fiction, but pretended ignorance of the whole affair.

After several days, authorities sent him and Cox to Washington in an army ambulance. Mudd was held in Bryantown. Detectives traveling with them tried, without success, to get Jones drunk. Jones was constantly interrogated during the six weeks he was in prison, but both he and Cox denied they knew anything about Booth or the assassination. He was eventually released from Carroll Prison and was never called as a witness because his simple country manners were interpreted as stupidity. A week after Jones was freed, authorities released Cox. For his years of Rebel service, Jones earned $3,500 — in worthless Confederate bills.[25]

Later in life, he revealed that plans to capture the President went back to 1863 and that everything had been ready, but conspirators delayed action that year because roads were bad. Jones may have been wrong about the year; but his detailed account was corroborated by statements of M. E. Martin which were hidden away in War Department files.[26] Few suspected this inconspicuous Maryland farmer to have been an essential link in Booth's escape.

XVI
Conflicting Evidence

As the funeral train, draped in black mourning crepe, bearing a picture of Lincoln on the cowcatcher, pulled out of the Washington station, a clearer picture of the intrigue began to emerge. The Government had identified most principal conspirators and had pieced together the general plot through hundreds of witnesses.

Not all information was accurate, however. Newspapers speculated wildly as to Booth's whereabouts. Some reported that he had been recognized in Reading, Pennsylvania; others stated he had been arrested in Philadelphia. A writer for the *National Intelligencer* made the best guess. Soon after the assassination, he wrote that Booth had headed for Port Tobacco and planned to cross into Virginia.[1]

One enterprising reporter got hold of the revealing letter Booth left with his brother-in-law John Clark. Publication of the document led some Copperhead papers, such as the *New York News* and the *Chicago Times*, to assume that the assassin had acted alone. Authorities felt that release of this type of information hampered the search. Also, Stanton wanted to centralize control. Therefore General Augur, acting under Stanton's direction, issued an order prohibiting those engaged in the investigation from divulging information, except to the War Department.[2]

Stanton's distrust of the Ford brothers increased, and on April 20, Henry Clay Ford was again questioned in prison. He confirmed what was already known about Booth's presence in the theater on the morning of the assassination, but added one significant detail. He noted that Booth had also visited the theater early in the afternoon during rehearsal. Apparently Booth wanted to determine the best moment to shoot and escape. Investigators had wondered how he was able to flee across the stage, cluttered with props, actors and stagehands, without being stopped. Evidently his knowledge of the positions of stage scenery and actors made possible his dramatic escape.

At this point Spangler was only one of several theater employees under suspicion, but Henry Ford's testimony further implicated him. Ford told of often seeing Spangler with Booth and described Spangler as "low and vulgar,—very vulgar in conversation."[3] Ford may have accused the stagehand to divert attention from himself and his brothers. Obviously Booth needed the cooperation of someone in the theater, but it was never determined who failed in his assignment to turn off the gaslights when Booth fired.

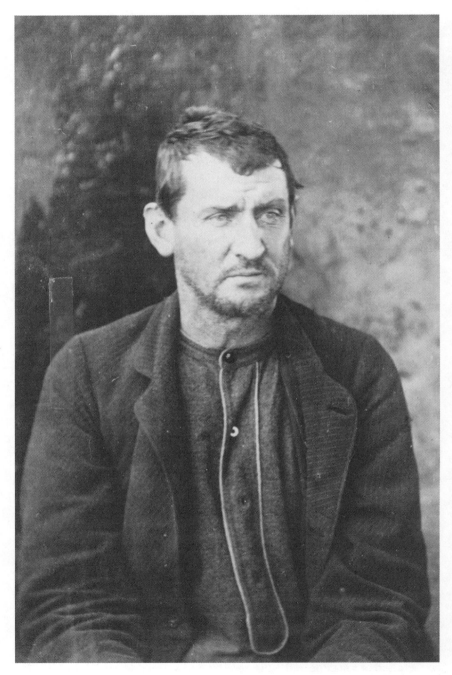

Edward Spangler. This suspect had previously worked for the Booth family and was, at the time of the crime, a carpenter and scene shifter at Ford's Theatre (Library of Congress).

Investigators gathered further evidence against David Herold from his sister June. She revealed that Herold was away from home often in March, sometimes for more than a week at a time, but added that he was home nearly every night in April. On the day of the assassination, he ate breakfast at home but did not return for supper and had not been seen by his mother or sisters since.[4]

The 23-year-old, baby-faced Herold was the only son in a household with six daughters. Like Mary Surratt, the widowed Mrs. Herold ran a boarding-house. Here the resemblance ended. Mrs. Herold watched her son closely and questioned him repeatedly about his activities—so much that he grew resentful and evasive. His older sisters doted on their brother, admitting freely that he was pampered. Nevertheless, his mother insisted that he get home by ten o'clock each evening if he did not want to be locked out. This did not bother David as he had a key, although his mother eventually took it away.[5]

Some observers felt that Mrs. Surratt was accused of a crime her son committed. Mrs. Herold was in a similar position, yet she was never jailed or even suspected. The conspirators occasionally met at Mrs. Herold's boardinghouse, even as they did at Mrs. Surratt's. There were significant differences, however. Mrs. Herold never fraternized with them. They never came to her house when her son was not at home, and there was no evidence that she was connected with questionable activities. Furthermore, she cooperated with investigators.

Detectives constantly uncovered bits of evidence that did not fit easily into the puzzle. One piece was the so-called "Etta letter." Dated April 13, a day before the murder, the nearly illegible postmark seemed to be April 18 or 19, and it did not come to light until April 20 or 21. Some investigators thought it a fraud because of the postmark, but the wording did not fit any fraudulent scheme. "I too have the blues ever since the fall of Richmond," confessed the writer, adding that if anything should happen, "let me know and I will join you (as agreed upon) in the house of our mutual friend . . . [name illegible]. Don't let anything discourage you." The letter contained an account of the writer's disagreement with her landlady which resulted in her moving from the house. There followed a few more illegible words and then the signature, "Etta . . . Amen!!!Sam."[6]

The letter interested Colonel Foster, who immediately sent a telegram in code to the superintendent of police in New York City (the letter seemed to have been postmarked there), asking him to check anyone there who fit the description. New York City police began a search of "every public and private house of prostitution," particularly the ones frequently visited by Booth, but found no one named Etta, nor anyone who had left her landlady as a result of a misunderstanding. They did discover that Booth had lived there with Sally Andrews and Anne Horton. After 18 hours of constant searching, the superintendent wired Foster that he thought the letter was a hoax. "A letter written the 13th and postmarked the 19th tells its own story," he concluded.[7]

Adding to the mystery was the suicide of a man who had in his possession a slip of paper with the name Starr on it.[8] Police knew that Booth's mistress in Washington was Ella Starr. Washington newspapers carried stories of

Booth's relations with Ella, and she had been questioned briefly several times, but the similarity of the name "Etta" to "Ella" apparently was never considered.

The War Department opened a message found in the Washington post office, postmarked April 20, addressed to Anna Surratt. The letter, mailed from Steubenville, Ohio, Stanton's hometown, came from Anna's cousin, Belle Seaman, and seemed innocent. Seaman expressed deep regret that John had been accused of the attempted assassination of Secretary Seward and acknowledged that she had received a letter from him postmarked Montreal.[9]

While mourners gathered at railroad stations and along the tracks to catch a glimpse of the funeral train passing slowly across the country, the mood of the Nation's capital remained subdued. Mrs. Lincoln remained in the White House, but President Johnson had moved from his room in the Kirkwood House to the residence of Samuel Hooper, just a few blocks east of the Surratt boardinghouse. Johnson's family resided in Nashville, Tennessee. John Surratt was hiding in Canada and Booth and Herold were making their way to Virginia. Authorities had Mudd, Atzerodt, Payne, O'Laughlin, Arnold, Lloyd, Weichmann, Spangler and Mary Surratt in custody.

Superintendent William Wood intensified his efforts to claim a share of the reward. As Stanton's friend and one well acquainted with the search area, he wrested permission from the Secretary of War to go after Booth. Wood was convinced that rumors of Booth's escape to Pennsylvania, or Upper Maryland, were a hoax. He believed, as did most others, that the assassin was south of Washington. The superintendent was in a unique position—trusted by Stanton, and considered a friend by Zadoc Jenkins. Jenkins' daughter Olivia was in the Surratt boardinghouse when soldiers raided it and was jailed with the other inhabitants. Wood persuaded Stanton to release her.

Having secured Olivia's freedom, Wood rode to her father's house in Prince Georges County. If Jenkins knew anything, Wood thought he could discover it. He arrived too late; officers had already placed Jenkins under arrest. When Wood finally contacted Jenkins, the suspect told him to question Gabriel Thompson and he would "learn something."[10]

For all Wood's trouble, he got nothing but a dubious tip. Thompson never really figured in the plot and knew nothing. Jenkins, a longtime Rebel, had given his friend a false lead. Thompson's son recited to the superintendent a long, ridiculous story. The superintendent seemed to realize he was on a cold trail and changed his direction toward Samuel Mudd's house. By that time Mudd, too, had been interrogated.

Wood at one time appeared anxious to defend his friend Jenkins and Jenkins' sister, Mary Surratt, but after having been given the run-around, he developed more doubts. When he happened to hear Wells question Lloyd about Mrs. Surratt's visits, he became convinced of her guilt. He wrote a report to Major Turner on April 23, declaring, "You can take all precautions necessary now with Mrs. Surratt for she was beyond the question of doubt in the conspiracy."[11] Wood was not one to condemn his friends carelessly. In the same report, he pronounced Mudd truthful.[12]

Continually working under the apprehension that the conspiracy formed part of a larger operation directed by desperate Confederate leaders, Stanton remained inordinately fearful. Everything was done in strict secrecy; prisoners were kept closely guarded. In hindsight, these precautions appear excessive, but during the period following the President's death, no precaution seemed too extreme.

Amid other duties, Stanton did not overlook the need for a secure place to confine the accused assassins. Expecting to capture Booth alive, he ordered the commandant of the Washington Navy Yard:

> If the military authorities arrest the murderer of the President and take him to the navy yard, put him in a monitor and anchor her out in the stream, with strong guard on vessel, wharf and in navy yard.[13]

He advised the commandant to prepare the vessel immediately and to keep it ready day and night. Stanton further insisted that any prisoner sent to the ship be heavily ironed "to prevent escape or injury to himself."[14] These orders, received within a few hours of Lincoln's death, show clearly that the Secretary of War desired the assassin and his accomplices captured and kept alive. Far from attempting a cover-up as some have claimed, Stanton wanted every detail revealed.

The first suspects, Michael O'Laughlin, Lewis Payne and Sam Arnold, were already confined on the ironclad *Saugus* in double irons. About midnight on April 23, guards imprisoned George Atzerodt and Hartman Richter on the vessel. Stanton preferred to move his prisoners at night. Later he ordered that a ball and chain be attached to each of Payne's legs and that Richter be transferred secretly to another ship. He ordered that no one be permitted to communicate with the prisoners without a pass signed jointly by himself and Secretary of the Navy Welles.

The next day he demanded even tighter security. To prevent prisoners from communication, he directed that canvas bags be placed over their heads and that Payne be secured to prevent self-destruction. The suffocating bags had one hole for breathing and eating but contained no slits for eyes. Stanton also transferred Spangler from Old Capitol to the growing group of prime suspects aboard the prison ships.

Atzerodt, visibly frightened, insisted to the Captain of the *Saugus* that he was innocent of any crime. All the accused except Lewis Payne made similar claims. The prisoners seemed to regard themselves as innocent because they had not fired the fatal shot. Atzerodt declared he had actually saved Vice-President Johnson's life because he had refused to carry out orders to kill him.[15] The carriage painter from Port Tobacco was at least partly correct. He may have saved the Vice-President's life. If Lewis Payne had been given the job, he would likely have completed it.

George Atzerodt was a different sort. He was one of those individuals for whom petty crime came easy. He felt no remorse, because vice was his way of life, but not murder. Brutality was not natural for him as it was for Payne. Atzerodt revealed his muddled understanding of the crime and consequences in that he had made no plans for escape. While others frantically sought safety

George Atzerodt. One of several photographs taken on the prison ship shows the suspect's obvious concern (Library of Congress).

either by leaving the scene or cleverly disguising their roles, Atzerodt wandered aimlessly through the city. Later he realized that he was involved with crafty men who had placed him in danger of hanging.

Of all the conspirators, Atzerodt's plea of innocence seemed the most plausible—plausible because of his mental condition. The dull Atzerodt did not fully comprehend the conspiracy. When he did, he refused his part.

Atzerodt had already signed one confession, but he wanted to talk. In his almost unintelligible German accent he told Captain Monroe of a visit to Port Tobacco by John Surratt about three weeks earlier. Surratt announced that Booth was going to open a theater in Richmond and that Booth had a vessel to run the blockade but that he needed Atzerodt's aid. Atzerodt accompanied Surratt to Washington where he met Booth, who explained that he was to assassinate Vice-President Johnson. According to Atzerodt, he quickly refused the assignment. In his conversation with the captain, Atzerodt gave the impression that he knew of the plot to kill three weeks before it occurred.[16] (In other confessions he claimed he had learned of assassination plans only a few hours before the crime.) After his refusal to participate in murder, Atzerodt declared that he returned to Port Tobacco. A short time later, Surratt again visited Port Tobacco and once more tried to involve him; again Atzerodt refused.

When Captain Monroe questioned him about a knife found in his room, Atzerodt said Herold had given him a knife and a revolver. Asked if he knew of plans to assassinate the President, the unhappy immigrant replied that he had heard it spoken of, but said he did not believe it. Monroe sent this testimony to Burnett immediately.

As the Secretary of War's power increased, he even tried to dominate the new President. Within a week of Johnson's swearing in, signs appeared of inevitable conflict. Judge Hughes prophetically confided to Orville Browning that "Mr. Stanton and President Johnson will not agree . . . Johnson is determined to be master."[17]

Col. Henry Burnett, whom Stanton had summoned to take charge of the investigation, gradually relieved the Secretary of War. Subordinates continued to refer major decisions to Stanton for final approval, however.

Even as Burnett examined a copy of Atzerodt's confession, he continued to follow other leads. For instance, he ordered the arrest of Thomas J. Raybold, who had charge of renting private boxes at Ford's Theatre. Although Raybold denied he had sold any private boxes on the day of the murder, authorities confined him to Old Capitol. Detectives later learned he had sold tickets for the President's box to Booth for March 15. Booth's invited guests that evening included Lewis Payne and Anna Surratt.

Upon examining the evidence, Burnett ordered Dr. Mudd transferred from the Bryantown jail to confinement in Washington. In Samuel Mudd's first prison statement he declared again that he had not recognized Booth. But under continued probing, the doctor admitted for the second time that he had met Booth once, several months prior to the assassination. He revealed he had helped Booth buy a horse blind in one eye (the same horse that Atzerodt claimed he owned and that was found, fully saddled, wandering loose near the Capitol on the night of the murder). The doctor expressed ignorance of Booth's whereabouts at the present time.

Mudd's denial that he knew the men was weak, considering that Booth and Herold stopped only at houses of known sympathizers and proudly identified themselves as the assassins. Mudd was evasive; yet at this stage he was not a prime suspect. Even so, Wells noted in his report that the doctor was either "*ignorant or wilfully conceals the facts.*"[18]

Wells also interrogated one of Dr. Mudd's black servants who made the interesting observation that the man with Booth had asked specifically for Sam Mudd's residence. Obviously the pair were not looking for just any doctor's house. The servant added that when the men left, they headed for the swamp.

Lt. Edward P. Doherty commanded the contingent of 25 cavalrymen who searched successfully for Booth (National Archives photo no. 2181, Brady Collection).

After soldiers failed in their search for Booth in Maryland, LaFayette Baker figured the fugitives must have crossed into Virginia. He realized they could not have traveled toward Richmond (as originally planned) because the city was in Federal hands. Baker surmised that the only logical route was toward the southwest. He marked the principal crossings of the Rappahannock and decided to search that area. On Sunday morning, April 23, Baker requested from Major Eckert a telegraph transmitter and an operator. That evening, Baker sent two detectives and the telegraph operator on the steamer *Keyport* to Port Tobacco. The operator was not for Baker's exclusive use, but was also available to other investigators.[19]

The quest for Booth, as well as the rewards, intensified. Later that day, O'Beirne began to track Booth in the same region. He accidentally noticed a slight indentation in the ground. Looking more closely, he discovered the mark was repeated every few feet. Assuming it had been made by Booth's crutch, he and his men followed the trail several miles. O'Beirne then telegraphed Stanton that Booth must be near Port Royal, Virginia.[20]

In the meantime, an elderly black man had revealed to telegraph operator Theodore Woodall that two suspicious men, one of them lame, had gotten into a boat to cross the Rappahannock near Swan's Point. Instead of sending this information over the wires, which would have passed through the War Department, Woodall personally escorted the man to Baker's headquarters in Washington, where he repeated the story. Baker realized that he had the best lead on Booth's flight. He later claimed that the unidentified black man gave the same report to soldiers in the area several days earlier, but they did not believe him.

Armed with this clue, Baker asked Gen. Winfield Hancock for a detachment of 25 calvarymen. Accordingly, Lieutenant Doherty of the Sixteenth New York Cavalry and his men left Washington on Monday, April 24.[21] Baker also sent his cousin, Luther Baker, and his chief detective, Col. E. G. Conger.

Later, when LaFayette Baker was fighting for a larger share of the rewards, he claimed he had calculated Booth's approximate location and marked it on a map for Conger and Luther Baker. He belittled the army's role, arguing that it was needed merely to protect his men and not to aid in the capture of Booth.

The investigation in the Washington area also continued without letup. Two officers, Captains Potts and Newcomb, searched the Surratt house again and found a scrap with words "Gen. Suratt, CSA." This paper was probably forged, as the name Surratt was spelled with only one "r," a mistake no one of the family would have made.

Honora Fitzpatrick, released from Carroll Prison, was attending a church bazaar when she was called aside and told she was wanted at the Provost Marshal's office. Frightened, she sent for Father Jacob Walter, who evidently assured her the request was genuine. Officers again questioned her about activities in the boardinghouse and sent her back to Carroll Prison.[22] What new evidence authorities found against Fitzpatrick is not known. Most likely they held her as a witness of the activities in the Surratt house, which was gradually emerging as the conspirators' rendezvous.

XVII
"Tell My Mother
I Died for My Country"

Lincoln's funeral train arrived in New York City on April 24. Black crepe draped every building as the casket, drawn by sixteen white horses, passed slowly through the streets to City Hall. All along the route to Springfield throngs of mourners gathered to pay homage to their former leader. In Cleveland, citizens erected a giant pavilion, and Chicago prepared a great reception at the Cook County Courthouse. Early in May, after lying in state in Springfield, Lincoln's body, and that of his little son Willie, were interred amid elaborate ceremonies.

Lincoln's burial did not settle the Nation's unrest. Mrs. Lincoln continued to occupy the Executive Mansion; she never fully recovered from the shock of seeing her husband shot. President Johnson, who did not move into the White House for several weeks, conducted the Nation's business from temporary offices in the Treasury Department. Johnson was content to let the War Department conduct the investigation, and for a while, at least, the Government as well. John Hay and John Nicolay, Lincoln's private secretaries, were busy arranging the dead President's papers and getting the offices ready for the new tenant.[1]

Reports constantly poured into the War Department from around the United States, Canada and even Germany. O'Beirne telegraphed Stanton from Port Tobacco of his progress. A black woman living in the alley behind Ford's Theatre told of having seen Maddox, Spangler and Booth in conversation.[2] Detectives questioned Mrs. Surratt again, apparently as a result of Lloyd's confession. Government agents in Baltimore forwarded information on the search of the Girard house. Officials received a report on the chemical examinations of two questionable letters. And thousands of police, army troops and self-appointed detectives maintained a constant alert.

Even with all these leads, Atzerodt remained one of the most valuable sources. Detectives questioned him repeatedly. Each time, he told basically the same story but added significant details. When he was interrogated on April 25, he recounted how John Surratt had taken him to the Surratt boardinghouse where he first met Booth. He told of Booth's taking him to another boardinghouse to meet someone who claimed his name was Wood. The description given by Atzerodt was a perfect picture of Lewis Payne—"a strong, stout man—no hair on his face—rather good looking—wild look in his eyes—he carried a toothbrush with him—."[3] Strange that the shaggy little German should remember that Payne carried a toothbrush. Others also noted this unusual characteristic. Apparently Atzerodt was unaware that Payne and other suspects were being held on the ironclad with him.

This confession provided a glimpse into Booth's activities on the morning of the murder. According to Atzerodt, Booth sent Herold to ask him to go to Surrattsville. Herold said that Booth had some things there and wanted him "to see after them. They were in Mrs. Surratt's old house."[4] Atzerodt agreed to go, but changed his mind. When he made this statement, he probably did not know who had made this vital trip and certainly was unaware that some of the "things" had been found in "Mrs. Surratt's old house." He was also ignorant of Lloyd's confession a few days earlier. Atzerodt's statement made it clear that someone had to advise Lloyd to be ready that night. His refusal to make this indispensable journey placed Mary Surratt decisively in the conspiracy activities. The Government realized that whatever excuse might be fabricated, the purpose of the trip was to prepare for Booth's escape. Even if Atzerodt had made that fateful trip, Mrs. Surratt would still have been implicated, but it was this crucial journey on the day of the murder that presented the strongest evidence against her. Atzerodt asserted that at one time Herold had been designated to kill the Vice-President.[5] But Herold backed out, apparently because he wanted a less-risky task.

Detectives asked Atzerodt if he thought Mrs. Surratt had been involved. He replied that he did not know. Later, he changed his opinion. Booth had kept Atzerodt, as well as Arnold, Payne and O'Laughlin, ignorant of some aspects of the operation. He told them only what was essential to carry out their assignments.

As Atzerodt was dicussing Booth and Herold, soldiers drew nearer to their hiding place at Garrett's farm. While the crippled Booth was studying a map of his possible escape route to Mexico, troops sent down from Washington passed by the farmhouse. Both fugitives saw the soldiers. As Booth and Herold hurriedly planned their next desperate move, the cavalry troop continued on its way to Bowling Green, Virginia. There Colonel Conger found Willie Jett in a hotel. When Conger and two of his men burst into Jett's dark room, the startled Confederate soldier jumped out of bed. Conger yelled, "Is that you Jett?" Receiving an affirmative reply, the Colonel announced that he wanted to talk to him. Conger was dressed in civilian clothes, so the Confederate had no way of knowing which side he was on, but assumed that he was a Southerner.

"Where are the two men who came with you across the river at Port Royal?" Conger demanded.

Jett whispered nervously, "Can I see you alone?"[6]

After Doherty and Luther Baker left the room, the Rebel said that he knew who Conger was looking for and that they were about three miles away at Garrett's farm. When Conger replied that he had just come from Garrett's, the Confederate seemed embarrassed. Jett said he thought the detective had come from Richmond, observing that if Conger had already passed Garrett's, the men must not be there. Conger responded that he would return to check it out.

That evening at the farm, Booth tried to buy a horse from Jack, one of Garrett's sons, but was refused.[7] Garrett did promise, however, to take the two men to Guinea's Station the next morning. The Garretts later claimed they knew nothing about Lincoln's murder, much less the identity of their two visitors. Booth, using the name Boyd, had told them he was a wounded Confederate soldier. The presence of strangers would not necessarily have raised questions in this area frequented by spies and blockade-runners. Yet the Garretts could not have been ignorant of the assassination considering that Lincoln had been dead more than a week. Even in rural areas the assassination was the major topic of conversation, and the Garrett farm was only 75 miles from Washington. Richard Garrett later admitted that he had heard about the murder the day before Booth arrived and that they discussed the assassination with the man they thought was Boyd.

Whatever the case, Booth seemed safe, at least for the night. He gave Jack $10 in advance for his promised help. Then Booth and Herold went to sleep in a tobacco barn 150 feet behind the house. The boys locked the men in because they were afraid they might steal their horses.

Taking Jett with him, Conger and his men started back to Garrett's farm, arriving about 3:00 A.M. Lieutenant Baker and Jett approached the house in the dark as Conger quietly deployed his men around it. As soon as the guard was in place, Baker aroused Garrett.

"Where are the men who stopped at your house?"

"They have gone."

"Gone where?"

"Gone to the woods."

"Where abouts in the woods have they gone?"[8]

After Garrett's initial lie, he sensed his predicament and began to explain that the men had come to his house without his consent and that he had not wanted them to stay. Conger, who had by this time joined the interrogation, cut him short, saying he did not want to hear any long stories. Garrett obligingly began his explanation again. Conger, exasperated, told one of the soldiers to bring a rope, and threatened to hang Garrett on the spot. One of Garrett's frightened sons ran forward begging Baker to spare his father.

"I will tell you where the men are," he blurted out, adding quickly, "they are in the barn."

Satisfied, Conger ordered soldiers to surround the barn. At approximately 3:30 A.M. Baker told one of the Garrett boys to go into the barn and get the arms from the men. After some hesitation, the youth entered the dark, silent barn. Soon he came out explaining that the injured man cursed him and threatened to shoot him for his betrayal. Conger directed Baker to order the men out within five minutes, or he would set fire to the barn.

Booth, unable to see what was happening, demanded to know who the soldiers were. Then for nearly thirty minutes, he haggled. Finally Baker decided to give Booth and Herold another fifteen minutes. All the time, Booth was asking questions in a delaying tactic. He wanted to know who they were and, not being told, suggested they back off about 100 yards and let him shoot it out. Then, in his theatrical manner, Booth called out, "Well, my brave boys, you may prepare a stretcher for me."

For nearly an hour, the dispute disrupted the predawn quiet. Finally the bargaining was over. Conger ordered the Garretts to pack pine branches around the barn. Booth could hear the activity and dimly make out figures moving around. He warned the Garrett boys to keep away or he would shoot them. There were a few more warnings before Booth yelled out that there was "a man here who wants to come out."

Baker answered, "Very well; let him take his arms and come out."

Soldiers could hear an exchange between Booth and Herold but could not understand the words clearly. Conger heard Booth curse and call Herold a coward and order him to "go, go; I would not have you stay with me." After a few more words, Herold came to the door and called to Baker, "Get me out."

"Hand out your arms."

"I have none."

"You carried the carbine, you must hand it out."

Booth broke in, "The arms are mine; I have got them."

"This man carried the carbine and must bring it out," Baker responded.

"Upon the word and honor of a gentleman, the arms are mine; I have got them."[9]

Tired of the delay, Conger ordered Baker to forget about the carbine and get Herold out. The defector thrust his hands out of the partially open barn door and Doherty, grabbing one, led him out. (Baker later claimed that he pulled Herold out.) The officer then searched the prisoner, asking him if he had any papers. "Only this," declared Herold as he pulled a piece of a map from his pocket.

Conger wasted no time starting the fire. The dry straw blazed rapidly, transforming the darkness of the early morning into bright orange and yellow. The sudden inferno seemed to surprise Booth. Conger, looking through the cracks, could see Booth's shadowy form staring in bewilderment toward the barn door. The doomed man walked back to a corner of the flaming barn, still clutching a rifle. He looked around, frantically, apparently wondering if the fire could be put out, but the barn was becoming a flaming tomb. Conger started around to the barn door. Before he got halfway, he heard a pistol shot. Hurrying to the door, he found Lieutenant Baker in the barn trying to lift the dying Booth. Conger exclaimed, "He shot himself." Baker claimed that was not so. When the two men raised Booth, they could see blood running from a wound in his head. Again Conger declared, "Yes, he has shot himself."

Baker, becoming agitated, stated defiantly that he had not. Baker's concern about the shooting seems to have been motivated in some way by a desire for reward money. In the confusion, he may have thought he could get more credit for the capture if Booth's death was not thought of as suicide.

Lieutenant Doherty, who had custody of Herold, also heard the shot. He dragged Herold back into the burning barn as detectives were examining

Richard Garrett's house. Booth died on the front porch (Osborn H. Oldroyd).

Booth's fallen body. After he pulled Herold out of the barn a second time, Herold pleaded, "Let me go, I will not leave."

The officer refused; then Herold asked who had been shot in the barn. "You know who it is," Doherty replied.

Herold vowed that he did not, insisting that the dying man had said his name was Boyd. "His name is Booth," Doherty corrected, "and you know it." "No, I did not," Herold maintained.[10]

Tired of the useless argument, the Lieutenant tied Herold's hands to a tree and proceeded to attend Booth.

In the meantime, soldiers had moved Booth a safe distance from the fire; it was too late to save the barn. At first, Booth appeared to be dead, but gradually he opened his eyes and began to move his lips. Conger called for water to put on Booth's face, which seemed to revive him a little. The officer put his head close to the dying man's in order to hear Booth's feeble whisper, "Tell my mother I died for my country."[11] Conger repeated the words and asked if this was what he wanted to say. "Yes," came the faint reply. Soldiers then carried the assassin to the Garretts' front porch and laid him on a straw mat.

The once pompous actor could not speak above a whisper. There were no more theatrics; what he wanted was water and comfort. First he wished to lie on his face, then on his side, but not finding a satisfactory position, he begged to be turned on his back again. Booth gave some indication that he thought he might live. He asked Conger to apply pressure on his throat and then tried to cough. Apparently he thought there was blood in his throat. The colonel asked him to put out his tongue, which he did. Not seeing blood on it, Conger convinced him there was no blood. At that point Booth seemed to give up. "Kill me, kill me," he pleaded. Officers assured him they did not want him to die but rather to recover.

A physician who had been summoned arrived while Booth was still breathing, but could not save him. The mortally wounded man asked to have his hand raised and shown to him. "Useless, useless," he muttered.[12] The light of the approaching dawn gradually revealed the tragic scene. Booth's pulse was almost gone. About every five minutes he would gasp for air; occasionally a little twitch was apparent. He died four hours after he shot himself.

Booth's body showed evidence that he had shaved his mustache and had allowed his beard to grow, apparently in an effort to change his appearance. His hair was also cut shorter than usual.

As soon as the doctor pronounced Booth dead, Conger left Baker in charge of the body and of Herold, telling him to wait for an hour, then get some conveyance to transport them to Washington. Doherty sewed the body up in a blanket and ordered a black man to take it to Belle Plain where a boat was waiting. Soldiers transported Herold and Garrett's sons to Washington. In the confusion, the Rebel Captain Jett escaped.

By the time of the postmortem examination, the actor's face had been transfigured into a haggard semblance of its once imposing lines. Blood discolored his features and his hair was matted and dirty as if he had not combed it since the assassination.

About 5:00 P.M., on April 26, Conger arrived at LaFayette Baker's head-quarters and, in a low whisper, privately informed him that Booth had been killed and Herold captured. Baker, ecstatic, sprang to his feet, ordered a carriage and rushed with Conger to the Secretary of War's house. They burst into Stanton's room shouting, "We have got Booth."[13] Stanton, despondent over the tedious progress of the manhunt, was lying on a sofa when Baker entered. On hearing the news, he put his hands over his eyes and remained silent and motionless. After a few moments, he got up coolly and put on his coat. Baker laid the articles taken from Booth's body on a table—his two pistols, a belt, a knife, a compass covered with candle wax, a pipe and a diary. Conger informed Stanton of the details of the capture, after which the Secretary directed Baker to go to Alexandria to meet the boat with Booth's body.

Officers also found on Booth a bill of exchange on a Montreal bank. (He still had $455 in his account.) Jacob Thompson, the Rebel leader in Canada, had deposited $180,000 in the same Montreal bank on April 6, 1865, a few days after the surrender of Richmond. On April 8, he drew the money out and on April 11, closed the account. Thompson left Montreal on the day Lincoln was shot.

That evening at 10:40, the *John S. Ide* arrived with Booth's body and Herold aboard. An hour after midnight on April 27, soldiers transferred them to the ironclad *Montauk*. Authorities secured Herold in double irons. After placing Booth's rapidly decaying corpse on the deck, soldiers guarded it

An accurate representation of Booth's burial under the stone floor of the ammunition room in the Arsenal Penitentiary.

constantly. At ten the next morning, Stanton sent passes for Surgeon General Joseph K. Barnes and several others to board the ship to identify the cadaver.[14] Conger, Baker, and Doherty had previously made positive identification.

The War Department wanted to establish unequivocally that Booth had not escaped. Dr. J. Frederick May, who had operated on Booth a few months earlier to remove a tumor, told Dr. Barnes that if it was Booth, there would be a scar on the left side of his neck, three inches below the ear. Barnes testified that when he examined the corpse he found such a scar. In the course of the examination, he cut the section of vertebra from Booth's neck through which the bullet had passed. (It was later exhibited in the Army Medical Museum.)

With the passage of time, as impostors appeared claiming to be the assassin, myths developed concerning the identity of the man killed in Garrett's barn. In spite of these sensational stories, the identification was beyond doubt. Charles Dawson, chief clerk at the National Hotel where Booth frequently lodged, identified the body aboard the gunboat. Dr. G. L. Porter, an army surgeon, found the initials "J.W.B." tattooed on the right hand. The identification was so certain that not even Herold's defense counsel questioned it.

None of the prisoners, who might have benefited from proving that the cadaver was not Booth's, raised any question about it. They knew that Herold had been with Booth when the actor was killed. Even Herold, who previously claimed that his companion was named Boyd, spoke of Booth by his real name while returning to Washington. He later denied that he had been a willing accomplice, but he did not deny that the man shot was Booth.

A few years later, when the Booth family disinterred the body, rumors circulated that the assassin was still alive. Family members, careful to make sure they were burying the right corpse in the family plot, had Booth's dentist check the teeth with his record, adding further proof it was John Wilkes. A member of the Garrett household stated that the man shot was the same one who had come to his house. The dying Booth asked if Jett had betrayed him, a natural inquiry for Booth, but not for anyone else. Captain Jett himself saw the wounded man and identified him as Booth.

Objects taken from the body were the best proof. When Booth went to the barn to sleep, he could not have realized that he would never leave the farm alive. On his cadaver soldiers found a personal diary, identified by numerous witnesses as containing entries in Booth's handwriting. The diary also contained pictures of several of Booth's girl friends. The carbine he carried was later identified by Lloyd as the one he had given to Herold and Booth on the night of the murder.

When Conger was caring for the dying man, he found a pin, set with a small stone, attached to Booth's undershirt. It was engraved "Dan Bryant to J. W. Booth."[15] Bryant was one of the originators of minstrel shows and a friend of the Booth family. At the Surratt trial, the pin was exhibited and identified by Conger as the one he had taken from Booth's body.

Officers found six personal letters on Booth's body in addition to the articles mentioned earlier. The letters were addressed to Booth's friends—John Ford and actors and employees of Ford's Theatre. Strangely, no one knows what information these important papers contained or what happened to them. However, this may explain why Stanton was so determined to keep John Ford in prison. Mysteries still linger around the events and persons involved in the assassination, but it is certain that the man who shot the President was himself mortally wounded in Garrett's barn.

After identification, authorities planned to seal the corpse in a secure box. But at 2:45 that afternoon, Col. LaFayette Baker suddenly whisked the body from the ship in great secrecy. The detective worked so quickly that he left the box prepared for Booth's remains on board. Navy Yard Commandant Montgomery complained to Stanton about the irregular action but never received a reply. Stanton was clearly in charge of the Navy Yard as well as of the army. He ordered General Augur to station an army guard at Navy Yard day and night.

Stanton's fear extended even to Booth's dead body. Navy historian H. B. Hibben, referring to the cadaver, wrote that Stanton's "arbitrary restrictions in regard to it and the enjoinment of secrecy in regard to the disposition of it were strained to a degree that amounted to disrespect to the commandant."[16]

Stanton successfully thwarted many citizens' morbid desires to see Booth's body. A *Washington Star* reporter predicted correctly that the remains "will probably be deposited in a place that gives the most obscurity for it."

Before the corpse was taken, a naval officer boasted that he had a lock of hair, cut from Booth's head. This news infuriated the Secretary of War, who requested Secretary of Navy Welles to provide names of all persons who had access to the body. Lt. Commander E. E. Stone, in charge of the ship, replied that some naval officers and a lady had visited the boat. The hair, however, had been cut off by Surgeon Barnes' assistant. Stone was exonerated of any misconduct.

Baker's men quietly carried the cadaver down the Anacostia River late that night to the Arsenal Penitentiary where, on Stanton's orders, soldiers secretly buried it under a stone floor. The Secretary of War, fearful that Booth's body might be made the object of curiosity, was successful in keeping the burial location unknown until the Booth family claimed it several years later.

XVIII
Filling in the Gaps

With Booth's death and the capture of Herold, the Government had partially avenged the President's murder. They might have terminated the investigation, but the War Department had uncovered such an extensive plot it could not call a halt. Several individuals wrote they had information linking Booth to Confederate leaders. Henry Von Steinacker wrote a reavealing letter, complete with convincing details, names and dates, to Brigadier General Schaeff, who passed it on to Maj. W. B. Lane, who eventually forwarded it to authorities in Washington. Von Steinacker wrote that a Lieutenant Cockrill of Charleston, Virginia, played a part in the conspiracy. The writer said that while serving in the famous Stonewall Brigade, he heard the assassination discussed. Von Steinacker offered to help the Government convict Rebel leaders.[1]

Read, scrutinized and underlined, the letter became the basis for an embarrassing fraud. Ordinarily the Government would have checked Von Steinacker's story, but the accusations were exactly what Judge Holt and Secretary Stanton were looking for. Holt already possessed evidence that Confederate leaders had formed a conspiracy to disrupt Northern cities and throw the Union into confusion. Von Steinacker's letter proved, to his satisfaction, that the Lincoln murder was part of the broader scheme.

Another document, written by John Deveny at the same time, was similar to Von Steinacker's disclosures—that Booth had been working with Rebels in Canada. Deveny also offered his services in identifying the culprits. His plausible revelation was never considered.[2] Perhaps this burst of information, coming the day after the assassin's death, appeared too bogus.

Even before Booth's death, investigators suspected his brother, Junius Brutus, an unstable, disappointed actor, similar to John Wilkes. Among the assassin's possessions, police found a questionable correspondence from Junius Brutus in which he referred repeatedly to the latter's "oil business." Detectives knew that "oil business" was a cover used by the conspirators. As Booth actually had stock in an oil project, the term could be applied with several meanings. The letter, however, seemed to use the term in reference to the conspiracy and linked the "oil business" to the fall of Richmond.[3]

On April 25, Burnett began a search for Junius. He first sent a telegram to Gen. Joseph Hooker in Cincinnati, requesting that he look for the actor there and if unsuccessful, determine where he was. Burnett finally arrested Junius Brutus in Philadelphia and sent him to Washington.

After John Wilkes' death, Junius was called from prison to explain his letter. He admitted visiting his brother frequently, one time in Washington less than two months before the murder. John Wilkes visited Junius a month later in New York City, during the period when John Wilkes was completely absorbed with the conspiracy. Junius told detectives he was trying to get his brother to leave the "oil business" and get back to his acting career. Almost certainly during these visits John Wilkes, who talked freely of his plans, confided in this brother.

The Government never seriously suspected John Wilkes' more famous brother, Edwin. While Edwin was in no way associated with the conspiracy, he seems to have suffered more than other members of the family. Several years after John Wilkes' death, Edwin came to claim his brother's body.

The Branson boardinghouse in Baltimore was in some way involved in the conspiracy. Baltimore was second only to Washington as a base for the plot. Samuel Arnold and Michael O'Laughlin lived there; Lewis Payne first came in contact with the conspirators in Baltimore and John Wilkes Booth often visited the city. Even so, attention would not have been drawn to the Branson house except for an unpredictable incident.

Joseph Thomas committed suicide in Baltimore on April 24. Authorities discovered that Thomas had been staying at the Branson house; they knew that Payne had lodged there also. Further investigation revealed that after hearing of Payne's arrest, Thomas and his wife moved out. He declared that he "was fearful there would be trouble at Mrs. Branson's house."[4] Stanton had already investigated Thomas, even before he knew of his suicide and hasty burial. He wrote immediately to Gen. Lew Wallace, in charge of military affairs in Baltimore, to exhume the remains and subject the body to thorough examination. He also ordered that the boardinghouse be searched and the occupants arrested, thus unraveling another bizarre thread in the conspiracy.

Boardinghouses, particularly in such strategically located areas as Washington and Baltimore, served as rendezvous for Southern spies. Confederate couriers knew which landlords had "Secesh" sympathies. Some of these Rebel havens occasionally advertised in local papers with such tantalizing leads as "Boarding House with pleasant Southern exposure," or "House operated by genteel Southern family." Some more notorious places, however, avoided open publicity, relying rather on more discreet word-of-mouth advertisement. By whatever method, these houses attracted all sorts of Rebels.

The Branson boardinghouse was such a place. On April 27 (or 28), Mrs. Branson, her daughters and their boarders, were placed under house arrest until May 23, when they were summoned as witnesses.

Mrs. Branson, like Mrs. Surratt, denied she knew anything about the plot, but her daughters were more communicative. Margaret had been a nurse at the Union hospital at Gettysburg in 1863. There she had met Lewis Payne, whom she said was called "doctor." While in the hospital, she and several others were suspected of strong Southern sympathies. Samuel Bond, the hospital steward, believed that she had come there after the Battle of Gettysburg expressly to care for wounded Confederates. Soon after this encounter, Branson left the hospital under questionable circumstances.[5]

At the same time Margaret left, eight or ten Rebels fled, and authorities thought she was responsible.[6] Very likely Payne escaped at that time. About six weeks later, he visited Margaret at her mother's boardinghouse under the name Lewis Powell. She did not see him again until he reappeared in January of 1865. On this visit he used the name Payne, asserting that his father was a Baptist preacher. He told Margaret that his two older brothers had been killed in the war. Branson seemed interested in the Confederate soldier and invited him to accompany her to church.

Under interrogation, she admitted she had never taken the oath of allegiance to the Union and that she had friends in the South. Detectives inquired about the connection between Payne and Thomas. She described the two as on speaking terms but not close. Margaret did reveal, however, that the previous March, Payne, in a fit of anger, had knocked a black servant down and kicked her.

Things had changed since Payne's prewar days in the South. Slaves had just been emancipated in Maryland. Furthermore, the military controlled the area around Baltimore. The servant, therefore, reported Payne's treatment to the Provost Marshal's office. Colonel Woolley immediately arrested Payne at the Branson house. The Rebel gained his release by signing the oath of allegiance and promising not to return south of the Mason-Dixon line. (He had the oath with him when arrested at Mrs. Surratt's house.) Payne wrote Margaret only once, about a month before the assassination.

It was not Margaret, however, but her fiery sister Mary whom Payne was really interested in, and who, apparently, was in love with him. Margaret introduced her to the handsome Rebel. When authorities questioned Mary, the investigator, trying to trick her, asked what kind of uniform Payne wore when she met him. Mary, one of few witnesses unintimidated by army officers, replied that she did not think he had on Rebel garb, then added coyly, "a Confederate uniform is gray, isn't it?"[7]

Following this little joke, Mary revealed enlightening glimpses of Payne's background and of her mother's boardinghouse. Payne was not the illiterate backwoodsman he pretended to be. Although he complained of his lack of education, he spent much time in the boardinghouse playing chess with Maggie and other boarders. He often spoke of the Confederate guerrilla leader John Singleton Mosby and revealed that he had served in Mosby's command with Harry Gilmore's unit. (The persistent Mosby did not disband his troops until a week after the assassination.)

Mary confirmed her sister's assertion that Payne's real name was Powell and that his father was a Baptist minister. However, Payne was not always honest, even with Mary; he misrepresented his hometown as Frederick, Maryland.

The interrogator inquired if she was a Southern sympathizer, a dangerous fact to admit, especially in connection with the Lincoln assassination. She responded defiantly that she had always been a Rebel. The intrepid girl volunteered that she had sent provisions to Confederate prisoners of war, although she claimed she had obtained permission first from authorities.

Mary spoke more openly than her sister throughout the interrogation. She admitted she had seen Payne talking to Joseph Thomas, which contrasted with Margaret's statement that Payne hardly talked to anyone. Margaret tried to minimize her relations with Payne; Mary was boastful: "I think I was with him more than anyone else—even more than my sister."[8] She told of ten or twelve dates she had with the young Confederate, including a visit to her cousin and attending church. She described numerous visitors to her mother's boarding-house, giving the clear impression that it served as a rendezvous for blockade-runners.

When officers arrested Payne for mistreating the servant, Mary proceeded to the Provost Marshal's office to obtain his release. She confessed freely that she had lied to the officer in charge, Lieutenant Smith, declaring that Payne had never traveled north, when she knew that he had made at least one trip to New York City. After his release, he visited the Branson house and left again for New York. From New York he traveled to Washington in time for the assassination. He corresponded with Mary, and she wrote to him. She seemed to be the only person sincerely concerned for the brutal suspect.

Mrs. Surratt's boardinghouse was similar to the Branson place. The Surratt house, ostensibly providing much-needed income for the widow, was not a boardinghouse in the usual sense. Only trusted friends stayed there. Seldom, if ever, did anyone apply for lodging who was not already known to the family. Boarders were invited personally. Weichmann, who seemed to be a Southern sympathizer, was invited to stay there. Mrs. Surratt's coreligionists, Mr. and Mrs. Holohan and their family, were trusted acquaintances and relatives of her neighbor Wallace Kirby. These and Honora Fitzpatrick were the only paying boarders. Olivia Jenkins, Mrs. Surratt's niece, was an infrequent visitor. John Surratt seldom spent much time there and, of course, did not pay. Payne was evidently invited by John, since on his first visit he asked for John Surratt or Mrs. Surratt by name. Atzerodt did not find the place by accident. The mysterious Mrs. Slater and the notorious blockade-runner Augustus Howell were not ordinary, casual guests, but used the location as a contact point. The house on H Street in no way fit the needs of a widow struggling to survive.

Most rooms were occupied, but only because the boarders were spread around. Boardinghouses at that time were flexible, often keeping four or five persons in the same room, if not in the same bed. Usually Anna and Honora slept in Mrs. Surratt's bedroom. The landlady had space for additional boarders if the tenants had doubled up as was common. Weichmann shared a room and bed with John Surratt, but as John was frequently absent, Weichmann's room could have been occupied by more gentlemen. When the girls slept in Mrs. Surratt's room, that left space for boarders in the attic room.

On November 30, 1864, the following advertisement appeared in the *Washington Star:*

For rent, 2 furnished rooms in a private family at 541 H Street between 6th and 7th, available for 4 gentlemen.

Again on December 8, and December 27, 1864, Mrs. Surratt published a similar notice. After that, she made no effort to acquire paying guests.

Records of the District of Columbia Recorder of Deeds show that John H. Surratt, Sr., acquired the property on December 6, 1853, from A. A. and Sarah K. Gibson. The three-story brick house stood on a narrow lot 29 feet wide and 100 feet deep. In 1860, Surratt borrowed money on the realty from Henry Naylor. In January 1865, Mary Surratt again mortgaged the house, this time to John F. Givens. There was also a $1,000 indebtedness on the property owed to James Harvey.[9]

From the standpoint of economics, there was no reason for Mary Surratt to move to Washington. Due to scarcity of rooms in the city during the war, the house on H Street could be profitably rented. Also, for a mother protecting her emotional daughter, the farm was less hazardous than the city filled with thousands of undisciplined recruits. In 1864, Maryland passed an ordinance freeing slaves, but this had little effect on the Surratt household. They were slave owners, but not dependent on slaves to operate the farm. She rented the farm and country house for only $600 a year and still owed money on both houses—money she did not have.

John Wilkes Booth visited the Surrattsville area in the fall of 1864, ostensibly inquiring about farms. About that time Mrs. Surratt first proposed the move to Washington. During his first trip to Lower Maryland, Booth met John Surratt and began an active enlistment of conspirators. A safe, convenient rendezvous in Washington was absolutely necessary for the operation Booth was concocting. Mrs. Surratt's house served perfectly. John Surratt later confessed that he had been a Confederate blockade-runner for more than three years when they moved to Washington and that after the move his activities increased.

The date of the Surratts' move cannot be determined exactly. Anna told detectives that she went to Washington on October 1, 1864.[10] John arrived in November, but Mrs. Surratt did not leave the farm until December.

A letter from John to Weichmann on September 21, 1864, contained a suspicious reference to the move:

John Surratt is neither dead nor drafted though he runs the gauntlet of both . . .

I shall be in Washington as soon as possible, in fact I intend to stay up some few days in order to recuperate.

Possibly we move up sooner than we anticipated on account of certain events having turned up.

Miss _____ moved to Washington, says she is glad Mr. Surratt intends moving to town.

. . . .

I am very happy to state that I escaped the draft. I surely hope you may do the same.[11]

John Wilkes Booth opened an account in a Montreal bank used by Confederate leaders shortly after Surratt wrote these words. The exact day Booth first met John Surratt is unknown. But in his diary, Booth noted that the conspiracy had been in an active planning stage for six months, which would place its inception around October.

While in New York, Booth sought to enlist Samuel Chester to turn off the gaslights in Ford's Theatre, but plans were not rigid at this early stage. It would take several months of scheming, collecting equipment such as boats and guns, working out escape routes and recruiting collaborators. The Surratt boardinghouse was included in these plans.

On November 12, 1864, John Surratt, who was still spending time in Surrattsville, wrote to Weichmann, who was living in the boardinghouse. The letter was among the first documents referring to the plot, albeit vaguely.

> Sorry I could not get up hill today. . . . Hope you are getting along well. How are times and all the pretty girls.
>
> . . . .
>
> I'm interested in the bedstead. How's Kennedy? Tight as usual I suppose. Been busy all week taking care of securing the crops.
> Next Tuesday goodby Surrattsville, goodby ye God forsaken country. Old Abe, the good old soul—may the Devil take pity on him![12]

"Old Abe," obviously the object of an emerging plot, must have raised at least some questions in Weichmann's mind.

Surratt's movements by this time did not go unnoticed by the Government. His name appeared several times in the Union Provost Marshal's file. Officials simply designated his crime "rebel."[13]

Stanton wanted the conspirators captured, tried and hanged before Lincoln's burial—an unreasonable goal. Nevertheless, he could claim that when Lincoln's body was laid in the grave, the chief conspirators, except one, were dead or captured. He wanted the prisoners tried quickly. Interrogators worked intensely during the last days of April. Stanton ordered them not to bother with insignificant crimes and to concentrate on those directly involved in the conspiracy. Detectives asked detailed and often tricky questions to separate the principal conspirators from relatively harmless citizens.

The prison housed numerous suspects who had not shown proper respect for Lincoln's death. Authorities confined a Miss Lewis in Carroll Prison because she had not draped her mother's house in mourning. When questioned about this oversight, she complained she had no money for black cloth, whereupon the Government furnished the material and hung it for her. As soon as soldiers left, she tore it off. Enlisted men returned and again draped the house. Again the young lady ripped it down. She repeated this process three times before the exasperated men finally arrested her.[14]

Late one night, officers awakened Honora Fitzpatrick in Carroll Prison to inquire if she knew Mrs. Holohan. The half-awake girl managed to mumble "No." This sudden midnight interview revealed more than the unorthodox methods of Government detectives; it showed that the young lady's automatic response was to deny everything. The detective paused and suggested that she think a moment about her answer. Her interrogator, turning to trickery, asked what church Mrs. Holohan attended. Without thinking, Honora gave the name. The detective went further, "Who is her Father confessor?" The sleepy girl, realizing her mistake, but not wanting to make it worse, responded bluntly, "Indeed, I do not know. I never asked her."[15] The purpose of this interrogation is not known.

After Booth's death, reporters became fascinated by his incredible escape. Their digging revealed that the first reliable information had come from John Lloyd. When the public learned of his confession, Mary Surratt's name became widely associated with the crime for the first time.

On April 29, the *Washington Star* printed the account of her visit to her country tavern on the afternoon of the murder and her order that Lloyd have two carbines ready for men who would pick them up that night. The paper narrated details of the guns suspended by ropes between the joists in an unused section of the house. At the time this story leaked, guards were watching Lloyd closely in prison, so the information must have come from soldiers who were present when the guns were found.

The monitor *Montauk*, on which officers held David Herold, remained anchored off the Washington Navy Yard, within sight of his mother's house. The boyish-looking Herold's small frame made him appear younger than his 22 years. Detectives learned he had lived for several years with a Washington druggist named Ward, to whom he was apprenticed. There he first learned of medication prescribed for Secretary Seward, knowledge later used by Payne to gain entrance to the Seward home. After his father's death, Herold moved back home with his mother and sisters.

During his interrogation by John Bingham on April 27, Herold volunteered very little information. He repeated the same excuse used by Lloyd and Atzerodt—his drinking made him too intoxicated to remember the crime. Herold explained he spent most of the day trying to sell a horse to Judge Parker and later traveled to Surrattsville to pay John Lloyd two dollars. On the way back to Washington, about 11:30 P.M., he met Booth on the road. Herold made no attempt to deny that the man was Booth. He stated that Booth requested his company back to the country for a good time. Herold replied that he had to return home, but Booth argued that the gates across the river were already closed. Booth had been drinking and insisted that Herold accompany him. At the time, Herold affirmed, he did not know Lincoln had been shot, so he accompanied the actor. The following day, on hearing that a man named Booth had shot the President, he told his companion, "Either you or your brother did it."[16] Herold claimed that Booth denied knowing anything about it. Herold then asked why he was armed. Finally Booth admitted that he had, indeed, shot the President and told Herold that now he was implicated, and if he tried to run away he would shoot him.

Herold reminded Bingham that Booth's last words before he was shot were, "Let the young man out. He is innocent."[17] For those who believed that a trapped or dying man's final utterances deserved special consideration, it might have been convincing. Several conspirators attempted some noble deed in their final desperate hours, especially if it involved deceiving the Government.

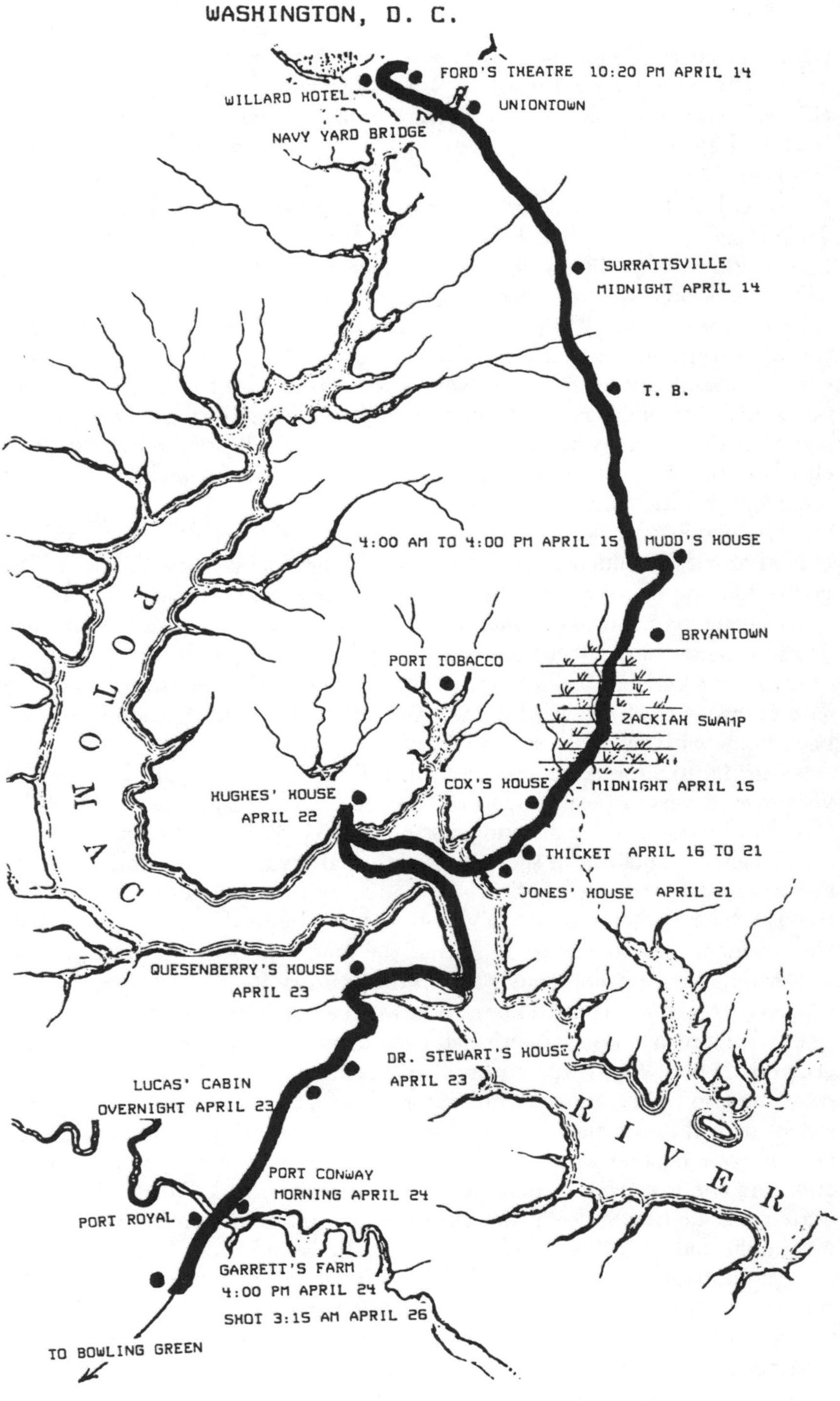

WASHINGTON, D. C.

FORD'S THEATRE 10:20 PM APRIL 14

WILLARD HOTEL
UNIONTOWN

NAVY YARD BRIDGE

SURRATTSVILLE
MIDNIGHT APRIL 14

T. B.

4:00 AM TO 4:00 PM APRIL 15   MUDD'S HOUSE

BRYANTOWN

PORT TOBACCO

ZACKIAH SWAMP

HUGHES' HOUSE
APRIL 22

COX'S HOUSE   MIDNIGHT APRIL 15

THICKET   APRIL 16 TO 21

JONES' HOUSE   APRIL 21

QUESENBERRY'S HOUSE
APRIL 23

DR. STEWART'S HOUSE
APRIL 23

LUCAS' CABIN
OVERNIGHT APRIL 23

RIVER

PORT CONWAY
MORNING APRIL 24

PORT ROYAL

GARRETT'S FARM
4:00 PM APRIL 24

SHOT 3:15 AM APRIL 26

TO BOWLING GREEN

POTOMAC

Herold's tale was as good as any. Even though he had been caught with Booth, it was his word against others. His account was as plausible as that of Mrs. Surratt or Dr. Mudd. Only the facts condemned him.

He claimed ignorance of others involved—a falsehood he could have avoided had he known that Atzerodt, O'Laughlin and Arnold had already confessed and that the Government had his companions in prison. He was also ignorant of Lloyd's confession about two men stopping for guns. Herold was unaware of almost everything that had transpired since the murder. In hiding with Booth, he had access to only a few newspapers, and he had been kept isolated from other prisoners since his capture.

Herold casually mentioned a letter Booth had left, signed by most of the conspirators. This was the second reference to the document which Booth had given to John Maddox, to be published in the *National Intelligencer*.[18] The diary found on Booth's body also referred to the letter. The assassin had anxiously searched newspapers for its publication during his first days in hiding. Finding no trace of it, he complained bitterly that even the newspapers were against him.

Herold filled his testimony with insignificant and deceptive details. Had not the investigation been thorough, these misleading clues might have confused detectives. As it was, they simply noted Herold's statements as craftiness.

Herold did provide one otherwise unknown glimpse into the crime. He revealed how Booth gained access to the presidential box. From the time Booth climbed the steps of Ford's Theatre until he lay dying on Garrett's porch, he only communicated at length with one man—David Herold. Apparently only four persons knew how Booth got past the President's guard: Booth, now dead, the guard protecting the box (who said nothing), a witness in the theater and Herold. The latter reported that Booth simply pulled a letter (the witness said a card) from his pocket and showed it to the guard.[19] What the letter contained is not known, but the guard was sufficiently impressed to allow the well-known actor to pass unchallenged into the dark hallway.

The interrogation of Confederate spy Augustus Howell was less enlightening than Herold's. Union forces had captured Howell and held him in Carroll Prison for nearly a month before the assassination. Confined in a cell on the third floor, Howell was treated well at first with accommodations much like those of John Ford. Nevertheless, he contacted the assistant superintendent, a rotund little man named Charles H. Wilson, requesting better treatment. Wilson refused to help. Finally Howell found an opportunity to speak to Superintendent Wood. The superintendent immediately gave orders to furnish the Confederate spy with everything needed to make him comfortable.[20]

Wood was an enigma, obviously corrupt, and unusually friendly to Southern prisoners; his actions were seldom consistent. His method of examining

Opposite: Booth's escape route. The conspirators had carefully considered possible escape routes. Even though the original kidnap scheme had to be altered, Booth's first stops seemed to have been planned beforehand.

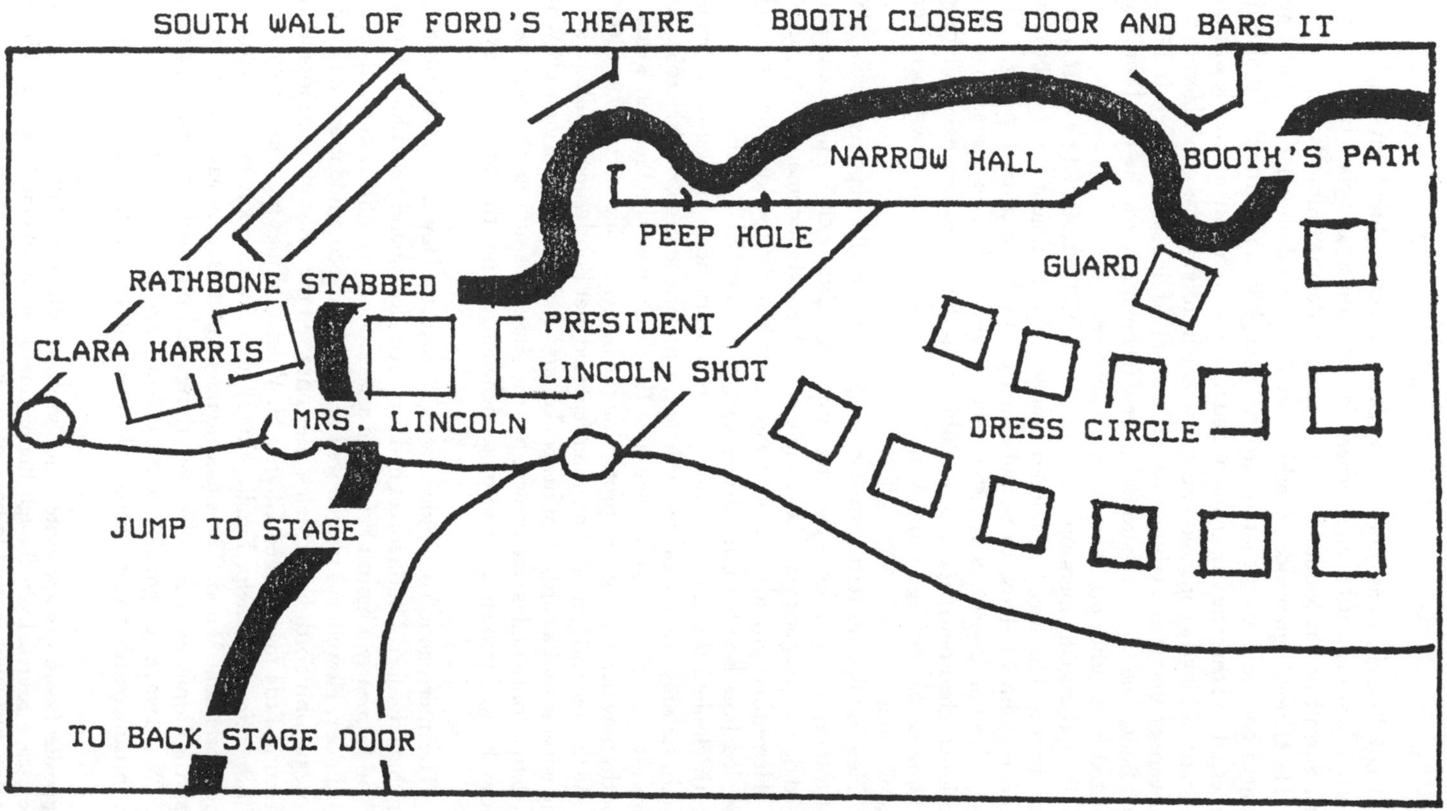

SOUTH WALL OF FORD'S THEATRE   BOOTH CLOSES DOOR AND BARS IT

BOOTH'S PATH

GUARD

NARROW HALL

DRESS CIRCLE

PEEP HOLE

PRESIDENT
LINCOLN SHOT

MRS. LINCOLN

RATHBONE STABBED

CLARA HARRIS

JUMP TO STAGE

TO BACK STAGE DOOR

suspects was low-keyed and gentle, and, while generally unsuccessful, he did as well as Detective Baker. Whatever the case, Southerners seemed to regard him as their friend.

There was a limit to Wood's support, however. About two weeks after the assassination, Howell, who up to that time had enjoyed certain liberties, was suddenly called out at 2:00 A.M., put in irons and thrown into solitary confinement. He blamed this abrupt change on Weichmann's statement about seeing him at Mrs. Surratt's house. His deduction was probably correct, but he was incorrect in condemning Weichmann for all his troubles. Investigators had several statements linking him with the Surratts.

Howell sharply denounced Weichmann as a turncoat. He regarded the clerk as a Southern sympathizer. The spy accused Weichmann of passing information about Government prisons to him. In fact, Howell reported that Weichmann had purposely obtained his job with the Commissary General of Prisoners in order to secure information for him and Surratt.

Howell soon complained again to Superintendent Wood, requesting that his handcuffs be removed. This time the amicable superintendent did nothing. Only orders from Secretary Stanton could make the change.

A few days later, Wood sent for Howell. On entering Wood's office, he found the superintendent talking with the detested LaFayette Baker. Colonel Baker pretended disinterest in the proceedings as Wood put questions to the spy. Howell, aware of the investigator's aim, took delight in thwarting their attempts. He particularly resented the devious Baker, whose pretense of friendly concern was an all too obvious effort to win confidence. Wood continued his gentle probing. Baker, standing back, watched the process but took no part. Getting nowhere, the superintendent released the prisoner. The next day he sent for Howell once more and again quizzed him about his visits to the Surratt boardinghouse. This time, with Baker absent, Howell admitted freely that he had called on the Surratts.

Following this interrogation, Howell was caught trying to communicate with Mrs. Surratt from the prison yard as she stood at her cell window. He vowed that he had made no attempt to talk with her, but, nevertheless, officers denied him the privilege of walking in the prison yard, and he remained handcuffed until after the trial.[21]

Government investigators had in Howell a definite link between Mrs. Surratt and the Confederate spy system. Several witnesses supported this undeniable fact. Detectives questioned Howell repeatedly, hoping to learn the names of other visitors to the house on H Street. Howell labeled these frequent sessions torture; the War Department called them interrogations. Whatever they were, they proved unfruitful.

As a last resort, the Government sent James A. Gregory, a United States detective and former Rebel, to interrogate Howell. Gregory pretended to be

Opposite: Booth's path to Lincoln's box. A guard stopped Booth at the entrance to the hall but allowed him to enter. Inside, Booth barred the hall door closed, looked quickly through the peep hole, entered the box and shot the President.

SURRAT.   BOOTH.   HAROLD.

War Department, Washington, April 20, 1865,

 # $100,000 REWARD!

THE MURDERER

Of our late beloved President, Abraham Lincoln,

IS STILL AT LARGE.

$50,000 REWARD

Will be paid by this Department for his apprehension, in addition to any reward offered by Municipal Authorities or State Executives.

$25,000 REWARD

Will be paid for the apprehension of JOHN H. SURRATT, one of Booth's Accomplices.

$25,000 REWARD

Will be paid for the apprehension of David C. Harold, another of Booth's accomplices.

LIBERAL REWARDS will be paid for any information that shall conduce to the arrest of either of the above-named criminals, or their accomplices.

All persons harboring or secreting the said persons, or either of them, or aiding or assisting their concealment or escape, will be treated as accomplices in the murder of the President and the attempted assassination of the Secretary of State, and shall be subject to trial before a Military Commission and the punishment of DEATH.

Let the stain of innocent blood be removed from the land by the arrest and punishment of the murderers.

All good citizens are exhorted to aid public justice on this occasion. Every man should consider his own conscience charged with this solemn duty, and rest neither night nor day until it be accomplished.

EDWIN M. STANTON, Secretary of War.

DESCRIPTIONS.—BOOTH is Five Feet 7 or 8 inches high, slender build, high forehead, black hair, black eyes, and wears a heavy black moustache.

JOHN H. SURRAT is about 5 feet, 9 inches. Hair rather thin and dark; eyes rather light; no beard. Would weigh 145 or 150 pounds. Complexion rather pale and clear, with color in his cheeks. Wore light clothes of fine quality. Shoulders square; cheek bones rather prominent; chin narrow; ears projecting at the top; forehead rather low and square, but broad. Parts his hair on the right side; neck rather long. His lips are firmly set. A slim man.

DAVID C. HAROLD is five feet six inches high, hair dark, eyes dark, eyebrows rather heavy, full face, nose short, hand short and fleshy, feet small, instep high, round bodied, naturally quick and active, slightly closes his eyes when looking at a person.

NOTICE.—In addition to the above, State and other authorities have offered rewards amounting to almost one hundred thousand dollars, making an aggregate of about TWO HUNDRED THOUSAND DOLLARS.

a Southern sympathizer, but the prisoner easily saw through the guise and revealed nothing. Authorities, gaining little, eventually gave up. Howell never divulged the identity of Mrs. Slater and, although he certainly knew of the plan to kidnap Lincoln, denied it.

Detectives scrutinized no one more closely than Louis Weichmann. His position continued to be precarious, and he knew it. Early in the investigation, several persons informed authorities that Weichmann was probably connected with the crime. Gilbert J. Raynor, who had a desk in front of Weichmann's at the Commissary, came forth belatedly to tell authorities that the young man had bragged he could make $20,000 to $30,000 in some dishonorable enterprise. Raynor informed detectives that Weichmann brought John Surratt to the office one evening and introduced him to various workers.[22] In his many interrogations, Weichmann never mentioned this fact.

The Government had arrested a few prime suspects against whom it had strong evidence. Payne, Atzerodt, Arnold, and Herold were certain to be tried. Herold, Booth and John Surratt were the three pictured on reward posters; Booth was dead, Surratt was still at large but, if caught, would surely go on trial. Authorities were not yet certain which other prisoners should be tried, including O'Laughlin, Dr. Mudd, Mrs. Surratt, Anna Surratt, Weichmann, Spangler, Mr. and Mrs. Green, John Ford, Junius Booth, the Bransons, Lloyd, Maddox, Cox, Jones, Parr and a few Confederate leaders.

The Government did not look for scapegoats; it did not need any. It had uncovered a large conspiracy. If anything, authorities wanted to avoid prosecuting too many. For this reason, a few, against whom officials had slight evidence, were not investigated thoroughly.

The investigation left many loose ends, but hundreds of statements were still being scrutinized by lawyers. Those who appeared most guilty were questioned repeatedly. Intensive interrogation aimed at filling in the gaps. The War Department did not want the guilty to slip through its dragnet. Colonel Wells interrogated citizens of Lower Maryland again, seeking those who had helped Booth escape. He was convinced that Osborn, Swan, Sam Cox, Austin Adams and Thomas Jones had helped Booth. The evidence was especially strong against Cox and Jones.

In Baltimore, not only were the Bransons implicated, but also Edmond Murphy, J. B. Henderson and B. J. Early. The latter three had accompanied Michael O'Laughlin to Washington on the night of the murder and stayed in the city while he apparently conferred with Booth.

The Government continued to open mail sent from or received by any suspect and all letters sent to or from Canada. By the end of April, officials had opened about 500 letters. Many were suspicious; some were written in invisible ink, which was revealed by chemicals. No charges were made as a result of those investigations, however.[23]

Opposite: Early reward posters had the wrong picture for John Surratt, the photograph of Herold was outdated and "Surrat" and "Harold" misspelled. (Later posters corrected pictures but continued the misspelling.)

XIX
"I Do Not Know, Sir—
I Declare I Do Not Know"

Late in April, the War Department commissioned Col. H. S. Olcott to supply conclusive facts on suspects confined at Old Capitol and Carroll prisons. Burnett instructed him to examine the suspects and report his findings.[1] On the 28th and 29th, Olcott conducted the most thorough examinations to date. They were indispensable in drawing up charges. The findings also helped the War Department determine which prisoners to try.

Olcott employed several interrogators, including the superintendent of Old Capitol Prison and Col. Robert S. Foster. Different agents often questioned the same suspects. Scribes tediously recorded the process in longhand, although frequently misspelling names and leaving out questions.

Conscious that they were dealing with Rebels involved in an attempt to destroy the Federal Government, interrogators did not play games. They used all legitimate means to uncover the facts. Yet, of those questioned, only John Ford and Sam Arnold accused the Government of brutality, and their acccusations were weak. Arnold complained of cruel physical treatment, such as the inhuman hoods, cold showers and the miserable cells, but even he could not point to ruthless questioning.

Olcott and his assistants first interrogated Samuel Cox. He confessed that Booth had come to his house but denied he helped him, swearing that he shut the door in the assassin's face. Nevertheless, he obviously had not voluntarily reported Booth's visit. Cox admitted that after the emancipation of his forty or fifty slaves, he turned against Lincoln.[2] Freeing the slaves was the chief complaint of most prisoners. The Government placed no charges against Cox.

In his interrogation of John Ford, Olcott queried him on his opinion of the strange letter from Junius to his brother, John Wilkes. Ford defended Junius, asserting that he had heard Junius talk about the need for John Wilkes to leave the oil business and get back into acting, adding that Junius was very loyal. He affirmed his own innocence and swore that he knew none of Booth's associates. This denial appeared suspect considering that workers around Ford's Theatre correctly identified several of Booth's friends.

Ford complained that the assassination hurt him and predicted correctly that his name would be "forever associated with the murder."[3] Somehow he convinced Olcott of his innocence. Perhaps it was Ford's dignified bearing, which Olcott admitted impressed him, or maybe the impresario's prominent standing in the city influenced the officer. Whatever the reason, Olcott recommended that Ford be released. Stanton, however, remained unconvinced and refused the request, leaving Ford in Old Capitol.

In the extensive interrogation, the Government included the unassuming 19-year-old Honora Fitzpatrick. Detectives had already questioned her frequently but never extensively. Nora, as she was called, moved early into Mrs. Surratt's Washington house. Her father, James Fitzpatrick, a collector for various Washington banks, had sent his daughter to board with her friend Anna.

Precisely when she moved in is uncertain. She told Superintendent Wood it was October 6, 1864. Yet she informed another interrogator that she started boarding there September 6, 1864.[4] The more likely date is October 6. Apparently only Nora and Anna occupied the entire three-story house until Weichmann came a few weeks later. Anna's brother John then joined them. Later Mr. and Mrs. Holohan moved in with their two children. Apollonia Dean, a nine-year-old girl, came next but only lived there briefly. Finally Mrs. Surratt and her niece, Olivia Jenkins, arrived toward the end of December.

In contrast to her earlier hesitancy, Fitzpatrick now opened up. Her responses were not unduly devious or obstinate, but seemingly straightforward. Sensing this change, detectives worked on her constantly. Nora repeated what others had already admitted—that Booth came to the house very often. About three or four times a week, she remarked. Detectives posed a routine question about those who frequented the house—"Did they meet apart from the other boarders?"

Casually, hardly realizing the implications of her statement, she replied, "I know sometimes they were up at Mrs. Surratt's room."

"How often?"

"I don't know how often, but I know they went up there."

"Who went up there?"

"Sometimes Mr. Booth went up there, and sometimes 'Port Tobacco' and then Wood [Payne] sometimes would."[5]

This was extremely damaging testimony, and although Fitzpatrick was not an important witness at the trial, her seemingly ungarnished answers left detectives little doubt about Mrs. Surratt's part. One would assume she was talking about John Surratt, rather than his mother, had she not previously stated that John Surratt was at home only "a few days." Booth spent more time at the house than John Surratt did. By this time investigators knew that the dwelling on H Street was the conspirators' principal meeting place and that John Surratt's mother probably had more to do with the actual direction of the operation than her son.

Authorities still remained perplexed about misleading statements concerning three men who visited the house to change clothes and then left quickly. Interrogators tried repeatedly to identify the mysterious guests. They questioned Nora about them, but she could not recollect any such visitors.

"Don't you remember Mrs. Surratt getting up to let somebody in?" the inquisitor pressed.

Fitzpatrick again responded negatively, although trying to be helpful.

Her testimony slightly contradicted Weichmann's description of events. Weichmann had stated that Mrs. Surratt was apprehensive and that she sent everyone to bed early on the night of the murder. Fitzpatrick said, "I remember Weichmann laughing and talking in the parlor. I was up with him until—I think about eleven o'clock."[6]

When quizzed about Mrs. Surratt, Nora stated that, although Anna was sick and went to bed early, Mrs. Surratt stayed up and seemed lively and talkative. The bewildered investigator wanted to know if Mrs. Surratt was laughing more than usual or if she noticed any change in her attitude. Nora answered that she had not noticed any particular change. The interrogator wondered why Nora had not recognized Payne the night of the arrest. She avoided a direct answer and replied merely that she had been frightened. The suspect obviously did not want to compromise the Surratts, but neither did she want to be caught in a lie. Recognizing her equivocation, the examiner inquired directly if she would have told anybody that she recognized Payne if she had been asked. Again she avoided a direct answer. Nora said enough by her evasiveness and the subject was dropped.

The Government uncovered a suspicious telegram from John Surratt to Preston Parr in Baltimore dated March 14, 1865. The communication read, "Immediately telegraph if my friend is disengaged and can see me this evening in Washington." Parr responded, "Will be on the 6:00 P.M. train."[7] Parr, whose china shop served as a meeting place for the conspirators, was arrested and sent to Washington. He requested an early hearing, complaining that he had epilepsy and needed to get the investigation over with. However, on April 29, when Foster and Olcott were busy interrogating suspects, Parr informed Foster that he would have difficulty testifying that day because he was ill.[8] When Foster insisted, Parr would only admit that he had known Surratt for about two years. The Government felt certain that Parr and his wife had had a part in the conspiracy, but since they could not prove it, released them. The exact part played by the Parrs was never known.

Colonel Foster's interrogations led him to believe that Holohan and Weichmann might be involved. At this time, both were under surveillance but not actually imprisoned. Foster concluded that they should be confined, at least Weichmann. This ended Weichmann's privileged treatment for a while.

Anna Surratt remained the most difficult suspect to label. Detectives learned that she had hit Weichmann and left him bruised because of his condemnation of slavery. Examiners believed that she was not above lying to protect herself and her family. It became clear that Booth charmed her. Papers with Booth's name written over and over in her handwriting, as well as his picture, were found among her possessions. The attachment was not entirely absurd. Anna, pictured by many contemporaries as a girl of 16 or 17, was in fact 22 years old—old enough to make a match for a dashing 28-year-old actor.

Although Anna was devoted to her mother, Mrs. Surratt lavished her love on her younger son John, giving little attention to her daughter. Anna's interrogation indicated her amazing ignorance of what was going on and yet showed that she had enough judgment to recognize incriminating questions. She would cleverly sidetrack these probes, yet some answers seemed extremely simple—even moronic.[9]

During one interview, Anna told detectives that she moved to her mother's Washington house on October 1, 1864, nearly three months before Mrs. Surratt joined her. She spoke of other boarders, including a Mr. Dowing, Atzerodt, the Holohans and Payne, whom she called Wood. Anna declared that neither she nor her mother liked Payne, who by that time had been identified as Seward's attacker.

When asked what she did not like about Payne, she responded, "I did not like his eyes,—something peculiar about them—I was always expressing my likes and dislikes when I see persons..."

"But why did you dislike his eyes?"

"I don't know."

Anna then remarked that Payne did not look like a preacher to her, although he had said he was one.

"Was he a very handsome fellow?"

"I do not know—I have not seen any remarkably handsome men since I have been in Washington. I didn't like him."

The young lady's answers seemed immature for her age. They were certainly misleading, as Booth, for one, was described by contemporaries as strikingly handsome. The detective continued, "When did you next see him?"

"I have not seen him since."

"Didn't you see him the night you were arrested?"

Anna was evasive, if not untruthful, "I did not look at that man that came at all."

"Not when we thought he was a Surratt."

"Oh, I saw him then, but I didn't recognize him then because he had changed."

The detective suggested that maybe it was because he had changed clothes. "Well," noted Anna, "he looked different but there was something about him—like somebody that I had seen."

"Wasn't there a conviction in your mind that he was the very man that you had seen who pretended to be a Baptist preacher?"[10]

Anna expressed her right not to answer a question for the first time. Her mother had said that she did not recognize Payne and therefore Anna could not admit that she had. She remarked hazily, "I [never] shall forget my feelings that night."

"Would you ever forget that eye or the look he had?"

"No, sir."

"Would you ever forget that he had been at your house before?"

"They did not look like the eyes of the man that was at our house."

The detective questioned how Payne had paid his bill and who had handled the cash at the boardinghouse. Then he asked, "How often did Booth come to your house?"

"I do not know."

"About how often?"

"I could not say—he came often—he never asked for anybody in particular—he usually saw the whole family."

The inquisitor, wanting to establish the connection between Booth and Mrs. Surratt, inquired, "Did he always see your brother when he came?"

Her careless response could only hurt her mother: "No, sir, my brother was not at home much when Mr. Booth used to come there."

"On the night the President was murdered, what time did you retire?"

"We retired as usual—we usually retire about ten o'clock."

The interrogator, already aware this was not so, asked, "Did you at that particular occasion retire at nine o'clock or between nine and ten?"

"I think that was the hour." Anna then explained that her mother slept in the room next to the parlor on the lower floor. She added that on that night she (Anna) slept on the third story. Usually, she said, she and Nora Fitzpatrick slept with her mother—three in a bed. But on the night of the assassination her mother informed Anna that she would have to sleep in the upper story. According to Anna this was because her cousin, Olivia Jenkins, had come to Washington to attend Easter services. Anna noted that Weichmann slept in the back room on the second floor and that the Holohans occupied the front room on the second floor. "That night," she revealed, "the servant slept up in the third story in the room next to me. There was no other rooms occupied that I know. There was a little girl boarding there and she had gone away to see her mother."[11]

Anna's explanation was particularly revealing, yet the Government did not pursue it. Detectives already had Weichmann's statement that Mrs. Surratt sent the girls to bed early that night and that she had stayed up pacing the floor. Weichmann knew, of course, that Mrs. Surratt would deny it, but he also knew that some other residents could back him up, if they would. Nora Fitzpatrick did not support Weichmann's statement, but Anna unknowingly did. She had opportunities to talk with her mother after their arrest and certainly had guidance in her evasive answers. But in the matter of when they retired on the night of April 14 and where they slept, she did not know how to answer. In this case she not only revealed that she had gone to bed early, but what was far more important—that Mrs. Surratt, who usually had the two girls sleep in the bed with her, had sent them as far away as possible, to sleep in the attic. The servant girl was also moved to the third floor. When detectives searched the house about three in the morning, they found the girls in the upstairs rooms. Suspicion of Mrs. Surratt resulted, in part, from numerous revealing accounts such as this, by those trying to defend her.

The interrogator wanted to know the whereabouts of her brother John. Again, Anna revealed more than she wished. "Ma did not tell me any particulars about where he was going—I did not think she knew any more than I did." Anna's pitiful reply seemed truthful. She was undoubtedly beginning to realize that her mother may have known more than she did.

The question of three men having come to the house came up again.

Government agents continued their obsession with this "mystery." Anna swore that no one came on Saturday or Sunday, to her knowledge, except Mr. Kirby, who came alone, and the three men, Weichmann, Holohan and Detective McDevitt. She said they came there both Saturday and Sunday. They came back and went upstairs to change clothes, according to Anna. Long before this clear statement, the Government should have realized that these were the three men referred to by the servant girl.

The investigator did not linger on the subject, but got back to Payne. "How do you explain the man who came there the night you were arrested?"

"I cannot say anything about it."

"Calling your mother by name?"

"I cannot explain anything about it."

"When he came saying that he came to see her, calling her by name, and saying he had been sent there."

"Indeed, I cannot explain anything about it. If I could, I would."[12]

This was all poor Anna could say. She must have thought about it, but explain it, she could not. Even those who wanted to believe Anna and her mother had difficulty accepting the Surratts' denial that they recognized Lewis Payne. His distinctive size and shape made him easy to identify, even from a distance. Witnesses who had seen Payne only briefly readily described his features. His face, clean shaven and youthfully handsome, was as readily recognizable as his large muscular form. Detectives wondered how so many strangers could describe Payne accurately and identify him quickly, while those of the Surratt household claimed not to know him. He had been in the Surratt house on several occasions. According to Weichmann, Mrs. Surratt visited Payne's apartment when he lived in the Herndon house. Anna attended a play with him at Ford's Theatre. His voice and form were familiar to all the boarders.

With these doubts in mind, interrogators tricked Anna into discussing Payne's appearance. Anna discussed his first visit under the name Wood and his second as Payne and began to describe his changed appearance. Suddenly she realized her portrayal revealed she remembered him very well, and she quickly retracted her words in confusion.

Throughout the ordeal, Anna gave the impression of a young lady completely dominated by her mother, anxious not to betray her. Her responses when arrested, during several interrogations and at the trial, revealed a frightened, bewildered girl who had some knowledge of treasonable activities which she did not completely comprehend. This seemed to befuddle her. She obviously loved her mother and brother and did not want to believe what gradually became obvious.

The interrogator asked one more question about John, "Did your mother assist him when he was postmaster?"

"Yes, sir—when he would go away sometimes she would make out the bills."[13]

With this, soldiers escorted Anna back to her cell. Next to Mary Todd Lincoln, she was the most pitiful living victim of the whole episode.

Detectives questioned John Lloyd frequently, particularly about Mrs. Surratt. Authorities called him from his prison cell again on April 28 and quizzed him about the two questionable trips she made. Regarding the meeting in Uniontown, when she mentioned "shooting irons," Lloyd declared that she first talked to him from her buggy in such a way that he could not understand her. "Finally she came out and asked about the fire arms."[14] Possibly Lloyd did not intend to, but he partially exonerated Weichmann because it seemed Mrs. Surratt tried to hide her conversation from him. Exactly what Lloyd and Weichmann knew remained uncertain, but their frequent interrogations made clearer that their roles in the intrigue were more circumstantial than deliberate.

Each query drew bits of information. When questioned about John Surratt, Lloyd revealed that he saw him the last time about March 25, "when he came here with his mother. She did not stay here but went back to Washington. They had another lady with them."[15] Lloyd referred to the "French lady." Later witnesses confirmed this visit.

XX
"Any Statement You Make Will Be Used"

Olcott's final examination of Mrs. Surratt provided critical evidence. As previous testimony had begun to implicate her, Secretary Stanton ordered the Colonel to interrogate her again, particularly in relation to Lloyd's most recent confession.

Because of her sex, officials did not subject Mary Surratt to the isolation imposed on other prime suspects. She remained in Carroll Prison, where she had contact with others. Although unaware of the exact statements Lloyd and Weichmann made, she realized they had been questioned repeatedly.

Authorities were reasonably successful in keeping suspects ignorant of others' revelations, but occasionally prisoners compared notes. Guards tried, unsuccessfully, to keep inmates from communicating, but this was practically impossible. Fleeting, whispered words passed among them. They signaled, sometimes amicably, occasionally menacingly, from their windows to the yard below. During one of these periods, Weichmann heard that Lloyd had implicated him. Thus, Mrs. Surratt had a vague idea several suspects had accused her.

As he initiated his crucial interrogation, Olcott reminded the prisoner that her answers were extremely vital. Informing her that the Secretary of War had personally requested the examination, he advised her of her rights, warning "You are a woman of too good sense not to know that it is better to refuse to say anything than not to tell the truth." The landlady remained unaffected, maintaining the same disdainful attitude which appeared to be purposely obstructive. Mrs. Surratt answered every question, at times evasively, sometimes answering questions not asked, occasionally with a curt "I don't remember," but never refusing to respond.

Her attitude did not reflect a picture of innocence, but rather one of self-confident defiance. She believed her son had successfully avoided entanglement in the actual crime and was safely hidden in Canada. Her indifference fused with an indomitable attitude which often characterized Southern womanhood during the rebellion. Women spies, almost invariably, thought of themselves as noble preservers of the Southern way of life which necessitated slavery. A common trait of intense hatred of the enemy, combined with a certain self-righteousness, led them to justify almost any crime. Mrs. Surratt was a typical domineering slaveholder.

She had ample reason to be detached and confident. She had a reputation as a pious woman, and the United States Government had never executed a woman. Relatives and friends as well as her church would support her. It was strictly her word as a religious woman against that of a few traitors and ruffians. As the conspirators had sworn to strict secrecy, the Government could gather little evidence against her. Furthermore, by this time, she knew that Booth was dead, which may have strengthened her sense of security.

Before getting down to the questions, Olcott reminded Mrs. Surratt of her rights a second time. Years before *Miranda V. Arizona*, he advised, "You are at liberty to decline answering, but you will understand any statement you make will be used in your trial."[1] The officer dispensed this seemingly modern advice in part because chivalry demanded treating women gently, and partly for legal considerations. It was not yet certain whether the suspects would be tried in a civil or a military court. Stanton apparently wanted to avoid future legal loopholes for the accused. That other suspects were not "read their rights" seems to indicate, however, that the main consideration was her sex, rather than legalities.

As usual, a stenographer, who recorded the interrogation, accompanied Colonel Olcott. The Government used these notes in determining whom to try, as well as in developing the prosecution's case. Officers promised none of the chief suspects preferential treatment for turning state's evidence. Interrogations were occasionally severe and even tricky, as in the questioning of Honora Fitzpatrick, but the Government offered no lenient treatment or favors in return for information. (However, a prison guard unofficially promised Atzerodt less severe punishment for his cooperation.) Stanton preferred, rather, to threaten harsher punishment for deception. Authorities warned Lloyd, Weichmann, and Mrs. Surratt of the consequences of lying.

The interrogation started where it always did for Mary Surratt—with her son. "When was the last time you saw your son John?"

"Monday week—previous to Mr. Lincoln's being murdered he took dinner at home."

"Had he been living constantly at home before that?"

The landlady explained that the family had only been living in Washington for three or four months, their business being still mostly in Maryland. Therefore, John would often be gone for a week. "I thought it better for him to be in Maryland than here where there were restaurants and bad company. I thought this was not the place for a boy," she affimed in conclusion.[2]

Mrs. Surratt assumed responsibility for her son's absences—to get him away from "bad company" in the city. It was a weak alibi, considering that John had spent much of his time with companions such as Atzerodt and Herold, drinking in the public bar which she had operated in her country home. This pious expression of concern rang false. She showed no particular anxiety for her daughter, whom she sent alone to live in the city.

The interrogator wanted to determine not only if John had been away long enough to run Rebel mail to Canada, but also if she knew of his clandestine activities. Mary Surratt chose her words carefully. She generally couched her denials in terms which, in her mind, must have seemed technically correct. She denied knowledge that her son had done "anything prejudicial to the public interest." But the "public interest" meant one thing to a slaveholder and another to the Federal Government.

When asked previously about John's absence, she had sworn he had never been away long enough to go to Richmond. After more than a week in prison, she had time to rethink her answers. This time she freely admitted that John had been away from home frequently, working on the farm. Her answers were in no way those of a widow, pitifully ignorant of her wayward son's activities, but rather those of an intelligent woman, fully conscious of her evasive role — coolly sparring with her interrogator.

Olcott moved to other questions concerning John. "Up to that Monday how long has he been there continuously?"

"That day he came from the country he had been gone a week. Perhaps a few days more I think. He left home Saturday week before the Monday he came home. He was only Monday to dinner. He went away after dinner."

Although she did not answer the question, she indicated that John had the habit of stopping at home only briefly between trips.

"Where did he go?"

"He didn't tell me where he was going," responded Mrs. Surratt. She proceeded to tell of her efforts to get John to buy his way out of the draft, and scolded him because he had not cooperated. Her son, irritated, left the house with Weichmann, according to the witness. "When Mr. Weichmann came back," she declared, "I asked him where John was and he told me that he had bid him good evening and said that he was going away."

"You have never seen him since that time?"

"I have never seen him since."[3]

This account appears only in this pretrial statement. The prosecution never brought it up again, nor did Weichmann mention it. In some measure, it tied Weichmann to John's activities. It made John's leaving home the result of a family squabble. It gave his mother an excuse for not knowing where her son was for more than two weeks and placed him away from the scene of the crime. Previously Mrs. Surratt had reported that John was in Canada, but she avoided the subject this time, perhaps because of strong suspicion that the "Canadian Confederacy" was responsible for the conspiracy.

Answering the next questions concerning Atzerodt, she explained that she could only survive by taking boarders. She had enjoyed a good living on her farm, however, and had not been forced to move. The Washington house provided her very little money.

Her explanation of how Atzerodt found the boardinghouse was an obvious deception. "I advertized in the Star several times. I was down in the country and when I returned I found him there. He lingered several days." She knew Atzerodt had come as John's friend, and that the few ads she placed in the paper were published in November and December of 1864. Atzerodt did not show up until March 1865. She did not advertise in any paper in 1865.

Her explanation of Atzerodt's leaving was also inaccurate. None of her boarders corroborated her story. "I found in his room bottles of liquor when I came home. I told him [John] I did not want this man to board. That he kept bottles of liquor."[4] Everyone associated with John drank—frequently in her house. For a woman who had kept a tavern in her own country residence, this was unconvincing. Weichmann had told authorities that Atzerodt was asked to leave because the rough, uncouth immigrant was not good company for Anna.

Her inquisitor turned to the Surrattsville trips. Olcott wanted to know how many times she had gone to Surrattsville the week of the murder.

"Twice."

"Who went with you?"

"The gentleman who boards with me, Weichmann, he drove me down in a buggy."

Mary Surratt testified that she stopped at her country house, but when asked about her conversation with Lloyd, she was evasive. "I do not remember any particular conversation, Mr. Lloyd was not at home until I was going to start."[5]

Detectives had already questioned Lloyd; she evidently wanted to minimize any conversation with him as incidental. Lloyd had sworn that the brief discussion, about having the guns ready, seemed to be the whole purpose of her trip. The Government now had both of the Spencer repeating rifles hidden in Mrs. Surratt's country house, one found with Booth and a second discovered still concealed there. Not only Lloyd's word, but a whole series of interlocking facts made Mrs. Surratt's explanation crucial. No one knew this more than she. But, unaware that the incriminating Spencer rifles had been found, the questions suggested only that Lloyd must have revealed something of her inculpating conversation.

Olcott inquired about the time of the conversation. Reluctant to state the hour precisely, she answered "Friday evening." The interrogator pressed on, "Was it the day of the murder?"

"Yes, sir."

"About what time?"

Mrs. Surratt explained that she did not start back home until after dinner. She then volunteered information about a letter she had received from Calvert in relation to a piece of land. "The parties wanted me to show my deed. I only wanted to say that the deed would be ready when the parties paid me the money. I got the letter that morning."

Olcott had asked nothing about the reason for her trip, but she seemed anxious to get this fact in the testimony. Her lawyers, however, later gave a different purpose for the trip and said nothing about the deed. B. F. Gwynn, a notorious Rebel, also took pains to assert that he and Mrs. Surratt had conferred about a real estate transaction, but he had another explanation. It appears the Calvert letter was to have been used as a cover for the trip but that the conspirators failed to coordinate their stories.

"What time do you drive?" continued Olcott.

"Usually late, after Mr. Weichmann comes from the office."

"What time did you get dinner that day?"

"Only took lunch about one o'clock."

The interrogator, still trying to pin her down on the exact time, assumed she must have started after one o'clock.

"How long does it take to drive down there?" he questioned.

"About one and a half hours."

"How long did you stay at Lloyd's?"

"I do not remember."

"About how long?"[6]

Olcott got to the central point. Mrs. Surratt started the indispensable journey about three hours after Ford had notified Booth of Lincoln's intentions, and she arrived back in Washington approximately two hours before the murder. The widow answered, "I think we started from there about five o'clock to the best of my knowledge. When I got there I learned that Mr. Nothey, the man I had business with, had gone to Marlboro..."

This statement was false. He had not gone to Marlboro—he remained at his home only three miles away.

"I remained there as long as I could to see whether he would return. In this I had a letter written to Mr. Nothey stating what he could do." Mrs. Surratt later mentioned another letter she wrote to Gwynn. "Just as I was about to start, the captain drove up. I told him my business and left the letter also."

In these statements she lied about situations easily disproved.

All other witnesses swore that Mrs. Surratt had not previously arranged to meet anyone at her tavern that day, but that she waited until Lloyd came home about 6:00 P.M. and then left immediately after a hasty conversation.

"How long a conversation did you have with Lloyd?" Olcott inquired.

"Only a few minutes conversation. I did not sit down. I only met him as I was going home."

"Where was Mr. Weichmann?"

"He was there."

Everyone who saw her with Lloyd, and even Lloyd himself, testified that the short conference was private and that Weichmann could not have heard it. Olcott pressed the issue, "He heard the conversation?"

"I suppose he did. I don't remember."

"What did the conversation relate to?"

"He spoke of having fish and oysters. He asked me whether I had been to dinner... said he could give me fish and oysters. Mr. Weichmann said that he would return home as he was in need of his bread and butter."

"What did you say about the shooting irons or carbines?"

"I said nothing about them."[7]

To the suspect it probably seemed that it was her word against Lloyd's. That was not the case. Eventually she had to confront the fact that Booth had stopped by her Surrattsville house about midnight and had found the Spencer rifles, whiskey and binoculars ready. It would have been impossible to retrieve the rifles quickly from their hiding place after dark, and Lloyd could not have been prepared for the midnight visitors without having been alerted that afternoon. He had only one visitor—Mary Surratt. Detectives discovered later that she had also delivered a small package to Lloyd, which she subsequently admitted. This transaction would have involved conversation relating to more than "fish and oysters." Yet she revealed nothing in her pretrial testimony about the package containing binoculars.

Colonel Olcott continued, "Did you tell him to have the shooting irons ready? That there would be some people there that night?"

"To my knowledge no conversation of that kind passed."

"Did you know any shooting irons were there?"

"No, sir, I did not."[8]

After a short discussion about Weichmann, the Colonel asked how Payne found his way to her boardinghouse. Mrs. Surratt repeated her statement concerning Atzerodt, that he had come as a result of newspaper advertisements. Regardless of her knowledge of John's activities, she knew that the only time she advertised was more than three months before Payne showed up, asking for her son by name.

The deception was too obvious and the interrogator picked it up, "What time did he come?"

"I don't remember—several weeks ago."

"Was it before the inauguration?"

"I think it was in February—I do not remember and would not like to state it."

With a touch of sarcasm, Olcott observed, "You could tell by the advertisement in the paper?"

"Yes sir, he said he saw we had rooms to rent, and he wanted to get rooms and board. He was a stranger to me. I had never seen him before."

"What sort of man was he?"

Mrs. Surratt described Payne as a short, stout man. "He seemed to be a young man so quiet and odd," she added.

"Did your son have any acquaintance with him?"

"Not that I know of."

In answer to further inquiries, Mrs. Surratt explained that Payne claimed his name was "Wood." He described himself as a Baptist preacher, noting that he had to return to Baltimore to preach.

"How long did he stay?"

"A few days. He came some day during the week and left on Friday for Baltimore. He remained in his room most of the time."

"What was he doing?"

"I never go into my boarders' rooms anymore than if I were not there."

The suspect got careless here. She had previously testified that she did not want Atzerodt in the house because she found liquor bottles in his room.

Olcott then approached another damaging part of her experience. "Do you recollect the man who came to your house at the time of your arrest?"

"I do not. I thought he was someone calling for the gentleman there. I never noticed him."

This answer was inconsistent with later explanations. She said nothing about not seeing well, an excuse her lawyers emphasized.

"Did you look to see whether it was this man, Wood?" asked the officer.

"I only saw a stranger. I never saw him before. I never thought it was the Wood who was at our house."

The questions turned to John Wilkes Booth. "When did you get acquainted with Booth?"

"Some months ago."

"Who brought him to the house?"

"He came to the house and asked whether my son was in. We always found him pleasant. His visits were short. I never knew anything about his private matters at all."

The widow answered more than she was asked but did not answer the question. Booth was one of the most famous stage personalities of the day— why should he frequent a second-class boardinghouse? Although Olcott had suspicions of Booth's motives, he was willing to listen to a plausible explanation. "Were his visits always visits of courtesy?"

"Yes, sir."

"Any business discussed?"

"No, sir. No political affairs. I do not think that his longest stay was over an hour."

"What part of the day did he use to come?"

"Sometimes in the day and sometimes in the evening."

The landlady evidenced no concern that the murderer of the President had been a frequent and unexplained visitor at her house.

"Did not an attachment spring up between him and your daughter?" Olcott continued.

"Not particularly I should suppose. Not that I knew of."

"He was a handsome man?"

"He was a handsome man and gentleman. That is all we knew of him. I did not suppose that he had the devil he certainly possessed in his heart."[9]

Olcott, pursuing this lead, asked if Anna "thought favorably" of Booth. "If so, she kept it to herself," the mother responded curtly. Anna, however, did not keep it strictly to herself. She bought a picture of Booth, which her brother objected to, and as mentioned earlier, she wrote the name Booth repeatedly on papers found in her room. Mary Surratt insisted, however, that Booth did not pay attention to anyone in particular.

The interrogator wanted to know how long John had known Booth. She responded that although she was not quite sure when her son met Booth, she was certain that Weichmann was with him when they met at the National Hotel. Mrs. Surratt's reference to Weichmann's presence at this meeting raised serious questions. The Government still had doubts about Weichmann's part and did not uncover details of this critical encounter until later. Intrigued, Olcott asked incredulously, "Mr. Weichmann was well acquainted with Mr. Booth before they came together?"

"I do not know. I think Mr. Weichmann was with my son when he was introduced."

Mary Surratt should not have known of this supposedly secret meeting. She was not present, and she pretended ignorance of her son's activities. Mary Surratt inadvertently gave herself away in this exchange. Being aware that Weichmann had told what he knew, she made an effort to involve him with Booth. However, Weichmann's friendship with Booth also involved her son, whom she had strenuously protected throughout the interview. In this predicament, she seemed willing to mention the vitally important secret meeting of Booth, her son and Weichmann. This encounter, which also involved Dr. Samuel Mudd, was an early planning session which only participants should have known about. This was not John's first encounter with the famous actor, as he pretended. He subsequently admitted that he had known Booth for several months.

After a few evasive answers about Kirby's visits to her boardinghouse, Olcott asked when she had first heard of the President's murder.

"When the gentleman called at my house next morning."

"What time?"

"Just about day."

"A few hours after the assassination?"

"I suppose so."[10]

Several questions about her knowledge of the assassination plot, which she denied absolutely, ended a most revealing interrogation. Before the interview, officials considered putting her on trial, but, had she been convincing or even helpful, she might have escaped indictment as did the mothers of other suspects.

The War Department had damaging evidence against the widow before this interrogation, but Americans, particularly Southerners, were strongly opposed to harsh treatment of women. Even the War Department preferred not to include a woman in its indictments. Booth had been killed and the Government already had several suspects to try. If the Nation thirsted for vengeance, it had enough blood to shed without including a woman.

The matronly widow, however, remained unbending as if challenging the Government. She had no idea of the massive evidence accumulated against her. Although Mary Surratt realized that Weichmann probably revealed all he knew, she was not aware how much her fearful boarder perceived. Always calm and self-assured, she gave the impression of defiance rather than of cooperation in solving one of the most tragic crimes in American history. Olcott's findings left the Government no alternative. Even so, authorities requested another opinion before making the final decision.

XXI
The Final List

Olcott next interrogated Sam Chester, whom he believed a valuable witness because he appeared uninhibited. He talked not only as a man acquainted with the plot from its inception, but also as one certain of his own innocence. Chester explained that conspiracy plans crystallized in late November, 1864. Other accounts also indicated that, although the conspiracy was conceived about September, it did not take definite form until November. At this time, Booth began to scout around the side roads between Washington and Port Tobacco.

Chester confirmed that the conspirators originally planned to abduct Lincoln and his Cabinet. Booth asked him to guard a theater door; he was not certain which theater. According to Chester, the scheme involved between 50 to 100 persons—all bound by a solemn oath.[1] Undoubtedly the investigation failed to uncover all the participants. Chester thought that Confederate leaders knew of the plot. Olcott recommended that Chester be released on bond.

Olcott moved on to S. J. Sheet, Booth's neighbor, whom he believed knew something of the conspiracy, but nothing could be proved. His part, if any, is uncertain.

James Maddox, a wardrobe custodian at Ford's Theatre, trembled violently as Olcott examined him. He vowed he had never had five minutes' conversation with Booth. Although Maddox energetically proclaimed his innocence, Olcott felt that he was involved; yet he was not indicted.[2]

While Olcott conducted his inquisition, Foster sent a report to the War Department stating, "It seems extremely improbable that Weichmann was ignorant of the entire plot, if he was not an accomplice."[3] He based this conclusion on testimony of clerks who worked with Weichmann. Furthermore, Foster noted that officers found in Weichmann's room large quantities of envelopes with the official frank of the office of the Commissary General of Armies.

After Weichmann's return from Canada and his arrest on Sunday, April 30, soldiers took him to Carroll Prison and subjected him to another examination, this time by Superintendent Wood. He told Wood he was 22 years old (some evidence seemed to indicate he was only 21), a student of divinity, and that he had left college in 1862. He repeated his previous accounts, but this time severely condemned his fellow prisoner, Augustus Howell. Obviously he had learned through the prison grapevine of Howell's accusations against him. He mentioned Mrs. Surratt's conversation with Lloyd at Uniontown, but vowed the only part he heard was her desire to get Howell out of prison. Wood, however, remained convinced that Weichmann must have heard more.

Two days later, officers took Weichmann from his prison cell and lined him up with other suspects. Lyman Bunnell scrutinized the group to determine if he was the man Bunnell had seen with Booth near Ford's Theatre on the night of the murder.[4] He was not, but detectives remained suspicious.

Next, Colonel Foster interrogated the clerk again in prison. this time the suspect described Mrs. Slater as a petite lady who always covered her face with a veil. Howell first brought her to Mrs. Surratt's house, according to the suspect. The last time, she came in the evening and asked for Mrs. Surratt. John Surratt was not home at the time. Other witnesses, as well as Howell himself, subsequently confirmed Mrs. Surratt's close association with Confederate spies including Howell and Slater.[5]

Within two days of this interrogation, authorities took Weichmann to Stanton's office and again questioned him. Face to face with the awesome Stanton, Weichmann repeated practically the same account he had given many times before, but this time he had more explaining to do. Stanton inquired about the package Mrs. Surratt had taken to her country house. The prisoner replied that she had told him it contained china dishes. Then Weichmann showed the Secretary a letter from Bishop John McGill to support his story that he had been interested in going to Richmond to further his theological studies. Weichmann must have taken this letter with him when he first left the boardinghouse, because he produced it several times after his confinement.

Stanton questioned him about a dispute with Anna Surratt over politics. Weichmann confessed that Anna had hit him in an argument about slavery and because he had gone "downstairs with blue pants on."[6] But he seemed reluctant to talk about it. Actually Weichmann refrained from any mention of Anna Surratt if he could avoid it. Stanton wanted to know more about Anna Ward and Mrs. Slater. The young clerk said little about Ward but told the Secretary that he had learned from Mary Surratt that Slater was a blockade-runner, and that she had accompanied John Surratt to Richmond. He claimed that John Holohan could confirm these facts. Naturally, Stanton wondered why Weichmann had not previously mentioned these unusual activities. He responded that he had revealed his suspicions to Captain Gleason several weeks earlier. Stanton, satisfied, returned Weichmann to jail.

After the interview, Weichmann wrote Colonel Burnett that the interrogation "terrified me so much yesterday that I was almost unable to say anything."[7] Unfortunately, he also told his fellow prisoners about the frightening confrontation, which they later used against him. Nothing in the official transcript indicated the interrogation was threatening. The questions were direct, designed to clarify doubts about Weichmann. The Secretary of War's power and reputation were such that he could have intimidated even the most intrepid. No doubt the young suspect was aware that his future was in Stanton's hands.

The Government still did not trust Weichmann, and he was soon questioned again, this time by Judge Advocate Burnett. Later Weichmann sent a letter to Burnett, responding to accusations leveled against him by friends of the Surratts. He wrote that he wanted all guilty parties brought to justice. But he begged Burnett not to confound the innocent with the guilty; then he proceeded to demonstrate that he belonged among the innocent. He revealed some additional facts he had previously forgotten. These included a letter to John Surratt, sent in the name of James Sturdy and signed "Wood," some additional suspicious remarks by Mrs. Surratt, and more about Howell—who sometimes went by the name Spencer.

He explained that he had told Brooke Stabler that Surratt had gone to Canada because that was what he had been told. There were, however, discrepancies between his account and Stabler's version. Weichmann testified he talked to Stabler about 7:30 on the morning after the shooting. Stabler claimed it was five o'clock. Judging from the time he later met Holohan, Weichmann's conversation with Stabler must have taken place close to five, but this was not a serious error.

"Would you please allow my clothing to be sent to me. I have not had a change for four weeks," he scribbled at the end of his confession.[8] A little exaggeration perhaps, but Weichmann was careless in calculating time. The Government waited another two weeks before sending his clothes. Weichmann signed his statement "Weichmann" although his name was previously spelled with only one "n." For convenience, he continued this latter spelling.

Olcott's interrogations led him to conclude that Sam Cox, Sam Chester, S. J. Sheet, Mary Surratt, James Maddox and Anna Surratt knew something about the murder plot. He changed his mind again about John Ford and now included him among the guilty. In compliance with instructions, he sent Burnett a detailed account of his examinations. Among other things, he wrote that Mrs. Surratt's manner throughout the interrogation was "cool and collected."[9]

The Government accepted most of Olcott's report but was still uncertain about Spangler, Mudd, and a few others. Officials had some evidence of Mudd's involvement, but they had practically nothing against Spangler. Yet detectives were convinced that someone in the theater helped Booth. Someone had to prepare the hole in the door, get the wooden bar, place it in the right spot, carve out a niche and then paper over it. They also knew that in the original plan, someone was assigned to turn off the gaslights. The three most suspicious men around the theater were Spangler, Maddox and James Gifford. They possessed little evidence against any of them, however.

Gifford was chief carpenter at the theater. When questioned by Wood, he stated that although he usually prepared the President's box, on the day of the crime, he sent Spangler to remove the partition between two boxes, making one larger box in order to accommodate the President's party.[10] This statement led the Government to release Gifford and hold Spangler. Even so, the evidence against him remained flimsy.

Dr. Samuel Mudd presented a more complicated problem. The opposite of Spangler, he was cultivated and intelligent, but the evidence against him was serious. Mudd finally admitted that he had met Booth once when the actor came to see him about purchasing his farm and ended buying a one-eyed horse from a neighbor. The doctor, however, repeatedly denied that he had met with Booth, John Surratt and Weichmann in a Washington hotel before the murder. The story of Booth wanting to buy his farm, while farfetched, was at least plausible. Also Mudd could have seen the famous actor once several months earlier and not have recognized him instantly on the night of the murder. But to admit that he had spent several hours with Booth and John Surratt in private conversation would have been particularly incriminating. Mudd realized this and fought the accusation.

Louis Weichmann had told police about the secret meeting and may have influenced the Government to hold the doctor. Weichmann's accusation was probably in response to Mrs. Surratt's testimony that he was present at the first meeting between John Surratt and Booth.

Stanton sent Assistant Secretaries Dana and Eckert to question Payne. They found the gladiator silent and unmovable. Dana, thinking the effort useless, soon left. Eckert, however, continued several days trying to gain Payne's confidence. Eckert stayed with Payne almost constantly, sometimes sitting for hours in the hot ship without a word passing between them. During this time, officers came to photograph Payne. The prisoner tried to hide his face and kept moving his head from side to side to keep the photographer, using slow emulsions of that time, from getting a picture. Angered by Payne's obstinateness, one officer struck at him with a sword. Eckert intervened, contending the officer had no right to hit the prisoner or even to photograph him. Payne seemed to appreciate this defense. Stanton upheld Eckert and, sensing that the two giants would get along together, placed the prisoner in Eckert's custody. From that day, Eckert took a particular interest in Payne and talked to him frequently, but gained little information.

Payne eventually admitted, albeit reluctantly, that he knew about an attempt to burn one Northern city in November 1864, and was supposed to take part in the operation. After a while, Payne asked for some tobacco, which Eckert got for him. As the prisoner's hands and feet were heavily ironed and a canvas bag covered his head, Eckert cut off a piece of tobacco and placed it through the slit of his hood.[11]

The Government finally decided against prosecuting several suspects known to have aided Booth's escape or to have obstructed justice. Included in this group were Sam Cox, Thomas Jones, John Lloyd, and James Maddox. Others, who certainly knew of the conspiracy, but against whom detectives gathered no hard evidence, included Booth's brother, Junius Brutus, John Ford, Booth's mistress, Ella Starr, Anna Surratt and Sarah Slater. The Government held these in prison except for Ella Starr and Slater, who was soon apprehended.

The Government left the final decision mainly to H. L. Burnett, who was faced with the dilemma of trying a woman. After considering the facts, Burnett

Thomas T. Eckert, chief of the War Department telegraph office. Eckert, a big, strong individual, seemed to feel a special kinship for Lewis Payne, also endowed with a large physique (Library of Congress).

informed Stanton of his opinion. In a little more than two weeks of frantic investigation, the War Department narrowed the list of the active, living conspirators to nine. Authorities held eight in custody, and detectives were searching for the other—John Surratt. Stanton confined most prime suspects on two ironclad ships anchored in the Potomac. Mrs. Surratt and Dr. Mudd remained in the Old Capitol Prison complex. On April 29, Stanton directed General Hancock to transfer all prisoners on the ships, except Celestino, to the military prison in the Arsenal.[12]

Stanton deliberately set aside investigation of those indirectly involved in order to prosecute those who took active roles. While not entirely successful, Government officials came close. They indicted David Herold, George Atzerodt, Lewis Payne, Mary Surratt, Samuel Mudd, Michael O'Laughlin, Samuel Arnold and Edward Spangler.

XXII
Care That They Not Escape

Stanton, closely guarding his prisoners, ordered Hancock to observe the following rules:

1. No person shall have access to the prisoners—or have any communication with them without my personal permission—except the Gov. (of the prison and the medical officer that may be assigned for medical duty).
2. The Gov. will inspect the cells at least twice every day.
3. A medical officer will be assigned to make an inspection twice a day. This inspection to be made in the presence of the Gov.
4. Prisoners will be supplied with nothing but necessary food and water—unless by special order (great care that they be given nothing by which they may take their own lives or escape).
5. Details inside and outside left to you but no communication verbally or in writing with prisoners.
6. Remove prisoners from ironclads after 8:00 tonight (April 29, 1865). Cells have been prepared for them.
7. You (General Hancock) are to inspect the condition of the prison once a day and submit an official report to the War Department.
8. Colonel Baker will help move the prisoners—also he will have 4 detectives not in military service who will be on duty inside the prison.
9. Do anything else to prevent the escape of the prisoners alive, or their cheating the gallows by self destruction.
10. Same conditions for others that may be captured and sent to prisons.[1]

That night at 10:30 the *Keyport* steamed out to the ironclads. The clanking of chains overhead awakened Arnold. After a short interval, an officer ordered him to prepare to move; next he felt hands grab him by each arm and guide him roughly to the deck of the *Monitor*. With his head covered, he was not sure what was happening, but he thought that he was being led to another vessel. The other prisoners, undergoing similar experiences, knew from the movement and noise that they were being transported to a side-wheel steamer. They moved Mudd about the same time from Old Capitol.

Colonel Foster sent an additional report to Burnett concerning the arrest of Mrs. Surratt. He stated that information derived from the servant girl about three men visiting the boardinghouse on the day after the murder led to her arrest. Opinions expressed by both Olcott and Foster influenced the Government to include Mrs. Surratt among those indicted. Foster also felt that, because Honora Fitzpatrick owned a picture of Booth, she and Anna should be detained.

Authorities always had a problem handling women spies and blockade-runners. The War Department had not expected its extensive conspiracy dragnet to ensnare a woman. To put a woman on trial for the murder of the President would surely occasion a great outcry. The evidence collected against Mrs. Surratt, however, was too strong to ignore. Stanton, who had maintained a no-nonsense attitude toward women blockade-runners during the war, even in opposition to President Lincoln, was not ready to back down now. Neither was the new President.

Soon after Foster made his report, Stanton directed the following order to the warden of Old Capitol Prison:

> You will deliver to Colonel Baker, Mrs. Surratt, a prisoner in your custody together with any effects she may have.
>
> by order of the Secretary of War
> (signed) Jas. A. Hardie[2]

In contrast to Mary Surratt and Dr. Mudd, Payne seemed resigned to his fate. In the first moments after his capture, he frantically looked for a way to escape but came to the conclusion it was hopeless.

Major Eckert remained with Payne as the prisoners were moved from the ironclads. He noticed the young man's feet had swollen so he could not put on his shoes. Officers eventually provided a pair of slippers for him and the other suspects through the Major's efforts. As the suspects neared the gangplank, each prisoner had to lower his head to avoid hitting a large iron crosspiece. In the dark, with his head covered, Payne could not see the obstacle. Eckert thoughtfully pushed Payne's head down to help him pass. The Rebel must have appreciated Eckert's many kindnesses because he soon told the officer enough details of Booth's plot to suggest that the chief conspirators had been captured, except John Surratt. As usual, however, Payne refused to directly implicate anyone. Eckert now had the information he sought. At last, he could assure the anxious Stanton that the Government had nothing more to fear from the conspiracy.[3]

Two marines and a detective guarded each prisoner. Guards prohibited the suspects from speaking to each other. On board the *Keyport*, soldiers of the Veterans Reserve Corps took over from the marines. The trip was short, the destination being the Arsenal. Close to midnight, the ship docked at the wharf. The grotesquely hooded, chain-clanking figures were escorted by eerie lantern light through the darkness to the Arsenal Penitentiary. Soldiers pushed the miserable prisoners up several flights of steps and locked them in damp, narrow cells. For some, this was to be their last earthly dwelling place. For others, midnight transfers became a custom. Arnold complained, "Midnight actions had followed my every footstep from the moment the military arm of the United States Government had touched my body."[4] The entire operation was carried out with military precision and in the strict secrecy typical of Stanton's methods.

The next night, Sunday, April 30, as women inmates at Carroll Prison were visiting, they heard a voice from the street below shout, "Double the

An artist's rendition of the suspects' transfer to the Arsenal prison. Male prisoners were ushered into the Arsenal more or less in this fashion, but Mrs. Surratt was not taken to the prison until the next night – without chains or hood (Library of Congress – USZ62-6950).

guard!" Instantly they feared mob action. A few minutes after additional guards had surrounded the prison, several men burst in with the curt message, "Mrs. Surratt, you are wanted." Apparently she anticipated the notice and began to get her few things ready. In contrast to her composed, deliberate demeanor, her daughter became hysterical. Anna clung to her mother, begging to accompany her.

Mary Surratt had gained a reputation for thoughtfulness toward other prisoners. As she left, she kissed her fellow inmates and then asked Mrs. Virginia Lomax to pray for her. One prisoner tried to pull Anna away gently, but the terrified girl grabbed frantically at her mother even as guards led Mrs. Surratt down the dingy stairs to the waiting military carriage. The prisoners watched in silence for a few moments, except for Anna, who continued to sob piteously. They left the distraught girl kneeling by her iron bedstead, wringing her hands in anguish, and crying over and over, "Oh, Mama, Mama." Soldiers carried her mother to the Arsenal Penitentiary to join the seven men already confined there.[5]

For weeks following this episode, Mrs. Lomax heard the sound of Anna's slippered feet restlessly pacing back and forth in the room above hers. Hour after hour, Anna moved about aimlessly, seldom speaking. Sometimes she would become delirious, sometimes dazed, but in whatever state, she paced the floor. Prisoners feared Anna might lose her mind.

Rumors spreading through the prison made the young woman's condition even worse. Some suggested that guards took Mrs. Surratt aboard a gunboat that would be taken out to sea and sunk. Others pictured all the indicted

The Washington Arsenal. The buildings, initially used as an arsenal, were later converted into a prison. The conspirators were confined and tried in this area (Library of Congress).

suspects laden with heavy iron balls fastened to their heads which kept them bent over both day and night. Inmates tried to keep these rumors from Anna, but she heard the whispering and insisted on knowing what was being said. When told, she became even more uncontrollable. Eventually, guards kept Anna from communicating with anyone.[6]

In time, she was again allowed to converse with others. But there seemed little hope for the young lady whose father was dead, one brother still unaccounted for in the Confederate army, another brother a hunted fugitive, and whose mother was charged with murder, not to mention Booth, her secret interest. Anna gradually regained some stability and briefly considered entering a convent because she feared she no longer had a home. Anna might have seemed a more logical suspect than her mother. She was a young temperamental secessionist who knew something of her brother's activities and who was infatuated with Booth. But Anna was not put on trial.

As the suspects were adjusting to the dismal Arsenal, related activities continued elsewhere. The army tracked Jefferson Davis closely; legal specialists prepared for his trial; *Harper's Weekly* advertised photographs of John Wilkes Booth for 25 cents; W. C. Wemyes of 575 Broadway, New York, also had the assassin's picture for sale and "assassination medals" were available for 25 cents each, or five dollars for one hundred.

The Government continued its search for other possible conspirators and increased its fight against malcontents. Realizing that the area of Lower Maryland, and the little town of Port Tobacco in particular, were still the seat of subversive activity, H. H. Wells decided to renew his investigation of the region. He distributed a printed notice warning that a large number of inhabitants around Port Tobacco,

> having heretofore rendered themselves notorious for their hostility to the Government, many of them engaging in blockade running, supplying the enemy with goods ... and more recently aiding in the murder of the President, are notified they must take the oath to show loyalty. Also they are not allowed to wear any Rebel uniform or display the Rebel flag.[7]

Citizens of the area took the threat more seriously when a local newspaper reminded them that, without taking the oath of allegiance, no one could exchange property or engage in any occupation or trade.

General Augur, having heard several references to Anna Ward in the recent interrogations, sent an officer to the Catholic convent at 10th and G streets to search her rooms, confiscate her papers and conduct her to the War Department. Although it was known that John Surratt had written to Ward, officers found none of his letters in her possession.[8] No other arrest of significance followed this.

Baker's Secret Service Bureau played a major role in preparing for the trial. He and his detectives had responsibility for procuring, recording and arranging testimony. Baker helped subpoena more than 200 witnesss, most for the prosecution, but many for the defense.

Although the War Department completed its list of suspects, some pieces in the puzzle did not quite fit, and some actions taken by the Government defied logical explanation. On April 30, Colonel Ingram arrested Sarah Antoinette Slater on orders of General McPhail. Burnett, who was by this time in charge of the entire investigation, told Ingram to send her to his office. She admitted having known a Rebel blockade-runner named Samuel Sharp, whom she had met in Richmond at the beginning of the war. Officers immediately arrested Sharp and sent him to Washington. Authorities did nothing with either of them.[9]

Mrs. Slater's release defied explanation considering that several witnesses, including Weichmann, swore she was a Rebel agent known as the "French woman." She served as a major link between the Confederates in Richmond and those in Canada. She accompanied Mrs. Surratt and John on a suspicious sojourn into southern Maryland. Mrs. Surratt returned to Washington alone while John and Mrs. Slater journeyed on to Richmond. This event took place immediately before the city fell to Union troops. Mrs. Slater could probably have revealed much about Mrs. Surratt's role in the conspiracy.

At the time of Lincoln's murder, Dr. George L. Porter, a young army physician, had been stationed with his wife and little daughter at the Arsenal grounds for nearly a year. On April 30, the Secretary of War ordered him to report for special duty.

Knowing military routine, the surgeon noticed that most of his orders were given verbally. After some thought, he concluded that the turbulent conditions in Washington caused the secrecy. The army trusted no one. Written messages could fall into the wrong hands. While the 27-year-old doctor preferred not to answer the summons, he obeyed promptly.[10]

His specific duties, however, were outlined in writing.

Surgeon General's Office
Washington, D.C.
April 30, 1865

Sir: By direction of the Hon. Secretary of War you will report to General
Hartranft, U.S. Vols., for the daily inspection of prisoners under his charge.
Should medical attendance by required you will give it.

While engaged on this duty you will be careful not to answer any questions
addressed to you by the prisoners nor allow them to make remarks not connected with your professional duties (to you).

The fact of these inspections will not be communicated to anyone and your
daily official reports will be made directly to General Hartranft, who is in
command at the Penitentiary, Arsenal Grounds, Washington.[11]

Dr. Porter could not provide the Arsenal prisoners with all the comforts
they wished, but he tried to rectify some glaring abuses. He examined them
each day, making sure their physical needs were met. The Government housed
about 20 prisoners in the Arsenal in addition to the eight conspiracy suspects.
In his first report, he recommended that inmates be given slippers and that the
hoods be padded.

Because the accused were confined to an area of the Arsenal that had been
closed for years, the air had become stale and unhealthy. The doctor suggested
that ventilation be improved by breaking out the glass in the upper row of windows. Porter recommended daily cleaning of the cells and airing the bedding.
"The food that is furnished is good and abundant," he observed.[12]

The physician's suggestions brought immediate action. Sam Arnold
acknowledged that about a week after he was hooded, guards removed his
hood, and they took him from his cell and ordered him to bathe himself.
Officials provided clean clothes and a new style hood, but he complained that
he almost died as a result of the bath. The cold water, he complained, caused
his whole body to tremble. A detective, seeing him shaking, asked if he was ill.

What Arnold intended as criticism actually indicated the care, however
rudimentary, given the inmates. Perhaps the Government tried to avoid
criticism of prisoner treatment that Union soldiers directed against Confederate prisons. At this time, the Government held in Old Capitol Capt.
Henry Wirz of Andersonville infamy. And within a few months they hanged
him for his cruel handling of Union prisoners. Officials buried Wirz in the
Arsenal penitentiary. To the thousands of Union soldiers who languished in
Andersonville prison, Arnold's complaint would have seemed extremely
trivial.

Guards usually required prisoners to wear canvas hoods all day, every day,
from April 25 to June 10, except in the courtroom. Occasionally, however, the
suspects managed to remove the covers. Arnold's lawyer told of one visit to
his client when he observed the hated hood lying on the cell floor. Dr. Porter
thought the device would be less irritating if padding was added around the
eyes and ears. The stuffing made the hoods worse however. Arnold complained
that the extra cotton pushed his eyeballs back in their sockets.

The physician reported his relations with prisoners were cordial and that they "all behaved well and gave no trouble," except for Mary Surratt. When first confined in the Arsenal, she refused to eat, "evidently intending to provoke an attack of sickness." Attendants tried to force her, but she would not cooperate. Finally Dr. Porter assured her that, as he was professionally responsible for her health, he would employ the necessary means to supply her with the required nourishment. Eventually she yielded.

The suspects' basically good health during their confinement on some of the hottest days of the year indicates the doctor's effectiveness. Although Mary Surratt received preferential treatment and remained overweight, she complained of various ills.

After the Government transferred prime suspects to the Arsenal, others implicated remained behind bars in Old Capitol. Officials continued to detain actors from the company of *Our American Cousin*, but they were not actually confined in prison. Since they had engagements in Cincinnati, they requested permission to leave. Col. LaFayette Baker knew of no reason to hold Laura Keene and her troupe, but Stanton refused to release them. Eventually, however, repeated pleas on their behalf brought freedom.[13]

Instructions on the prison record book revealed that officers watched certain inmates more closely than others. A notation by James Maddox's name read, "close confinement." For some unexplained reason, there was a special instruction by Honora Fitzpatrick's name recommending to keep her apart from other ladies and to have no communication with them.[14] Perhaps detectives felt they could obtain more information from her than from Mrs. Surratt or Anna, and, for a while, they succeeded. But evidently someone did manage to reach her because her testimony during the trial was obviously more guarded. Officials released Olivia Jenkins early along with her uncle, John Jenkins.

Prison records reveal that authorities imprisoned John Holohan on April 29, a day after Weichmann. This contradicts Holohan's later testimony. At the trial, he presented himself as a valued Government aide contrasting himself to Weichmann, whom he pictured as being highly suspect and closely watched. The Government seems to have been equally suspicious of both men.

From his jail window, Weichmann could see other inmates in the exercise yard. A few hours before the military transferred Mrs. Surratt to the Arsenal, he got her attention. She responded by kissing her hand. Just what this signal meant is not certain, but soon after, a male prisoner whispered to Weichmann, "You have to say nothing of anybody of the female gender when asked."[15] Weichmann understood this warning as coming from Mrs. Surratt, but it was too late. He had already stated a great deal about one of the "female gender."

John Ford continued to fight for his freedom. He based his repeated pleas on his absence from Washington on the night of the crime, having been given permission by the War Department to go to Richmond. Superintendent Wood frequently recommended that he be freed. After Stanton's constant refusals, Ford sent requests to Holt, Augur and Ingram. If he could not be freed permanently, he begged for a two-day parole to visit Baltimore. He promised to leave something as security. With a sick wife and six children to care for, his need was real, especially after being confined 25 days.[16] Stanton refused his appeal, but he tried again a few days later. Ford lamented that he was a victim of circumstances and wanted to know why he had been held without being told the charges.

John Ford's case was not typical. Secretary Stanton did release many prisoners. He finally ordered the superintendent to free James and Henry Ford and Thomas Green upon their taking the oath of allegiance. However, Wood wrote back that the men were no longer in Old Capitol. Apparently someone had allowed them to go free without Stanton's permission—a serious violation.

Early in May, Foster and Olcott turned over to Burnett 17 packages of letters and papers. Police Superintendent Richards sent Burnett the hat worn by Lincoln and Booth's spur. Not every piece of evidence was given to Burnett, however. When he asked LaFayette Baker for the items found on Booth and Herold, Baker replied that he had given them to Stanton, including Booth's diary.

The Secretary of War ordered Foster and Olcott to deliver to Burnett all other relevant material. As a result, Burnett received the following items:

> Sword from Surratt house, 541 H Street
> Suit of clothing worn by Holohan
> Coil of rope 81 ft. long and a carpet bag taken from Ned Spangler
> Pair of boots worn by Weichmann taken from Surratt house
> Portrait of Weichmann taken from Surratt house
> Carbine left by Booth at house of Lloyd
> Clothing worn by Payne and personal articles in his possession at the time of
>   his arrest, including
>   cap made from sleeve of undershirt
>   pocket compass
>   2 toothbrushes
>   3 pieces of tobacco
>   package of pistol cartridges
> Package of papers taken from J. W. Booth's room, secret Confederate cipher,
>   letter to Booth from "Sam"
> Hat and pistol left by attacker of Secretary Seward
> Trunk and contents from Surratt house[17]

The Government eventually assembled 98 exhibits.

While Burnett gathered papers and materials Judge John Bingham busily accumulated testimony taken during the investigation. The War Department already had most of the statements. Superintendent Richards had previously informed Burnett that the Police Department had no more testimonies to forward. Judge Olin replied that he had given all statements taken by him to Secretary Stanton.

Stanton gradually allowed Burnett to coordinate the case so that when the trial began, the Secretary of War had little part in it. His word remained the final authority, however. At this point, Stanton was practically running the country, and the conspiracy trial was only one of his many concerns.

Carrying out his duties, Burnett recalled scores of witnesses to check their stories. He reexamined Daniel J. Thomas, who declared he was ready to swear that Dr. Mudd had told him three weeks before the assassination that Lincoln and other Cabinet officers were to be murdered. Thomas, however, was a notorious liar. On May 4, officers sent Sam Cox to Burnett, but somehow Cox convinced him that he knew nothing about the conspiracy.[18] Guards also took Louis Weichmann to be questioned again by Burnett. A week before the start of the trial, the Government remained uncertain about Weichmann and Cox.

XXIII
"... And Others Unknown"

On May 2, Stanton advised Holt that the President wanted a list of persons in Canada and Richmond against whom there was evidence of complicity in the assassination. Stanton requested that the list be given to the War Department that very morning.[1] Holt had short notice, considering the importance of the request, but Stanton knew that Holt had been investigating Confederate activities in Canada for a year.

Holt had made a report to the Secretary of War seven months before the assassination concerning Rebel plots. On October 17, 1864, the *New York Tribune* had reported Holt's statement that "the cold-blooded assassination of Union citizens" would not surprise him. The *Tribune* further reported that "Green H. Smith confessed that the 'secret assassination of United States officers, soldiers, and Government employees has been discussed in the councils of the order and recommended.'"[2] The paper headlined the sensational report, "HIGHLY IMPORTANT REVELATIONS," "The Great Conspiracy Against the Union—Secret Armed Organization to Defeat the Government and Aid the Rebels."

The Government had known of secret organizations affiliated with the Confederacy operating in Illinois, Indiana and Missouri. These groups used such names as the Mutual Protection Society, the Circle of Honor, the Circle and Knights of the Mighty Host. Generally known as Knights of the Golden Circle, they had grown rapidly since the fall of 1863.

Holt's report included the names of leaders in each state, the origin and history of each organization, its size, rituals, oaths and purposes. The lengthy, detailed account left little doubt about the existence of armed organizations dedicated to overthrowing the Federal Government.[3]

Holt felt, therefore, that Confederate leaders in Canada had plotted Lincoln's assassination and he promptly answered the President's request. He stated that the Bureau of Military Justice had testimony implicating Jefferson Davis, George Sanders, Beverly Tucker, Jacob Thompson, William C. Cleary and Clement C. Clay.[4]

The President gave Judge Holt the additional responsibility of drawing up the actual charges against the accused—a complicated and time-consuming task. Not only did the conspiracy include many in custody, but preliminary evidence indicated others, not yet captured, might be directly involved.

The Judge Advocate carefully avoided loopholes in stating the charges and

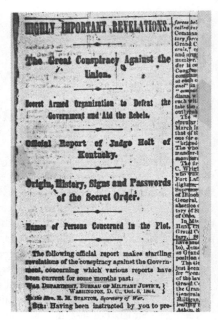

Left: Judge Advocate General Joseph Holt. A Kentuckian and one of few Southern leaders to support the Union, his influence was second only to Stanton's in the investigation (Brady Handy Collection. Library of Congress—BH83- 1802). Right: Before the assassination, Holt reported to Stanton the existence of widespread conspiracies throughtout the Midwest. This report, published in the "New York Tribune," October 17, 1864, affected Stanton's judgment.

specifications. In the first draft, he left blank spaces in which to add other names as detectives uncovered new evidence. On the original copy of the charge against known suspects, Holt penciled in "and others unknown." He later scratched this out and inserted the names Davis, Sanders and Thompson. Holt seemed determined to include his former fellow Cabinet members. Undoubtedly his personal vendetta against several former associates influenced his selection of those charged with the crime.

When Holt first visited the Nation's capital during Buchanan's administration, Jacob Thompson, a fellow Southerner, was Secretary of the Interior. His influential friend helped get Holt named Commissioner of Patents. Thompson also claimed to have been instrumental in Holt's appointment as Postmaster General. As a Cabinet member, Thompson may have been consulted on Holt's appointment, but it was not likely that he played an important part in his selection.

Shortly before Thompson resigned, because of the supply ship sent to Fort Sumter, he sent a dispatch south, warning that the Federal Government had dispatched the vessel with reinforcements. The command in Charleston Harbor, once alerted, hurriedly prepared and, as the *Star of the West* sailed into view, let go a volley of cannon fire, forcing its retreat. From that moment Holt and Thompson became determined enemies, their hatred intensifying through the years. Thompson accused Holt and Gen. Winfield Scott of employing a "concealed trick" in commissioning the *Star of the West.*[5] Holt fought back – using the medium which would become his chief weapon in the future – by writing a vindication to the *Washington Intelligencer.*

Holt now labored over the exact wording of the charges to make them legally binding. In the first draft, he strangely included Stanton's name on a list of the assassins' intended victims, but upon further consideration, scratched it out. Holt carefully added to the final draft the words "existing armed" rebellion.[6] The Judge correctly anticipated questions as to the jurisdiction of the Military Commission and wanted it understood that the Commission was dealing with a crime committed during time of war.

The Secretary of War, apparently double-checking Holt, requested Burnett to gather information on the Knights of the Golden Circle. That same day Burnett sent Stanton a long report of their activities. He reiterated much of what the Government already knew about the uprising of Southern sympathizers in the North to gain release of Rebel prisoners. Burnett also reported that the name, Knights of the Golden Circle, had been changed after the war started and that the assassins belonged to the organization. Actually, only O'Laughlin was known to have been a member.

Although Stanton asserted the request originated with the President, the Secretary of War introduced the list in the Cabinet meeting.

Stanton prepared his own statement to accompany Holt's document. He urged the Government to offer rewards for the arrest of those named.

Stanton requested the opinions of the Cabinet on the risky charge against the former President of the Confederacy. Several accepted the Secretary's accusation immediately; others hesitated. But being assured by Holt's claim that the Government possessed concrete evidence against those named, the Cabinet agreed and ordered reward posters printed. Neither the Senate, the House nor the President pushed this questionable indictment – Stanton and Holt did.

President Johnson then issued the following proclamation:

BY THE PRESIDENT OF THE UNITED STATES
OF AMERICA
A PROCLAMATION

Whereas it appears, from evidence in the Bureau of Military Justice, that the atrocious murder of the late President, ABRAHAM LINCOLN, and the attempted assassination of the Honorable WILLIAM H. SEWARD, Secretary of State, were incited, concerted, and procured by and between JEFFERSON DAVIS, late of Richmond, Va., and JACOB THOMPSON, CLEMENT C. CLAY, BEVERLY TUCKER, GEORGE N. SANDERS, WILLIAM C. CLEARY, and other rebels and traitors against the Government of the United States, harbored in Canada: –

Now, therefore, to the end that justice may be done, I, ANDREW JOHNSON, President of the United States, do offer and promise for the arrest of said persons, or either of them, within the limits of the United States, so that they can be brought to trial, the following rewards: –

One hundred thousand dollars for the arrest of JEFFERSON DAVIS.
Twenty-five thousand dollars for the arrest of CLEMENT C. CLAY.

Jacob Thompson, Secretary of the Interior under Buchanan, resigned to serve the Confederacy. He was included in the reward for Lincoln's assassins (Library of Congress – BH82-5261).

Twenty-five thousand dollars for the arrest of JACOB THOMPSON, late of Mississippi.

Twenty-five thousand dollars for the arrest of GEO. N. SANDERS.

Twenty-five thousand dollars for the arrest of BEVERLY TUCKER.

Ten thousand dollars for the arrest of WILLIAM C. CLEARY, late clerk of CLEMENT C. CLAY.

The Provost Marshal General of the United States is directed to cause a description of said persons, with notice of the above rewards, to be published.

In testimony whereof, I have hereunto set my hand, and caused the seal of the United States to be affixed.

Done at the city of Washington, this second day of May, in the year of our Lord one thousand eight hundred and sixty-five, and of the independence of the United States of America the eighty-ninth.

ANDREW JOHNSON.

By the President:

W. Hunter, Acting Secretary of State[7]

The front pages of many leading newspapers carried announcements of the enormous rewards. Officials rapidly printed and distributed reward posters. In less than a week the General in command at Macon, Georgia, advised other military leaders in Atlanta and Augusta to circulate the posters in their areas. Leaders throughout the Nation took similar action.[8]

The accusations against Confederate leaders brought immediate protests. Edward Bates expressed surprise but assumed the Government had strong evidence against Davis. Further, Bates felt the Government acted unconstitutionally in attempting to try the conspirators in a military court. This view, coming from the previous Attorney General, raised questions of what might have resulted had Bates remained the Nation's chief legal adviser a few months longer. He believed his successor James Speed to be a weak man and called him a "poor imbecile."[9]

W. C. Cleary, one of the accused, wrote that he had no part in the plot to kill Lincoln. Jefferson Davis, fleeing through the South, did not pause to respond. George Sanders and Beverly Tucker protested their innocence and addressed a strong letter to Johnson denouncing his proclamation. They vowed they had never heard of Booth, and that anybody who claimed they were involved "blackened his soul with diabolical perjury."[10]

The rewards animated a widespread search for the accused Confederate leaders. Jefferson Davis at this time kept only a few steps ahead of his pursuers. The famous photographer Mathew Brady volunteered his services in capturing Davis, offering a life-size picture of Davis and other Confederate leaders to help bring them to justice.

The Government's act of linking top Confederates to the assassination provoked editorial comments across the continent. Canadian newspapers published the well-known fact that John Surratt was hiding north of the border, thus giving credence to the contention that Booth received support from Confederates in Canada. The *New York Tribune* placed the blame for Surratt's escape on United States detectives and denied Confederate complicity. Although admitting that Booth might have contacted Rebel leaders, the paper expressed doubt they would get involved in such a crime.[11] The pro–Southern *New York World* asserted there was no evidence to link Rebels in Canada with the crime. The *Toronto Globe*, however, cited Booth's visits to Canada and Surratt's escape to Montreal as evidence. Most Northern papers doubted that Rebel leaders knew of the conspiracy. The *Philadelphia Inquirer* announced that the Government should have very concrete evidence before it accused Davis.

The greatest outcry against the accusations came from the *Montreal Gazette* which ridiculed the "evidence in the Bureau of Military Justice."[12] The *Gazette* could not believe that a civilized Government would issue such a proclamation without extremely good evidence. The paper darkly suggested that the "evidence" had better be strong because such an act of murder was inconsistent with the whole life of the former President of the Confederacy. It further predicted that if the charge against Davis could not be proved, the United States Government would be guilty of the most infamous libel in human history.

Gerrit Smith, well-known abolition leader, branded the charges against Davis "insane."[13] Most newspapers in England disapproved of the accusations.

Jefferson Davis, President of the Confederacy, learned he had been accused of complicity in the assassination as he fled through the Carolinas (Library of Congress — BH82-2417).

Strangely, in the debate over the guilt of Confederate leaders operating from Canada, the United States made no demand before the trial for the surrender of Tucker or Sanders, who were known to be living in Canada.

Not everyone worried about solving the conspiracy; self-serving businessmen continued their commercial pursuits unabated. Orville Browning, former Senator from Illinois, law partner of Thomas G. Ewing, Sr., and a political influence in Washington, persisted, as during the war, to support men accused of plotting against the Government. However, without the backing of his martyred friend, Lincoln, he was forced to turn to Stanton. On the day Rebel leaders were accused, he sought Stanton's permission to transport Confederate cotton from the Red River. This was, presumably, the same cotton Mrs. Lincoln's half sister had tried to get through the blockade for months.

Stanton refused, saying he hoped the boats carrying the cotton would be seized and confiscated.

The Secretary of War must have gained satisfaction from news of Gen. George Washington Singleton's business ventures. For months Singleton had bought Southern goods, hoping to sell the contraband in the North. In this operation he had received permission, if not the wholehearted support, of President Lincoln and General Grant. With the sudden fall of the Confederacy, all of Singleton's purchases were destroyed, and he suffered total loss.

Shortly before the trial opened, the War Department received one more valuable document. John Clark, brother-in-law of John Wilkes Booth, belatedly revealed that Booth had left a sealed envelope with him in November of 1864. When Booth again visited the Clark home the following January, he made some changes in the manuscript. The Clarks thought no more about it until the day after the assassination. That day Booth's grieving mother visited them in Philadelphia. The following day, the Clarks remembered the envelope and opened it. Another visitor, Junius Brutus Booth, arrived from Cincinnati three days later. The Clarks grew apprehensive about the Booth clan gathering in their home, especially at Junius Brutus's arrival. John Clark then delivered the envelope to the United States marshal. The marshal held the revealing letter two weeks before passing it on to the War Department.

The document, dated simply 1864 and addressed "TO WHOM IT MAY CONCERN," explained Booth's motive.

> Right or wrong, God judge me, not man. For be my motive good or bad, of one thing I am sure, the lasting condemnation of the North.
>
> I love peace more than life. Have loved the Union beyond expression. For four years have I waited, hoped and prayed for the dark clouds to break, and for the restoration of our former sunshine. To wait longer would be a crime. All hope for peace is dead. My prayers have proved as idle as my hopes. God's will be done. I go to see and share the bitter end.
>
> I have ever held the South were [sic] right. The very nomination of Abraham Lincoln, four years ago, spoke plainly of war—war upon Southern rights and institutions. His election proved it.
>
> . . . .
>
> This country was formed for the white, not for the black, man. And looking upon African slavery from the same standpoint held by the noble framers of our Constitution, I, for one, have ever considered it one of the greatest blessings (both for themselves and us) that God ever bestowed upon a favored nation. Witness heretofore our wealth and power, witness their elevation and enlightment above their race elsewhere. I have lived among it most of my life, and have seen less harsh treatment from master to man than I have beheld in the North from father to son. Yet Heaven knows, no one would be willing to do more for the negro race than I, could I but see a way to still better their condition.[14]

Booth's words made clear his support of slavery. Slavery also motivated Payne's wild acts, Dr. Mudd's assistance to the rebellion, the Surratt family's long promotion of the Confederacy, as well as the treasonable activities of O'Laughlin and Arnold. The only conspirators not fully devoted to maintenance of slavery were Herold and Atzerodt.

Booth's friends claimed he became unbalanced mentally because of his brooding over the fate of the South. But his letter, although revealing Booth's faulty reasoning, does not picture a crazy man, but rather a man with misplaced loyalties. After discoursing further on slavery, Booth continued:

> I have also studied hard to discover upon what grounds the right of a State to secede has been denied, when our very name, United States, and the Declaration of Independence, both provide for secession. But there is no time for words—I write in haste. I know how foolish I shall be deemed for undertaking such a step as this, where, on the one side, I have many friends and everything to make me happy; where my profession alone has gained me an income of more than twenty thousand dollars a year, and where my great personal ambition in my profession has such a great field for labor.[15]

Why Booth wrote "in haste," as he was writing more than three months before he consummated his crime, is not clear.

The manuscript indicated Booth's crime did not result from disappointment in his career. Actually the 28-year-old actor's career was, in some ways, on the ascendancy in spite of his throat problems. A popular and sought-after actor, he turned from a promising career to support the Southern cause. Booth continued his epistle:

> On the other hand, the South have never bestowed upon me one kind word; a place where I have no friends, except beneath the sod; a place where I must become either a private soldier or a beggar. To give up all of the former for the latter, besides my mother and sisters, whom I love so dearly (although they so widely differ from me in opinion), seems insane, but God is my judge. I love justice more than I do a country that disowns it; more than fame and wealth; more (Heaven pardon me if wrong), more than a happy home. I have never been upon a battlefield, but oh, my countrymen, could you all but see the reality or effects of this horrid war, as I have seen them (in every State, save Virginia), I know you would think like me, and would pray the Almighty to create in the Northern mind the sense of right and justice (even should it possess no seasoning of mercy), and that He would dry up this sea of blood between us, which is daily growing wider. Alas, poor country, is she to meet her threatened doom?[16]

Booth constantly expressed love for his mother and, in this case, for his sisters, but pointedly left out his brothers.

He gave himself away in writing that he had never been on the battlefield. Feeling, as he did, the need to fight for the South, he must have felt some remorse not serving the Confederate army. Booth apparently preferred to be remembered for one radical act rather than to die in a soon-forgotten skirmish. In this document, as well as in his diary, he betrayed his desire to perform some spectacular act, covering it in patriotism. In describing the Union's downward course the actor waxed poetic:

> day by day she has been dragged deeper and deeper into cruelty and oppression, till now (in my eyes) her once bright red stripes look like bloody gashes on the face of Heaven. I look now upon my early admiration of her glories as a dream. My love (as things stand today) is for the South alone.

Booth concluded with a description of his project. These revealing lines show that murder was not his original plan. Perhaps this is one reason the letter was never presented as evidence in the trial.

> Nor do I deem it a dishonor in attempting to make for her a prisoner of this man, to whom she owes so much of misery. If success attends me, I go penniless to her side. They say she had found that "last ditch" which the North have [sic] so long derided, and been endeavoring to force her in, forgetting they are our brothers, and that it's impolitic to goad an enemy to madness. Should I reach her in safety and find it true, I will proudly beg permission to triumph or die in the same "ditch" by her side.
> A CONFEDERATE, DOING DUTY UPON HIS OWN RESPONSIBILITY.
> J. Wilkes Booth.[17]

This letter was the last significant evidence gathered by the War Department before the trial. The preliminaries were over. The investigation had required strenuous efforts in a relatively short time. The Government now faced a difficult prosecution.

XXIV
"A Horrid Sight"

President Andrew Johnson turned to James Speed for advice on the imminent trial. Speed confronted the central question of deciding on the proper judicial body to conduct the proceedings. Having been Attorney General only a few months, he remained unsure of himself and became easy prey for domineering politicians. Lack of a great legal reputation added to his insecurity. Thus, he soon fell under the influence of William Seward and Edwin Stanton. Both of these powerful Cabinet members courted him until he was reduced to a "mere tool—to give such opinions as were wanted."[1]

James Speed and his famous brother Joshua had been longtime friends of the slain President. This friendship was one reason Lincoln appointed him Attorney General, a position he continued to occupy for 16 months under Lincoln's successor Andrew Johnson. In many ways, Speed maintained strong principles, yet he possessed a legalistic mentality that gave little room for mercy. On April 28, at the prodding of the War Department, he advised the President it was proper to try the conspirators before a Military Commission rather than before a civil court.

This crucial decision spawned fierce debates before, during and after the trial. Brilliant men argued both sides and continue to do so. Although there were several opposing views concerning the legality of a military trial, Secretary of War Stanton had no doubt that jurisdiction properly belonged to the military court. President Johnson, rather than Stanton, requested Speed's opinion.[2] However, the persuasive Secretary of War influenced both Johnson and Speed. The Attorney General, however, took full responsibility for the decision. Armed with Speed's opinion, the Government prepared for a military trial.

The Government never put the question of a Military Commission before the full Cabinet. If it had been, it might not have been approved. Several members, including Gideon Welles and Hugh McCulloch were in favor of a civilian trial. Seward, Stanton, Speed and probably President Johnson favored a trial by military court.

Some evidence indicates that even Attorney General Speed was not originally in favor of a Military Commission. Gideon Welles felt that Stanton had pressured him. Welles, disgusted, stated that "the rash, impulsive, and arbitrary measures of Stanton are exceedingly repugnant to my notions and I am pained to witness the acquiescence they receive. He carries others with him, sometimes against their convictions as expressed to me."[3]

The argument over the Commission's legality centered on one primary issue — military jurisdiction over civilians. The problem was left unsettled during the war. President Lincoln, in a letter June 12, 1863, to critical Democrats in Albany, New York, had declared that certain military arrests and military proceedings against civilians were constitutional. The United States Supreme Court considered the case of Clement Vallandigham, who was tried by a Military Commission in 1863. The Supreme Court decided that it had no jurisdiction over the case. It, therefore, left the problem of military trials of civilians unsettled, if not actually recognizing their legality.

Edward Bates, who preceded Speed as Attorney General, was particularly upset that Speed had been "wheedled out of an opinion" and thought that the conspirators should not be tried by a military court. The former Attorney General noted in his diary:

> Such a trial is not only unlawful, but it is a gross blunder in policy: It denies the great, fundamental principle, that ours is a government of *Law*, and that the law is strong enough, to rule the people wisely and well; and if the offenders be done to death by that tribunal, however truly guilty, they will pass for martyrs with half the world.[4]

Bates had experienced enough Cabinet meetings to know how things were managed. "I do not doubt," he wrote, "that that determination was the work of Mr. Stanton." He incorrectly surmised, however, that President Johnson would only allow the Military Commission to serve as court of inquiry and that the defendants would eventually be turned over to civil courts. Such was not the case; Johnson depended heavily on Speed and Stanton at the time.

Precedent could not serve to defend the legality of the conspiracy trial as no real precedent existed. The Constitution did not cover problems arising from civil war. The question of when the war was actually over further complicated the issue. No formal peace treaty or armistice date ended the fighting.

Other problems arose from the nature of the crime. The conspirators planned the crime while the war still raged and committed it as the conflict was coming to a conclusion. The Government investigated and tried the suspects after the fighting had ended. Some legalists felt that since the war was then over, the whole concept of martial law and emergency military measures were unnecessary.

On May 4, less than a week before the scheduled start, Salmon P. Chase, Chief Justice of the United States Supreme Court, wrote President Johnson concerning the military government in Virginia. Chase advised him that the military government should remain supreme until the President "should see fit to declare the insurrection at an end."[5] While the situation in Virginia did not match that in Washington, Chief Justice Chase obviously remained unsure that all hostilities had ceased.

The murder definitely intertwined with the War for Southern Independence as the South viewed it, or the Rebellion as designated by the Union. Even the nature of the conflict had some bearing on the legality of the court. In any case, confessions of the conspirators showed clearly that their basic

James Speed. A personal friend of President Lincoln, who appointed him Attorney General, Speed ruled, with Stanton's support, that the conspirators should be tried by a Military Commission (Library of Congress—B813-2080).

motive was support for the Southern war effort. It was a partisan assassination foolishly connected, in some vague manner, to defeat the Federal Government. No group had ever plotted a crime of this nature and magnitude against the United States.

Military Commissions were practically unknown in the United States. The Constitution contained nothing about them. They grew out of martial law— which, itself, did not fit American thinking. A commanding General usually administered martial law and military courts. Military Commissions differed slightly from courts-martial, although similar rules governed both. Martial law, however, did not violate provisions in the Constitution which guaranteed trial by jury under *normal* circumstances. In fact, martial law was an indispensable element in preserving the Constitution in time of crisis.

The Constitution did not fully provide for extreme emergencies in which the Nation's enemies were also fellow citizens. The Civil War was both a war and a rebellion. Difficulty in clearly defining military lines compounded already tough questions. Frequently, as in the Nation's capital, surrounded by slave states, the enemy existed within defense lines. Some of the Nation's most dangerous foes did not wear enemy uniforms. Military courts tried blockade-runners, traders in contraband, Confederate spies and bushwhackers, as well as uniformed soldiers.[6]

Ordinarily, martial law and military courts, as distinct from courts-martial, operate only in time of war or under emergency conditions when the regular civil courts are closed. However, unlike military law, regulations concerning martial law varied with the exigencies of the times, the nature of the population and the imminence of danger to the Nation. The necessity for martial law and military courts is not easily defined. The Nation's security must be in critical danger to justify their use. Under such conditions, military courts are not only acceptable; they are obligatory.[7]

Exactly when conditions meet these criteria were naturally interpreted differently by various factions. Citizens with Southern sympathies, even though loyal to the Union, generally objected to a military court trial of the conspirators. Union authorities, however, viewed the assassination of the Commander-in-Chief in wartime by Southern sympathizers as a crime so treasonable as to warrant trial by a military court. Even some strong advocates of Constitutional rights recognized the need of military courts in time of imminent danger. Others, however, agreed with the view expressed years earlier by the Duke of Wellington that martial law was no law at all.[8]

President Andrew Johnson sought the advice of the highest legal authority in the land. The decision was not arbitrary in spite of Stanton's influence, but one carefully considered. Four years of devastating war obviously colored the deliberation, but critics of military courts were also influenced by the same horrible war. One legal expert of that period admitted the question was extremely complicated and that "many years must elapse before the history of these times can be justly written."[9] More than 100 years later, the question remains unresolved.

On May 1, 1865, President Johnson announced the Attorney General's opinion that the suspects were subject to the "jurisdiction of, and lawfully triable before a Military Commission;..."

The President, consequently, ordered the Assistant Adjutant General to "detail nine competent military officers to serve as a Commission for the trial." In addition, he directed Judge Advocate General Joseph Holt to designate Assistant Judges Advocate to help him conduct the trial. The President named Maj. Gen. John F. Hartranft to serve as special Provost Marshal General to provide protection for and give military assistance to the Commission. Johnson then requested that the Commission establish its rules and get on with proceedings without delay.[10]

The Government had performed well. It had accumulated evidence quickly and efficiently. Without aid of the telephone, rapid transportation, electronic picture transmission, vast criminal files, radio, computer printouts, or other modern investigative devices, the authorities had tracked down all but one prime conspirator.

Preparations for the trial created furious activity. The War Department sent telegrams to military officers throughout the country requesting them to subpoena witnesses. Authorities also returned approximately 500 letters addressed to Canada which inspectors had opened. Cartographers prepared maps tracing Booth's escape route.

Asst. Adj. Gen. W. A. Nichols announced on May 6 the names of those selected to serve on the Military Commission: Maj. Gen. David Hunter, Maj. Gen. Lewis Wallace, Bvt. Maj. Gen. August V. Kautz, Brig. Gen. Albion P. Howe, Brig. Gen. Robert S. Foster, Bvt. Brig. Gen. Cyrus B. Comstock, Brig. Gen. T. M. Harris, Bvt. Col. Horace Porter and Bvt. Brig. Gen. Federick H. Collier. Later orders relieved Collier from duty and substituted Lt. Col. David R. Clendenin. Brig. Gen. Joseph Holt, Judge Advocate General of the United States Army was appointed Judge Advocate and recorder of the Commission. In spite of some critics who called the Commissioners second-rate, they were for the most part exceptional individuals.

War Department Special Order Number 211, which named members of the military court, also ordered the Commission "to meet in Washington, District of Columbia, the 8th day of May, 1865, at 9 o'clock A.M. or as soon thereafter as practicable."[11] The Commission met as directed but could not conduct business because two of its members were absent.

August Kautz, one of the absentees, was a German-born hero of the war who had been brought to the United States by his parents at the age of four. Like several other members, Kautz had trained at West Point. He had the distinction of commanding a division made up of former slaves whom he marched into Richmond as the city fell.

The ambitious, egotistic, twenty-seven-year-old Kautz, found time during the war to produce two books published by Lippincott. After Lincoln's assassination, he applied for a leave of absence to settle his courtship of Charlotte Tod. Instead of being granted a leave, to his dismay, the military ordered him to Washington and detailed him to serve on the Commission. Heavyhearted, he implored his superiors to relieve him. Burnett denied the request. He then took his case to General Grant. At first Grant seemed inclined to give Kautz leave for "an affair of the heart," but later changed his mind. After four years of war, Kautz's chief concern remained his wedding day, and he continued to plead for release, all to no avail.

Because of disgust at his plight, Kautz did not even know where the Commission was to convene. Accompanied by his friend Gen. Philip Sheridan, he sought directions from Stanton, but finding the Secretary out, he skipped the first short meeting. The day was not a total loss, however. Kautz used the free time to have his picture taken by Mathew Brady.[12]

Even though the Court had been unable to transact business on May 8, the day had significance for those indicted for the murder. Gen. John F. Hartranft delivered a copy of the charges and specifications to each of the accused in his or her cell. For the first time they learned the formal accusations against them. All were charged:

> For maliciously, unlawfully, and traitorously, and in aid of the existing armed rebellion against the United States of America,... combining, confederating, and conspiring together with one John H. Surratt, John Wilkes Booth, Jefferson Davis, George N. Sanders, Beverly Tucker, Jacob Thompson, William C. Cleary, Clement C. Clay, George Harper, George Young, and others unknown, to kill and murder within the Military Department of Washington, and within the fortified and intrenched [sic] lines thereof, Abraham Lincoln....[13]

The charge also included conspiracy against Andrew Johnson, William Seward and Ulysses Grant. The indictment pointedly stressed treason and conspiracy in aid of the existing rebellion.

In a conspiracy, all directly involved are held to be equally guilty. In the case against Mary Surratt, for instance, it was not necessary to prove that she pulled the trigger, but only that she took an active part in the conspiracy which resulted in the President's death. The specific charge against her was that she:

> did, at Washington City, and within the military department and military lines aforesaid, on or before the 6th day of March, A.D. 1865, and on divers other days and times between that day and the 20th day of April, A.D. 1865, receive, entertain, harbor, and conceal, aid and assist the said John Wilkes Booth, David E. Herold, Lewis Payne, John H. Surratt, Michael O'Laughlin, George A. Atzerodt, Samuel Arnold, and their confederates, with the knowledge of the murderous and traitorous conspiracy aforesaid, and with intent to aid, abet, and assist them in the execution thereof, and in escaping from justice after the murder of the said Abraham Lincoln, as aforesaid.[14]

Hartranft read similar detailed charges to each suspect.

On Tuesday, May 9, 1865, a dreary, rainy day, all Commissioners finally met in a makeshift courtroom in the old Arsenal Penitentiary. The gloomy Arsenal consisted of several aging red-brick buildings, construction of which had begun during the presidency of John Quincy Adams and had been completed during that of Andrew Jackson. It had served to house prisoners on Greenleaf Point in southwest Washington. During the Civil War, women manufactured munitions there, but a few buildings were reserved for war criminals.

The public developed a morbid curiosity about the large main edifice, Old Penitentiary, because of a rumor that John Wilkes Booth's remains lay buried under its stone floor. The three-story structure was high, a little more than 300 feet long and approximately 50 feet wide.[15] The Government confined suspects and tried them in this edifice. A high brick wall linked it to several other structures on the Arsenal grounds. The entire complex stood on a slender strip of land jutting out into the water at the confluence of the Potomac and the Anacostia.

Guards confined the accused in cells scattered throughout the prison. A small door separated the area occupied by male prisoners from that of females.

John A. Bingham. Famous for his oratorical abilities, this former Republican Congressman from Ohio was an Assistant Judge Advocate for the trial.

The section for women prisoners contained 64 cells, all the same size as those of the men. Heavy iron doors with a grating at the top were set in 18-inch-thick cell walls. A small aperture at the bottom of the door provided drainage. The cells measured a little less than eight feet deep, four feet wide and seven feet high, with a heavy vaulted roof. They clustered around a large central room with thick walls, small barred windows and a door on the south opening into the prison yard.

A large room on the third floor of the northeast corner of the Old Penitentiary served as a makeshift courtroom. Authorities cut a doorway between this room and the cell block so prisoners could have easy access to the courtroom. Against the west wall, carpenters erected a platform about a foot high, surrounded by a plain wood railing.

All members of the Military Commission, even though several harbored severe misgivings, complied with disciplined military assiduity and took their posts in the courtroom. At 10:00 A.M. Judge Advocate General Holt, in somber tones, presented his Assistant Judges Advocate, the Honorable John A. Bingham and Col. H. L. Burnett.

Following these introductions, guards guided the accused into the courtroom for the first time. The parade of men, barely able to walk, shuffling in with their hands locked in iron bars, their feet shackled, some chained to iron balls, and their heads covered with black hoods, presented a spectacle "never to be forgotten" as Benn Pitman wrote 28 years later.[16]

B. Brig. Gen. Cyrus B. Comstock recorded in his diary the dreadful impression made on him as the prisoners, "staggering and clanking," were led in by guards. "It was a horrid sight."[17]

The vision of the suspects stumbling into court, their eyes completely covered so they had to be guided to their seats, also shocked Horace Porter. Guards sat between each prisoner. Mrs. Surratt, who was neither hooded nor chained, was seated in a chair on the courtroom floor near her defense counsel rather than on the raised platform.

This special treatment of the lone woman suspect was only one of many distinctions made in handling the accused. Heavy iron bracelets, joined by a solid metal bar about ten inches long, confined all but one of the male prisoners. Authorities allowed Dr. Samuel Mudd more freedom, his hands being joined by a flexible chain rather than the rigid bar. Officers did not handcuff Mary Surratt at all. The prisoners' ankles, except those of Mrs. Surratt, were chained together; in addition to ankle chains, Lewis Payne and George Atzerodt had heavy iron balls attached to their legs. Guards carried the balls when the prisoners entered and left the courtroom. After the first day, the male inmates' heads were uncovered before they entered the courtroom, but the canvas hoods were replaced as soon as they left. Mrs. Surratt was never hooded.

This day, the hoods remained until after guards seated the men. Their eyes adjusted painfully to the first burst of light as they stared wildly around the room. Lewis Payne, in particular, reacted like a man demented. The others, after becoming accustomed to the light, appeared dejected and hopeless. Mrs. Surratt sat, leaning back in her chair, with her unmanacled feet stretched forward. Throughout the proceedings, she kept up a soft moaning sound, frequently requesting water, which was dutifully provided.[18]

General Kautz, not realizing Mrs. Surratt was to be tried, expressed surprise when soldiers guided her in. "One of them was a woman," he recorded in his diary.[19] In addition, Kautz complained about what he deemed unnecessary secrecy and mystery which surrounded the proceedings. The Commission was still unable to accomplish much and adjourned at 1:30.

After adjournment, the Judge asked the suspects if they desired to employ counsel. All replied that they did. Herold requested Frederick Stone, Joseph Bradley and J. M. Carlisle. Bradley, a prominent Washington lawyer about fifty years old, had a reputation as a Union supporter during the war when he headed the Washington Bar. He had taken the oath of allegiance, a mark of loyalty. He refused, however, to accept Herold's case (two years later he served as a counsel to John Surratt).

J. M. Carlisle, a member of the Washington Bar, was about 45 years old and one of the most able lawyers in the capital. He had refused to take the oath required of all who practiced law in Washington and therefore had to abandon his clients. His only law practice had been limited to appearances before the United States Supreme Court under Chief Justice Roger Taney, where the oath was not required. As the oath was mandatory in the military court, Carlisle could not take the case.[20]

Frederick Stone, a middle-aged attorney of some prominence from Port Tobacco known for his Southern sympathies, gladly accepted Herold's case.

Payne requested Mason Campbell of Baltimore. Mrs. Surratt wanted United States Senator Reverdy Johnson and her close friend William Wallace Kirby. Dr. Mudd asked for Robert James Brent of Baltimore. The other prisoners did not know anyone to select.

Burnett immediately sent either telegrams or hand-delivered messages to the lawyers requested. Mr. Brent informed Dr. Mudd that he was unavailable because of another case, but he suggested his partner, Richard T. Merrick. Merrick, however, also refused, although he was more sympathetic to John Surratt's later request. Mason Campbell, the son-in-law of the late Chief Justice of the United States Supreme Court, Roger Taney, refused Payne's request.

Dr. Mudd, still without counsel, desired the services of his cousin, Henry Clark. Clark was not an attorney, but he agreed to help Mudd find one.[21] Apparently either he or the accused contacted another cousin, G. D. Mudd, who answered the summons to consult with the doctor. Mudd also asked Burnett to contact Dr. James E. Morgan about serving as his counsel. The lawyer responded that he barely knew Mudd and declined to talk with him.

After several days, Dr. Mudd and a few other prisoners had still failed to secure lawyers and were holding up the proceedings. Frederick Stone eventually agreed to defend Mudd as well as Herold. In addition to Stone, Mrs. Mudd was later able to employ Thomas Ewing, Jr., for her husband's defense.

Ewing, a well-known Union general, was the son of the renowned lawyer whose name he bore. He had strong connections in Washington and, after running unsuccessfully for the Kansas seat in the United States Senate, began a law practice. His friends were surprised and concerned that he would risk his reputation defending one of the conspirators. Ewing, however, had personal motives. When he accepted Dr. Mudd's case, his brother-in-law, Gen. William T. Sherman, was in a bitter struggle with Stanton. The attorney viewed the military court as another evidence of Stanton's arbitrary and dictatorial methods, and hoped to thwart the Secretary of War.

All prisoners had difficulty finding lawyers, but Payne had a particularly hard time, being rejected repeatedly. Mrs. Surratt was also pressed to secure a defense counsel. Mr. Kirby, whom she requested, had the reputation of a country gentleman. He knew the rules of civil law but was not a lawyer by profession and preferred not to represent his friend. Sen. Reverdy Johnson, her other choice, wavered in making up his mind but finally agreed to serve. He claimed that his slowness was due to other commitments rather than to any hesitancy to defend her. Johnson had previously agreed to serve as counsel for a railroad in Pittsburgh, but the case was postponed, thus making it possible to help Mrs. Surratt.

Richard T. Merrick, who had already turned down Dr. Mudd, seemd willing to defend Mrs. Surratt but was prevented by his wealthy father-in-law, J. C. McGuire.[22] Later, Merrick helped defend Mrs. Surratt's son, John, which she would probably have preferred. She also requested the services of J. F. Zimmerman, but he declined to have anything to do with her case.

Union General Thomas Ewing risked his reputation to defend the suspects. His foster brother and brother-in-law, General William Sherman, was embroiled in a feud with Stanton, thus intensifying Ewing's motivation (Library of Congress — BH83-3729).

Several lawyers, though refusing to be associated with the trial publicly, helped behind the scenes. Merrick, for instance, served as advisory counsel for Dr. Mudd, although this was not widely known. Orville Browning also helped Ewing in the defense of Mudd and Arnold.

The suspects had more to worry about than securing lawyers. Some had not changed clothing for days. Herold's sisters were able to bring him a few articles, and Dr. Mudd managed to keep himself looking respectable. Somehow Payne acquired an old sailor suit, which he wore with a tight knit undershirt every day. Friends supplied Mrs. Surratt with clothes, but satisfactory attire remained a problem for the prisoners.

Cyrus B. Comstock, among the other Military Commissioners, listened to Judge Holt explain rules for conducting the trial. A brilliant 34-year-old general, graduating first in his class at West Point, Comstock became an army engineer and served in several campaigns before becoming senior aide-de-camp to General Grant. Serving in Vicksburg when he heard of Lincoln's assassination, Comstock noted in his diary, "Death is too good . . ." for those responsible, and in passing, added, "It will cost the South, very dear."[23] A few days later, authorities ordered the general to Washington. For several weeks, as the investigation proceeded, Comstock whiled away the time in his office, then on May 8, officials called him to serve on the Commission. This was his opportunity to

General Horace Porter was originally appointed to the Military Commision, but after attending the first session, he managed to get released from this duty (National Archives, photo 4150 – Brady Collection).

administer the revenge he had written about. Yet that evening, he wrote in his diary, "Wish I could get off. They ought to be tried in civil court."[24] Comstock particularly objected to the rumor that the trial was to be held in secret.

After Holt's initial remarks, Comstock openly expressed his misgivings about the court's jurisdiction. The Judge assured him that the Attorney General had already decided that the military had jurisdiction in the case. Dismissing Comstock's further objections, Holt proposed limiting the defense counsel to five-minute arguments. Confirming Comstock's suspicions, Holt next recommended that the sessions be held behind closed doors.[25] Secret sessions were necessary, according to the Judge, because if the evidence were made public, it might prevent the arrest of others implicated. Moreover, he explained, some witnesses would not give evidence in public. Holt already had several false witnesses who sought to hide their identities by testifying in secret.

Comstock spoke up courageously against these proposals. He knew Holt worked closely with Stanton, and he had personal knowledge of Stanton's methods. He had previously witnessed a severe confrontation between Stanton and Grant.

Holt was not accustomed to having his proposals opposed, especially by a young officer. Comstock, however, was not the only one to oppose Holt's restrictions; another officer, General Horace Porter, also spoke out. The 28-year-old Porter, son of a former governor of Pennsylvania, had studied at Harvard and graduated from West Point. He had a distinguished military record, having been wounded twice in battle. Less than two months earlier, the army breveted him brigadier general in recognition of meritorious service. Porter had also served as aide-de-camp on Grant's staff. Like Comstock, he objected to the military trial.

When the Commission convened the following day, Comstock and Porter were delighted to find orders excusing them from court duty. Later in the day, Stanton sent word explaining that since they were members of Grant's staff, and Grant had been an object of the assassination plot, it was necessary to remove them from the Commission.[26] This explanation seems a manufactured excuse for eliminating uncooperative Commissioners.

That same day, after court adjourned, Pres. Andrew Johnson made the action official by issuing Special Order Number 216, dismissing Comstock and Porter. Their places were filled by Bvt. Brig. Gen. James Ekin and Bvt. Col. C. H. Tompkins.

Years later, after Porter had served as personal secretary to President Grant, he wrote that officials relieved him because of defense objections that he would be biased. Actually the defense had no opportunity to object, because he was removed before any defense counsel attended the sessions.

The official trial record, prepared by Benn Pitman and endorsed by Holt, pointedly left out the questions raised over the court's jurisdiction and the debate about rules.[27]

The next day dawned dismal and rainy. The now-purged Commission proceeded with its business although most prisoners remained without legal counsel. The court was officially sworn in. An impressive array of brass sat around the large table located along the north side of the courtroom. General Hunter, as president, sat at the east end. To his right were Wallace, Ekin and Tompkins; to his left, Kautz, Foster, Harris, Howe and Clendenin. At the foot of the large table stood two smaller ones where Holt sat with his assistants, Bingham and Burnett. Officers displayed the evidence on one of these smaller tables.[28]

A court official read the lengthy charges individually to each prisoner after which he asked each how he or she pleaded. Every suspect responded "Not guilty." For want of defense counselors court adjourned early.

This pleased the enamored Kautz; his mind was not on the military trial. He tried to find time to write his fiancée but was unable to finish the letter. He did have time, however, to make an entry in his diary: "We are likely to have a long siege of duty on the Commission."[29]

In spite of criticism, the military was, perhaps, the only branch of Government prepared to deal with the complexities of such an unprecedented trial.

As president of the Military Commission, Gen. David Hunter was the most prominent member of the tribunal (Library of Congress, Portrait File – B814-C-4449).

The War Department received vicious letters, some condemning the accused and some threatening Government leaders, including the President. These dangers, both actual and conjectured, caused the Government to take unusual precautions that would also have been necessary in a civil court. Excitement reached such a peak authorities feared mobs might try to lynch the accused or attack the Commission.

On May 10, they passed an order to provide protection. No trial in American history had been conducted with so many soldiers standing guard. A sergeant and eight mounted men reported to the residence of General Hunter each morning to escort him to the courtroom, to remain on duty until court adjourned and then to accompany him home again. The same arrangement provided protection for Judge Holt, except that in his case, only six

Opposite: Commissioners and Judges. Standing: Harris, Wallace, Kautz, Burnett. Seated: Clendenin, Tompkins, Howe, Ekin, Hunter, Foster, Bingham, Holt (Library of Congress).

soldiers stood guard. The other Commissioners, including special Judges Advocate Bingham and Burnett, were assigned only four men. In addition, thirty soldiers reported daily to General Hartranft at the Arsenal, prepared for any emergency. A noncommissioned officer and ten soldiers guarded every block between the Arsenal courtroom and Pennsylvania Avenue. These sentries served as escorts in the event that anything happened to the regular bodyguards. These additional soldiers accompanied hundreds of others assigned to guard the prison and the courtroom.[30]

In the absence of any Confederate attempt to interfere with the trial and the lack of mob action, these precautions seem ridiculous. Yet this could not have been known in the spring of 1865.

War-related problems demanded Secretary of War Edwin Stanton's time. Battles still raged in small, isolated campaigns and the logistical problems associated with discharging thousands of troops needed attention. Reconstruction and military governments in the South required guidance. In addition, the Secretary of War maintained an increasingly ugly fight with General William T. Sherman—a struggle with ties to both the murder investigation and the conspiracy trial.

During the Civil War, spy activities and Confederate plots constantly threatened the inhabitants of Washington. Noah Brooks wrote that it would be impossible to give a later generation "any adequate idea of the uneasiness that pervaded Washington, or of the morbid sensationalism which characterized the conversation and conduct of the loyalists who were constantly haunted by suspicions of secret plotting all about them."[31]

After the assassination, this uneasiness became even more intense, especially with Secretary Stanton, who imagined plots against his life. Ohio Senator John Sherman, the General's younger brother, and Stanton's neighbor, described the atmosphere in Washington as "charged with terror." The Senator explained that Stanton "was under the influence of a well-grounded fear that his life was in danger."[32] At the time, the army still chased Jefferson Davis. Stanton, believing that Davis was behind the conspiracy, feared that somehow the Confederate President might escape and continue his intrigues.

Stanton felt that Sherman was not aggressive enough in pursuit of Davis, and he objected to the General's having ordered Gen. George Stoneman to withdraw from Salisbury, North Carolina. According to the apprehensive Stanton, this would "probably open the way for Davis to escape." Intensifying his fears was a dispatch the Secretary received from Richmond that Davis and his cohorts hoped to "make terms with General Sherman, or some other commander by which they will be permitted, with their effects, including this gold plunder, to go to Mexico or Europe."[33] Many believed the Rebel leader had carried away huge amounts of gold.

As the trial began, the Government continued to gather evidence. Detectives questioned David H. Cockerill, who had served four years in the

Confederate Army as a lieutenant in the Stonewall Brigade. Judge Joseph Holt had already learned from Henry Von Steinacker that, while assigned to the Stonewall Brigade, he heard Booth talk about Lincoln's assassination. Cockerill admitted he knew Von Steinacker but declared that he heard no talk of secret societies or of assassination plots circulating. He claimed he had never heard of Booth before April 16. At this point it was one man's word against another's.

Cockerill's subsequent account created later problems. He gave a long detailed account of how Von Steinacker had stolen his horse and fled to Spotsylvania. The Lieutenant dispatched a sergeant to apprehend him. They arrested Von Steinacker and returned him to be tried by court-martial. The court sentenced him to two years' imprisonment as a horse thief but later released him.[34] Cockerill gave dates, places and names that could easily have been checked. Instead of verifying the account, Joseph Holt ignored it and called Von Steinacker to testify at a secret session before the newly appointed Military Commission. But Holt failed to mention Von Steinacker's questionable character. The Judge was to pay severely for this oversight.

XXV
Abhorrence of All Things Secret

The trial and continuing arrests did not completely dominate life in the capital city. Although Ford's Theatre remained closed, surrounded by a military guard, Grover's Theatre reopened appropriately with *Uncle Tom's Cabin*. Citizens pushed efforts to raise money for a monument to Lincoln.

Problems relating to the aftermath of war occupied most Government workers. Loyalists who wanted to retaliate against "certain obnoxious persons who left the city to take part in the rebellion against the Government" held a mass meeting. They passed a resolution that "while disclaiming all feeling of personal animosity against them, we cannot contemplate their familiar faces without evicting a feeling of profound regret" that the traitors do not go somewhere else to live.[1] Tension and bitterness continued to divide the capital.

Some signs, however, indicated war mentality was gradually decreasing and business as usual was returning to Washington. Dr. S. B. Sigersmond had just returned from Paris with his concoction, Essence of Palmetto, which could cure a toothache without even touching the tooth. Another doctor discovered a great Indian medicine which provided an unfailing cure for dimness of vision, loss of memory, old age, insanity and constipation. The Patent Office approved the application of Henry Goodyear for extension of a patent for hardening rubber which made a material that was a substitute for bone, wood or ivory.

Paradoxically, John Wilkes Booth's picture still sold throughout many cities in the North. Authorities prohibited its sale in Philadelphia but not in Washington.

Since the death of her husband, Mrs. Lincoln had developed severe depression and seldom left her room in the White House. By May 10 she had sufficiently recovered for workmen to begin packing her effects.

Secretary of State Seward gradually mended, but his wife became seriously ill. His daughter remained mentally distressed and his son continued to suffer.

Soldiers waiting to be paid and preparing for the last grand parade gathered rapidly around the Nation's capital. Armies camped on all sides of the city and workers prepared additional grounds for the daily influx. General Grant, whom Burnett had telegraphed requesting that he appear at court, occupied a room in the city. Sherman and his army were en route.

Reminders of the war still scarred the Nation. The *Philadelphia Inquirer* advised readers that if they planned to visit the battlefields to obtain the remains of deceased family members, they should first get suitable coffins from undertakers at home.[2]

Detectives assigned to the assassination investigation made a few insignificant arrests. J. H. Blackburn, alias Dr. Tumberty, was apprehended in Washington. In Poughkeepsie, New York, authorities jailed Robert Cox because of his friendship with Confederate agent Sanders in Canada.

The prospect of large rewards caused growing tensions among would-be claimants. A false rumor spread that Major O'Beirne had been imprisoned for denying Col. LaFayette Baker's part in Booth's capture. Arguments over the reward money continued for years.

Some pockets of scattered resistance persisted even though the war was finally over. The notorious John Singleton Mosby, with whom Payne rode, had already disbanded his men, but he continued to hide out somewhere in Virginia.

Authorities removed restrictions on movements of civilians around the capital. Telegraph lines reopened to the South, and workers busily drilled for oil in Pennsylvania. Elias Howe was earning $250,000 yearly on his sewing machine. Even in devastated Richmond, business picked up.

General Grant ordered that "all paroled prisoners of the late Rebel armies now confined or detained at Alexandria, Va.," be returned to their homes.[3] The accused conspirators, held at the Arsenal Penitentiary just across the river, were not so fortunate.

While the Arsenal inmates selected lawyers, Federal troops in south Georgia closed in on another suspected conspirator. Jefferson Davis had begun his desperate flight on Sunday, April 2. During morning worship services, a sexton at St. Paul's Church approached Davis in his pew and whispered that he was wanted immediately. Upon receiving news of Lee's unexpected withdrawal from Petersburg and of the subsequent precarious situation around Richmond, he hastily called a Cabinet meeting. He informed members that the city would have to be evacuated. Davis ordered the removal of Confederate archives and the destruction of everything that could not be carried.

Only the railroad to Danville, Virginia, remained open, and it was in danger. Davis told Government leaders to meet him at the station at 8:00 P.M. Rebel leaders had trouble pushing through the confused crowds to the train. Near-hysteria gripped the excited multitudes, who were held back by soldiers as Davis and his Cabinet, along with a few select supporters, scrambled aboard. Mounted horsemen guarded the train as it pulled out around midnight, leaving the burning city in the hands of frenzied mobs. Within a few hours, the Confederate capital, which had valiantly withstood the onslaught for nearly four years, fell into Federal hands.

On the train, Davis discussed the possibility of establishing a new capital at Danville. In an attempt to show confidence in Confederate paper money, Rebel leaders exchanged $40,000 in silver coins for paper notes (at an exchange of two silver dollars for 70 paper dollars).[4] Thousands of faithful Confederates fled to the new capital. On April 5 at Danville, President Davis sought to animate his followers with brave words. Even though faced with temporary defeat, he admonished, "again and again we will return until the baffled and exhausted enemy shall abandon in despair his endless and impossible task of making slaves of a people resolved to be free."[5]

Davis, however, was out of touch with General Lee, as well as with reality, and he waited in vain for the arrival of Lee's forces. After several anxious days, the dismayed leader learned of Lee's surrender.

The Confederate President then fled with his dwindling supporters to Greensboro, North Carolina, where they were met by unreceptive citizens.[6] All that was left of the once proud Confederacy was one small train on a dead-end track.

In Greensboro, Davis conferred with Gen. Joseph Johnston, John C. Breckinridge and Gov. Zebulon Vance. Still determined to resist, the leader asked the governor to help him continue the fight west of the Mississippi. Vance refused. General Johnston sought to dissuade his President, warning that "it would be the greatest of human crimes for us to continue the war."[7] He did not convince Davis, but at least he gained permission to write to General Sherman requesting terms for peace.

Davis, discouraged with this reception in Greensboro, seldom left the train. With a small, ragged military escort he pushed on toward Charlotte. Unable to travel farther by rail because the tracks had been destroyed, the desperate band took off in wagons and on horseback through Salisbury to Charlotte. There Davis learned of Lincoln's assassination and the $100,000 reward that had been placed on his head. But a much needed rest was interrupted by the approach of Gen. George Stoneman's men. Sherman had ordered Stoneman from Salisbury to join his forces. This move seemed foolish to Secretary Stanton, and it may have been. Apparently it allowed Davis to move southward through Yorkville to Abbeville, South Carolina.

Here his escorting generals finally convinced their defeated leader that the Confederacy was hopelessly lost. Nevertheless, accompanied by 2,000 cavalrymen, he rode on relentlessly toward Washington, Georgia.

He made no further effort to keep together the remainder of his depleted Cabinet. George A. Trenholm, Secretary of the Treasury, and George Davis, Attorney General, resigned and fled on their own. Judah Benjamin, Secretary of State and "the brains of the Confederacy," left the group and escaped to Florida and on to the Bahamas, eventually getting to England. Stephen R. Mallory, Secretary of the Navy, separated from Davis at Washington, Georgia, and fled to La Grange, where his family lived. John Breckinridge, former Vice-President of the United States, also abandoned the lost cause at Washington and escaped to the Florida Keys. Eventually he reached Cuba and from there made his way to England.

After General Johnston negotiated a peace settlement with Sherman, Federal troops made greater efforts to capture Davis. Officers ordered three of Stoneman's brigades to track him down. They crossed the Savannah River to the west of the little band of fugitives, cutting them off from the Mississippi. Davis then turned due south, apparently heading for Florida. Little hope

As Confederate Secretary of War (and he was later Secretary of State), Judah P. Benjamin had charge of secret operations in Canada.

remained, however, as the Federal cavalry formed a dragnet through which he could not escape.

On May 5, 1865, as Union soldiers approached, Davis selected fifteen soldiers to accompany him farther south. The rest of the cavalrymen surrendered.

Following a tip, Col. Henry Harnden, commanding the First Wisconsin Cavalry, arrived on May 8 at a campsite that had been occupied by Davis only a few hours earlier. On May 9, Harnden's forces reached Abbeville in southern Georgia and learned that Davis camped nearby. By that time, other Union forces were moving toward the area.

At 2:00 A.M., May 10, Harnden sent a detachment, which joined with troops under Colonel Pritchard, to surround the Rebels.[8] Just before dawn, Union soldiers encircled the Confederate camp. They thought that between ten and fifty heavily armed bodyguards protected Davis and, therefore, expected strong resistance. At dawn the Federals attacked. As the Union soldiers surrounded all sides of the camp, they rushed in not realizing they were shooting at each other. Actually, Davis had only about a dozen soldiers with him. In the confusion of the dim light, Union troops killed two of their own men and wounded others.

During the fighting, Lt. J. G. Dickinson noticed "three persons dressed in female attire" walking toward the woods. The lieutenant ordered them to halt, but they kept moving. A Corporal Munger cut off their exit. On detaining the three, Union soldiers discovered Mrs. Davis and a woman companion. The third captive was Jefferson Davis. A loose-fitting woman's cloak covered the humbled Rebel President's Confederate uniform, and a black shawl hid his face. The soldiers had assumed that Davis was a woman until they noticed his high boots beneath the cloak.

Later, Mrs. Davis claimed that her husband made no attempt to disguise himself. She explained that he happened to grab up a woman's cloak in his hurried escape attempt and that she simply threw her shawl over his head. This episode animated Northern cartoonists for years.

In Washington, the trial had just started. The military could have rushed Davis back to the capital to stand trial with his supposed coconspirators. Instead they took him by ship from Savannah to prison in Fortress Monroe. Why—only Stanton knew.

Stanton insisted that the Government's relocation of Davis be kept strictly secret. Other Cabinet members advised him that it was impossible to keep everything secret—that news reporters were certain to find out Davis' destination. Stanton replied that he controlled the telegraph service and that he could suppress anything.

After court officials read the charges and specifications to the accused, the Associated Press wanted to print them. Stanton preferred to make them public, but Judge Holt opposed it. Special Judge Advocate Burnett, left in an awkward position, consulted Stanton about the decision. Burnett explained that Holt was "decidedly against any publication of the charges" and was in favor of giving the press only a very brief synopsis of the proceedings. "What should I do?" Burnett wrote. The Secretary of War scribbled a brief note on the back of Burnett's letter. "You should be governed by the opinions of Judge Holt. You will consider yourself under his direction."[9]

Stanton, busy with other matters, had turned the trial over to his trusted friend. He continued to wield power as Secretary of War, but he did not interfere with the trial. He never visited the courtroom or made any known attempt to influence either the proceedings or the outcome.

The man who did exercise control was Joseph Holt. The 58-year-old Holt, appointed Judge Advocate General of the Commission, was one of the most respected and honored men in the Union. Born in Kentucky of poor parents, Holt nevertheless graduated from college and studied law. He opened his first law office in 1828 in Louisville. His successful practice there and later in Vicksburg, Mississippi, provided him financial security—enough to spend several years touring Greece, Egypt and Europe. On his return, Holt became interested in national politics, taking part in the presidential contest which resulted in the election of Franklin Pierce in 1852. In the following campaign, he supported James Buchanan who subsequently appointed him Commissioner of Patents, a position he held until commissioned Postmaster General in 1859. The threat of war brought him other advancements.

On the last day of the year in 1860, President Buchanan was compelled by pressure from his Cabinet to adopt a more stringent attitude toward belligerent South Carolina. Holt joined with Stanton, who was then Attorney General, in backing stronger measures against the South. Buchanan appointed Holt Secretary of War after John B. Floyd of Virginia resigned. Almost immediately Holt set in motion efforts to send provisions to beleaguered Fort Sumter. As a result, the *Star of the West* sailed toward Charleston harbor on January 5, 1861. Rebels fired on the ship after it arrived in the harbor on January 10, and Holt became a hero in the North.[10]

Other Southerners in Buchanan's Cabinet then began to resign. Howell Cobb of Georgia gave up his position as Secretary of the Treasury, and Jacob Thompson resigned as Secretary of the Interior. (Holt later accused Thompson of complicity in the assassination.) He blamed Holt for sending what he thought were reinforcements to Fort Sumter and demanded unsuccessfully that the President dismiss him.

Holt, a Southerner, like his predecessor in the War Department, had proved his loyalty to the Union. Noted reporter Lawrence A. Gobright commented after Holt took over as Secretary of War, "Mr. Holt, I see that you have, for the first time in our history, hoisted the National flag over your Department."

"Yes," Holt responded, "I did not feel as if I could work for the country without the old flag flying over my head."[11]

Praised throughout the Union for his strong stand, he spoke in Boston and New York to enthusiastic crowds. Much credit for keeping Kentucky from joining the Confederacy was correctly attributed to Holt's efforts. Newspapers praised his work and bands serenaded him. Magazines published articles eulogizing him as a keystone of the Union. His name became better known than Stanton's at the time. Neither realized the war would become the bloodiest conflict in United States history. The nature of the combat greatly increased the importance and power of both men.

When Lincoln became President, he named his own Cabinet, which did not include Holt, a conservative Democrat. Lincoln, however, saw the importance of keeping Holt in the Nation's service, as Southern conservatives were needed to hold border states in the Union. When it became known that Simon Cameron planned to resign as Secretary of War, Lincoln wanted Holt for the position again. Radicals in the Republican party, however, forced the President to appoint Edwin Stanton. Far from creating jealousy between Holt and Stanton, the two became warm friends. Holt admired Stanton; the two had the same disposition and conservative war views.

After Congress passed a law making disloyalty and offering aid or comfort to Rebels punishable crimes, President Lincoln took the measure a step further and brought the crimes under martial law, thus putting its enforcement under military control. Lincoln entrusted fellow Kentuckian Joseph Holt, whom he had just appointed Judge Advocate General, with carrying out this radical departure.

Holt immediately extended martial law not only around Washington, but throughout the Nation. The acts of Congress, which created the office of Judge Advocate, stipulated that his duties would involve regulating courts-martial and Military Commissions. In this position, Holt worked closely with Stanton as well as with President Lincoln.

As Judge Advocate, Holt sought to establish the authority of courts-martial and Military Commissions over civilians as well as over military personnel.[12] Gen. Henry Halleck had paved the way by insisting that civil offenses in time of peace often became military offenses in time of war. A military offense can, therefore, be committed by either civilians or by military personnel. According to Halleck, such offenses should be tried by military tribunals. Halleck's opinions carried weight not only because of his high military rank, but also because of his recognized brilliance. He had graduated third in his class at West Point and was known as "Old Brains."

Holt was aided in his effort to strengthen military courts by Frances Lieber. The "Laws of War" on which military law developed were not rules established by statues such as the "Articles of War," but rather grew out of custom and had remained mostly unwritten. On April 24, 1864, the Adjutant General's office published a compilation of these laws prepared by Lieber. During the compilation, he often conferred with Holt.

Partly as a reward for Holt's enthusiastic efforts, the Government commissioned him Brigadier General and head of the newly created Bureau of Military Justice. Thus when he was named to conduct the conspiracy trial, Holt could look back on a successful career in law, politics, and the military. He had held several Cabinet positions and was even mentioned as a possible presidential candidate. This was to change.

Lincoln's authority to suspend the writ of habeas corpus excited debate and criticism even within his own party and created factions active in the conspiracy trial. Holt and Stanton supported the suspension of the writ and were leaders in prosecuting the conspirators. Republican Senator John Sherman of Ohio opposed the late President's suspension on constitutional grounds. He associated closely with those who defended the suspects. United States Senator from Maryland Reverdy Johnson had gained a following by supporting personal liberties, but, strangely, he supported Lincoln's right to suspend the writ of habeas corpus. Johnson's actions, in this case, seemed inconsistent with his entire career and may be explained by his attempt to remain loyal to the Union in the midst of disruption and dissent in Maryland. Reverdy Johnson became a defender of the conspirators.

Thus before the trial began, legal factions had already been established. The trial, in many ways, served as a testing ground for differing views of executive prerogatives as well as of military authority.

Once officials announced the date of the trial, newsmen began to speculate that it might be closed to them. At first, the New York Times stated that the trial would be open. When the Times discovered the Government planned to exclude reporters, it printed a scathing editorial. Referring to the Government's contention that a public trial might prevent the arrest of others implicated, the reporter observed that difficulties in the capture of others should not be made a pretext for "introducing into our criminal procedure so extraordinary an anomaly as trial by a Military Commission for a capital offense with closed doors. . . ." Only one condition—that of war—could possibly have justified this kind of proceeding, and the war had finally been declared over on the very day that the trial began, the editor wrote. Would people really believe that peace had been restored, the paper queried, "when a most atrocious crime has to be tried and punished by a military court, sitting in secret in the national capital, and in a country in which all secret things, and above all, secret trials, have always been held in abhorrence."[13]

The *Times* unaccountably reversed itself the next day, observing that the Government had seen fit to try the assassins by military tribunal in secret so that it might publish its own disclosures. The paper apologized again a few days later for the "ill-judged language of an article accidently inserted."

Most leading newspapers, however, consistently opposed a secret trial. The *Philadelphia Inquirer* reported that the press could only read the trial record taken by official stenographers. The *Philadelphia Bulletin* noted simply that the Government intended to keep the trial closed to the public.

Many reporters objected to the military court, but their chief concern was that they were excluded. If a group of Rebels had rushed in upon General Grant at his headquarters and killed him in cold blood, the *Washington Daily Chronicle* asked, would they have had a trial by jury? The murder of the Commander-in-Chief was the same thing according to the paper.

Under the bold-type heading SECRET MILITARY TRIALS, Horace Greeley's *New York Tribune* observed:

> There is a curious old document in existence known as the Constitution of the United States, which formerly had the force and effect of law in that large portion of our country not specially dominated by slave powers. Under the rule of our present Cabinet it seems to have gone out of fashion and, since Mr. Stanton's accession to the control of the War Department, it has become practically obsolete.[14]

That paper, in a long, harsh article criticizing the trial, insisted that the Rebellion had been suppressed and that the Government had no right to take away the writ of habeas corpus.

The *Washington Chronicle* responded by asking if Greeley thought he knew more than the Attorney General.

The *Tribune*, in a seemingly inconsistent article, reported on the trial, by court-martial, of a civilian named B. S. Osborn. The Government charged him with the relatively minor offense of having given intelligence to the enemy. The alleged crime had taken place in New York in the latter part of 1864. Osborn contended that the military court did not have the right to try him and pleaded the 5th Amendment as a civilian over whom the military had no jurisdiction. The *Tribune* did not condemn the military court in this case.

Actually there were several military trials of civilians in progress at the time. Congressman Benjamin Harris from Maryland was under the scrutiny of a Military Commission for harboring Rebels. And the Government put

Mrs. Bessie Perrine, a Baltimore civilian, on trial before a military court, accused of assisting Confederate cavalry in plundering a town between Baltimore and Philadelphia.

Influential individuals, as well as newspaper editors, objected to the military court; some sought to intervene through the President. Henry Winter Davis, a radical Maryland politician, wrote the President that the military trial would be a disaster and that the President should halt the proceedings at once. That most conspirators came from Maryland may have influenced Davis. Lincoln's friend and well-known liberal statesman Carl Shurz also opposed the military trial, particularly after hearing the rumor that it would be held in secret.[15]

Proceedings opened on schedule, Thursday morning, May 11. The court admitted defense attorneys after they took the required oath of allegiance. Following the preliminaries, the Commission allowed them time with their clients. Reverdy Johnson had not yet appeared, but he sent one of his young assistants, Frederick Aiken, to converse with Mrs. Surratt. Aiken, a 28-year-old native of Massachusetts, passed the bar in Vermont before coming to Washington. John Clampitt, a 25-year-old graduate of Columbia College (now George Washington University), another inexperienced associate of Johnson's, collaborated with Aiken in Mrs. Surratt's behalf.

General Thomas Ewing, Jr., a tall, handsome, 35-year-old Washington attorney, was present as counsel for both Arnold and Mudd. He had already distinguished himself as a lawyer before the war and added to his legal honors by serving courageously in the Union army, rising to the rank of general. Thus the glitter of military brass did not intimidate Ewing. In addition to his own ability, he relied on the advice of his venerable 75-year-old father.

The senior Ewing had served in several Cabinet posts under two different presidents and at the time of the conspiracy was recognized as one of the most respected lawyers in America. Thus the younger Ewing had access to sound advice.

Frederick Stone, Mudd's other counsel, was also present. Stone came from one of Maryland's most honored families. One of his early ancestors served Lord Baltimore as governor of the colony. His great-uncle, Thomas Stone, signed the Declaration of Independence. Stone also represented Herold.

Walter E. Cox, 39 years old, a graduate of Georgetown University and Howard Law School, appeared as attorney for O'Laughlin. Payne, Spangler and Atzerodt could not yet secure legal counsel. Holt gave defense lawyers copies of the charges, which they swore to keep confidential.

Several days had passed since the court first convened. It remained closed to the public and had not yet examined any witnesses. The delay aggravated the generals. Kautz could not get interested in the proceedings. He complained about the absence of defense counsel. What really worried the young general was a letter from Charlotte Tod. His fiancée insisted on postponing their marriage until November. She also accused Kautz of making unfounded statements. The letter so unnerved Kautz that he thought all hope of ever marrying Tod had vanished. He longed to see her personally and get the matter

Thomas Ewing, Sr. This venerable old attorney (and his partner, Orville Browning) guided his son's efforts on behalf of the accused assassins (Library of Congress—USZ621-15572).

settled, but that was impossible as he had to remain on duty in Washington. Kautz was in no mood to sit in judgment of anybody.

After court adjourned Sen. Reverdy Johnson finally requested a pass to talk with Mrs. Surratt and determine if he should serve as her counsel. He approached his 69th birthday as a public servant, highly respected for more than a generation. Johnson had been United States Attorney General in Pres. Zachary Taylor's Cabinet and had served in the United States Senate off and on since 1845. As Senator he served as a member of the Peace Congress in 1861 and 1862 and later urged quick readmission for Southern states. At the time of the trial he was a Democratic Senator from Maryland. Johnson had gained recognition as an outspoken and independent thinker. He disregarded party labels, preferring to follow his own course. After the conspiracy trial, President Johnson appointed him ambassador to England.

By this time Mrs. Surratt's notoriety had created strong sentiment against her. Only a few weeks before she had been an object of curiosity, if not of pity. The *New York Tribune* now described her as chief among the conspirators

One of the most enigmatic Washington politicians, Reverdy Johnson was a pallbearer at his friend Lincoln's funeral and then defended one of the accused assassins (Library of Congress—BH82-29).

occupying "a place in the front rank."[16] On its front page, the *New York Times* called her the "female fiend incarnate," adding that the Government seemed "to have the rope coiled around her neck."[17]

The *New York World* published an amazingly accurate list of the suspects eventually tried, even before they were charged. In a strangely mixed metaphor, the *World* identified Mrs. Surratt as the anchor and the rest of the boys as disciples who "relied upon Mrs. Surratt and took their 'cues' from Wilkes Booth."[18]

Ben Perley Poore, a perceptive reporter for the *Boston Evening Journal*, carefully followed the investigation and trial. He identified Mrs. Surratt as one of the chief conspirators who had "unquestionably nursed the plot with malignant care, although it would rather appear that she sent her own son out of the way when the time for action came."[19]

When court convened on May 12, most prisoners except Payne and Spangler had lawyers. George Atzerodt's detective brother John had been able to employ W. E. Doster.

Ironically, John Atzerodt, who sought out and paid for a lawyer to defend his brother, was also the detective who led arresting officers to Atzerodt's hiding place. These events troubled the Atzerodt family. As immigrants, they regretted their association with the President's murder, yet they felt a compulsion to defend a family member. Other families, such as Booth's and Herold's, were torn by a similar divided loyalty, but not so deeply.

Since Payne and Spangler had little hope of obtaining lawyers, Burnett asked Doster to take Payne's case also. At first the attorney refused, knowing Payne had little chance, and the defense of Atzerodt would demand his full attention. He eventually agreed to serve temporarily.[20] Payne never acquired another counsel, leaving Doster to do the best he could for both clients. Although Payne had no way to pay, Doster, who had served bravely as a colonel in the Union army, did his best to defend him. The difficult and almost hopeless task took courage.

According to Doster it was a contest in which a few lawyers were on one side, and the whole United States on the other. Even among the conquered Southern people, the accused had few friends. Many Southerners, anxious to forget their defeat and eager to exhibit a new spirit of loyalty, condemned the conspirators or ignored the whole legal process.

The lawyer knew nothing about his client's background and Payne refused to help. Although Payne had earlier tried to defend himself, by this time he had given up hope. He gave no indication that he even wanted defense counsel. Spangler still had no lawyer.

After formal recognition of Doster on May 12, the Commission called its first witness, Henry Von Steinacker. But they heard his testimony in a special secret session. Holt insisted that his statement was too sensitive to be made public. Questioned by Holt behind closed doors, Von Steinacker's testimony seriously incriminated Confederate leaders.

He told of serving in the Confederate army for several years as an engineer in the Topographical Department and claimed he was on Gen. Edward Johnson's staff. Von Steinacker then related a convincing story of helping a sick soldier find his way back to Virginia after the battle of Gettysburg. While in Virginia he happened to encounter a man named Booth.

Handing the witness a photograph of Booth, Holt asked if he recognized the man.

"There is a resemblance; but the face was fuller."

"You think it is the same person, but he had a fuller face than this?"

"I believe it is."

He explained that he visited with Booth for 18 or 20 hours.

Then Holt asked, "Will you state what Booth said to you in regard to any contemplated purpose of attack upon the President of the United States? State all that he said."

Von Steinacker gave a long account of Booth's confidence in the ultimate

Confederate victory. According to the witness Booth predicted that "Old Abe Lincoln must go up the spout, and the Confederacy will gain their independence anyhow."

"What did you understand by the expression, he 'must go up the spout,' from all that Booth said?"

"It was a common expression, meaning he must be killed. That I understood always."

Von Steinacker continued, under Holt's prompting, to link Booth with Confederate leaders. The Government had a powerful witness who made an indelible impression on the court. One Commissioner wrote in his diary at the end of the day that he was convinced Davis, Thompson and Clay were all involved in the conspiracy.

Following Von Steinacker's secret hearing, guards led the prisoners into the courtroom. The Commission then interrogated witnesses in the presence of spectators. Reporters, however, were still excluded.

G. W. Bunker, an employee of the National Hotel, provided the Court with a record of Booth's stay. Booth apparently did not visit Washington during the month of October 1864. However, according to Bunker, he registered at the hotel on November 9, occupying Room 20, and left on an early train on the morning of the 11th. The witness then gave further detailed account of Booth's visits. He was in Washington on November 14 and 15 and December 12 through 16, then on December 22 and 23 and again on December 31 through January 10, 1865. He arrived again on January 12 and stayed until the 29th occupying Room 50½. He was back on February 22 staying in Room 231. This time he came with John P. Wentworth and John McCullough.[21]

Other sources indicated that Booth visited the capital for Lincoln's second inauguration on March 4, which Bunker affirmed. Booth's name, however, did not appear on the hotel register, but the witness stated that "his account commences March 1, without any entry upon the register of that date." Bunker testified that Booth paid $50 on his account on March 21 and left the city on the 7:30 P.M. train. He arrived again on March 25 and occupied Room 231 and left the next afternoon. Booth came to Washington for the last time on April 8. This time he occupied Room 228. According to Bunker, the name directly below Booth's on the register was A. Cox. This person gave no home residence. The part of the hotel register containing both names had been cut out prior to the trial.

Gen. Ulysses S. Grant took the witness stand to prove that Washington, D.C., and Maryland were areas directly involved in the fighting and, consequently, under martial law. Aiken, cross-examining the popular hero, asked, "Are you aware that the civil courts are in operation in this city, all of them?"

General Grant agreed that while this was true, martial law had been extended to Washington and much of Maryland.

One of the last witnesses that day was Samuel Chester, an actor and longtime friend of the assassin. He gave a clear picture of Booth's *modus operandi*. After a few preliminaries, Judge Advocate Holt questioned him about the date of a conversation he had with Booth sometime in November 1864.

Chester claimed he did not remember the exact date, but that it was early in November. He recalled that Booth had vowed never to act again in the North and had taken his wardrobe to Canada. However, in answer to another question, Chester admitted that Booth did act again in the play *Julius Caesar* which the Booth brothers presented in New York City on November 25, 1864.

November 25 was a day to remember in New York City. The presentation of *Julius Caesar* was a sensation because it was one of a few times all three Booth brothers performed together. Junius Brutus appeared as Cassius, Edwin as Brutus and John Wilkes was Marc Antony. John Wilkes, ever competitive with his brothers, shaved his mustache for the performance and threw himself into the part with relish. To his delight, he received the greatest applause. Their proud mother watched her famous sons.

This performance in the Winter Garden was interrupted, however, when firemen burst into the theater. The fire proved to be a false alarm, and the audience, convinced there was no danger, allowed the show to continue.

The next morning, New York papers announced that the fire had actually broken out next door to the theater and was one of dozens deliberately set.[22] Later, detectives learned that Confederate agents, working out of Canada, started the fires.

John Wilkes played more than the role of Marc Antony. He was recruiting partners for his abduction scheme and likely was aware of the planned Confederate sabotage of the city. Chester related a long account of Booth's efforts to coerce him to take part in a large conspiracy to capture the heads of Government, including the President. The plan was to take them to Richmond. Chester pleaded that he had to think of his family and could not cooperate. Booth offered money for his family and then threatened him. According to the witness, he stood firm and refused any part. Holt then inquired, "Did he indicate to you what part he wished you to play in carrying out this conspiracy?"

The witness replied that he was to open the back door of the theater at a given signal.

"Did he indicate at what theater this was to occur?"

"Yes, he told me Ford's Theatre; because it must be someone acquainted or connected with the theater who could take part in it."[23]

Before Chester finished, he revealed that Booth had lots of money to start with but ran short of funds later on. Booth said that he or someone else would have to go to Richmond to obtain means to carry out their design.

The Government called other witnesses before concluding. The long session lasted until six that evening. Before the day was over, however, reporters, convinced they were to be excluded, consulted with General Grant. Grant, impressed, accompanied them to the White House to see the President. Andrew Johnson, backed by public pressure, was able to force the Military Commission to abandon secrecy.

Opening the trial to the public decidedly influenced the outcome. Reporters thronged to the Arsenal. Guards admitted them after they exhibited passes signed by General Hunter. Officers set up a special table for their use on the south side of the courtroom.

Many papers which had previously criticized the Commission printed the testimony in full. The *New York World*, a bitter critic, had predicted that the trial would be kept secret because Stanton would find his case difficult to prove. Later, it printed all of the incriminating evidence against the prisoners with little comment.

Reporters who attended the sessions regularly and made daily comments were L. A. Gobright of the Associated Press; U. H. Painter, the *Philadelphia Inquirer*; W. R. Shaw, the *Boston Transcript*; G. B. Wood, the *Boston Advertiser*; W. Warden, the *New York Times* and W. Croffut, the *New York Tribune*. They published the best coverage—particularly the *Philadelphia Inquirer*—which gave the most accurate account. Washington papers such as the *Star*, the *Intelligencer* and the *Chronicle* also sent reporters. *Harper's Weekly* and *Leslie's Illustrated Newspaper* had artists sketch courtroom scenes.

Larger newspapers recorded the testimony day by day, describing in detail the proceedings. Many papers printed the complete testimony, frequently giving it the entire front page. A crowd always gathered around the press table. Even small papers occasionally dispatched reporters. For weeks the trial covered space comparably given to sports and entertainment by present-day newspapers. Without the insatiable public appetite and the gargantuan efforts of the periodicals to satisfy it, the basic facts of the conspiracy might have been obscured. Even so, some details were never brought to light.

Opening the trial to the press lessened, to some extent, the complaint against the Military Commission. Still, several publications, particularly the Rebel-oriented *New York News*, never let up. The *News* constantly branded the court-martial a "military murder" weapon. Most newspapers (even Democrat papers), finding little to complain about in the conduct of the trial, reported it favorably. Their descriptions of the courtroom demeanor of the counsel and Commissioners naturally had a restraining effect on overzealous participants.

Opposite: Artist's rendition of the trial prepared for "Frank Leslie's Illustrated Newspaper," Vol. XX (Library of Congress—USZ62-2221 and USZ62-6948).

XXVI
Justice in Epaulets

The Arsenal building stood in an isolated area almost due south of the Capitol, a mile and a half from Pennsylvania Avenue. Horse cars serviced the first mile of dirt road from town. One had to walk the rest of the way. Sentries, questioning each pedestrian, stood at intervals along the last half mile.

Soldiers guarding the prison concentrated around the entrance gates. Visitors entered through the east door of the main building where officers checked passes. Spectators then climbed a wide stairway to a small second-floor waiting room. This area, as well as the stairway and the halls, was staffed with orderlies serving as messengers under the court's command. Off to the side was one of several rooms where witnesses waited before being called. Carpenters had built a new stairway from the second floor leading to the 40- by 50-foot courtroom on the third floor.

A platform on which the accused sat extended across the west end of the courtroom. Near the corner, behind the prisoners' dock, a newly cut doorway led to the cells. A heavy wooden door studded with bolts secured the passage. Two other doors opened off the south side. The one nearest the prisoners was permanently closed; the other led into a room where witnesses waited. The defense counsel occupied three tables in front of the prisoners' dock. In addition to the tables designated for Commissioners, Judges and defense lawyers, another served for official reporters and newspaper correspondents.

Government painters had whitewashed the improvised courtroom in preparation for the trial. Heavily barred windows provided light, and workers added several gas fixtures in case sessions extended into the night. Carpenters constructed plain pine furniture for participants and visitors. Two stoves, a water cooler, some hard-bottomed chairs and the inevitable cuspidors completed the furnishings. No pictures or adornments decorated the plain walls. The room was austere, but neat and serviceable.[1]

Officers, seated with military erectness around their table, presented an impressive sight in their trim dress uniforms with gold braid—in marked contrast to the miserable-looking prisoners.

General Hunter, presiding over the tribunal, looked the part of the veteran officer he was. His bronzed, scarred face reflected years on the battlefield. Hunter took the proceedings seriously, leaning forward on his elbows to hear every word, occasionally showing his impatience with unnecessary delays and irrelevant testimony.

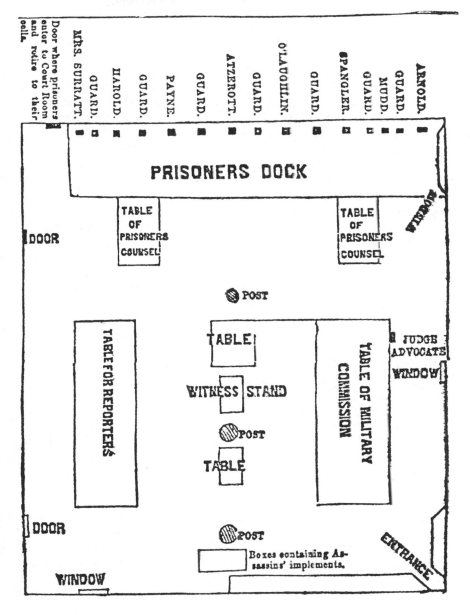

PRISONERS DOCK

MRS. SURRATT.
GUARD.
HAROLD.
GUARD.
PAYNE.
GUARD.
ATZEROTT.
GUARD.
O'LAUGHLIN.
GUARD.
SPANGLER.
GUARD.
MUDD.
GUARD.
ARNOLD.

Door where prisoners enter to Court Room and retire to their cells.

DOOR

TABLE OF PRISONERS COUNSEL

TABLE OF PRISONERS COUNSEL

WINDOW

POST

TABLE

WITNESS STAND

POST

TABLE

TABLE FOR REPORTERS

TABLE OF MILITARY COMMISSION

JUDGE ADVOCATE

WINDOW

DOOR

POST

WINDOW

Boxes containing Assassins' implements.

ENTRANCE

Contemporary diagram of the Arsenal courtroom showing the arrangement during the second or third session. Officials later moved the witness stand closer to the prisoners' dock. (Position of the prisoners' door is incorrect.) (From Pitman's trial account.)

General Wallace sat next to Hunter. Wallace was known best, at the time, for his decisive battle with Rebel General Jubal Early at the Monocacy River near Frederick, Maryland. Although Wallace lost that conflict, he won respect for slowing Early's advance toward Washington and was credited with saving the capital. (Wallace is best remembered today as author of *Ben Hur*.) These two generals were the most noteworthy of the distinguished Commission.

Judge Advocate Holt, the Government's chief interrogator, referred constantly to a mass of notes taken in the preliminary investigations.

At a small table, near the entrance, sat the strikingly handsome Gen. John Hartranft, who would later become governor of Pennsylvania. After distinguishing himself in the war, the army assigned him to special duty as Provost Marshal for the trial. He stayed busy during the proceedings, signing passes and daily supervising prisoners.

The witness stand was located between the two main tables and faced the military court. The stand was a plain raised platform about a foot high with a simple arm chair and surrounded on three sides by a railing. Rules required witnesses to face the Commissioners, thus forcing them to turn their backs to the lawyers located near the prisoners' dock. Frequently witnesses unconsciously turned toward the lawyers while testifying, invariably bringing a sharp rebuke from Hunter.[2]

Sessions usually opened at 10:00 each morning. Guards ushered in the defendants one by one, their chains clanking. Arnold entered first and took his seat at the north end, next to the window. O'Laughlin followed, then Atzerodt, Spangler, Payne, Herold and Mudd. Mary Surratt entered separately. The order seldom varied. The prisoners remained separated with guards seated between them. Mrs. Surratt maintained her privileged position near the counsel for several days before officials moved her chair back closer to the prisoners' platform. Further objections to even this special treatment eventually forced her to sit with the others. On the first day that reporters attended court, Mrs. Surratt tottered in wearing a heavy black veil. During the entire session she kept her head bowed, resting it on her right hand. Some reporters thought they detected an effort to evoke pity.

In contrast, Atzerodt and Payne seemed deliberately unconcerned, although Atzerodt constantly leaned over the rail to converse with his counsel. Payne directed a cool, assured stare at each person in the room, one by one. He wore a close-fitting, collarless, blue woolen undershirt with no vest or coat. He sat towering above the others with his head thrown back against the wall defiantly. Dr. Mudd made an effort to distinguish himself from the rest, dressing in a vest and coat and maintaining a dignified, above-it-all attitude. Except for Payne, the prisoners were rather small, Atzerodt being the shortest.

The Government planned no surprise tactics or clever maneuvers. Evidently it intended to present its strongest evidence in the first few days. This simple plan proved to be effective because few people outside the War Department knew of the mammoth evidence accumulated. Presentation of its strongest testimony on the first day reporters were present left the public little doubt about the strength of the Government's case.

The Commission followed, with only slight changes, the pattern set early. President Hunter opened each session, followed by a roll call of the Commissioners. D. F. Murphy, one of the official court stenographers, then read the complete record of the previous session, which often took all morning.

The widely acclaimed officers on the Commission obviously considered themselves superior to the common crowd. Several members of the defense counsel, particularly Reverdy Johnson and Thomas Ewing, Jr., exhibited similar self-esteem.

Johnson, recognized as one of the leading lawyers in the Nation, was not only a United States Senator but a friend of presidents. He was already well known to several Commissioners—Gen. Lew Wallace for one. As a military commander in Maryland, Wallace exercised powerful influence at the time Johnson was serving that state in the United States Senate.

Johnson had previous conflicts with other members of the Court, including Judge Advocate Holt, Assistant Judge Advocate Bingham and the Commission president, Hunter. In September 1862, Hunter was president of the court-martial of Gen. Fitz-John Porter and Holt, the Judge Advocate General, assisted by the Hon. John A. Bingham. The situation paralleled that of the conspiracy trial. In the Porter court-martial, Reverdy Johnson served as legal counsel for Porter, who was accused of disobeying orders of his commander, Gen. John Pope, during the Second Battle of Bull Run. The Court found him guilty on three charges, dismissed him from the army and forever disqualified him from holding office in the Federal Government.

Holt wrote a review of the case in January 1863, and President Lincoln approved the sentence. Reverdy Johnson responded with a severe criticism of Holt's review.[3] In one acrimonious exchange, the Senator accused General Hunter of being unfit for his position. Johnson also published a pamphlet belittling Hunter's military qualifications, stating that he had been removed from commands twice for mistaken policy. At the Lincoln conspiracy trial, Holt, Bingham and Hunter showed they had not forgotten Senator Johnson.

The Secretary of War had also clashed with Johnson, who on one occasion requested an order from Stanton releasing a Marylander, Judge Carmichael, from Fort Delaware. Stanton signed the release, but then countermanded it. He did not trust the Senator, who in turn had no confidence in the Secretary of War.[4] These and other personal antagonisms affected the trial.

Reverdy Johnson, a maverick, enigmatic man, supported the Union while his own border state leaned toward the Confederacy. Yet, while he opposed secession, he constantly supported individual Rebels. Johnson's efforts on behalf of disloyal citizens were well known. Gen. Benjamin Butler called him a rank secessionist and criticized the Senator for trying to conceal his Confederate sympathies.[5]

On one occasion, Johnson advised Bernard Boyard of Delaware that he need not feel obligated to take the oath of loyalty. Johnson, himself, did take the oath, albeit under protest, apparently because he did not want to appear disloyal.

Whatever Johnson's true sentiments, it was through his personal intervention that many Confederate prisoners were released from Union prisons. General John A. Dix, attempting to be charitable, wrote that Johnson was not discriminating in the list of prisoners he wanted freed.

What particularly aggravated many public leaders was Johnson's practice of charging for his services. In April 1864, he accepted a $1,000 fee for clearing a blockade-runner named Maddox. The Senator made no attempt to hide the fact. He admitted it openly on the floor of the United States Senate, although he maintained that he personally was loyal to the Union.[6]

In regard to slavery, Johnson tried to be consistent but was placed in an awkward position since he represented Maryland, a slaveholding state that remained in the Union. He avowed his hatred of slavery but did not believe the Federal Government had the right to interfere with it where it already existed, even during time of war. The Senator was a close friend of President Lincoln. His views on slavery, while similar to Lincoln's, were probably the cause of his eventual denouncement of Lincoln and support of McClellan in the presidential campaign of 1864. In spite of this break, Johnson served as pallbearer at Lincoln's funeral.

Several Commissioners basically distrusted Johnson because of advice he had given after the Maryland Constitutional Convention of 1864. The Convention had drawn up a new constitution abolishing slavery in the state. Furthermore, it prescribed that each voter had to take the oath of loyalty in order to vote on the new constitution. Johnson had fought vigorously against the oath on grounds that it was unconstitutional. In order to vote, Johnson advised his constituents to take the oath even though they held private reservations.

In a pointed letter distributed a few weeks before the vote, Johnson again advised Marylanders to take the prescribed oath, even falsely if necessary. It was the only way Marylanders could protect their rights, Johnson added. Citizens adopted the new constitution and abolished slavery, but Johnson's questionable recommendations, coupled with his practice of accepting remuneration for seeking the release of Confederate prisoners, made him appear a deceitful opportunist.

Johnson's fight against the seizure and punishment of citizens without a trial and his opposition to arbitrary military arrests brought him into additional conflict with Gen. Lew Wallace. In Somerset County, Maryland, a Democratic candidate had been elected by a majority of several hundred votes. General Wallace, however, ordered him not to take his seat because he had raised a Rebel flag on his property three years earlier. The candidate denied the charge but was nevertheless arrested and jailed. Friends appealed to President Lincoln, who telegraphed an order for the politician's release, but the man had already been sent south. In this case, Johnson supported Lincoln.[7]

The Senator was consistent in his adherence to the new Maryland constitution, abiding by the document in the face of severe criticism. He was not, however, hesitant in criticizing Lincoln for the President's failure to abide by the Constitution of the United States. Johnson was to face his adversaries again in the military courtroom.

The stage was set as the trial, now open to reporters, got underway on Saturday, May 13. After a court reporter read the short proceedings of the previous day, Holt stated that the names of defense counsel needed to be placed on record.

"Do I understand Mr. Johnson as appearing for any of these prisoners?" Holt inquired.

Reverdy Johnson, present for the first time, responded that he was not sure whether he could serve as counsel or not. He was very busy, he claimed, and not certain if he could stay as long as necessary. If, however, the court were to grant him permission to leave at any time, he might be able to serve.

Ignoring Johnson's appeal, Commission president Hunter interrupted, declaring gravely that he had a note from a member of the Court. He then read the paper, which raised objections to Johnson's serving as Mrs. Surratt's counsel because "he does not recognize the moral obligation of an oath that is designed as a test of loyalty."[8]

Senator Johnson appeared stunned by Hunter's remarks but not intimidated. He asked boldly if he might know which member objected. General Hunter responded sharply, "Yes, sir, it is General Harris, and if he had not made it, I should have made it myself."[9] Hunter then referred to the letter in which Johnson seemed to promote deception in regard to oath-taking.

These opening remarks previewed the clash of ideologies and hostilities that were to be unleashed during the trial. Jarring conflicts existed between military authority and civilian rights, between loyal Unionists and Confederates, and between Republicans and Democrats. Women's rights became a minor, but real, issue, and there were undertones of strain between Catholics and Protestants, even though the Government cautiously avoided the religious issue. All these tensions influenced the proceedings but did not alter the outcome of the trial.

This first clash developed between Union militarists, represented by the Commissioners, and the States' Righters, represented by a civilian, Reverdy Johnson. Neither side wasted time in drawing the battle lines. For the moment, the prosecution of the prisoners was laid aside.

The awesome phalanx of blue-uniformed generals did not intimidate the Senator. Johnson answered that he did not object to the question being raised. "The Court will decide if I am to be tried."

Hunter, warming to the challenge, ordered the courtroom cleared. Johnson objected, "I hope I shall be heard."

General Aiken, entering the fray, advised, "I think it can be decided without clearing the court." General Wallace moved that Johnson be heard. The motion carried.

A shrewd infighter, Reverdy Johnson wanted to know if the letter alluded to concerning the loyalty oath was in the courtroom so that it could be examined.

"I believe it is not," Hunter replied curtly.

Johnson declared that it would be difficult for him to speak on the subject without having the letter before him, because the Commissioners might twist his words. No member of the Court recognized "the obligation of an oath more absolutely than I do," he proclaimed. Growing more belligerent, Johnson challenged the generals, declaring that his life would stand up to the morality of any member of the Court. Because of his eminence, he could get by with this confrontation of the venerable military leaders. With the exception of counselor Thomas Ewing, Jr., he was the only person to stand up boldly to the military judges. After proudly relating his faithfulness to the Union, he majestically proclaimed:

> I have lived too long, gone through too many trials, rendered the country such services as my abilities enabled me, and the confidence of the people in whose midst I am has given me the opportunity, to tolerate for the moment — come from whom it may — such an aspersion upon my moral character. I am glad it is made now, when I have arrived at that period of life when it would be unfit to notice it any other way.[10]

Then, repeating his assertion that he recognized the obligation of oaths, Johnson launched an attack on the legality of the Maryland Constitutional Convention, stating almost verbatim his previous opinion that "there was no moral harm in taking an oath which the convention had no authority to impose." Growing bolder with each sentence, he affirmed, "I mean it as no reflection on any member of this Court when I say, that upon a question of that description, I feel myself at least as able to form a correct opinion as any of the gentlemen around the table."[11]

Then pointing to Mrs. Surratt, seated demurely veiled a few feet away, Johnson stated that he was in the courtroom at the invitation of that lady, whom he had never seen or heard of before. He declared that he knew nothing of the facts — only that Mrs. Surratt had told him she was innocent. Johnson indicated that he took the case because of his profession and, not losing the opportunity to take another jab at the generals, added that it was "not inferior to the noble profession" of which they were members. The Senator affirmed that he was defending Mrs. Surratt voluntarily and without pay, although he detested the fiendish plot that had brought about the death of his friend Lincoln as much as anyone on the Commission. He was not there "to protect anyone whom, when the evidence is offered, I shall deem to have been guilty, even her." This statement had significance in the light of Johnson's later attitude.

General Harris, distinguished and battle-scarred himself, was not impressed. He acknowledged that Senator Johnson had long been eminent for his service to the country, but the General strongly objected to the Senator's interpretation of the sanctity of oaths. Harris felt the Senator's explanation was unsatisfactory. He energetically pressed the point that Johnson had declared the oath to have been unconstitutional and illegal, with no binding effect.

Johnson shot back that he had said no such thing and that if Harris thought so, the General was "under a misapprehension." Generals were not accustomed to back talk; Senators, however, were not inclined to accept abuse either. The match was even. After more words passed between them, the president of the Commission intervened.

A Virginia-born physician, Gen. Thomas Harris had served heroically in the Union army before his appointment to the Military Commission (National Archives photo 1580-A, Brady Collection).

But Reverdy Johnson would not be silenced. He reiterated that he had not meant the oath was to be taken lightly. But even if that were the case, he asked,

> Who gives to [the] Court the jurisdiction to decide upon the moral character of the counsel who may appear before them? Who makes them arbiters of public morality or of my professional morality? What authority have they under their commission to rule me out or any other counsel out...?[12]

This was the real point, and, although it seemed to satisfy some Commissioners, it did not convince General Harris, who, controlling his anger, responded calmly. He intended nothing personal, he explained, but the case of the Maryland constitution was of more than little importance. Radical changes had been proposed so that the main purpose of the constitution was to blot out slavery. Harris declared that disloyal voters opposed the changes and he understood that Senator Johnson advised them to take the oath even though they did not mean it. As for judging the moral standing of the counsel, the Court had no right, the General admitted, but the order constituting the Court stated that all lawyers must exhibit a certificate showing that they had taken the loyalty oath, or they must take it in the presence of the Court. If the Senator felt the oath could be taken without any moral obligation to fulfill it, then, he defeated the purpose. Harris insisted that his concern was not to measure character, but simply to raise the question of the sanctity of oath-taking.

Johnson, not fully comprehending Harris' point, snapped that the Court had no authority to administer the oath to him. He boasted of having taken the oath in the United States Senate, in the circuit courts and in the United States Supreme Court. Johnson then declared "It would be a little singular if one who has a right to appear before the Supreme Court of the land, and who belongs to the body that creates courts-martial, shall not have the right to appear before courts-martial."[13]

The military officers could not miss the expression "who belongs to the body that creates courts-martial." It clearly reminded them that a civilian body, the Congress, created both courts-martial and generals.

General Hunter had heard enough. "The day has passed," he stated firmly, "when freemen from the North were to be bullied and insulted by the humbug chivalry of the South."[14]

The Court took a welcome recess for half an hour then went into secret session. When it resumed, General Harris withdrew his objection. All ended amicably, Harris declaring that Johnson's explanation removed any question in his mind. Johnson magnanimously agreed to take the oath, but the Commission decided it was unnecessary.

With the opening skirmish ending in a draw, the Commission called its first witness. John Lee, a military detective, testified that he broke open the door to search Atzerodt's room in the Kirkwood House. The prosecution exhibited numerous small articles wrapped in a coat, which the witness identified as items found in the room. They included an account book in the name of Mr. J. Wilkes Booth, a revolver and two bowie knives. On cross-examination Lee admitted that he had never seen Atzerodt, so far as he knew, and did not find the suspect's signature in the room. Lee's testimony was corroborated by a later witness, Robert Jones, the hotel desk clerk who identified Atzerodt as the man who had rented the room and who had signed the hotel register.[15]

The prosecution then called Louis J. Weichmann. As he entered the courtroom, he faced his former associates for the first time since their arrest. He took the witness stand a few feet from Atzerodt, who sat chained hand and foot. The last time he had seen Atzerodt was at Howard's livery stable a few hours before the assassination. He caught a glimpse of Lewis Payne, sitting erect, his wild eyes glaring at the spectators, and the boyish-looking Herold, whom he had known for two years, slouched in his chair, apparently indifferent to it all. Weichmann recognized the young farmer-physician, Sam Mudd, whom he had met once. Also on the prisoners' dock were several men whom he had never known—O'Laughlin, Arnold and Spangler. The motherly Mrs. Surratt was still separated from the other prisoners. As officers swore in Weichmann, the suspects must have realized that the words of this man could determine their future.

During the swearing-in process, Mrs. Surratt showed no emotion. She had been particularly kind to Weichmann, and he often accompanied her to church. As he testified, she sat only a few feet away, dressed in deep black. Her posture changed little during the proceedings. Members of the Court and spectators, who had hoped to get her reaction to the testimony through her facial expressions, were disappointed as her face remained hidden under her heavy black veil.

Before Weichmann's interrogation, very few knew the facts concerning Mrs. Surratt, their only information being a few uncomplimentary newspaper speculations. Those who had heard vaguely of the pleasant landlady were inclined to feel sorry for her. This attitude was to change.

XXVII
On Trial but Not in Chains

Judge Holt opened his lengthy inquisition asking Weichmann about his background. The witness stated that he was a clerk in the office of Col. William Hoffman in the Commissary General of Prisoners, a position he had held since January 8, 1864. He knew John Surratt as a fellow divinity student at St. Charles College. Both left school in 1862, but Surratt renewed their acquaintance in Washington in January 1863.[1]

His opening testimony raised a question which was never fully answered. Why had Surratt and Weichmann abandoned their divinity studies in 1862 — a crucial war year. The Government did not draft divinity students or otherwise force them into military service. The obvious explanation was they left school because of the war — an answer that needed further clarification, especially in Weichmann's case. He took a teaching position and Surratt returned home to southern Maryland to become a Confederate spy.

Holt continued, "When did you begin to board at the house of his mother, Mrs. Surratt, a prisoner here?"

Weichmann replied that he moved to the boardinghouse at 541 H Street on November 1, 1864.

"You speak of Mrs. Surratt, who is sitting near you there?"

"Yes, sir; she is the lady."

Holt shifted abruptly to questions about the doctor. "State when you first made the acquaintance of the prisoner, Dr. Samuel A. Mudd?"

Weichmann replied that he first met Dr. Mudd about January 15, 1865. He swore that as he was passing down 7th Street with John Surratt, someone called "Surratt, Surratt." This man proved to be an old acquaintance of Surratt's, Dr. Samuel Mudd of Charles County, Maryland.

Holt asked if the witness referred to the prisoner at the bar.

Weichmann, pointing to the doctor, answered, "Yes, sir; that is the gentleman there. Mr. Surratt introduced Dr. Mudd to me; and Dr. Mudd introduced Mr. Booth, who was in company with him, to both of us."[2]

In a few minutes Weichmann had touched on two of the accused. His testimony concerning Dr. Mudd was devastating — if true. The defendant's counsel was surely aware of the implications.

Mudd's defense rested on the plea that his treatment of Booth's leg had been merely an act of mercy performed on a man he had not recognized, having met him briefly only once before. If Weichmann's statement was true,

Mudd's alibi would collapse. Weichmann's words identified Mudd with John Surratt. Even more damaging, he pictured Dr. Mudd as actively bringing together the two principal conspirators early in the plotting.

According to the witness, after Mudd introduced the well-known actor, Booth took the group to his room at the National Hotel and furnished them with wine and cigars. Soon Booth and Mudd stepped out into the hallway and held a private conversation. After a while the doctor returned and asked Surratt to come out with them, leaving Weichmann alone in the room for about 20 minutes. When they returned, Mudd apologized, saying they had private business with Booth who wished to buy his farm. Weichmann stated that Booth then drew some lines on the back of an envelope and showed them to Surratt and Mudd.

Leaving this revealing account abruptly, the prosecution again centered on Mrs. Surratt. "You continued to board at Mrs. Surratt's?"

"I boarded there up to the time of the assassination."

"After this interview at the National, state whether Booth called frequently at Mrs. Surratt's?"

"Yes, sir."

"Whom did he call to see?"

"He generally called for John H. Surratt, and, in his absence, called for Mrs. Surratt."

Holt wanted to know if the meetings were held apart or in the presence of others. Weichmann answered, "Always apart, I have been in company with Booth in the parlor with Surratt, but Booth has taken Surratt to a room upstairs, and engage[d] in private conversation up there: he would say, 'John, can you spare me a word? Come upstairs': they would go and engage in private conversation, which would last two or three hours."

"Did the same thing occur with Mrs. Surratt?"

"Yes."[3]

Asked if he knew Atzerodt, Weichmann indicated that he did and pointed out the defendant among the prisoners. Atzerodt, he said, had visited Mrs. Surratt's house ten or fifteen times, always inquiring for John or his mother. He first came to the house about three weeks after Weichmann first met Booth. The ladies there nicknamed him "Port Tobacco" after the village he came from.

According to Weichmann, he and Surratt met Atzerodt on the corner of 7th Street and Pennsylvania Avenue at the time Booth was playing Pescara in *The Apostate*. Booth had given Surratt tickets to the play. On learning this, Atzerodt wanted to go with them. At the theater they met a fellow-boarder, John Holohan, and David Herold.

The officer asked if he recognized Herold among the prisoners. As Weichmann pointed to the prisoner, Herold nodded his head in recognition and giggled boyishly—the first show of emotion among the accused. Herold maintained a playful attitude throughout the trial.

Weichmann stated that after the play Atzerodt and Herold went their own way but that he and Surratt later ran into them again in a restaurant talking with Booth.

The line of questioning switched to horses. "Do you know where Surratt left his horses in this city?"

The witness replied that Booth kept two horses in Howard's stable on G Street between 6th and 7th streets. This was directly behind Mrs. Surratt's house. When asked if he had ever seen Atzerodt at the stable, he replied that he saw him there about 2:30 on the day of the assassination. Holt wanted to know what Atzerodt was doing. Weichmann explained that while he (Weichmann) was renting a horse and buggy for Mrs. Surratt he heard Atzerodt trying to hire a horse. The stable manager refused Atzerodt's request.

Holt questioned, "Was this horse that was kept there Surratt's or Booth's?" The witness responded that on the Tuesday before the assassination Mrs. Surratt wanted him to drive her into the country and sent him to see Booth at the National Hotel in order to get Booth's buggy. He then testified that "Booth said he had sold his buggy, but he would give me ten dollars, and I should hire a buggy for Mrs. Surratt, and spoke of the horses he kept at [Howard's] stables. I then said they were Surratt's; he said they 'were mine.'"

"Did Booth give you ten dollars?" asked the interrogator.

"Yes, sir."

"Did you drive her out?"

"Yes, sir."

Holt inquired about their destination, and the witness replied, "To Surrattsville; we left at ten and reached there at twelve; that was on Tuesday, the 11th."

When asked if they returned that same day, Weichmann said, "Yes, sir; we only remained half an hour; Mrs. Surratt said she went for the purpose of seeing Mr. Nothey, who owed her money."[4]

Weichmann related a few details of the trip, but the Government never fully probed the implications. How and why, for instance, did Weichmann take off work all day Tuesday to accompany Mrs. Surratt to the country? Getting a day off from a Government job during the war years was difficult.

Judge Advocate Holt went on to question the witness concerning the second trip to Surrattsville. "Will you state whether, on the following Friday, that is, the day of the assassination, you drove Mrs. Surratt to the country?"

"Yes, sir," said Weichmann. "We left about half-past two o'clock in the afternoon. She herself gave me the money on that occasion, — a ten-dollar note; and I paid six dollars for the buggy."

Asked where he drove her, the witness answered, "Surrattsville, arriving there about half-past four." Weichmann then explained that he went into the tavern kept by John Lloyd, Mrs. Surratt's tenant, while Mrs. Surratt went into the parlor.

"What time did you leave on your return?" inquired the Judge.

Weichmann revealed that he left about 6:30, explaining that the trip back to Washington took about two hours when the roads were good.[5]

In a real sense Weichmann was on trial, although not in chains. For nearly every answer there were several witnesses who could be called to test his veracity. At this time, he was held in Old Capitol. Weichmann realized his precarious position. If his testimony was proved false on any significant point, he would not only be discredited as a witness, but might spend the rest of his life in prison, or worse.

Weichmann's statement about the visit to Surrattsville only a few hours before the murder could be verified by a number of individuals—inhabitants of the boardinghouse, employees at Howard's stables, as well as several people at Surrattsville. Considering that many possible witnesses were closely associated with Mrs. Surratt, if not related to her, Weichmann might have expected them to dispute his chronicle. The defense counsel contended vigorously that the trips were in no way related to the assassination, but Weichmann had not intimated that they were. He simply stated what had happened, as he remembered it—and he remembered well.

The Government attempted to get some incriminating statement about all the accused on this first full day of public trial rather than focus on one. Accordingly, Judge Holt moved on to Lewis Payne. "Will you state whether you remember, some time in the month of March, of a man calling at Mrs. Surratt's where you were boarding, and giving himself the name of Wood, and inquiring for John H. Surratt?"

The witness testified that he opened the door for the man, who inquired for John Surratt. When told that John was not in, the man then asked to see Mrs. Surratt. "I accordingly introduced him" explained Weichmann, "having first asked his name. He gave the name of Wood."

Weichmann pointed to Lewis Payne when asked if he recognized Wood among the prisoners, thus identifying all of the accused he knew.[6] Weichmann had seemed cowardly to the conspirators, too weak to be included in their daring undertaking. He was not timorous, however, in testifying against them.

As Payne maintained his rigid posture and fierce stare, Weichmann calmly related the details of the suspect's visits. He had first come to the house on H Street about eight weeks before the assassination. Three weeks later he visited again, this time representing himself as a Baptist preacher.

When asked if anyone recognized him as having been there before under the name Wood, Weichmann responded that he did not recognize Payne until one of the girls called him Wood. The prosecution did not press this point, which implied that at least some of the women recognized Payne after having seen him only briefly three weeks earlier, even though he came in a different costume, presenting himself as a different person.

The interrogator wanted to know if the witness had observed any effort of Payne's to disguise himself. This question was designed to give Weichmann a chance to explain his own suspicious conduct, as well as to further implicate the prisoner. He explained that Payne shared his room while at the Surratt house and that one day he saw a false mustache on the table. He threw it into his own box and noticed that when Payne came in he looked around for the mustache. Weichmann admitted that he did not tell Payne he had hidden it among his own things. The officer forced Weichmann into making this confession because detectives had found the mustache in his trunk. Weichmann's action was questionable, and several defense lawyers caught it.

False mustaches were common disguises during the Civil War, especially for spies. Weichmann wanted to explain why he possessed one, even at the expense of appearing to be a thief. His explanation was weak. So weak, in fact, that it left the impression that he was not as innocent as he claimed. The defense later made the most of his vulnerability.

Weichmann, not deterred, however, continued to narrate Payne's suspicious activities. He testified that he once found John Surratt and Payne in a third story room playing with bowie knives, guns and spurs. A previous witness had identified a spur found in Atzerodt's room at the Kirkwood. Holt asked if it was one that Surratt and Payne had at the boardinghouse. Witnesses' identification of exhibits played a significant part in the trial, but it was often difficult and sometimes they made mistakes. Weichmann was usually cautious, but when questioned about the spur, he identified it unequivocally as one he had seen. However, when shown a bowie knife found in the same room of the Kirkwood, he hesitated. "I do not recognize that as the bowie knife. It was a smaller one."

"But you know the spur? You are satisfied as to that?" countered Holt.

"Yes, sir," replied Weichmann, "there were three spurs similar to this in a closet in my room when I was last there; and those three I am sure belonged to the eight that had been purchased by Surratt."[7]

Holt showed Weichmann a revolver, identified by the preceding witness as one detectives found in Atzerodt's room and asked if he had seen it before. Weichmann, a little slow to answer, said he thought so. The Judge Advocate, helping him avoid a mistake, asked if the barrel was round, or octangular. Taking the hint, Weichmann declared the barrel was octangular, although about the same size as the one on exhibit. Holt fed the witness questions related to Weichmann's previous revelations to detectives.

An episode which revealed the conspirators' cautious planning concerned the effort of John Surratt to obtain a room for Payne at the Herndon house. This boardinghouse, run by Mrs. Martha Murray, was in the general vicinity of Mrs. Surratt's. The conspirators, not wanting to draw excessive attention to Mrs. Surratt's house, although she had rooms available, made arrangements to have Payne stay at Mrs. Murray's.

When quizzed about it, Weichmann responded that Anna Ward had previously spoken to the landlady about engaging the room. Although she did not mention Payne's name in the transaction, the inquisitive Weichmann later found out from Atzerodt that the room had been secured for Payne.

The Government had already questioned both Murray and Ward but placed no charges against either. Detectives found no evidence against Martha Murray other than the natural tendency for Southern sympathizers to find lodging in the boardinghouses where they felt most welcome. With Anna Ward, the situation was different. She had been close to the Surratts for years and at least one of John's questionable letters to his mother had been sent through her. The Government knew these facts but decided not to arrest her.

When asked if he knew Arnold or O'Laughlin, Weichmann replied that he did not. He was then questioned about details relating to the Surratts.

"What knowledge have you, if any, of John H. Surratt having gone to Richmond?"

Weichmann recounted an adventurous story starting about the 17th of March, 1865, when a woman named Mrs. Slater came to the house and stayed there overnight. This lady then went on to Canada and returned. On Saturday, the 23rd of March, John Surratt drove her into the country about eight in the morning. He had hired a two-horse team at Howard's stables. "He left in the company with Mrs. Slater; and Mrs. Surratt was also in the buggy," according to the witness.[8]

Weichmann related what he vowed he had heard from Mrs. Surratt. According to this secondhand account, John, his mother and Sarah Antoinette Slater had driven to southern Maryland where Mrs. Slater was to have met Augustus Howell, who was to escort her back to Richmond. However, Howell had been captured by Federal troops. Because of these abrupt changes the Surratts accompanied her on to the Potomac where Mrs. Surratt parted company, while John continued on to Richmond with Mrs. Slater. He started back from the Confederate capital the day before Federal troops captured it.

Although the Military Commissioners were not aware of it, Holt had already seen Mrs. Surratt's denial of these events. When questioned in prison she had steadfastly defended her son, stating categorically that John could not have been engaged in any questionable activities against the Government, because he had never been away from home long enough. Later Holt was to use these discrepancies.

Weichmann's testimony definitely pictured Mrs. Surratt as a participant in her son's activities. Other witnesses related a similar account. It happened that on her way back from the Potomac, Mrs. Surratt had been seen by several persons.

Further questioning dealt with John Surratt's return from Richmond and subsequent trip to Canada. Holt finished his lengthy interrogation with two questions about Mrs. Surratt—both revealing. "Do you remember, early in the month of April of Mrs. Surratt's having sent for you, and asking you to give Mr. Booth notice that she wished to see him?"

After an affirmative response, Holt inquired about the nature of the message Mrs. Surratt wanted to communicate. "She merely stated that she would like to see him, and for him to come to the house," replied Weichmann.

"Did she state that she wished to see him on private business, or any expression of that kind?" quizzed the Judge.

Weichmann answered, "Yes, sir; she said, 'Private business.'"[9]

When Weichmann delivered the message, he found actor John McCullough in the room with Booth (a fact McCullough later denied). Booth agreed to go to Mrs. Surratt's that evening and did.

Some question arises as to why Mrs. Surratt felt free to use Weichmann as her errand boy. Actually, she did not use him when her son was around. At the time in question, April 2, John was not available; he was returning from Richmond. She must have felt that Weichmann, a pleasant, harmless person, was sympathetic to the Confederate cause.

Holt saved the most devastating question for last. Weichmann had already mentioned how he obligingly obtained the horse and buggy for Mrs. Surratt on the day of the murder. What the Judge had not brought out was that when Weichmann returned from the livery stable with the rented buggy, he found Booth in the parlor talking with her. In response to Holt's question about preparations for the trip, Weichmann told of Booth's untimely visit and then added that immediately after this, he (Weichmann) and Mrs. Surratt set out for Lloyd's tavern in Surrattsville.

Weichmann's testimony left the Court with an astounding picture of the assassin taking time, in the midst of his frantic preparations, to talk with Mary Surratt. This conversation took place several hours after Booth had learned that Lincoln would attend Ford's Theatre. It was less than eight hours before he would shoot the President – less than ten hours before he and Herold would stop at Mrs. Surratt's property in Surrattsville to pick up the guns, the field glasses and whiskey that Lloyd had ready for him.

Weichmann had finished the first part of his ordeal, and he was turned over to Reverdy Johnson for cross-examination. Throughout Weichmann's damaging testimony, Senator Johnson was sitting quietly a few feet away at the table designated for the defense counsel. Unlike the other lawyers, he had not had an opportunity to seriously study the case, and this was his first day in court. He had spoken briefly with Mrs. Surratt and knew her side of the story but was otherwise familiar with only the well-publicized events. His subsequent questioning of Weichmann, therefore, was as much for his own understanding as it was to impress the Court. In spite of his considerable ability, the brevity of his preparation put him at a disadvantage.

His cross-examination was extremely poor; with one exception, he failed to deal with critical issues. For the most part, he simply asked for a repetition of Weichmann's previous testimony. Johnson brought out no new facts, did not shake the witness's testimony on a single point, and, if anything, strengthened the case against his client.

He opened by asking the witness how long he had lived at Mrs. Surratt's. Weichmann patiently repeated his previous answer; he had boarded there since November 1, 1864.

Johnson asked about the size of Mrs. Surratt's house and if she rented rooms and provided board. Weichmann answered that the house had six large rooms and two small ones which Mrs. Surratt rented and that she furnished board.

The counselor then wanted to know about John Surratt's absences from home, especially his trips to Canada. This, too, had alredy been discussed, but Weichmann obligingly went into more detail, reciting that sometimes he was at home and sometimes not. He recalled that during the winter of 1864, especially in November, John Surratt spent most of the time in the country. "His stay at home has not been permanent at all, because he would sometimes remain at home half a week, and go into the country the other half; and sometimes he would be three or four weeks at a time in the country," he noted.[10]

Johnson continued to push the question of John's trips. Had he been away from home anytime during the winter of 1864–65 long enough to have gone to Canada and returned without Weichmann's knowing about it? Weichmann answered, "Yes, sir."

The question was curious, obviously motivated by conversation with his client. Mrs. Surratt's greatest concern was to protect her son. One of the few times she shed a tear was when it appeared that John was riding off on a harebrained scheme to kidnap the President. She seldom exhibited emotion for her hysterical daughter or for herself. The one time the widow mentioned her personal correspondence was when she told Weichmann she had received John's letter from Canada, dated April 12, 1865. Her most emotional encounter with interrogators involved her insistence that John was in Canada at the time of the murder. Yet the questioning by Johnson in no way proved that John Surratt was in Canada on the night of the assassination. It did indicate that Mrs. Surratt's contention that John had never been away from home long enough to have gone to Richmond was false. Perhaps Johnson wanted to satisfy himself about John's activities.

The cross-examination proceeded in a new direction when Johnson tried to link Weichmann with the conspirators. Was Weichmann on "intimate terms" with John Surratt, he asked. If he expected a denial or an indefinite answer, he was surprised.

"Very intimate indeed," affirmed the witness calmly. Throughout the trial Weichmann frankly claimed strong friendship with John Surratt. He generally praised the character of both John and his mother.

The lawyer relentlessly pushed his efforts to show that Weichmann must have known more about the plot than he was telling. "Were you in the habit of seeing John H. Surratt almost every day when he was at home, at his mother's?" he queried.

"Yes, sir," Weichmann answered politely. "He would be seated at the same table."

"Was he frequently in your room, and you in his?" persisted Johnson.

"He partook of the same room, shared my bed with me, slept with me," admitted Weichmann without hesitation.

"And during the whole of that period you never heard him intimate that it was his purpose, or that there was a purpose to assassinate the President?"

"Never, sir."[11]

Making no progress, Johnson shifted his interest to Mrs. Surratt's two trips to Surrattsville. He had come to a crucial point in Mary Surratt's defense. Weichmann had just answered questions about the trips, but Johnson went over them again to show that she had good reasons to make these visits. When asked the purpose of the first trip on Tuesday, April 11, Weichmann responded that Mrs. Surratt had said her business was to see a Mr. Nothey about $479 he owed her. The timid clerk added cleverly, "And the interest on it for thirteen years."

This last statement could not have escaped Johnson's attention nor did it elude the observation of the Military Commission. Mrs. Surratt's reason for the abrupt, urgent trip was to collect a debt about which she had done nothing for thirteen years. The money was to be collected because she needed to pay an equally long-standing debt of her own to Charles Calvert. Mrs. Surratt had, on other occasions, met her obligations by borrowing money on her boarding-house. She never attempted to explain why this old debt had to be settled immediately. Her seemingly sudden compulsion to collect the money involved inconveniencing her boarder, seeking a loan of a buggy from a famous friend, taking Weichmann off his job, making two time-consuming trips and ultimately spending nearly $20 in the unsuccessful effort. She might have waited for the return of her son to take care of such business, especially since John passed by Nothey's house nearly every week. Some of her contemporaries suggested that she would have saved money and time by simply handling these business affairs through the mail. To the Court, at least, it appeared she had more urgent business to transact in Surrattsville.

Reverdy Johnson did not bring up Mrs. Surratt's meeting with John Lloyd on her first trip and Weichmann did not mention it. He next quizzed Weichmann about the other trip. "Did she state to you what her purpose was in making the second visit?"

"She said, when she rapped at my room on that afternoon, that she had received a letter from Charles Calvert with regard to this money that was due her by Mr. Nothey," responded Weichmann.

Johnson wanted to know if it was the same debt. Weichmann said it was.

The lawyer inquired more about the letter, "Did you see it?"

Weichmann replied, "No."

After trying to satisfy himself about the nature of the letter and just exactly why Mrs. Surratt had to make the trip, Johnson questioned, "Did you take anything with you, any weapons of any sort?"

"No weapons," answered the witness. He explained that she took two packages. One consisted of some papers about her property and the other was a package about six inches across. He said the second package "looked to me like a saucer or two, two or three saucers, wrapped in paper. That was deposited in the bottom of the buggy and taken out by Mrs. Surratt when we arrived at Surrattsville."[12]

Weichmann's last answer was interesting in the light of subsequent events. He spoke only of an unidentified package. Apparently he was still unaware what it contained, although he did know that John Wilkes Booth had given it to Mrs. Surratt just before she left. John Lloyd had already revealed the package contained a pair of binoculars. When soldiers shot Booth, they recovered the binoculars from his body.

Weichmann tried to answer as favorably as possible about Mrs. Surratt without jeopardizing his own position. He said nothing about Booth having given her the package. Although Holt already knew what it contained and its source, Johnson was ignorant of the contents or how the landlady got it. Before the day was over he and the Court were to find out.

After a few repetitious questions about their return to Washington,

Johnson inquired, "Who came to the house between the period of your return and three o'clock on Saturday morning when the detectives came? Anybody?"

"There was someone that rang the bell; but who the person was I do not know," Weichmann responded.

The lawyer, apparently surprised, asked who answered the door. When told that Mrs. Surratt did, he wanted to know more about the visitor. "I heard steps going into the parlor, and immediately going out, and going down the steps," explained Weichmann.

This incident seemed to excite Johnson. "How long was that after you had got back from Surrattsville?"

"It must have been about ten minutes. I was taking supper at the time."

"That was before ten o'clock, was it not?"

"Yes sir; it was before ten o'clock."

"Before what is understood to have been the time of the assassination?"

"Yes, sir. The assassination is said to have taken place at half-past ten. It was before that time."[13]

Mrs. Surratt must have been disturbed to hear her lawyer bringing up the unidentified person who visited her shortly after her return and soon before the murder.

Johnson's next question also harmed Mrs. Surratt. He wanted to know if people were in the habit of going to her house for rooms and staying for a day or two. This gave Weichmann an opportunity to present more damaging testimony against his former landlady if he had wanted to hurt her. He knew, for instance, that Confederate agents stopped there. But in his answer he avoided any reference to these questionable guests. He answered simply that "Mrs. Surratt had a great many acquaintances, was always very hospitable," and that some persons "coming from the country" had a habit of staying with her.

Inquiring about Atzerodt's short stay at the boardinghouse, Johnson asked if there had been any drinking in Atzerodt's room. This question may have seemed irrelevant, but the lawyer had a purpose, even though it backfired.

When Mrs. Surratt made her several statements to detectives, she put undue emphasis on her refusal to allow Atzerodt to stay at her house because she found liquor bottles in his room. This gave the impression she was a proper landlady who, far from encouraging conspirators to congregate in her house, actually refused to allow one of them to remain there. Obviously Mary Surratt thought it an important point in her defense. She must certainly have discussed it with her lawyer, who was now trying to get from Weichmann an admission of its truth. Unfortunately, Weichmann did not know about the incident, neither did Anna, nor did anyone else.

When Johnson first asked about Atzerodt's drinking, Weichmann misunderstood the question and thought he was asking if Atzerodt had company in his room, and started talking about Atzerodt's entertaining a guest named Howell. The venerable old lawyer became aggravated. Every question he asked seemed to hurt his client; he was getting nowhere. He snapped at the witness, "What I asked was, whether there was any drinking in the room."

Weichmann responded apologetically, "Yes, sir," still not realizing the drift of the interrogation.

"Were they noisy at all?" questioned Johnson.

Weichmann said they were not. The lawyer pressed him about the motive for Atzerodt's leaving. Weichmann guessed it was because John Surratt arrived, "as near as I could judge. He said he wanted to see John, and, as soon as he saw John, he left."

Johnson, not satisfied, questioned why Atzerodt left. Still trying to cooperate, Weichmann mentioned that he heard "Miss Anna and Mrs. Surratt afterwards say, that they did not care about having him brought to the house."

Still pursuing the wrong course, Johnson asked why the Surratts didn't want Atzerodt in their house. Weichmann replied, "The way Miss Anna Surratt expressed it, she said she did not care about having such sticks brought to the house; that they were not company for her."[14]

These answers thwarted Johnson. He was accustomed to presenting his arguments before such august bodies as the United States Senate and the United States Supreme Court, but he got nowhere with Weichmann.

However, the veteran was not completely defeated; he came back with his most telling attack—questioning Weichmann about taking Payne's false mustache. "Why did you not give Payne his mustache?" asked the counsel. Weichmann responded weakly that he did not care to have false mustaches lying around his room. Johnson reasoned, "It would not have been about your room if you had given it to him, would it?"

"No, sir."

"That would have taken it out of your room; but, to keep it out of your room, you locked it up in a box, and kept the box with you?"[15]

Weichmann muttered unconvincingly, "Then, again, I thought no honest person had any reason to wear a false mustache." In all of his many hours of testimony Weichmann never gave a more ridiculous response.

Apparently satisfied with this exchange, Johnson allowed the military court to ponder Weichmann's position and changed his line of interrogation.

After a few relatively harmless questions about John Surratt and his mother, he ended his cross-examination in an effort to establish her religious devotion. Weichmann accommodated him; he described his former landlady in flattering terms. Her character was "exemplary and ladylike in every particular" and he "generally accompanied her to church every Sunday."

Her lawyer asked, "As far, then as you could judge, her conduct, in a religious and in a moral sense, was altogether exemplary?"

Weichmann agreed that his landlady attended mass at least every two weeks and was regular in attendance up to the assassination.[16]

What he did not mention was that her urgent trip to Surrattsville and the assassination of the President took place on Good Friday, a day not usually devoted to unnecessary business pursuits by the pious. Weichmann's eagerness to concur that Mrs. Surratt was faithful in her religious duties was hardly enough. Pious spies, religious blockade-runners and refined, ladylike saboteurs served well in Confederate secret operations. Johnson's defense did not greatly influence the Commission. Nevertheless, he seemed satisfied and turned the witness over to Thomas Ewing, Jr.

Weichmann's testimony had its greatest effect directly on Mrs. Surratt's case, but because of his incidental acquaintance with four other suspects, his statements also touched them. For this reason several lawyers subjected him to repeated cross-examination. If any counselor had discredited Weichmann's testimony, it would have damaged his credibility against all defendants.

Ewing had just one object — to destroy Weichmann's statement concerning the meeting of Dr. Mudd with Booth and John Surratt. He cross-examined aggressively.

Mudd had claimed the only time he had seen Booth, other than on the night of the assassination, was late in 1864 when Booth wanted to buy a farm (Mudd stated at one time that Booth wanted to buy a *horse*). The additional meeting mentioned by Weichmann was critical, but the exact date was of little consequence.

Ewing opened with a question concerning dates. "What time was it that you said Dr. Mudd introduced Booth to yourself and Surratt?"

The witness indicated it was about January 15. When asked if he had any way of fixing the date, he reasoned, "I could fix the exact date if reference could be had to the register of the Pennsylvania House, where Dr. Mudd had a room at that time."[17]

His mention of the Pennsylvania House was a skillful move. The witness challenged the defense to check it out. Since authorities held Weichmann in prison, he was not at liberty to examine the register. His answer was also a subtle reminder that it was ridiculous to ask him about the exact date when he admittedly gave only an approximate time. Also, if the counsel had genuine interest in the exact date rather than in a polemic sparring match, he could have easily verified it.

Ewing ignored the suggestion and continued to stalk his prey. The polite young witness did not back away from the challenge.

"Are you sure that it was before the 1st of February?"

"Yes, sir, I am sure."

"Are you sure it was after the 1st of January?"

"Yes, sir."

"Why are you sure?"

From a letter he received about January 16, explained Weichmann. Also he asserted the room that was occupied by Booth at the hotel had been previously occupied by a Congressman who had not returned from Christmas recess.[18]

By this time, Ewing must have realized that Weichmann was an observant witness, not easily tricked. But Ewing was a clever interrogator and a good lawyer, not quickly discouraged; he continued the confrontation over the exact date. "You are certain that it was after the Congressional holiday vacation?"

"Yes, sir."

The lawyer and witness then entered into a long and fruitless exchange over how he remembered the date. Weichmann insisted that he thought the date was after the Congressional Christmas recess but added, "I do not recollect that fact as distinctly as I do recollect the conversation about the purchase of the farm."[19]

The lawyer's interrogation was becoming absurd. Certainly he must have known that the exact date was relatively trivial. But Ewing's last question indicated that he was trying to equate Weichmann's confusion about dates with a possible confusion about what happened. Even though Weichmann's answers left no doubt about the approximate date, Ewing insisted that Weichmann indicate some personal "memorandum" by which he fixed the event. Weichmann suggested for the second time that there should be no problem about the date at all as it could "probably be fixed by reference to the register at the Pennsylvania House." Mudd, he reiterated, had a room in that hotel at the time. This seemed to satisfy Ewing, but there is no indication that the hotel register was ever checked.

Ewing finally changed the subject and eventually got around to the actual meeting between Mudd and Booth.

"You went directly to Booth's room?"

"Yes, sir."

"How long, in all, did you stay there?"

"That I cannot say exactly. I suppose the conversation must have lasted about three-quarters of an hour."

"You say that Dr. Mudd wrote something on a piece of paper?"

The 22-year-old clerk corrected the counselor, "I say that Booth took an envelope out of his pocket, and took a pencil; and he drew, as it were, lines on the back of this envelope."

Weichmann further clarified that while Booth was drawing, Surratt and Mudd were watching "and they were engaged in deep conversation, — private conversation: it was scarcely audible."[20]

Ewing, following Reverdy Johnson's lead, tried to prove that Weichmann must have heard some of the conversation.

"You were in the room at the time?"

"Yes, sir."

"How close were you to them?"

Pointing to Judge Holt, who was about eight feet away, Weichmann responded, "I was as close to them as that gentleman sitting at the far window is to me."

"What was the conversation about?"

"That I do not know."

"You said it was 'scarcely audible': was it not, in part, audible?"

"It was an indistinct murmur."

Apparently not believing the witness, Ewing asked again if he heard the conversation. Again Weichmann replied, "No, sir. I heard none of the conversation."

"Which one went out with Dr. Mudd first?"

"Booth."

"Are you sure?"

"Yes, sir."

"How long were they out together?"

"As near as I can judge, not more than five or eight minutes."

"Where did they go?"

"They went into a passage right along the room,—a dark passage,—a passage that leads to the front of the room there."

Dr. Mudd, sitting close by on the prisoners' dock, knew that his future depended upon Ewing's ability to find some inconsistency in the witness's statements. The lawyer tried his best; he belabored every little detail. How did Weichmann know that Mudd and Booth stopped in the passage outside the room, he questioned. Weichmann responded that he did not know for certain because they closed the door, but from their movements it seemed that they remained outside.

"What makes you think so?" queried the lawyer.

"Because I did not hear any retreating footsteps," replied the witness.

When asked if he listened to hear retreating footsteps, he answered, "Yes, sir. I listened. If they had gone downstairs, a person would have naturally supposed that a noise would have been made with their feet; and then, again, they did not take their hats."

By this time, both the prisoners and the defense counselors must have become aware that this witness was observant and not easily intimidated. Mrs. Surratt and Dr. Mudd, in particular, surely realized that they had underestimated the curiosity of the young man.

Thomas Ewing continued his interrogation without bringing out any significant fact or causing Weichmann to falter. The witness made no attempt to attack Dr. Mudd's character or even to associate him with the assassination. He stated positively that Dr. Mudd had never visited Mrs. Surratt's boarding-house and that the doctor, when talking about the war, "spoke like a Union man."

After an interval, Ewing got back to the subject of the controversial meeting. The lawyer wanted to know if Booth had been talking while he was drawing lines. Weichmann replied, "Yes, sir."

"And Mudd and Surratt were attending?"

"Yes, sir, they were all three sitting around the table; and they were looking at what Booth was marking with his pencil, and talking."

"Are you sure they were looking at what Booth was marking? Or were they simply attending to what Booth was saying, their eyes resting on the paper?"

Then the lawyer showed some agitation. "Did you observe it close enough to swear as to that?" This served to remind the witness that he was under oath—and under suspicion.

How could he be so sure of the direction in which Dr. Mudd's eyes were focusing after three months, Ewing inquired. Weichmann met the challenge with a flash of defiance: "They looked at the envelope, and they looked at the motions of the pencil, I could swear to that."

"Their eyes were on the envelope?"

"Yes, sir, their eyes were on the envelope."

"And Booth was talking at the same time?"

"Yes, sir."[21]

Apparently Ewing did not expect such definite responses, because his next question repeated one asked previously about how close Weichmann had been to Booth and Mudd. Although attorneys often asked Weichmann the same questions, he usually answered without showing annoyance. This time, he reminded his interrogator that he had already responded to the query. General Ewing ended his fruitless interrogation with a rather irrelevant question about the size of the hotel room and then turned the cross-examination over to Frederick Stone.

As attorney for both Herold and Mudd, Stone asked Weichmann about his first meeting with Herold two years earlier at Mrs. Surratt's country house and one visit Herold had made to her Washington house. In the course of his response, Weichmann indicated that Spangler, O'Laughlin, Arnold and Mudd never visited the Surratt boardinghouse; that Herold had been there only once and that Atzerodt visited often but only stayed a short time and that Booth never stayed overnight. This was subsequently corroborated. Stone's interrogation ended an amazing day in the courtroom.

The proceedings entered their second week as detectives continued to gather evidence, arrest and interrogate suspects. In Richmond, Government officials busily gathered up every document they could find. By the middle of May, papers of the Confederate archives filled 93 boxes. Judge Holt eagerly awaited their shipment, hoping to uncover strong evidence incriminating Rebel leaders. Even as soldiers cleaned up the Confederate capital, pockets of Rebel resisters in Texas vowed to continue fighting until Maximilian could come to their aid.

XXVIII
A Large Boot,
Slit Down the Side

Officials made a few changes in the courtroom before the session convened at ten o'clock on Monday morning, May 15. They moved the witness stand toward the center of the room to enable both Commissioners and reporters to hear better, but it did not help defense counselors. To ensure an accurate record, the Government employed the reporting corps of the United States Senate, under the direction of R. Sutton, to record the proceedings. The Murphy family, D. F., J. D. and E. V. Murphy, helped transcribe the events. The Judge Advocate General employed Benn Pitman, assisted by Robert Bonyinge, to make his own record and oversee the entire operation.

A Court official opened the proceedings by reading the testimony of the previous session, which lasted until 2:30 in the afternoon. Hearing the overwhelming evidence for the second time had a sobering effect on the defense counsel as well as on the prisoners. During the reading the suspects appeared listless, some even hopeless. Payne's wild glare even moderated at times. Mrs. Surratt and Dr. Mudd, however, maintained their steadfast, stoic composure.[1]

Edward Spangler, who, up to this point, had not secured a lawyer, was added to the clients represented by Ewing. Spangler, following the example of other suspects, asked through his counsel that his plea of "not guilty" be withdrawn in order that he might plead the jurisdiction of the Court. After the Court granted permission, Ewing again argued that the Military Court had no jurisdiction in the case. Holt overruled the contention. Ewing, following the pattern set by other lawyers, then asked that Spangler be granted a separate trial. The Judge perfunctorily denied the request.

O'Laughlin, represented by counsel for the first time, went through the same process with the same negative results. Consequently, both men reversed their pleas to "not guilty."

Hearing the interrogations repeated, the defense detected a weak point in Weichmann's testimony and requested further cross-examination. The Commission deliberated the point briefly, then acquiesced, but stated that in the future, rules would be established and observed governing cross-examination. The Court then called for a recess.

Weichmann had stated that while in the buggy with Mrs. Surratt on

Tuesday, he had not overheard her conversation with Lloyd. During the recess, Mrs. Surratt apparently reported to her counsel that Weichmann had heard it. The point, while not absolutely crucial, was important. On numerous occasions Weichmann seemed to have been involved in the conspirators' affairs. If the defense could prove that he had actually heard the conversation, he would be linked more closely to the plot. On the other hand, if Mrs. Surratt had something to hide, she would have deliberately spoken in such a way that Weichmann could not have understood her. In the cross-examination, it became evident that Mrs. Surratt had leaned out of the buggy to speak to Lloyd in such a manner that Weichmann might have heard sounds but could not have understood them. But Weichmann's explanation was somewhat contradicted by Lloyd's account of the incident.

Apparently Weichmann's testimony convinced Reverdy Johnson, because he never again took an active part in the proceedings. He had given up an important case in Pittsburgh to serve as Mrs. Surratt's lawyer, yet, after the first few days, he usually stayed away from the courtroom. Johnson's departure damaged her chances because it appeared he was acting on his promise not to represent anyone, not even Mrs. Surratt if the evidence should show that person guilty.

Although he gave up active defense of the lady, he never retreated from his attacks on the Military Court. As the most prominent defense lawyer, he had more to lose in his association with the accused. Johnson left Mrs. Surratt's defense to his two young, rather inept, assistants, John W. Clampitt and Frederick A. Aiken.

Aiken had worked as correspondent for the New York Times before he moved to Washington to become Secretary of the National Democratic Executive Committee. He later turned to criminal justice, but was relatively inexperienced when he took this case.

Clampitt, a young stump speaker for the Democratic party, was born in the District of Columbia. He had practiced law only a short time when he was called upon to defend Mrs. Surratt.

Several reporters noticed Johnson's apparent abandonment of his client. But his departure was even more obvious to fellow lawyers, some of whom, like Thomas Ewing, Sr., severely criticized him. The Boston Journal predicted correctly that Johnson would not assume Mary Surratt's defense, but would advise her counsel. The Boston Advertiser noted that Johnson did not appear at court on May 16 and that there was a rumor he had withdrawn from the case.[2]

It impaired Mary Surratt's defense, for without saying so in words, the lawyer indicated by his actions that he doubted her innocence. Mrs. Surratt's supporters spread rumors that Reverdy Johnson quit because his feelings were hurt over his argument with General Harris. No one who knew Johnson's character could have believed that the old warrior, toughened by the scars of hundreds of legal skirmishes, would quit because of a wounded ego. But as a man of some principle he was willing to defend anyone, regardless of the crime, only if he believed him or her to be innocent.

Atzerodt had stated before the trial that someone had been assigned to follow and kill General Grant. Some speculators began to link John Surratt with the task, but it was not certain that John was in Washington at the time. The only other member of the conspiracy who could have followed Grant was O'Laughlin or possibly Herold.

Testimony by David Stanton, son of the Secretary of War, seemed to point to O'Laughlin. Judge Holt asked the witness to "look upon the prisoner, O'Laughlin, and state to the Court whether you ever saw him before, and if so, when and where."

The witness declared that he had seen him.

"Which is he?" asked Holt.

"That is him; he sits there between two soldiers," came the response.

"State when and where you saw him."

Stanton replied, "The night before the assassination; at the house of the Secretary of War; I simply saw him there; he remained some moments till I requested him to go out."

The Judge asked about the conversation. Stanton responded that the stranger wanted to know where the Secretary of War was.

"Was General Grant there that night?" questioned Holt.

Young Stanton testified that General Grant was in the room and that the visitor left when asked to. When asked what time this occurred, the witness replied, "At ten thirty; there was a crowd there; and a band there serenading General Grant and the Secretary of War."[3]

Testimony strengthened the Government's case but was unexciting. Later in the day, the Court learned more of Booth's activities immediately before the murder. The Commission put Peter Flatterkelt on the witness stand and asked him if he knew J. Wilkes Booth.

"Yes."

"What is your business?"

"I keep a restaurant near Ford's Theatre."

"State whether or not you saw Booth in your restaurant on the evening of the 14th of April."

"Yes; he was there just about ten, or a little after that, that night."

Flatterkelt then explained the circumstances. "He just walked into the bar and called for some whiskey; I handed him the bottle of whiskey and a tumbler; I did not give him water at once, as is usual; he called for water, and I gave it to him; he put some money on the counter, and went right out."

The witness reiterated that his restaurant was next to Ford's Theatre and pointed out that he saw Booth leave the bar alone.

"How many minutes was it after he went out before you heard the report?" asked Holt.

"I did not hear the report of a pistol."

"How long before you heard the President was assassinated?"

"I think from eight to ten minutes, as near as I can come at it."[4]

The Court next called John M. Buckingham to the stand. Holt inquired, "In what business were you engaged during the month of April?"

"At night I was door-keeper at Ford's Theatre; during the day I was employed in the Navy Yard," replied the witness. He testified that he knew Booth and saw him around the theater. In response to a question about Booth's actions on the night of the murder, Buckingham recounted how Booth came into the theater about ten o'clock and walked out again. Two or three minutes later he returned and asked Buckingham what time it was. "I told him to step into the street and he could see," Buckingham stated.

The witness described how Booth "came out immediately and walked up the stairway leading to the dress circle; that was the last I saw of him until I saw him leap on the stage and run across the stage with a knife in his hand; he was uttering some sentence, but I could not hear what it was so far back."[5]

Capt. Theodore McGovern was sworn in to answer the prosecution's questions about Booth's entrance into the President's box. After admitting he knew Booth "by sight," McGovern told the Court that as he was seated in the narrow aisle leading toward the door of the President's box, a man passed by, causing him to push his chair back. The individual "stood leisurely taking a survey of the house." He then took a pack of visiting cards and, selecting one, handed it to a guard at the door to the President's box. Then in a moment or two, the witness said he saw Booth go "into the box and close the door of the lobby leading to the box."[6]

Maj. Henry Rathbone's testimony followed with a graphic account of his effort to stop the assassin. These statements had little to do with the individuals on trial, but they gave the Court a clearer understanding of the murder.

The Government determined to keep the accused from communicating and coordinating their stories. It was reasonably successful, but most defendants did talk freely with their lawyers, who could have planned a unified defense. Unfortunately, they chose to work independently.

As some newspapers printed trial testimony in full, it was widely accessible. The witnesses in prison were transported under guard in army vehicles to the Arsenal courtroom, which gave them opportunity to exchange a few furtive words. Sometimes, therefore, they were able to coordinate their testimonies.

Soon after Weichmann had testified, he and Lloyd were riding together to the Arsenal. Weichmann mentioned he had testified that he had not been able to hear Lloyd's conversation with Mrs. Surratt. Surprised, Lloyd replied that the conversation had not been conducted in a low voice. These two witnesses never made their stories agree, but they had opportunity to do so.

At the conclusion of the session on May 15, Holt suggested that the Court visit Ford's Theatre. He, therefore, requested the Commission to meet informally at the theater the next morning at 9:30. Accordingly, the members gathered there on Tuesday morning. An announcement of the intended visit appeared in the *Washington Chronicle*, causing a large crowd to assemble for a glimpse of the dignitaries.

The theater had been left exactly as it was on the night of the assassination,

Contemporary sketch of the rear of Ford's Theatre. Booth ran through the back door into this dark alley, grabbed the horse "Peanuts" was holding and galloped away.

except for the blue silk regimental flag of the Treasury Volunteers on which Booth's spur had caught and the rocking chair in which Lincoln sat. Someone had taken them. Relic hunters had scavenged the area for small removable articles. The seats and everything else in the theater were covered with dust.

The Court first investigated the alley behind the theater and the tavern to the south and then the third story over the tavern, formerly used as a sleeping room by John Ford and his brother Henry. They closely examined the door to Lincoln's box and the wall in the hallway where the brace had been placed. The Commissioners noticed that the notch where the brace was wedged had been previously covered with paper to conceal it.

They checked the doors at the back of the theater and spent time reenacting Booth's escape. Nothing had been moved on the stage since the tragedy. The officers observed the carpenter's bench in the alley behind the theater where "Peanuts" had snoozed while minding Booth's horse. Farther down the alley they examined the stable used by Booth. They looked at the property room and the carpenter shop, as well as the passageways under the stage and out to the orchestra.

Satisfied with its investigation, army ambulances carried the Court back to the Arsenal, escorted by a detachment of West Virginia Cavalry. The Commission had spent only a few hours at the theater and arrived at the courtroom in time for a long session.

General Kautz continued to correspond with his fiancée, but his responsibilities at the trial gradually demanded more time. Court sessions frequently lasted from 10:00 A.M. until 6:30 or 7:00 P.M. Kautz usually spent the evening hours with his military friends, especially Gen. Phil Sheridan. As a member of the Commission, however, he was gaining notoriety, and even received requests for his autograph. This attention helped ease the pain of his floundering romance.

As Court sessions became more interesting, Kautz's romantic relations also improved. His joy was dimmed, however, when the army transferred General Sheridan to Texas to deal with Kirby Smith, the last major Confederate holdout. Kautz started to correspond with another admirer, which further revived his romance with Miss Tod. She apologized for her indifferent attitude and all seemed right with the world. A few things were not entirely right. The General was disgusted that Bingham's constant objections slowed the trial proceedings.

Kautz and his fellow Commissioners felt free to discuss the trial with friends. They were not restrained by the isolation which governed civilian juries. The Commissioners read newspapers and kept up with public opinion. Some of Kautz's military friends expressed their dissatisfaction that the trial was military rather than civil. His mind was not entirely on the proceedings, however; he was busy working on a new book, which, along with "temptations of the city," vied for his attention.[7]

Payne's background remained a mystery, even to his lawyer. He had confided in Eckert but tried to extract a promise that the officer would not testify against him. The prisoner never gave Eckert significant information, but he did reveal some details not otherwise known. He mentioned a gambling house on Monument Square in Baltimore which was a rendezvous for the conspirators. One of the leaders was a physician who lived on Fayette Street near the Square. With this information, Eckert consulted the doctor for some imaginary ailment. When the physician went into another room to write a prescription, Eckert quickly pocketed the doctor's photograph from the mantle and took it back to Washington. Payne identified the man in the photograph as one of those involved. So far as is known the Government never pursued this lead.[8]

Another secret meeting place Payne revealed was on D Street in Washington. Eckert also visited this location and found a few papers, but, again, nothing that was used in the trial.

On May 16, several distinguished guests, including Maj. John Hay, Lincoln's secretary, and Bishop Matthew Simpson of the Methodist Church, visited the courtroom. Passes to the proceedings were so difficult to get that attendance became a status symbol.

The trial began, as usual, with prisoners shuffling and clanking into the courtroom, but this time there was a slight difference. Mrs. Surratt did not take her usual seat near the defense counsel's table, but on the platform with the other prisoners. The change indicated more than a mere rearrangement of seating; it clearly placed the widow with the other suspects. The absence of Sen. Reverdy Johnson was a silent reminder of her precarious situation. Even

A somewhat imaginary concept of the trial, showing the accused and the Military Commission, including the judges. It depicts the usual attractions—Mrs. Surratt hiding her face behind a fan and Payne sitting tall, staring at the Court.

the mannerisms of the dejected woman revealed her growing apprehension. Previously her movements seemed calculated to evoke pity, but on this morning, careful observers noted that her sorrowful expression appeared genuine.

The prosecution suggested the Court dispense with reading the previous testimony because the proceedings were being published daily and because the defense counsel was furnished with the official record. But the defense requested the proceedings be read each day. As a Court officer read the testimony, Mrs. Surratt rested her head on the rail in front of her. She seldom raised her head and then only to hold her forehead in her hands with her elbows on the rail.

One observer described Mrs. Surratt as "much downcast, her features showing unmistakable signs of mental wear and tear."[9] She dressed, as usual, in mourning black, her head covered with a black bonnet and her face hidden behind a veil. Some spectators thought they had seen her crying during the trial. They were probably mistaken, as Mary Surratt's face was hidden, and, furthermore, she did not cry in public.

Dr. Mudd, dressed in a black suit with a clean white shirt, paid more attention to the testimony than did the other prisoners.[10]

This morning the Commissioners turned instinctively toward Spangler. After examining the theater, they came to the conclusion that it would have been impossible for Booth to have shot the President, jumped onto the stage, recovered from the fall before more than a thousand spectators, crossed the cluttered stage, opened the back door, mounted his waiting horse and escaped without some prearranged help. They suspected Spangler of having provided that help. General Kautz observed that "an accomplice seemed absolutely necessary to enable Booth to accomplish his purpose." Knowing that his judges had just come from the theater, Spangler sat listlessly at the prisoners' dock and leaned back against the wall awaiting the day's hearings.

The stagehand did not have long to wait. The first witness called was a black youth, Joseph Burroughs, known around the theater as "Peanuts." He testified that less than an hour before the shooting, Spangler had given him Booth's horse to hold. Soon after Burroughs heard the pistol shot, he saw Booth limping out of the theater yelling, "Give me the horse." In his haste, Booth knocked the youth down and quickly galloped away. "Peanuts" also testified that Spangler had helped Harry Ford decorate the President's box earlier that afternoon and had been standing by the stage door as Booth escaped through it.[11]

William Browning, Andrew Johnson's secretary, swore that between four and five on the afternoon of the murder, a clerk at the Kirkwood House gave him a card from John Wilkes Booth which was intended for the Vice-President. Browning read the card for the court, "Don't wish to disturb you; are you at home? J. Wilkes Booth."[12] (Booth's obvious attempt to make sure of the whereabouts of the Vice-President was later used by Radical Republicans to implicate Johnson.)

Lt. Alexander Lovett was next sworn. Holt questioned him about his investigation of Dr. Mudd. The Judge asked what route Lovett had taken in pursuit of the murderer. The witness answered that he passed by Surrattsville and eventually came to the house of Dr. Mudd. When asked, the witness pointed out the doctor among the prisoners. "Did you stop there and make any inquiries?" quizzed Holt.

"I stopped there and made inquiries of his wife first. He was out," replied the Lieutenant.

When Holt wanted more details, the witness stated, "We first asked him whether there had been any strangers at the house; he said there had; at first he did not seem to care about giving us any satisfaction; . . . I asked him who the man was; he said he did not know, he was a stranger to him; he stated that they were both strangers. . . ."

In the continuing interrogation, Lovett revealed that Mudd had given him the impression that the men remained only a short time and left in the morning.[13]

Lovett described Mudd's house as being about thirty miles south of Washington, about one-fourth mile off the main road. He said that he and other officers remained at the house about an hour. When asked if Mudd continued to maintain that the men were strangers, Lovett replied, "Yes sir; that he knew nothing of them." According to Lovett, Mudd revealed that one of them called for a razor, soap and water to shave his mustache off. "I asked him if he had any other beard; he replied, 'Yes, a long pair of whiskers.'"

Holt inquired about how the men left. The army officer stated that Mudd "said one of them went away on crutches, and that he showed them a way across the swamp."

"Did he state what the wounded man had done with his horse?"

"He said the other one led his horse and that he had a pair of crutches made for him; I was entirely satisfied that these parties were Booth and Herold."

After Lovett testified that Mudd had told him the men were going to a place called Allen's Fresh, Holt returned to Booth's mustache. "Did he state for what purpose this man had shaved off his moustache?"

Lovett replied, "No; some of the other men along with me made the remark that this looked suspicious and Mr. Mudd then also said it looked suspicious."[14]

A point never raised was the disappearance of the rented horses on which Booth and Herold escaped. The Government had a reasonably good description of the animals. Booth and Herold admittedly arrived at Mudd's house mounted on two horses. Yet when they arrived at the Potomac, they were on foot. Defense counsel Walter Cox later claimed to know what happened to the horses, that he knew where a man named Frank Roby shot them.

Lovett's testimony concerning his first visit varied from later statements made by Joshua Lloyd and William Williams, both of whom testified that Mudd, at first, denied absolutely that anyone had come by his house.

Holt then asked Lovett if he made another visit to Mudd's house. The witness replied that he did, three days later, on Friday, April 21. When Dr. Mudd realized soldiers were going to search the house, he said something to his wife "and then brought down a boot and handed it to me; he said he had to cut it off in order to set the man's leg." The Lieutenant added that he turned down part of the boot and saw "J. Wilkes" written inside. He called Dr. Mudd's attention to the name, but the doctor vowed he had "not taken notice of that before."[15]

At this point the prosecution produced a large boot, slit down the front. The officers passed the boot around the table for each member to examine. On the inside near the top under the name of the maker they could clearly see "J. Wilkes."

Holt continued his questioning, "Did he at that time still insist that they were strangers to him?"

Receiving an affirmative reply, the Judge now approached a vital point. "Did he acknowledge at any subsequent period that he knew Booth?"

"Yes; he said subsequently that he was satisfied that it was Booth," responded Lovett. The witness explained to the Court that Mudd also reported that his wife claimed she saw the man's whiskers become "disconnected from his face."

"But," Holt interrupted, "he had stated to you distinctly before that he had not known this man?" Lovett acknowledged this was so.

Pressing forward, the Judge asked if, in any subsequent conversation, Dr. Mudd admitted that he had previously known Booth. "After I had arrested him and we had got on our horses and were going out, some of the men gave him Booth's photograph," replied the witness. Lovett then explained that Mudd acknowledged the picture looked a little like Booth "across the eyes." Shortly after this admission the doctor confessed he had previously met Booth in the fall.

Mudd told the army officer that "a man by the name of Johnson gave him an introduction to him."

Holt asked, "Did he state where he met Booth?"

The witness replied, "No; on being questioned by one of the other men he said he had rode with him in the country, looking up some land, and then he bought a horse."

Judge Holt then turned Lovett over to the defense for cross-examination. Mudd's counsel tried to show that his client had cooperated with the investigation, asking, "You say that Dr. Mudd gave you a description of these two persons?"

"Yes, sir; he gave me a partial description of them; he said that one was quite a young man, and the other had large thin whiskers," responded Lovett.

Mudd's lawyer, still stressing the doctor's cooperative spirit, inquired, "What did he say to you as to the resemblance between the photograph and its original?"

This time the officer's answer did not help. "In the first place he said that it had not looked like Booth; then he said it looked like him across the eyes."

Ewing's cross-examination began to indicate that Mudd had given his defense counsel a different story. "Did not Dr. Mudd then tell you, that since you were there before, the boot had been found in the room?"

"Not until after we were in the house some time."

"He then volunteered the statement?"

"Yes, he said something to his wife, and she went upstairs and brought it down."

"But did he not make the statement voluntarily?" the lawyer insisted.

"He did after one of the men told him that we would have to search the house," corrected Lovett.

"Are you sure he did not make the statement until after that was said?"

"I am."

Dropping the question about the boot, Mudd's attorney asked, "He said that he had shown those men the way across the swamp?"

"So I understood him."[16]

The defense counsel's effort to prove Mudd's helpfulness was unconvincing. Ewing brought up a few unimportant questions about the swamp and about Mudd's description of Booth and then, still trying to prove Mudd's cooperation, asked, "When you asked the Doctor how long those two men had stayed, he said they did not stay long?"

"At our first interview he told me they stayed but a short time, and afterwards his wife told me that they stayed until three or four o'clock, on Saturday afternoon," responded the witness. Ewing, frustrated, cut him short, "You need not state to the Court what his wife said."

"Well, I think he told me that himself, afterwards," admitted Lovett.

The lawyer changed the subject to questions about whether Mudd charged Booth for his medical services. The answers were inconclusive.

Ewing's cross-examination was ineffective thus far. He could not find a significant error in Lovett's account, and he could not refute the fact that Mudd had been misleading. He asked Lovett if others were present during the interrogation. The lieutenant named three soldiers who later took the witness stand.

The attorney continued, "When you were at Dr. Mudd's the second time do you not recollect that he told you the two men started from his house to go to the Reverend Mister Wilmer's?"

"Yes, sir," responded Lovett, adding, "but I paid no attention to that; I thought it was a blind for the purpose of throwing us off the track."

"But he said that?"

"Yes, sir, he stated that they inquired for Parson Wilmer's, and that they said they were on their way to Allen's Fresh."

The topic shifted again with Ewing asking "Are you sure it was not out of doors that you first asked Dr. Mudd for the razor?" Lovett admitted that it might have been outside, but he remembered having made the demand in the house.

But to Ewing, the real issue centered on the boot. He inquired again, "Are you sure that it was not before he got to the house he told you the boot had been found since you were there before?"

"He told me that in the house, not outside," the officer responded sharply.[17]

Frederick Stone wanted to question the Lieutenant. "When you went to Dr. Mudd the first time did you have any conversation with him before you went into the house?"

"I think not: I had a conversation with his wife."

Stone, also stressing Dr. Mudd's effort to cooperate, questioned, "As soon as you asked him whether two strangers had been there, he told you at once they had?"

Lovett answered, "Yes, sir," but he explained further that the doctor "was made aware of the nature of our errand, I suppose by a friend; he seemed very much excited and turned very pale when he was first asked about the two strangers, though he admitted they had been there."

The lawyer reminded the witness that Mudd admitted he had been introduced to Booth at church by a man named Johnson. But the Lieutenant insisted that at first Dr. Mudd had denied that he knew Booth at all.

"You say that Dr. Mudd seemed to be very much alarmed?" Stone continued.

"Yes, he turned very pale in the face and blue about the lips like a man who was frightened at the recollection of something he had done."[18]

Judge Holt, wanting to clarify Lovett's account, again interrogated, "You state that Dr. Mudd appeared very much frightened; did you address any threat to him?"

The army officer explained that he wore citizen's clothes at the time. Holt observed that Mudd's alarm was not in consequence of anything that the soldier had done or said. Lovett agreed and described the encounter in more detail. "He seemed very much concerned when I turned the boot inside out; some of the men present said that the name of Booth had been scratched out...."

Holt, wanting the Court to envision two men coming to the doctor's house after midnight heavily armed, continued, "You have stated that when you asked Dr. Mudd whether the two strangers had any arms, he replied that the one with the broken leg had a brace of revolvers: did he say anything about the other having a carbine or a knife?"

"No, sir."

"Did you understand him to say that this brace of revolvers was all of the arms the stranger had?"[19]

Ewing objected on grounds that it was a leading question. Judge Holt accepted the objection and rephrased his approach. "Will you state what was his manner? Was it frank or evasive?"

Lovett described Mudd as "very evasive." Just what the doctor reported in regard to arms carried by the strangers remained uncertain. Holt moved to another point. "I understand you to say that Dr. Mudd stated that he did not hear the news of the assassination of the President until Sunday morning, at church. At the time of this statement to you did he mention the name of the assassin?"

"No, sir."

The importance of the time that Dr. Mudd admitted he had first heard of the assassination became clear to his defense.

Again Ewing took over the interrogation, apparently to clarify this issue. "Did not Dr. Mudd, at your first interview, state that he heard the details of the assassination while at church, on Sunday Morning?" The witness stated that he did not think so. Lovett said he thought Mudd must have known of the assassination earlier "because the cavalry were all along the road, and everybody in the neighborhood knew it on Saturday."

Changing course, but still picturing Mudd as trying to be helpful, Ewing asked if the doctor had not told the officers that the strangers were going in the direction of Allen's Fresh in order to find the Rev. Dr. Wilmer's house. Again, Lovett told the Court that Mudd said the men inquired for Mr. Wilmer and that he took them across the swamp. Lovett continued, "I went to Mr. Wilmer's, and searched his house, but I was satisfied we would find nothing there, as I looked upon it as a blind to draw us off that way."

At this time, of course, neither the Government nor the defense actually knew which route Booth had taken. Only years later was it clear how much Dr. Mudd's statement hampered the search.

"In going from Dr. Mudd's to Mr. Wilmer's would you cross the swamp?" continued Ewing.

"Yes, sir, you can go that way."

"Did you follow the track of this man Booth and his companion?"

"Yes, sir, as far as I could."[20]

Several Commissioners sensed the weakness of Mudd's assertion that he did not know about the murder until Sunday morning, and they questioned Lovett more. His testimony revealed that everybody in the area knew on Saturday that Booth was the assassin. He further stated that if any person had valuable information, they could have found soldiers on any public road.

The Court called Joshua Lloyd, a soldier who accompanied Lovett to Mudd's house, to the witness stand. After being sworn in, he testified that when he first asked Dr. Mudd if he had seen any persons resembling the assassins pass that way, he said no. Lloyd stated that in his second interview Mudd changed his story, acknowledging that two men had stopped at his house. A Court officer then handed a photograph to the witness which Lloyd identified as the one he had shown Dr. Mudd. The soldier testified that on the second visit to Mudd's residence, both the doctor and his wife appeared very excited and worried. During the cross-examination, the witness again emphasized that Mudd at first denied having seen the supposed assassins.

Col. H. H. Wells, Provost Marshal of defenses south of Washington, took the stand. Having been responsible for the exhausting investigation, he appeared tired and worn. He had since requested to be retired from his position, but because of the trial his superiors refused.

The Judge asked the Colonel to chronicle his interviews with Dr. Mudd. He recounted his three different interrogations of the prisoner, the first occurring on Friday, April 21, a week after the murder, but before Booth's capture. Wells had ordered the doctor brought to his headquarters for questioning. According to Wells, the suspect repeated a long story about two men coming to his house. This time, however, Dr. Mudd added an extraordinary detail—he admitted that he made a trip to Bryantown to get a buggy for the strangers. Mudd also revealed, for the first time, that he had begun to have suspicions about the men in his house during breakfast, because he was not sure if one of their beards was real or false.

Under Ewing's cross-examination, Wells informed the Court that Mudd "did not seem willing to answer a direct question," and that unless Mudd was asked about a particular fact, he did not volunteer anything. Ewing asked, "You said that at the last interview he was much alarmed from some statement you made?"

"I said to him that he was concealing the facts," responded the officer, and that "I did not know whether he understood that was the strongest evidence that could be produced of his guilt at that time, and might endanger his safety."

The defense pried, "When was it that Mudd took you along the route which these two men took?" According to the witness, it occurred Sunday morning.

Ewing then inquired about soldiers' efforts to pursue the strangers. Wells described his attempt to follow their tracks. "They took the direct road, coming out by the doctor's house . . . the marsh was full of holes and bad places." He said he thought the men got lost because "they went from right to left, and kept changing on that way till they lost the general direction."[21]

Ewing tried to prove that Mudd had told of the suspicious men on the Saturday or Sunday after the murder. He asked if the doctor did not mention the men. The witness readily agreed that he did. But when the attorney sought to establish that Mudd informed authorities on Saturday evening or Sunday morning, Colonel Wells said he thought it was later.[22]

Ewing seemed to believe that his client had given some information to the Government earlier than Tuesday, April 18. Wells testified that Mudd finally stated that he had talked to his relative, Dr. George Mudd, about the visitors. "Did he not say to you in some one of your interviews that he told you that on Sunday?" questioned Ewing. The Colonel said his impression was that he mentioned them to Dr. (George) Mudd on Monday. Wells swore that he had warned Dr. Mudd, "One of the stongest circumstances against you is that you have failed to give us the fullest information of this matter." After that Dr. Samuel Mudd revealed he had mentioned the two strangers to Dr. George Mudd.[23]

That Sam Mudd told his cousin George Mudd about the men seemed vital to the counsel, but the Government contended that the facts were debatable. One fact not debatable was that Mudd had withheld crucial information from authorities at the time they were searching desperately for Booth. Ewing, seeking to demonstrate that the doctor may have been afraid, asked, "Was there not intense excitement in the town among the soldiers and the people?"

"Not among the soldiers," answered Wells. "They were calm enough; but among the people there was; they were going and coming all the time."

"In a state of angry and excited feeling?"

"There was no angry feeling exhibited, but there was an excited state of feeling evident."

The defense contended the soldiers must have been angry and excited, but the Colonel, admitting there may have been excitement, denied the troops were angry.

At this point Judge Holt broke in. "State at what time Dr. Mudd professed to have recognized Booth as the man he had been introduced to?" Wells responded that Sam Mudd admitted he recognized Booth while the suspicious men remained in his house.

Holt approached an extremely vital point. For Mudd to admit that he recognized Booth while still in his house and then go to Bryantown where he heard that Booth assassinated the President and still guide the fugitive to temporary safety could send the doctor to the gallows. Ewing, aware of this serious admission, requested the witness to quote Mudd's exact words when soldiers showed him Booth's picture. In the answer and further interrogation, it became clear that Mudd had recognized Booth while still in his house. But this did not satisfy Ewing. Again he insisted that Mudd had recognized Booth only after the men had left. And again Wells testified that it was before Booth left. "He gave it as a reason why he didn't remember him at the first, that the man was much worn and debilitated," stated the Colonel, adding that Mudd said the man made an effort to keep the lower part of his face disguised, but when he came to reflect he remembered it was the man he had been introduced to.

No other witness mentioned that Booth wore any disguise or sought to conceal his identity. Soldiers found no disguise on Booth's body nor did anyone produce the false beard, claiming it belonged to Booth.

Ewing wanted to know if the disguise was discontinued at anytime in Mudd's house. Wells said, "No, but the light of the day, the shaving of the face, the fact that he sometimes slept and at others was awake, gave him opportunities to recognize the man." When asked if Mudd ever denied that anyone had been in his house, Wells answered, "He certainly did not deny it to me."[24]

With this exchange, the Court adjourned to reconvene at ten o'clock the next day.

When Judge Holt recognized the significance of Dr. Mudd's visit to Bryantown, he ordered Colonel Baker to send two detectives to find witnesses to verify the trip. Baker reported back that the detectives had conducted a thorough search for witnesses but had not found any, adding that any further search would be useless. Ignoring Baker's suggestion, Holt persisted and eventually located witnesses, whom he used later.[25]

The convincing testimony of May 16 seriously implicated Dr. Mudd. The Government had still others lined up to corroborate Lovett's account.

There was nothing subtle about the Government's presentation. Stanton and Holt felt they had irrefutable evidence. The Judges brought in witnesses with little regard for order, except that they did seek to prove the complicity of Mrs. Surratt and Dr. Mudd early in the trial.

XXIX
"We Are the Assassins
of the President"

Before Court opened to the public on May 17, the Commissioners listened again to secret testimony of Von Steinacker. He related convincing stories of Booth's plots on behalf of the Confederacy, but his accusations were kept from the public.[1]

After the closed session, guards brought in and seated the prisoners. Arnold entered first. He had the most desirable spot, next to the window. Dr. Mudd, in addition to his customary gentlemanly dress, wore a white handkerchief around his neck to protect his throat. Upon entering, Mrs. Surratt talked for a moment with Aiken, then buried her head in her hands and closed her eyes. She sat on the southern corner of the prisoners' platform, separated from the others by the door to the cell area. On the few occasions when she raised her head, she would turn toward the wall, away from the witness stand. In contrast to Payne, she seldom scrutinized the audience. Mrs. Surratt seemed to suffer from the heat and sometimes fanned herself with a newspaper.

During the exhausting reading of the preceding testimony, the prisoners conversed frequently with their counselors. These sporadic discussions provided opportunity for suspects to refute the evidence or add to it. As several hours each day were spent this way, the accused had ample opportunity to consider the evidence and discuss the testimony. At one point, the Court suspended the reading briefly to allow Herold to leave.

The Hon. Ben Wade of Ohio and Judge Watts of New Mexico visited the courtroom this morning. Payne particularly fascinated the few women spectators. "Did you ever see such a perfect type of cutthroat?" one was heard to say. Another commented, "What a monster he is, to be sure."[2]

The prosecution continued its investigation of Dr. Mudd by calling as its first witness William Williams, one of three soldiers in Lieutenant Lovett's detachment. Williams, who had not heard the previous testimony, pictured Mudd as even more reluctant to aid in apprehending Booth. He swore that when he first asked if any strangers had come by the house, the doctor replied no. Even after repeated questions, Mudd continued to deny that he had seen anyone. "He denied altogether that there had been any strangers there, you say?" queried the prosecution.

"Yes," answered Williams.

After a few questions about who said what, the Judge again brought up the time Mudd had said he first heard of the assassination. Williams testified that it was at church Sunday morning. He also described Mudd as being uneasy and not willing to give any information without being asked specifically.

Williams told of the second visit to Mudd's when the doctor admitted that two men had visited his house, but he denied they were Booth and Herold. Williams continued, "I informed Mrs. Mudd that we would have to search the house, and then she said that one of the men had left a boot upstairs in bed and she went and brought the boot." He described the object as a long riding boot "with the New York maker's name and the name of J. Wilkes written inside; the boot was cut about two inches up from the instep."

The Judge asked, "Was Mrs. Mudd in the parlor when she made this declaration about the boot?"

"She was standing at the door."

"Where was Dr. Mudd?"

"He was in the parlor."

"Could he hear what Mrs. Mudd said?"

"I judge he could, he was no further than where you are sitting there."

Holt asked if she was the first person to mention anything about boots. (The trial transcript has "Booth" instead of "boots," which is inappropriate in this context.)

"Yes," said Williams, "I told her we should be compelled to search the house, and then she said that the men had left the boot there, and went up and brought it down."[3]

Both Stone and Ewing surely realized the importance of the time and manner in which the boot was revealed. They also noted a little discrepancy in the stories of Williams and Lovett. These variations were natural when four soldiers were interrogating two different suspects at the same time, but the defense wanted the situation clarified. "You were all together in one room?" asked the defense lawyer.

"Yes, sir."

"Did you or Lieutenant Lovett ask him about two strangers who had been at his home any time previous?"

"We both asked him."

"Which asked him first?"

"I don't remember."

When asked if Dr. Mudd gave the same reply to both soldiers, Williams said he thought so. But the lawyer wanted a more definite answer.

"His reply to me, on Tuesday, was that they had not been there; I think it was the same he said to Lieutenant Lovett," responded the witness.

"Do you remember on the Friday of the examination who asked him first?"

"I think it was Lovett."

"Do you remember whether he asked about two strangers, or about Booth and Herold?"

"About strangers, I think."

The next witness summoned, Simon Gavacan, supported the previous testimony and also strongly implicated Dr. Mudd.

In his cross-examination, Ewing questioned the soldier vigorously. As a rule, Generals on the Commission were able to frighten low-ranking soldiers in their interrogations, but the defense also used intimidation. General Ewing had the same advantage. The noncommissioned soldier on the witness stand was naturally conscious of his subordinate position. General Ewing, seeming to emphasize rank, asked the private who was in charge of the search party. Gavacan answered that Lieutenant Lovett was in charge of the cavalry detachment but that they went out under the orders of Major O'Beirne. Further attempts by General Ewing failed to confuse the witness as to the chain of command, so he got back to the boot, asking, "Did not Dr. Mudd himself bring the boot down to you?"

"No, sir, his wife brought it down," the soldier replied confidently.

"Who was it given to?"

"The one nearest the door."

"Did you, in point of fact, make a search of the house?"

"We did not go upstairs, when we found the boot and razor we considered it satisfactory evidence that Booth and Herold had been in the house."[4]

Having established a strong case against Dr. Mudd, the Government called Mrs. Emma Offutt, John Lloyd's sister-in-law, as a witness in its case against Mrs. Surratt. After being sworn in, and getting past the preliminaries, Holt questioned her about a meeting between Lloyd and Mrs. Surratt.

Mrs. Offutt said they met on a road "somewhere near Uniontown." Holt inquired about the conversation between Lloyd and the suspect, which the witness admitted hearing only in part. The Judge then asked, "Under what circumstances did the conversation take place?"

Mrs. Offutt told the Court, "Our carriages passed each other before we recognized who it was, and Mr. Lloyd went to her carriage, and they had a conversation which took place at her carriage, and not at ours."

The subject turned to Mrs. Surratt's trip on the day of the murder. Holt asked, "Were you at Mr. Lloyd's again on Friday, the 14th of April?" Mrs. Offutt said she was and, in subsequent testimony, told of seeing Mrs. Surratt conversing with John Lloyd. According to the witness the conversation took place privately in the yard.[5]

Under cross-examination by Aiken, Mrs. Offutt stuck by her story that she heard nothing and had no idea of what was going on. Aiken then inquired if she had heard Mrs. Surratt say anything about "shooting irons," to which Judge Advocate Bingham objected. The objection was sustained.

The Court turned its consideration to David Herold. The Government called William Jett, the Confederate soldier involved in Herold's capture. "Look at the prisoners and see if you recognize any or all of them," instructed the Judge.

"Only one of them, sir."

"Which one?"

"Herold."

"State when you first saw him."

Jett explained that since October 25, 1864, he had been in Maryland as a Confederate agent but that he had been wounded and was on his way home. He had gotten as far as Port Conway, where he saw a wagon on the wharf. After digressing a bit, Jett described Herold's request to be taken south. According to Jett, Herold identified himself and his crippled companion as the "assassins of the President." Jett then called to his Confederate friend Lieutenant Ruggles who was watering his horse nearby and another soldier named Bainbridge. About this time Booth came up, and Herold introduced him. Jett noticed that Booth's hand was marked with J.W.B. The men left together with Booth riding on Ruggles' horse. Booth announced that he wanted to go under the name Boyd. Jett told of being rejected once before the Garretts permitted Booth to spend the night. Herold accompanied the others on to Bowling Green and left the next morning.

When cross-examined by Stone, Jett stated that Herold wanted to go further south, but they had no facilities to help him. Under continued cross-examination, Jett testified that Booth was not present when Herold first bragged about being the assassins of the President. When Booth found out what Herold had confessed, he became agitated, saying he didn't want that revealed.[6]

Aiken took over and asked Jett if he had ever taken the oath of allegiance, to which he replied, "No, sir; but I am perfectly willing to do so."

The prosecution then called Lt. Col. E.G. Conger. Questioned by Holt, Conger related the story of Booth's capture and death at Garrett's house. "You left before he died?" asked Holt.

"No; I stayed there some ten minutes; after the doctor who was there said he was dead."

"You have seen the dead body since?"

"Yes."[7]

Then Conger slipped through one of the most controversial points of the trial. Court officials showed the witness and the Court a knife, cartridge box, pistols, pocket compass and carbine. Conger identified these as objects in Booth's possession when he died. One item not exhibited was Booth's diary, which Holt knew about, but did not mention. The defense failed to ask if these were all of the objects taken from Booth's body.

When LaFayette Baker later referred to the diary before a Congressional Committee, the War Department was blamed for having kept it secret. The so-called diary was not actually kept secret; several publications mentioned it freely as one proof that the man killed was Booth. Newspaper accounts referred to the diary as having been among Booth's effects. The day after Conger's testimony the *Boston Advertiser* noted that Conger did not refer to "the diary which had been so often mentioned in print."[8] Herold, of course, knew of the diary and could have brought it to his lawyer's attention, if he thought it had value to the defense.

Perhaps it should have been exhibited in court, but it did not contain startling revelations which could have altered the final verdict. Numerous documents, not exhibited at the trial, would have had a greater impact. The most important, perhaps, was John Surratt's letter from Canada which, although frequently cited, was never produced. The confession Booth left with his friend Matthews and the letter Booth left with his brother-in-law were never presented as evidence. Some documents were lost, destroyed, or hidden, but the diary, while not permissible as evidence, was not a secret.

Holt hastened to the next question. Pointing to the rifle, found with Booth, he asked, "Is that what is called a Spencer rifle?" Lieutenant Colonel Conger answered, "Yes" and described the weapon, as well as the pistols, as being loaded when brought to Secretary Stanton's office.

An officer then showed the witness a spur and a file which he was requested to identify. He recognized the file, saying, "That file was taken out of Booth's pocket; the spur is like the one he had on, but I could not identify it as the same spur."

He also identified a bill of exchange as found on Booth's dead body. Holt continued, "Do you recognize the prisoner Herold as one you took out of the barn?" Again Conger replied, "Yes." In further questioning, the witness revealed that soldiers discovered on Herold "a little piece of map of the State of Virginia, including a part of Chesapeake Bay." A portion of a map was shown to the witness, who identified it as the only property Herold had with him.

Stone, cross-examining Conger, asked if Herold had any arms. He answered, "No." Under further questioning Conger revealed that while the fugitives were still in the burning barn, he heard Booth speak harshly to Herold and call him a coward.

Each prisoner was naturally more attentive when his name came up in the testimony, but most made efforts not to react visibly. Herold was an exception, responding childishly to any testimony involving himself. When Conger stated that Booth called Herold a coward, the prisoner smiled sneeringly and twisted uncomfortably in his seat.

Stone continued his cross-examination. "How long were you at the barn?" Conger replied that it was about 2:00 A.M. when soldiers got to the barn. "Booth was shot and carried on the grass about fifteen minutes past three, so that we must have remained there about an hour and a quarter," he calculated.

"Was he carried almost immediately onto the grass after he was shot?" inquired Stone. The army officer responded, "Yes."

Stone, seeking to put his client in the best light, asked Conger if he did not hear Booth say that Herold was not to blame. The witness responded that he did not remember the exact words but added "I will tell you as near as I can what it was; he said, 'Here is a man who wants to come out,' and I think he added, 'who had nothing to do with it'; that is as near as I can remember what he said; after that Herold came out."[9] Herold showed a sense of relief when he heard the witness repeat Booth's words exonerating him.[10]

The Court took its customary short recess at 1:30. Guards escorted prisoners back to their cells to eat while the Judges, Military Commissioners, and their friends had a lunch prepared for them, as usual, in a lower room of the Arsenal.

Sergeant Boston Corbett, an unstable zealot, claimed he shot Booth. His assertion has been disputed for more than a century (National Archives photo 3475-A, Brady Collection).

After the break, the prosecution called Boston Corbett, credited with shooting Booth, to the stand. Corbett, a 33-year-old soldier, was a strange character. Born in London, he was brought to the United States when he was seven. His family moved constantly. While living in Boston, he joined the Methodist church. At his baptism he took the name of the city of his conversion. Corbett had been captured during the war and sent to the infamous Andersonville prison. He was later freed in a prisoner exchange. Of the fourteen Union prisoners sent to Andersonville with Corbett, only he and one other remained alive, and Corbett was near death at the time of his release.

He developed a reputation as a religious fanatic, when in fact he was mentally unstable. Corbett, constantly in the guardhouse, was forced to carry a knapsack full of bricks as punishment. But even in these circumstances he

kept a New Testament in his hands. At a dress parade, when Colonel But-
terfield cursed the regiment for some mistake, Corbett stepped out of ranks and
censored the colonel for his profanity. Guards promptly arrested him. On
another occasion, while on picket duty, Corbett figured his enlistment time
was up at midnight and advised his superiors that he would leave at that time;
he did. He was subsequently court-martialed and sentenced to be shot. Officers
reduced his sentence, however, and dismissed him from the regiment. Even his
supposed shooting of Booth was against orders.[11]

As Corbett mounted the witness stand he caused a sensation. He was
decked out in full uniform with high boots and wearing the pistol with which
he claimed to have shot Booth.

The prosecution had urged Corbett to make a short statement, but having
memorized a lengthy speech, he delivered a dramatic account of his part in
Booth's death. Undoubtedly Corbett knew of the large rewards offered for apprehension of the assassin.

According to the witness, Booth yelled out of the barn that there was "a
man in here who wants to surrender," and "I declare before my Maker this man
is innocent of any crime whatever." The actor could have made such a
proclamation. Like Mrs. Surratt, Booth frequently called on God to sustain
his declarations. The conspirators often swore to the innocence of their collaborators, in efforts to cheat justice, or perhaps to make amends for having
involved others in their downfall. He recited for the Court:

> I kept my eye on him steadily; he turned towards the other side; he brought
> his piece to an aim, and I supposed was going to fight his way out; I thought
> the time had come, and I took a steady aim upon him and shot him; the ball
> entered his head a little back of the ear and came out a little higher on the
> other side of the head....[12]

The Commissioners received his story with amusement, but obvious
disbelief. In spite of evidence to the contrary, Corbett was credited with having
shot Booth.

Physicians found that Booth had been shot by a pistol. Conger said he
heard a pistol shot. Yet Corbett carried only a rifle. Booth, when found dying,
had a pistol in his hand. Conger was convinced Booth committed suicide,
which is almost certainly the case.

After Holt finished with Corbett, Stone cross-examined him. "You say
that you judged from the conversation between Booth and Herold in the barn
that Booth was anxious to surrender?" he questioned. Corbett confirmed that
he thought so. In a verbal exchange with Stone the witness made an appeal
on his own behalf, "I also wish to state, with the permission of the Court, as
improper motives have been attributed to me, that I offered twice to Lieutenant
Colonel Conger and Lieutenant Baker to go into the barn and take these
men." The witness, growing more energetic, stated that it was less dangerous
to go into the burning barn than stand "before the crack exposed to his
fire."

Even at this early time, there was a question of who should get the credit
and the reward money for Booth's death. Corbett seemed to be making his

The Navy Yard Bridge. Herold and Booth fled across this structure about 11:00 P.M., April 14. Metro Police were delayed in chasing them for lack of horses, which the army controlled (Library of Congress—B8184-40466-2A).

claim clear to the Court. He concluded his colorful testimony declaring, "I did not fire the ball from fear, but because I was under the impression at the time that he had started to the door to fight his way through and that I thought he would do harm to our men if I did not."[13]

Authorities next called John Fletcher, foreman of Naylor's Livery Stable. Witnesses often involved several suspects in their testimony. This one not only told of Atzerodt's activities, but also of his own frantic search for Herold.

Fletcher gave a detailed account of his pursuit of Herold through Washington and out to the Navy Yard Bridge. He related how the guard at the bridge told him of allowing two men to pass over into Maryland, one of whom matched Fletcher's description of Herold. Since the guard would not allow him to cross the bridge and return the same night, Fletcher went back to Washington. At about one in the morning, he heard of Lincoln's assassination. He told of going to General Augur's headquarters and of informing the General of his pursuit of Herold and of the two men who had crossed the bridge under suspicious circumstances. He said nothing about Augur's failure to follow up on this early lead. Fletcher also mentioned that he recognized a saddle and bridle in Augur's office.

Soldiers brought into the courtroom a saddle and bridle. The witness identified them as ones he had seen at the General's office. The prosecution then asked more about Atzerodt. "Did he call at 10 o'clock precisely?"

"Yes."

"Did he speak about anything wonderful that night?"

"He said if this thing happened I would hear of a present."

After Fletcher testified, the Commission requested that he go to headquarters' stables on 17th and Eye streets to examine the one-eyed horse picked up on the night of the murder. Later that day, Fletcher returned and was questioned about the horse. He confirmed it was the horse Atzerodt rode. Stone's cross-examination failed to shake Fletcher's testimony and, if anything, made Herold's part in the plot more certain.

One of the most important witnesses could not speak—the large, dark-brown, one-eyed horse. If this horse could have communicated, he could have solved much of the crime by himself. The animal was found, straying near Camp Barry, three-fourths of a mile east of the Capitol, by Lt. John Toffey about 12:30 A.M. the morning Lincoln died. Toffey delivered the horse, which seemed to be lame, to General Augur.

At this point, Judge Holt and John F. Coyle, one of the editors of the *National Intelligencer* and a close friend of Booth's, got involved in a rare exchange. Since boyhood, Coyle had known both John Wilkes and his father. The document that Booth entrusted to John Matthews was to have been delivered to Coyle for publication.

Coyle's interest in the proceedings prompted him to get permission to visit the Court. Almost as soon as he sat down, Colonel Burnett recognized him and called him to the witness stand. Coyle declared years later that he had not been summoned to Court as a witness and that the whole incident surprised him.[14] After the usual questions about where he lived and worked, Judge Holt asked if he had received a letter from Booth. Coyle replied that he had not. Holt then requested the witness to state if he had been acquainted with J. Wilkes Booth. To this Coyle responded casually that he had known him. Holt became more specific. "Did you know him intimately?"

"Not at all,'" Coyle lied.

Holt then read from a small leather-bound book, stating that, on the night of the assassination, Booth had written a long letter justifying the drastic action he was about to take and left it with one of the editors of the *National Intelligencer*. Holt interrogated the witness the second time about receiving Booth's letter. Coyle again vowed that he had never heard of any such document. Holt, not satisfied, pressed the witness further, "Are you quite certain that no such paper was ever received at the office?" For the third time, Coyle swore that he knew nothing about Booth's letter.

Surprisingly, this unusual dialogue went unnoticed by the defense counsel as well as by most reporters. The small leather-bound book from which Holt read was Booth's outdated diary. Few newspaper accounts mentioned the event at all. One of those that did reported merely that Holt declared that Booth had made a statement about a letter before he died, but the paper reported nothing about the diary.[15]

Later, in talking with Matthews, Coyle heard about the document. Although he was never a suspect in the investigation, Coyle had clearly been on friendly terms with Booth, Matthews and others involved in the conspiracy.

Hezekiah Metz, a farmer living in Montgomery County, about 22 miles north of Washington, took the stand. He testified that Atzerodt ate at his house on Sunday after the murder. His words added little of importance except for his casual mention that the conspirator talked about a man who was to have killed Grant. Ordinarily, officers gave little credence to this type of rumor, but Metz was testifying under oath about a matter not affecting him personally. The remark surprised the Court as well as the defense. Doster, seeking to protect the absent John Surratt, quickly cross-examined Metz. "Was anybody else present and talking with you when he made the remark about somebody following General Grant?"

"Yes, sir," responded the witness, "there were a couple of young men; we were all in the room together; I was about three yards from Atzerodt when he made the remark."

"Was not this the answer—that a man must have followed General Grant to kill him?"

"No, sir, it was not spoken in that way; it was, that if the man who was to have followed him had done so, General Grant would have been killed."[16]

Even though the Court paid little attention to the statement, it is almost certain that one of the conspirators was to have killed Grant. The designated killer was never identified. At first glance it seems that only O'Laughlin or John Surratt could have been given this assignment, but there is a real possibility that the pusillanimous Herold might have been designated. Booth wrote in his diary soon after the murder about someone failing in his assignment. If Booth had not seen the newspapers when he wrote this, he must have referred to Herold, as he was the only conspirator Booth could have known about.

The next witness, a young man named Thomas L. Gardiner, interrogated by Holt, was asked, "Have you any knowledge of the horse having been sold by your father, and if so, to whom?" Gardiner corrected the Judge, "He was sold by my uncle, George Gardiner, to a man by the name of Booth."

Under Holt's questioning the witness stated that the sale took place the latter part of November. He revealed that his uncle lived just over a quarter of a mile from Mudd's house and that Booth came to buy the horse with Dr. Samuel Mudd. "Describe the horse," Holt asked

"He is a dark bay horse, and is blind in the right eye."

A member of the Commission broke in, "Were you at your uncle's when Booth and Mudd came to buy the horse?" Gardiner said he was. He told the Court that although Dr. Mudd and John Wilkes Booth left together, he did not think the doctor had any part in the purchase.

Stone cross-examined him, "Where did Booth take the horse?"

"At his request I took the horse, next morning, to Montgomery's stable in Bryantown," stated Gardiner. Under further questioning the witness declared that Booth said he wanted the horse for a buggy to use traveling over lower Maryland to look for land.[17]

The young Gardiner, under Stone's continued cross-examination, testified that Booth had been in the neighborhood on other occasions before that.

During the winter of 1864-65 when the conspiracy was taking shape, Booth owned several horses, including the one-eyed horse, which he moved from stable to stable in the city in order not to attract attention. On the night of the murder, however, Booth and Herold escaped on rented horses; Payne rode the one-eyed horse.

Andrew Kallenbach, Mrs. Surratt's neighbor in Surrattsville, was brought in to testify. According to Kallenbach, Zadock Jenkins had seen an officer come to subpoena him (Kallenbach) as a witness. When Jenkins found out that Kallenbach was to testify at the trial, he threatened to kill anyone who might speak against him or anyone in his family—meaning his sister, Mary Surratt. Jenkins vowed that anyone testifying against him should swear strongly enough to have him hanged, because if he, Jenkins, were to be set free, he would kill the witness.

After a few statements by John Toffey, the Government ended another revealing day. After the first few sessions, the public had a reasonably clear picture of the conspiracy and its leaders. By May 17, a reporter for the *Boston Advertiser* had already picked out the four who would eventually hang.

A month after the murder, the Nation's attention still focused on events associated with the crime. French diplomat de Chambrun was surprised that the Government allowed cross-examination of witnesses by the defense. "Great liberty is permitted lawyers for the defense. They interrogate the witnesses quite as they please." The Frenchman could not understand all the dialogue, but followed well enough to realize that some lawyers "brought forth unexpected answers which were disastrous to their clients...."[18]

De Chambrun's greatest concern was not the trial, but Emperor Maximilian's activities in Mexico and the United States' response. From the French point of view, Texas had "recently been detached from Mexico." Maximilian, in his constitutional decree, had omitted any mention of the northern border of Mexico. At the same time, Confederate diehards vowed to continue their fight in Texas and join forces with Maximilian. This worried the French statesman, who felt that the United States would not permit Texas to return to Mexico. At that moment General Sheridan was on his way to Texas to stamp out lingering Rebel resistance and make sure that Texas remained in the Union.

Throughout the investigation, incidents occurred which remain unexplained. Some seemingly suspicious reports were false leads, others were unrelated to the conspiracy, but a few seemed relevant.

One such event occurred in New Haven, Connecticut. There a man, arrested for stealing money from a hotel, offered to return not only the stolen money, but also to give his captors a gold watch to set him free. On being released, he left behind a carpetbag which he wanted sent to a Mr. Myers. Authorities turned the carpetbag over to police, who, upon examining it, found a photograph on the back of which was written, "Meet me in Washington on the 10th, J. W. Booth." Experts inspected the signature and found it genuine. Another suspicious paper discovered in the carpetbag was a pass signed by General Sheridan's Adjutant General to permit a Mr. Lemos to pass through military lines and return. Detectives decided that Lemos should be questioned but could not locate him. Although he was known in the community, several weeks of searching failed to turn up any trace of the man.

The first documents found in Confederate archives began arriving at the War Department. Examination of the papers failed to link Confederate leaders with the conspiracy.

The defense counsel began to worry about their pay. Dr. Mudd had agreed to pay General Ewing. Sen. Reverdy Johnson had announced that he would donate his services, but other prisoners had difficulty securing money. Interested individuals in Baltimore, recognizing the problem, raised funds for attorneys' fees. This was not enough to pay the bills, however, and the question of money continued to plague the lawyers.

Excitement over the coming Grand Review began to compete with interest in the trial. By the middle of May, all the hotels were booked. Thousands of military officers had already crowded into the city, but enlisted men, unless they had special permission, were not allowed to visit the Nation's capital.

XXX
Confessions, Blockade-Runners and Secret Ciphers

On May 18, when Court sat, the heat was so intense that the door leading to the prisoners' cells was left open to permit ventilation. An armed guard stood by the doorway. The proceedings, published on the front pages of newspapers throughout the country, brought out multitudes. They packed the courtroom and both spectators and witnesses, including several ladies, filled the adjoining rooms. Little Tad Lincoln sat among the visitors.[1] About twenty reporters crowded into the room, eager for a firsthand account.

Some prisoners began to show the effects of stress, particularly O'Laughlin and Mrs. Surratt who sat next to each other, separated only by the doorway. As the day progressed, the heat became even more oppressive. A guard had to provide water in a large metal dish for the suspects. Mary Surratt alternated between burying her head in her hands with her elbows on the wooden rail, and fanning herself. Herold showed his disdain by propping his slippered feet on the railing. He appeared dirtier each day and acted more childish. Some observers thought he was trying to impress the Court that he was a half-wit and thereby escape punishment.[2] The other prisoners seemed listless, except for Payne, who maintained his usual rigid, monolithic position, staring at the Court, "towering like an Egyptian pyramid," as one visitor observed. O'Laughlin seemed utterly despondent. A surprising condition, considering that he and Spangler had the least evidence against them.

The mild-mannered Dr. Mudd, with his blue eyes, thinning sandy hair and high forehead, continued to appear out of place among the rough-looking suspects. The young doctor sought daily to give the impression that he should not even be on trial. One spectator noted that Mudd seemed to view the whole trial proceedings "with the air of a man who felt sure of himself."[3]

The accused, except O'Laughlin and Mrs. Surratt, indulged freely in laughter, which occasionally broke the tension. The simple, expressive testimony of former slaves especially amused the prisoners.

The trial was hard on guards, who stood for more than three hours during the reading of the previous testimony and even longer during the interrogations. When the proceedings were lengthy, they were relieved periodically.

Holt directed the calling of witnesses, conducted the principal interrogations and generally managed the proceedings. He guided the trial admirably, try-

Members of the Court: J.A.G. Joseph Holt, Gen. Robert S. Foster (Commissioner), Asst. J.A. H. L. Burnett, Col. C. R. Clendenin (Commissioner) (Library of Congress–BH831-1324).

ing to be impartial, and moving the testimony along, not allowing examinations to get sidetracked. Several newspapers criticized the military aspect of the Court but praised the Judge for his fairness. Even the *New York World* noted that Holt worked hard as Judge. Gullibility, however, marred his otherwise competent leadership.

Reporters began to notice the numerous celebrities involved. The *Tribune* observed that the trial involved three Presidents: one killed – Lincoln, one accused of the conspiracy – Davis, and one marked for death – Johnson.[4] The paper could not have known that Grant, who was also a target, would be a future President, and that Gen. Winfield Hancock would be a presidential candidate. The trial, however, involved many other notables – Cabinet members, military heroes from both sides, Senators and those who in the future would become famous authors and governors.

Reporters also observed Reverdy Johnson's continued absence. Pro-Southern papers seemed particularly disturbed. The *New York World* complained that he was missing and the *Detroit Free Press* stated, with apprehension, that "Reverdy Johnson takes but a little part in the trial."[5] Some claimed he had deserted Mrs. Surratt. Her other defense counsel, however, continued as though nothing had happened and tried to minimize the effect of his absence. Perhaps in an effort to prove reporters wrong, Johnson appeared in the courtroom on May 18, but did little and never returned.

The testimony of Louis Weichmann constituted the strongest evidence against the conspirators. Enough proof existed without Weichmann to convict several prisoners, but his testimony tied it all together. He avoided some subjects, however. He never mentioned John Surratt as having been in Washington on the day of the murder, and he clearly shielded Anna Surratt. Apparently he knew nothing about Arnold, Spangler or O'Laughlin and made no effort to involve them.

Some observers wondered how Weichmann could have seen so much and suspected so little. One spectator thought Weichmann must have been a Government agent, planted among the conspirators, but his subsequent treatment by the Government made it evident that this was not so. Officers kept Weichmann constantly under guard when he appeared as a witness. And while waiting to testify, soldiers surrounded him. These precautions served primarily to protect his life, not to prevent his escape. The defense soon realized, that to save their clients, they would have to destroy his credibility.

On the 18th they had their opportunity. After the reading of the previous day's record, A. R. Reeve, a New York telegraph operator, testified concerning a message sent to Weichmann by Booth, asking him to contact John Surratt. Weichmann then took the stand for several more hours. As the young man stood before the Court this time, he seemed unsure of himself and was noticeably nervous as the cross-examination began. As the interrogation progressed, however, he gained confidence.

Holt started the examination by asking him to explain the telegram alluded to by Reeve. Weichmann admitted he had received the message and that he passed the information on to Surratt, who refused to enlighten him about its content. Weichmann stated that he sometimes picked up letters at the post office for John Surratt addressed to "James Sturdy."

Guided by Holt, he testified about the attempt to capture Lincoln on his way to the Soldiers' Home. One day after work, he asked a Negro servant in the boardinghouse where John Surratt was. The servant replied that "Massa John had ridden out about two o'clock in the afternoon, with six others, on horseback." Later when Weichmann went down for dinner, he found Mrs. Surratt weeping. She said, "John is gone away; go down to dinner, and make the best of your dinner if you can." After eating, while Weichmann was reading, John Surratt came in excitedly. In fact, Weichmann testified, he "rushed into the room. He had a revolver in his hand,—one of Sharpe's revolvers, a four-barreled revolver, a small one; you could carry it in your vest-pocket,—and he appeared to be very much excited." Weichmann asked what was the matter. Surratt replied, "I will shoot anyone that comes into this room; my prospect is gone, my hopes are blighted; I want something to do; can you get me a clerkship?"[6]

Weichmann recounted how about ten minutes later Payne also rushed into the room, pistol in hand. Fifteen minutes after that, Booth entered, holding a whip. All were talking excitedly. Finally, when Booth noticed Weichmann's presence, the other three went upstairs to a back room where they stayed for about thirty minutes. Then they left the house together.

Although not brought out in the trial, the investigation had discovered details of the original kidnap conspiracy. The conspirators planned to transport Lincoln and other Government leaders to Richmond by using a relay of fresh horses stationed along the way. If this scheme failed they had an alternate plan ready. It included hiding Lincoln in the old Van Ness mansion on 17th Street, near the confluence of Tiber Creek and the Potomac.

This mysterious two-and-a-half-story brick mansion was built by Gen. John Peter Van Ness about 1820. A high brick wall surrounded the house, situated on a large, secluded lot. Known as one of the finest homes in Washington, it was famous for the lavish entertainment that took place within its walls. A cellar, dug under the house, could be entered through a trap door in the floor. The area had been used variously as a wine cellar, an ice house and a slave prison. Apparently the conspirators intended to hide Lincoln in this cellar. When General Van Ness died in 1847, the wealthy Thomas Green bought the house. Green, a dedicated Southerner, had two sons serving in the Confederate army. The Government kept the residence under surveillance during the war years and raided it several times. Following the assassination, soldiers searched the mansion and arrested its occupants when they found incriminating letters.[7]

After Holt's examination failed to bring out any shocking revelations, the defense bombarded Weichmann. Aiken cross-examined him about Mrs. Surratt's meeting with Lloyd at Uniontown. Weichmann stated again that he had not understood the conversation. Reverdy Johnson asked one insignificant question and left the rest of the cross-examination to Ewing. Ewing's questions about Booth's performance in *The Apostate* and the dates of the conspirators' activities were also unproductive.

Aiken renewed his attack. "How did you learn anything with reference to the antecedents of Mrs. Slater?"

"Through Mrs. Surratt herself," Weichmann replied. Under further interrogation the witness testified that Mrs. Surratt told him that Mrs. Slater came to the boardinghouse with "this man Howell." Aiken quizzed, "Are you certain beyond all doubt that Mrs. Surratt ever told you that Mrs. Slater was a blockade-runner?"

"Yes, sir," he maintained without hesitation.

"Had you before that time ever seen Mrs. Slater at the home of Mrs. Surratt?" continued the lawyer.

"I myself saw her only once; I learned she had been to the house twice," Weichmann responded. Aggravated at his inability to break the witness, Aiken snarled, "Never mind what you learned; you saw her only once."

"Only once," Weichmann obligingly responded.

After a few questions the young lawyer wanted to know if Weichmann had any personal conversation with Mrs. Slater. Trying to set the stage for the few words he had with the suspicious woman, Weichmann answered, "She drove up to the door in a buggy, the bell rang, and Mrs. Surratt told me to go out and take her trunk; there was a young man in the buggy with her; that was all the conversation I had with her."[8] He added that she had her "mask down, one of those short masks that ladies wear." Unable to understand the term "mask," one of the generals asked Weichmann to explain what he meant. He replied that he was trying to indicate a heavy veil.

Following a few inquiries about the time of this incident, Aiken asked exactly what Mrs. Surratt said in regard to Mrs. Slater. The witness answered, "She said that this woman was from North Carolina, and that if she got North, there would be no danger for her because, being French, she could immediately apply to the French Consul: that was about the only language I can remember."[9]

The inexperienced lawyer had hurt Mary Surratt's defense. He turned the interrogation over to Doster, who referred again to Weichmann's previous testimony about John Surratt's part in the early kidnap attempt. "You remarked that Mrs. Surratt was weeping bitterly; did she state the cause of her grief?" he inquired.

"She merely said go down and make the best you can of your dinner; that John had gone away: John, when he returned, said to me that he had on three pairs of drawers; I thought from that that he was going to take a long ride," responded Weichmann.

Doster, unable to dent the testimony, gave up and allowed Aiken to try a third time. Implying that Weichmann must be a tool of the Government, he asked, "By whom were you called upon to give your testimony in this case?" The witness said he was called by the War Department, specifically by Judge Burnett.

Aiken then got to an often disputed point. "Were you arrested?" Weichmann testified that he voluntarily surrendered to Superintendent Richards on the morning after the murder. He added that he told the police chief that he "knew of these men, Payne, Herold and Booth, visiting Mrs. Surratt's; I stated also what I knew of John Surratt."

Weichmann paid no attention to the hard stares the prisoners directed at him, and the interrogation continued without a pause.

"What was your object in doing this?"

"My object was to assist the Government."

"Were any threats ever made to you by any officer of the Government, if you did not give this information?"

"Not at all."

"Were any inducements held out to you by any officer of the Government?"

"Not at all."

At this point the witness tried to explain why he seemed so eager to turn on his previous friends, testifying that he had seen in the morning papers a description of the man who attacked Secretary Seward. "He was described as a man who wore a long grey coat," stated Weichmann. "I had seen Atzerodt wearing a long grey coat; I went down to Tenth Street, and met a gentleman, to whom I communicated my suspicions, and then went and delivered myself up to Superintendent Richards of the Metropolitan Police force." He admitted telling Richards where Atzerodt, Payne and Herold had been staying.[10]

Aiken touched on a subject that was to be debated for years—that Weichmann had been arrested on suspicion of murdering the President and that, under severe threats, he had been forced to testify against other conspirators.

No evidence exists that he was formally arrested, however. He was nevertheless placed under guard and later detained at Carroll Prison, partly to satisfy Stanton and partly for his own protection.

The lawyer pressed the issue. "Did you ever say previous to your surrendering yourself and going to the office of Colonel Burnett, that you were fearful of being arrested?" Weichmann responded calmly, "I myself had a great deal of fear; being in this house where these people were. I knew that I would be brought into public notice."[11]

Weichmann's indirect but logical explanation annoyed the defense. The inexperienced lawyer barked, "I am not asking what you had to fear; but what you said."

Up to this point the Judges listened patiently, but Bingham had endured enough of the counsel's badgering. "You had better allow him to answer in his own way," he advised quietly.

Aiken backed down and changed the subject to Henri St. Marie, a questionable friend of both Weichmann and Surratt. The lawyer tried to show that Weichmann had discussed his sympathy for the Confederacy with St. Marie. Before Aiken could get down to details, a recess was called for lunch, allowing Weichmann a break.

When court reconvened, Aiken took up where he had left off. Bingham again objected to the cross-examination on the grounds that the questions concerned immaterial subjects and secondhand evidence. Bingham explained that if Aiken "proposed to ask the witness whether he himself was guilty of any treasonable practices, nobody would object to it."

In accepting the objection, the counsel responded, "As the Judge Advocate would not object to any questions . . . with respect to his [the witness's] own conduct," he would "address a few interrogatories to that effect." Aiken then asked, "Did you give notice to St. Marie that he would probably be arrested by the Government?" The witness explained that he did not notify him because "St. Marie rose one morning early and left; he afterwards enlisted in a Delaware regiment, and was taken prisoner and lodged in Castle Thunder."

Aiken, determined to trap Weichmann, had obtained reports from Confederate spy Augustus Howell about Weichmann's Southern sympathies and directed his questions to this topic. "Are you a clerk in the War Department?" he quizzed. Weichmann admitted that he had been. The lawyer then designed his interrogation to show that Weichmann had been friendly with a known Confederate blockade-runner and even offered to reveal the number of Southern prisoners held by the Union armies. Weichmann denied the insinuations, telling the Court that far from working with Howell, he actually exposed his suspicious activities to Captain Gleason. The lawyer asked if the witness ever talked to Howell about going south.

"I told him that I would like to go south; that I had been a student of divinity, and would like to be in Richmond for the purpose of continuing my studies."

"Did he offer to make any arrangements in Richmond with a view to getting you a place there?"

John W. Clampitt, one of Mary Surratt's defense counsel. Clampitt did the best he could for his client, but his inexperience was a handicap.

"No, sir."[12]

At this time Howell, one of the stongest witnesses against Weichmann, languished in Carroll Prison less than two miles away.

Aiken gave up temporarily and turned the cross-examination over to his partner, John Clampitt, who pursued the same point.

"Was it your desire to go to Richmond for the purpose of continuing your theological studies?"

"Yes, sir."

"For what reason?"

The Court objected to Clampitt's second question, and Aiken took over the interrogation again. He continued to hammer at Weichmann's questionable relationship with Howell. "While you were in the War Department did this man, Howell, teach you a cipher?" Aiken questioned. The witness admitted that Howell "showed" him the Confederate cipher.

"What was his purpose?" inquired Aiken.

"No particular purpose," replied Weichmann nonchalantly.

Aiken suggested that Weichmann planned to correspond with Richmond using the cipher. Weichmann knew that he had left the secret cipher alphabet in his box and that detectives must have found it among his possessions. He explained lamely that he operated the code to write a poem of Longfellow's and that was the only time he used it.

"Is that all the use you ever made on the cipher?" asked Aiken incredulously.

"Yes, sir, I never had a word of correspondence with Howell, and never saw him the second time until I saw him in prison," swore the hard-pressed witness.[13]

Following a question about the possibility of Weichmann's having overheard the conspirators' conversations, Aiken got back to the subject of the Confederate code. He wanted to know if Howell gave Weichmann the key to the cipher. Reluctantly, the witness admitted that he had. Aiken pressed ahead, "He taught you it, did he not?"

"I made no use of it whatever, except on that particular occasion, when I showed it to Mr. Cruikshank."

"That was not an answer to my question; he taught you the cipher, did he not?"

"Well; yes, sir."[14]

The witness was now definitely on the defensive. The prisoners on the dock remained silently attentive as the counsel pursued his advantage confidently. "Now, according to the best of your recollection, how soon was that after his return from Richmond?" he questioned. Weichmann, obviously uneasy, tried to defend himself. "He had returned from New York," he corrected, not from Richmond. Then, forgetting about the question, the squirming witness swore that it was the "first and only time I ever saw the man in my life." He quickly added that Howell "was well acquainted with Mrs. Surratt, and his nickname around the house was Spencer; he had been at the house a day or day and a half before I met him."

After one more brief question about the cipher, the lawyer moved on to another weak point in Weichmann's position. He wondered why the suspects were so free and unreserved while talking in his presence. Weichmann replied that the prisoners only spoke on general topics and never about "their private business" in his presence. Aiken was unconvinced. "Do we understand you as stating to the Court that in all of your conversations with them you never learned of any intended treasonable act or conspiracy of theirs?"

"I never did; I would have been the last man in the world to have suspected John Surratt, my schoolmate and companion, of the murder of the President of the United States," Weichmann declared.[15]

Aiken concentrated on the defense's strongest point, but Weichmann had regained his confidence. The lawyer continued his energetic interrogation about Weichmann's close relationship with the conspirators and his failure to notify authorities. Weichmann claimed convincingly that he had notified the Government. He avowed that he had told Captain Gleason of the War Department about the secret dispatches and blockade-runners, and even speculated they might try to capture President Lincoln. At this response Aiken brightened up. "You did, then, hear of a proposition of that kind?"

"I did not hear, but it was freely discussed in the papers," Weichmann shot back.

Now, growing more confident, he suggested that if the attorney would look at the *New York Tribune* of March 19 [1865], he would see the capture plot mentioned. "It was just a casual remark," explained Weichmann.

"How came you to connect the matter of the capture of the President, of which you read in the newspaper, with any of these parties?" the lawyer wanted to know.

Judge Bingham objected to the question as being wholly immaterial or irrelevant. The Court sustained the objection. Aiken asked again about his "intimate personal relations with the prisoners at the bar." Somewhat more relaxed, the witness maintained that his relations were not intimate. "I met them merely because they boarded at Mrs. Surratt's house; I met Atzerodt and went to the theatre with him; I looked upon him as did everyone in the house as a good-hearted country-man."[16]

Surprisingly, Aiken then reversed his argument. He had endeavored to prove that Weichmann must have known of the conspiracy and should have reported it, but since Weichmann had informed Captain Gleason, this argument had no value. Aiken now attempted to show just the opposite—that a man of strong character would not have betrayed a friend. "But you were a schoolmate with John Surratt?" he noted.

"John had been my companion for seven years," the witness agreed.

"Did you still profess to be a friend of his when you gave the information you did to the War Department?" interrogated Aiken.

Weichmann, on more solid ground now, announced proudly that he was John's friend until he felt the Government might be in danger. "I preferred the Government to John Surratt." He admitted he did not know what John Surratt contemplated. Surratt had revealed only that "he was going to engage in cotton speculations and in the oil business."

"You did not know what he was contemplating; why then did you forfeit your friendship to him?"

"I never forfeited my friendship; he forfeited his friendship to me."

"How so; by engaging in cotton speculations?"

"No, sir, by placing me in the position in which I am now; I think of the two I was more a friend to him than he to me."[17]

This response not only confounded the defense, it won the admiration of the Court. General Harris commentated years later on the young clerk's ability to stand up to the grueling cross-examination.

It was not quite over, however. General Ewing still wanted to take another jab at the witness, who had deflected most thrusts all day. "You spoke of reading a publication in the *Tribune* of March 19th, referring to a plot to capture the President?" Ewing questioned.

"Yes, sir," Weichmann responded.

The attorney, trying to fix the date of John Surratt's "ride in country," asked if the escapade took place before or after the *Tribune* article of March 19. Weichmann thought it was after. Then the lawyer wanted to know if Weichmann talked to Captain Gleason after Surratt's mysterious venture.

"Yes," confirmed the witness. He explained that after that "ride," his suspicions "were not so much aroused as before it because neither Payne nor Atzerodt had been at the house since; the only one of them who visited was the man Booth."

"Have you ever seen the prisoner, Arnold?" Ewing questioned.

"No, sir," he responded.[18] A few words more about meeting Dr. Mudd, and the Court released the witness. He had stood the test.

The Judges recalled John Greenawalt to the stand. His testimony was followed by that of a black man, James Walker. Both testified about Atzerodt's stay at the Pennsylvania House, but neither added anything significant.

The next witness of consequence was J. L. McPhail, Provost Marshal-General of Maryland. Holt interrogated him about his conversation with Atzerodt in prison. Doster objected on the ground that the confession had been made under duress. Holt then asked under what circumstances Atzerodt had made his confession. McPhail responded, "I received information that he desired to see me, and I went to see him accordingly; I found him in a cell in prison in irons."

Doster arued that the condition of the prisoner was such as to intimidate him and that to make his confession under such circumstances was improper for use as evidence. He cited several authorities to sustain his objections. McPhail explained that it was not his idea to talk with Atzerodt, but that the prisoner's brother and brother-in-law were assigned to McPhail's force and they had asked him to see Atzerodt. Nevertheless, the Court sustained Doster's objection.

The Military Commission was not entirely impartial. They sustained many more objections by the Government than those by the defense, but the officers made an effort to be fair. The Judges remained conscious of the presence of reporters. They also read the daily news accounts of the Court's action, so they could not afford to be high-handed, even if they had wanted to.

After the Court sustained his objection, Doster began a cross-examination which brought out the very things to which he objected. "Did he describe the knife," he asked, "or name the place where he threw it?"

McPhail replied, "He said he threw it away just above the Herndon House, which is on the corner of Ninth and F Streets." A dagger, thought to have been Payne's, had been found at 9th and D streets.

Doster continued, "Did he also say where his pistol was?"

"He stated that it was at Matthews & Co.'s, Georgetown, in possession of a young man named Caldwell," responded the police officer.

"Did he state how he got it there?"

"He said he went there and borrowed $10 on the pistol, on Saturday morning, April 15th."

"Did the prisoner mention to you a certain coat containing a pistol and bowie knife, and exchanging it in the Kirkwood House, and if so did he state who it belonged to?"

"He stated that the coat at the hotel belonged to Herold."[19]

Herold's counsel jumped to his feet yelling, "I object to that testimony." Spectators laughed audibly at the sight of lawyers fighting among themselves.

One flaw in the defense was its inability to work in harmony. Doster especially made himself offensive by delaying the proceedings with absurd and irrelevant questions and by frequently exhibiting objectionable and impudent attitudes toward the witnesses.

The Commissioners, turning now to Arnold, asked McPhail to identify his handwriting. Walter E. Cox, counsel for Arnold and O'Laughlin, wondered how Arnold's handwriting could be so easily identified. "How did you become acquainted with his handwriting? State that first," demanded Cox.

"He once placed in my hand a written statement."

"What instrument did he place in your hands?"[20]

McPhail answered calmly, "A confession."

This pronouncement produced a visible shock among all the prisoners except Mrs. Surratt and Spangler, neither of whom had been associated with Arnold. McPhail went on to explain that the confession had been turned over to Secretry of War Stanton, and that Arnold had mentioned names.

The Government then presented Arnold's confession. The reading of the document caused the accused notable distress and was especially embarrassing for Arnold. By this time, the suspects knew that George Atzerodt had confessed something, even though his entire statement was not permitted in the trial record. In addition, they were aware Atzerodt had been questioned for several days while in prison. But the defendants had no idea that Arnold had freely and voluntarily confessed.

The Government called other witnesses to tell of Arnold's friendship with Booth and of his subsequent arrest. One otherwise insignificant witness, Littleton Newman, testified that as early as September 9 or 11 Arnold had received a letter containing money that seemed related to the conspiracy. This revelation placed the beginning of the plot earlier than usually thought.

Eaton G. Horner took the stand to testify about Arnold's arrest and his subsequent oral confession. Cox objected to cross-examination by fellow-counselor Ewing. Cox did not want any confession mentioned that might implicate other prisoners. Ewing and Cox got into a heated dispute that eventually had to be settled by the Judges, who ruled the oral confession was admissible evidence. The witness then pulled a paper from his pocket and read the names of those Arnold had implicated in his oral confession: John Wilkes Booth, Michael O'Laughlin, George Atzerodt, John Surratt and Lewis Payne, whom Arnold knew by the alias "Moseby." Before this, Payne had not been associated with Arnold.

The witness stated that when officers questioned Arnold about others who might have been involved, he indicated that Booth had letters of recommendation to Dr. Samuel Mudd and Dr. William Queen. The net was slowly being drawn around Mudd, but Queen, whose name came up several times in the investigation, was never seriously questioned. Fortunately for Queen, Booth stopped at Mudd's house rather than his. A long cross-examination followed, but it failed to shake the witness.

Why Arnold confessed so quickly and freely, after joining other conspirators in swearing never to reveal anything, puzzled some. He claimed later that he thought O'Laughlin had already confessed, but O'Laughlin was not even in custody at the time. Arnold, who had been out of touch with the

Benn Pitman, brother of the developer of the popular Pitman shorthand system, was responsible for preserving records of the trial testimony.

conspirators for more than three weeks, felt that Booth deliberately implicated him. But more importantly, Arnold's father had written a letter encouraging him to tell all. Arnold was the only conspirator who had considered his parents' advice not to get involved, albeit belatedly. Undoubtedly this had an influence on his quick confession. Then, too, he was the only conspirator to have written proof of his break with Booth.

The perceivable tension of the prisoners, brought on by these unexpected confessions, was relieved momentarily by a humorous description of the plot. The witness quoted Arnold as having described his part in the kidnapping to have been catching the President when he was thrown out of the theater box after the gaslights were turned off. The prisoners relaxed and laughed at the idea of the small-statured Arnold catching the lanky President.

O'Laughlin, however, did not even smile — he realized for the first time that his longtime friend's confession could lead him to the gallows. He sat, stony-faced, as others enjoyed their laugh. Mrs. Surratt, suffering from the heat, also failed to enjoy the humor.

The Military Commission could usually rest at the conclusion of the testimonies, but court stenographers were just beginning their labors. Throughout the trial Benn Pitman began his daily task about an hour before court convened and did not finish until ten or eleven at night. He made a longhand copy of the day's proceedings from shorthand notes he and six assistants had taken. Two additional copies of this original were printed by old-fashioned letterpress. Soldiers assisted in making the press copies. The War Department kept one copy and one was used by Pitman in compiling his book. Workers later made additional reproductions from these first transcripts for use of defense lawyers and the Commission.

This tedious work was done without the help of typewriters or carbon paper, much less modern duplicators and word processors. Although Pitman usually completed his task before eleven each evening, other helpers labored all night preparing the official transcript to be published in the *National Intelligencer*. They rarely finished before five in the morning.

A special vehicle driven by a soldier and followed by two mounted cavalrymen carrying loaded rifles escorted Pitman daily to and from the Arsenal. This extra precaution not only protected Pitman, but also the records.[21]

XXXI
"Yes, That's the Man"

When not in the courtroom, the defendants were confined in the prison area formerly used by female inmates. The cells, in three different tiers, were scattered far enough apart to make communication impossible. An attendant constantly stood guard at each cell. Even in the cells, the men were usually required to wear the close-fitting, padded hoods.

The usual unappetizing prison diet varied somewhat for Mrs. Surratt, who was allowed toast and other food from the officers' mess. Officials did not require her to wear a hood, and she remained unmanacled. In spite of this preferential treatment, Mary Surratt was ill, or pretended to be. She passed the time reading a prayer book.

Dr. Mudd continued to give attention to his appearance and, like Mrs. Surratt, occupied much of his time reading religious books.

O'Laughlin felt the desperation of his situation deeply and shuffled back and forth in his cell. He was a pitiful sight—his head hooded, his feet and hands shackled with irons.

Payne displayed the same cool, devil-may-care, reckless spirit in his cell as in the courtroom. At this point neither the Government nor his lawyer knew the background of this mysterious young warrior, but they suspected that his real name was not Payne.

Arnold was usually quiet and pleasant and gave little trouble in court or in his cell. Spangler, however, maintained a lighthearted, talkative attitude. He had a great appetite and usually wanted more to eat. In spite of orders to the contrary, guards generally obliged the talkative stagehand.[1]

The prisoners shuffled to court at ten o'clock on May 19. The weather was a little cooler, to everyone's relief. Each day more spectators crowded the courtroom. This morning they again overflowed into two adjoining rooms. There was not even standing room.

Curious observers, showing a morbid interest in the accused, picked out the different conspirators from newspaper descriptions. Mrs. Surratt, her eyes closed behind her veil, hid her face still farther behind a palm-leaf fan which she seldom moved. She appeared to pay no attention to the proceedings. Arnold was also indifferent, Payne, defiant and Atzerodt, fearful. O'Laughlin looked thoroughly broken, Spangler, stupid and Herold, childish. One visitor described the anguished Atzerodt as a man with "a villainously low forehead, pinched up features, mean chin, sallow complexion, snaky eyes of greenish

309

blue, nasty twisted mustache, head sunk into his shoulders and with a
crouching figure making up the disagreeable presentment."

Herold looked a little better in court this day; he had washed his face and
brushed his hair a little. He appeared "less like an imbecile."

While Herold laughed and giggled, Payne continued to attract the most
attention. His large, erect figure and his constant impudent stare startled every
new visitor.[2]

The first witness, Col. J. H. Taylor, identified a letter found in Booth's
trunk, written in Confederate code.

The prosecution then called witnesses to describe the attack on Secretary
Seward and to identify Payne. The first, William Bell, Seward's young black
servant, identified Payne and related the story of Payne's intrusion. Doster
made a feeble effort to shake the young man's identification. "How old are
you?" he questioned.

"I don't know exactly; I reckon between nineteen and twenty," Bell replied.

"How long had you been at Mr. Seward's?"

"Three months."

"Have you ever been to school?"

"Yes, four or five years."

"Where precisely was this man standing when you had this conversation
with him?"

"He was just inside the door; I had closed the door."

Doster asked if the visitor gave him a package of medicine, to which Bell
said no. When the lawyer suggested that the man talked rough, the witness
corrected, "He did not talk rough, he had a very fine voice when he came in."
Then Doster apparently tried to lead the young black servant into a careless
description of the intruder. "You say you recognize that man as the prisoner
at the bar; state what there is about the man that resembles the man you saw
that night," he quizzed.

Bell gave a surprisingly detailed description. "I noticed his hair, his pantaloons and his boots; that night he was talking to Mr. Fred Seward nearly five
minutes." He added that the man "had on very heavy boots, black pants, light
overcoat and a brown hat; his face was very red at the time he came in; he
had very coarse black hair."

"Have you seen the same boots on this man?" questioned Doster.

"Yes, the night they captured him," Bell responded without hesitation.

"Have you seen the same clothes on him?"

"I have seen the same pantaloons; he had on black pantaloons."

"And would you infer from the fact that he wore black pants that it was
the same man?"

"No, I know from his face."[3]

The youth then described how he had identified Payne among three men
at Augur's office on the night of his capture. Doster tried to show that the identification was rigged.

"Did either of the two men they showed you before look like the man?"

"No, one had moustaches, the other whiskers."

"Were they as tall as this man?"

"No, they were short; they didn't look at all like this man."

Doster suggested that the reward money might have influenced Bell's identification by asking if he had heard of the reward for Payne. The witness admitted he knew of rewards for the capture of others but not for the supposed assassin of Secretary Seward.

"Did anyone offer you money before this man's apprehension?"

"No, sir."

"Did anybody threaten you?"

"No, sir."[4]

Recognizing Payne was no problem due to his size and unique features, yet the defense continued to question the identification.

Major Seward, son of the Secretary of State, next took the stand. In a faltering voice, he narrated a graphic account of Payne's attack. His moving testimony profoundly affected the courtroom as well as Payne.

As Payne fled the Seward house, screaming, "I'm mad," he assumed that his wild attack had killed the Secretary of State. Even though newspapers carried reports on Seward's condition, Payne remained unaware that his mission had failed until the witnesses referred to Secretary Seward. He realized then, for the first time, that Seward was still alive. This surprising report stunned and noticeably disappointed Payne. His reaction not only revealed his character, it indicated the isolation of the prisoners. Far from feeling relief that he had not killed the Secretary, he was crestfallen because he had failed in his assignment. Payne viewed the attack as his duty as a Confederate soldier. He knew he faced death in any case, but he would have been more satisfied dying for having completed his duty than to face the gallows a failure.

After several police officers related their experiences in arresting Mrs. Surratt and finding Payne at her door, the defense again brought up the process of identifying him. His identification seemed important, not only to Payne's lawyer, but also to Mrs. Surratt's counsel.

Maj. H. W. Smith, who led the arresting party, testified that he had asked Mrs. Surratt to come and see who the man was. The widow, on seeing Payne, threw up her hands and exclaimed, "Before God I do not know this man and have never seen him."

The defense made no effort to deny Mrs. Surratt's remarks, but they tried vigorously to prove that she had not recognized him as the man who had stayed in her house, visited with her family and eaten at her table. The question was of little importance since the Government had stronger evidence, but the defense had a better opportunity to protect her at this point than on more serious charges. Thus, the defense made identifying Payne a major issue, and one in which Mrs. Surratt's lawyers scored a few points.

In his cross-examination, Aiken exhibited a large, dirty, grey sack coat to Major Smith. The Major promptly identified it as the one Payne wore on the night of his arrest. Actually an innocent mistake had been made by the Judge Advocate. When Aiken asked that the witness be shown the coat worn by

Payne, the Judge accidentally picked up the wrong one from the exhibit table. The witness carelessly, but very positively, identified the wrong garment. When the counsel noticed the mistake, he made the most of it. Shrewdly, he asked the witness to repeat his identification.

"How do you know that coat to be the one Payne had on?"

"By the way anyone would recognize such an article, from memory."

"What marks about it do you recognize?"

"The color and general look of the coat."

"Are you sure the coat he had on was not what is called Confederate grey?"

"I am very sure, as I said before, this is the coat."

"Then you are certain it was not a Confederate grey coat Payne had on when you arrested him?"

"I have said I am certain this is the coat."

"Will you answer my question?"

The Major, irritated with the young, impudent lawyer, snapped, "I have already testified on that point, and I do not know whether I am called upon to testify three or four times."[5]

Aiken calmly walked over to the trial exhibits and picked up another coat, smaller, cleaner and a different grey. Major Smith suddenly realized that he had absolutely identified the wrong one. He admitted the second coat was actually the one Payne wore. He recognized it by the buttons. The Major tried in vain to explain that the second coat was identical to the first one except for the buttons. He alibied that the light was so bad in Mrs. Surratt's hallway that it was difficult to see the coat. This was exactly what Aiken wanted. If Smith could not identify the coat, how did he expect Mrs. Surratt to have recognized Payne?

Aiken played on this point. Suppose you see a gentleman dressed up presenting himself as a Baptist preacher and then two months later see the same man with a dirty shirt sleeve on his head and a pickax in his hand—would you recognize him? Smith claimed that he would if he was familiar with his looks.

"You would recollect that, but you could not recollect a coat you had only seen a short time before, nor distinguish it from another so different in appearance as these are," chided the lawyer.

"It is very hard to remember, as anyone may well know, the color of a coat seen in the night time," answered the Major feebly.[6]

The official account, released to the press, did not report this embarrassing episode and most reporters failed to mention it. The defense won a minor victory, but it had little effect on the Court. The Commission evidently perceived the difference between a man and a piece of cloth; men can be recognized, even in the dark, by their voices, mannerisms or sizes.

Seward's servant, brought back to identify Payne, weakened Aiken's case. Bell's easy identification revealed more than looks; it revealed something of Payne's personality. Judge Holt ordered the manacles taken off Payne's wrists so that he could put on the coats and hat. There was a short delay, as General Hartranft ordered his soldiers to this task, and the prisoner seemed to enjoy the brief freedom afforded him. When he stood up, the courtroom became curiously silent. As everyone turned toward this strange giant, the initial silence was broken by whispers of admiration, mingled with expressions of horror and disgust. Payne remained completely relaxed and unconcerned. Occasionally an involuntary smile altered his otherwise tight-set lips, suggesting that he might be enjoying the attention.

The suspect first tried on the grey coat and then put the longer garment over it. Guards handed him the slouch hat which he put on. When the Judge directed him to face the witness, Payne turned abruptly toward the young black man, glaring as if to challenge him. They looked steadily at each other for a moment without a word uttered in the hushed courtroom. The youth held his ground. When Holt finally asked if he recognized the man, the witness blurted out excitedly, "Yes, that's the man, that's him." Payne smiled.

The young servant then described how the attacker had worn his hat turned down over one eye and stated that his eyes had been "pretty fiery." The witness, turning toward Payne again, shook his head and exclaimed, "Oh, he knows me well enough, don't you see, he knows me?"[7]

Payne laughed and the Court joined in. The servant's excited exclamation brought relief to a tense moment. Despite the humor, it recalled a tragic scene.

Sgt. George Robinson, the male nurse who had been attending Seward, took the stand. Holt again directed Payne to stand up while he listened to a detailed description of the destruction and horror he had wrought. A look of shame gradually replaced Payne's usually defiant, haughty expression as the witness gave a vivid demonstration of the accused's effort to stab and kill the defenseless Secretary of State in his sickbed. A noticeable flicker of remorse seemed to cross the prisoner's face as the witness, reenacting the crime, raised the knife Payne had used in his bloody attack. As spectators turned toward Payne, the stoic defendant, straining to contain his emotion, stood, like a statue, staring at the witness.

Soldiers again removed the irons from Payne's wrists, and Holt ordered him again to put on the two coats and the hat which he had dropped when he fled. This time, as Robinson identified him, Payne showed no emotion other than a defiant sneer.

The remaining testimony dealt mostly with the arrest of Mrs. Surratt. Officers Morgan, Smith and Wermerskirch testified they found pictures of Booth and of Confederate leaders Jefferson Davis, Alexander Stephens, and General Pierre G. T. Beauregard in the Surratt residence. They also found a card with the Virginia motto, *sic semper tyrannis*. The defense sought to prove that homes of many loyal citizens contained such pictures.

Holt interrogated Capt. W. M. Wermerskirch, one of the three principal arresting officers. "State whether or not on the 16th of April you were at the house of the prisoner, Mrs. Surratt, in this city."

The Captain, speaking with a decided German accent, gently corrected the General. "No, sir; I was there on the night of the 17th." As the interrogation progressed, the Captain affirmed that he was present when Major Smith asked Mrs. Surratt if she knew Payne. "What did she say?" questioned the Judge.

Wermerskirch stated that she held up her hands (raising his hands to demonstrate). According to the officer's testimony Mrs. Surratt said, "So help me God, I never saw him before, and I know nothing of him." Asked if he recognized Payne, the witness pointed to Payne and replied, "That is the man yonder."

"Is that woman there Mrs. Surratt?" inquired Judge Holt.[8]

Wermerskirch looked at the heavily veiled lady seated on the prisoners' dock and remarked that he could not see her face. Each time the Judge requested witnesses to identify Mrs. Surratt, she had to be reminded to raise her black veil. Bingham asked her to remove it once again. As she did so, the crowd turned to catch a glimpse of her face. She stared back without blinking or blushing. After Wermerskirch's identification, the prisoner slowly and deliberately replaced the veil.

Unfortunately for his client, Aiken's cross-examination brought a few damaging details that Holt had missed.

"Did you make any search of the premises while there?" Aiken questioned.

"I did."

"What did you find?"

"I found a number of photographs, papers, bullet moulds and percussion caps."

Aiken made it worse, asking where the officer found the percussion caps. The Captain reported they were found in Mrs. Surratt's room. He also discovered a bullet mold there. The lawyer asked a few insignificant questions about the bullet mold and the location of Mrs. Surratt's room, then inquired about photographs found there. The witness stated that several photographs were in her room, but he didn't know whom they represented. "Did you find any of Davis or Stephens there, or any of the Rebel leaders?" questioned the lawyer.[9]

Captain Wermerskirch, a cautious man, made a slight correction in terms, "Yes, but not exactly photographs; they were lithographs, cartes de visite in the same style as photographs."

The interrogator turned around and whispered to his client, Mrs. Surratt, and then asked, "Did you not find pictures of Union generals there?"

Wermerskirch's astonishing response was, "No, sir, none—there was a picture of McClellan."

The stunned counsel inquired indignantly, "Well, sir, was not he a Union General?"

The witness, a little confused, admitted, hesitatingly, "I don't exactly know, I believe he was employed on our side."

That Captain Wermerskirch did not recognize one of the Union's greatest and most popular generals, who had run unsuccessfully against Lincoln for President of the United States only a few months earlier, shocked the Military Commission. Apparently, however, it did not destroy Wermerskirch's credibility.

Mrs. Surratt, who had shown little interest in the proceedings, began to reveal some anxiety as the Court examined the photographs. Aiken continued his interrogation. Attempting to show that such pictures were no sign of disloyalty, he noted that "dealers expose these for sale throughout the country." The witness admitted to having seen some in Baltimore 18 months earlier, but observed that they were "prohibited to be sold by the Commanding General at that time."

"Have you not seen photographs of the leaders of the Rebellion in the hands of persons known to be loyal?" Aiken quizzed.

"Not frequently."

"Well, did you ever see them?"

"Perhaps I did."

"Have you ever seen photographs of Booth in the hands of loyal men?"

Wermerskirch replied sarcastically, "Only in the hands of those who took an interest in having him arrested."

Aiken interrogated him more about the pictures, then returning to Mary Surratt, asked, "What remark did you make to her when you were ready to take her from her house?"

Wermerskirch corrected his inquisitor, stating that it was Major Smith who talked with Mrs. Surratt. That when Smith said the coach was ready to take her away, she asked him "to wait a while, and she knelt and prayed a little; she knelt down, but whether she prayed or not I can't say."[10]

Suppressed laughter rippled through the courtroom. Mary Surratt, not amused, turned around and, quickly raising her veil, glared angrily at the witness. Whatever her defects in character, this Catholic convert took her faith seriously.

Her lawyer, ignoring Mrs. Surratt's displeasure, moved on quickly to the next question. "How was Payne dressed when he came in?" he questioned. The witness described him as wearing a dark coat and "pants that seemed to be black." He had what appeared to be a shirt sleeve on his head.

Taking a portion of a sleeve from the exhibit table, the lawyer inquired, "Is this the article?"

"It looks like it," responded the officer. "He was full of mud to his knees."

Aiken had been so successful in tricking Major Smith with Payne's coat, he thought he would try it again with the Captain, who did not know about Smith's ordeal. "Do you think you could recognize the coat he had on if you should see it now?"

"Yes," came the reply. The guards again put a coat on Payne.

"Do you recognize it now? Is that the coat?" Wermerskirch, not falling for the trick, replied, "I think it was longer and darker."

The makeshift cap was then placed upon Payne's head, the first coat removed and the other one put on. The witness responded, "That's the coat and that's the way he had the headdress on."

Failing in his stratagem, Aiken questioned, "Are you sure you recognize the man?"

The witness replied confidently, "Yes, sir; that is the man."

Aiken again went through his spiel about the problem of recognizing a man dressed in his shirt sleeves who had previously been presented as a Baptist minister and asked the Captain if that would not be difficult. The witness replied, "I declare I don't know how a Baptist minister does look." Wermerskirch's homey response caused an outburst of laughter. The idea of the prisoner impersonating a Baptist minister was so ludicrous that it brought a slight smile even to Payne's face.

The numerous spectators in the room obviously affected the proceedings. Lawyers and Commissioners, as well as prisoners, reacted to the attention. The crowd was becoming so large it hampered progress. Some critics suggested that officials should stop giving passes or the trial would be seriously disrupted.

In spite of interruptions, Aiken persisted in his line of reasoning. "You think you would recognize a person in such a change of garb in a dim gas light." Wermerskirch responded clearly, "If I were asked to look at him and identify him I think I would." He explained that the "prisoner had taken no particular pains to disguise himself; his face looked as it is now, and I would recognize him if he put another coat on and covered himself with mud."[11]

It was a good response, which the lawyer did not dispute. Aiken, passing on to another subject, inquired about a black bag found in Mrs. Surratt's house and concluded his interrogation.

Holt wanted to make sure the Court understood that the bullet molds had been found in Mrs. Surratt's room, so he asked the Captain to reconfirm his earlier testimony. This done, Mrs. Surratt's lawyer retaliated with the weak excuse that lots of people kept percussion caps and bullet molds.

The Government's case grew stronger each day. Witnesses testified on every detail, however insignificant. As noted, the defense was hampered because it did not coordinate its presentations, but even if it had, it could not have sustained a strong, logical defense of Herold, Payne or Atzerodt. Mrs. Surratt, Dr. Mudd, O'Laughlin, Arnold and Spangler were the only suspects lawyers could really help, but they did not bother much with O'Laughlin or Spangler.

The Government called Lt. G. W. Dempsey to the stand and showed him a colored print of three female figures representing Spring, Summer and Autumn and asked if he had ever seen it. "I saw that picture in the house of Mrs. Surratt, in the back parlor," he testified. When asked if he examined the illustration, he said he did and found underneath it "a likeness of J. Wilkes Booth, a side-face view."

Officers showed the witness a picture of Booth and asked, "Is that it?"

"That is the same face, but the picture I found was side view."

The defense objected to the interrogation, but the Court overruled the objection.

Aiken cross-examined the witness: "Have you ever been in the habit of seeing pictures of Booth, or the leaders of the Rebellion exposed?" Dempsey explained that he had been a prisoner in the South for 15 months and had seen many "leaders of the Rebellion personally and in pictures."

"I mean in the loyal states," corrected the attorney.

"Very few, sir, except in the newspapers."

Asked if he had seen illustrations of Confederate leaders in loyal newspapers, the witness replied that maybe he had seen a picture of Davis. "How about pictures of famous actors?" inquired the attorney.

"I am not a theatrical character and can't say that I have never noticed it, but I have seen pictures of Forrest and Macready."[12]

Mary Surratt's case was not unique. At the time of the conspiracy trial, the Government was judging another woman, Eessie Perrins, before another Military Commission. The defense used the same arguments against military jurisdiction in both cases. Mrs. Perrins' lawyers argued that their client was a fine, well-educated woman who would be out of character associating with cutthroats and thieves. Similarly, Mrs. Surratt's counsel postulated that her sex and piety were inconsistent with the charges against her.

The prosecution turned briefly to Dr. Mudd's case. Miss Blise, a black woman, indicated that she had seen Dr. Mudd in Bryantown about four o'clock with another man the day after the murder. When asked about the exact time, she said that she could not be exact because it had been a cloudy day and she could not see the sun. (Timepieces among poor people were not common in 1865.) Miss Blise's statement concluded the testimony for that day, and court adjourned.

Payne had seldom spoken to anyone since his confinement, and he never complained. On one occasion, as one of his guards, John Hubbard, was leading him back to his cell, Payne declared that he was tired of life and wished they would hurry up and hang him. At the conclusion of this day's dramatic accounts of Payne's attack on Seward, he felt moved to speak again. As John E. Roberts was replacing the irons on him Payne admitted that the Government was "tracing" him pretty close and that he wanted to die. While the other prisoners did not want to die, they must have realized that the Government was also "tracing" them pretty close.

Battle-weary soldiers streamed daily into the hills around Washington in preparation for the victory parade. On May 19, the War Department issued a special order rescinding the prohibition against army officers visiting the capital without special permission. Authorities wanted to give officers an opportunity to witness the Grand Review. The capital, however, remained off-limits for noncommissioned soldiers.

Other signs indicated the pain and grief of the assassination were beginning to heal. Mrs. Lincoln moved out of the White House and Secretary Seward visited the State Department for the first time since the attack. His son Frederick was permitted out of bed, although confined to the house.

Even though Jefferson Davis did not stand trial with the other accused, the Government showed indications of prosecuting him in a civil court. Gov. Joseph E. Brown of Georgia was held in Old Capitol Prison as a witness against Davis.

The *Boston Transcript* speculated on the movements of another conspirator, stating that John Surratt had probably sailed for England on the *Peruvian* which left Quebec on May 13. It suggested that someone should arrest him in Liverpool on his arrival.[13] The suggestion was premature; Surratt did not slip out of Canada until four months later when he did sail on the *Peruvian* to Liverpool. The Government was aware of the move but did nothing to apprehend him. Another nearby activity was related to the conspirators. The Booth family sent a representative to Washington in an unsuccessful attempt to obtain the assassin's body.

Court did not sit until eleven o'clock on Saturday, May 20. By that hour the heat was stifling. Soldiers opened windows as wide as possible and kept the door leading to the cells open. Guards with glistening bayonets at the ready stood at every exit. A mild-looking, middle-aged gentleman with a rosebud in his lapel sat close to the prisoners' exit peering through his spectacles at the morning newspaper. Except for the large bunch of keys dangling from his waist, he did not look like a jailer, but even as he read, he kept a watchful eye on the prisoners, especially on Herold, now seated by the door.

Herold generally sprawled all over the platform, sometimes propping his feet on the rail, sometimes twisting around in his seat, but always grinning without comprehension. Occasionally he would slide down on his knees and whisper between the rails to spectators seated near the prisoners' dock. The jailer would methodically advise him to get back into his chair. Herold generally obeyed without a word.

Many in the crowded courtroom had come to Washington to view the parade scheduled for the following week. The press of spectators became so great they pushed in front of the prisoners' dock. The defense counsel had to request General Hunter to keep a passageway open between them and their clients. The spectators included several dignitaries from foreign countries, among them Lieutenant Colonel Le Comte and Counsel General John Hitz, both of Switzerland.

The first witness, Assistant Secretary of War Charles Dana, told of an instrument used by the Confederacy to send coded messages which he had found in the Richmond office of the Confederate Secretary of State, Judah Benjamin. The machine was a type of wheel which could be turned to substitute one set of letters for another.

Major Eckert then testified that some letters found in Booth's trunk were written in the same code. An official read two of the decoded letters. The first, dated October 13, 1864, said:

> We again urge the necessity of our gaining immediate advantages. Strain every nerve for victory. We now look upon the re-election of Lincoln in November as almost certain, and we need to whip his hirelings to prevent it. Besides, with Lincoln re-elected and his armies victorious we need not hope even for recognition, much less the help mentioned in our last. Holcombe will explain this. Those figures of the Yankee are correct to a unit. Your friend shall be immediately set to work as you direct.[14]

The Holcombe referred to was surely James Philemon Holcombe, the 44-year-old Confederate Commissioner to Canada during the last two years of the war. The letter definitely linked Booth with Confederate leaders at the time conspiracy was being formed.

The second dispatch, dated October 19, was similar. The first letter was sent from Canada to Richmond; the second from Richmond to Canada. Some false evidence connected Booth with Confederate leaders, but these letters were genuine. The Confederacy had used Booth as a spy, much as it had used John Surratt. Some of this testimony seemed superfluous to the case at hand. But the Government had named Davis and other Rebel leaders in the conspiracy charge, and even though they were not present, officials tried to prove their connection to the scheme.

After Gen. Alexander J. Hamilton's description of Rebel efforts to destroy Northern shipping, the Government produced witnesses who placed Mudd in Bryantown on the Saturday after the murder. Frank Bloyce (or Blice or Blise), a black man from Charles County, Maryland, testified that he had seen the doctor in Bryantown between three and four o'clock. This testimony was not especially damaging to the prisoner, because Mudd had admitted going to Bryantown with Herold to get a buggy for Booth. What Mudd denied, however, was that he had known anything about the assassination until Sunday morning at church.

The prosecution then interrogated J. H. Ward. He testified that the day Lincoln died he went to Bryantown, which was just a few miles from his home. As soon as he got to town, about one o'clock, he noticed the soldiers' great excitement. He thought the troops were going to search each house, and, as his wife was home alone, he hurried back to be with her.

The defense objected. The Court overruled and Ward continued, "I must explain the facts because I know but little." Ward explained that the village was under martial law and people wanted to get home. The Judge asked if he saw Dr. Mudd. "I can't say, the excitement was so great; I can't say I saw the doctor," he replied. Questioned further about Mudd's presence, the witness vacillated, "I would not like to say positively, but it occurs to me from faint memory that he was there; the excitement has been so great ever since that time that I can not say positively."

Under continuing interrogation the witness testified that he knew about the assassination and heard that the assassin was a man named Booth or Boose. Asked when he first heard, Ward answered, "It was, I think, between one and two o'clock, it was a cloudy day, and I never paid any particular attention, but I think it was one and two o'clock."

The Judge inquired, "You say some said it was Booth and some said it was Boose that was spoken by some soldiers with whom the English language was not conversant?"

"They would call him Borth, Booths and Boose; those who had an amalgamation of the languages said it was Booths," explained the witness.

The interrogator wanted to know where Ward first heard that the President had been assassinated. "At home," responded the witness. "I wanted to tell you it was through the authority of the darkey."

"Who was the darkey?"

"Charles Blice, the brother of the fellow whose testimony had just been taken."[15]

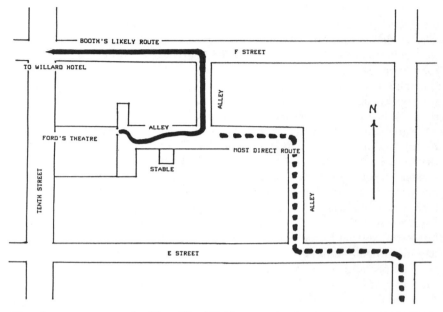

The shortest route to the Navy Yard Bridge was southeast. However, witnesses saw Booth turn north out of the alley. Which direction he turned on F Street is not known, but most likely he headed west.

These statements severely damaged Mudd's contention that he had heard nothing about the murder on Saturday. The next witness, Lt. David Dana, testified that he pursued the assassins to Bryantown, arriving there before one o'clock Saturday. According to Dana, news of the assassination had already spread, and John Wilkes Booth was thought to be the assassin.

Next, Joseph B. Stewart testified that he was in the theater when Booth shot Lincoln, and discussed his efforts to catch the assassin. Asked about Booth's escape through the stage door, he swore that he saw several people around the closed door. Near the door, he testified he passed a person "who didn't seem to be moving about."

"Look at the prisoners and see if you recognize the man."

"I see but one face that would recall him to mind," Stewart answered. When asked which one, the witness pointed to Spangler, "That one."

The Judge ordered Spangler to stand up. Stewart hesitated, "That one looks more like the man than any other there." He tried to explain that in the darkened area, and because of his position, he could not characterize the man's features well.

"I didn't observe so far as to have a clear impression of his visage; he was turning from the door towards me."

In cross-examination, the defense asked, "Was it the passageway between the scene and the green-room, about two and a half feet in width, through which Booth ran?"

"I don't know where the green-room is. I never was there, but if I had a plan of the building, I could point it out."

Assistant Judge Advocate Burnett handed Stewart a plan of the theater. The witness pointed out the routes that both he and Booth took and marked the spot where he saw the man. The witness stated that by the time he got through the door, the assassin was leaning forward in his saddle. With his left foot apparently in the stirrup, he was getting his horse under control for a forward movement.[16]

Stewart stated that Booth turned *west* onto F Street, after riding north out of the alley behind the theater. His most direct route to the Navy Yard Bridge would have been to head south through a vacant lot behind the theater and then east along E Street and across the Capitol grounds to the Potomac, which was southeast of Ford's Theatre. Evidently Booth headed out in the opposite direction. (Most writers picture Booth turning *east* on F Street.)

Booth had prepared the details of his escape—his horse was saddled and Herold was prepared to accompany him. Herold apparently was waiting for Booth when Fletcher saw him about 10:30 P.M. near the Willard Hotel, which was four blocks west of Ford's Theatre. When Fletcher ordered Herold to return the horse, the conspirator galloped off to the Navy Yard Bridge. Booth had likely planned to head northwest in order to evade possible pursuit and then turn south at the Willard Hotel, meet Herold, turn east on Pennsylvania Avenue, and gallop toward the Navy Yard Bridge.

Robert Campbell, a teller at the Ontario Bank in Montreal, testified concerning Jacob Thompson's bank account which Confederates had opened there in May 1864. The witness stated Thompson's account contained $649,000. Campbell also knew Booth, who had a small amount in the same bank. He remarked that Thompson's account was closed on April 11, 1865, and that Booth's account still contained about $400.

Holt informed the Court one more witness needed to be heard, but, because of the sensitive nature of his testimony, the Commission would have to question him in secret. Officers therefore cleared the chamber and spent the remainder of the day in closed session.[17]

XXXII

Empty Sleeves Dangling in the Spring Air

While the Court continued its interrogations, experts busily sifted through captured Confederate archives. In addition to documents previously found in Richmond, the Government discovered five tons of Confederate papers in Charlotte, North Carolina. Before Lee evacuated Richmond, the Rebels burned some papers, but they boxed most of their documents and sent them to Charlotte for safekeeping. As soon as Union soldiers found them, they sent the archives to Washington where experts scrutinized them for evidence against Davis and other leaders.[1]

Other events only indirectly related to the trial included President Johnson's long-delayed occupation of the White House. Perhaps reflecting on the fate of his predecessor, he took out a $20,000 life insurance policy. Belle Boyd, the notorious Rebel spy, was thrown out of her hotel in England, penniless. And the Confederate navy surrendered at Mobile—the war was over at last.

One of the "greatest military displays of the world" was planned for the next two days, May 23 and 24. For weeks, excitement had been building for the Grand Review. Engineers constructed a pontoon bridge to enable troops to cross back into Virginia from Georgetown after the parade.

Sherman had appeared in Washington the previous Saturday and paid his respects to President Johnson and General Grant. When Sherman and Grant appeared together on a balcony at the Willard Hotel on Sunday, a crowd gathered quickly and called for speeches. The generals did not respond. Sherman's homesick, weary troops spontaneously honored him in a farewell salute as bands played "Hail to the Chief." The "Chief" in this case was Sherman, who watched from the balcony smoking his ever-present cigar.[2]

Workmen were busy cleaning up Pennsylvania Avenue and putting finishing touches on the reviewing stands near the White House. But even as the armies prepared for their day of glory in Washington, 3,000 emaciated prisoners of Andersonville were still waiting in Jacksonville, Florida, for transportation home. The Government had sent two hospital ships for those in greatest need, but as the ships could only accommodate 500 soldiers each, the rest had to wait.

The Government was able, however, to find a ship in which to transport

A former Senator from Alabama, Clement C. Clay served the Confederacy as a member of the secret service in Canada. Holt included him on the list of Lincoln's assassins.

Jefferson Davis north. Rather than bring him to Washington for trial, they shipped him to Fortress Monroe in Virginia. Officials were slow in moving Davis from Georgia. The conspiracy trial had not gotten under way until three days after soldiers captured Davis. If authorities had desired, they could have brought him to Washington by May 13, the first full day of court.

The military also confined Clement Clay in Fortress Monroe, but they did not allow him to communicate with Davis. Secretary Stanton issued an order that no one be permitted to see the ex–President of the Confederacy without special permission from the War Department.

The Government was dilatory in apprehending another fugitive, John Surratt. Newspapers constantly reported Surratt's presence in Canada, yet authorities seemed reluctant to pursue him. The usually reliable *Philadelphia Inquirer* wrote that he was probably hiding in a Catholic convent near Montreal.[3] Surratt was not in a convent, but was hiding with Catholic priests near Montreal, a fact undoubtedly known to the War Department.

As court opened on Monday, May 22, Commission president General Hunter announced that it was necessary to recall some important witnesses whose testimony had been taken behind closed doors the previous Saturday evening. He ordered the courtroom cleared. When the doors were later opened to the public, the room filled quickly with spectators, among them numerous women.

George Bancroft, the eminent historian from New York, had written influential friends that he would like to see the Review and attend the conspiracy trial. He was assured a pass to the courtroom.[4] In addition to Bancroft, other visitors included Senators Lane and Chandler, and the flashy young General, George Custer, with his beautiful bride.

The tremendous crowd inconvenienced court reporters and others there on legitimate business. Spectators had to stand on their toes to catch a glimpse of the prisoners as they entered. As usual, Payne attracted the greatest attention, especially from the ladies. Next in popular interest were Mrs. Surratt and Herold. Dr. Mudd did not excite much attention apparently because he did not fit the preconceived image of the conspirators. The doctor, usually dressed in a dark business suit, this time wore a brown linen coat. He continued to project the countenance of a successful, cultured physician, only accidentally involved with the ruffians around him. The Court could not forget, however, that a man even more successful, cultured and famous pulled the trigger that killed the President.

One reporter noticed a change in Mrs. Surratt's attitude. "It is not fear, not the excitement of a mighty doubt, but the withering blasting woe," caused by more than 30 hours of testimony which were sufficient to paint upon her face "some horrifying sorrow."[5] The newsman may have allowed his imagination to control his pen. The widow actually continued much as before. She remained in her corner of the room, continued to dress in black and to hide her face behind the never-absent veil and palm-leaf fan. Occasionally she would raise her head to smooth her dark hair and to keep it from falling in her face, and at the same time try to catch a quick glance at the courtroom without appearing to stare.

Newspaper reports of the trial were readily available in the courtroom. Spectators often brought papers with them in order to compare drawings to the prisoners. These papers, of course, were supposed to be withheld from the accused. Stanton had prohibited any contemporary reading material, but nothing could keep defense counsel from revealing news to their clients.

After the reading of the previous day's testimony, Honora Fitzpatrick took the stand and was questioned by Judge Bingham. Fitzpatrick did not produce any surprising revelations. She testified she had seen Booth, Atzerodt, Payne, and of course, John Surratt, in the boardinghouse, and mentioned having attended Ford's Theatre with Surratt and Payne. The young lady recalled that Booth visited the box, but she couldn't remembr which box they occupied.

Following a recess, Capt. E. P. Doherty again related details of Booth's capture. He reported how Herold had at first denied that he knew who Booth was and that Herold claimed he met the man accidentally about seven miles from

Washington. Under Stone's cross-examination, Doherty told about Booth's claim that Herold was innocent.

The next witness, William Cleaver, testified that Booth kept a one-eyed horse at his stable on 6th Street. He said the actor sold the horse to Arnold. This one-eyed horse had now been connected with Mudd, Booth, Atzerodt, Surratt, Payne and Arnold.

Marshal McPhail then testified that O'Laughlin served in the Confederate army about a year but that he took the oath of allegiance sometime after the battle of Antietam.

Dr. F. S. Verdi, the next witness, pictured the bloody scene he found at the Seward house. In cross-examination, Doster asked a curious question about Payne's attack on the Secretary. "Have you not at some time before this trial stated that the wounds received by Mr. Seward had a tendency to aid in his recovering from the former injury?"

"No, sir; I have heard that such an opinion was expressed, but I do not know by whom; that was not my opinion."[6]

The Government interrogated Joseph Burroughs again, but he revealed nothing new. James Maddox testified next. Authorities called these two witnesses to reinforce their weak case against Spangler.

Bingham interrogated Maddox. "Did you see Spangler that night?"

"Yes, sir."

"State at what time you saw him during the performance."

Maddox made it clear that Spangler was not absent from his assigned position, because if he had been, someone else would have had to make the scene changes.

"If he had been away for what length of time?" Bingham questioned. Maddox claimed that if he had missed one scene, directors of the play would have known it. "One scene sometimes lasts two minutes," he explained.[7] The witness indicated his belief in Spangler's innocence, but Bingham wasn't satisfied. "Have you ever seen Spangler wear a mustache?" the Judge inquired.

"No; not since I have known him, and I have known him two years next month."

"Where were you at the moment the President was assassinated?"

"At the first entrance leading to the lefthand box."

"Did you see Spangler there shortly before?"

"Yes, sir; I think I did; I saw him in his proper position as I crossed the stage after the second scene of the third act was on."[8]

The Government then, digressing from prosecution of the prisoners, brought in a series of witnesses to recite the barbarous activities of the Confederate Government. Later in the day the Commission got back to the suspects but revealed little of importance.

After court adjourned, Judge Holt explained that because of the parade and otherwise crowded conditions in Washington, it would be difficult for Commission members, as well as witnesses and guards, to get to the courtroom the next day. He therefore suggested a two-day recess. The Military Commissioners knew that their fellow officers, their comrades in arms and their friends were to be honored by a grateful Nation, and they were eager to join the festivities. Having all led victorious armies with distinction, the temptation was great to call off the trial. But the dutiful officers did not yield, deciding rather to meet as usual the next day.

During the last few days, the defense and the prosecution frequently engaged in casual conversation. Informal talks took place around the tables during the recesses and occasionally after court adjourned. Aiken was seen waiting for an interview with the Secretary of War in the latter's office after the session on May 22. It is uncertain what this flurry of interchange signified.

Spangler's growing dread of the gallows led him to ask his lawyer about his chances. Stone, conferring with Bingham about the matter, nonchalantly speculated that the Government did not have a real case against Spangler. Bingham just smiled.

That night, as soldiers escorted the Commissioners to their homes, they could sense the excitement of the coming parade. Carpenters were still at work, preparing the capital for the big event. Fire engines hurried around washing dirt off Pennsylvania Avenue, the only paved street in the city. The Nation's capital, after four years of Civil War, was dismal. On the eve of the Grand Review, hordes of soldiers and visitors made conditions worse.

The War Department had ordered a review of the armies by the President and his Cabinet as a fitting climax to the victory and as an expression of the Nation's appreciation. Even though combat-weary soldiers wanted to get home, they reluctantly camped on the outskirts of the city to await the celebration.

For nearly a week the capital engaged in elaborate preparations. Colorful symbols decorated public edifices. Flags hung on private buildings and patriotic mottoes and garlands of flowers were displayed everywhere. Carpenters erected a large reviewing stand on Pennsylvania Avenue in front of the White House.

The Army of the Potomac, Sherman's troops and Sheridan's cavalry encamped around Washington, but the War Department had dispatched Sheridan to the Rio Grande to initiate a campaign against Maximilian, whom the French had enthroned as Emperor of Mexico.

Crowds arrived early, stationing themselves at prime locations along the parade route. Space of any kind was scarce. Citizens had been warned for days not to come to the capital as all hotels and boardinghouses were crowded. The warning went unheeded, and every train puffing into the city bulged with celebrants. Even sitting space in unoccupied carriages or wagons sold for a dollar a night. Windows overlooking Pennsylvania Avenue cost $10 an hour during the parade (more than a week's pay for an average clerk). A spectator could rent a window for a day for $50 to watch 21 miles of soldiers parade by.

General Grant was the first to enter the reviewing stand. Members of his staff, including Colonel Porter, who had originally been delegated to serve on the Military Commission, accompanied him. Grant, seeking to avoid attention, had walked through the grounds of the White House to the stand. However, the crowds recognized him immediately and shouted their admiration.

The reviewing stand soon filled with Government dignitaries including the President, Cabinet members, Supreme Court justices, state governors, United States senators and representatives.

A signal gun fired at nine o'clock sharp starting the grand procession. Armies marched according to seniority. The Army of the Potomac, the first organized, led the march from the Capitol down Pennsylvania Avenue toward the White House. Martial music provided by numerous bands added to the excitement. War songs, familiar to both civilians and soldiers, filled the air. The crowd responded most enthusiastically to "When This Cruel War Is Over," and "Tramp, Tramp, Tramp, the Boys Are Marching."

A little more than a mile south of the parade route the Military Commission pushed doggedly forward with its grim work. Day after day the generals had gathered in the stifling courtroom dutifully performing their task. Stoically they tried to ignore the victory parade they had helped make possible. It was not a pleasant assignment, but military discipline demanded faithfulness to duty.

On the first morning of the Grand Review the courtroom was nearly empty. The prisoners became more relaxed and seemed to enjoy the attention of the few gaping visitors. Herold playfully ran a straw across his mouth during the hearing. The officers could easily hear the music in the distance. Arnold and Mudd, nearest the open window, ignored the legal proceedings and stood up to look out.

The generals, however, pressed on with the trial. For two weeks not one had missed a single hour, but this reminder of the Grand Review was getting to them. Each one had led troops in bloody battles to hold the Union together. Gloomily they remained cooped up in the Arsenal while their fellow officers were enjoying the adulation of the wildly cheering throngs.

The uninhibited rejoicing on Pennsylvania Avenue was in striking contrast to the gloom and hopelessness of the prisoners securely manacled in the courtroom. They were not the only ones to miss the victory celebrations, however. Mrs. Lincoln and little Tad were absent. They had returned to Springfield.

Some of the witnesses summoned by the Court could not get across 4½ Street to the Arsenal because of the parade. The lack of witnesses gave the Commissioners an excuse to call off the sessions for two days, as Holt had previously suggested. The prisoners were led back to their cells, except for Herold, who was given permission to write a letter. He lingered behind in the courtroom with a guard, his hands free of the dreaded handcuffs so he could write. The generals hurried off to Pennsylvania Avenue.

After the early adjournment, a rumor spread that the trial was delayed, not because of the victory parade, but because the two extra days would give the Government more time to examine 15 tons of Rebel documents that had just arrived at the War Department. A large clerical force had already methodically examined other Confederate papers, hoping to find enough evidence to "hang the entire Rebel Government."

May 24 was a beautiful 70-degree spring day. Again, with military precision,

**William T. Sherman. The stubborn General became embroiled in a personal
quarrel with the Secretary of War that affected attitudes in the trial (Library of
Congress—BH832-796).**

a gun sounded at nine o'clock sharp signaling the start of the final day's parade.
Multitudes waving flags and flowers lined the streets and almost blocked the
parade route. This day Gen. William T. Sherman headed the procession. The
General, attended by his staff, rode slowly and grandly down the Avenue. As
he neared the Treasury Building, he looked back on magnificent columns of
men holding glittering muskets, looking "like a solid mass of steel, moving with
the regularity of a pendulum." It was a glorious moment for the outspoken
leader.

A few days earlier he had telegraphed his wife in Lancaster, Ohio, to bring
their eight-year-old son, whom the General hardly knew, to be with him in
Washington. Mrs. Sherman's brother, Thomas Ewing, Jr., was defending the
conspirators. Her father, the Hon. Thomas Ewing, Sr., accompanied her. (The
senior Ewing was later selected Secretary of War in Stanton's place, after the
impeachment of Johnson failed.) General Sherman, reared by the Ewings, was
closer to the Ewing children than he was with his own brother, Senator John
Sherman, from whom he had been separated during his youth.

When Sherman's father, an Ohio judge, died, he left 11 children, aged three
months to 18 years. The children were separated to be reared by various
families. The family of Thomas Ewing, Sr., who lived near the Shermans in

Lancaster took William. Judge Sherman had helped Ewing early in his career, and he was eager to repay the kindness. Thomas Ewing, Jr., and William Sherman grew up as brothers. Sherman eventually married Ellen Ewing, making Thomas, Jr. both his foster brother and his brother-in-law.

Someone had notified Sherman that Secretary of State Seward, still convalescing, had removed enough bandages to view the parade from his window. The General rode over toward Seward's house overlooking the southeastern corner of Lafayette Square to doff his hat to the Secretary. Seward gratefully returned the salute.

Sherman's approach to the reviewing stand was particularly stirring. All bands, in unison, struck up "Marching through Georgia," resulting in wild demonstrations honoring the hero. The General walked his horse, decorated with garlands, past the stand, his sword raised in salute to the Commander-in-Chief. The President and all in the stand rose to their feet in recognition of the leader. The General then turned into the White House grounds, where he dismounted. He proceeded to take his place with his wife and son in the reviewing stand. As was customary, he shook hands with the assembled dignitaries. When he reached Stanton, his friendly countenance changed abruptly; he angrily faced the Secretary of War and turned away brusquely.

This ugly incident was tied to the conspiracy trial. Stanton, though not directly active in the trial, exercised authority over the participants and, in the minds of many, was the man most responsible for the prisoners' plight. To further complicate matters, Ewing's father was advising his son in the defense of the conspirators and at the same time trying to patch up difficulties between his foster son and the Secretary of War.

The rift between Sherman and Stanton had deep roots. The General had harbored a hatred for the Secretary of War for nearly a month because Stanton had reprimanded him publicly in the press. Sherman refused all attempts by General Grant, a concerned third party, to work out a reconciliation.

Stanton, accustomed to bullying even the most powerful, was tangling with a man as obstinate and almost as mighty as he. While Stanton's no-nonsense sternness had complemented Lincoln's easygoing nature, Stanton and Sherman were too much alike. Both were hardheaded prima donnas. Both expected unquestioned obedience, and, beneath imperturbable exteriors, both were sensitive to criticism. Both were competent and indispensable to the war effort. Few men had served their country more sacrificially than Stanton and Sherman, each in his own way. As the war drew to a close, Sherman, especially, expected laurels rather than censure.

Reporters were at first reluctant to publicize the acrid dispute that had developed between the two. Historians barely mentioned the controversy at the time. Stanton never dwelt on the conflict; as with other difficulties that troubled his life, he preferred to forget it.

The clash began in the closing days of the war, after Sherman had completed his astounding march to the sea and his subsequent drive through the Carolinas. While reforming his forces at Goldsboro, North Carolina, preparatory to a confrontation with Confederate General Joseph E. Johnston, he received word of Lee's surrender. Sherman continued to ready his army for a move against Johnston, but the Confederate General avoided a fight, and on April 14 (the day Lincoln was shot), Johnston asked for peace terms.

At one time, when Sherman seemed to be eclipsing Grant in power and glory, Stanton visited Sherman in Savannah, Georgia. The Secretary of War appeared to be courting favor with the popular General. With Grant's subsequent success in capturing Richmond, and the surrender of Lee, Stanton apparently shifted his favor to Grant.

Grant authorized Sherman to offer Johnston the same surrender terms Grant had given Lee. Sherman had also met with President Lincoln in the final months of the war. He knew that the now-deceased President had told the Peace Commissioners at Hampton Roads that, other than preserving the Union and abolishing slavery, he was willing to accept lenient peace terms.

Sherman did not follow Grant's terms to Lee exactly, but he undoubtedly thought that what he offered was in keeping with Lincoln's expressed wishes. In any case, his surrender terms were not binding. They were conditional upon the approval of the Federal Government. Unfortunately for Sherman, he was unaware of the more rigid guidelines which Lincoln had later ordered Grant to offer Lee.

Lincoln's death and Stanton's growing power also worked to Sherman's disadvantage. The General made the mistake of not consulting either President Johnson or the Secretary of War before he submitted actual surrender terms to the Confederate General. Sherman believed he was on safe grounds, however, because he thought Stanton had given him a free hand in working out the surrender.

He was far from safe, however. The assassination hysteria had dramatically altered the situation. A week after Lincoln's death, the lenient terms Sherman offered Johnston were telegraphed to Stanton. Enraged, the Secretary immediately called a special Cabinet meeting. As all official communications passed through his office rather than the President's, he did not even bother to let President Johnson exercise his prerogative in calling the meeting. At this point, Stanton was stronger than the President.

Sherman's easy terms caused the suspicious Secretary of War to lose his temper. Convulsed with anger, he harshly denounced Sherman in the Cabinet meeting, insinuating that the General might be cooperating with the Confederates, and might even try to take over the Federal Government. Attorney General Speed joined Stanton in his emphatic denunciation of Sherman. Stanton's wild actions resulted from the intense pressures of authority beset by abnormal fears.

Stanton called on General Grant to explain Sherman's terms to the hastily assembled Cabinet. The entire Cabinet, as well as Grant, quickly rejected Sherman's surrender terms. Stanton had a message sent immediately to Union troops in the South to disregard the surrender treaty and not to obey Sherman's orders. He decided that Grant should personally inform Sherman of the Government's decision.

The Cabinet's main objection was that Sherman had overstepped his authority and included strictly civil matters in his offer to Johnston. The Secretary of War ordered Grant to advise Sherman strongly that generals in the field should not take upon themselves the authority to decide civil and political questions. Although unhappy with his assignment, Grant left at once for North Carolina.

During the next few days, Stanton and his colleague Speed kept the entire Cabinet agitated with intemperate stories of Sherman's "grave mistake." The Attorney General, like the Secretary of War, also imagined that Sherman might have designs to take over the Government. "Suppose," Speed speculated, Sherman "should arrest Grant when Grant arrived at Raleigh...."[9]

During this time, Stanton and his friends repeated the "positive evidence" dug up by Judge Holt about a widespread conspiracy involving Confederate leaders. Secretary of the Navy Welles later recalled the excited atmosphere in which these Cabinet meetings were held. "Strange stories," he wrote, "were told us and it was under these representations, to which we then gave credit, that we were less inclined to justify Sherman."[10] Just exactly how Holt's supposed evidence implicating Confederate leaders would reflect on Sherman's terms was not made clear. Presumably, the Cabinet feared the surrender offer was so lenient it might allow Rebels to continue their grand conspiracy against the Government. Speed's words suggested that he thought Sherman might be involved in it.

A confused and fearful atmosphere continued to pervade higher Government circles, and many suffered as a result. Welles wrote,

> I think we have permitted ourselves, amid great excitement and stirring events to be hurried into unjust and ungenerous suspicions by the erroneous statements of the Secretary of War. Speed adopts and echoes the jealousies and wild vagaries of Stanton who seems to have a mortal fear of the Generals....[11]

To say Stanton had a "mortal fear" of generals was going too far. He had a "mortal fear" of no one. General Grant recalled that when he was in command of the Union armies, Stanton, "owing to his natural disposition to assume all power and control in all matters that he had anything to do with," had boldly taken control of the armies. Stanton prohibited any order being issued by the Adjutant General's office until he had approved it. Because of this procedure a number of Grant's orders were held up for several days. Grant eventually complained about this to Stanton, who backed off for a while, but "soon lapsed again and took control much as before."[12]

Sherman, however, was not so easily controlled. Grant hurried to Raleigh, hoping to see Sherman without either Johnston's or Sherman's soldiers knowing about the visit. Grant told Sherman that the terms had been rejected at Washington and he would have to renegotiate them. Sherman, following orders, renegotiated the surrender, making the terms the same as Grant's to Lee and considered the matter closed.

In a highly irregular move, Stanton gave the correspondence relating to the incident to New York newspapers. The papers published Stanton's version, which presented Sherman in the worst light. When Sherman read the *New York*

Senator John Sherman. Brother of General Stanton's neighbor, and he was in the middle of rivalries that influenced the trial (Library of Congress – BH826-3214).

Times, he was furious. He wrote General Grant that Stanton was incorrect in thinking that his (Sherman's) orders to Stoneman had aided Davis' escape. On the contrary, Sherman wrote, "Davis was between us, and therefore . . . by turning toward me he [Stoneman] was approaching Davis. . . ." He added bitterly, "Even now I don't know that Mr. Stanton wants Davis caught, and as my official papers, deemed sacred, are hastily published to the world, it will be imprudent for me to state what had been done in that regard."[13]

Stanton's account stated that Confederate leaders hoped "to make terms with General Sherman, or some other commander, by which they will be permitted, with their effects, including this gold plunder, to go to Mexico or Europe." The insinuation that he might have been bribed enraged Sherman.

Stanton, however, genuinely believed that Sherman's actions were disastrous and that the officer's lenient terms favored a Rebel plot. He commented to Orville Browning that Sherman's treaty was the worst thing that had happened during the war. According to Stanton, Sherman had thrown away all they had been fighting for and had afforded Davis a chance to escape.

Sen. John Sherman, Stanton's neighbor, got along well with the domineering Secretary, but these insults to his brother were too much. He made no effort to defend the surrender terms, but he did support his brother against Stanton's charges of treason and corruption. The Senator, unlike the General, however, was forgiving and excused Stanton's extreme reactions as the result of the Secretary's fear for his own life. Guards still remained around homes of Cabinet members. Stanton overreacted to Sherman's treaty as he did to many crucial issues in the aftermath of the assassination, but seldom in American history would such a reaction be more excusable than in the last two weeks of April 1865.

Sherman had expected Stanton to apologize, and when he did not, Sherman refused all efforts at reconciliation. Feeling he had been publicly insulted, he was determined to insult Stanton publicly. The occasion presented itself at the Grand Review. The General and his family had joined Sen. John Sherman in the reviewing stand on the first day of the parade, but that day he had no opportunity to offend Stanton.

On the second day Sherman got his revenge, which at least satisfied him. According to Sherman's account, Stanton extended his hand, "but I declined it publicly and the fact was universally noticed."[14] The General, anxious to publicize the incident, exaggerated the importance of his vengeful conduct. Stanton took little notice, having become accustomed to insults.

Exactly what happened is debatable. Horace Porter, who criticized the military trial and was no friend of Stanton's, saw the episode and confirmed Sherman's version. Charles Dana, Assistant Secretary of War, gave a different story. He sat directly behind Stanton and, being aware of the tensions, watched closely as Sherman came to the reviewing stand. He wanted "to see what General Sherman would do in passing before Mr. Stanton. . . ." Dana declared that Sherman was entirely mistaken when he wrote that Stanton offered his hand. "The Secretary made no motion to offer his hand, or to exchange salutations in any manner. As the General passed, Mr. Stanton gave him merely a slight forward motion of his head."[15]

This report is more in keeping with Stanton's nature. The stubborn Secretary of War was likely to have remained as cool as Sherman. The two leaders stayed in the reviewing stand for more than six hours together without exchanging a word.

However it happened, the defiant General snubbed the hardheaded Secretary of War. Those on the stand noticed the affront and discussed it all over town. While newspapers had previously tried to minimize the rift, this public rudeness could not be ignored. The press tended to criticize Sherman. His conduct did not characterize a great man and did not raise Sherman in public esteem. Several accounts praised Stanton for his composure.

The feud did not lessen the enthusiasm of the crowds absorbed in the spectacle of the "greatest army in the world." If not the greatest, it was, in Sherman's estimation, a display of the "most magnificent army in existence." Sherman's armies had performed their duty to preserve the Union in Tennessee and Georgia. Even though leaving a large portion of it desolate, they had marched nearly 2,000 miles in hostile country.

Prisoners in Old Capitol could not avoid hearing the loud music and wild cheers. They understood that even if the trial was suspended, it was only temporarily. The following day it would start again. How much this boisterous reminder of the war, coming as it did in the middle of the legal proceedings, influenced the outcome, no one knows. But it certainly did not help the cause of the accused.

Visitors from across the Nation, drawn to Washington by the Grand Review, found their way to the courtroom after the two-day recess. The crowd on May 25 was so large that most spectators remained only 10 or 15 minutes. After a good look at the prisoners they left, making room for others.

One observer, disturbed by the shoving and talking, complained that "the most important trial of the age is degenerating into a most undignified exhibition of a half-dozen criminals to an unmannerly populace—and if no restriction is put on the visitors the Court might as well give up its operations altogether."[16] The noise, at times, was so great that the Court could not hear the witnesses. Col. LaFayette Baker visited the courtroom frequently to help his deputies control the crowds. Baker's men worked with four other high-ranking officers stationed at the Arsenal. On this day General Hartranft sat inside the railing with the Military Commissioners because of the conditions.

The prisoners, except Arnold, seemed more haggard as the trial dragged on. Apparently, he felt the testimony favored him. O'Laughlin remained the most downcast. The two-day recess, however, had given guards time to get the men shaved and cleaned up; they even wore clean shirts.

The accidental discharge of a guard's musket in an adjacent room created a little excitement. The loud shot unnerved the crowd, and the Judges recessed long enough to check on the cause.

After the commotion died down, the first witness testified that he had found a naval revolver among Arnold's possessions at Fortress Monroe. The Government then produced more witnesses who described the awful conditions in Southern prisons.

Getting back to the assassination, Judge Holt interrogated George Magee. Holt asked if Arnold had ever been in the Confederate army. General Ewing objected vigorously to the question, explaining that Arnold was on trial for conspiracy in the assassination. "He is not on trial for having been in the military service of the Confederate States," declared Ewing emphatically.[17]

The emotional victory parade obviously had not dampened the Union General's energetic defense of an ex–Confederate soldier.

Southern-born Holt countered Ewing with his own argument. "I think the testimony in this case has proven what I believe to be sufficiently demonstrative, how kindred to each other are the crimes of treason against the Nation and the assassination of its Chief Magistrate."

The murder of the President, he continued, was preeminently a political assassination. "Disloyalty to the Government was its sole, its only inspiration," he added. "When, therefore, we shall show, on the part of the accused, acts of intense disloyalty, the bearing of arms in the field against the Government, we show the presence of an animus towards that Government," concluded the Judge.[18]

Bingham came forward with legal examples supporting Holt's position. The Court overruled Ewing's objection, and the witness answered that he was not certain that Arnold had served in the Confederate army.

The Government produced a series of witnesses dealing with Dr. Mudd. Assistant Judge Advocate Bingham questioned Mary Simms, "State whether you know any of the prisoners." Pointing to Mudd she answered, "I know that one, Dr. Samuel Mudd."

"State whether you were his slave, and lived with him."

"I was his slave, and lived with him four years; I left him about a month before last Christmas; I was free then."

Bingham inquired about Mudd's attitude toward President Lincoln. The girl replied that Mudd didn't like the President.

"State who visited him."

"A man by the name of Surratt visited him; also a man named Walker Bowie."

"Who called this man Surratt?"

"Dr. Sam Mudd and Dr. Sam Mudd's wife called him Surratt."

When Bingham solicited a description of Surratt, she responded, "He was young looking, rather slim, neither very tall nor short; his hair was rather light, at least not black."[19]

Descriptions of Surratt varied. Some witnesses described him as tall, while others remarked that he was small, but Miss Simms' description was very accurate.

"State where he slept when at Dr. Mudd's house."

"All of his men slept in the woods."

"State how many were with him when they slept in the woods."

"There was a Captain White, from Tennessee; Bennett Gwynn, Andrew Gwynn and George Gwynn."

The Court knew the notorious Confederate Ben Gwynn was the man Mrs. Surratt had visited on the first of her two trips to Surrattsville. "How did they get victuals to eat while they were in the woods?" continued the prosecutor. The witness explained that sometimes the soldiers went in the house with Dr. Mudd to eat. At such times he posted his slaves "at the door to watch if anybody come along." Sometimes he sent the witness into the woods with victuals for the men. In that case she would "stand behind a tree to watch when the Rebels would come out and get them." When asked, she admitted seeing John Surratt with the soldiers. Mary Simms also revealed that when the men wanted to talk privately, they would go "upstairs in a room." Her testimony was particularly damaging to the doctor. She pictured him as receiving and sending letters and clothing to the Rebels in Virginia.

Bingham got to a more personal subject. "Did you hear Dr. Samuel Mudd say anything about sending anybody to Richmond?" The witness stated, "I heard him say something about sending my brother to Richmond; when he bought my brother he said he would have something for him to do in Richmond."

"What did he say he would have for him to do?"

"To build batteries."

"Was your brother a slave?"

"Yes, sir."[20]

The judges did not always take black witnesses seriously, yet Mary Simms answered questions convincingly. The former slave did not mention the date Rebel soldiers visited Dr. Mudd, but she did give names and showed clearly that Mudd had been aiding Confederates. Ewing's cross-examination failed to reveal any flaws in her testimony.

Eleazer Eglin, brother of the previous witness, came to the stand. After identifying Dr. Mudd among the prisoners, Holt questioned him. "Were you his slave?"

"Yes, sir; I left him in August 1863."

"State whether he said anything to you about sending you to Richmond."

Ewing objected to the question, but Holt claimed that it was necessary, to show the accused was disloyal. The objection was overruled. Holt repeated the question and the witness responded, "He told me that when I got so that I could travel he would have a place for me in Richmond." The former slave confirmed much of his sister's testimony, describing how Mudd fed and cared for the Rebel soldiers.[21]

The next witness, Sylvester Eglin, another brother and a slave of Mudd's father, also testified that he and Eleazer were to have been sent to Richmond.

L. Washington, also one of Dr. Mudd's slaves, stated that his master disliked President Lincoln and told of Confederate soldiers being aided by Dr. Mudd in secret. The facts mentioned by these former slaves were later substantiated, even by defense witnesses. The only real differences involved questions of time. Some did not mention the year Mudd concealed the troops, but others made it appear that the activities occurred in 1864. The defense later disputed the date but could not alter the facts. Washington told about efforts to warn the Confederates. "Dr. Mudd set the children to watch while they were at dinner; the children said they were coming, and these men jumped up from the table and ran out the side door."

Ewing attempted to undo the damage. "How many times did you notice these men in the woods?" The former slave replied, "They were there for a week or more, and I saw them seven or eight times; they all then went away together in the night."

"Do you know their names?"

"I think one was Andrew Gwynn; I do not know the names of the others."

When asked who else saw the Rebel troops, Washington responded, "The woman, Mary Simms, who was on here just now, saw them; her and another woman were in the room; I don't know any white person who saw them, except Dr. Mudd and his wife."[22]

Mylo Simms, a young boy, also Mudd's former slave, was called. This time defense lawyer Stone, whose family had lived for generations in the same area as the Mudds and who had owned slaves himself, cross-examined the witness. "Did you work in the house or in the field?" he questioned.

"In the field, but sometimes when I was at the house I took the horses."

"How old are you?"

"I reckon about fourteen years."

Stone asked how he could be sure that John Surratt visited Dr. Mudd if he didn't even know him. The former slave answered the former slave owner unwaveringly and convincingly, "Dr. Mudd would say, 'take Mr. Surratt's horse and carry him out to the stable and feed him.'"

The lawyer questioned him about other visitors to the Mudds' house, many of whom were involved in the assassination. Answering a question about Andrew Gwynn, the witness testified, "I saw him at Dr. Mudd's father's house; I never saw Andrew Gwynn at Dr. Mudd's house."

"Who was with Andrew Gwynn?"

"[Jerry] Dyer."

"When was the last time you saw John Surratt at Dr. Mudd's?"

"Last winter."

"Did he stay all night?"

"Yes."[23]

The Government had previously identified Gwynn, Dyer and Surratt as suspects.

Stone's interrogation did not help the doctor's plight, but Mudd was a difficult client to serve. Even though the testimony was going against him, he refused to confide in his legal counsel.

William Marshall, another former slave, took the witness stand. "State whether you were the slave of and lived with Dr. Samuel A. Mudd," solicited the Judge.

"I married near him."

"Do you know Ben Gardiner, one of his neighbors?"

"Yes, Ben Gardiner was my wife's master."

The Judge asked about a meeting between Gardiner and Mudd. Marshall, describing the conversation, stated that Gardiner talked of Confederate victories at the Rappahannock. According to the witness, Gardiner "said that 'in a short time he [Lee] would take the Capital, and Washington, and have Old Lincoln burned up in the house'; Dr. Mudd said he would not be surprised."[24]

Marshall continued, relating a convincing story of Mudd's support of the Confederacy.

Another of Mudd's former slaves, Rachel Spencer, then swore that the doctor hid soldiers on his farm in the summer of 1864, among them Andrew Gwynn and Walter Bowie. Stone's cross-examination attempted to show that the slaves had faulty sense of time. "You say you saw them there in the summer; was it the first day of the summer or the last?" he questioned.

"I do not know; it was warm weather; they all came together and went together; I believe they stayed at the spring for about a week."

As Stone knew the citizens and their political views in that area, he asked about some of Mudd's neighbors. "Was Mr. Best living there that year?"

"Yes; to the best of my knowledge he came there the winter before."

"Do you know whether Mr. Albion Brooke was living there at the time these men were there?"

"Yes, he did."

"Did Mr. Best and Mr. Brooke also see these people?"

"Yes, sir."

Exact times and years were difficult for slaves, and the defense made it a point to quibble over dates.

Judge Bingham, noting some carelessness in the last statement, wanted to clarify it. "Do you know whether Albion Brooke ever saw them or not, or did you merely suppose he did?" Rachel Spencer answered firmly, "He saw them."

"Did he tell you he saw them or how did you know it?"

"He used to go with them; they were all together."

"Do you know whether Mr. Best ever saw them or not?"

"I am not positive whether he did or not."[25]

These questions terminated the prosecution's first round. The Government turned the case over to the defense but reserved the right to introduce further testimony. The early evidence strongly incriminated the suspects. The Associated Press reported that "a review of the evidence deeply implicates Mrs. Surratt, Dr. Mudd, Atzerodt and Spangler; of the guilt of Payne and Herold there is perfect proof; and the evidence but slightly implicates O'Laughlin and Arnold."[26] Except for the evidence against Spangler, which was weak, the writer correctly summarized the case.

XXXIII
In Defense of Mary Surratt

Following a rare consultation, defense laywers agreed to collaborate in presenting their cases. They decided to introduce testimony in behalf of Mrs. Surratt first. Aiken advised the Court that counsel would not consider testimony closed in regard to any of the accused until all defense testimony had been given.

The strategy in behalf of Mary Surratt became obvious with the calling of the first witness. Father B. F. Wigget was president of Gonzaga College, located just a few blocks from the Surratt boardinghouse. He was one of five priests called in her defense. Defense strategy attempted to present Mrs. Surratt as a devout Catholic mother incapable of participating in the horrendous crime. The lawyers played on sentiment, motherhood and religion. It was the only defense she had, and it had promise. Mary Surratt's counsel tried to ignore the evidence against her as much as possible.

The Confederacy used women spies successfully throughout the war. Many had been caught, but none hanged. The women were not in uniform and did not carry arms. When captured, they trusted in the Nation's traditional chivalry.

This strategy had worked in all other cases, but this case was different. The Federal Government had never hanged a woman, but then it had never tried a woman for complicity in the murder of the President. The enormity of the crime, not public hysteria, put the widow in danger.

Using priests as witnesses had both advantages and disadvantages. Even though lawyers could select questions favorable to Mrs. Surratt, the priests would not lie. After identifying Father Wigget, Aiken began the case for the defense. "Are you acquainted with the prisoner, Mary E. Surratt?"

"I am and have been for ten or eleven years."

"Has that acquaintance been of an intimate character?"

"I know her very well."

Aiken opened with the tactic stressed constantly in Mrs. Surratt's case— her piety. In response to several general questions about her Christian devotion, the priest testified she was highly thought of. The interrogation turned to Weichmann. "Are you acquainted with Louis J. Weichmann?"

"Only very slightly; I saw him a few times; I am not well acquainted with him."

"State whether, from your knowledge, he has ever been a student of divinity."[1]

Bingham objected. The attorney countered that he expected to show that Weichmann misrepresented his vocational aims and could not be trusted. The Court upheld the objection.

The defense harped repeatedly on this questionable point. The term "student of divinity" could be variously interpreted. Both John Surratt and Louis Weichmann had attended a Catholic school whose students were generally preparing for some responsibility within the Roman Catholic Church, although they made no formal contract or public announcement of their future plans. Surratt denied that he was preparing for the priesthood, while Weichmann declared that such were his intentions. His personal correspondence bore this out.

Aiken, trying another approach, asked, "Was there in the city of Richmond a Catholic Theological Institute?"[2] Again Bingham objected.

Bingham's repeated interruptions caused growing resentment. He allowed little latitude in the evidence given by the defense, objecting at every possible point. Even the Boston Advertiser, which usually praised the Judges' conduct, criticized Judge Bingham. His overbearing legalism contrasted to the leeway the defense granted the prosecution. For instance, several days were taken up with testimony concerning Southern atrocities and brutality in Rebel prisons, Numerous witnesses related accounts of Confederate plots to burn Northern cities. The defense counsel listened quietly to this interesting, but somewhat irrelevant, testimony. The Government contended these statements proved the brutality of Confederate leaders and concluded, therefore, that the murder of the President was altogether within the realm of the Southern mentality. None of the evidence, however, related directly to the case.

After Bingham's repeated objections, the defense changed the subject. The lawyer asked, "In your acquaintance with Mrs. Surratt have you ever known of a defective eyesight on her part?" Apparently not realizing that Mrs. Surratt used poor eyesight as an excuse for not recognizing Payne, the Reverend Father replied that he did not realize she had bad eyesight. This first inept effort by Mrs. Surratt's lawyers characterized her defense.

Holt's cross-examinations quickly annulled any good impression left by Aiken's questions. "You say you know the character of the prisoner, Mrs. Surratt, for Christianity is good; have you any personal knowledge of her character for loyalty?"

"No; my intercourse with her has never extended to political affairs."

"You have had intercourse with her as her pastor during the Rebellion, have you not?"

"I am not her pastor."

Holt's interrogation revealed that Father Wigget had slight knowledge of the prisoner's political sentiments. "Have you ever since the Rebellion heard her utter one loyal sentiment?" he continued. The priest said he could not remember.

"Can you state whether it is not notorious among those who know anything of her, that she is intensely disloyal?" Again Father Wigget responded that he did not remember anything about it.[3]

The testimony of Father Francis E. Boyle, pastor of St. Peter's Catholic Church in Washington, followed the same lines. The clergyman stated that he had met Mrs. Surratt about nine years earlier, but that he had "merely met her casually some three or four times since then." He maintained she was spoken of as "an estimable lady."

"In all your acquaintance with her, did you ever hear her utter a disloyal sentiment?" Aiken questioned weakly.

"I never did."

It must have seemed to the Court an act of desperation for the defense to produce a character witness who admitted he only knew the accused slightly. Under cross-examination, Holt needed only one question – "Have you ever heard her utter a loyal sentiment?"

"I never heard much of her sentiments at all; I saw her so little, and at such long intervals, that I could not undertake to say what her general character for loyalty is."[4]

Another cleric took the stand. The Reverend Charles H. Stonestreet, pastor of St. Aloysius Catholic Church in Washington, testified that he had been acquainted with the suspect for more than 20 years. The defense repeated the usual question about her "general reputation as a Christian and a lady." "I have always looked upon her as a proper, Christian lady," affirmed the priest.

Aiken continued his routine. "Have you in all your intercourse with her ever heard her utter a disloyal sentiment?" As with the previous clergymen, he vowed that he had never heard her utter a disloyal sentiment, but he added, "There was no question of the kind at the time I knew her."

Judge Holt's cross-examination was short. "State whether you have probably seen her since the beginning of the Rebellion." The pastor made an extraordinary admission. "I do not remember having seen her at all; I have no knowledge whatever of her character for loyalty except what I have seen in the papers."[5] The clergyman further acknowledged that he had hardly seen her in the last 14 years. The opening defense, instead of being a powerful statement in favor of the prisoner, gave the impression that she was trying to hide behind her church. The priests, however, did not fit well in the scheme. They answered only what they knew about the widow, for whom they must have truly felt sympathy. Out of a sense of pastoral duty, they said what they could in her behalf, but nothing more.

Several reporters criticized this tactic as an effort to introduce religious influences into court procedures. Actually, ecclesiastical questions boiled beneath the surface. Soon after the assassination, some individuals introduced a religious element. Government authorities received letters accusing the Catholic Church of involvement. As the investigation progressed, it became evident that many suspects were Catholics. Letters to newspapers occasionally asserted that John Surratt was harbored in some Catholic institution or home in Washington; some more accurately mentioned Canada.

Occasionally the Catholic Church was described in unflattering terms. Benjamin Wood, editor and proprietor of the *New York Daily News*, was paid by the Confederate Government to publish his Copperhead paper. On May 5, 1865, he wrote that the *New York Tribune* charged the Roman Catholic Church with complicity in Lincoln's assassination. While newspapers agitated religious themes, and unfounded rumors caused tensions, the Government avoided the explosive issue.

Even before the assassination authorities had accumulated evidence showing what appeared to be Catholic support of the Confederacy. Investigators of the secret mail route from Richmond to Montreal discovered that many letters were carried by women dressed as nuns. Detectives later uncovered evidence that John Surratt obtained information from a Mr. Cullahan, one of the editors of the *Constitutional Union*, a small Washington paper. Cullahan furnished Surratt news about Federal armies, which he obtained from professors at Georgetown College, a Catholic institution in Washington.

The Government came across Honora Fitzpatrick's slightly suspicious correspondence. This young lady's presence in the Surratt house was never convincingly explained. She did not seem to have any business in Washington and made frequent trips to Baltimore, another center of the conspiracy. Early Easter Sunday morning, less than 24 hours after Lincoln's death, and a day after detectives first searched the boardinghouse, she wrote, "Dear Grandmother, . . . the only news I could get from you was through Father H____." (The priest's name was removed by the Government.) The next day, a letter posted from Baltimore to Fitzpatrick read, "My dear Nora, Father Dougherty will be in Washington on Wednesday. Go down to St. Patrick's about 1:00 to see him— don't put it off."[6] Someone wrote this note before the public knew about the women in Mrs. Surratt's house and before any were suspects. The communication had no signature. That night police arrested Nora and the other boarders.

The pastor of St. Patrick's, Father Jacob Ambrose Walter, spent a lifetime criticizing the Government for its treatment of Mrs. Surratt. No evidence indicates that the Government interrogated Father Dougherty or investigated the circumstance of this correspondence, but the Secretary of War denied the priest's request to see Mary Surratt a few days later. Stanton kept the suspicious letters hidden in War Department archives and seemed anxious to avoid confrontation with the Catholic Church.

Another incident known to the War Department, but not revealed to the public, involved Father N. D. Young, pastor of St. Dominic's. The priest testified on behalf of Mrs. Surratt but also seemed concerned about John Lloyd, one of the chief witnesses against her. On May 12, just as the trial started, he requested permission to give spiritual comfort to Lloyd in Old Capitol Prison. The Government did not allow him or any other visitor to see the prisoners at that time. But the timing of his request raised questions—it was the day before Lloyd was to testify against Mrs. Surratt. Father Young made no effort to visit Mrs. Surratt.

When detectives arrested Rebel blockade-runner Ben Ficklin, they discovered in his possession a letter from the bishop of Richmond, Father John McGill. He was the same Catholic prelate with whom Weichmann was corresponding. The letter was addressed to The Most Revered Dr. McCloskey, Archbishop of New York, and dated March 28, 1865. McGill wrote:

Most Rev. Dear Sir

Mr. B. F. Ficklin who has been a most liberal friend of our little orphans during the past years of difficulty, although not a member of our church, and who, as I am informed visits the North on business of his own not connected with the troubles of the day, will present you these lines of introduction. Any courtesy you may be able to extend to him will be well bestowed, and will be appreciated by yours very truly in Xt.

J. McGill
Bp. of Richmond[7]

Authorities imprisoned Ficklin, but they never questioned Bishop McGill and made nothing of this connection.

Stanton was well aware of the Catholic hierarchy's support of the Union. During the draft riots in New York City in the summer of 1863, Stanton received invaluable aid from Archbishop John Hughes, McCloskey's predecessor. The Secretary of War invited the influential prelate to Washington to discuss the tense situation. On returning to New York, the Archbishop, the most powerful Catholic in America, appealed to both clergy and laity to support the Federal Government. One of the Archbishop's last public appeals supported the Union. He used his great influence to bring order to New York City.

Federal leaders realized that some Catholics and some Protestants supported the Confederacy and that some backed the Union. The Government sought to convict conspirators and keep religious tensions out of it. Political authorities as well as spiritual leaders, both Protestant and Catholic, admirably kept this potentially eruptive issue subdued.

The Lincoln murder case could easily have aroused strong religious resentments. The testimony, particularly for the Government, made little or no reference to church affiliations of the suspects. The defense, on the other hand, deliberately attempted to inject religion. An article published later by Father Jacob Ambrose Walter could have inflamed religious passions, but the Archbishop controlled the situation. Circumstances also helped keep spiritual sentiments in balance. The most bitter arguments pitted Protestants against Protestants and Catholics against Catholics. The Government's chief witness, Weichmann, was a devout Catholic.

Following the series of priests, Aiken interrogated Eliza Holohan. She told the Court that she boarded with Mrs. Surratt from Februray 7 until April 16. Mrs. Holohan testified, under Aiken's prodding, that she saw Payne at the boardinghouse twice, but that he called himself Wood. She and her family moved from the Surratts' house the day after Lincoln died. The prosecution overlooked this suspicious move, but it had significance, because at that time, Mrs. Surratt had not been accused of anything. There was no compelling reason for anyone to have left. But, as in the case of the Branson house, boarders who suspected something clandestine hastened to move.

Aiken asked how she came to know Payne at the Surratt house. "Indeed I do not know anything about it; I went into the parlor and was introduced to him as Mr. Wood; I never changed a word with him at all," she stated.

"Did he represent himself a Baptist preacher?"

"I asked Miss Ann Surratt who he was; she said he was a Baptist minister; I said I did not think he would save many souls."

The packed courtroom burst into laughter. Even Payne could not suppress a broad grin. Mrs. Surratt remained solemn. During the questioning of her former boarder, Mary Surratt—who usually covered her face—made an even greater effort to hide herself. Aiken continued, "Did Mrs. Surratt keep a boardinghouse?" Her answer was surely unexpected. "I do not think she did; only my family and another young lady boarded there."

The counsel had tried to indicate that the accused was a simple landlady— an innocent victim of her boarders. Mrs. Holohan's answer surprised the counsel. They seemed to support the prosecution's contention that the boardinghouse was a convenient cover for the real purpose of providing a rendezvous for Rebel spies and blockade-runners.

Aiken dropped this approach and began to focus on her friendship with Mrs. Surratt. But Eliza Holohan was hesitant to claim close association. She acknowledged that her landlady was kind but claimed she hardly knew her.

Concerning John Wilkes Booth, Aiken asked, "Did he spend most of the time when he came there in company with Mrs. Surratt?"

"I think he did; he would ask for John Surratt, and if he was not there he would inquire for Mrs. Surratt." Few statements could have hurt Mary Surratt's cause worse. It also confused Aiken. Holohan was supposed to defend the suspect, but she was not sure what answers were expected and took her cue from the questions. The inexperienced lawyer was careless in forming his inquiries.

Aiken wanted to prove Mrs. Surratt's vision was poor and tried to suggest this in his next question. "Have you learned anything while boarding with Mrs. Surratt of her defective eyesight?"

"I never saw her read or sew after candlelight," Mrs. Holohan replied weakly.[8]

The attorney's next interrogation indicated that Mrs. Surratt attended church faithfully; then he turned the witness over to Holt for a short but impressive cross-examination. "You say you never saw Mrs. Surratt sew or read after dark: have you not often met her in the parlor at gas-light?" the Judge queried.

"Yes."

"Did she ever have any difficulty in recognizing you within the parlor by gaslight?"

"No, sir."

Aiken generally ignored the critical issues, centering his defense on secondary ones. Interrogating Honora Fitzpatrick, he belabored the point of Mrs. Surratt's dislike for Atzerodt, which, although probably true, had little bearing on the case. The defense asked why Atzerodt left the boardinghouse. "I do not know under what circumstances; I believe Mrs. Surratt sent him away," testified Fitzpatrick.

"Are you aware of his getting drunk in the house and making a disturbance?"

"I am not; I heard he had bottles up there, but I didn't know anything about his getting drunk."

"What room did you occupy in the house?"

"I slept in the same room with Mrs. Surratt and her daughter, Anna."

As has been noted, on the night of the murder, neither Anna nor Honora slept in Mrs. Surratt's room; they were sent to an attic bedroom. The prosecution never probed this unnatural move.

Aiken then dealt with the question of Booth's picture in Mrs. Surratt's bedroom, which the witness stated was not hers. The lawyer showed Fitzpatrick a picture, asking if she was aware that Booth's likeness was placed behind it. "No," she replied.

Honora admitted, however, that Booth's photograph was openly displayed in Mrs. Surratt's room, but when detectives searched the house, they found it hidden behind the other picture.

After a few questions about Weichmann, the interrogation turned again to Booth. "When did you last see Booth there?" inquired the attorney. The young witness claimed it was on Monday before the crime (a visit not known previously).

Asked the same thing about John Surratt, she vowed she had not seen him since "the night that he left the house, two weeks before the assassination."[9]

These questions, intended to exonerate John Surratt, actually pushed his mother closer to the gallows. George Townsend, who followed the investigation closely, noted that one of the most damaging points against Mrs. Surratt was the fact admitted by all boarders—Booth was in frequent communication with her during John's absence, and John was often absent. The age-old story of a mother suffering because of her son's waywardness seemed reversed. Several witnesses suggested that the mother influenced the son rather than vice versa.

The Military Commission did not overlook this earlier unmentioned visit of Booth on the Monday before the murder, the day before her first trip to Surrattsville (witnesses from Surrattsville testified that she also visited her country house on Monday).

After Honora Fitzpatrick described how the landlady had difficulty recognizing people, Judge Holt asked more specifically, "Did you ever know Mrs. Surratt to have difficulty in recognizing her friends in the parlor by gaslight; did she always recognize you?"

"She did."

Examining photographs of Confederate leaders taken from the house, the witness testified that they did not belong to her.[10]

Having finished with Fitzpatrick, the defense called Bennett F. Gwynn. He swore he delivered a letter from Mrs. Surratt to Mr. Nothey on the day of the murder. His testimony would have been more effective if Mudd's former slaves had not mentioned him as a strong supporter of the Confederacy. Other citizens around Surrattsville also labeled Gwynn a notorious Rebel.

Capt. George Cottingham, another defense witness called by Aiken, told the Court that after officers arrested Lloyd, he denied knowing anything about the conspiracy. The witness recounted how Lloyd expressed dread that if he were to confess, they would murder him. Cottingham added that he assured Lloyd "if he was going to free himself by letting these parties get out of it, that was his business, not mine; I then put him in the guardhouse; he seemed to be much exicited...."

Again Aiken's unskilled examination hurt his client, especially when he asked about guns in the house Lloyd rented from Mrs. Surratt. Cottingham stated that he was in the house when Lloyd confessed and cried out, "Oh, Mrs. Surratt, that vile woman, she has ruined me." Cottingham then said to Lloyd, "You stated there were two carbines, and that Booth could not carry his; where is that carbine?"

These answers astounded Aiken, but he continued with the interrogation, asking who heard this conversation. Cottingham testified that Mrs. Surratt's brother was in the same room. The officer explained further that Mrs. Surratt's country house had long been a "head-quarters for Rebels and blockade-runners during Lloyd's occupation of it."

The lawyer became still more puzzled at Cottingham's response but continued to ask the wrong questions. When asked if Lloyd had mentioned his "difficulty" to anyone else, Cottingham replied, "Yes, he did; he cried and threw his hands over his wife's neck and howled for his prayer book; Mr. Lloyd's wife and Mrs. Offutt were there and heard all the conversation in that room; I told them to brace up."[11] Flustered, Aiken dismissed the witness in disgust.

Unbeknown to the Court, Aiken had been tricked into calling Cottingham as a witness for the defense. A few hours before Cottingham appeared on the stand, he had a casual conversation with Aiken. In answer to the lawyers' inquiries during that meeting, Cottingham had explicitly and repeatedly stated that Lloyd, in his first confession after being arrested, had not implicated Mrs. Surratt.[12] The detective was accordingly called as a witness for the defense, but rather than testify about the first confession, he referred to Lloyd's subsequent statements in which he strongly accused Mrs. Surratt.

Elated, Judge Holt asked what precise language Lloyd used in reference to the prisoner. "It was 'Mrs. Surratt, that vile woman, she has ruined me; I am to be shot!' He meant by that, I suppose, that his guilt was so great there was no hope for him."[13]

Lloyd's exclamation that he would be shot reflected what the conspirators expected, if caught. Thus far the defense had only complicated the position of Mrs. Surratt.

Witnesses were next called to testify in favor of O'Laughlin. B. J. Early told of being with the accused and some other friends in Washington on the night of the murder. While O'Laughlin was hardly angelic, his activities seemed relatively innocent except for one suspicious trip. Early testified that on the day of the assassination,

> Henderson went into a barber's shop to get shaved; O'Laughlin then asked me to go with him to the National Hotel; when we got there he went to the

desk, telling me to wait, and he would detain me only a few minutes; I went as far as the door; he left me standing there, and came back again in three to five minutes, and after that we went back to Lichau's and thence up the avenue.[14]

Nothing in the rest of his testimony implicated O'Laughlin.

A man named Murphy, another of O'Laughlin's friends, related a similar story of the group carousing in Washington on the night of April 14. He was followed by four other witnesses who gave convincing testimonies about O'Laughlin's relatively innocent activities on that momentous night. Whatever role he may have played in the conspiracy, O'Laughlin had a solid alibi on the night of the shooting. He apparently saw Booth, or tried to see him, for a few minutes in the National Hotel, but beyond that he spent the night drinking. The Government's case against O'Laughlin continued to be weak.

The confused Aiken recalled Captain Cottingham to the stand, starting a bizarre episode. The lawyer admitted his private conversation with Cottingham and threw himself upon the consideration of the Court. Judge Bingham objected, as usual, but Judge Holt permitted Aiken to interrogate Cottingham again. "State again the precise language that Mr. Lloyd used in his confession with reference to Mrs. Surratt," asked Aiken. Again Bingham objected, so Aiken appealed directly to Cottingham, "I will ask the witness if he did not make a different statement to me with reference to Mr. Loyd's confession?" Judge Holt this time objected, but after a short discussion it was withdrawn.

Captain Cottingham unblushingly admitted that in his confidential interview with Aiken, which had not been under oath, he had purposely deceived him. According to the Captain, Aiken invited him to have a drink. During the conversation, the lawyer asked if he was a Catholic. Cottingham said no. Then Aiken said he had heard that Lloyd had confessed something to Cottingham, and he wanted to know what it was. Aiken informed the Captain he would call him as a witness and wanted more details of Lloyd's confession, but Cottingham declined.

Aiken, continuing his interrogation of Cottingham before the Court, asked, "What did you tell me this afternoon?"

"I told you a lie; you were trying to pick it out of me," responded the Captain proudly, "and I told you that you might call me into court, and I would state what I told you, a lie, and now I state that I did do it."[15]

A burst of laughter indicated the spectators approved of Cottingham's deception. However, it completely confused the counsel and further distressed the black-clad widow huddled in the corner.

Cottingham appeared delighted with himself, stating that as a detective, lying was his business. One observer, not happy with the trickery, wrote indignantly, he "hoped that such outrageous acts are not part of our detective system."[16] Two more brief testimonies ended the long session.

The testimony was calamitous for Mrs. Surratt and Dr. Mudd. Mary Surratt, in particular, must have sensed the disaster of her first day's defense. Most reporters ridiculed her long-awaited justification. The *New York Times* commented on what it called Aiken's "corrupt proposals" to Cottingham.[17] Her lawyers miscalculated, according to the *Boston Journal*, in parading the Catholic clergymen.[18]

Many expressed resentment against the blatant introduction of strong religious sentiments into a case already fractured by sectional and political divisions. The move might have been positive if the priests had touched on material facts, but each admitted that he knew nothing about Mrs. Surratt's political views. One reporter noted that of the ten or twelve witnesses for Mrs. Surratt, none gave any factual evidence in her behalf. This view summarized the feelings of close observers. In an article titled "Injured Innocents?" the *New York Times* deplored the use of church attendance as a cover for treason, describing the tactic as pure hypocrisy.[19] Even the *New York World* belittled the testimony of ecclesiastics, observing, "They were silent on Mrs. Surratt's loyalty since the Rebellion."[20]

Again on May 26, spectators so packed the courtroom many could not find seats. After the laborious reading of the previous day's testimony, Aiken applied for the recall of Von Steinacker, who had testified in a secret session. Aiken complained that this procedure deprived the defense of cross-examination. Judge Holt asserted that the witness had been discharged without any objection from the counsel; but Aiken claimed he later found evidence that Von Steinacker was a notorious liar. Holt promised obligingly that the Government would try to locate him.

The defense recalled B. F. Gwynn. This time Gwynn read the letter Mrs. Surratt had given him to deliver to John Nothey.

> SURRATTSVILLE, MD., April 14, 1865.
>
> Mr. John Nothey.—Sir;—I have this day received a letter from Mr. Calvert, intimating that either you or your friend have represented to him that I am not willing to settle with you for the land. You know that I am ready and have been waiting for you for the last two years, and now, if you do not come within the next ten days, I will settle with Mr. Calvert and bring suit against you immediately. Mr. Calvert will give you a deed on receiving payment.
>
> (Signed) M. E. Surratt
> Administratrix of J. M. Surratt[21]

Mrs. Surratt's defense then turned again to several Catholic clergymen. The first, Father Peter Lanihan from Charles County, Maryland, said he had known the accused for about 13 years, and, that in his estimation, she was a good Christian woman. Judge Bingham, irritated by the procession of priests, interrupted harshly, "We do not want your estimation, but her general reputation."

The witness responded, "Her character stands in the neighborhood where she lived as a good Christian woman." Regardless of the impression on the Court, Mrs. Surratt was pleased. Her previously gloomy countenance brightened noticeably as the priest testified.

Holt's cross-examination was short. "Have you ever heard her express a loyal sentiment?"

"I do not remember that I have."

"Is not her reputation that of a disloyal woman?"

"I think not; she never expressed that sentiment to me; I may have heard her general reputation for loyalty or disloyalty spoken of, but I do not remember it."[22]

Father N. D. Young, who had previously tried to visit Lloyd in prison, took the stand. The clergyman repeated much of what the other four priests had testified, but he hedged even more, claiming he hardly knew the prisoner. Holt didn't even bother to cross-examine him.

George H. Calvert had testified earlier about his letter to Mrs. Surratt; the defense interrogated him again and read the letter for the Court.

> RIVERSDALE,
> April 12, 1865. — Mrs. M. E. Surratt
> Dear Madam: — During a late visit to the lower portion of the county I ascertained of the willingness of Mr. Nothey to settle with you and desire to call your attention to the fact in urging the settlement of the claim of my late father's estate. However unpleasant, I must insist upon closing up this matter as it is imperative in an early settlement of the estate, which is necessary. You will, therefore, please inform me, at your earliest convenience, as to how and when you will be able to pay the balance remaining due on the land purchased by your late husband.
> Yours respectfully,
> (Signed) GEORGE H. CALVERT, JR.[23]

The document added to Mrs. Surratt's defense, but Calvert's weak testimony did not.

The defense next called W. L. Hoyle; he claimed only "a store acquaintance" with the prisoner and knew nothing of her political views.[24]

Mrs. Surratt's lawyers had scoured the area around Surrattsville for neighbors willing to testify in her behalf. Their inability to find anyone other than Hoyle, who knew practically nothing of the prisoner, divulged more than his words. When asked to describe John Surratt, the witness guessed he was about six feet tall.

Bingham had only one question: "Do you know he was over five feet nine inches in height?"

"Not positively."

Mrs. Surratt's counsel rested and turned the interrogation over to Cox, O'Laughlin's lawyer. He called P. H. Maulsby, the prisoner's brother-in-law. Maulsby described how O'Laughlin had helped his brother in the produce and feed business in Washington. To Cox's inquiry if he knew J. Wilkes Booth, Maulsby admitted proudly, "Yes, intimately. Mrs. Booth owns the property right opposite my house. Michael and William were schoolmates of John Wilkes Booth. They attended the school of J. M. Smith, not very far from the house." He further testified that O'Laughlin had been Booth's friend almost 12 years.

The witness tried to tell of O'Laughlin's arrest but was interrupted so often by Bingham's technicalities that his testimony lasted until 1:00. The Court then took its usual recess, to reconvene at 2:00.

Resuming his testimony, Maulsby narrated his efforts urging O'Laughlin to turn himself in to the Government on Monday morning, April 18. At this point, the prosecution abruptly interrupted the defense's case to introduce witnesses who again described brutal conditions in Confederate prisons.

When the defense resumed, John Nothey, who lived about three miles south of Mrs. Surratt's country property, was called. He testified that he had bought land from Mrs. Surratt's deceased husband many years earlier. He admitted he had only met the widow one time—in Surrattsville, at her request, on Tuesday, April 11. He did not see her on the day of the murder, but she sent him a letter by Gwynn.

The prosecution did not bother with a cross-examination, apparently not considering these letters worth refuting. They seemed too obviously staged as a cover. The first letter (from Calvert), dated April 12, was written the day after Mrs. Surratt first contacted Nothey, which made the timing suspicious. Mrs. Surratt wrote the second note on the afternoon of the assassination. Strangely, she penned the letter in Surrattsville, only a short distance from Nothey's house, which seemed absurd.

Mudd's lawyer introduced several witnesses whose unconvincing testimonies ended the day's proceedings.

XXXIV
A Loyal Citizen?

Spectators learned to avoid the tedious reading of the previous day's testimony by arriving about noon. Some enterprising visitors found a way to assure themselves a seat. They pushed in confidently with pencil and paper in hand to the reporters' table. Usually they presented themselves as representatives of some small-town newspaper.

The rage for relics also afflicted spectators, but little in the courtroom could be carried away as souvenirs. Relic hunters had to be satisfied with taking the nearly empty spools of red tape used by the Court. They eagerly divided it into short lengths, which they distributed among themselves. But the craze became more extreme each day. Visitors began to chip away at chairs, tables and everything in sight. One spectator noted that the passion for relics threatened to destroy the courtroom furniture. Women visitors, in particular, wanted a hair from a suspect's head. A rush toward the dock as the prisoners entered became so disruptive that one observer expected "to see some enterprising lady clipping away at the long hair of Payne or Herold."[1]

Mrs. Surratt's spirit changed noticeably on May 27. She still appeared in her usual mourning dress and bonnet, but this day she lowered her palm leaf fan and gazed freely around the room for the first time. The testimony in her favor, though not impressive, seemed to please her.

The defense concentrated primarily on Mrs. Surratt and Dr. Mudd—the only defendants claiming absolute innocence. Spangler proclaimed his innocence, but since the case against him was weak, his counsel had little to refute.

Samuel Mudd's defense took a different course from that of Mary Surratt. His obvious contact with the conspiracy centered on his having set Booth's foot. As a physician, his defense easily explained this as an act of mercy. Therefore, his lawyers concentrated on discrediting witnesses who testified to Mudd's other links to Booth. Mudd's well-known Southern sympathies and support of the Confederacy created another problem for lawyers who sought to picture him a loyal citizen.

The prosecution interrupted the main thrust by calling witnesses who coupled Rebel leaders in Canada to the infamous St. Albans raid. The defense then tried to destroy the veracity of David Thomas, who had previously testified against Mudd.

Dr. Mudd's lawyers relied heavily on his relatives as character witnesses;

numerous witnesses named Mudd took the stand. Ewing called Jeremiah T. Mudd, a third cousin of the accused, who refuted the testimony of Thomas, claiming that Thomas was deceitful. Ewing asked, "From your knowledge of his reputation for truth would you believe him under oath?"

"I do not think I could; it had been my impression that—"

"You need not state your impression," Bingham broke in. General Ewing, tired of Bingham's interruptions, ignored him, instructing the witness to proceed. A bold move that he got by with. Mudd simply repeated his last statement; he would not believe Thomas even under oath.

Bingham wanted to know on what evidence the witness based his judgment. A ridiculous exchange followed, typical of Bingham's style.

"How many people did you ever hear speak of his general reputation for truth before the taking of this testimony the other day?"

"I heard several speak of it."

"How many, ten?"

"I think so; I will not say positively; I am speaking now from what I have heard generally."

Bingham insisted that he name ten, or even five. The witness mentioned Dr. George Mudd. "When did you hear Dr. George Mudd speak on the subject?" questioned the prosecutor. Then Bingham hounded the witness for names in a long, fussy inquisition over trifles.

"If you cannot name two men who ever assailed his character for truth, how can you come to the conclusion that his general reputation for truth is bad?"

"Well, I heard a number say so."[2]

The defense interrogated Ben Gwynn again, this time in Dr. Mudd's defense. He admitted hiding on Mudd's farm but disputed the date. "State what occurred in 1861, when you were in the neighborhood of Dr. Mudd's house?" solicited Mudd's lawyer.

"I was with my brother Andrew J. Gwynn, and Jerry Dyer; about that time General Sickles came over into Maryland, arresting everybody; I was threatened with arrest, and left the neighborhood to avoid it," explained Gwynn.[3]

Gwynn paused, apparently expecting another question; Ewing urged him to continue telling about his experience. But Bingham objected on the basis that what had been done in 1861 was not the issue. The Court sustained the objection and took a recess until two o'clock.

Bingham's unending interruptions became so unbearable that Ewing complained to Judge Holt. The Judge, agreeing, advised the Court that he wanted all the evidence presented and hoped that frivolous objections would cease. Bingham took the Judge Advocate's criticism gracefully and protested less frequently.

Government detectives continued their anxious search for concrete evidence linking Confederate leaders to the murder. Officials eagerly examined confiscated Confederate documents but failed to find proof. In desperation, they searched Beverly Tucker's former home in Richmond, where his wife still resided. Detectives tore the house apart in the mad search. They took all his papers but discovered no incriminating evidence.[4]

A related legal action occurred a few miles from the courtroom. The grand jury of the District of Columbia got around to indicting Jefferson Davis and John C. Breckenridge for high treason. They decided not to try Davis for the assassination but for the attack in July 1864 against Washington. The Government held Davis in prison, but officials were still searching for Breckenridge.

When court reconvened, Ewing continued his interrogation of Gwynn. "State where the party of whom you have spoken as being in the pines got their meals and slept."

"They slept in the barn, near the spring, on bedding furnished from Dr. Mudd's and were furnished with meals by Dr. Mudd; we remained there about four or five days."

The witness admitted that Mudd gave them clothing and took them to his house "almost every day."

Asked if John Surratt was part of the group, Gwynn said no. The Union General now serving as a defense counsel must have been disturbed by Gwynn's casual account of his disloyal activities, but he continued without showing it. "What induced the party to go to the pines to sleep?"

"To avoid arrest, I did."

"What reason had you for supposing you would be arrested?"

"Almost everybody in our neighborhood was being arrested, and I understood I would be, too; so I went down there," he admitted. Gwynn admitted again that he and Andrew Gwynn were brothers.[5]

Judge Holt took over the examination. "You spoke of the universality of arrests in 1861; did you understand that they were confined to persons suspected of disloyalty and disloyal practices?" Gwynn, making no pretense of loyalty, responded frankly, "They were generally; there were several volunteer companies there whose members were arrested."

Holt requested clarification of the nature of the volunteer companies in which Gwynn served as captain. Gwynn explained their purpose "of protecting the neighbors; at that time there was a good deal of disaffection among the blacks; it was thought to be a proper time for raising companies through the country; I therefore petitioned Governor Hicks, and he gave me a commission."

"Was it not understood they were organized to stand by the state in any disloyal position she might take against the Government of the United States?"

"Yes, sir, I so understood it; they arrested several members of my company, and, as I understood there was a warrant for my arrest, I left."

"You slept in the pines for the sole purpose of escaping arrest?"

"Yes, sir."

"Dr. Mudd, I suppose, concurred fully in your sentiment and the sentiments which pervaded the local organizations?"

**Beverly Tucker. As a member of the so-called "Canadian Cabinet," the Govern-
ment included him on the reward poster (Library of Congress – USZ62-61751).**

"I do not know what his sentiments were at the time."[6]

Holt turned the witness back to the defense counsel, who inquired, "Do
you know whether Dr. Mudd was a member of any of those volunteer companies?"

"I think he was a member of a company gotten up in Bryantown."

Shocked, Ewing questioned in disbelief, "Are you sure of that?"

"I do not know positively; I think so," came the reply.

His lawyer had thus astonishingly established Mudd's membership in a
military organization opposed to the Federal Government.

Jeremiah (Jerry) Dyer, a former slaveholding neighbor of Mudd's and
friend of the Surratts, was interrogated next. Dyer denied that he personally
had heard Mudd say he would send any of his slaves to Richmond, but he admitted that "I heard, when I got down in the country, that such a report had
been started there by a certain man in the neighborhood; I never heard Dr.
Mudd say any such thing."

Ewing, continuing on the wrong track, asked, "Do you know Andrew
Gwynn?"

"Very well."

"Do you know where he has been since 1861?"

"He has been in the Rebel army."

These answers, unfortunately given in response to the defense's examination, indicated strong and widespread Confederate affiliations among
slaveholding families in southern Maryland, including the Surratts and the
Mudds. After a few questions about John Surratt, Ewing asked about Mudd's
slaves, Milo Simms, Rachel Spencer, Elvina Washington, Eleazer Eglin and

Mary Simms. Having spent several years fighting against slavery, the Union General could not bring himself to use the term "slaves" and substituted the word "servants" in his interrogation. Dyer supported previous testimony about his seeking refuge on Dr. Mudd's farm. He said that to avoid arrest, "I came to Dr. Mudd's and stayed about there, sleeping in the pines between his house and mine several nights; we were two nights very near his spring."

"Where did you get your bed clothing?"

"At Dr. Mudd's house."[7]

The defense counsel had laboriously brought out details that could only injure the prisoner. Perhaps he was determined to prove that Dr. Mudd's former slaves were incorrect about the dates. But the effect of Mudd's having aided men seeking refuge from Union forces damaged him, whether it occurred in 1861 or 1864.

Later Ewing quizzed Dyer, "Do you know whether a watch was kept at Dr. Mudd's house when you were there?" He responded with his usual openness, "I recollect telling the children to keep a lookout and let me know."

Ewing shifted to a safer subject—the reputation of Daniel Thomas. Dyer testified he would not believe him even under oath. When questioned about Mudd's reputation, the witness declared that it was good. "What is his reputation as a master over his servants?" Ewing inquired. Dyer responded, "I have always considered him a very kind humane master; I have not known anything to the contrary with the single exception of his shooting that boy."

Ewing didn't want any more talk about "shooting that boy" and concluded his inquiry.

Judge Holt cross-examined the witness but did not pursue the point. Holt continued the subject of Thomas, seeking to show that he was an outspoken loyal supporter of the Government in a neighborhood supporting the Rebellion, then questioned Dyer's loyalty to the Government in 1861. The witness was not so open this time, "I hardly know how to answer the question; circumstances have changed so since then; at that time everything was confusion and excitement, and I can hardly answer the question."

A member of the Commission inquired about Dyer's sentiments in the war. Dyer claimed his views had changed some.

"What time did your sympathies undergo a change and what produced that change?"

"I do not know; the only thing I objected to was the emancipation of the slaves; that I thought was wrong."[8]

He hit the heart of the problem—the loss of slaves had embittered both Mary Surratt and Samuel Mudd.

Stone took over the defense and called William T. Bowman. The witness stated that Booth came to Charles County ostensibly to buy land. The lawyer argued that Booth's first contact with Mudd was strictly for business reasons. That Booth had business dealings with the doctor all admitted now, but what business? Booth had a letter of introduction to Dr. Mudd, and "buying land" seemed a camouflage.

Augustus G. Howell, the next important defense witness, testified that he had known Mrs. Surratt about one and a half years. Asked why he went to her boardinghouse, he replied unconvincingly, "On a visit as much as anything else, I had no business there in particular."

"What was your reason for not going to a hotel?"

"I knew them, and thought I would spend the time better there than at a hotel."

The defense wanted to know if Howell had possessed enough money to have gone to a hotel. Again he answered weakly that he did not think so.

The counsel then made a strong effort to discredit Weichmann. "After you made the acquaintance of Mr. Weichmann did you show him any cipher?"

"I showed him how to make one, then he made it himself."

"Was it simple or complicated?"

"I could tell the cipher if I saw it."

Bingham had an orderly display a cipher from the exhibit box.

"Was it like that or similar to it?"

"It was like this but this is not the one, I think."

"Did Weichmann give you any information with regard to the prisoners we at that time had on hand?"

The question was objected to and waived.

"Did you have any communication with Mr. Weichmann with regard to his going south?"

"Yes, sir, I had."

"State what it was and what he said."

"He said he would like to go South."

Howell explained that Weichmann had definite Confederate sympathies. Although Weichmann may not have indicated such a preference, he did want to go south.

The defense got back to the question previously objected to. "Did Weichmann give you a full return of the number of prisoners?"

"Yes, sir; he stated to me the number that the United States Government had, and the number they had over what the Confederate Government had: I doubted it, but he said he had the books in his own office to look at," responded Howell.

Under cross-examination by the prosecution, the witness stated that his family lived in Prince Georges County, Maryland, and that he knew Mrs. Surratt when she lived there. "What has been your occupation for the last year and a half?" questioned the Judge.

The defense objected to the question but it was overruled.

"I have had no particular occupation since I've been out of the army."

"What army?"

"The Confederate army."

"What portion of the army did you serve in?"

"In the First Maryland Artillery till July, 1862; I then left the service."

The prosecutor knew, of course, that Union troops had captured Howell running the blockade and wanted to get this fact before the Court and the public. He asked about Howell's activities since he left the Confederate army.

The witness said he really hadn't been doing anything. "Haven't you been making trips to Richmond?" inquired the interrogator.

"I've been there, sir."

"How frequently?"

"Some times once in two or three months; I've been there twice since the first of April, twelve months ago."

"And those two times were when?"

"In December last and in February."

"Did you go alone in December?"

"There might have been some gentleman with me."[9]

Without identifying the "gentleman," the Judge inquired about Howell's friendship with the Surratts. "How often have you visited them; how often did you go to Richmond after you became acquainted with them?"

"About half a dozen times," he admitted.

After a few questions about Weichmann, the prosecutor came back to the Surratts. "Did you ever talk with Mrs. Surratt about being at Richmond?"

"I might."

"Did you or did you not?"

"I disremember; I can't say positively."

"Weichmann knew you had been there?"

"Yes, sir."[10]

Reporters, and presumably the Court, noticed the Confederate agent's most revealing admission, that he might have talked to Mrs. Surratt about being in Richmond.[11] Such an admission concerning other prisoners would have done no harm, since they were aware of Howell's work; several admitted they knew him. Mrs. Surratt, however, based her case on complete ignorance of the whole affair. Yet one witness after another (some inadvertently) gave the clear impression that she knew about, and collaborated in, treasonable activities against the Government.

The defense took a risk in putting the confessed Confederate collaborator on the stand. But it was their best chance to discredit Weichmann. Howell justified the gamble to some extent, although he confirmed the Government's contention that Mrs. Surratt's house was a stopping place for Confederate agents.

After interrogations relating to his work, the Judge asked, "Were you known by your friends as a blockade-runner?"

"I don't know."

"What name did you go by besides the name you have given here?"

"They sometimes called me Spencer."

"Well, is that your name?"

"My name is A. S. Howell."

"What is the S. for?"

"Spencer."

"Why did you not give it when asked for it under oath?"

The witness asserted that he thought A. S. Howell was enough. A comical exchange followed with the prosecution wrangling to force Howell to state his full name, but he insisted on using his initials. Giving up, the interrogator changed the subject. "When were you arrested?"

"In March."

"How recently had you then come from Richmond?"

"I had not been in Richmond for three weeks."

Howell remained evasive, as when asked where he obtained the cipher used for sending Confederate messages. He got it from a magician's book, he claimed somewhat flippantly.

The questions turned to Mrs. Slater. Howell admitted he knew her but never met her at Mrs. Surratt's house. "Did she accompany you to Richmond?" he was asked.

"Partly."

He swore that he met her accidentally and didn't know her business. Again the Judge quizzed, "Did you meet her at Surratt's house?"

"Not till after I had met with her on the Potomac."[12]

Howell caught himself in a falsehood, having previously testified that he had never met Mrs. Slater at Mrs. Surratt's. Under continued cross-examination, the Judge practically demolished Howell's previous testimony, forcing him to admit that he accompanied Mrs. Slater partway to New York City and met her when she got back at Mrs. Surratt's house. "Did she go in?"

"No, sir; she stayed in the buggy."

"Who was with her?"

"A young man."

"Who was he?"

"John Surratt."

The prosecution wanted to know about Weichmann's and the Surratts' knowledge of Howell's trips to Richmond. "They knew you had been in Richmond?"

"They knew I was from Richmond sometime previous."

"Did you have any conversation with Mrs. Surratt about the matter?"

"I don't know, sir."

After Howell reluctantly revealed that he met Mrs. Slater in Richmond after which John Surratt accompanied her, the Judge inquired, "Do you know what her business was in Richmond?" Knowing the Government could not punish him much more than it had, he replied in his usual impudent fashion, "No, sir; I didn't inquire."

"You only know that soon after you saw her at Mrs. Surratt's, you saw her at Richmond?"

The witness refused to answer, and the prosecution continued. "What other of your friends did you meet at Mrs. Surratt's?"

"I don't know that I met any."

"Did you meet Atzerodt there?"

"I think Atzerodt was there."

When Howell was asked about Payne, he professed not to know him, but when the Judge inquired if he knew any of the other prisoners, he responded, "I think I have seen two."

"What two?"

"Atzerodt and Dr. Mudd."

"Where did you see Dr. Mudd?"

"At Bryantown."

"Tell us where your acquaintance first commenced with Dr. Mudd?"

"I have known him a long while, but I have not lately seen him."

The Confederate spy testified that he did not deliver messages to the doctor, although he had been in his house but only stayed "an hour or two."[13]

The testimonies of both prosecution and defense witnesses were gradually picturing a large network of spies, blockade-runners, Southern sympathizers, former Confederate soldiers and conspirators working together and protecting each other. The names Surratt and Mudd figured prominently in this network which centered in Prince Georges and Prince Charles counties, Maryland.

After cross-examination, Ewing tried to salvage something from Howell's startling revelation. "I wish to ask whether you ever saw Dr. Mudd about Bryantown."

"Yes, sir, I have been about Bryantown a good deal before the war; was raised in the county."

"You have seen Mudd before the war?"

"Oh, yes, sir."

"Were you ever at Mudd's house at any other time since the war?"

"I don't think I have been, sir."

Ewing inquired again about Howell's conversation with Weichmann and then surprisingly observed, "How come you to remember that conversation and not be able to remember the conversation with Mrs. Surratt, or anybody else in the house?"

"Well, sir, it just came to my mind by the question being so pointed."

Judge Burnett, who seldom took part, told the witness that Weichmann belonged to a company of men for the defense of Washington and queried, "Don't you know that he was turning you over to pick out of you about your visits to Richmond? Don't you know he tried to find out what your objects were?"

"If he did he didn't succeed."[14]

Spectators laughed at Howell's reply, but it was a significant admission that he hid his clandestine activities from Weichmann. Burnett, who had interrogated Weichmann during the pretrial investigation, retorted that Weichmann probably knew more about Howell than the witness thought. After a few final words by Aiken, the Court adjourned until the following Monday at ten.

Weichmann was held in Carroll Prison when Augustus Howell gave his somewhat damaging testimony. The *Washington Intelligencer* carried the testimony in full, so Weichmann could easily learn what Howell had said. Unlike some of the more secure witnesses, he quickly defended himself. On May 28, he wrote to Judge Advocate Burnett giving his version of the events. He branded Howell a notorious blockade-runner, which no one disputed, and tied Howell's activities to the Surratts, even before their move to Washington.

He also told Burnett that Howell had threatened him since the two had been in Carroll Prison. When authorities first sent Weichmann to prison, Howell warned him not to say anything against him.[15]

Covering all imputations, Weichmann took pains to refute Howell's reference to his proposed theological studies in Richmond. To clarify his position, he turned over to Burnett a letter he had received from the Bishop of Richmond. How he managed to have this letter with him in prison is a mystery. The Government had supposedly confiscated Weichmann's personal possessions and sent them to the War Department. Presumably he requested someone in the War Department to search his letters. Apparently he retrieved the document and kept it with him, because he also showed it to Stanton. If that was so, he was given privileges denied others.

In a moment of self-pity, Weichmann explained that his testimony on behalf of the Government had made him many personal enemies. Even the defense counsel, he wrote, had heartlessly accused him of having no human feelings. Weichmann added that "no person could have had more respect and love for Mrs. Surratt than I, but when they place me in a position to tarnish my reputation and make me suspected as an accomplice in President Lincoln's death, the sympathy ceases forever."[16]

Weichmann maintained this position until his death, claiming the Surratts had betrayed him. He went too far, however, when he contended that John Surratt had undoubtedly sworn to kill the President, and that he, Weichmann, had sworn to avenge his death.

He insisted that if he had the chance, he could redeem his character ten thousand times against the accusations of Howell. Yet when he got to the most damaging testimony against him, his rebuttal was weak. The conversation which Howell claimed to have had with him about Confederates in Northern prisons was false according to Weichmann. The number of Rebel prisoners had been published in the papers anyway, he maintained. Furthermore, he added that he had never looked in the book at the office to ascertain the number, because he "did not keep that particular book."[17]

Of the accusations leveled against him, Howell's charge that Weichmann had given him the number of Southern prisoners held in the North was one of the most serious. It was clearly treasonable and also plausible. While working in the Bureau of Prisons, Weichmann had contact, however briefly, with a known Confederate spy. The number of prisoners and where they were held were valuable information. That newspapers published some general information was true, but it did not include detailed listings and locations. Weichmann surely knew the dangerous position in which Howell's testimony placed him, yet he could only come forth with the lame excuse that he did not "keep that particular book." Furthermore, he never denied that Howell taught him the secret Confederate cipher. He acknowledged that he used it, but only to translate poems. While this may have been true, it was suspicious.

XXXV
A Growing Weariness

As the trial entered its third week, pockets of die-hard Confederates continued fighting in the West. The last of these troops, under the direction of Gen. Edmund Kirby Smith, had set up an almost independent country west of the Mississippi known as Kirby Smithdom. Under his supervision this region sold large shipments of cotton abroad and used the proceeds to build factories, making the area almost self-supporting. His forces remained a matter of concern until they finally surrendered toward the end of May.

A week after the Grand Review thousands of soldiers loitered in the streets of Washington, brawling and creating disorder. The problem of some 200,000 unoccupied troops crowding the city was even more acute because of poor lighting. Frequently whole city blocks remained dark because the gas company failed to light the lamps. Authorities sought to move the soldiers across the river to Virginia, but it took time.

The conspiracy trial was practically ignored in the Old Confederacy. Trial coverage in the South consisted of an occasional small notice copied from Northern papers, and no Southern reporter attended the sessions. The *Atlanta Intelligencer* mentioned the tragedy of Lincoln's murder but had only a few lines concerning the Military Commission.

The *Natchez Courier* used black borders when it announced the death of Lincoln and described the gloom which pervaded Natchez but had only one short article on the conspiracy hearing.

In the North, one pro–Southern paper not only criticized the defense's strategy, but also complained that "while the evidence for the prosecution took the widest latitude the defense was checked by technical objections at every point."[1]

Toward the end of May a tall, muscular man from Maryland's eastern shore called at Doster's office wanting to visit Payne. He had seen the prisoner's description in newspapers and thought he might be his younger brother who had escaped from a private mental asylum. The family physician had seen Payne at the trial and also believed that he was the missing man. Doster was hesitant. He felt it might be a trick, but, noticing some resemblance between Payne and the visitor, he told him he could see the prisoner the next morning at court, that only Stanton could permit him to visit Payne earlier. The man insisted on taking Doster to Secretary Stanton immediately. The lawyer, apprehensive about dealing with a family with a strain of insanity, went along.

Stanton refused the request. The stranger, ignoring the Secretary, rode out to the Arsenal anyway, but General Hartranft barred his entry.

The next morning, May 29, the man arrived early at the prison but was able to see the accused only as he entered the courtroom. Payne did not recognize the person staring at him. Reluctantly, the stranger realized that the prisoner was not his brother and left disappointed.

Soon after court reconvened, one of Mrs. Surratt's lawyers, John Clampitt, again requested the recall of Henry von Steinacker. Judge Holt had previously promised to find him but accomplished nothing. Clampitt had taken little part thus far, insomuch as the moody widow continued to make his task difficult by failing to communicate with him.

Defense lawyers had investigated Von Steinacker's secret testimony and believed it was false. The defense presented its allegations against Von Steinacker in written form, declaring that Oscar Heinreichs, on General Johnson's staff, gave Von Steinacker a job as draftsman in the Confederate army. Von Steinacker, who had previously been court-martialed for stealing a horse, was again accused of stealing and again was court-martialed.[2]

According to the document Clampitt read to the Court, Von Steinacker "stole some clothing north of Richmond and escaped ... to Winchester." Clampitt explained that he wanted to refute Von Steinacker's account of a meeting of the Second Virginia Infantry at which Booth had allegedly discussed the assassination plot. He stated that Von Steinacker escaped to Winchester, Virginia, pretending that he was " in charge of the dead body of Major Henry K. Douglas, Assistant Adjunct-General on General Johnson's staff; who is now present before this court, alive and well."[3] The paper was signed by Reverdy Johnson, Fred Aiken and J. W. Clampitt.

Holt declared that he had tried to locate Von Steinacker but could not locate him. In his usual courteous manner, Holt agreed that he would willingly recall him, if he could be found.

Gen. Lew Wallace, irritated by what he perceived to be a criticism of Holt, affirmed that the Judge had never refused to issue a summons for any witness. General Hunter inquired if anyone knew Von Steinacker's location. Aiken replied that the Government released Von Steinacker from prison at Fort Delaware in order to testify before the Court but that no one knew his whereabouts at the moment.

The Commissioners seemed a little edgy. Wallace wondered what connection the defense request had with the defense of Mrs. Surratt, anyway. Aiken explained, "We wish to prove that Mr. Booth was not in Virginia at the time stated by Von Steinacker; that no such meeting of Confederate officers, as he alleges, took place; that no plans for the assassination of President Lincoln were discussed."[4]

Furthermore, Aiken pointed out, even had such a plan existed, Mrs. Surratt would not have known about it. Judge Holt interrupted to explain that it would not be necessary to recall the witness to prove that. Aiken answered that the defense was trying to show that Von Steinacker could not be believed under oath.

Holt again declared his willingness to bring Von Steinacker back if possible but added he did not want Clampitt's paper included in the Court records because it was so defamatory. By this time, Wallace was furious that the Court's secret witness had been so slandered. His fury may have been heightened by a nagging suspicion that the Commission had been tricked by Von Steinacker. Whatever the reason, he chided the defense angrily for its accusations against Von Steinacker. "It is very discreditable to the parties concerned, to the attorney, and if permitted, in my judgement, will be discreditable to the court."

Clampitt, a quiet lawyer who seldom raised his voice, would not be bullied this time. He responded in a most eloquent speech.

> May it please the court, as one of the counsel for Mrs. Surratt, we are here standing within the portals of this constituted temple of justice, and here for the purpose of defending the very citadel of life, and we feel it to be our duty to use every exertion in our power, consistent with forms that obtain before a court, to impeach and destroy the testimony of any witness whose testimony can properly be impeached, and we do it for the purpose, if possible, of shielding the accused. It is, at the same time our bounden duty, and an obligation that we owe to our client, that we should spread before the court the character of the witness on the part of the prosecution who had made this explanation. I hope it will be satisfactory to the court.[5]

Lew Wallace, still agitated, answered curtly, "It is not satisfactory to me for the reason that he has in no instance been denied the privilege which he has sought by that paper." General Howe broke in, "Neither has he shown any connection of the paper with the case of his client."

Aiken came to his colleague's aid, stating that the defense did not want to call Von Steinacker as a witness, "but we had presented this paper in accordance with a strictly legal form."

Wallace interrupted, "Yes, I understand that."

After more haggling, the Court voted that the defense request should not be included in the record, and nothing can be found in the official account about this episode.[6]

Actually Von Steinacker had duped the esteemed members of the Court. The devious Rebel requested freedom from prison to testify and then vanished without a trace. He was never located again. Having exhausted the subject, the Court got down to the business at hand.

The defense called several individuals who swore that Dr. Mudd had not been in Washington on the dates indicated by Weichmann. Ewing's defense was effective at this point. However, the witnesses he secured, even though carefully rehearsed, occasionally slipped up. Julia A. Bloyce, one of Mudd's former slaves who, at the time of the trial, was serving another master in the same county, took the stand. "Did you ever know of his whipping Mary Simms?" Ewing asked.

"No, sir, he never struck her that I know of."

Why did she leave the house, the lawyer wanted to know. "One Sunday evening Mrs. Mudd told her not to go away, but she would go; the next morning

Among the Commissioners, Gen. Lewis Wallace (above) was second in importance to the president, David Hunter (Brady Handy Collection. Library of Congress).

she [Mrs. Mudd] struck her with a little switch; I do not think she hurt her, as the switch was a small one." She added that Mary Simms was a liar, anyway.

The most effective witness for Samuel Mudd was his third cousin, Dr. George Mudd, a respected physician with unquestioned loyalty to the Union. However, Ewing selected his words carefully. "State whether you know his [Sam Mudd's] reputation in the neighborhood in which he lives for peace, order and good citizenship."

"I know of no one whose reputation is better in that regard; it is very good."

Ewing avoided asking about Mudd's reputation for loyalty to the United States.

After a lengthy argument erupted between Ewing and Holt over procedural matters, the witness stated that Dr. Samuel Mudd had told him at church on Sunday that some suspicious characters had visited his house. George Mudd passed this information on to Lieutenant Dana on Monday morning. These statements strongly favored the prisoner's case, but they were in contrast to Sam Mudd's reluctance to tell the whole truth the following day to officers.

Nevertheless, Ewing, making progress, asked, "At the time he imparted this information to you, was anything said about communicating to the military authorities?" Dr. George Mudd testified that he told his cousin he would have to talk to authorities. Sam Mudd seemed agreeable but preferred not to make the events public because he "feared for his life, on account of guerrillas that might be infesting the neighborhood."[7]

Dr. Samuel Mudd told soldiers another story. If Dr. George Mudd had remained in the house while detectives interrogated his cousin, he might have corrected the differences, but he deliberately left when the officers began the questioning.

George Mudd, continuing his testimony before the Court, was questioned about the character of D. J. Thomas. This was one point the defense could win and they continued to hammer away on it. George Mudd said he thought Thomas was insane.[8]

Judge Bingham cross-examined the doctor, requesting sarcastically, "Be good enough to tell the court what works you have read on insanity." The witness patiently explained that he had read Taylor's book on insanity. This didn't satisfy Bingham, who questioned, "Do you wish to state here today that Daniel Thomas is so crazy that he does not know how to tell the truth?"

"No, sir; I mean to say there seems to be a mental and moral insanity."

"Are you prepared to swear that he is so crazy that he does not know how to tell the truth when he is under oath before a court?"

"I am not."[9]

Questions regarding types of insanity, whether "moral" or "mental," led the Court to inquire further, "What is the form of insanity under which Mr. Thomas labors?"

"There is no specific form that I know of, except at times a peculiar excitement and inability to appreciate matters and things as other people do," testified the doctor. By way of explanation he added that "it is not monomania; it is what is called aberration of the mind; there is a certain form of insanity which exacerbates and remits, but I do not know that it has any particular name or belongs to any particular form of insanity."

Dr. George Mudd's knowledge of mental problems was not as sophisticated as that of modern psychiatrists, but he told the truth as he understood it, not only about Daniel Thomas, but also about his cousin Samuel. When questioned again about Dr. Sam Mudd's reputation for loyalty, his answer differed from his previous response. "From my association with him, I have had to consider him as sympathizing with the South." Even with this frank admission, the witness continued to support his cousin, saying that he was temperate in his views and had taken the oath.

George Mudd stated that he personally administered the oath in 1864 and

was impressed with the reverence Sam Mudd showed, "making a decided contrast to many others to whom I administered the oath on that occasion; so far
as I know he has obeyed the provisions of that oath."[10]

Members of the Court were aware that 1864 was late to be taking the oath
of allegiance and that the oath was a prerequisite for voting on a new Maryland
constitution which would abolish slavery. Reverdy Johnson had already been
accused of advocating taking the oath in order to vote, even if one did not intend to keep the promise. Dr. Sam Mudd, as a slaveholder, apparently wanted
to vote on the new constitution and was thereby forced to take the oath.

During the trial, Mrs. Mudd could only stand by helplessly as Daniel
Thomas lied repeatedly about her husband, but in reality, he benefited the
doctor. Reporters and others recognized Thomas as a prevaricator, but his obvious falsehoods strengthened Mudd's defense. Judges might assume that other
witnesses also lied about the suspect. Thomas's character was so questionable
that his own brother admitted he would not believe him. Years after the trial,
police arrested Thomas and put him in prison for pension frauds. He died in
the penitentiary.

How much Mrs. Mudd knew of her husband's activities is debatable. She
obviously knew something, but probably not much. She was not present when
her husband first met Booth at church. After church Booth, Mudd and
another man named Thompson visited in the Mudd home together until evening. Apparently Mrs. Mudd only saw Booth at suppertime. Later that evening, Booth evidently slept in the house of a neighbor, and she did not see him
again until the next morning at breakfast. Possibly she did not recognize Booth
on the night of the murder or realize the consequences of his staying in their
house.

The investigation was particularly hard on Mrs. Mudd after her husband's
arrest. Soldiers guarded the farm and used her house as headquarters for
William Wood and other detectives. During the day they were out searching
for Booth and Herold, but they spent the night in the Mudd house. Mrs.
Mudd, with her four small children, was predictably frightened until a cousin,
Sylvester Mudd, realizing her situation, came to stay with them. As soon as
the soldiers received word that Booth had been killed, they left the farm and
headed back to Washington.

The Government later sent Lt. Luther Baker to bring Mrs. Mudd to
Washington to testify. She refused to go with him but promised she would be
in Washington at the designated time. When Mrs. Mudd later reported to
LaFayette Baker's office, he told her to go to a hotel and send him the bill. She
preferred staying with a cousin, however, to which Baker made no objections,
requesting only that she be at his office the next morning at 10:00. Arriving
at the appointed hour, the doctor's wife explained to Baker that she had four
little children at home with no one to care for them. He instructed her to wait
at his office until 2:00 P.M., and if he had not sent for her by that time, she
could go home. Baker did not call her, so she hired a carriage to return home.
Mrs. Mudd was never called as a witness.[11]

Following a few insignificant statements, the lawyer had another opportunity to defend the doctor. H. L. Mudd, Jr., the prisoner's brother, endeavored to prove that the accused could not have been in Washington on the days mentioned by Weichmann. An incidental result of his testimony was a dispute over the prisoner's farm. The defense contended that Booth's purpose in visiting with Mudd was to buy his land. This was a flimsy argument considering Booth's obvious objective at the time. The prosecution maintained Dr. Mudd did not own any land. Although a small point, lawyers debated it hotly. The witness declared that his brother owned a 400–500-acre farm. Judge Burnett quizzed, "Do you mean that he owns it?" The witness contradicted himself testifying, "Father gave it to him; he never had any deed for it; he is simply there as a tenant; my father owns it."

Ewing tried to correct the impression that Mudd's father owned the land. Under questioning, the witness changed his story again. "I have always understood that the farm was set apart for him by his father; it is known as his farm."

"Do you know of your brother having sold and received the proceeds of any land belonging to your father?"

"Yes, sir; the land on which Mr. Forey now lives he bought from my father; the house was burnt down and my brother sold the farm."

"Who held the title?"

"My father, sir."[12]

Later Ewing recalled this witness to have him correct the impression that Dr. Mudd was only a tenant. But the evidence remained that he did not own the land he supposedly wanted to sell and, in fact, did not sell the farm, but lived there many years later. Booth's clear purpose in talking with Dr. Mudd for hours on several occasions was not to buy a farm. The defense called other witnesses, who added nothing of importance, and court adjourned.

Although it did not excite great attention from the press, events occurring outside the courtroom were to have an indirect bearing on the trial. Political observers realized that strong-willed President Johnson would eventually clash with Secretary of War Stanton. Johnson could not easily dismiss Stanton during the assassination investigation, yet a complete reshuffling of the Cabinet might have averted future conflicts.

Johnson was conscious of the unfortunate consequences that had beset Pres. Millard Fillmore when he hurriedly appointed a new Cabinet at the death of Pres. Zachary Taylor. Fillmore's efforts to reverse the trend of his predecessor through Cabinet changes lost him his party's support and eventually caused his downfall as well as the disintegration of the Whig Party. Johnson wanted to avoid such disastrous results. With Fillmore's sad example in mind, he decided at first not only to retain Lincoln's Cabinet, but also to try to cooperate with the radical section of the Republican Party.

The President could not foresee the changes which would inevitably affect his administration. He gradually modified his early harsh treatment of the South, however, thus alienating Radicals. At the same time Stanton, who began his career as a proslavery Democrat, cast his lot more solidly with Radical Republicans.

Johnson, persuaded somewhat by the recuperating Secretary of State, believed as President he had responsibility for directing the Reconstruction program. While the President possessed many weaknesses, he did not lack tenacity. He determined to take the reins of Government and guide Reconstruction. Thus on May 29, he issued his Proclamation of Amnesty and Pardon. This pardon, conditioned upon taking the prescribed oath, and encumbered by restrictions, was a definite first step taken by the President with Seward's blessing. However, Radicals opposed it, and this was to create problems for Johnson as it probably would have for Lincoln.

Johnson's program essentially followed Lincoln's lenient plans for Reconstruction, but it brought the President into direct conflict with the Radical-controlled Congress. Several leaders in the conspiracy trial, including Bingham, Speed and Stanton, later fought with the President over his Reconstruction efforts.

By the end of May social conditions in Washington became intolerable. Hotels remained packed. Soldiers continued to crowd the city, routinely getting paid, drunk and robbed. Thieves and scoundrels of all sorts swarmed around discharged soldiers, selling them bad whiskey and generally fleecing them. General Grant was forced to issue an order closing all saloons.

Out at the Arsenal things progressed a little more orderly, but not much. Multitudes thronged the courtroom again on May 30. The noise of rustling silk, as elegantly dressed ladies passed in and out and around each other searching for seats, distracted the Judges and lawyers. Detectives from Colonel Baker's force tried to maintain order the best they could.

Although the proceedings attracted large crowds, public interest in the trial began to wane. Most people had already come to some conclusion on the basis of early evidence. Newspapers, which during the first week or ten days printed every word of testimony, began to publish condensed versions, and eventually they mentioned only the highlights.

The Commissioners and the Judges also grew weary, particularly as the heat increased, crowds expanded, and testimony became monotonous. The Generals seldom violated regulations regarding dress, however. Even on the hottest days they appeared in full uniform, pressed and polished. But the heat steadily drained them of their rigid military bearing. The generals appeared less solemn and impressive as they leaned back in their chairs or sat casually with their heads bent sleepily over the table. One visitor noted that "members of the Commission sat about in various negligent attitudes, and a general disorder was evident."[13] However, an occasional remark or significant new evidence revived interest.

The courtroom became suffocating by the time the previous day's testimony was read. Two of Herold's younger sisters, about 16 and 18 years old, sat in front of the counsel table listening to the record. The prosecution began by calling witnesses again to show the connection of Confederate leaders to various acts of brutality and presumably to the assassination plot.

The prosecution then questioned Jacob Ritterspaugh, a carpenter at Ford's Theatre. He testified that Spangler hit him on the mouth and ordered him not to tell which way Booth had gone. Spangler, who usually expressed little interest in the trial, shook his head in disbelief.

Cross-examined by Ewing, the witness swore that he was in the center of the stage when the shot was fired and that Spangler was near him. "He was standing there, and seemed to look pale." Ewing asked if Ritterspaugh realized what had happened immediately after the shot. "Not right away," answered the witness. "I did not know what had happened until I heard somebody halloo 'stop that man; the President is shot.'"

"When you came back whereabouts was Spangler?"

"In the same place where I left him."[14]

Dr. Stewart, who had chased Booth, was the only previous witness to seriously implicate Spangler. He had testified that a person wearing a mustache stood by the door when Booth fled the theater and could have caught the assassin. Ritterspaugh's testimony, however, showed that Spangler was in the center of the stage when Booth went through the door on the left side.

The defense then recalled several witnesses to correct their previous statements. The only important change was in the testimony of Mudd's brother-in-law, Jeremiah Dyer. He had stated under oath that he had never gone to Richmond, but this time he admitted that he had. Bingham asked, "Who were the parties whom you accompanied to Richmond at the time of which you speak?"

"Ben Gwynn and Andrew Gwynn."

"That was after the Rebellion commenced?"

"Yes, sir."

"Did you see Jefferson Davis while you were in Richmond?"

Dyer admitted that he saw Davis but never spoke to him. "What business took you to Richmond?" Bingham inquired.

"I went there to avoid arrest."

"You preferred to fall into the hands of the enemy?"

"I regretted very much the necessity of going there."[15]

Bingham took advantage of the witness's confession to rehash his admitted association with Dr. Mudd. In referring to Dyer's testimony given previously, Bingham had him repeat his statement about Dr. Mudd's hiding Confederates.

Ewing objected to any further examination of Dyer, declaring that these facts were already established, but General Hunter wanted to pursue the point.

Hunter asked Dyer if he had not previously sworn that he was loyal and had remained so during the war. Judge Bingham supported Hunter, declaring that such was also his understanding. Hunter inquired, "Did you not belong to an association hostile to the Government of the United States?"

"I belonged to a cavalry company," Dyer hedged.[16]

The prosecution thus established that the witness had misrepresented his position under oath—a slight setback for the doctor.

Another defense witness, Marcellus Gardiner, was a friend and neighbor of Dr. Mudd. His testimony did not impress the Court because he denied that the name of the assassin was generally known on Sunday. Practically all witnesses, both Government and defense, had sworn that Booth was widely believed to have been the assassin on Saturday.

XXXVI
"Where Is Ma?"

Although Mary Surratt's lawyers were thwarted in their efforts to have Von Steinacker recalled, they were not entirely defeated. They located the general under whom Von Steinacker had served. Gen. Edward Johnson, confined at Fort Warren as a prisoner of war, had been brought to Washington to defend Jefferson Davis before another Commission, though not the civil court earlier considered. At the end of May the Government temporarily detained him in Old Capitol Prison.

The Government had decorated the 49-year-old, Virginia-born Johnson for gallantry in the Mexican War, and he had been highly honored before joining the Confederacy. While serving as a Southern general, Union troops captured him at Spottsylvania's "bloody angle." They later exchanged him and he fought again in Hood's division. The persistent warrior was captured again at Nashville.

As the Confederate General approached the witness stand, the battery of Union generals bristled. Even before Johnson could be sworn in, General Howe objected.

Howe complained that Johnson had been educated at the National Military Academy at Government expense and for many years had been a commissioned officer in the United States Army. It was well known, the Commissioner continued, that a condition for receiving a commission was the taking of the oath of allegiance to the Federal Government. Furthermore, he remarked, Johnson had led a charge in 1861 that killed Howe's men. General Howe was highly indignant that the defense had brought the Confederate General before the Court "with his hands red with the blood of his loyal countrymen, shed by him or by his assistance, in violation of his solemn oath." Howe pronounced Johnson's presence an insult to the Commission and demanded that he be ejected from the courtroom.[1] General Ekin rose to second the motion.

Aiken retorted that he was not aware that a person was disqualified from becoming a witness because he had borne arms against the United States. He reminded the Court that Willie S. Jett, who had also fought for the Rebels, testified for the prosecution. He pointed out that Jett, by his own admission, had never taken the oath of allegiance.

The usually silent General Kautz inquired, "Does this person appear here as a volunteer witness?" Aiken said no.[2]

Edward Johnson. When this Confederate general was called by the defense to testify, Union officers on the Commission bristled ("Harper's History of the Great Rebellion").

Judge Advocate Holt reminded the Commission that, as a rule of law, before a witness can be "rendered so infamous as to become absolutely incompetent to testify he must have been convicted by a judicial proceeding." Other evidence could affect his credibility, but not prohibit his testifying, "however unworthy of credit" he might be. Johnson waited patiently during the debate.[3]

After a few moments' reflection, General Wallace recommended that Howe withdraw his objection, not for the sake of the "person introduced as a witness," but for the sake of the investigation. Howe withdrew his objection and the Judge Advocate swore Johnson in.[4]

The Confederate leader related his story in a self-possessed, albeit somewhat nervous tone. He faced the Court with what appeared an "air of defiance," but which may have been a natural bearing for a general accustomed to command.[5] He described his capture in the Battle of Nashville and his current condition as prisoner at Fort Warren in Boston Harbor.

Aiken began the interrogation. "State to the court how, when, and under what circumstances Von Steinacker presented himself to you."

"In the month of May, 1863, a man accosted me in Richmond, in Capitol Square, by my name and the rank I bore in the United States Army, as Major Johnson; he told me he had served under me—"

Bingham interrupted angrily, "What has that to do with it? There has been no inquiry made as to his services under you—."

"Well, " faltered Johnson, "he met me in Richmond and applied for a position in the Engineer Corps, stating that he had served under me previously; that he was a Prussian by birth, and an engineer by education, and he would like to get in the Engineer Corps in our service."[6]

"You need not tell what he said," Bingham interrupted again, using every opportunity to badger the witness.

After other delays by Bingham, General Johnson gave the Court some idea of Von Steinacker's questionable character. Aiken asked, "Have you a personal knowledge of the fact of Lieutenant David Cockerill losing a horse?"

Bingham spoke up again, "I object. We do not propose the question of horse stealing here, it is not in the issue."

"The charge was made in the paper presented, that Von Steinacker had been guilty of horse stealing, and I understood we were to be permitted to prove any allegations in that paper," responded the frustrated Aiken.[7]

Judge Burnett, supporting Bingham, argued, "Anything that is legitimate and competent to be proved. We did not go further." The Court, obviously embarrassed by its blunder, did not want to hear the truth about Von Steinacker and sustained the objections.

Aiken inquired if Von Steinacker had been subject to a court-martial. Judge Bingham objected again. The court-martial record would not be of any value, he complained, because there were not "any courts in Virginia in those days that could legally try a dog."[8] A surprising assertion considering the questions raised about the legality of the Military Commission. The Court, however, sustained the objection.

General Johnson, continuing his account, denied he had ever heard of the secret meeting of officers of the Stonewall Brigade that Von Steinacker mentioned or of any talk of assassination. Johnson's testimony had little effect because of Bingham's constant interruptions, but the Military Commission had failed inexcusably in not investigating Von Steinacker's character.

Reporters were more impressed by Johnson's revelations. Several papers contended that his testimony threw grave doubt on Von Steinacker's credibility.[9] The Philadelphia Inquirer, however, criticized the Confederate General's testimony, saying that the Court "permitted the witness a momentary triumph which should not have been permitted him."[10]

The Commission next faced another well-known Confederate officer, Maj. H. K. Douglas. This witness was more outspoken than General Johnson. Aiken interrogated, "Do you recollect, after the return of your army from Gettysburg, where it was encamped?"

"I was wounded at Gettysburg, and left in the hands of the enemy; I was a prisoner for nine months," Douglas reported. He then swore that he never saw Von Steinacker after Gettysburg but that he did get "a letter from him immediately after I returned to camp."

"Do you know of any secret meetings ever being held in your camp, at which the assassination of President Lincoln was discussed?"

"No, I do not."

"Were you acquainted with J. Wilkes Booth, the actor?"

"No."[11]

A Commissioner asked the witness if he had ever been a member of the United States service. "No," he responded. Douglas then made a bold request. "With the permission of the court, I would like to make a statement." General Howe interrupted, "I object to the prisoner making any statement."

General Foster, being more lenient, suggested that the witness "be allowed to make his statement."

The unbending Hunter became surprisingly permissive. "If no further objection is made the witness will proceed with his statement."

Douglas informed the Court that accusations against the "Stonewall Brigade" were unfounded. The soldiers of the brigade had a reputation for gallantry, he boasted, and could not have been employed as assassins of President Lincoln. "In their behalf I only wish to say that I do not believe they knew anything about or in the least sympathized in any such unrighteous or unsoldierly action," he concluded.[12]

Oscar Heinreichs, another Confederate witness, confirmed the statements of both Johnson and Douglas, and that ended the strange affair of Von Steinacker.

The testimony did not directly affect Mrs. Surratt, but it helped thwart the Government's efforts to connect the defendant with a large conspiracy that supposedly had roots back to Jefferson Davis.

The defense turned to witnesses more directly concerned with Mary Surratt. Thomas (some accounts say Joseph) Nott, the bartender at her country house, stated that John Lloyd had been drinking on the day of the murder, but he did not alter previous damaging statements about Lloyd's meeting with Mrs. Surratt.

Bingham cross-examined the witness. "Did you see him tie the buggy of Mrs. Surratt?" The defense had contended that Lloyd was too drunk to know what he was doing. The bartender hedged, "With assistance he did; I do not know whether Mr. Lloyd, Mr. Weichmann or Captain Gwynn tied it; they were all there...."

Clampitt quizzed, "Where did you first see him that afternoon?"

"Driving around the kitchen; he came round to the front of the house while Mrs. Surratt was there."

"Did you hear any conversation that took place between Mr. Lloyd and Mrs. Surratt?"

"I did not."

"How close were they to the buggy?"

"Probably fifteen or twenty yards off."[13]

Judge Bingham wanted to make sure that the Captain Gwynn mentioned was the same Ben Gwynn who had testified before the Court and who had been identified as hiding at Dr. Mudd's farm. "What Captain Gwynn was that who was at Mrs. Surratt's buggy?"

"Captain Ben Gwynn."

Thus far Mrs. Surratt's defense was less successful than Dr. Mudd's. Too many witnesses had seen her in what appeared to be suspicious circumstances.

The next witness, J. Z. Jenkins, was Mrs. Surratt's brother. Aiken questioned him but did not mention his blood relationship to the prisoner until it was brought out under cross-examination. Jenkins tried to exonerate his sister, telling of the letter from George Calvert and picturing Lloyd as too drunk to know what was happening. "Was Mrs. Surratt upon the point of going away when Lloyd drove up?" asked Aiken.

"Yes; she had been ready to start for some time before Lloyd drove up; she had business with Captain Gwynn, and when he came she went back and stopped."

"At what time did you leave?"

"About sundown, I judge."

His testimony raised more questions. According to Jenkins, his sister's purpose in making the trip was to contact John Nothey. Yet she had not asked Nothey to meet her. She wasted more than two hours at Lloyd's with her brother and Captain Gwynn without requesting anyone to send for Nothey or to drive her to Nothey's place just three miles away. After waiting at the house, she left immediately after Lloyd's arrival and her brief, private talk with him.

These facts were uncontestable. Even the defense did not deny the events as first described by Weichmann and later substantiated by Lloyd and Jenkins, among others. Even if Weichmann had harbored Southern sentiments, and if Lloyd had been drunk, as the defense sought to prove, it did not alter the undeniable activities of that crucial day.

Jenkins, nevertheless, supported his sister as best he could. He told of her care for Union soldiers and their horses without concern for remuneration. He mentioned the prisoner's bad eyesight. The defense lawyer pushed him too far, however, when he asked if he remembered a time when Mrs. Surratt "gave the last ham she had to Union soldiers." Mary Surratt's brother could not remember that imagined kindness. Jenkins swore that Mary Surratt was very loyal to the Government and that he had never heard her say anything disloyal.

The prosecution cross-examined him rigorously. After getting him to reluctantly acknowledge that Mary Surratt was his sister, Burnett asked, "Are you now under arrest?"

"I am. I was arrested and brought here last Thursday week."

"Where were you on the evening of the day previous to your arrest?"

"At Lloyd's Hotel."

Burnett asked about a Mr. Coltenback, whom Jenkins admitted he knew.

"Did you have any conversation with him at that time in reference to this trial?" the Judge questioned.

"Yes, sir, we were talking about the trial."

The witness revealed that he told Coltenback that he (Jenkins) would check the newspaper account of his (Coltenback's) testimony. Burnett wanted to know if Jenkins said anything else to Coltenback.

"Not that I know of; I might have told him that my sister found [was fond of?] his family."

"What relevancy had that to the conversation?"

"I disremember how the conversation commenced."

"Did you at that time and place say to Mr. Coltenback that if he, or anyone like him, undertook to testify against your sister, you would see that they were got out of the way?"

Jenkins denied that he said "anything of the kind," and the Judge asked, "Did you say you would send any man to hell who testified against your sister?"

"I did not."

"Did you use any threats against him if he appeared as a witness against your sister?"

Again the witness swore that he said nothing like that, but only reminded Coltenback that Mary Surratt "had raised his family."

"Did you call him a liar?"

"I disremember."

"Was there any anger exhibited in that conversation?"

"I did not mean it if there was."

After a few words about John Surratt, Judge Burnett came back to Coltenback. "How did you learn that Mr. Coltenback was to be a witness?"

"He told me himself."

Asked if he threatened Coltenback, Jenkins said not to his knowledge.

"Wouldn't you know it if you had?"

"I think I ought to; I do not think I did use any, only in reference to the public press; I told him I would look at his statement."

"And if you found in the public press that he had testified against your sister what did you say?"

"I do not recollect."

Burnett discussed points related to Ben Gwynn and then asked if Jenkins had been loyal to the Government during the war.

"Perfectly loyal, I think."

"How did you stand when the question of the secession of Maryland was under discussion?"

"I spent $3000 to hold her in the Union, and everybody in that neighborhood will testify."

When asked if he had ever taken part in any way against the Government, Jenkins swore, "Never, by act, word, aid or sympathy with the Rebels."[14]

The ease with which some witnesses lied created a problem in sorting the evidence. Many statements were corroborated by accumulated evidence. But most witnesses would shade the truth when their lives were in danger—and when their story could not easily be checked. Close relatives of the accused often gave false statements, which, if not outright lies, were at least distortions.

Soon after Jenkins testified about his absolute loyalty, Judge Holt received a letter from an indignant neighbor of Jenkins stating that the witness was a noted Rebel—a fact well known to the Court.

The War Department received numerous letters accusing people of Confederate sympathies. Few signed their allegations or offered to testify. Yet William A. Evans volunteered to testify that Jenkins was a Rebel and that his whole story about spending money for the Union cause was false. Evans declared Jenkins to be one of the strongest supporters of the Confederacy in Prince Georges County. He mentioned others, including Mr. Roby, willing to take the stand concerning the notorious pro–Southern character of Jenkins.

The defense next called Anna Surratt. Even though she had been in prison for six weeks, the young woman presented a neat, even haughty, appearance as she approached the witness stand. Anna was a tall, slim girl, 22 years old, but her nervous, immature actions made her seem younger. She had a high forehead, gray eyes, a thin pointed nose, thin lips, a narrow chin and light brown hair confined in a net. In court she wore a black silk dress and a white straw hat with a black veil. Under normal circumstances, she might have been considered attractive. These were not normal circumstances, however, and she could only be described as pitiful.

In the crowded courtroom a group of ladies standing in front of the prisoners' platform blocked Mrs. Surratt from Anna's view. Her mother added to the difficulty by keeping her head bowed.[15]

Gently, the defense lawyer began his interrogation with an innocuous question. "Can you state from your knowledge whether or not Atzerodt was given to understand that he was not wanted at the house?"

"Yes, sir; mamma said she did not care to have strangers there, but we treated him with politeness, as we did everyone who came to the house."[16]

Dutifully she told of her mother's poor eyesight, although when arrested, Anna had also denied recognizing Payne. Lawyers said nothing about Anna's inability to see well.

The young lady spoke in the sharp, clipped tone of a fearful girl trying to appear certain of herself. Exhibiting a feeling of wounded innocence, she was spiteful toward the Commissioners and made a point to demonstrate her scorn for Weichmann.

"Do you know Louis J. Weichmann?" questioned the defense.

"Yes."

"Was he a boarder at your mother's house?"

"Yes, sir."

"How was he treated there?"

"Too kindly."

The attorney suggested that Mrs. Surratt often sat up and waited for him when he was out late. "Yes," confirmed Anna, "just as she would wait for my brother; Weichmann engaged a room for Atzerodt; when he came, Weichmann and he used to make private signs for each other."[17]

Anna's air of insulted dignity during her interrogation gradually softened under Judge Advocate Holt's considerate handling of the proceedings.

The defense lawyer asked about Payne and again she made an effort to implicate Weichmann. "It was Weichmann went to the door, and it was Weichmann who brought Payne in there. . . ."

The witness repeated that her mother did not like strangers coming to the house, a curious statement considering that she supposedly ran a boarding-house. When asked if she was acquainted with Booth, the young woman replied indifferently, "Yes, sir, I have met him." She followed this understatement with a misrepresentation.

"When was he last at your house?"

"On the Monday before the assassination."

Anna should have known this statement to be false, but she was uncertain what the counsel was trying to prove. She was apparently oblivious to previous statements by several witnesses that definitely established Booth's visits on Tuesday and Friday. Aiken courteously guided the now-confused young lady to retract her statement about Booth's last visit. "Did your mother go to Surrattsville about that time?"

"Yes, sir; on Friday, the day of the assassination."

Aiken asked if the carriage was ready to go when Booth arrived. She answered, "Yes, I think he came and found her about to go; and she had been speaking about going a day or two before that on a matter of business, and she said she was obliged to go." Thus Anna, guided by her mother's lawyer, incredibly confirmed Weichmann's very damaging account of Booth's suspicious visit.

Anna tried earnestly to cover every angle, as though she had been rehearsed, but her contradictions were obvious.

"How long did Booth remain?"

"Not over a few minutes; he never stayed long when he came."[18]

Anna was deeply aware of her total dependence on her mother, especially now that her brother was a fugitive. The interrogators, conscious of her unhappy position, directed their questions with appropriate compassion. The witness recounted how the picture "Spring, Summer and Autumn" had been given to her by Weichmann and how she had hidden Booth's picture behind it on her brother's advice.

Some observers surmised a romantic link existed between Anna Surratt and Louis Weichmann. Yet neither the prosecution nor the defense ever suggested such a romance. Whether by design or by accident, the ages of the two young people were reported incorrectly. Anna was usually pictured as a young girl about 17, when in fact, she was 22. Weichmann, on the other hand, was said to have been about 27, when he was actually 22.

As Weichmann told it, most overtures for him to join the Surratt household had come from the Surratts. John first invited him to visit their house in the country. Mrs. Surratt befriended him during his several visits there. Then, when she opened her boardinghouse in Washington, Weichmann was invited to be one of the first boarders. During the month of November, Weichmann, John Surratt and Anna, along with Honora Fitzpatrick, were the only persons in the house. Weichmann was intelligent and scholarly but somewhat shy and a little awkward. Even so, he would have been a good prospect for the immature, high-strung Anna.

During the period of plotting in February 1865, Weichmann was being pursued by a girlfriend from New York named Clara. He exchanged letters with Clara, relating that his real interest was Anna Surratt. Clara responded that she hoped he had gained the heart he "seemed to court." Weichmann also wrote to Clara of his plans for an "appointment abroad." To this impressive-sounding news, Clara expressed interest in knowing if perhaps Lou would be passing through Philadelphia or New York City.[19] This trip, planned for July 1865, was a youthful boast, but the suggestion seemed strangely similar to John Surratt's frequently stated intent to leave the country.

Clara often included questions about Anna along with a clear indication of her own attraction to Weichmann. One letter ended, "reply please, especially about Miss S__tt." Clara wanted to know if Louis was sure that Anna returned his interest. She sadly answered her own question, "I know and feel Miss S__tt is worthy of you and they were all favorably disposed toward you I believe. Most sincerely, your friend Clara."[20]

Years later John C. Martin, a friend of Captain Gleason, reported that Louis was interested in John Surratt's sister, but he did not elaborate.[21]

Nothing indicates that Anna reciprocated Weichmann's attention. Weichmann was hopeful, but he never hinted that he had any romantic interest. Two years after the trial, he told reporter George Alfred Townsend that he felt that he had been supplanted by Booth in his friendship with John Surratt.[22] This frank confession may have applied even more so to Anna. It was a revealing, symbolic irony that Anna concealed the portrait she bought of the dashing actor behind the gift of her timid suitor.

Although Anna had never shown any particular interest in Weichmann before the assassination, she showed extreme contempt toward him on the few occasions when she saw him after her arrest. She did not hesitate to turn on any male acquaintance in an effort to protect her mother. Anna unhesitatingly branded both Booth and Payne crazy. While her evaluation may have been true, she had not thought so before the murder.

Weichmann's love for Anna influenced his words at the trial. Although his testimony was not vicious or purposefully hateful toward the Surratts, he did not avoid facts damaging to Mrs. Surratt. Not so in Anna's case; he mentioned little evidence that might have been harmful to her, even while Anna went out of her way to condemn him.

Two years later, however, Weichmann's affection cooled. Constant insults and libelous attacks by Anna and her friends forced him to fight back. During John Surratt's trial, Weichmann brought out facts about Anna that he had hidden previously. He pointedly testified that, on the day after the assassination, Anna remarked that Lincoln's death was no worse than that of any "nigger's."

Weichmann's unrequited love had turned sour. Throughout the rest of his life, he had little to say about Mrs. Surratt's daughter. A few years after the trial she married another man, Dr. William P. Tonry. Weichmann never married.

The interrogation continued with Anna being asked about pictures of Confederate heroes. "Did you own any photographs of Davis and Stephens?"

"Yes, sir, and General Lee and General Beauregard and a few others; I don't remember them all."

When asked where she got them, Anna replied, "Father gave them to me before his death, and I prized them very highly on his account."

"Did you not have photographs of Union Generals?"

She hesitated, looked anxiously around the courtroom for her mother, then replied, "Yes sir; of General McClellan, General Grant and Joe Hooker."[23]

Mrs. Surratt, obscured by the crowd, made no effort to make herself more visible. Anna, growing noticeably more agitated as the interrogation proceeded, searched more frantically for her mother. Her eyes darted from one corner of the room to the other. She began to answer slowly, as if thinking about something else, as she continued to glance around the room.

When Aiken turned the interrogation over to Ewing, the young lady became even more frightened. Ewing asked, "What year did your brother leave college?" Anna, dazed, responded mechanically and incorrectly, "In 1861; the year my father died." While answering she muttered to herself, "Where's mama?" Still searching uneasily for her mother, she repeated more audibly, "Where's mama?"

Although Miss Surratt was a high-strung young woman, she was not stupid. She was guilty of several errors such as her statement about Booth's last visit and the one about when her brother left college, but these could be blamed on the emotional strain.

Ewing continued his considerate interrogation as members of the Court and visitors realized something was wrong.

"What year were you in school at Bryantown?"

"From 1854 to 1861, the 16th day of July was the day I left."

"Did you ever see Dr. Mudd at your mother's house at Washington?"

"No, sir."[24]

Now Anna showed definite signs of distress; the veins and muscles in her face and throat became distended. She had trouble concentrating on the questions. In this pitiful state she continued to answer mechanically, searching more earnestly all the while for her mother. Mary Surratt could not see her daughter's agony but could hear her confused answers, yet she made no effort to reveal her position. She sat, immobile, in her corner, hidden by spectators and her heavy black veil. Anna started to tap her foot impatiently on the stand. It was now obvious to everyone that Anna was on the verge of emotional collapse.

All eyes turned toward the poor girl, who seemed completely indifferent to their gaze. The defense counsel and the Judges stopped the proceedings. Her interrogator advised her quietly that she could retire, but Anna, dazed, continued to linger on the stand frantically looking for her mother.

Ewing, trying to be helpful, began to ask what he considered comforting questions in an effort to keep Anna occupied until an officer could lead her away. "Is Surrattsville on the road between Washington and Bryantown?" he asked quietly. Her face flushed and her eyes filled with tears as several men approached to help.

By this time Hartranft, a considerate officer, came forward to help her, but Anna, recognizing the General as her mother's jailer, struck out at him. The understanding General did not force the frightened girl but sought the aid of Henry Douglas, the Confederate officer, who, after testifying earlier, had lingered around the courtroom to watch the proceedings.[25] As she rose to go, she answered Ewing's last question, "Yes," as if in a trance, then added in a sharp, pathetic voice, "Where is mama?"

Holt, in an effort to calm her, said softly, "That is all," and tried to get her to leave, but she resisted, searching frantically. As Douglas and Aiken dragged her from the witness stand, she still looked around wildly. In the confusion, Anna dropped her small white handkerchief. One of the generals picked it up for her, but she snatched it rudely from his hand without a word and turned away. Aiken sought to comfort Anna by assuring her that she would soon see her mother and guided her trembling through the crowd.[26]

For some reason the lawyer tried to avoid letting Anna see her mother as he led her away. They passed within a few feet of Mrs. Surratt as they pushed through a narrow passageway which had been cleared through the crowd. Approaching the door leading into the waiting room, Anna pleaded again, "Where is Ma?"

This was not a theatrical act and the Court knew it. Tears of sympathy moistened the eyes of many spectators. Throughout the emotional ordeal, Mary Surratt never made a move; her veil continued to hide her face. One observer noted that on entering and leaving the courtroom, Anna had been careful to keep her skirts from touching Yankee officers. After her daughter was gone, Mrs. Surratt wept audibly, covering her face with her hands.[27]

When Anna reached the waiting room, she collapsed. Officers quickly shut the door and sent for a doctor. General Hartranft asked Douglas to carry the exhausted girl down to his office. There Anna became hysterical. Completely losing control of herself, she tore at her hair and sought to rip her clothing. Hartranft got some of the women in the area to care for her until the doctor arrived. The physician gave her a sedative, and she was soon asleep.[28]

Government prosecutors had treated Anna with marked consideration.

Henry Kyd Douglas. This young Confederate soldier testified at the trial then helped calm Anna Surratt. (From Douglas' book 'I Rode with Stonewall.")

They avoided cross-examination and let her answer in her own way without interruption. A reporter for the *Philadelphia Inquirer* asked Bingham why there had been no cross-examination. The usually legalistic Judge explained that it would have been cruel to subject the girl to any more questions, as she already had "a greater load of sorrow upon her than she could bear."[29]

Anna, indeed, had more than she could bear. She never fully recovered. Her father had died just a few years before; her mother had been arrested and tried for conspiracy. She, herself, was in prison. one of her brothers was a fugitive, while the other, a Confederate soldier, remained conveniently absent; her secret love had been shot to death; her uncle had been put in prison and her would-be admirer had apparently betrayed her family. There was little left for Anna. It was truly "a greater load of sorrow" than she could bear.

Later that day, General Augur sent the following order to Superintendent Wood: "You will immediately release and set at liberty the person of Anna E. Surratt, now in your custody."[39] But where could she go?

Anna and her mother were not the only ones grieving. Government workers were asked to contribute one dollar for the support of Mrs. Lincoln, who by this time had regained enough strength to move to Chicago. But her mental condition remained precarious.

After Miss Surratt was helped from the room, a subdued Court resumed its interrogations. Witnesses called to testify about Atzerodt's activities added nothing that could help his cause. Of all the prisoners, Atzerodt had to accept the most abuse. Hardly anyone spoke a complimentary word about him.

He was generally described in the lowest terms. The prisoner, sitting chained and silent, had no way to escape these derogatory remarks. When the testimony concerned him, he would usually try to crouch behind the railing and hide. The unhappy suspect bowed his head even deeper in shame every time a witness called him a coward. This seemed to hurt most.

Capt. Frank Monroe, who had charge of the prisoners aboard the monitors, took the stand. Atzerodt's counsel paused after he introduced Monroe and asked permission to give the Commission a written request from Atzerodt. The prisoner desired to have his confession to Captain Monroe admitted as evidence. The counsel admitted that he had no legal right to insist upon the confession being read, but he hoped the Court would accept a little change in the rules on behalf of his client. The battle-hardened soldiers might have been softened by Anna's grief, but they were in no mood to bend the rules. Judge Holt, dismayed, announced, "I think it is greatly to be deplored that counsel will urge such matters upon this Court as they know and admit to be contrary to the law."[31]

The Commissioners agreed that the confession could not be heard and the witness was dismissed. The next few testimonies added little to the proceedings and the Court adjourned after a hectic day.

Throughout the trial Ewing kept a notebook in which he recorded the names of possible witnesses and the subject of their testimony. One entry read, "Nellie Starr 62 Ohio Ave. See her and find if Booth did not tell her that the conspiracy was to capture the President."[32]

The Court summoned Ella Turner (Miss Starr's real name). Complying with the request, she went to the Arsenal on three different days and waited in the witness room. Although Booth's mistress had been interrogated frequently, she was never put on the witness stand.

Ewing also planned to call C. D. Hess, manager of Grover's Theatre, but changed his mind. Hess was to have testified that during the week of the assassination, Booth had wanted him to plan a special program and invite President Lincoln.[33] Ewing apparently intended to show that even a few days before the assassination, Booth still did not have concrete plans.

Many soldiers and visitors who had thronged the city to see the Grand Review lingered around Washington. Some combined business with pleasure and took the opportunity to buy horses or mules from the Government. The animals were mostly condemned as unsound, but the sales attracted large crowds because of low bargain prices.

Other temptations bombarded the recently discharged troops to part them with their money. One advertisement appealed to soldiers to buy a Waltham watch before returning home because the watch would be more useful than "a pocket full of silver dollars." Commerce in Lincoln relics continued at a fast pace, but only the wealthy could afford big items. Dr. F. B. Brewer bought Lincoln's family coach and harnesses. Women concerned with the latest fashions could purchase a new invention, the "duplex elliptic or double-spring skirt," advertised as the greatest invention of the age, promising new flexibility to hoopskirts.[34]

Rumors circulated about the trial had some basis in truth. One indicated that Payne's lawyer intended to put him on the stand as a witness for the defense of other prisoners.[35] Ample precedent existed for such action and Holt did not oppose the move. Payne also seemed willing.

This unusual tactic was consistent with Payne's attitude toward the proceedings. He realized soon after the trial began that he had little hope. But Payne had a noble streak mingled with his brutal nature. During the war he saved the lives of two Union soldiers, and yet a few months later, he ruthlessly beat and kicked a black servant girl. It was his nature to make a savage attempt to kill Secretary Seward and then gently submit to arrest. Payne would have been pleased to save his fellow conspirators. However, he never testified.

The prisoner known as Lewis Payne remained a mystery. The public knew nothing of his background. He did not even communicate with his lawyer. The last week of May he surprised Doster by requesting that three witnesses be called for his defense—a lady and a doctor living in Warrenton, Virginia, and a minister residing in Florida.

The Court uncovered little of significance on May 31. But during the opening proceedings, it became clear that Payne's attitude had changed. He seemed genuinely concerned for the first time. Rather than sitting in his customary upright posture, he leaned forward in his seat, his face alternately pale and flushed. He drew a sigh of satisfaction when the Court announced that it would summon his witnesses.

Following the preliminaries, the defense presented Hartman Richter, in whose house Atzerodt had been arrested. All he could say in Atzerodt's defense was that he did not resist arrest.

The defense called William Arnold and later Frank Arnold, brothers of Sam Arnold. They added nothing.

The testimony of John T. Ford showed that at the time Booth was seeking Samuel Knapp Chester's help, he was also trying to get Ford to employ Chester at the theater. Evidence showed that Booth had planned to use Ford's Theatre several months before he murdered the President.

Henry Clay Ford, the next witness, may not have intended to, but his testimony practically sealed Spangler's fate. "Did you receive any suggestions from anybody as to the preparation of the box?" the prosecution inquired.

"Only from Mr. Raybold and from the gentleman who brought the third man down there."

Asked what Spangler had to do with the decoration, he replied that he removed the partition between the two boxes making one box.

"Was it usual to remove the partition on such occasions?"

"Yes, we always removed it when the President came there."

In his further testimony Henry Ford revealed that Lincoln attended the theater often in the spring and winter.

"Was Spangler in the box during the time you were there decorating it?"

"No, he was at work on the stage at the time: I called for a hammer and nails, which he handed up to me."

Ford stated that Spangler was aware the President planned to see the play that night. Then the defense attorney asked a question that hurt Spangler. "Do you know whether there was any penknife used in the preparation of the President's box?"

"I used a penknife in cutting a string by which the picture is tied; I forgot it, left it there."

The interrogator turned to the chair brought from Henry Ford's sleeping room to the box. Ford remarked that it was part of a set of furniture originally kept in the reception room, "but the ushers were in the habit of lounging in it, and I took it into my room."

This famous chair, now belonging to the museum of another Henry Ford (in Dearborn, Michigan), became the subject of controversy. John Ford's widow later claimed it was part of her personal furniture.

Henry Ford also testified that Booth often rented box number 7 "which was part of the box occupied by the President nearest the audience." According to Ford he procured that box four or five times during the season.[36]

Even though several witnesses testified that Spangler remained at his assigned place throughout the play, Ford's reference to the penknife pointed to Spangler as the most likely source of the hole in the door to the President's box. A few other interrogations followed and court adjourned until Friday.

XXXVII
Guilt and Insanity

Anna did not leave prison smiling. She had no family and no real home. Her maternal grandmother still lived, but she was seldom spoken of by the Surratts and had little contact with them. Soon after gaining her freedom, Anna tried to retrieve items taken from her mother's house. She asked authorities to return the letters and papers belonging to the family. The Government waited until after the trial to return her letters. Some larger items, including a sword, two pistol cases, a box of detonator caps and a trunk, were not returned until later in August 1865. Authorities then turned them over to the Holohans, with whom Anna was staying.[1]

Reporters noticed several important documents and witnesses the prosecution had not presented in Court. A writer for the *Boston Advertiser* named Wachusett noticed that the prosecution had left out much of what Booth said and did. Incriminating letters, such as one from his brother Junius Brutus, were known to exist but were never presented. The Government did not call the Garretts, in whose barn Booth and Herold were captured, and with whom Booth discussed the assassination. Wachusett observed acutely that "a diary found in Booth's pocket is not opened for our information." He noted that the diary explained Booth's motives and was written by him before the murder. The reporter complained that it was "only mentioned once by Holt."[2] Actually Holt's brief reference to Booth's diary went unnoticed by the defense.

The prosecution never produced other revealing items such as the map Booth used and the crutches Dr. Mudd made. What was left of one crutch the Garrett family kept.

Some articles associated with Booth became prized possessions and were not turned over to the Government. Fifteen years after Booth's death, when one of the Garrett boys was studying at the Southern Baptist Theological Seminary, he wrote to Government officials informing them that he had the crutch. Garrett also kept the map which Booth had marked, showing his proposed escape route to Mexico, a lock of Booth's hair, and the mattress on which the assassin died.[3]

E. D. Wray, who picked up Booth's hat and gave it to the Government, wanted it back. He wrote officials begging to keep it when the trial was over.

During the trial, P. T. Barnum offered an incredible $1,500 for Booth's hat. Benn Pitman, court reporter, heard of the offer and wrote to Lincoln's pastor, the Reverend Dr. P. D. Gurley, to prevent the sale. Barnum never got the hat.[4]

Thursday, June 1, was declared a day of humiliation and prayer by President Johnson in respect for his predecessor. Citizens observed the day with varying degrees of mourning. In Washington, all Government offices closed and churches held religious services, but most stores, having an eye on soldiers' money, stayed open. Saloons closed—except for the back door.

President Johnson attended a service at the Lutheran Church. The pastor, J. G. Butler, chose the text, "Shall the throne of iniquity have fellowship with thee, which frameth mischief by a law" (Psalm 94:20). He equated the "throne of iniquity" with the Confederate's evil Government. Later this same pastor was called upon to comfort one of the conspirators.

The courts had just decided the case against B. G. Harris. Harris, a member of Congress from Maryland, was convicted of aiding the Rebels. He hid two Confederates near Leonardtown, Maryland, and advised them to violate their parole by returning South. The Government sentenced the Congressman to three years' hard labor, but President Johnson pardoned him. Harris's crime occurred in the same area and about the same time that Dr. Mudd was aiding Booth and Herold. Undoubtedly news of Johnson's generous action encouraged defense lawyers.

During the conspiracy trial, when it seemed that Mrs. Surratt's case was improving, Herold confided to Doster, "That old lady is as deep in as any of us."[5] It was an astonishing declaration because the prisoners tended to cover for one another, or at least did not implicate others unnecessarily. Atzerodt and Arnold had already confessed, but they had done so when first arrested and were seeking to excuse their own actions. Their confessions, once made, were repeated, but Herold had made no confession. In stating that Mrs. Surratt was in as deeply as any of them, he obviously included himself and others on trial.

Doster claimed that Atzerodt and Payne declared that Mrs. Surratt was innocent, but if Atzerodt did, it would have been a contradiction to his other statements. Payne happily obliged fellow conspirators, except John Surratt, with a confession of their innocence.

Mrs. Surratt's case fluctuated more than those of other suspects, but in general, she appeared more guilty with each day's testimony. When she realized the mounting evidence against her, she became concerned for her life and asked Frederick Stone to join Aiken and Clampitt in her defense. Guards brought her from her cell into the courtroom to confer with Stone. General Hartranft, who was in charge, motioned to the guard to move to the other side of the room where he remained looking out the window, thus allowing the lawyer privacy with his new client.[6] Actually Stone took little part in Mrs. Surratt's defense.

After weeks of watching her, one writer described Mary Surratt as "a graduate of that seminary which spits in soldiers' faces."[7] Despite her seeming guilt, the reporter noticed that she still attracted sympathy.

According to the *New York World*, Samuel Cox was called to the War

Department and questioned by Stanton but never put on trial, although he aided Booth and Herold and threw detectives off their trail. The article included its own italicized explanation, "*Perhaps the fact that Coxe [sic] is known to have visited Secretary Stanton some days previous to the assassination may account for it.*"[8] This was the first effort to connect Stanton with the crime. Coming from a paper strongly critical of the Government in general and of the Secretary of War in particular, it carried little weight. Cox was only one of hundreds of suspects questioned and released, many of whom were guilty to some degree.

The length of the trial and the increasingly hot weather began to take their toll. General Hunter, who sat at the end of the table opposite Holt, was not physically up to his responsibility. Through much of the testimony he shut his eyes—either to think or to sleep. Other generals, seated around the table, took a few notes but seemed tired, even bored. General Wallace, considered second in importance to Hunter, and later author of the religious best-seller *Ben Hur*, gave the impression of being intolerant and severe.

While reporters sometimes criticized the Commission on constitutional grounds and occasionally spoke harshly of Stanton or Holt, they avoided insulting the military leaders outright. On June 2, however, the consistently critical *New York World* printed a vicious attack:

> The composition of the court is of the worst possible description. There is not a man composing it who ever achieved any honorable distinction in the service, or who is regarded with favor by his brother officers. Hunter, the president, as everybody knows, what part of him is not fool is knave.
> ... General Lew Wallace, for a young man has made the most proficiency in official flunkeyism of any man of the time. He is neither soldier, scholar, judge nor gentleman. Kautz is a good natured, harmless Pennsylvania Dutchman who knows as much of the nature of a legal proposition as the horse he has killed by useless hard riding.[9]

The paper considered other members too inconspicuous to warrant comment. The descriptions were not only insulting; they were untrue. Because of this attack, a rumor spread that the Court would exclude the *World* reporter from the trial. The Commission did not bother, however, and he was admitted as usual.

Another explosive action occurred outside the courtroom. The *Cincinnati Commercial* shocked the Commissioners by publishing much of the evidence taken in secret sessions.[10] Upon investigation, the Government discovered that Benn Pitman, who had given himself the title of Official Recorder of the Commission, was the culprit. Pitman, in charge of the original drafts of the proceedings, was under oath not to divulge any information without special permission. In violation of his oath, he made a synopsis of the secret testimony and mailed it to the *Commercial*. Judge Holt, exasperated at this breach, had no alternative but to order the publication of all suppressed material and to call for another secret session.

A curious personality brought to light as a result of the newspaper revelations was a man known as Sanford Conover. This individual first appeared at Holt's offices early in May but up to this time had operated in secret.

Charles A. Dunham, alias Sanford Conover—alias James Watson Wallace, was born in the small town of Croton, New York, sometime between 1830 and 1837. His father, a tanner, was a man of respectability and some wealth. Young Dunham worked with his father until he was about 20 years old, then went into the brick business, which failed. At the outbreak of the Civil War, he tried to raise a regiment in New York City, but that failed also. Dunham then moved to the western part of the state and, according to some evidence, tried to recruit for the Confederate army.

Conover—the name by which he is best remembered—later served with Confederate forces as a war office clerk in Richmond. In December 1863, he abruptly left and went back to his native state. After a short interval, he turned up in Washington, D.C., where he became a local correspondent for the *New York Tribune*. In October 1864, Conover journeyed to Montreal, Canada, as a reporter for the *Tribune*, using the name James Watson Wallace and pretending to be a Southerner.

In some way, Conover managed to become acquainted with Confederate leaders in Canada, among them, Jacob Thompson. Conover testified in Montreal on February 11, 1865, in behalf of Confederate soldiers who had escaped to Canada after their raid on St. Albans, Vermont. He later admitted that his testimony was entirely false, but Confederate leaders were unaware of his craftiness.

Canadian authorities had arrested the St. Albans raiders and detained them. The United States demanded that they be returned for trial, but the Confederate Government contended that the raiders were not subject to extradition on grounds they were regular soldiers of a sovereign belligerent Nation. To back up this contention, Confederate leaders had to prove the raiders were bona fide soldiers on a mission of war.

Conover later claimed his only responsibility in the proceedings was to identify the signature of James A. Seddon, the Confederate Secretary of War. In his statement before authorities in Canada, Conover related an elaborate story of his service with the Confederate army as a major and of his eventual capture by Union forces.

Under the name J. Watson Wallace, Conover sent a letter dated March 20, 1865, to Confederate agents in Canada with a proposition to blow up the Croton Dam on the Hudson River above New York City. According to Conover, this would "deprive the city of its sole source of supply of water," and he promised to make the destruction "appear entirely accidental." Rebel authorities turned down his offer.[11]

After the United States Government accused Davis, Thompson and Clay of participation in the conspiracy, Conover sensed another opportunity to put his talent for glib prevarication to work. He contacted Judge Holt, promising that he could supply the exact evidence Holt needed. He offered to testify against Confederate leaders, especially those in Canada, providing it be done behind closed doors. Conover explained his demand for secrecy claiming that if Rebels found out, they would kill him. Holt eagerly accepted his offer.

In a closed session with Holt, Conover told of a discussion among

Confederate leaders in Montreal in January or February 1865 concerning the assassination plot. After his secret session on May 22 with the Military Commission, Conover returned to Canada under the name he used there, Watson Wallace. When Pitman unexpectedly released the suppressed testimony, it was quickly published in Canada. Confederates in Canada demanded that "Wallace," suspected of being Conover, explain how he could have told such lies in Washington.[12]

For a less-imaginative criminal this predicament could have created problems; for the mendacious Conover it would be solved with other fables. Under the alias Wallace, he appeared on June 8, 1865, before William H. Kerr, attorney for the St. Albans raiders. He denied under oath that he had ever used the name Conover or that he had given any statement in Washington. He charged that a man named Conover impersonated him.

Two days later, the *Montreal Telegraph* published his affidavit. According to the article, "Wallace" vowed that he could prove he was not Conover if given a chance to appear before the military tribunal in Washington. He also offered a $500 reward for the capture of Conover, that "infamous and perjured scoundrel who recently personated [sic] me." Within days, the *New York World* printed these contradictory statements.[13]

In less than a week, a report indicated that "Wallace" had been arrested for being a common loafer in Montreal. This time he confessed that he was really Conover. Hearing this astonishing news, Holt immediately sent for Conover. For several days authorities could not find him. When finally apprehended, the Government brought him back to Washington. Again, he insisted on a secret hearing, which not only freed him from cross-examination, but also ensured his perjured statements would not get back to Canada.

This time, Conover had another fiction ready—Pitman caused all the trouble by making public the secret testimony. Conover's life, he vowed, was endangered because Rebels in Canada captured him and made him swear that he had lied to the Military Commission.

Now everybody was confused—except Conover. The military officers reminded him that his Canadian statement—denying his Washington testimony—had been signed before a notary public. Unperturbed, Conover affirmed that he had indeed signed such a denial but contended that the Confederates held a gun at his head, threatening to kill him. With these contradictory falsehoods, the Commissioners should have at least been skeptical, but, with Holt's blessing, they exonerated Conover. The Court, however, labored the first few weeks of June trying to ascertain the truth in his many conflicting statements.

Anna Surratt, now released from Old Capitol Prison, was permitted to sit close to her mother during the proceedings. Guards, however, did not allow them to converse, but just being at her mother's side seemed to soothe Anna. Dressed in deep mourning, she remained on a bench close to the prisoners' dock with a look of "indescribable yearning."

The heat grew so stifling that officers finally had to disregard regulations and unbutton their coats. The temperature did not seem to affect Dr. Mudd, who still dressed the part of a gentleman, but he watched the proceedings unsophisticatedly chewing a wad of tobacco.

Women visitors increased at Court. Herold gave more attention to them than to his defense. One observer noted that Herold's casual attitude gave the impression "that if an assassination is productive of so little fun, he will have nothing to do with another one."[14]

After the reading of the previous day's record, defense witness Thomas Raybold explained why one of the doors to the President's box was loose. He and other witnesses supported Spangler's assertion that the suspicious rope found in the defendant's bag was used at the theater. Louis J. Carland testified that Jacob Ritterspaugh told him that Spangler had said, "You don't know who it was; it might have been Booth, and it might have been somebody else." The defense wanted to show that Spangler might have spontaneously uttered words in defense of a friend but was not guilty of taking part in the intrigue.

One witness revealed that Atzerodt had a "tender regard" for a woman in the country. These words caused the prisoner to double himself up, hide his face and try to disappear behind the railing. He remained in this animal-like position until the Court's attention focused on another subject.[15]

Attorney Stone, now serving Mrs. Surratt, questioned James Lusby. Stone made a point of demonstrating that Mrs. Surratt's conversation with Lloyd had only been accidental since she had been getting ready to leave when he happened to arrive. The defense witness, however, did not support that impression. He declared that Mrs. Surratt seemed to have intentionally waited near the house while Weichmann remained in the buggy driving around aimlessly. Stone queried, "What was Lloyd's condition at that time?"

"He was very drunk I thought; I reached Surrattsville about one minute and a half before he did; I drove up to the bar-room door; he went up to the front door."

"Did you see the prisoner, Mrs. Surratt, there that day?"

"I saw her as she was starting out to go home."

"Was she all ready to go home at the time Lloyd drove up?"

"Yes, the buggy was there waiting for her and she left about fifteen minutes afterwards."

The picture emerged of Mrs. Surratt waiting all afternoon and then leaving 15 minutes after Lloyd arrived. This evidence could not help her case.

Judge Holt realized that if Lusby went to the bar on the north side of the house, he could not have seen Mrs. Surratt in the back on the south side. He questioned, "You drove up on one side of the house and Lloyd went round to the other side, didn't he?"

"Yes, there was a front yard he went through when I went into that bar-room and got a drink."

"Did you see Mrs. Surratt when you first came? You didn't see her in the barroom, did you?"

"No."

"You didn't see her until you got your drink?"

"I disremember whether I got my drink when I first saw her or not."[16]

The defense had constantly stressed Lloyd's drunken condition. Holt attacked this point. "You say Lloyd was drunk; how do you know that fact?"

"I have seen him before."

"Did you see him drinking?"

"Yes; and I took drinks with him."

"Which drank the most?"

"I never measured mine."

Holt wanted to know if the witness was as drunk as Lloyd was. He said he didn't think so. The Judge suggested that after Lusby got his additional drink he must have been as drunk as Lloyd. "I don't know," remarked Lusby. "I never tried to pass even with him; I did not say I was drunk; I don't know whether I was, though I had drank with him right smart that day."

Burnett's cross-examination got closer to the truth. "Mr. Lloyd was sober enough, wasn't he, to drive his own horse and to take his fish, etc. into the kitchen?"

"He drove his own horse; I didn't see him go to the kitchen."

"Did you see him fix Mrs. Surratt's buggy?"

The witness remarked that he didn't know anything about that, but he described his return from Marlboro with Lloyd. "How far is it from Marlboro to Surrattsville?" inquired Burnett.

"About twelve miles; it is a fast drive of about two and a half hours."

"Did you stop to get any drinks on the road?"

"No."

"Then he was two and a half hours without getting any drinks before he came to Surrattsville?"

"Yes, sir."[17]

The defense witness had helped destroy Mrs. Surratt's case.

During the trial the Court examined more than 300 witnesses; only two made any effort to defend Payne. One was Margaret Branson, called by Doster after Payne mentioned her as a possible witness. Her appearance in court must have brought satisfaction to the stoic Rebel.

The young lady, interrogated by Doster, appeared eager to testify.

She described her service as a voluntary nurse in Gettysburg immediately after the battle. There she met Payne, whom she described as "very kind to the sick and wounded. I don't know if he was a soldier. He had on no uniform." Branson added, "He went by the name of Powell and the name of Doctor."

The witness stated that she remained at the hospital about six weeks. Doster asked, "In the hospital, where he seemed to be attending the sick and wounded, were the patients both Confederate and Union soldiers?"

"Yes," she replied. "I left the hospital the first week in September; I met Payne again some time that fall and winter; I do not remember when." She mentioned that the short meeting of only a few hours took place in her house in Baltimore.[18]

The lawyer inquired if Payne had told her where he was going. Bingham objected on grounds that the declaration of the prisoners could not be used as evidence.

Doster then revealed that he intended to enter a plea of insanity for Payne. This disclosure startled both the defendant and the Court. After the initial shock, Payne smiled as though he thought the proposal ridiculous. Of all things, he did not want to be perceived as insane, particularly on the testimony of Branson, and he refused to cooperate with his counsel in supporting the plea. Doster's suggestion also astonished Judge Bingham, who scorned the theory that

> a man might take a knife large enough to butcher an ox, rush past all the attendants in the house wounding and maiming them, stab a sick man in his bed again and again, and escape punishment on the ground that the acts were too atrocious for a sane man to commit. . . .[19]

Nevertheless, Doster labeled Payne's actions insane. He argued that Payne made no attempt to conceal his awful crime. He left his pistol and hat at the scene and threw his knife away where it could easily be found. Payne departed so slowly that a man on foot could follow his horse. According to Doster, instead of escaping, Payne turned his horse loose and wandered about the city, "finally going to the house of all others where he would be liable to be arrested."

The evidence against Mrs. Surratt had even influenced the defense lawyers, including Doster. He rephrased his statement, but he still inferred it was an act of insanity to return to the Surratt house.

Getting back to Branson, he tried to show Payne's erratic behavior. Asked why Payne left her mother's boardinghouse, she responded, "We had a Negro servant who was exceedingly impudent to him." Bingham interrupted, "You need not state what passed between the girl and that man."

Doster seldom spoke back to the Judge, but this time he challenged him, "This witness is just to state that."

"Why?"

"It is for you to show why she should not."

Bingham, backing down, muttered, "Well, let her answer it."

Doster's victory was worthless. Branson, avoiding the details of Payne's wild behavior, answered simply, "He was arrested by the authorities and sent north to Philadelphia."

Neither Doster nor Burnett in his cross-examination could persuade Payne's faithful friend to tell exactly what occurred. The next witness did. Margaret Kaighn was called and questioned by Doster.

"State whether you are a servant in the home of Mrs. Branson."

"Yes, sir."

"Did you see the prisoner Payne there?"

"Yes, he came there in January or February and stayed till the middle of March."

Doster then inquired about the controversy between Payne and the Negro girl. The witness recounted Payne's request that the girl clean his room, and her refusal. He called her names, slapped her and struck her, according to Kaighn.

"Did he not throw her on the ground, stamp on her body and try to kill her?"

"Yes."

"Did he not strike her on the forehead?"

"Yes."

The witness stated that as a consequence the Negro girl "went to have him arrested."[21]

Doster called Dr. Charles Nichols, superintendent of the Government hospital for the insane, and besieged him with a series of hypothetical questions about Payne's behavior. The Military Court was patient with the attorney and unusually attentive to the doctor's answers. Payne sat motionless as his actions were pronounced insane.

Doster questioned, "Is not long, continued constipation one of the physical conditions accompanying insanity?" The doctor agreed that "constipation frequently precedes insanity...."

"If this same person I have described had been suffering from constipation for four weeks, would that be an additional ground for insanity?"

"I think some weight might be given to that circumstance."

Then Doster described Payne during the trial as never speaking until spoken to at a "time when all his companions were peevish and clamorous." He claimed that Payne never expressed a want when all others had many. According to the lawyer, Payne remained unconcerned when other prisoners became nervous and anxious. He then questioned, "If he continued immovable except a certain wildness in the movement of his eyes, would it not be additional ground for believing him to be insane?"

"I think it would."

If such a man, inquired Doster, when questioned about his crime, should say "he remembered nothing distinctly but a struggle, with no desire to kill, would not that be additional ground for suspicion of insanity?" Again the doctor obligingly responded, "I think it would."

Doster associated slavery with insanity, much to the Court's displeasure.

> If one of these same men should own slaves and believe in the origin of the institution, fight in its defense, and believe that he had also fought in defense of his home and friends, should attempt to assassinate the men who were the leaders of those he believed were killing his friends, would not that give rise to the suspicion that he was laboring under a fanatical delusion?[22]

Burnett objected, asserting the question was irrelevant.

The lawyer announced that he had a dozen additional questions but that his chief concern was to buy time. He explained that he had sent for a witness in Florida who had not yet arrived, and he did not want to conclude his defense without him. Doster was referring to Payne's father.

The prosecution introduced Charles Dawson, a hotel clerk. He told of an unusual letter sent to the National Hotel, addressed only with the initials "W. B." Pitman read the letter to the Court.

> SOUTH BRANCH BRIDGE, April 6, 1865.
> —Friend Wilkes:—I received yours of March 12th, and reply as soon as practicable. I saw French Brad and others about the oil speculation. The subscription of the stock amounts to $8,000, and I add $1,000 myself, which is about all I can stand. Now, when you sink your well go deep enough. Don't fail. Everything depends on you and your helpers. If you can't get through on your trip after you strike ile [sic], strike through Thorton's Gap and cross by Cacco pond, Romney, and down the branch, and I can keep you safe from all hardship for a year. I am clear of all surveillance, now that infernal Purdy is beat.[23]

The writer indicated that the letter could not be understood if lost but advised the recipient to burn it. It was signed "Lou." According to the postmark, it was mailed at Cumberland, Maryland, on May 8, although it was dated April 6.

The Government received scores of suspicious letters, most of them fakes, but this one seemed genuine. The Government began an immediate search for those mentioned.

Joseph Nott, Lloyd's bartender, took the stand again, but he denied knowing anything about the affair. Several persons then testified about the condition of the President's box.

The prosecution called six or seven witnesses who swore that Mrs. Surratt's brother, Jenkins, spoke harshly against the Government after 1862. At the start of hostilities, he appeared to favor the Union cause but changed drastically when he lost his slaves. With this testimony court adjourned.

XXXVIII
Rebel Complicity?

Life in the Nation's capital changed slowly. Gen. James Longstreet was one of many former Confederate leaders seeking pardons in Washington. The plight of blacks in the capital city improved a little. But thousands still lived in pitiful makeshift shacks. Fights broke out almost daily between white soldiers and freed blacks.

Peacetime growth and development gradually affected other areas. Philadelphia made special arrangements for blacks on trains and horse cars. The Union Passenger Railway Company added cars to its line to accommodate integration. The destitute South lived begrudgingly with forced change. In no place did real equality exist, but the long process had begun.

For several weeks detectives had investigated a mysterious inscription scratched on a windowpane of the McHenry House in Meadville, Pennsylvania. The inscription read, "Abe Lincoln departed this life August 13, 1864, by the effects of poison."[1] Some attributed the writing to Booth, who visited the region at that time. The mystery was cleared up, however—for those who accepted his word—by a gentleman who recalled that on the 13th or 14th of August a rumor circulated that an attempt had been made to poison the President. The man confessed that he and a friend had occupied Room 22 in the hotel and that his friend, upon hearing the news, believed it and scratched the words with a diamond.

On June 3, Anna Surratt again sat near her mother. Dr. Charles H. Nichols took the stand to give his professional opinion of Payne's sanity. Doster's questions dragged on so long that Burnett finally interrupted. Spectators, also weary of the tedious technical explanations, clearly approved of Burnett's action. One observer became so disgusted with Doster's boring interrogation he speculated that if this was the best Washington attorneys could do, they were far below the level of Philadelphia lawyers.[2]

Later witnesses often disagreed with earlier testimony. Occasionally a witness would contradict himself. The truth could usually be discovered, but the Court had to sift it out. The process involved the primary interrogation, cross-examination, reexamination and seemingly endless repetitions.

The Commissioners took into consideration the background of witnesses. Former slaves who no longer worked for their masters, for example, were more inclined to tell the truth than freed slaves still employed by their former owners or another master in the neighborhood. Thus, their testimonies often conflicted.

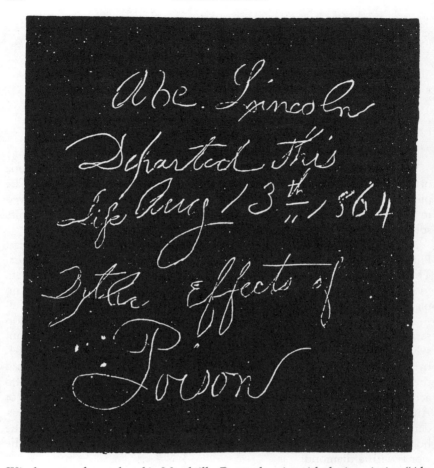

Windowpane from a hotel in Meadville, Pennsylvania, with the inscription "Abe Lincoln Departed This Life Aug. 13th, 1864 By the effects of Poison."

This morning Ewing called more freed slaves to testify on behalf of Samuel Mudd. Susan Stewart, a servant of John Miller, lived a few miles from Dr. Mudd. Under Ewing's guidance, Stewart stated that the day after the shooting, she saw the doctor *going* to Bryantown by himself. The prosecution sought to prove that at that time Mudd had already been to Bryantown and was *coming back*. Under cross-examination, Bingham questioned, "This was on Easter Saturday afternoon?"

"Yes, sir."

Not pleased with the answer, Ewing quizzed, "Did you see which way he was coming, whether he was coming from Bryantown or not?"

"No, sir."[3]

Another former slave, Charles Bloyce, took the stand in Mudd's defense. The witness still worked for the doctor. Bloyce easily answered Ewing's leading questions. He pictured Mudd as a fine man, especially kind to his slaves. He claimed that the doctor's former slaves who had testified against him were liars.

Referring to Mary Simms, one of Mudd's former slaves, Ewing asked, "Do you know what the colored folks about there think of her as a truth-teller?"

"The folks there said she was not much of a truth-teller; that she told such lies they could not believe her."

The lawyer, pushing his attempt to discredit the previous damaging testimony of Mudd's slaves, inquired about Mylo Simms. The witness declared, "I used to think myself that he was a liar, because he used to tell me lies sometimes."

Asked about Dr. Mudd's treatment of his slaves, Bloyce stated, "I would call him a first-rate man; I never heard of him whipping or saying anything to them; they did pretty much as they pleased."

"Did you ever hear him threaten to send any of his servants to Richmond?"

"No, indeed, I never heard one of they [sic] say a word about it."

Under Judge Bingham's cross-examination, the witness gave a different impression.

"Did you ever hear anything about his shooting any of his servants?"

"I did hear that."

"You thought that was first-rate fun?"

"I don't know about that."[+]

A roar of laughter filled the packed courtroom.

The prosecution presented lawyer Marcus P. Norton of New York, who had lodged at the National Hotel when Booth stayed there. The defense counsel's objection to Norton's testifying was overruled. Norton's testimony about seeing Booth, Atzerodt and Mudd meeting together was not credible. The defense later annulled most of his narrative.

The defense hammered at Daniel Thomas's testimony against Mudd. The prosecution countered, showing that defense witnesses were mostly Southern sympathizers who opposed Thomas because of his loyalty to the Union. But the evidence against Thomas's veracity was overwhelming. Even if he were telling the truth about Mudd, which was unlikely, his credibility was so damaged by the barrage of testimony against him that it held no weight. Ewing had searched urgently for individuals to buttress his successful refutation of Thomas.

Anna Ward was the next witness of importance. Anna Surratt had previously testified that Ward was with her when she bought a picture of John Wilkes Booth.

Aiken began with the usual questions about Mrs. Surratt's eyesight, then questioned, "Did you receive a letter from John H. Surratt not long since?"

"I did."

"Where is that letter?"

"I gave it to his mother; I presume it has been destroyed."

"The defense requested that Ward tell of the circumstances of John Surratt's efforts to get a room at the Herndon house. "He called one afternoon and asked to see me," responded the witness.[5]

Judge Bingham stopped her. "You need not state that conversation."

Aiken snapped, "Very well, then, we turn the witness over to you. Perhaps you may want to make some inquiries yourself about the matter."

Bingham made the best of it. "Have you been in the habit of visiting often at Mrs. Surratt's?"

"Occasionally," she responded, "up to the day of the assassination; that was the last day I visited her."

Bingham induced the witness to admit that Mrs. Surratt easily recognized her, both by sight and by voice. The relatively unimportant question of Mrs. Surratt's poor eyesight remained a major dispute.

The Judge's inquiry returned to Payne's room at the Herndon house. "Did you go with him or go alone to the Herndon house to obtain a room?"

"I did not obtain a room, I simply went there to ascertain if there was a vacant room," responded Ward, assuring the Court she did not know for whom she was seeking the chamber.

"Have you met any of the prisoners at the bar?" Bingham inquired.

"I can't see them well enough to answer; I do not think I have." She did admit to meeting Booth at Mrs. Surratt's house.

Bingham turned the interrogation back to the previously mentioned letter. "You got a letter from John H. Surratt, postmarked Montreal, Canada, East?"

"Yes."

"When did you receive it?"

"I received two from him; the first, on the day of the assassination; I do not recollect the date of the second; there was a very short interval between them."

In response to the Judge's interrogation, the witness remarked that she delivered one letter to Mrs. Surratt and one to Anna and had not seen them since. Asked if she answered the letters, she testified, "Neither of these; he wrote me two letters at the same time, enclosing the letters for his mother; I answered those addressed to me." Ward stated that the correspondence arrived "very soon after the President's assassination." She did not know what happened to any of the letters because she gave them all to Mrs. Surratt.[6]

Mary Surratt had told officer McDevitt, who searched the house a few hours after the crime, that she had received a letter that day from her son in Canada. When McDevitt requested to see the correspondence, Mrs. Surratt claimed she could not find it. She also mentioned the same document to Weichmann but did not allow him to read it. She even kept the two letters addressed to Anna Ward, but none of these communications was ever found by detectives. Mrs. Surratt was careful, however, to save the letters which would serve her purpose. She produced in court the message from Calvert asking about payment of her debt. John's need to correspond with his mother through Ward seemed suspicious. The prosecution did not press this point, but then, it did not have to.

In the last few minutes of the session, Doster requested that

> the testimony for the defense be not considered as closed until George Powell, the father of Payne, and other witnesses who had been summoned from Florida, who would testify in respect to Payne's antecedents and the tendency on the part of the family to insanity, should be present.[7]

These words created a flurry of interest among the Commissioners and spectators.

Bingham, astonished, inquired, "Then are we to regard that as an authentic statement that the prisoner's name is Powell?" The counsel answered sarcastically, "I have stated that his father's name is Powell, and I take it for granted the inference will be drawn that, that is the name of the prisoner."[8]

Judge Burnett was willing to wait for Doster's witnesses, but the president of the Court, General Hunter, felt that ample opportunity had already been allowed and refused to grant more time. It did not make any difference; Payne's father made little or no effort to go to his son's aid.

On Sunday, June 4, Anna Surratt obtained permission to visit privately with her mother. Mrs. Surratt welcomed her daughter warmly but not enthusiastically; she still maintained her reserve. Poor Anna, uninhibited, ran through the silent courtroom straight to her mother's arms and burst into tears. She remained crying in her mother's arms fully ten minutes. Mother and daughter spoke not a word. Only Anna's sporadic sobs broke the silence. The guard, overcome, finally walked away.

They remained together for about two hours until Mrs. Surratt called the guard and requested that he take Anna away. She indicated that her daughter was tired. During the episode Anna wept almost constantly, but her mother shed no tears. The guard, Capt. Christian Rath, took Anna home, concerned about the seeming hardheartedness of her mother. On his return, another guard revealed that almost as soon as Anna left, Mrs. Surratt fainted. Anna visited her mother's cell as well as the courtroom almost daily after that.[9]

Public interest continued to wane in the first days of June. The failure of witnesses to appear hampered the proceedings. Newspapers reported less about the conspiracy proceedings and speculated more on the proposed trial of Jefferson Davis. The Cabinet, divided almost equally on whether Davis should be tried by a civil or a military court, eventually decided on a civil court.

Many unfounded rumors circulated, mostly about Mrs. Surratt. She had two daughters in prison according to one story; one of them had gone mad and died. The *Washington Star* investigated the rumor and declared it false.[10] Another report stated that Mary Surratt had taken poison and was dying. Upon examination, the *New York Times* also found that story to be untrue.

The press, fascinated with Payne, speculated about his background. One article reported that Payne did not know who his parents were. He had reportedly declared, "I don't know my name. I was stolen from my parents when I was quite young."[11]

The growing antagonism between President Johnson and Secretary Stanton also created a rash of rumors. One tale made it seem that Stanton was ready to resign and that he already opposed the nomination of Johnson in the next presidential election. Some real evidence indicated that Stanton was attempting to blame the President for the military trial. Stanton had refused to sign his name to the order establishing the Court, thus forcing Johnson to do so.[12] A confrontation between the two determined leaders appeared imminent.

Early in June the Government released several suspects from Carroll Prison, including Samuel Cox and Thomas Jones. Colonel and Mrs. Green, owners of the Van Ness house where Lincoln was to have been hidden, were also set free.

Guards opened the few small windows on June 5, but that did not relieve the oppressive heat. Most prisoners, Judges and lawyers wore lighter clothes. Dr. Mudd, alone, persisted in his meticulous grooming, complete with coat and tie. General Hunter again had to request women visitors not to stand between the prisoners and their lawyers. Anna Surratt sat, as usual, near her mother.

More government witnesses branded Zad Jenkins a notorious Rebel. Their testimony corroborated previous statements that he made a show of Union loyalty until he lost his slaves. William Evans stated that on one occasion Jenkins created a disturbance at the polls in order to keep Union men from being elected.

Evans, a New School Presbyterian minister, admitted that he was forced to leave his church in Prince Georges County because he was loyal to the Union in "a very disloyal neighborhood." He had known J. Z. Jenkins about 15 years. He testified that while Jenkins pretended to be loyal, he exhibited strong sympathy for the Rebels. The Reverend Mr. Evans maintained that he did not know "a loyal man in that neighborhood except for Mr. Roby, his son, and a few others."[13]

"We were in danger all the time, so much so that I had to call upon General Augur for a guard," the witness affirmed. The minister presented a gloomy picture of conditions in Prince Georges and St. Marys counties. But he tended to exaggerate, and his testimony did not seem entirely reliable.

John L. Thompson, who boarded at Mrs. Surratt's house in Prince Georges County, was more convincing. He swore that he had known Jenkins for as long as he could remember, adding, "His disloyalty is open and outspoken." Thompson testified that Jenkins drew a knife on him in a quarrel. According to the witness, Jenkins "hated that Government." He revealed that he lived with Mrs. Surratt's family for two years and declared that Mrs. Surratt's conversation was against the Government.[14]

Ewing introduced witnesses who swore that Dr. Mudd had been with them at the time Weichmann testified he had met Mudd and Booth in Washington. But Ewing produced too much evidence. Fanny Mudd stated that her brother came to their father's house before breakfast on March 2, 1865. Another sister, Emily Mudd, also swore under oath that the doctor visited their father's house before breakfast on that day and tarried a long time in order to see another sister who was sick. But a little later a black servant, Betty Washington, swore that on the same day, Dr. Mudd cut brush and remained on his own farm all day. So many witnesses testified to having seen the doctor all day long at different places that it seemed the defense had overstated its case. Judge Holt, noticing this error, cross-examined Washington. "On the 2nd of March Dr. Mudd took breakfast at home, did he?"

"Yes, he took his breakfast at home, and he took dinner and supper at home too that day."

Ewing realized the discrepancy too late to correct it, although he tried. "Are you certain he took breakfast at his house the day after Ash-Wednesday?"[15] Judge Bingham objected to the question and was sustained.

Carroll Prison Superintendent William Wood presented the day's most revealing testimony. Clampitt constructed his questions to present Wood's friend, Jenkins, in a favorable light. "Do you believe Mr. Jenkins to be a consistent loyal man?" Wood hedged, "I do: I do not believe he is a friend of the Administration, on account of the Negro question, but outside of that he is a loyal man."

Cross-examined by Holt, Wood changed his testimony abruptly. "Has not Mr. Jenkins been for some time past bitterly hostile to the Government; and if that is so, do you not consider that disloyalty?" asked Holt.

"I have had very little to do with him lately, and have not regarded him as sound as I did formerly; in the last election he voted for Harris, I believe, and associated with that sort of men."[16] Wood was in a bind, being a close friend of Jenkins and also Stanton's subordinate.

The next witness revealed nothing important, and court adjourned.

A thorough search of Confederate archives failed to turn up conclusive proof that the Rebel Government was directly involved in the conspiracy. But evidence showed that during the last 15 months of the war, Confederate leaders were entangled in savage secret activities, including the burning of civilian buildings.

Rebel archives revealed that on February 12, 1864, the Confederate Congress, in secret session, voted to organize special "bodies for the capture and destruction of the enemies' property."[17] This decision had to be authorized by Congress, which implied that the "capture and destruction" referred to more than usual battlefield maneuvers. Less than a month later, in another secret session, the Confederate Congress adopted a bill to provide for the establishment of a Bureau of Special and Secret Service.

The Confederacy had maintained a type of secret service before, but the new Bureau was to include special services and had relatively strong financial backing. Appropriations for the Confederate State Department for the period ending June 30, 1864, included $500,000 for secret service operations. This was by far the greatest expense in the State Department; the second largest was $29,400 for "Foreign Intercourse."[18] These expenses coincided with the arrival of several important Confederate agents in Montreal, Canada. A few months later, John Wilkes Booth opened a bank account in the same Montreal bank used by the Rebels.

Even before Confederate activities became highly organized in Canada, Jefferson Davis promoted secret exploits there as shown in this revealing Confederate dispatch, dated March 22, 1864.

A Mrs. _____ from Maryland, whose only son is in a Federal prison writes the President that she desires to go to Canada on some secret enterprise. The President favors her purpose in an endorsement. On this the Secretary endorses a purpose to facilitate her design and suggests that she be paid $1,000.00 in gold from the secret service fund.

She is a Roman Catholic, and intimates that the bishops, priests and nuns will aid her.[19]

Some have suggested that the document might have referred to Mrs. Surratt, but she did not fit the conditions described.

Union leaders kept track of many Confederate movements through a double agent—a Rebel messenger who passed Confederate dispatches through Washington. Union offices had little trouble in deciphering the simple Confederate codes. The intercepted messages enabled Federal officers to copy an early dispatch from Clement Clay in Canada addressed to Judah Benjamin, at that time Secretary of State, in Richmond. The letter revealed that Rebel agents were using Canada as a base of operations against Northern cities.

Early in 1864, a Rebel spy in Canada wrote to Jefferson Davis that the Confederacy should enlarge its work there so as to create confusion and increase support in England. In reply, Secretary Benjamin contacted Jacob Thompson.

Union authorities intercepted a dispatch addressed to Thompson, dated April 7, 1864, only a month after the Bureau of Special and Secret Service had been authorized. It read, "If your engagements will permit you to accept service abroad for the next six months, please come here immediately."[20] It was signed "Jefferson Davis."

On April 27, another decoded message to Thompson read:

Sir: Confiding special trust in your zeal, discretion, and patriotism, I hereby direct you to proceed at once to Canada, there to carry out such instructions as you have received from me verbally in such manner as shall seem most to the furtherance of the interest of the Confederate States of America, which have been entrusted to you....[21]

Jefferson Davis signed this letter and sent a copy to Clement Clay.

The Confederate Government passed its most confidential messages verbally. Thompson's orders were top secret, which may account for the absence of any written documentation of his operations.

Thompson reached his new post in May and was soon joined by former United States Senator from Alabama, Clement Clay. Two weeks later, J. P. Holcombe, who was already in Canada helping Rebels escape from Northern prisons, joined the others. Confederates set up headquarters at the Queens Hotel in Montreal. In addition to these men, the so-called "Confederate Canadian Cabinet" included Beverly Tucker (a former circuit judge in Virginia), George N. Sanders, William C. Cleary and George Harper. At one time, approximately one hundred Confederate agents lodged in the Queens Hotel.

By the end of May 1864, Thompson was well established in Montreal. At first he sought to influence Northern politics by peaceable means but soon turned to more extreme measures. He worked through Southern sympathizers such as Clement Vallandigham and the Wood brothers of New York and Washington.

Fernando Wood, mayor of New York City when the war broke out, recommended that the city secede from the Union. Later his constituents elected him to the United States Congress. His younger brother Benjamin, also an outspoken supporter of the South, purchased the *New York Daily News* in 1860, and as its editor, lashed out at the Federal Government. His assaults became so vicious that Stanton suppressed the *Daily News* for 18 months. Even after the paper resumed publication, it continued to agitate defiantly in favor of the Confederacy.

Thompson, working with these men, as well as with such Northern Rebel organizations as the Sons of Liberty, planned the release of Confederate prisoners in Chicago and the capture of Federal ships on the Great Lakes.

On August 4, 1864, in the embryonic stage of the conspiracy to capture Lincoln, the Confederate war clerk, J. B. Jones, sent the following dispatch: "Thompson from Canada says work will not begin before middle of August. I do not know what sort of work. He says much caution is necessary."[22]

Unfortunately, it is not known to whom the telegram was addressed or who composed it. It could not have referred to the destruction of Northern property, which had begun several months earlier.

A double agent brought one letter to Washington which, after being deciphered, revealed the Rebels' intent to set fires in New York City and to stir up trouble in Chicago. The fires mentioned earlier when Booth was acting in New York were part of this effort, but since Federals were notified of the plot, they averted a major disaster.

Secretary of State Seward believed that Booth had been encouraged by Confederate Secretary of State Benjamin. Evidence indicated that Benjamin directed the Bureau of Special and Secret Service. However, Confederate activities in Washington were more likely directed from nearby Richmond than from Canada. Furthermore, according to some sources in Montreal, Booth was not cordially received by Southern leaders in Canada, who thought he might be a spy. This view revealed more than it denied, because whatever Booth's reception by the Rebel leaders, it was an admission that he was, at least, in contact with them.

As Benjamin later escaped to England he was never questioned about his role in the plot. On April 6, 1865, three days after the fall of Richmond, Union Assistant Secretary of War C. A. Dana searched Benjamin's Richmond office. He found a secret cipher key, some books and other papers, but nothing that could tie Benjamin to the plot against Lincoln. If the former Confederate Secretary of State had been involved, he would not likely have left incriminating evidence. At the time of the assassination, there was no functioning Confederate Secretary of State.

The *New York Evening Post* reported that the two main proofs tying Jefferson Davis to the conspirators were the cipher found in Booth's trunk and a paper, written in code, found in Davis' home. But these were not conclusive proofs.

One of the strongest indications of Confederate complicity was Arnold's letter suggesting that Booth check with Richmond before carrying out his new scheme. The letter definitely tied Booth's operation to Richmond, but it also showed that his change in plans was not known to Confederate authorities. Booth's friend Chester testified that he thought Southern leaders knew of the plot. Confederate agent Jones, among others, admitted he was aware of the conspiracy.

Several close observers believed that evidence – apart from the obviously false testimony of Von Steinacker and Conover – strongly implicated the Confederate Government in the original kidnap conspiracy. One correspondent wrote that the evidence was enough to indicate that the plot "was known and cherished in Richmond, aided pecuniarily from the treasury of the Rebel Government, and through the means of its agents in Canada."[23] The correspondent specifically excluded from his report the fraudulent secret testimony.

As the trial entered its concluding phase, editors of the *Atlantic Monthly* were preparing an article concerning Rebel plots to invade Chicago. The writers felt their research would sustain the Government's theory that Confederate leaders in Canada had directed a widespread conspiracy. Realizing that the story would probably not be published until after the trial, they sent proof sheets to President Johnson. He passed them to Burnett and he on to Holt.[24]

Author James Gilmore contended that the plot, which had been formulated in Richmond, was to have been carried out by Jacob Thompson in Canada. According to Gilmore, Rebels planned the initial attack against Camp Douglas. Confederate prisoners confined there were to be freed by Rebels from Canada and "Butternuts" from Missouri, as well as by several thousand Southern sympathizers in the vicinity of Chicago. At that time, Chicago had a population of nearly 200,000. Camp Douglas comprised 60 acres of flat, sandy land near the city, enclosed by a wooden fence 14 feet high.[25]

This makeshift arrangement was vulnerable. Only 700 Union soldiers guarded approximately 8,000 Rebel prisoners, among whom were many undaunted guerrillas who had served under the dashing raider John Hunt Morgan. To make security even more precarious, prisoners chiefly operated the camp. They served the meals, distributed clothing, handed out ammunition to guards, kept records and filled most of the jobs.

According to the audacious plan, prisoners freed at Camp Douglas would liberate other Confederates held elsewhere in Illinois and then fan out through Indiana and Ohio. The scheme depended on support from large numbers of Southern sympathizers in the Midwestern states. The uprising would include robbery, arson, and even assassination. If successful, the daring intrigue was expected to break the Union, thus providing independence for the Confederate States.

Looking back on the actual outcome of this gargantuan effort, it appears ridiculous. In 1864, however, when Rebels conceived the plot, it did not seem entirely futile. Large segments of Southern supporters in Illinois and Indiana backed the plan. In addition, many loyal Unionists wondered openly if

Southern states should not be allowed to follow their independent course. However, presidential elections later that year proved that a majority in the Union supported Lincoln's leadership. Nevertheless, McClellan's respectable vote also indicated many citizens were willing to follow another course. The Chicago conspiracy was born of such hopes.

The plot took definite form early in 1864. By May, when a new commandant, Col. B. J. Sweet, took charge of Camp Douglas, the scheme was already in operation. Sweet soon noticed that many letters received by prisoners were written on long sheets of paper which contained surprisingly little writing. Considering the scarcity of paper, he correctly surmised there must be a reason. In June he subjected some suspicious-looking correspondence to a heat treatment which brought out messages in the seemingly blank spaces. In the revealed portions were numerous vague references to a coming celebration on the Fourth of July. Colonel Sweet questioned this outburst of patriotism on the part of Southerners. He then realized that the National Democratic Convention was scheduled to meet in Chicago on the 4th. The city would be crowded with delegates, presenting a perfect time for attacking the camp. The Commandant quietly replaced Rebels in charge of camp operations with his own soldiers and infiltrated the camp with spies pretending to be Confederate prisoners. He learned that the Rebels planned a huge celebration on Independence Day with a large bonfire to be lighted just outside prison walls. The prisoners were then to fire a salute to the Old Flag but were to substitute real bullets for the blanks. A group of Southern sympathizers in Chicago called "The Society of the Illini" worked with the inmates. The Commandant quickly sent men to infiltrate this group, which at the time numbered several hundred.

Nothing happened, however, because the Democratic Convention postponed its meeting to the 29th of August. By that time, Colonel Sweet was in full control. Well-placed men kept abreast of the conspiracy, and the guard was increased. The Commandant, nevertheless, wrote his superior officer on August 12, informing him of conditions at Camp Douglas. He told of squads of Rebels who had gradually slipped into Chicago from Toronto and reported that there were at least 5,000 armed men in the city waiting for the signal to join Confederate prisoners in a general insurrection in Illinois and Indiana. His report was not alarmist, but it expressed concern that such action, if successful, could have serious consequences.

Sweet was not alone in his apprehension. Lt. Col. B. H. Hill, commanding the military district of Michigan, also uncovered some details of the conspiracy. On August 16, Hill wrote the commanding general of the northern area what he had learned from a Rebel officer. According to Hill, about 200 armed Confederate refugees had assembled in Toronto, supplied with money and tickets to Chicago; another 150 Rebels had already arrived clandestinely in Chicago. Confederate Capt. Thomas Hines, who had masterminded the escape of Gen. John Morgan from an Ohio Penitentiary, directed the Chicago operation. Hill also learned that Confederate leader George Sanders and a Colonel Hicks were in Toronto making final preparations. His informant told of a plan similar to the one already uncovered by Colonel Sweet. This time the attack was set for August 29 in conjunction with the new date of the Democratic Convention. Leaders later changed these plans, however, and that date also passed without incident.

Captain Hines continued to direct the oft-postponed assault on Camp Douglas. He and other Confederates assembled at Chicago in November 1864 to carry out their daring scheme. Men supporting them slipped into Chicago in small groups by various railways.

An informant reported to Colonel Sweet that the camp was to be attacked Tuesday night, November 8. The Commandant alerted his men, and, at two o'clock the next morning, police raided various private houses where Confederate leaders had assembled. Captain Hines evidently sensed danger and escaped, but police captured several of his subordinates, including Col. George St. Leger Grenfel. Col. Vincent Marmaduke, Brig. Gen. Charles Walsh of the Sons of Liberty and the notorious Capt. George Cantrill of Morgan's command were captured at Walsh's house. Authorities also arrested Buck Morris, treasurer of the Sons of Liberty. Detectives found two cartloads of loaded revolvers and 200 loaded muskets and ammunition. Many guerrillas escaped in the darkness, however.

At 4:00 A.M., November 7, Colonel Sweet reported that the Rebels had the ability to raise a force larger than his little garrison of prison guards. The raid uncovered plans to take advantage of the excitement of election night to release the prisoners, cut telegraph wires, seize arms and ammunition, take control of Chicago and initiate a general insurrection in the Midwest.

A writer for the *Chicago Tribune*, learning that the near-diastrous conspiracy had been broken up, wrote on November 8, 1864, "A shiver of genuine horror passed over Chicago yesterday."[26] Further investigation proved that Jefferson Davis and Jacob Thompson had instigated the plot.

The conspiracy included a vast disruption of Northern cities, beginning with Chicago. Rebels planned to rob banks, destroy railroads, burn public buildings and demolish grain elevators. They had marked fire hydrants and assigned a group to open them, thus diminishing the water supply.

In addition to liberating prisoners in Camp Douglas and sacking Chicago as a signal for the uprising in Illinois and Indiana, there was to be a coordinated attack on Nashville by Hood's army while Buckner moved against Ohio, Bowles against Indiana and Walsh against Illinois. The plot involved the capture of some Union leaders and the assassination of others. These accounts may have been exaggerated, but the principal facts were true.

Detectives uncovered information indicating that Jacob Thompson was provided a large sum out of the Confederate treasury for these operations. Constant communication between Richmond and Montreal underscored Confederate complicity. The South resorted to desperate actions in the last year of the war. Officials never definitely established proof connecting the Chicago plot with Booth's original conspiracy, but the same troubled spirit animated both reckless projects.

George Alfred Townsend, who researched the Lincoln murder minutely, concluded that Booth had undoubtedly "sought and obtained counsel in Canada." Townsend discounted the false testimony and based his judgment on the best information available. But he deduced that Booth had received very little monetary support from the Confederacy; perhaps only $200 in gold. "This is too paltry a sum with which to charge the Rebel Government," he concluded.[27]

Townsend's financial calculations seem to have been inaccurate. Booth lived comfortably, if not luxuriously, for six months without obvious means of support. During that time, he purchased numerous items for the conspiracy and supported several followers (albeit feebly), none of whom had steady work. Shortly before the fall of Richmond, Booth suddenly ran out of money. Arnold complained to Booth that because he needed more money he was forced to part company with him. Booth sold his horse and buggy and used rented horses for his escape. When captured, he had practically no money, although a few funds remained in his Canadian bank account. This bank tied him with Canadian Confederates; he had no legitimate business in Canada.

Even though Confederate leaders knew of and probably encouraged the original kidnap scheme, it was almost impossible for them to have taken part in the assassination. The Confederacy had virtually collapsed before Booth definitely decided upon murder.

Involvement in plans to capture an enemy President in time of war was significantly different from taking part in a conspiracy to kill the President after the fighting was over. Confederate leaders indignantly denied they had anything to do with the assassination, but they did not deny they had known of the proposed kidnapping. It is inconceivable that such plans, carried out in behalf of the Confederacy by its confessed agents, were not promoted by Confederate leaders.

XXXIX
What He Knew and When

Col. H. S. Olcott wrote Burnett from New York to remind him of evidence he might be overlooking. He told of finding a paper in Anna Surratt's handwriting with the name "J. Wilkes Booth" repeated many times as well as the words "Shall Virginia call on her sons in vain?" Olcott stated there were strong indications the "plot was discussed in the family and well understood."[1] He explained that Burnett could find the paper in a black valise. The Government had confiscated the valise, which contained many objects besides these papers, including a photograph album, eight pictures in a case, a bullet mold, a bank book, a small book owned by Anna, part of a spur, 21 card photographs, the program of a concert given in benefit of St. Aloysius Church and 108 letters. Olcott suggested that the handwriting could be verified by Honora Fitzpatrick. Authorties, however, never bothered to investigate Anna, apparently feeling she had suffered enough.

The trial became tedious and monotonous by the second week of June, but the generals and the prisoners were more relaxed. The courtroom was so stifling and crowded on June 7 that one of the women spectators fainted.

Mrs. Surratt seemed to grow weaker each day and eventually had to be lifted into her chair. Some thought that she pretended at least part of her sickness. Mrs. Surratt had been a robust, active lady before the trial and seemed to change noticeably the day the testimony started. But her physical infirmities were not entirely pretense. She sat in a corner with little ventilation and insisted on wearing coarse black clothes and on covering her face with a heavy veil. Crowds pressing around Mrs. Surratt increased her misery, not only by making the heat worse, but also through thoughtless comments. Day after day, the widow endured insulting remarks.

After the preliminaries and a few insignificant testimonies, Ewing announced that, although he had called 13 additional witnesses, none was present. He wondered if the Government had sent the subpoenas. Judge Burnett, who had conscientiously and efficiently searched for all witnesses requested, answered curtly that "the subpoenas in each case had been promptly issued and sent to General Augur's Headquarters, with the direction of the Secretary of War that they be served forthwith."[2] In the absence of witnesses, the morning session adjourned.

When court reconvened, the Government presented several persons to vouch for Weichmann's character. In its cross-examination the defense could not effectively challenge either Weichmann's character or the major points of his testimony.

John Holohan, next on the stand, supported part of Weichmann's statement. "I was dressing myself one morning about half-past seven o'clock and saw Mrs. Slater getting into an open carriage; Mrs. Surratt was on the pavement at the time, talking to this lady."[3] He told of seeing John Surratt for the last time on April 3 when the witness gave Surratt $60 in paper money for $40 worth of gold coins. Aiken cross-examined Holohan. "Can you state whether Weichmann gave himself up after the assassination, or whether he was arrested and taken to the police office?"

Burnett objected that the question was not legitimate to cross-examination. Without arguing, Aiken asked, "Did you accompany Weichmann to Canada?" Again Burnett objected. The counsel dropped the subject and inquired, "Who were the first parties who entered Mrs. Surratt's house the night after the assasination?"

Colonel Burnett again interrupted, "You need not state that." Aiken, unruffled, continued, "State if you have any knowledge of John H. Surratt being in this city since the 3rd of April?"

"None."

"Did you see Weichmann at three o'clock Saturday morning, April 15th?"

"I did."[4]

The Colonel broke in, "All is outside a proper examination." Aiken, now exasperated by the repeated interruptions, argued that "the counsel for the defense had not objected to any testimony, legal or illegal, sought to be introduced by the Government, and they claimed the same liberality...."

Burnett denied the Government had presented any illegal evidence. Defense counselors then asked for a break in the proceedings. They conversed together, seeking a means to overcome the frustrating legal bickering. Because he was himself a General, Ewing thought, perhaps Colonel Burnett would be less likely to interrupt him. He, therefore, asked permission to question the witness. With Burnett's consent, Ewing resumed the interrogation, repeating the same question, "State whether Weichmann gave himself up after the assassination of the President."

The Colonel, not intimidated, stopped the General as he had Aiken. Burnett explained, "Mr. Aiken had been excluded from asking the question because he had stated that he had close[d] his evidence upon this point and he desired now to see whether the court would allow the same list of questions to be turned over to the counsel for another prisoner."

General Ewing, ever conscious of his rank, was ready with a little advice himself. He declared that the Colonel's reprimand was "Unnecessary and exceedingly out of place." Furthermore, he said, it was not the business of the Court to know where he got his questions, and the Assistant Judge-Advocate had stepped beyond the proprieties of his position when he undertook to get that information. Ewing declared that the questions were originally written by him and given by Aiken to use.[5]

Burnett, also aware of his position, reminded the General that it was only through his courtesy that Ewing was allowed to interrogate the witness. That said, he withdrew his consent. Holt tried to end the dispute by doubting the right of Burnett to withdraw his consent. The Judge eventually settled the argument in Burnett's favor, ruling that Ewing was out of order "till the foundation had been laid of asking the question first of Mr. Weichmann himself."

Ewing continued, "Did you go with Weichmann to Canada and back?" Holohan cleverly answered so as to include the material previously objected to. "I did; he appeared to be a good deal excited; he was much excited the morning after the murder." He continued by informing the Court that the first persons who entered Mrs. Surratt's boardinghouse were officers McDevitt and Clark about 2:00 A.M. Weichmann opened the door for them. His concluding statement contradicted Weichmann's version: "I took Weichmann down myself to Superintendent Richards the morning after; he did not express himself as wishing to be delivered up."[6]

The next witness, James McDevitt, described his investigation at Mrs. Surratt's house. "A lady put her head out of one of the upper windows and asked who was there; we asked if Mrs. Surratt lived there, and she said she did." McDevitt related that Weichmann opened the door dressed "in his shirt, pants and stockings." In narrating his trip to Canada with Weichmann in his care, the witness told the Court, "He had abundant opportunity to escape while in Canada, and in fact, I left him in Canada and returned to New York."[7]

Whether Weichmann had been arrested or not did not greatly affect Mrs. Surratt's case, but her lawyers continued to probe the issue. Under cross-examination by Aiken, McDevitt revealed more details. "When I left him in Montreal he was in company with officer Bigley, but he could have escaped, for he went out once with a citizen of Montreal, accompanied by an officer, to identify some parties at St. Lawrence Hall."

Bingham objected to any more questions as immaterial, pointing out, "Everybody knew that when Weichmann was taken within a foreign jurisdiction he was free."

After a short statement by J. Z. Jenkins, the defense questioned Andrew Collenback again about Jenkins' threat. Collenback swore that Jenkins threatened to give him the worst whipping he ever had if he found out Collenback was testifying against him "or anyone connected with him." Both Cottingham and Lloyd heard the warning.[8]

James Judson Jarboe, called by the defense, was a rough-looking character. A court had previously tried and acquitted him for killing a Union man. Questioned by Ewing, he denied that he had ever been in Mrs. Surratt's house. Under cross-examination by Bingham, Jarboe admitted he was acquainted with John Surratt, J. Wilkes Booth and David Herold and that he had met Mrs. Surratt in prison. The witness claimed he did not know why he was arrested and wanted to know if he had been called as a witness or was on trial himself. Bingham, ignoring the question, continued to probe the witness about his support of the Rebellion.

"I do not think I have joined in any jollification in honor of Rebel victories, I could not expect the success of the Rebellion."

Ewing objected to what he called the Judge's "inquisition." Bingham countered that the witness did not have to answer if he thought it would "criminate" him. Jarboe broke in, "I hardly know what will criminate me here," bringing a big laugh from spectators.

Bingham pressed his interrogation. "State whether you made an assault upon a man on election day, about four years ago, and what you did to him."

"Are you going to try me for that, because I have been tried for that twice."

Again spectators were amused. Things were loosening up in the conspiracy trial.

Bingham's inquisition did not relate directly to the assassination, but he was allowed to continue. "State whether you attacked a man down there about four years ago, and killed him."

"There was a pretty smart attack made on me; I understand the man was killed, but I do not know who did it." A little exasperated, Jarboe protested that he had already responded to these questions before and didn't think he should have to answer them again. Anyway, he added, "I could not tell whether somebody killed him or not."

"Did you have a hand on it?"

Jarboe did not answer, and Bingham continued, "What was the man's name that was killed?"[9]

Again the witness remained silent. It was the first time in the trial that a witness refused to answer the awesome Judge. Bingham knew where to stop and dismissed Jarboe.

The defense brought Anna Surratt back to the stand for some unknown reason. She added nothing, and the prosecution wisely refrained from cross-examining her. Court then adjourned.

No witnesses appeared for the defense on June 8, although several had been summoned. Ewing declared that he had called eight persons in behalf of Mudd; Doster said he still had six to interrogate.

Holt asked for the names of those requested by the defense who had not answered the summonses. Doster mentioned several, including Justice Abram B. Olin of the District of Columbia Supreme Court. Doster protested that he did not want the Justice arrested, but Holt insisted that he would use compulsory means to secure the Judge, remarking, "Those who administered the law ought certainly to show obedience to it."[10]

The Government sought diligently to obtain witnesses requested by the defense, paying their transportation and daily expenses. Burnett prepared an order, endorsed by the Court, empowering Hartranft to arrest and bring before the Commission all delinquent persons named by the defense.

The Government then called Francis R. Farrell, a neighbor of Dr. Mudd. He testified that the doctor had come by his house after the assassination. Following objections by the defense, the witness told of a very revealing meeting between four and five o'clock on that Saturday. "I was in my house," he testified, "when Mr. Hardy, who was at the yard gate with Dr. Mudd, hallooed to me that the President was assassinated and Seward and son injured...."

The witness testified that he asked the doctor about it and "he said it was so...." These surprising words contradicted Mudd's sworn statements. Farrell then said that he asked Mudd the assassin's identity. Dr. Mudd replied it was a man named Booth. The witness testified that Hardy asked Mudd "whether it was the Booth who was down here last fall; the doctor said he did not know whether it was so or not, as there were three or four by the name of Booth; if that was the one, he knew him; the doctor said he was very sorry the thing had occurred."[11]

These statements were damaging. The conversation referred to by Farrell occurred immediately after Dr. Mudd had helped two heavily armed, late-night visitors on their way after attending them for 12 hours. The supposed strangers carried with them their pistols, knives, a Spencer rifle, a compass, field glasses, a cartridge belt with ammunition and a map.

Farrell's testimony demonstrated clearly that Mudd knew that Booth, a man whom he admittedly had business dealings with, was the suspected assassin. Even more detrimental was proof that the prisoner knew of the murder on Saturday, while he swore repeatedly that he did not hear about it until Sunday. Dr. Mudd possessed information that could have helped the Government capture the assassins that afternoon, if not sooner.

These facts did not depend on Farrell's word alone. John Hardy, the neighbor with Farrell and Mudd, took the stand. Hardy was unaware of the questions the Judge asked Farrell or how he answered, but he presented the same general picture. He stated he lived near Mudd, and that, on the day after the crime, he met the doctor about 200 yards from his (Hardy's) house. Mudd talked about the terrible news that the President, Seward and Seward's son had been "assassinated by a man named Boyle. Booth's name was mentioned somehow, and he said he did not know which of the brothers it was."

Hardy swore that the conversation occurred shortly after sundown on April 15th. According to the witness, Mudd mentioned nothing about two suspicious men having come to his house after midnight. Hardy testified he had seen Booth at church the previous fall, and that "at the time of the conversation with the prisoner, I asked him, when Booth's name was mentioned, whether it was the same Booth who had been down there before, and he said he did not know."

Under Ewing's cross-examination, Hardy's account caused more harm. "The conversation I have mentioned was commenced by the prisoner; he said he had got the news from Bryantown, where he had been; he seemed to feel all the sorrow he expressed in regard to the assassination...."[12]

The witness again swore that Mudd had not mentioned any questionable callers having spent the night and most of the day in his house.

These two witnesses were not trying to malign their neighbor; they were simply relating a conversation. They could not have known that Mudd had sworn repeatedly that he was unaware of the assassination until Sunday or have any idea of Booth's involvement. Strangely, the defense made no effort to impeach the extremely damaging statements of Farrell or Hardy. If the Military Commission had any lingering uncertainty about what Mudd knew, and when he knew it, the doubts vanished.

One witness who might have helped Samuel Mudd was his wife, but the defense never called her. He was the only prisoner to have a spouse, and some question arises as to why she was not put on the stand—perhaps because some testimony against the doctor also involved his wife.

Sarah Frances Mudd was always more cooperative with investigators than was her husband. But how much she knew is uncertain. After the trial, she wrote a long account of the events. According to her story, Dr. Mudd first met Booth in November 1864, at the Catholic church in Bryantown, Maryland. A man named John Thompson of Baltimore introduced him saying that Booth wanted to buy a good riding horse. A witness also named John Thompson had previously testified about Mrs. Surratt. He said he had lived in Surrattsville for two years and knew the citizens of that area. Whether he is the same man referred to by Mrs. Mudd is not known. Dr. Mudd had sworn that his dealings with Booth were about buying his farm. From the doctor he bought neither a horse nor a farm.

Nellie Mudd, the doctor's daughter, described life on their Maryland farm as deteriorating because their slaves "became imbued with the idea of freedom...."[13] As a result they did not want to work. After Lincoln's 1862 Emancipation Proclamation went into effect on January 1, 1863, the Negroes became almost useless in Maryland, even though that state was not included in the emancipation. When slavery was finally abolished by the new Maryland Constitution, Mudd's daughter complained that their slaves "almost uniformly refused to work for their former owners, even for highly remunerative wages." Nellie Mudd observed sadly that they had to pay their former slaves "twice the value of their services" to keep them around the farm.[14] All of these changes distressed the family and, according to many accounts, heightened the usually gentle physician's opposition to Lincoln's policies. Neighbors knew that Dr. Mudd had helped Southern sympathizers hide on his farm.

Under these conditions, it was not unnatural for Booth to expect that the doctor might be interested in his scheme to abduct Lincoln. Certainly Booth expected Mudd's cooperation, because he had a letter of introduction to him. At this time, Booth did want to buy a horse, but he was also seeking a possible escape route for the kidnapping. The doctor's house, 30 miles from Washington, conveniently off the main road, near the swamps, evidently fit Booth's needs.

Mudd's casual meeting of a stranger at church who wanted to buy a horse was not unusual. But the doctor's subsequent actions coincided with Booth's admitted activities in planning the conspiracy. Dr. Mudd did not have a horse for sale. According to Mrs. Mudd, instead of introducing Booth to the man who did want to sell one, Mudd spent the afternoon with Booth and did not get home until evening. The doctor invited his new-found friend in for supper and, after eating, they visited some more. As previously mentioned, Booth apparently spent the night with Dr. William Green. Several witnesses testified that Booth had letters of introduction to both Drs. Mudd and Green. The next day, Mudd helped Booth buy the one-eyed horse from his friend George Gardiner.[15]

The army supplied ambulances to escort members of the Court to and from their residences each day. One of Kautz's neighbors, apparently a Southern sympathizer, complained that the ambulance that waited to pick up the General infringed on space in front of his house. Kautz thought it a silly complaint but, to avoid a conflict, requested the army escort to wait for him on Pennsylvania Avenue. Another irritant to Kautz was the constant tardiness of Judge Holt.[16] Even the president of the Commission, General Hunter, became annoyed about it.

On June 9, the Commissioners met early at Gardner's Gallery to have their portraits made. After the pictures, they convened at the courtroom but made little progress for lack of witnesses. The suspects' chances were further hurt by constant bickering among their counselors. The weather remained so stifling they were happy to adjourn early.

That night Kautz heard Anna Dickinson lecture on the death of Lincoln. Dickinson, though only 22 years old, had gained recognition as a public speaker in her teens. A fiercely outspoken abolitionist, she had addressed groups in army camps and hospitals during the war. Her violent views shocked Kautz, who concluded that she "would make an indifferent wife."[17] The lecture, however, did not influence his feeling toward conspirators.

At this time a mystifying exchange apparently took place between Stanton and Sen. Jacob M. Howard, Republican from Michigan. A letter from Detroit dated June 12, 1865, seemingly from Howard, said,

> For God's sake, my friend! Don't let Attorney General Speed fail to get Jacob Thompson's book from Clery. I am sorry Speed returned without them. Clery is not worth much, but the books are valuable as evidence and history will fix upon the Confederate leaders a stigma which no time can wash out. I beg the Cabinet to *get them* [italics in original]. Clery will burn them or give them to Thompson.[18]

What seems to have been another appeal opens with the underlined words *Burn this slip.* The letter, which may have been from Stanton but which was probably from Howard, was saved among Stanton's papers. It reads:

> Clery is poor and in distress and probably as vile a scoundrel as lives—but tell Speed to use all the money necessary to overcome his scruples if he has any and to procure the books—*It is right and just* [italics in original] but of course none of you people should be connected with it—I can manage that. I feel almost provoked that Speed went off without them. I would have got them *anyhow* [italics in original].[19]

The note was not signed. Exactly what happened in this mysterious endeavor is unknown, but nothing about the books came out in the trial.

Apparently Thompson's books had been destroyed and with them, Holt's chance to link the Canadian Confederates to the plot against Lincoln.

For a month, Orville Browning had persistently approached Stanton in behalf of B. F. Ficklin, who had been arrested on suspicion of complicity in the assassination. Day after day Browning beseeched the Secretary without apology; Stanton, in characteristic fashion, put him off. On Wednesday, June 14, Browning again urged the hardheaded Secretary to release Ficklin, who by this time had been in jail for nearly two months. Stanton said he could not let Ficklin go until all the trial evidence was in. Unfazed, Browning was back the next day; again the Secretary said no. On the 16th, Browning approached him again, and again Stanton denied his request. But the following week the Government released Ficklin.[20] Stanton had kept his word to wait for all the evidence, but he had, through it all, respected Browning's efforts.

At approximately the same time, Stanton directed General Hancock "to make any arrangement that can be done for comfort of Mrs. Surratt." He ordered that she be furnished any food or necessity she desired. The War Secretary added, "Such changes or additions to her furniture as may add to her comfort are also authorized—having due regard to the security."[21]

Dr. Gray, an authority on the treatment of prisoners, was requested by Stanton to examine the inmates and help oversee their care. The doctor had served as medical superintendent of the New York state mental hospital at Utica and gained a reputation for providing humane treatment.

Gray, with the help of Dr. Porter, visited each cell and made recommendations to Stanton. They suggested that the Government provide the men with a small box or stool to sit on and that Mrs. Surratt be given a chair. They requested officials to supply pillows and reading materials, other than newspapers, and asked that the men be given a small portion of tobacco after each meal. The doctors also recommended that O'Laughlin, who seemed to be suffering the most, be moved to a cell where he could get more light.[22]

Gray and Porter felt that the prisoners' diet was adequate and they found sanitary facilities suitable. The only other recommendation made was that authorities give inmates an hour of exercise in the open air each day. Stanton passed the recommendations along to General Hancock, requesting that he carry them out. Years later, Arnold, one of few who wrote about his prison experience, noted that about the middle of June the Government allowed prisoners to exercise two hours a day in the prison yard.

After talking with the suspects and ministering to their needs for nearly two months, Porter became convinced that Mary Surratt was "the only one who properly estimated the enormity of the crime and intelligently and deliberately ventured her own life to destroy that of those she had been taught to believe had brought about the calamities of the Confederacy."[23]

The physician felt that Mrs. Surratt believed that, even if apprehended and her guilty actions fully revealed, she would escape severe punishment because of her sex. The doctor pointed out that Union forces had caught many women spies, and they all escaped the death penalty. "Female spies during the war," he wrote, "were the most effective members of the Confederate Secret

Service and the natural results of this mawkish, unmilitary and unjust senti-mentality caused the death of many hundreds of Union soldiers."[24]

Government threats to arrest subpoenaed witnesses who had failed to ap-pear brought results. At least Judge Abram Olin responded. Questioned by Doster, he testified that he doubted the veracity of Mr. Norton, a previous witness. Olin's statement had little value, as Norton's testimony was superfluous.

The defense called Honora Fitzpatrick back to the stand. She claimed that on the night of their arrest, she did not recognize Payne until they were all together in General Augur's office. This point was irrelevant, however, because Honora had not confronted Payne until they arrived at the office. Mrs. Surratt refused to acknowledge that she had ever seen him before, even after staying with him for several hours in Augur's office. According to Fitzpatrick, she did not hear Mrs. Surratt deny that she recognized Payne, only that she denied Payne was her son John. So far, the defense had been unable to provide convincing evidence in favor of the accused, and they were running out of witnesses.

Government pressure continued to get results, and more defense witnesses reluctantly appeared in court. On June 10, both Doster and Ewing, as well as Cox and Aiken, had testimony to present. In spite of the heat and the tiresome proceedings, the courtroom was jammed with curious visitors, including Anna Dickinson.

Guards had shaved Herold's mustache and cut his hair, changing his ap-pearance but not his conduct. He continued to act like a mischievous child, apparently expecting soon to be free.

Daniel E. Morris, a defense witness, tried to soften the previous testimony against Mudd, stating that many people in Byrantown thought the culprit was Edwin, rather than John Wilkes Booth. His testimony was neither important nor persuasive, considering that John Wilkes was the only Booth in the Washington area for the six months preceding the assassination. His testimony was further discounted when he admitted his opposition to the Government's abolition of slavery.

The last witness called in behalf of Mudd was L. A. Gobright, an eminent reporter for the Associated Press. He backed up the defense's contention that Booth was not definitely named as the murderer until Saturday morning. Gobright testified that, when at Ford's Theatre, 40 minutes after the crime a difference of opinion still existed as to whether the assassin was Booth. "During the short time I remained there," he said, "I was not at that time satisfied that Booth was the assassin."

In his cross-examination, Bingham declared, "But you became satisfied during the night that it was Booth, and telegraphed that fact."

"I did not so telegraph that night."

"You became satisfied, the next day, that Booth was the assassin?"

"It was so announced the next morning in the official Bulletin."[25]

Gobright apparently had no effect on the Court, but he negated the myth that telegraph lines out of the city had been cut.

Ewing then announced the termination of his defense of Mudd, Spangler and Arnold.

Doster still had not received the report of Dr. Nichols about Payne's sanity, and he was waiting for Payne's father. Bingham reminded Doster that he had already had 40 days to secure his witnesses, which seemed ample time. Judge Holt kept the trial moving, however, by introducing several persons to prove his long-held view of Rebel atrocities. There being no other witness, court adjourned early.

XL
"... What a
Phenomenon He Was"

The Government did not treat the prisoners gently, but neither was it extremely brutal. They had only cold water for bathing, which was common in summertime. Authorities provided clean clothing and devised a new type of hood to be less irritating, but it proved even more uncomfortable. Guards removed the hated devices permanently about June 18.

During the trial, someone provided Bibles for the prisoners, but according to Arnold, officials confiscated them. This may have been true, but, on the day of the executions, Payne still had his.

The early adjournment of court gave the inmates their first opportunity to exercise in the prison yard free from the hoods and manacles. Every subsequent day, they enjoyed several hours of relative freedom, the first in nearly two months—the last for some. They were carefully guarded during these periods and were able to communicate only by facial expressions.

One guard watching over them was a young soldier, Alfred Gibson. He had enlisted in the 215th Pennsylvania Infantry when he was 16 and soon became a clerk for General Hartranft. At the time of the assassination, Gibson and the General were stationed at Fairfax Court House. When General Hancock ordered Hartranft to the capital to take command of the Arsenal Penitentiary, Hartranft took his clerk. Gibson, one of four turnkeys guarding the inmates, occasionally pitched quoits with them in the prison yard.[1]

One day Arnold noticed guards taking Atzerodt from his cell to the outer prison where they removed his irons. This led Arnold to think that Atzerodt had made a confession. Actually, Atzerodt had confessed no more than Arnold, but the suspects could not be sure what others had revealed.

As the prisoners were brought in on Monday, June 12, spectators noticed some changes. Payne's long hair had been cut close to his scalp. Spangler now appeared the most woeful. He exhibited his fear of hanging in nervous movements of his body and hands. Spangler constantly moved his ironed hands back and forth along his legs and fidgeted nervously with his fingers. He watched each witness anxiously, even those not directly concerned with him.[2]

The defense still had difficulty inducing some witnesses to appear, and those who did testify seemed hesitant. Doster eventually persuaded Mr. and

Mrs. John Grant from Warrenton, Virginia, to appear. They swore they had seen Payne save the lives of two Union prisoners.

Aiken found a witness whom he expected to strengthen the testimony about Lloyd's drinking. H. R. Sweeney asserted that he and Lloyd had been drinking on the day of the murder, but his testimony seemed forced and unconvincing. According to Sweeney, he and Lloyd drank from the same bottle as they were riding along the road from Marlboro, but he admitted he was on horseback while Lloyd drove a buggy.

During the recess, Arnold remained in the courtroom to visit with his father. The conversation deeply moved the elder Arnold. When the father parted, he was seen wiping away tears; the son turned his face to the window.

Aiken had told the Court that he was ready to close his argument, but he changed his mind. He had visited the area around Surrattsville and discovered new evidence. Judge Holt advised the Court to extend the time to hear the new evidence, adding that the Government also had additional witnesses.

Holt then called Horatio King, one of his longtime friends. King said little, but his appearance indicated the ease with which individuals could be introduced, in the closing days, to support any view. Court adjourned early for lack of additional witnesses.

Several newspapers published reports that Mrs. Surratt had been brought into court with her feet chained. It was not true, and no reporter claimed to have seen the irons, but other papers copied the notice. The Government did not bother to refute the rumor and it gained momentum. Toward the end of the trial, some papers, including the *New York Times*, questioned the accusation.[3] This developed into a lingering dispute not settled until years later when both General Hartranft and Mrs. Surratt's lawyer declared she was never chained in any way.

The Lincoln legend began even as the trial was in progress. A group of citizens searched through Kentucky and found what they professed to be the log cabin in which Lincoln was born. They took it to Chicago where it was reconstructed and exhibited on the corner of Randolph Street and Wabash Avenue.

The only remaining issue in the trial was the insanity plea. Dr. Nichols was prevented, because of his wife's death, from examining Payne. Therefore, Dr. James C. Hall, a well-known physician who had helped attend Lincoln, examined the prisoner. He reported, inconclusively, that Payne's physical condition was normal except that his eye had "no intellectual expression." The doctor noticed that the prisoner's head "was not symmetrical, the left side being much better developed than the right; the pulse was about thirty strokes above the natural average."[4]

Holt, cutting through the medical jargon, asked if the examination showed "reasonable grounds for believing that he is insane." The medical examiner stated there were; no sane man could exhibit "such utter insensibility which the prisoner manifests." The doctor explained that Payne made no attempt at deception and answered his questions without attempting to mislead him.

Judge Holt could not believe the witness and sought to guide him to another conclusion. "I understand you to say, that what you have discovered as peculiar in the condition of Payne, is not insanity, but extreme insensibility?"

Dr. Hall obliged, acknowledging that he could not discover actual insanity. But, he maintained, Payne had a "feeble, inert mind; a deficiency rather than a derangement of mind; a very low order of intellect."

Anxious to influence the physician's final evaluation, Holt questioned, "From the whole examination you have made, do you regard the prisoner, Payne, as sufficiently sane to be responsible for his acts?"

Again Dr. Hall hedged, explaining that he had not completely made up his mind. He thought Payne was not entirely sane but could not be positive. The doctor indicated, however, that insane people have a high pulse rate and "the prisoner's pulse was thirty odd strokes above the ordinary standard."[5]

As the examination seemed inconclusive, the Court appointed additional physicians to test the suspect: a Dr. Stevens, Surgeon General Barnes and a Dr. Norris. No evidence indicates that these men had ever studied mental disorders, but the two were eminent surgeons.

The defense of Payne was almost impossible. He had pleaded not guilty, and under this plea the rules of court-martial left the defense only two alternatives. Either they had to show that the prisoner was not the man whom witnesses had pointed out as Seward's attacker, which was hopeless, or they had to show he was insane. The second course also presented problems. The prisoner could not be put on the stand, thus the Court could not see for itself what manner of man he was.

During the first weeks of court, Payne hardly communicated with his counsel. He sat upright with his head against the wall and his manacled hands resting on his knees, seldom stirring.

Soon after Seward's servant identified him, Payne asked Doster what the next day was. The lawyer replied that it was Sunday. The prisoner requested Doster to come to the Arsenal and talk with him. Officials set up a private interview for the next day in the courtroom. Payne and his counsel conversed alone, except for sentinels stationed outside the door.

Payne gave Doster a brief and disconnected story of his life for the first time. After relating something of his past, Payne inquired about Frederick Seward. He expressed genuine sorrow that he had hurt him and wanted to apologize. In the next few weeks Payne repeatedly expressed regret for his attack on Frederick, but he never showed any remorse for his vicious attack on Secretary Seward.

After gathering some details of Payne's life, Doster passed the information to the Government, hoping this might help prove his client insane. But the Commissioners were never permitted to talk to the prisoner to determine for themselves "what a phenomenon he was."[6] Experts called to examine Payne were not authorities on mental problems and were of little help confirming the lawyer's alibi. All the examining surgeons swore Payne was sane. Doster felt that in a civil court, in which specialists rather than army doctors would be called, his client would have been declared unable to distinguish between right and wrong. The lawyer concluded that the Military Commission was afraid to "call civilians who made insanity a specialty."[7]

One member of the Commission, General Harris, was a physician. He had suggested, even before Doster thought of the insanity plea, that Payne showed symptoms of mental imbalance. Payne's abnormal constipation aroused Harris' attention. For weeks, the Court realized that Payne had apparently avoided the natural function of the body. Harris explained knowingly that "this was a general accompanying symptom of the early stages of insanity."[8]

After Doster's insanity plea, Anna Surratt told him that Payne's conduct at their house "was that of a perfect fool."[9] But Anna's evaluation was in contrast to all others who met him at the boardinghouse. They described Payne as quiet and gentlemanly. Anna was unbalanced herself during this period. Between fits of crying and hysteria, she denounced nearly everyone connected with the trial except her mother. Doster wanted to question her in court about Payne's conduct but decided against it because of her unstable condition.

The lawyer, desperate to find someone to confirm his client's unnatural behavior, again sent for the Bransons of Baltimore. But this time, they seemed so frightened he could obtain little helpful information. They declared that Payne was quiet and orderly, except for the time he beat the servant girl. Margaret Branson, apparently the only one willing to testify, even sought to minimize the beating. Surely Margaret's efforts gratified the beleaguered prisoner who, even at the price of his life, did not want to be thought of as insane.

One guard volunteered to swear that Payne was crazy; Doster put him on the stand. But the guard surprised the counselor by only testifying that Payne thought detectives were "tracking him pretty close."[10] Doster avoided using Government personnel after that.

Eventually Payne told his lawyer hitherto-unknown conspiracy details. Posing as a messenger from Seward's personal physician was suggested by Herold, who had worked in the apothecary which Seward's physician used. After the attack, Payne abandoned his horse, threw away his overcoat (stained with blood from his own finger which he cut in the struggle) and wandered through the woods. He climbed into a cedar tree and hid there for two days. Being overcome with hunger, he made his way to Mrs. Surratt's house because she was the only person he knew. This latter statement was untrue. He had boarded at the Herndon house for several weeks prior to the assassination. This would have been the logical place to go, as he was not a suspect at the time. Booth and Herold had definite plans for their escape, but Payne and Atzerodt had not the vaguest idea of where to hide.

A rumor spread that if Payne were sentenced to death, Secretary Seward would ask for his pardon. On hearing the report, Payne ignored it.

The military court wearily continued its task during the hot days of June. Everyone wanted to get the trial over with, but on June 13 new developments added a little interest. The Washington Star had published an account of the "mysterious" letter which the Court had read early in June. In the meanwhile, the Government had identified the persons mentioned and located them. The *Star* asserted that those named claimed the whole thing was a fraud perpetrated by a man named Purdy.[11] Counselor Cox read the account in court, chiding the prosecution for not informing the defense that the letter was false. Holt quietly assured the lawyer that the matter was still being investigated and that the defense would have opportunity to question those involved.

General Kautz gave special attention to testimony accusing Confederates of attempting to start fires and set off explosives in Northern cities, and believed it. Kautz and other Commissioners never doubted that such testimony was relevant to the case. They connected the conspiracy with other acts of Rebel terrorism. If the Confederates could plot the destruction of Northern cities, then the death of the President was not beyond their conception.

On June 15, the Commission met for another picture, this time at Brady's studio. That evening, Kautz and his colleague Gen. James William Denver discussed the "error" of trying the conspirators by a military court.[12] Holt had tried to rid the Commission of all dissidents, but he failed to correctly evaluate General Kautz.

Gen. James W. Denver, a 48-year-old Washington lawyer, took unusual interest in the trial. An energetic man, he had served in the state legislature of California and had been governor of Kansas. Before the war, he was Commissioner of Indian Affairs, as well as a promoter of the Union Pacific Railroad. Denver, Colorado, was named for him. He expressed his views readily, severely denouncing the Military Commission as being both irregular and illegal. Apparently his friend Kautz did not disagree, because the two Generals, despite their age difference, maintained an unfaltering friendship.

Two defense witnesses, John and William Hoxten, were supposed to testify that Zadoc Jenkins was a loyal man. But they admitted that "the report in the neighborhood now is that he is not loyal."[13]

In an effort to counteract overwhelming evidence against Mrs. Surratt, Aiken reexamined Lloyd and his sister-in-law Emma Offutt, but not, significantly, Lloyd's wife. Lloyd repeated his earlier devastating testimony. The lawyer then explained to the Court that when Mrs. Offutt testified earlier, she had not recovered from a sickness and had taken laudanum. Her mind, he said, was confused, and she now desired to correct her testimony. After a short conference between Aiken and Bingham, the witness swore that her previous testimony was incorrect, that, in fact, Mrs. Surratt did hand her a package saying "she [Mrs. Surratt] was requested to leave it there." This conversation took place four or five hours before the murder.

This supposedly new evidence further damaged Aiken's client. This bruising interrogation was the last effort made in Mary Surratt's behalf. It revealed that the month-old trial had not altered the original evidence. Mrs. Offutt admitted that she had seen Mrs. Surratt and Lloyd in a private conversation outside the house on the afternoon of the murder. After three brief testimonies, the defense closed its case, except for the report on Payne's sanity.

Court-appointed physicians visited Payne's cell the next morning. The prisoner had heard statements about his mental condition and was determined to prove his sanity. The idea of being thought insane had a profound effect on Payne. He did not object to being described as a cold-blooded killer, but he did not want to be looked upon as crazy.

On the last day of the regular session, Payne entered the prisoners' dock radically changed. Instead of taking his usual seat, he sat on a little ridge used by the prisoners to rest their feet and hid himself behind the railing. This was no effort to prove himself insane; he wanted to avoid the visitors' gazes while the doctors discussed his supposed deficiencies.

Dr. Hall announced to the Court that he asked Payne the same questions as previously and that he answered them as he had before, but even more promptly. Holt, impatient with the long, inconclusive diagnoses, demanded, "are you now prepared to express an opinion whether or not, in your judgment, the prisoner is a sane and responsible man?"

"I am now prepared to say there is no evidence of mental insanity," Dr. Norris responded, backing his colleague's opinion.[14]

Surgeon General Barnes testified similarly, and Dr. Porter, in charge of the prisoners' medical needs, vowed that Payne "was a sane and responsible man."[15]

That terminated the pertinent evidence, although two days later, the Court considered the mysterious letter in the *Washington Star* again. The Government brought in Robert Purdy, mentioned in the letter. He testified that he knew the persons involved in writing the document. The communication was genuine, he conceded, but the Court was too weary to pursue the matter. They had spent more than a month interviewing nearly 400 witnesses in trying eight persons. Only the summation arguments remained.

Up to this point, the Government had not interfered with press coverage. But on June 14, officials arrested John Mitchel, a reporter for the *New York News*, because of his unrestrained article against the Court and confined him in Fortress Monroe. Mitchel, an Irish immigrant, was strongly pro–Confederacy.

Two days later, testimony showed that Benjamin Wood, proprietor and editor of the *New York News*, had been paid by the Confederate Government to publish inflammatory articles against the Union. Although authorities had suppressed his paper previously, Wood had since been elected to the United States Congress. But his persistent opposition to the war had caused Congress to bring charges against him.[16]

D. S. Eastwood revealed that a check for $25,000 was issued on August 17, 1864, to Benjamin Wood against the account set up by the Confederates in Canada. He added that at the suggestion of Jacob Thompson, the name Eastwood was substituted for Wood. The Court examined documents showing Confederate payments to Wood over several months. The last payment was made March 21, 1865, two weeks before the fall of Richmond.[17]

The *Constitutional Union*, a Washington newspaper, was one of many that branded Conover's testimony false. The paper added prophetically that President Johnson probably did not want to hear the cry "'hang, hang,' because that same crowd may raise the same cry against him tomorrow."[18] Judge Bingham, the strongest advocate of severe punishment for the conspirators, was to preside over the impeachment trial of President Johnson three years later.

XLI
Education for Murder

The Government had to settle questions about Weichmann before it could conclude the case. Someone had introduced a list of accusations against Weichmann early in the trial which seemed to implicate him. The list was almost identical to one that John Brophy later sent to President Johnson. Burnett had ordered Weichmann to answer the charges. About the middle of May, after Weichmann had been on the witness stand twice, he answered Burnett's questions one by one. The first accusation concerned his remark at work that he could make "$30,000 as easy as dirt."[1] Weichmann admitted having made the statement but claimed the clerks were joking about the lottery and easy money, and his remark was just foolish talk.

Weichmann was also accused of indicating that his testimony before Stanton had been made under duress. But he maintained to Burnett that Stanton had treated him kindly, never saying that Stanton threatened him. Possibly, however, Weichmann gave the impression to fellow prisoners that Stanton had scared him, for that is what he had written to Burnett previously.

He answered a question which came up repeatedly about whether he and Surratt were "students of divinity." Weichmann declared that he had been a student of divinity. He admitted that perhaps he should have used the expression "ecclesiastical student" for Surratt.

One serious charge was that he had proclaimed privately and had even written to President Johnson that Mrs. Surratt was innocent. He answered, "*I do not believe she is innocent*" (emphasis in the original). "I partly made a promise to her friends," he said, "which on account of circumstances I do not deem it prudent to fulfill."[2] He never explained this statement. He had been in Government custody since the day Lincoln died and had had little opportunity for long conversations with her supporters. But he did have a few occasions to briefly discuss the assassination in the prison exercise yard.

It seems that Mrs. Surratt's allies wanted him to either modify his testimony or make some statement about her innocence, but he did not intend to keep the promise "on account of circumstances." This is the only reference Weichmann ever made to the "promise to her friends." Asked about his attitude toward the draft, he wrote that he had paid $100 to join an exemption club.

When Weichmann explained carelessly that Howell's colleague, Mrs. Slater, was in contact with the St. Albans raiders, he revealed more than he should have known. This had not been publicly stated before. Weichmann could not have obtained this information without being aware of the nature of the activities in the house on H Street.

Weichmann disputed two insignificant points. He stated that Howell had lied when he denied that he (Weichmann) had worn blue trousers. Weichmann also included the letter from Bishop McGill, which he kept with him, to prove that he intended to go to Richmond to prepare for the priesthood. He admitted that there was no Catholic seminary in Richmond but argued that a seminary was not always necessary for theological training. Howell's testimony was a "put up job," he wrote. By this time, Weichmann had begun to realize more clearly that the Surratts and their friends were determined to tarnish his reputation and "make me suspect as an accomplice...."[3] He had answered, although sometimes ineptly, all charges against him, but the Government remained suspicious.

Mrs. Surratt's supporters continued to raise the same accusations after the trial and forced Weichmann to respond to them repeatedly. Still, officials did not entirely trust him. Federal authorities such as Stanton, Gleason, Burnett and Holt treated him with contempt. And old friends had come to hate him for what they considered a betrayal. The trial left Weichmann in a wretched position.

The defense had tried to prove that while Weichmann was in Canada, he had not wanted to return voluntarily to the United States. The Judges contacted William Kelly, the officer who brought Weichmann and Holohan back. Kelly wrote on June 7, 1865, that he never told Weichmann that he was under arrest and that Weichmann did not want to return until he found John Surratt. Weichmann told Kelly that because of the circumstances, he was sure he would be locked up when he returned to the United States but that he was willing to suffer anything to help the Government.

After testifying, Weichmann continued to work with the Government, sending authorities new evidence which had not surfaced before. He recalled Mrs. Surratt's nervousness on the night of the murder ("she paced the floor of her parlor and counted her beads").[4] And because of the distracting conversation among the boarders, she asked everyone to leave the parlor and go to bed.

Weichmann reluctantly brought Anna more and more into suspicion. He surmised that it must have been Booth who quickly stopped at the Surratt house shortly before the murder, because the next morning at breakfast, Anna remarked, "Think of that man Booth having called at this house not more than an hour and a half before the assassination."[5] Anna frequently used the expression "that man." She referred to Payne as "that man" and constantly spoke of Weichmann as "that man." The mysterious visit was denied by other boarders at a later trial, however.

While Weichmann was aiding the Government, Federal authorities were not giving him much help. They had held him in custody almost two months without income. When released from jail in June, he asked Burnett to request his back salary at the Commission for the month of April.

More important than funds to Weichmann were friends. The trial also left him without friends. Weichmann's parole limited him to the Washington area. He soon realized that his testimony had caused his former friends not only to shun him, but also to ridicule and even harass him. Weichmann wrote Burnett again on June 16, this time begging that his parole be extended to Philadelphia so he could visit his parents. Weichmann pleaded, "I am here almost without friends," whereas in Philadelphia he could be with his parents and sisters, "who have never yet deceived me ... my sisters who love their unfortunate brother so much...."[6] He sought more than "one sympathizing heart"; he was looking for safety.

Authorities extended his parole to Philadelphia, but after a few weeks there, he wrote a long letter to Secretary Stanton documenting all the help he had given the Government. He described how he had helped McDevitt, Colonel Baker and General Augur. He mentioned that he had found photographs of Surratt and Herold and had helped in the apprehension of several conspirators. Then he complained that the trial had made it impossible for him to continue his theological studies and ruined him, leaving him "without money of which I am utterly destitute." Weichmann added that he would be interested in getting a job in the customs house or post office in Philadelphia or Boston. But better still, he inferred, a gift of cash would help now "that you are about to distribute the rewards."[7] He signed his letter "Louis Weichmann," adopting the spelling of his surname that reporters had used.

Stanton did help him get a job in the customs house but left him out of the rewards although, as Weichmann claimed, he had done more than any other person to bring the conspirators to justice.

Court opened on June 19 to hear the final summation arguments. In addition to the usual crowd, four of Herold's sisters, dressed in mourning, sat near their unconcerned brother. Mrs. Surratt was allowed to sit in the passageway between the courtroom and the waiting room in order to get a little fresh air.

As the session opened, Aiken announced he was not quite prepared to present his summation but that Reverdy Johnson's long-awaited argument in behalf of Mrs. Surratt was ready. Johnson, himself, did not attend court, but sent Clampitt to read his paper.

This was not the first time Johnson had presented these points publicly. He had delivered a shorter version of precisely the same views in a Senate debate on March 3, 1865, just before Lincoln's second inaugural. In his first presentation, the United States Senate voted against him. The arguments basically denied the right of Military Commissions to try civilians.

Johnson's paper was astonishing for what it left out. In the several hours it took to read, only one short part related to Mary Surratt's innocence, and even then he mentioned no facts. He simply tried to show that Mrs. Surratt was too fine a Christian lady to become involved in an assassination.

Johnson's defense closed by stating: "As far, gentlemen, as I am concerned her case is now in your hands." This admonition could have given no comfort to the widow. His summation was no real plea in behalf of his client and never once proclaimed her clearly innocent. Soon after Clampitt presented Johnson's argument, Mary Surratt complained of illness, and guards had to take her from the courtroom.

Frederick Stone prepared the next summation in behalf of Herold. Stone was also absent, and James Murphy, one of the official court reporters, read Stone's paper. Stone admitted that Herold must take the consequences of having aided and abetted in Booth's escape. But he pleaded that his client was a weak, trifling and cowardly boy and he trusted that the Court's justice would be tempered with mercy. It, too, was a poor defense.

In the light of later sensational books declaring that Herold and Payne were victims of mistaken identity, these defense pleas take on special value. Even though their lives depended on it, neither Herold or Payne challenged the Court's identification. They questioned the Court's interpretation but never claimed to be other than the persons named in the charges.

Walter Cox next offered his statements in behalf of Arnold and O'Laughlin. He admitted that his clients took part in the original conspiracy to capture the President but denied they had anything to do with the plot to kill him. This concluded the days' proceedings. These flimsy arguments must have sobered the prisoners as soldiers led them back to their cells.

As the Judges pondered these final statements, Secretary Seward's wife died. She had been in poor health before Payne's attack, but the added strain of caring for her wounded husband and son worsened her condition.

By this time, both Stanton and Holt possessed overwhelming evidence that Sanford Conover was a notorious perjurer. Canadian officials had found papers among his possessions which proved him completely unreliable. This information they passed on to Holt through the State Department. Gen. John Dix also informed Stanton of the findings. Among Conover's papers they discovered conclusive evidence that he had served as a Confederate agent in Canada. He was also the Montreal correspondent of the *New York Times*, the *New York World* and the *New York News*, under three different names.[8] Both the *World* and the *News* were pro–Southern. Both Holt and Stanton already knew most of this, or at least suspected it. They did not know that Conover had been imprisoned in Richmond as Charles A. Dunham, which the Canadians correctly discerned to be his real name. Nor did they know that he had written an atrocious article on Lincoln's assassination for the *Montreal Telegraph*. Canadian officials also reported to Holt that the man's character and reputation were so bad that no weight should be given his words unless corroborated by others. Even with this conclusive evidence against him, Conover continued to dupe Holt.

Court convened on June 20th at 2:00 P.M. to hear Ewing's presentation in behalf of Spangler. The prisoners took their usual places, except for Mrs. Surratt, who again sat in the passageway. Ewing opened the session announcing that none of the evidence proved Spangler had met Booth in recent years except in the theater. Describing Spangler as peaceful and good-natured, he took up each point, such as the rope found among the accused's possessions and demonstrated that they had no relation to the assassination. Ewing's defense

Orville H. Browning, a close friend of Lincoln's. His questionable business negotiations with Rebels irritated Stanton. Browning advised defense counselor Ewing behind the scenes (Library of Congress—BH82-4272).

was clear and systematic on every issue. The man supposedly helping Booth escape across the stage had been described as having a black mustache. The lawyer suggested that if the redheaded Spangler had worn a black mustache, people would have laughed.

Spangler had worked as a stagehand changing sets at Ford's Theatre since it opened. As a longtime friend of Booth, he willingly performed chores for him but was in no way connected with the plot, according to his lawyer.

Ewing's argument was convincing. Many witnesses swore that Spangler had been where he was supposed to be—at his job—when the assassination occurred. Booth had wanted Spangler to hold his horse, not help him by opening the door or clearing the way for his escape. As far as Booth knew, when he knocked down the youth holding his horse in the dark alley, it could have been Spangler. The lawyer pointed out the stagehand's innocent conduct after the assassination. Ewing concluded that a grand jury would not bring Spangler to trial on such superficial evidence.

Ewing, however, ignored Ritterspaugh's testimony that Spangler had hit him and told him to say nothing about Booth's escape. It was a difficult charge to disprove, but it seemed to be the spontaneous reaction of a friend rather than that of a conspirator. The more serious intimation that Spangler had bored the hole in the door to Lincoln's box he could not refute. This failure the Court did not miss.

Orville Browning assisted Ewing in preparing his final arguments for Spangler and Dr. Mudd. Browning, similar in many respects to his friend, the slain President, was born in Kentucky and later moved to Illinois where he practiced law. He assisted Lincoln in the establishment of the Republican Party and actively supported Lincoln for the presidency. In 1861, Illinois Governor Richard Yates appointed him to fill the vacancy in the United States Senate left by Stephen Douglas' resignation, a position he held until 1863. As a law partner of Thomas Ewing, Sr., he exerted an ongoing influence in Washington affairs.

During the war, Browning, General Singleton and others including President Lincoln's sister-in-law, Mrs. Clement White of Alabama, entangled themselves in questionable commerce with the South. Stanton knew about these illegal operations but could do little as long as the President permitted them. Reporters, and occasionally Cabinet members, complained to Lincoln that Mrs. Clement White, half sister of the First Lady, was carrying contraband south, on passes signed by the President.[9]

Another of Mrs. Lincoln's half sisters, Emilie Helm, the young widow of Confederate General Ben Hardin Helm, was a guest at the White House during the war. Mrs. Helm, a dedicated Rebel, refused to take the oath of allegiance, which was required for travel between North and South. President Lincoln, however, telegraphed military authorities to allow his sister-in-law to enter Washington without taking the oath. It seemed to many loyal citizens that Lincoln used poor judgment in allowing a determined Confederate to remain a guest in the White House at the height of the bitter conflict. Gen. Dan Sickles complained earnestly to the President, and Helm finally left to avoid further embarrassment. Again she crossed the lines without taking the oath. Somehow Helm was able to obtain the President's help in negotiating the sale of 600 bales of cotton at the very time Stanton was jailing Baltimore merchants for lesser offenses.

About three weeks before the assassination, General Singleton and Emilie Helm visited Orville Browning in Washington to enlist his aid in passing her cotton through the lines. In addition, Singleton was personally involved in contracting for large quantities of merchandise stored in Richmond. By questionable maneuvering, he managed to visit Richmond ten days before its fall in order to save his goods.

On March 29, Browning and Singleton were still busy negotiating the shipment of this cotton. Singleton went to Baltimore, apparently to talk to merchants, while Browning conversed with authorities in Washington. He had already obtained Lincoln's approval, as well as Grant's support, for getting the contraband out of the South.[10]

Throughout this period, Browning was staying in close contact with the notorious Southern agent B. F. Ficklin, who crossed the lines to visit him about three days before Richmond surrendered. Union forces captured the Confederate capital, however, before Browning, Singleton, Helm and Ficklin could complete their business. On April 6, Browning conferred with Stanton "about sundry matters," apparently meaning the illegal cotton transactions. He found the Secretary of War absolutely opposed to his dealings. On April 12, Browning, still attempting to salvage something from his clandestine business, convinced Lincoln to give Singleton a pass to see General Grant. Browning also conferred again with Stanton, who severely condemned him for negotiating with the enemy.

On the fateful evening of April 14, Browning waited at the White House until 8:00 P.M. to talk to Lincoln about "Singleton's business," but he never got in to see him. The President "was going to the Theatre and was not up at his room after dinner." A few hours later, when Browning learned of the assassination, his first thought was the possibility of "summary vengeance upon those of us who have been suspected of sympathy with the rebellion...."[11]

His fear was well founded. The next day, the Government arrested his collaborator, Ficklin, on suspicion of complicity in the assassination. Browning immediately tried to secure Ficklin's release. On three consecutive days, May 11, 12, and 13, just as the conspiracy trial was getting under way, he visited Colonel Baker's office seeking to expedite the release of his friend. An assistant finally informed him that Ficklin "had been discharged sometime ago" and advised Browning to check at Major O'Beirne's office. There he learned that authorities still had Ficklin confined in prison and would not release him. Browning then began a constant barrage of O'Beirne's office, and when that failed, began to pester Secretary Stanton.

Personal relations among those associated with the trial were intertwined and complicated. Stanton was still involved in his dispute with Sherman, who was a close friend of Browning. General Sherman had to spend one night at Browning's house when in town for the Grand Review. After the parade, Browning sought to act as an intermediary between Stanton and Sherman. Mrs. Sherman seemed anxious to patch up the quarrel which her husband had allowed to fester. She confided to Browning that she would like to make a social call on the Stantons but was not sure how she would be received. On one of his frequent visits to Stanton's office, Browning obligingly expressed concern about the problems between the General and the Secretary of War. Stanton responded that as far as he was concerned, there was no difficulty—he held no ill feelings toward the General. Browning then mentioned the possibility of a visit from Mrs. Sherman. Stanton responded that he would be happy to receive her, affirming that he had always felt kindly toward the family. The subsequent meeting of Mrs. Sherman and the Stantons at their home was pleasant, but the General did not accompany his wife. The next day, the Shermans left Washington; the two hardheaded leaders remained unreconciled.

On June 13, Browning wrote part of the summation argument which Ewing was to use for Arnold. The next day and again on June 15 and 16, he was in

Stanton's office requesting Ficklin's release. The day after authorities set Ficklin free, Browning continued working on Samuel Arnold's defense.

Doster's unpreparedness on June 20 angered General Howe. The General declared sternly that the Court had already extended the time, and, that if Doster was not ready the next day, he would have to file his argument. General Ekin disagreed; he felt the case was so important he was willing to grant all of the time the counsel needed. Even the usually austere General Hunter sided with Ekin.

Ewing announced that he could not be prepared for Mudd's defense before Friday, June 23, because he had 250 pages of evidence to evaluate. The Court, therefore, voted to extend the time.

The next day, Doster presented an unexpectedly energetic defense summation in behalf of Payne. Doster freely admitted that his client was sane and that he had attempted to kill the Secretary of State. He reviewed Payne's youth, molded by Southern customs, and pictured his horrifying experiences in battle. Eloquent and dramatic in his efforts, he pictured Payne's desolate condition at the time he became involved with Booth:

> Penniless and friendless, the earth seems to reject him and God and man to be against him. This is the work of civil war. His education is now completed. Slavery had taught him to wink at murder. The Southern army had taught him to practice and justify murder. Guerilla warfare had taught him to love murder. Necessity had taught him resolution to commit murder. He needs no further education; his four terms are complete, and he graduates an assassin. And of this college we the reunited people of the United States have been stern tutors, guides and professors. It needs now only that someone should employ him.

Doster concluded by arguing that Payne had killed no one, and that if put to death "we shall have the anomaly of the victim surviving the murderer, and, under the laws, he can be punished only for assault and battery, with intent to kill, and therefore imprisoned."[12] This passionate and emotional defense Payne may not have fully appreciated.

After an hour's recess, Doster delivered his summation in favor of Atzerodt. He presented yet another confession of his client, making a total of at least four confessions by Atzerodt. His first statement had been made to Provost Marshal McPhail at the time of his arrest. Another he gave to Captain Monroe aboard the ironclad. He later confessed to Colonel Wells and made a fourth admission to his lawyer. These statements were virtually identical. They all acknowledged that Booth and Surratt recruited Atzerodt to help capture Lincoln. They gave him the specific responsibility of providing a boat at Port Tobacco to carry the President across the Potomac. Just two hours before the crime Booth told him his new job would be to kill Vice-President Johnson. Atzerodt refused.

Other than Spangler, Atzerodt appeared to be the most innocent of malicious intent. According to Doster, Colonel Wells had promised Atzerodt that if he would point out the way Booth had fled, the prisoner would be reprieved. Atzerodt told Wells that he thought Booth had gone down to Prince

Charles County to cross the Potomac. Wells had no reason to doubt this clue, and it should have been taken into consideration in the sentencing. Atzerodt and Arnold were the only suspects to cooperate with the Government. From the beginning, Atzerodt freely revealed what he knew, and hoped that his numerous confessions would help him. But they were not admissible at the trial prior to Doster's closing remarks.

Aiken then read his defense. Two lawyers presented summations in behalf of Mary Surratt. Reverdy Johnson had said practically nothing about the prisoner, and neither did Aiken deal with the issues. In contrast to Ewing, who answered each accusation against Spangler, Aiken avoided the facts. He followed Johnson's lead, stressing Mrs. Surratt's Christian character, which he avowed was totally inconsistent with such a horrible crime. His closing remarks were both grandiose and threatening:

> Let not this first State tribunal in our country's history, which involves a woman's name, be blazoned before the world with the harsh hints of intolerance which permits injustice, but as the benignant heart and kindly judging mind of the world-lamented victim of a crime which would, in its ramifications of woe, arouse so many fates, would himself have counselled you. Let the heralds of peace and charity, with their wool-bound slaves, follow the fasces and axes of judgement and law, and without the sacrifice of any innocent Iphigenia, let the ship of state launch with dignity of unstained sails into the unruffled sea of union and prosperity.[13]

With this flowery plea, court adjourned. Aiken had to wait more than two weeks to learn what effect his speech had on the Commission.

On June 23, after a brief testimony by George Hutchinson concerning Confederates in Canada, Ewing gave his closing argument in behalf of Arnold. This second summation for Arnold was similar to Cox's previous statement, but Ewing brought out a new legal point. He claimed Arnold could not be held responsible for the conspirators' acts after he terminated his association with them, and quoted various legal precedents to support his view.

Following a recess, Ewing again challenged the authority of the military court to try the prisoners. Holt maintained the Court did have such authority. After a fruitless discussion, Ewing proceeded with his defense of Dr. Mudd.

Witnesses had given more favorable testimony for Mudd than for other defendants, yet Ewing's argument was relatively short and ineffective. Ewing spoke of the many witnesses who had lied about the doctor. Naturally he did not mention those caught lying in Mudd's favor. In contrast with his defense of Spangler and Arnold, the lawyer did not deal with facts, but rather treated the case in generalities.

In their closing arguments, defense lawyers refuted each accusation, when possible, and resorted to broad generalities on points not easily disproved. Ewing claimed that Mudd had been 30 miles from the crime. If he were in any way guilty, it was as an accessory after the fact, he argued. In dealing with the extremely serious accusation of the doctor's meeting with Booth and Surratt in Washington, the defense counsel stated unequivocally that no such meeting took place, leaving the Court to decide between Mudd's word and Weichmann's testimony. Many incriminating acts damaged Mudd's claim of innocence, but one of the most crucial was the vigorously denied Washington meeting.

All the arguments for the defense having been read, Bingham stated that he would begin the Government's summation on Tuesday, June 27. On the appointed day, however, Sanford Conover was brought back to Washington. General Dix had pressured the Canadians into releasing Conover from jail in order to deal with the havoc he had created in Washington. Bingham delayed his eagerly awaited remarks in order to hear from Conover.

Judge Holt read to the Court the affidavit made by "Wallace" in Montreal and his reward offer. Conover's seared conscience did not hinder him from further duplicity. He testified unashamedly before the Military Commission that the "Wallace" statements were false and that the reward was not serious. Furthermore, he added, he had been forced, at gunpoint, to sign the affidavit and offer the reward. He also confessed that his original statements in behalf of the Rebels in the St. Albans trial were incorrect. The Court was already aware of these confusing explanations, but hearing Conover repeat them convinced the weary Commissioners that he was telling the truth.

Joseph Holt began to have some doubts, but he chose to protect himself rather than to pursue the facts rigorously. On hearing Conover's confession that his St. Albans trial testimony was incorrect, Holt read Conover's St. Albans statements from a recent newspaper and inquired what part was false. Conover reversed himself again, asserting that the news account was "substantially" correct. The paper made no mention of his service with the Confederate army—a fact which Holt also failed to bring up.

As an experienced lawyer, Holt should have known that according to Canadian legal procedure, Conover's testimony had to be written out and signed by him before being incorporated into the official St. Albans trial record. Conover, now swearing under oath that his previous Canadian testimony was false, failed to explain why such errors were not amended before he signed the statement.

After the Commission questioned several witnesses brought by Conover, they began to see through the sham. One witness, Dr. James Merritt, testified that Rebels in Canada knew what was going on in the conspiracy trial even before it was published.

"By whom were they being posted?" interjected General Wallace.

Merritt responded that the Confederates had "friends in court; who, I don't know; I did not take for granted it was any member of the court."[14] This brought a little nervous laugh from the officers.

After examining Conover's witnesses, Holt dispatched Conover back to Canada to get an official copy of the St. Albans record. Why he sent a suspected perjurer several hundred miles for evidence he could have easily obtained by cabling the American ambassador, he never explained.

The Judge then announced that the Government had terminated its testimony and that his assistant, Judge Advocate Bingham, would deliver the closing statement. Ordinarily this important responsibility would have been performed by Holt as Judge Advocate General, but Stanton wanted Bingham for the task. Bingham at first protested that he was not up to the demand, but Stanton insisted. It took Bingham two days to present his summation. To his friends, it was brilliant; to the opposition, it appeared verbose.

Bingham systematically and legalistically argued for the legitimacy of the military tribunal. He based his impressive arguments on the Constitution, as well as on historic precedence.

Bingham admitted that civil courts were open in the District of Columbia, but only because of 50,000 Union bayonets. Furthermore, the military had carried out the whole process of preparing for the trial. The assassins could not have been arrested by a strictly civil process. They were pursued and arrested by military force, which would have been unthinkable except in time of war. Only the laws of war gave the President power to use military force in detaining civilians. Those same laws, according to Bingham, gave the President the authority to judge and execute civilians.

General Ewing, he said, had even tried and punished civilians in military courts and enforced martial law. Bingham asked rhetorically if the General placed himself under the "same stern judgment which he invokes against others." He did not settle the question absolutely, but his presentation was convincing.

Whether the Military Commission was strictly legal under the circumstances is still debated. But it was not clearly unconstitutional, and it did not open the floodgates for all kinds of abuses as some had prophesied.

Court adjourned before he finished his long argument, with the understanding that he would be heard the next day. On June 28, Bingham completed his 50-page summation, but Mrs. Surratt did not hear the Government's final arguments. She had been confined to her bed for several days.

Some observers were skeptical of her sickness, as she appeared to be the only prisoner who had not lost weight during the ordeal. President Johnson was also ill. Both of these infirmities came at convenient times and both may have had psychosomatic origins. They were, nevertheless, incapacitating.

Doster's arguments especially impressed Kautz, but he found Aiken's defense neither legal nor logical, though full of flowery language. He was also moved by Bingham's summation.

The evening before the Commission considered the sentences, General Denver visited Kautz. Their discussion lasted so long that Kautz returned to Denver's house to spend the night. Apparently Denver's strong objection to the military trial did not influence Kautz's decision.

The trial was over; all that remained was the verdict. The trial had lasted seven weeks. The prosecution examined 196 witnesses; 166 were questioned by the defense. Nearly 100 witnesses summoned failed to appear, most called by the defense. Court recorders filled more than 4,000 legal-size manuscript pages.

The trial did not demonstrate great legal expertise. Lawyers for both the prosecution and the defense were mediocre legal minds except for Reverdy Johnson and, to a lesser degree, Thomas Ewing. The Government could have presented a stronger case. Several important witnesses were not called such as the unnamed man in John Lloyd's carriage when he talked with Mrs. Surratt.

The Government never called Metropolitan Police Chief A. C. Richards. The War Department, jealous of Richards' early success, apparently did not want to hear about his investigation. Authorities did not fully investigate Booth's visits to Mrs. Surratt, either at noon or in the evening on the day of the murder. The questions and cross-examinations were often weak. In addition to its lack of legal thoroughness, the Government was negligent in its effort to apprehend John Surratt.

The defense counsel efforts were frequently inept, partly because most able lawyers refused the cases. Those who accepted the challenge failed to take aggressive advantage of what little opportunity they had. They could have questioned Weichmann's testimony about the time sequence in his getting the carriage for Mrs. Surratt's last trip to Lloyd's (lawyers did in a later trial).

The military nature of the court caused part of the problem. Another was the trial's speed. Eight defendants were tried in seven weeks. The hopelessness of the defense, as well as a sense of certainty on the part of the prosecution, led to carelessness. The prosecution foresaw no insurmountable problems. They did not have to convince an entire jury—only two-thirds of the Military Commission.

The public, however, was the final arbiter. Citizens eagerly devoured daily accounts in major newspapers throughout the North and Northeast, at least during the first few weeks. This audience had to be convinced, even if the military leaders did not. Fortunately for the Government, their strongest arguments came in the first days when more newspapers carried the entire proceedings.

When it was over, defense attorney Frederick Stone admitted that it "was a fair court and one of ability." He declared that Judge Holt "was a very able man. The court was courteous toward the defense." The lawyer concluded that the Government had performed its duty in drawing "the lines of justice pretty well."[15]

XLII
After Mature Consideration

The prosecution had presented the evidence, examined witnesses and delivered summation arguments, but the Commission still had to consider the findings and determine the punishment. The military tribunal took its responsibility seriously, knowing its decision would be the target of many editorials.

The Commission had been criticized from the beginning. Democrat newspapers produced the most criticism, although some came from Republican papers such as Horace Greeley's *New York Tribune*. The Court, ever-conscious of its critics, might have tried to relieve the pressure by handing out mild sentences. Yet, the senseless murder of the President and the bloody assault on the Secretary of State were borne of war hatreds. The military trial was an outgrowth of the Civil War, and the generals' attitudes reflected that fact. These battle-hardened leaders had seen men tried by courts-martial and hanged for less.

At 11:00 A.M., June 29, the Commission sat, as usual, in the courtroom of the Arsenal Penitentiary. A court official read the proceedings of the previous day and then cleared the room except for the nine Commissioners, Judge Advocate Holt and his two assistants. There were no prisoners, no spectators, no reporters, not even a court stenographer present. Guards locked the doors and took their stations at all entrances.

Exactly what went on in that large room during the next two days will never be fully known. Those present were sworn to secrecy and, as far as is known, kept their oath. A few pages from Judge Holt's personal papers reveal little more than the final decisions and the order in which they were discussed.

Deliberations began with the consideration of David Herold's case—the Government's strongest. Determining his sentence set the norm for those that followed.

The charges against Herold were read systematically and voted on one by one. The Commissioners considered each charge, noting at what points it considered the accused guilty or innocent.[1] The sentence as later read to the prisoner stated that:

> After mature consideration of the evidence adduced in the case of the accused, DAVID E. HEROLD, the Commission finds the said accused ... of the specification ... Guilty except combining confederating and conspiring with Edward Spangler, as to which part thereof
> ....NOT GUILTY.
> Of the Charge................................GUILTY.
> ....

436

Commissioners became more casual and relaxed in the courtroom as the trial progressed.

> And the Commission do, therefore, sentence him, the said David E. Herold, to be hanged by the neck until he be dead, at such time and place as the President of the United States shall direct; two-thirds of the Commission concurring therein.[2]

This first sentence gave an ominous portent of what was to follow. Exactly how much time the Generals spent deliberating Herold's sentence is not known. However, they considered evidence on seven suspects the first day, after starting deliberations around noon. Evidently they deliberated about an hour on each suspect. They considered the cases of Atzerodt and Payne next, in that order, both resulting in the same sentence—death by hanging.

In the final printed order, the Government listed Mrs. Surratt next. This was not, however, the order in which the Court actually considered her case. The Commission apparently first determined those it thought more certain to receive the death penalty. Herold, Payne and Atzerodt were never given much chance of escaping the noose. That Mrs. Surratt was sentenced next to last indicated the dilemma her case posed. The Court deliberated Dr. Mudd's case last; evidently it was even harder. Both he and Mrs. Surratt had constantly been given special treatment. When the moment of decision arrived, the generals observed this same deference.

After Payne, the Court considered O'Laughlin, Spangler and Arnold, in that order. They gave O'Laughlin and Arnold life sentences; Spangler got off with a six-year prison term.

Then came Mary Surratt's turn. As in the other cases, her sentence was preceded with the following: "After mature consideration of the evidence adduced,..." The Military Commission sentenced Mary E. Surratt "to be hanged

by the neck until she is dead, at such time and place as the President of the
United States shall direct; two-thirds of the members of the Commission con-
curring therein."[3]

The original indictment against Mrs. Surratt accused her of "maliciously,
unlawfully and traitorously" aiding the existing rebellion; conspiring with
Booth and the other prisoners, and also with Jefferson Davis and other Confederate leaders. The specific charge accused her, along with all the suspects,
of being part of the "traitorous conspiracy" which began around March 6 and
ended with the "discharge of a pistol then held in the hands of him, the said
Booth, the same being then loaded with powder and a leaden ball, against and
upon the left and posterior side of the head of the said Abraham Lincoln." The
charge pointedly described Lincoln not only as President of the United States,
but as Commander-in-Chief of the army and navy.[4]

The charge that she or any of the conspirators were working under orders
from Jefferson Davis or his Canadian colleagues was never conclusively proved.
The additional charge that she did on various days between February and
April "receive, entertain, harbor and conceal, aid and assist, the said John
Wilkes Booth" and other conspirators was clearly proved.[5]

That she did so "with intent to aid, abet, and assist them in the execution
thereof, and in escaping from justice after the murder of said Abraham Lincoln" there can be no doubt.[6] There may be, however, some doubt that Mrs.
Surratt had "knowledge of the murderous" intent of the conspirators. It was
this point that she continually stressed.

Almost certainly the conspirators spoke the truth when they admitted being involved in the plot to abduct, but denied knowledge of the plan to kill
Lincoln until a few hours before the assassination. From the time of their capture to the moment of execution, the prisoners were not allowed to converse
freely with one another. It is unlikely they would all have invented the same
story, although it made a logical alibi.

How much Mrs. Surratt understood about the final decision to kill the Nation's leaders may never be known. However, she knew more than the others
on trial. She was more astute than Atzerodt and Payne and certainly more
mature than any of them. When she learned, on the Tuesday before the
assassination, that Booth had sold his buggy, she had a clear signal that kidnap
plans had been abandoned. The only purpose of the buggy, according to the
conspirators, was the abduction of Lincoln. Any plans made without the
buggy had to be radically different. No one who knew Mary Surratt or even
followed the trial would accuse her of being unintelligent of gullible. She had
made her way in a man's world: managing a small inn with its tavern and post
office, taking care of her property in Washington, and getting along without
a husband in the rough, uncertain war years. She constantly denied participation in, or knowledge of, the plot to kill the President. Did this denial mean
that she did not pull the trigger?

The conspirators were unanimous in self-justification. Booth, even in the
darkest hours before his capture, was amazed that he had not been hailed a
hero. In his distorted mind, he imagined his bloody deed to have been a

sacrificial act in behalf of his country. Payne showed no remorse for what he considered his soldier's duty—no different from his murderous charge at Gettysburg.

The conspirators were also ready liars. Surprised by Union officers at the Surratt house in the middle of the night, with a pickax on his shoulder, Payne's natural response was to lie. He had come to dig a ditch, he declared without hesitation. Mrs. Surratt called on God as her witness when she swore that she had never seen Payne before. If she did not deliberately deceive, she was certainly mistaken.

Twisting the facts or imagining the circumstances in such a way as to convince themselves of innocence characterized the accused. All the conspirators pleaded not guilty to every charge. Obviously they had not expected such an extensive pursuit of the evidence. They surely had not expected that their private conversations and every suspicious movement would be examined closely by the Court and published throughout the land.

Thus, what the public viewed as conclusive guilt, Mary Surratt may have imagined to be innocence. The only thing she could possibly have been innocent of was an absolutely clear knowledge of the plot to murder at least four major heads of the United States Government, although she certainly knew that the plot involved several conspirators in violent actions. She had asked Lloyd to get the "shooting irons" ready—meaning rifles for more than one. It is barely conceivable that she was unaware of the details of the plot. Yet, by the admission of numerous witnesses, she spent many hours in private conversation with the assassin. Even her assistance in aiding the assassin's escape was more than enough to send her to the gallows.

She may have been ignorant of the law, which declares all directly participating in a conspiracy are responsible for the acts of each member. But this precept seems to have been common knowledge. Even the sluggish Atzerodt understood Booth's threat that he was in deep enough to be hanged. Any conspiracy to overthrow the Government during a time of war carried the death penalty, even if assassination were not involved. One man was even hanged for tearing down the American flag.

The Commission reviewed Dr. Samuel Mudd's case last. But because of the late hour, the generals agreed to meet the next day, June 30, at 11:00, to finish their deliberations. At the appointed time all members were present in addition to Judge Holt and his assistants Burnett and Bingham. They dealt promptly with Mudd's case, finding him guilty and sentencing him to life imprisonment.

Frederick Stone, Mudd's lawyer, stated later that the doctor gave "his whole case away by not trusting even his counsel or neighbors or kinfolks." Stone admitted that while Dr. Mudd denied knowing Booth, he actually "knew him well."[7] It was a preposterous denial when Booth had been in the doctor's house and had been seen in his company on several occasions by many witnesses. Stone recalled that the Government had made it clear that punishment would be death for anyone who withheld information. Years later the lawyer's views were echoed by Thomas Jones, the Confederate agent who helped

Booth escape. Jones affirmed that "there is no doubt but that in this original scheme [to kidnap the President] the late Dr. Samuel A. Mudd was to play some part."[8] Also some of Mudd's relatives acknowledged that the doctor was well acquainted with the assassin and that Mudd was probably part of the abduction plans.[9]

Mudd was saved from the gallows by one vote. The vote was 5 to 4 in favor of hanging him, but it took a two-thirds majority to apply the death penalty.[10]

If the death sentences had been handed down merely to satisfy the public demand for vengeance, the Commissioners could have satisfied it by one or two hangings. They might have hanged Payne and Herold as a good compromise. Payne was ready to die—few would cry over him. Herold was indifferent—he could be dispensed with, if necessary. Herold, like Payne, was young and unmarried. Both were undeniably guilty. If the Court were playing a political game with lives, that might have been the best option. If the cry for blood was stronger, they could have included Atzerodt, another lonely, insignificant man who would scarcely be missed. He was not a family man either. There was no reason—apart from justice—to hang Mrs. Surratt or imprison Dr. Mudd.

The verdicts were void of discrimination. During the trial itself, officials made distinctions in the treatment of the prisoners—the well-educated and prosperous Samuel Mudd they treated with greater consideration than the brutish, unlearned Atzerodt. Nevertheless, when the Court made its judgment, Mudd's sentence was not more severe than the evidence warranted, although in the minds of the majority, he should have been hanged with the other four.

In Mrs. Surratt's case, her special treatment was more obvious. As has been noted, while other prisoners were bound hand and foot with irons, she was not shackled in any way. Guards sat by the side of every prisoner except Mrs. Surratt. As the trial progressed and Mary Surratt appeared ill, authorities moved her from her original cell to a larger, more comfortable one, and her daughter was permitted to remain with her.

Like Dr. Mudd, she made a concerted effort to separate herself from her rough-looking companions. Other suspects had to face the unceasing glare of curious spectators while Mrs. Surratt was permitted to hide her face.

If preferential treatment was obvious during the trial, it was absent in the verdict. Many had expected Mrs. Surratt to be given special consideration, but on this point, the Commission was surprisingly modern. Equal guilt would require equal punishment, regardless of age or sex, the later mercy plea notwithstanding.

The military men found Spangler innocent of both the specification and the charge. But they judged him guilty, nonetheless, of "feloniously and traitorously" helping Booth escape.

The sentences were signed by Judge Advocate General Holt, President of the Commission Hunter, and by Assistant Judges Advocate Bingham and Burnett.

Before Holt dismissed the Commission, several officers suggested that

Gen. James Ekin suggested a recommendation of mercy in behalf of Mrs. Surratt. He wrote the clemency plea and was one of five Commissioners signing it. (Engraved by J. C. Buttre, Library of Congress.)

special consideration be given to Mrs. Surratt. No woman had ever been condemned to death by the United States Government. The war-weary officers
were conscious of the inevitable outcry against their decision. Five recon-
sidered the burden of hanging the widow they had just declared guilty, and
recommended clemency.

They drew up a petition stating that:

> The undersigned members of the Military Commission detailed to try Mary
> E. Surratt and others for the conspiracy and the murder of Abraham Lincoln,
> late President of the United States, do respectively pray the President, in con-
> sideration of the sex and age of the said Mary E. Surratt, if he can upon all
> the facts in the case, find it consistent with his sense of duty to the country
> to commute the sentence of death to imprisonment in the penetentiary for
> life.[11]

This slip of paper, signed by Hunter, Kautz, Foster, Ekin and Tompkins,
they attached to the findings and forwarded to President Johnson. It became
the most controversial document of the entire case.

The only personal account of the final meetings comes from Kautz's diary.
He noted that the Commissioners got along very well; there was little or no
disagreement on the sentences.

Mrs. Surratt's defenders later spread a false report that the Commissioners agreed beforehand to save her life by passing a death sentence and then adding the recommendation for clemency. If the Court had wanted to save Mrs. Surratt, they could have done what they did for Dr. Mudd—simply recommend a life sentence. The evidence, however, so conclusively placed her in the center of the plot that it was difficult to punish her less than Atzerodt or Herold. To escape the dilemma, the Commissioners sentenced the widow to death, thereby satisfying the demands of justice, and then allowed those who wished to sign a recommendation of clemency to the President. It seems they wanted to spare themselves public reproach for hanging a woman. The petition placed the final decision on the President; they could blame him.

The clemency note made no suggestion of innocence, but rather sanctioned mercy because of her "age and sex." However, she was only 42, although some reporters estimated her age as 45, or even 60. Not all favored clemency, and four refused to sign.

Judge Advocate General Holt, having finished his unpleasant commitment, announced there was no further business before the Commission and it adjourned *sine die*. If the generals thought it was all over, they were mistaken—especially Holt.

The Court recorded the sentences and, along with the recommendation for clemency, passed them to General Burnett. He guarded the findings, being careful not to reveal any information to court reporters. When Burnett arrived at his office on July 1, he attached the mercy plea to the end of the Court's findings and personally carried the papers to Judge Holt.[12]

Having completed his duty, Kautz had a photograph made for one of his girl friends, Sophie. His most urgent desire was to get out of Washington, and he began packing immediately, leaving on July 2. Kautz was not around for the executions. In spite of his slight interest in Sophie, he wasted no time in getting things patched up with Charlotte Tod. Within two weeks, she announced her willingness to marry him, and in less than six months, they were married.

The Court had been faithful to its task. Of the 12 members (nine on the Commission and three Judges Advocate), only one missed any session. He was absent only one or two days because of severe illness. But the Commissioners took no pleasure in the duties of justice. None attended the executions. A few, such as Burnett and Kautz, left town. Most stayed in Washington, but they had no desire to view the results of their decisions. Nor did they want to be pointed out as the men who decreed hanging a woman.

By July 3, rumor leaked that all prisoners had been found guilty. As members of the Court had been sworn to absolute secrecy until the official announcement could be made, this rumor must have been mere conjecture or come from secondhand sources. The report, while technically true, did not take into account differences in the sentences.

The first Independence Day celebration of the reunited states should have been an extravaganza, but the 4th was surprisingly subdued. P. T. Barnum spoke in Bridgeport, and a preacher gave an oration in Brookline, Connecticut. Mobs hanged Jefferson Davis in effigy in the once-rebellious city of Baltimore.

In New Orleans there were two celebrations—one held by hard-core Rebels in the Mechanics' Institute, and another directed by the Republican Party at the Customs House. Fireworks lighted Washington skies, but the only rousing orations came from the Colored National Monument Association. Frederick Douglass told a crowd south of the White House that the only way to settle racial problems was to give blacks voting rights. Sickness prevented President Johnson from attending the laying of a cornerstone for a soldiers' monument at the Gettysburg battlefield.

Even during the holiday festivities, petitioners besieged the ailing President. Mrs. Alexander Stephens stood among scores clamoring for his help. She sought a pardon for her husband, the former Vice President of the Confederacy. One group requested an audience in behalf of William Cozens, whose case was before a military court. They wanted it transferred to civil courts. Unsuccessful in gaining an audience, they deluged the President with telegrams.

Andrew Johnson's Reconstruction policies caused him the greatest concern. Petitioners with widely diverse sentiments advised him on the rights of blacks. Thaddeus Stevens warned Johnson that his restoration policy would "destroy the party and hurt the country."[13] Stevens wanted the President to leave Reconstruction to the Congress.

From the moment Johnson moved into the White House early in June, he did not step outside its doors until after the executions. Stanton's warnings of more conspiracies may have frightened the President, but throngs of visitors, well-wishers and petitioners kept him busy inside. He had little time for anything else.

By the first week of July, Johnson was exhausted and ill. He had to cancel most official duties and even postponed reviewing the verdicts of the Military Commission for several days. Governmental pressures and overwork related to the trial also indisposed Stanton.[14]

Between the trial and the executions, President Johnson received very few appeals in behalf of the conspirators, an indication that the Nation supported the rumored verdict. One complaint, however, came from Thomas Ewing, Sr. Even though he aided his son's defense, he was one of few men who might have influenced the President. He had previously advised Johnson that the military trial was unconstitutional. A few hours before the President was to review the Court's decision, Ewing appealed to him not to sign the trial documents. In the shaky, uncertain penmanship of an old man, Ewing reiterated his view that there was no possible legal foundation for the military court and predicted that the Commissioners would be criticized in the future. "You, I think, have never sanctioned by your signature the finding and sentence of these Commissioners against anyone not a spy—not taken in arms," the veteran statesman wrote.[15]

Ewing claimed that everyone knew that although the Commission was appointed in Johnson's name, the War Department set it up. "It is now in your power to set this matter right at once by dissolving all military commissions appointed to try civilians . . . set aside all their unexecuted sentences and transfer all the cases to the regular judicial tribunal."[16]

The next day, July 5, President Johnson requested the Commission's report.

That morning Judge Holt carefully briefed him at the White House. He was the only person to see the President on business that day. Guards were ordered not to allow anyone to disturb the discussion. Visitors were referred to the President's private secretary, Gen. R. D. Mussey, who handled their requests. More important matters were postponed until later.

After the meeting, Judge Holt went directly to Stanton's office with the President's decision. Burnett was in the Secretary's office when Holt arrived. After a few preliminary greetings, Holt remarked that he had just come from a conference with the President about the findings of the Court.

"Well," demanded Stanton anxiously, "what had he done?"

Holt replied that the President believed that Mrs. Surratt should be punished with the rest. Johnson felt that the request for clemency was based only on her sex and age. The President thought that everyone should learn that "if women committed crimes they would be punished." Otherwise, he reasoned, "hereafter conspirators and assassins would use women as their instruments. It would be a mercy to womankind to let Mrs. Surratt suffer the penalty of her crime."[17]

President Johnson remained secluded in the White House, refusing to see visitors until after the executions. He had been under a physician's care for several days. Reports indicated his health was improving, however.

On getting word of the President's decision, Major Eckert immediately sent for Capt. Christian Rath and ordered him to prepare for hanging four people. Eckert remarked, incidentally, that he thought only three would be executed. The sentences had not yet been made public.

Captain Rath, a novice at building gallows, made a crude sketch and put the Arsenal carpenters to work. What concerned the appointed hangman most was the rope. He determined to get one that would not break. The Captain decided on a ¾-inch 32-strand Boston hemp navy rope. Included in Rath's morbid responsibilities was preparation of four graves. Prison personnel, being superstitious, refused to dig them, so he detailed soldiers for the job.

Soon after the President approved the executions, General Hancock delivered the death warrants to General Hartranft. About noon, July 6, the two generals slowly climbed the steps to the second tier of cells on the north side of the Arsenal building. Their first stop was Cell 195. As gently as he could, Hartranft informed Payne of his fate. No others were present except a guard. Payne showed no emotion and said nothing.[18] He expected the decision. Perhaps Hartranft visited Payne's cell first because it was easier to inform him that he had only 24 hours to live than to tell the others. Even so, it was a gloomy task.

On the other side of the building on the same tier was Cell 161. When the death sentence was announced to its occupant, Atzerodt, he reacted profoundly, turning pale and quivering uncontrollably. He immediately requested his minister, his family and some friends. Since his confinement, only two people had come to see him—his brother and Marshal McPhail.

Still, that was two more visitors than Payne had received. Since his arrest no one had visited him. He later indicated that if any guests should come from

Baltimore, he would like them admitted. But he made it clear he would send for no one. Doster had summoned Payne's father from Florida, but he never came.

Next, the generals climbed to the third tier to inform Herold. He reacted nervously to the announcement and, drastically changing his previously frivolous attitude, begged for his family.

The last to be informed was Mrs. Surratt in Cell 200, also on the third level. Anna, who had been visiting her mother, had just left. Mrs. Surratt sat alone when the officers revealed her punishment. The devastating announcement had a greater effect on her than on the others. On hearing her sentence, especially the notice that the hanging was scheduled for the next day, the iron-willed woman broke down and wept. After recovering, she declared to the silent generals that she had "no hand in the murder of the President" and pleaded for more time. Then she requested that Father Wigget and Father Walter be sent for. In addition, she wanted to see John Brophy, a teacher at St. Aloysius School and her daughter. Anna was on her way out of the Arsenal when she heard of her mother's impending execution. She became so utterly overcome that soldiers had to remove her from the prison.[19]

On July 6th and 7th workers filled the Arsenal—carpenters building the scaffold, soldiers carrying lumber, and officers keeping a watchful eye from a vantage point in the shade. The most active place was the water pump where soldiers lined up to fill their canteens. On the west side of the Arsenal, troops lounged listlessly around twenty or more tents. They had just returned from Virginia where they had buried the dead of the Wilderness Campaign.

The suddenness of the proposed executions shocked the condemned prisoners. They had 24 hours to prepare for death. Two hours after they learned their fate, guards moved them to cells on the north side of a large cell block on the ground floor. They still did not occupy adjoining quarters, but were in the same general area.

The ground-floor room, approximately 30-feet square, around which the cells were located, was within hearing distance of workers busily constructing the gallows. Only one window, facing south, provided the little light that streamed past heavy bars. The ceiling, about 20 feet above the cement floor, permitted two tiers of cells on the northern end. Payne, Herold, Atzerodt and Mary Surratt awaited their fate in small cells on the lower tier, similar to those occupied by the male prisoners for more than two months. Mrs. Surratt had, for the last few weeks, occupied a more spacious and somewhat more comfortable room because of her physical condition.

Although physicians felt that Mary Surratt's sickness was not entirely physical, she was provided the best medical attention. Prior to this time her daughter had been with her almost constantly.

Sorrowful friends, relatives and clergymen soon filled the corridors and gloomy cells. Payne's only kin remained 800 miles away; as for friends, he had none, other than the Branson girls—and their fiery support had cooled. His closest associates, the guards, marveled at his endurance and uncomplaining nature. Doster tried to be a friend, which the prisoner seemed to appreciate.

When Doster visited in his new cell, he found Payne "crouched like a tiger at bay," his eyes red and glaring.[20] Payne could not pay his defense counsel, but he offered him all he had—a pocket knife. Doster declined the gift.

Authorities did not tell the other prisoners, Mudd, Arnold, Spangler and O'Laughlin, about the death decrees. They had a vague idea that some hangings were imminent but were left to guess their own fate. Sam Arnold imagined the executions were to take place in several stages and that those scheduled for July 7 were only the first with more to come. He feared that he and the others would be next.

In other areas of Washington, conditions were brighter. The War Department released Zebulon B. Vance, Confederate governor of North Carolina. He had originally opposed the secession of his state but later served as a colonel in the 26th North Carolina regiment. Eventually entering politics, he gained the title of war governor of the South because of his strong support of the Confederacy. At the War Department, Secretary Stanton was feeling better. He had recovered sufficiently to visit the President.

No strong sentiment existed in Washington concerning the accused before the sentences were known. A few people, however, questioned the military trial, particularly after Reverdy Johnson's summation argument. His widely published plea raised doubts about the trial's constitutionality.

Wild speculations had been spreading through the streets and hotels of the capital for several days. One rumor pictured President Johnson as dissatisfied with the military court and ready to order a new trial. Another story said that Secretary Stanton would resign on July 15. Most citizens, realizing that some decision had been made, became morbidly eager to know the outcome. When word of the findings leaked out, reporters mobbed War Department officers to get official confirmation.

The official report followed a few hours after the prisoners were informed. Evening papers splashed the news across front pages in bold type. The *Washington Star* published an extra edition. The *Washington National Republican* proclaimed that four of the conspirators were to be hanged, adding "Mrs. Surratt pleads for time." The *New York Tribune*'s headline read "PRISONERS FOUND GUILTY." The *Boston Advertiser* announced "ASSASSINS CONVICTED" and the *Philadelphia Inquirer* carried the simple headline, "JUSTICE!"

The published announcements created an immediate sensation. Animated discussions concerning the impending executions stirred the Northeast. The announcement in New York precipitated a spontaneous reaction. One Republican paper asserted that "every loyal man expressed himself satisfied with the verdict."[21] The *New York Tribune* reported a universal feeling of satisfaction with the judgments. Some even wondered why Spangler was not among those sentenced to hang.

A general feeling that the condemned were guilty mixed with apprehension about the haste of the executions. Some few still hoped the President would set aside the verdicts.

General Hartranft spent the afternoon sending for ministers and friends requested by the doomed conspirators. In his thoughtful, methodical way, he tried to make the prisoners' last hours reasonably quiet.

Stanton, too, tried to be helpful. He sent his assistant, Eckert, to the Reverend Dr. A. D. Gillette, pastor of the First Baptist Church in Washington, requesting that he visit the Arsenal to provide whatever spiritual consolation he could. Dr. Gillette readily agreed. The Secretary even dispatched his personal carriage to convey him to the Arsenal. Eckert presented the minister to the officers and then to the devastated inmates. But the prisoners had already made choices for pastors of their own denominations. Payne, the only Baptist among them, had eventually requested Dr. A. P. Stryker, an Episcopalian clergyman of Baltimore. But Dr. Stryker did not arrive until the next day, about an hour before the execution. He did, however, remain with the prisoner until the last moment. While the Episcopalian minister did not know Payne well, he had seen him at church several times with Mary Branson and had spoken to him at least once.

XLIII
Death Cells

A seemingly innocent event occurred early on the morning of July 6 which erupted in a dispute prolonged for decades. Before the Government had revealed the verdicts, the Reverend Father Jacob Walter arrived at the War Department seeking a pass to visit Mrs. Surratt. Gen. James A. Hardie, a convert to Catholicism, considered the priest's request.

Hardie, the 42-year-old Inspector General, had fought bravely in the Civil War before being brevetted Major-General. As assistant to the Secretary of War, Hardie had considerable influence. His ability to speak several languages, his broad education and courtly manners made him particularly helpful to Stanton. Hardie screened the throngs of visitors who daily sought audiences with the Secretary, deciding who would see him and diplomatically turning others away. Many, refused admittance to the Secretary's presence, were infuriated, but Stanton never reversed Hardie's decisions.

General Hardie received constant requests from Roman Catholics seeking favors on the basis of their mutual religion. One lady wrote that, because he was a Catholic, she wanted him to help get a position for her brother in the regular army. A Sister De Chuntel requested Hardie's intervention in behalf of one of her programs.[1] Archbishop John Purcell urged Hardie to use his influence to promote Henry Seton to Captain in the regular army.[2] Even Archbishop Martin J. Spaulding of Baltimore availed himself of Hardie's services, requesting his help in getting Union soldiers out of the property owned by the Sisters of Mercy in Fort Smith, Arkansas. Catholic priest Michael Farrea asked permission to visit Jefferson Davis in prison. The priest felt that Davis seemed much inclined to the Catholic Church.[3] The General was available and even anxious to render service to his adopted church.

In view of his helpful attitude, his public fuss with Father Walter seemed unlikely. The young priest did not know Mrs. Surratt personally, but, soon after her arrest, she sent for him. He refused to see her, claiming he did not want his name connected to the case until after the trial.[4] He paid little attention to the trial and did not seem aware of the enormous evidence against her. Before Mary Surratt knew the verdict, she again requested the priest. Hardie approved Father Walter's petition to visit the prisoner but had to request the pass from Stanton, who was out of his office. When Stanton returned, he authorized the pass but did not sign it. Hardie signed it and sent it to Father Walter.

Later, Hardie heard the President had approved the sentences and that Mrs. Surratt was to be hanged the next day. He realized that much tighter security would be enforced around the prison and feared the priest would not be admitted on his signature alone and would need a pass signed by the Secretary of War. The General dispatched a messenger to request Father Walter to wait until he could get a pass signed by Stanton. The messenger, an Irishman named Barry, tried to make it clear that the new pass would be offered only for the purpose of giving spiritual consolation.

Father Walter, assuming Barry to be a good Irish Catholic, began to lecture him on the widow's innocence. The clergyman based his reasoning on religious sentiment, with no reference to judicial evidence. He told Barry that no one could make him believe that a Catholic could go to church on Holy Thursday and commit murder on Good Friday. The young messenger, disturbed by the priest's emotional tirade, returned to General Hardie. He described the excited manner and language used by Father Walter. The General decided to call on the priest personally.

Taking the new pass, signed by Stanton, Hardie made his way to St. Patrick's Church. He informed Father Walter he was making this visit "as his well-wisher and as a friend of the Church," and entirely in a private capacity.[5] The General placed no restrictions on the priest's use of proper means to make his convictions known. But he admonished the earnest young cleric that potentially explosive conditions in Washington required unusual care and judgment. He cautioned that inflammatory remarks such as had been showered on Mr. Barry were unwise. Hardie, explaining that the previous pass might not be accepted by guards, offered the priest the other pass but stated that it must be used in good faith. The clergyman could employ all legal means to prove Mrs. Surratt's innocence. But he advised the clergyman not to abuse the privilege to spread his personal sentiments within prison walls.

Becoming increasingly agitated at the restrictions, Father Walter vehemently denounced the Government. He attacked what he called military tyranny in terms much stronger than "a prudent priest; a loyal citizen or a man of common sense" would have used.[6] Annoyed, the General warned him that he would not be allowed a pass if he did not promise to refrain from expressing his personal views on Mrs. Surratt's innocence. This brought forth another discourse by the priest on his responsibility to defend his flock and provide spiritual aid.[7]

Hardie turned to leave, feeling that the pastor was in no condition to provide proper religious counsel. He planned to send for another Catholic priest. Father Walter, realizing that his spiritual responsibilities were more important than his personal views, abruptly announced that he would refrain from making inflammatory statements. Hardie gave him the pass, and Father Walter kept his promise. Of course, he took every appropriate action to reach authorities in Mrs. Surratt's behalf and continued to agitate the question outside the prison.

The irate priest's superior, Archbishop Spaulding, helped calm the situation. After the clergyman had carried his fight to the public by publishing his

Left: As a faithful Catholic priest, Father Jacob A. Walter consoled Mrs. Surratt before her death. He continued, thereafter, to chastise the Government for her punishment. Right: James A. Hardie, Stanton's personal secretary. A prolonged dispute developed over Hardie's treatment of Father Walter (National Archives photo no. 158, Brady Collection).

version of the dispute in the *New York Tribune* and other papers, the Archbishop cautioned him to observe silence.[8] Before he was controlled, however, the priest had made a major issue of his efforts.[9]

His account, given to the press, varied from the facts. But Father Walter prolonged the controversy through newspapers, magazines and conferences for more than a quarter of a century, constantly changing his story.

On learning of the Court's findings, John F. Callan and John Holohan also sought Father Walter's help. That afternoon, the priest accompanied Anna Surratt and former Senator from Pennsylvania Thomas Florence, to the White House.[10] Florence, a Democrat, had been active in several reform movements before being elected to Congress. After his defeat in 1861, he retired from politics and began publication of a small Washington newspaper, the *Constitutional Union*. As a newspaper editor, he exerted some influence in the capital. Mrs. Surratt's supporters later used this paper extensively to proclaim her innocence.

In 1865 citizens could easily visit the White House for an interview with the President. No high iron fence surrounded the grounds, and the only guards stood inside the Presidential Mansion.

Preston King, a former Senator from New York, was a close friend of President Johnson. While serving as his White House deputy, he denied Anna Surratt's request to see the President (Library of Congress—BH82-5373).

Anna, Father Walter, and Florence ascended the stairs to a second-floor room next to the President's office. Preston King and Col. Reuben D. Mussey, the President's confidential secretary, met them. Father Walter demanded repeatedly to see the President; each time he was told to consult Judge Holt. He got the same negative results when he talked to Holt.[11]

A little later that day, after his unsuccessful attempt, Father Walter again called on Hardie for help. The General obligingly gave him a note addressed to the President's military secretary, requesting that the priest be given an audience with Johnson. Although the note was ineffective, at least Hardie made the effort.

Six months after this encounter, Preston King committed suicide by filling his pockets with rocks and jumping from a ferry into the Hudson River. Mrs. Surratt's sympathizers linked King's suicide to God's judgment on him for refusing to allow the priest to see President Johnson. Actually, King had been mentally unstable for years. As a close friend of the President and one who had helped him secure the vice-presidential nomination in 1864, King was a familiar figure around the White House, but he had little real influence. It was the President's secretary, Colonel Mussey, who, under orders, prohibited anyone from seeing the President. He was soon promoted to General.

At five o'clock that afternoon, July 6, Mrs. Surratt's lawyers, Frederick Aiken and John Clampitt, were in their office waiting for word on the verdicts when they were startled by the sound of newsboys yelling, "the execution of Mrs. Surratt."[12] The counsel expected an acquittal or, at most, a temporary confinement. The notice that Johnson had signed the death warrant so troubled the lawyers that they hardly knew what to do next. Perhaps more competent counselors would have been prepared for the death sentence, which many newspapers had predicted was inevitable. Apparently they relied too much on sentimentality.

Recovering from the jolt, they decided to go to the White House. They wanted to ask the President for a short reprieve for their client. Her spiritual advisers also hoped to gain for her a few days of life. Both lawyers and priests seemed to feel that the public's appetite for blood would be satiated with the execution of three men. If Mrs. Surratt could be reprieved until after the execution, her life might be saved.

This tactic probably would have worked. But the same maneuver could have been successful for any of the doomed prisoners, with the possible exception of Payne. If Herold's sisters had succeeded in their efforts to obtain a reprieve for him, there was a possibility he could have been saved. The same was true of Atzerodt. National sentiment did not demand four deaths. It did demand what it considered justice.

The question was one of relativity. Was the muddleheaded Atzerodt, who, once enticed into the crime, refused to cooperate when he realized it involved murder, more guilty than the woman, who, according to sworn testimony, promoted the conspiracy for several months. Or was Mary Surratt no more culpable than Arnold, who had relatively little to do with the planning and who left the conspiracy to take a job 100 miles away? Whatever the case of relative guilt, there was one huge factor in Mrs. Surratt's favor—she was a woman. If anyone were to be saved, it would probably have been she.

With this tactic in mind, the ever-ready Father Walter hurried back to the White House to see the President, this time accompanied by Frederick Aiken. They did not succeed. The President was adamant; he would see no one. The two did not even get up the steps. Walter and Aiken were met at the main door by King, who pointed to a guard of soldiers with fixed bayonets stationed at the foot of the staircase.

Mrs. Surratt was not the only conspirator represented at the White House that day. Herold's sisters also tried desperately to plead mercy for their brother, but with no more success.

One of the few communications sent to the President after announcement of the punishment was a telegram from James Miller, who requested a reprieve for David Herold. Another was an affidavit sent by the Surratts' close friend, John Brophy, seeking to impeach Weichmann's character.

Brophy's paper, received by the President, contained basically the same accusations Weichmann had already refuted several times—principally half-truths and distortions. In his first point he accused Weichmann of being a coward. His ninth charge stated that Mrs. Surratt cried when John went to Richmond. Number 13 noted that Weichmann had avoided the draft. Some allegations were false such as his second point asserting that Stanton had threatened Weichmann with death. The paper was hardly worthy of the President's time. Brophy could not have seriously believed that, after weeks of exhaustive investigation and thousands of pages of evidence, his rehashed charges had serious value. Perhaps he believed that his petition along with hundreds of others would have an effect. He probably never realized that his was one of only four or five appeals sent to Johnson supporting the condemned.

John Ford wrote one of these petitions. When Ford heard that Mrs. Surratt was to be hanged the next day, he stayed up all night writing to the President, urging him to suspend the death sentence until he could talk to him. About 3:00 A.M. Ford took a train from his home in Baltimore to Washington. Arriving in the Nation's capital, he hurried straight to the home of Montgomery Blair, who was still asleep.[13]

Blair, a Kentuckian, had served as Postmaster General in Lincoln's Cabinet but broke with the administration in 1864. At the time of the trial, he opposed the Government. Not being able to talk to Blair personally, Ford left his letter, imploring him to get it to the President as soon as possible. Ford then personally sought an audience with Johnson but found access to the Chief Executive blocked at every point. Blair, however, was able to get the petition to the President, but to no avail.[14]

Johnson and his advisers had much more evidence than the few prison rumors available to Ford. As the years passed, Ford repeated his belief in Mrs. Surratt's innocence, but the few elementary facts he presented were at variance with evidence presented before the Court. As late as 1889, Ford was still suggesting that those who knew something about the assassination might come forward to clear her name. No one did. On the contrary, all subsequent revelations further implicated her.

The President received several endorsements of his decision and a little contrary advice. Charles E. Sherman, who scribbled an illegible return address, wrote that he knew none of the prisoners but advised Johnson to read carefully Sections 2 and 3 of the Act of Congress of March 3, 1863, "before suffering the order for the execution...."[15]

The General Assembly of the United Presbyterian Church of North America supported the President and passed a resolution that traitors should be punished. The Assembly quoted Romans 13 and Ezra 7:26, "Whosoever will not do the law of thy God and the law of the King let judgment be executed speedily whether it be unto death or to banishment...." The Presbyterians obviously included leaders of the Confederacy as well as the conspirators. "Mercy to the great civil and military heads of this rebellion would be cruelty to coming generations," they advised.[16]

Father Walter persisted in his relentless efforts, but somewhat less energetically. In an interview with the editor of the *National Intelligencer*, John Coyle, he claimed he could say nothing as the War Department and Archbishop Spaulding had advised him to be silent. A timely visit by General Hancock brought about the muzzling of the clergyman. According to Father Walter, the War Department asked the Archbishop to forbid him to make any statements. This was not entirely accurate.[17]

The Surratt house at 541 H Street attracted large crowds. The Government closed the place after the arrests and stationed soldiers around it day and night. Guards permitted only persons with a pass from the War Department to enter. As daylight faded on July 6th, one light glowed faintly in an upstairs bedroom; the house itself was ominously quiet.

About eight o'clock a hack drove up to the front steps and Anna, accompanied by a gentleman (probably Mr. Holohan or Mr. Brophy), approached the deserted building. Anna appeared completely crushed as she climbed the steps and entered the front door; she almost fainted on several occasions, bringing tears to the eyes of curious spectators.

Large crowds of both young and old kept morbid vigil across the street until late that night. Some passers-by only wanted to catch a glimpse of the dwelling; others stood gazing at the mysterious residence. During the evening, at least 500 people visited the area. Washington has changed drastically since that time, but this troubled house still stands much as it did that night except that the outside steps Anna climbed have been removed. (At this writing it houses a Chinese restaurant.)

The melancholy scene at the Arsenal Penitentiary was heart-rending. A minister of his own Lutheran faith attended Atzerodt. Roman Catholic priests consoled Mary Surratt and an Episopalian minister talked to Herold. Although Stanton's call for Dr. Gillette may have seemed unnecessary, the Secretary wanted to avoid accusations that he was indifferent to spiritual needs.

One prisoner, not sentenced to hang, lived to cast doubt, however, on the Government's concern for their religious needs. Samuel Arnold, fearing he would be executed next, requested the busy Hartranft to obtain a Bible for him Hartranft informed Arnold's father, who secured a Bible through the YMCA, but Arnold complained that the condemned prisoners did not have enough time to read comforting Scriptures. However, the accused had spent several months in jail, allowing ample time to prepare for what was, at least for some, certain doom.

Dr. Gillette remained with the condemned all night, offering his services to each. All accepted his aid except Mrs. Surratt, who was well cared for by spiritual advisers. Dr. Gillette first called at Payne's cell. The lonely youth welcomed him and proceeded to tell the minister about his early life but revealed little more than what was already known. He confirmed that his father was a Baptist clergyman living at Live Oak Station, Tallahassee County, Florida. In addition to his two brothers, both killed fighting for the Confederacy, Payne had six sisters. None of his family came to his side or contacted him in any way. Payne finally revealed, for the first time, that he had enlisted in the

Confederate army at 16 and had been captured at Gettysburg. A youth of 20 (some accounts say 19), he had only a few hours to live.[18]

The muscular young man made special efforts to thank officers and guards for their kindnesses during his incarceration. He particularly desired the minister to inform Secretary of State Seward that he had no personal malice toward him. The attack, he confessed, was a matter of duty which he could not shirk. He was offered no pay for his bloody deed; the only compensation he expected was the approval of the Confederate Government. This twisted reasoning sounded darkly similar to Booth's explanation. Both expected their savage attacks would be widely praised in the South.

A death-cell statement by Payne — that the original plan was to capture and that assassination was not broached until the last moment — paralleled the testimony of other conspirators. This still left a question as to when Booth decided to kill Seward, Vice-President Johnson and General Grant. Most evidence pointed to a sudden change in plans a few days before the murder. The unexpected fall of the Confederacy, combined with Booth's compulsion to perform some spectacular deed, undoubtedly motivated this change. Even the personalities of the conspirators support this view. It is hard to imagine Atzerodt actually conspiring for weeks to kill the Vice-President.

Before leaving, Gillette asked who the other conspirators were. The unyielding youth still claimed ignorance of any names, although he thought that still others involved had not been apprehended. Booth, he confirmed, was the leading spirit. He sincerely regretted that his visit to the Surratt house brought suspicion on the landlady. He did not seem to realize that detectives had already arrested Mrs. Surratt before he arrived.

Payne informed the minister he had no conversation with Mrs. Surratt on the night of their arrest. It was a belated attempt to exonerate the widow and also avoid outright perjury. But like many witnesses', his words raised more questions than they answered. No one had claimed he had spoken to Mrs. Surratt that night; the crucial question was why he had chosen her house as a refuge.[19] In answer to this point, he explained to Dr. Gillette that he had wanted a suit of clothes to make his escape to Virginia. This disclosure still did not solve the problem. Why would this man, a casual boarder several weeks earlier, have expected to get a suit from a lady he hardly knew, especially when no one in the house matched his huge size?

Payne reserved his only denunciation for John Surratt, whom he condemned harshly. After more than an hour of earnest dialogue, Dr. Gillette left to console others.

The minister stopped next at the cell of David Herold. Herold's mother and six sisters were members of Christ Episcopal Church in Washington. He had already called for the family pastor, the Reverend Dr. Old. Nevertheless, Gillette spent a short time talking to the youth. Herold, having by this time composed himself, exhibited an attitude of careless indifference throughout the conversation, scarcely seeming to perceive his hopeless plight. Several of Herold's sisters were present. One of the older ones read to him from her prayer book. The Baptist minister offered a prayer, followed by another impassioned prayer by the same sister. Through it all, Herold remained untouched. In his conversation with Gillette, he confirmed Payne's account of the original plot to kidnap, insisting that his only part was to accompany Booth in the escape.[20] From all indications this was the only part the impressionable youth performed, although Booth had at first wanted him to assassinate Vice-President Johnson. In all of his death-cell justifications, he never made the slightest pretense to any mistaken identity. It would have been ludicrous, with his sisters by his side, to pretend he was not their brother, as some sensationalists have imagined.

Atzerodt could not, at first, name any clergyman to attend him. However, at Hartranft's suggestion, he requested the Reverend Dr. Butler, a clergyman of Atzerodt's Lutheran faith. Since it was not known when Dr. Butler could be present, the Baptist pastor offered his consolation early that evening. Atzerodt, acutely conscious of his fate, felt both the horror of the crime and of his approaching death. Every move and gesture indicated the fear which engulfed him. He appealed for more time to prepare for eternity. Like Mrs. Surratt and Herold, he continued to affirm his innocence. He admitted having been involved in the kidnap plot but vowed that when Booth suggested murder, he refused.

Atzerodt began to incriminate Mrs. Surratt, declaring bitterly that she was the cause of his ruin.[21] His denunciation was almost identical to that of John Lloyd. He acknowledged his worthlessness and wondered if his soul could be saved. The condemned man was terribly impressed with the divine retribution he faced and exhibited enormous fear of death. On the arrival of the Lutheran minister later that night, Atzerodt made his last confession, which newspapers later published. In it he strongly denounced John Surratt as having first involved him in the conspiracy.

This last confession matched earlier statements. In the first confession, he denounced Surratt and Booth and revealed, astonishingly, that both men had urged him from the beginning to assassinate Vice-President Johnson. Atzerodt left this part out of his last-hour confession. The Government hid his first statement for nearly 80 years presumably to perpetuate the Radicals' intimations that Vice-President Johnson was part of the conspiracy rather than its victim.

In several previous confessions, he had mentioned Mrs. Surratt's buggy ride with Confederate blockade-runners, the Slater woman and a Major Brown. He had previously declared pointedly that he thought Major Brown had nothing to do with the conspiracy. This remark, implying that Mrs. Slater, an associate of the Surratts, played a part in the plot, implicated Mary Surratt. His death-cell confession incriminated the widow even more.[22]

Atzerodt's words about the kidnap scheme were similar to the final statements of Payne and Herold which were later corroborated by John Surratt and Samuel Arnold. Undoubtedly in their last hours the convicted conspirators were getting close to the truth. But they seemed to miss the point — even a conspiracy to capture the President of the United States, in aid of the Rebellion, was punishable by death.

No word came from Mrs. Surratt's older son Isaac, who either remained unavailable in Texas or had fled to Mexico. He made no attempt to come to his mother's side. John Surratt acted even more cowardly. He disappeared in a priest's house in a little rural village outside Montreal. John later claimed that he tried to go to his mother's aid but found out about her death sentence too late.

Of the individuals involved in the Lincoln murder case, John Surratt was the most detestable. Other prisoners even condemned him. Witnesses repeatedly named John as co-leader of the conspiracy with Booth. One story circulated that John had promised to come to Washington to prove his mother's innocence if he could get immunity. The War Department supposedly turned down this offer. Whatever the case, Surratt remained safely hidden as his mother faced the gallows.

In the meantime, Mrs. Surratt's lawyers, continuing their frantic efforts, sought the aid of influential Washington personalities. This, too, failed. Still working feverishly as time grew shorter, her counselors met with her daughter. Together they approached Judge Holt to enlist his services. They thought that in the "unutterable woe of the poor girl, the pitying chords of sympathy might find a responsive echo in his heart...."[23] Kneeling before him, Anna tearfully begged Holt to implore the President for a three-day reprieve for her mother. The Judge eventually gave in. He told the group to meet him at the White House as soon as they could. Aiken had also submitted to Holt what the lawyer alleged to be important new testimony discovered after the trial and which he claimed would prove Mrs. Surratt's innocence.

The "new" evidence was the often-refuted list of accusations brought by John Brophy against Weichmann. It was not new to Holt, who knew Brophy's character and Weichmann's detailed denials, nor was it new to the President. Holt, nevertheless, took Brophy's statements to the President and gave him an evaluation of the so-called new evidence.

As Holt was leaving Johnson's office, the widow's supporters arrived. He declared flatly, "I can do nothing; the President is unmovable."[24] The Judge then informed the little group that the President had carefully examined the findings of the Commission and saw no reason to change the date of the executions.

The lawyers would not give up. Darkness already obscured the dirt streets when they decided to telegraph Sen. Reverdy Johnson at his home in Baltimore, requesting that he hurry to Washington to help stay the executions. A little before midnight the Senator wired back that it was late and there were no trains from Baltimore to Washington. (There were trains available, however, and John Ford was on one.) The Senator advised his colleagues to apply for a writ of habeas corpus and then take Mrs. Surratt bodily from the custody of military authorities.

This strategy had recently been tried successfully in Philadelphia. William Cozens, who, like Mrs. Surratt, was a civilian arrested by the military, applied for a writ of habeas corpus. His case was then transferred to the civil courts. Newspapers carried accounts of the Cozens case not only in Philadelphia, but also in Baltimore and Washington. While major differences distinguished the cases, Senator Johnson thought the tactic worth a try. But it was late; furthermore, the Surratt lawyers were not certain to whom they should apply for the writ. They knew that for any judge to defy the power of the military was risky. Even so, they began to prepare the petition.

The clock had already chimed the midnight hour. It was now July 7 – the day appointed for the hangings.

The legality of Lincoln's interrupting temporarily the habeas corpus writ was of crucial concern. Lincoln, true to his nature, was hesitant to take away personal liberties. But in the spring of 1861, he was faced with secessionist leaders in Maryland and surrounding Confederate states, thus isolating the national capital. In this dilemma, he had invoked suspension of the writ.[25]

Although the Constitution provides for setting aside habeas corpus when the public safety is threatened, a loud outcry arose against the President's action. It is not absolutely clear from the Constitution whether the President can act alone. Chief Justice of the United States Supreme Court, Roger Taney, a Maryland slaveholder, declared that the President did not have that authority. Taney felt that Congress alone possessed such power. The best legal minds on both sides ably argued the question. Surprisingly, Sen. Reverdy Johnson supported Lincoln in his controversial action.

The President first set aside the writ within military lines between New York and Philadelphia; later in successive stages, he extended the suspension. Before Lincoln could get Congressional approval for his action, Secretary Stanton on August 8, 1862, issued a similar statement on his own authority. Stanton's order further declared that anyone arrested for disloyalty would be tried by a Military Commission.

Several weeks later, on September 24, President Lincoln issued a more inclusive decree, ordering:

1. That, during the existing insurrection, and as a necessary measure for suppressing the same, all rebels and insurgents, their aiders and abettors, within the United States, and all persons discouraging volunteer enlistments, resisting militia drafts, or guilty of any disloyal practice, affording aid and comfort to the rebels against the authority of the United States, shall be subject to martial law, and liable to trial and punishment by court-martial or military commission.
2. That the writ of *habeas corpus* is suspended in respect to all persons arrested, or who are now, or hereafter during the rebellion shall be imprisoned in any fort, camp, arsenal, military prison, or other place of confinement, by any military authority or by sentence of any court-martial or military commission.[26]

In spite of Lincoln's kindly disposition, he felt that his first responsibility as President was to preserve the Union. On March 3, 1863, the United States Congress authorized the President to ban temporarily the writ when necessary for public safety. In the summer of 1863, obstructions to the draft became so serious that Stanton wrote to Lincoln, suggesting something be done to correct the problem. Within a few days the President issued a proclamation suspending the writ of habeas corpus throughout the entire country.

Andrew Wylie, justice of the supreme court of the District of Columbia. Wylie signed the writ of habeas corpus in behalf of Mrs. Suratt. (L. C. Handy Studios, Washington, D.C.)

At no time in American history has the suspension of habeas corpus embraced such a large territory or involved so many people. Lincoln's proclamation made citizens affording aid and comfort to Rebels against the authority of the United States, liable to trial in military courts. This made it possible to deal with obstruction of the draft but brought forth a clamor against the Government because of "arbitrary arrests." Those who backed Lincoln, however, thought that the suspension "was one of the most important executive acts of the war."[27]

Mrs. Surratt's attorneys worked late into the night preparing the writ of habeas corpus. They finished the petition shortly before two in the morning. It stated that Mrs. Surratt had been held by a military power since her arrest on April 17 and had been tried unlawfully by a Military Commission. Furthermore, the writ declared that she was being unlawfully detained by the military although she was a private citizen. Aiken and Clampitt signed the application and rushed to the house of Judge Andrew Wylie, of the Supreme Court of the District of Columbia.

Wylie was a Northerner residing in Alexandria, Virginia, when Lincoln became President. It was said he was the only man living in Alexandria who voted for Lincoln. Always an individualist, Wylie's open stand for Lincoln made him the subject of severe threats. After Lincoln's first election, a shot broke a glass the Judge held while sitting on his front porch. Soon after this incident, he moved from Alexandria to Washington. In 1863, Lincoln nominated Wylie to serve on the newly created Supreme Court of the District of Columbia. Stanton, a friend of the future Justice, influenced Lincoln's selection. For some reason, the Senate did not confirm his nomination, although it approved other Justices nominated by the President. Later, while the Senate was adjourned, the President commissioned Wylie as a recess appointment.

Wylie frequently dissented from the majority but consistently supported the oppressed. His vote regarding the return of a runaway slave named Hall was an example. The District Supreme Court was often called upon to return fugitive slaves, even while the war was raging to free them. Lincoln's Emancipation Proclamation applied only to slaves in the states in rebellion and did not apply to Northern or border states such as Maryland. Most Justices felt that Hall, a runaway slave from Maryland, should be returned to his master because of the fugitive slave law. Wylie, along with one other Justice, believed that the slave law was not applicable in Washington and that Hall should be freed. In the dispute that followed, Wylie fought to win the decision which allowed Hall to go free.[28]

Armed with their petition, Aiken and Clampitt tried to rouse the venerable old Judge. After hearing the door bell, Wylie stuck his head out of an upper-story window to ask what they wanted. The lawyers called back that they needed help of a judicial nature which could save a life. In a few minutes the Judge invited the counselors into his gas-lit parlor. The Judge, clad in his dressing robe, listened without comment as the lawyers read the petition. At the conclusion, with scarcely a word, Wylie asked for the papers and retired to another room. For several anxious moments the attorneys thought the Judge was going to reject their appeal. He soon returned, however, stating that he would sign the writ. But he warned that signing the petition might consign him to Old Capitol Prison.

His fears were exaggerated. In several recent cases, judges had defied the military by issuing similar writs. They were usually unsuccessful, but the judges themselves were always respected and never in danger. Wylie's endorsement required that Mrs. Surratt be brought before the District Supreme Court. The counselors hurriedly, yet fervently, thanked the daring Judge. They carried the papers to the clerk of the court, who made out the official writ.

Time became a crucial factor. It was 4:00 A.M., and still dark, when they delivered the writ to the United States marshal. The lawyers requested that it be delivered as soon as possible to General Hancock, Commander of the military district. Marshal David S. Gooding, complying with his duty, handed the writ to the General at the Metropolitan Hotel about 8:30 that morning.

After public announcement of the sentences, requests to attend the hangings deluged the War Department. The Government was anxious, however, to keep the executions a comparatively quiet affair. While it was impossible to exclude all the curious, officials made an effort to limit spectators. They admitted no one to the Arsenal grounds without a pass signed by General Hancock.

Members of the press had no trouble getting passes, but others found it difficult. The War Department received over 1,000 applications for admission. Hancock carefully reviewed them to make certain no one with strong Southern sympathies would be admitted. In addition, he rejected those known to have sought admission for mere curiosity. The Government issued about 100 passes—about one-fourth to reporters.

When Anna, exhausted and dejected, returned to the Arsenal Prison the night before the hangings, she found a scene of tragic activity. Officers and soldiers were swarming over the area preparing, in one way or another, for the executions. Family members, pastors and priests were offering what consolation they could. Pitiful and desperate scenes were being enacted in each cell. Dr. Gillette had finished his rounds but remained close by.

The sight of anguished sisters weeping over David Herold was particularly moving. Two were grown women; the others, younger ladies, but all were grief stricken. Throughout the ordeal, they remained tenderly attentive to their brother's needs. One brought a small basket of cakes and candies which General Hartranft had to examine before it was allowed in the cell. As they left late that night, they were sobbing uncontrollably. One of the older sisters quickly wrote a short note to her unconcerned brother and asked Hartranft to deliver it. Herold's nephew, a boy about 16, stayed behind to accompany him through the night.

The arrival of Atzerodt's aged mother was a scene of great sorrow and tenderness. The meeting of the terrified and confused son with his brokenhearted mother touched the hardened guards. Even though they had witnessed countless scenes of this sort, they could not contain their tears. There was something especially pitiful about this immigrant who never seemed to have had a chance and his grieving mother

Later that evening, an unidentified woman dressed in deep mourning visited Atzerodt. She carried a prayer book and seemed deeply concerned. The anonymous lady left after midnight, weighed down with sorrow.[29] Unaware of Atzerodt's romantic attachment, reporters described the mysterious visitor as his mother or sister. More likely it was Mrs. Wheeler, the woman he had been living with for years and the mother of his child.

Authorities gave Anna, who was now almost hysterical, permission to spend the last night with her mother. Fathers Wigget and Walter and also John Brophy remained there part of the night. Mary Surratt was a changed woman. Gone was her cool, detached attitude; she became completely distraught. She slept very little, if at all, requiring almost constant attention, suffering cramps and other pains all night.

Dr. Gillette returned to Payne's cell late that evening. After spending most of the night conversing with the minister, Payne slept reasonably well for about three hours. He changed slightly in his last hours. Under Dr. Gillette's care, he showed some spiritual interest. Although he maintained his stoic composure, he listened as the minister counseled with him about his eternal destiny.

Throughout the night guards could hear low, indescribable sounds of sorrow, consolation and confession, mingled with soft sobs and occasional uncontrollable outbursts of anguish. After midnight the darkened cells gradually grew quiet. Still, the soft whispers of spiritual counselors revealed heartfelt concern. Dr. Butler continued his efforts to console Atzerodt. Several priests spent much of the night with Mrs. Surratt and Anna, murmuring priestly consolation. After Herold's sisters left, he did not appear greatly concerned and soon dropped off to sleep. He probably had the best sleep of all the prisoners, but even his was limited to about four hours.

Late that night Payne, gradually softening, began to talk freely of his family and his spiritual pilgrimage. For the first time, the preacher's son broke his reserve, weeping, as he spoke of his mother. He chronicled pleasant times spent with his sisters and friends in the church of his youth. His father baptized him when he was 12, and he became an active church member. In defiance of his family's wishes, Payne enlisted in the Confederate army and, for a while, tried to maintain his religious convictions.

In his lengthy, early-morning conversation with Gillette, Payne admitted for the first time that soon after he left Seward's house he was gripped with a sense of horror at his deed. Life eventually became loathsome to him.

In spite of the young man's frankness in discussing his childhood and his sense of remorse, he maintained restraint when discussing the conspiracy. He continued to declare positively that he did not know the names of the principal men collaborating with Booth. Considering the sworn confessions of both Atzerodt and Arnold, Payne's reluctance to name others is hard to understand. Although, of course, he did not know exactly what they had confessed.

A few hours before this conversation with Gillette, Mrs. Surratt's friends had tried to get a declaration from Payne exonerating her. Brophy had urged Anna and Fathers Wigget and Walter to visit Payne and implore him for such a statement. After receiving permission to visit his cell, Anna pleaded with Payne; after she left the priests appealed to him. The obliging conspirator hedged a little, but apparently they got what they wanted. A little later Payne called Captain Rath to his cell. He declared it was his fault Mrs. Surratt was in trouble. The Captain related Payne's statement to Major Eckert. Early on the day of the executions, Secretary of State Seward summoned Rath. Rath repeated Payne's account and left convinced that officials were considering withdrawing her death sentence.[30]

Payne was the only conspirator to state that Mrs. Surratt had nothing to do with the assassination. This communication meant even less than Booth's declaration that Herold was innocent.

During the night the hangman took a rope to his room to make the nooses. He waited to prepare the noose for Mrs. Surratt until last. By the time he got around to it, he was tired of making the knot with the regulation seven loops and decided to use only five, thinking it would not be used anyway. Whatever the case, he figured, five turns would do the job as well as seven.

XLIV
Thirteen Steps

In the predawn hours, the cells were quiet. Most family members and clergymen had left. Occasional moaning came from Mrs. Surratt's cell. Atzerodt was restless but quiet. He remained agitated throughout the night, and, although he tried, he could not sleep. During the night, Atzerodt revealed that Booth first wanted Herold to kill Vice-President Johnson because Booth thought Herold had more courage than he. Atzerodt alternately prayed and cried. As morning dawned, he sat on the floor staring emptily into space—waiting.

Early in the morning, Herold's sisters returned, accompanied by their minister. About the same time, Father Walter carried Holy Communion to Mrs. Surratt's cell. He found the destitute woman lying on a crude mattress placed on the bare brick floor.

No one visited Payne except the uninvited clergyman. Even Mary Branson failed to show up. No brothers or sisters, no parents or friends came to comfort him—yet, as the morning light illuminated the cells on July 7, Payne was the most composed of all.

Later in the morning, Atzerodt also regained his emotional balance and continued to spend time in earnest conversation with Dr. Butler. Atzerodt's cell, Number 161, provided a view of the prison yard. He observed soldiers taking their places on the prison walls, but he could not see the gallows.

Guards brought the prisoners' breakfast as usual, but no one ate. Several newspaper accounts stated that Payne ate a hearty meal. This was pure guesswork by reporters, who had become accustomed to his defiant stare. They assumed the stoic youth would remain unaffected by the approaching hangman. Actually, Payne refused food on the morning of the execution.[1]

Anna left her mother early in search of General Hancock at the Metropolitan Hotel. The General could do nothing to save Mary Surratt although he tried to console Anna. These usually inflexible military leaders showed commendable gentleness in this difficult period. The condemned, except for Mrs. Surratt, thanked the officers publicly for their consideration. After the execution, however, Anna wrote Hartranft, expressing her appreciation for his thoughtfulness.

President Johnson did not reply to John Brophy's request for Mary Surratt's reprieve. But Brophy did not give up. In the morning, he pleaded with Payne, whom he did not know. Anna and the priests had previously beseeched Payne, and he had already made a statement to Captain Rath. Apparently, Brophy thought he could get an even clearer exoneration from him.

After Brophy left Payne's cell about 9:00 A.M., he begged General Hartranft to visit the prisoner to hear his statement. Hartranft obliged and was impressed with what he heard. The General wrote Brophy a note and furnished him with an army conveyance and swift horses. Hartranft told him to hasten to the White House and give the note to the President. Officials had scheduled the executions for sometime between 10:00 A.M. and 2:00 P.M., but Hartranft promised to delay it until he had an answer.[2]

Anna had already arrived at the White House at 8:30, accompanied by a female friend. Johnson had given orders that he was to see no one on the day of the execution. The doorkeeper stopped Miss Surratt at the foot of the stairs leading to the President's office and would not allow her to pass. She then begged to see the President's secretary, Colonel Mussey. When she saw the Colonel coming down the stairs she threw herself at his feet and grabbed him by his coat. Sobbing dreadfully, she implored him to help her mother.

Of the many extraordinary episodes witnessed by the White House staff, this was surely the most woeful. Mussey tried gently to tell the young woman he could not intercede as the President's order was firm—he would see no one. Anna remained weeping on the stairs as the Colonel slowly returned to his office. She was beside herself—without hope. Crying loudly, she proclaimed her mother's innocence. Anna stopped anyone who came near, pleading for someone to help her see the President. Guards remained at rigid attention, but with moist eyes, as Anna, in great anguish, continued her uncontrollable weeping, occasionally interjecting proclamations of her mother's goodness. "She is too good and kind to be guilty of such a crime," she cried.[3] These words echoed Mrs. Surratt's lawyers' arguments and would be repeated for years to come. Before she quieted down, Anna announced that if her mother were put to death, she wished to die also.

Exhausted and undone, Anna gave up. Soldiers gently persuaded her to take a seat in the East Room, and there she waited for several hours. Every time the front door of the White House opened, she jumped up, in expectation of help or some hopeful word.

Anna was still waiting when Brophy arrived. He also tried desperately to see the President but was stopped by Johnson's aides. He then begged for someone to pass Hartranft's note on to the President. This, too, was refused. Anna, clinging to Brophy, began to sob hysterically.

In another effort to save the widow, Ewing declared that the jurisdiction of the military court was illegal by referring to the Act of March 3, 1863, Sections 2 and 3. But no one listened, and this effort, like others, proved futile.

In the meantime, other supporters were working in behalf of Mary Surratt. Some had contacted the energetic young widow of Stephen Douglas. As Brophy and Anna stood hopelessly in the White House foyer, they saw a fine carriage drive up bearing the elegantly dressed Mrs. Douglas.

The 30-year-old Adele Douglas was the widowed Senator's second wife. Senator Douglas had waited three years after his first wife's death before

Adele Cutts Douglas, wife of the Democratic presidential candidate in 1860. She pleaded with President Johnson on Mrs. Surratt's behalf.

marrying the former Adele Cutts, who was 21 at the time she married. He was twice her age. Her father, James Madison Cutts, a government clerk, was the grandnephew of Dolly Madison. Her mother's family were prominent Roman Catholics in Maryland, and Adele, a devout Catholic, was educated in parochial schools in Georgetown. Her grandfather, John O'Neale, owned slaves and a large plantation near Port Tobacco. Adele's aunt, the celebrated Confederate spy Rose Greenhow, better known as Rebel Rose, had been confined in Old Capitol Prison with Mrs. Surratt.

As a young bride, Mrs. Douglas had traveled widely with her husband during the unsuccessful presidential campaign of 1860. Her husband's health was broken by rigorous campaigning, leading to his premature death. Instead of becoming first lady, Adele was left a widow.

Mrs. Douglas seems to have taken no personal interest in the trial. She is never mentioned as having visited the courtroom. Yet, Mrs. Surratt's friends could not have found anyone more able and willing to help than Adele Douglas. As the widow of a former presidential candidate, she wielded great influence. If anyone could get in to see President Johnson, it was this beautiful, strong-willed woman.

As Mrs. Douglas entered the White House, Brophy informed her of his futile efforts. Hearing this, she dashed past the readied bayonets and, sweeping the surprised guards out of her way, burst into Johnson's office. The astonished

President informed her that he had seen Brophy's statements about Weichmann, and they had no value. After a short discussion, she emerged, declaring solemnly there was no hope. Anna, still trembling, pleaded with Mrs. Douglas to see the President again. Brophy begged her to "show him Hartranft's note."[4]

The indomitable lady turned and again, pushing past the guards, pressed into the President's office. Johnson, however, remained firm.

Exactly what Hartranft's note contained is not known. Brophy later made copies of his own papers public, but he did not produce this piece of evidence. Neither was it found among the President's documents, although Brophy's petition was.

After Mrs. Douglas returned a second time without success, Brophy advised Anna that they had done all they could. It was now nearly 11:30. "Come with me if you would see your mother again while she lives," Brophy suggested.[5]

Soon after Miss Surratt left, two of Herold's sisters, dressed in black and heavily veiled, tried to see the President with the same negative results. They then sent a note to the President's wife, thinking that maybe a woman's heart might be touched. Mrs. Johnson, however, was ill and attendants thought it best not to deliver the message. In a last effort, the sisters asked to see Mrs. Patterson, the President's daughter. Officials also refused this request. At almost noon, with all hope gone, the sisters grimly started back to the dreaded prison cells.

Things were not going much better at the District of Columbia City Hall. Marshal Gooding interrupted the start of a trial in the civil court with the writ of habeas corpus, showing that General Hancock had seen the summons. The writ required that Mrs. Surratt be produced at court by 10:00 that morning. At the appointed hour, Mrs. Surratt's lawyers were waiting at the city hall, along with Judge Wylie, but there was no General Hancock and no Mary Surratt. The marshal announced that it was past 10:00 and that the General had not appeared in response to the writ.

At this point, District Attorney Carrington objected to the entire process. But Mrs. Surratt's lawyers refused to back down, declaring that their client should never have been tried by a military court. Carrington brushed aside the contentions, claiming that all he could do was assure the Court that the marshal had done his duty.[6]

In the meantime, General Hancock, having received the summons, conferred with both Attorney General Speed and President Johnson. At nearly 11:30 A.M., Hancock, accompanied by Speed, arrived at the District of Columbia courtroom to explain why he could not obey the writ.

When Hancock failed to bring Mrs. Surratt, Judge Wylie proceeded with the trial of Miss Harris. The trial, in progress for several days, was scheduled to convene that morning at 10:00. Miss Harris was charged with the murder of a clerk in the Treasury Department. The Harris case did not attract the attention of the conspiracy trial, although the public eagerly followed the sensational murder case.

As the execution hour drew near, excitement heightened. Rumors circulated that the President would grant a reprieve for Mrs. Surratt, and reporters learned of the recommendation for clemency. But as the public did not know the exact nature of this plea, it created a false hope.

Only minutes remained before the scheduled hangings. Anna and the young professor, Brophy, climbed into Hartranft's waiting army carriage and raced out 4½ Street toward the Arsenal. The streets of downtown Washington were almost deserted, but throngs of people congregated near the site of the execution.

A double guard had positioned itself around the Arsenal. The first sentry stood one-fourth of a mile north of the prison and other guards were posted along the main road toward the entrance.

As Anna and Brophy approached the Arsenal, crowds surged around the carriage, impeding their progress until the vehicle could not budge. A mass of people, all pressing toward the prison walls, engulfed them. There seemed little hope of getting back to the Arsenal. At that moment the carriage carrying General Hancock arrived. The General, recognizing Anna's tearstained face, jumped from his carriage and made his way to her. Brophy explained that Anna was trying to reach her mother before the execution. Hancock beckoned for an officer and soon had a squadron of cavalry surrounding Anna's carriage. They opened a path through the crowd, and in a few minutes, Anna was at her mother's side.[7] One person absent from her side was her son John. He remained hidden in Canada.

On the night of the murder, John Surratt probably lodged in the Brainard House in Elmira, New York. He later testified that Confederate leaders had sent him to survey the Union prison there. He claimed that he heard news of the assassination the next morning at breakfast. Surratt went immediately to the telegraph office in the hotel lobby to send a message to Booth. After writing the message he had second thoughts and asked the operator to return the telegram. The operator explained that he had to keep it on file, and Surratt walked off in disgust. This unsent telegram later played an important part in his trial.

By that time, the little village was in turmoil with church bells tolling and citizens speculating on the tragedy. Surratt left Elmira as soon as he could catch a train for Canandaigua, arriving Saturday evening. But because of the Sunday blue laws no train left Canandaigua until Monday morning. So he found a room at the Webster House, registering under the name John Harrison. Monday morning, he read in New York papers that he was accused of the assassination attempt of Secretary Seward. Surratt left for Albany at noon, arriving there Tuesday morning. From Albany he traveled to St. Albans, Vermont, and on to Montreal.[8]

By this time, soldiers closely guarded the border between the United States and Canada. Surratt passed undetected because he was wearing traditional Canadian clothes—an Oxford-cut jacket and a little Canadian cap. Shortly after noon on April 18 he registered at the St. Lawrence Hotel in Montreal and remained in seclusion. The next evening friends helped him find more secure lodging at a Mr. Porterfield's house. Porterfield, a Confederate agent, hid him

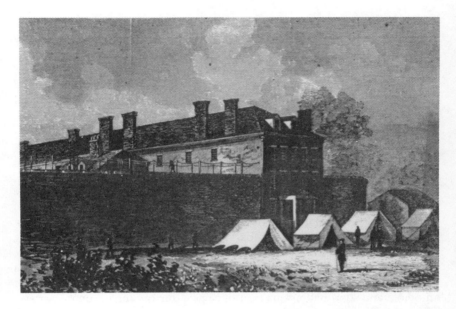

The Arsenal Penitentiary. A large room on the northeast corner of the third floor served as the courtroom for the trial. The executions occurred just inside the high wall.

several days. Later, Surratt was secretly driven to the Island of Montreal where he crossed the St. Lawrence River and was led to the house of Father Charles Boucher. The priest concealed him under the floor through a trapdoor. There he stayed until a rumor circulated that the priest was hiding a woman. Surratt then moved to the house of Father LaPierre. He remained with this priest about four months, never leaving his room until after dark.[9] John was hiding with Father LaPierre on July 7, 1865–the day his mother faced death.

In spite of efforts by General Hancock to keep the execution a relatively private event, approximately 1,000 spectators gathered to view the hangings. Hundreds of soldiers, stationed as guards along the walls and within the Arsenal, and prisoners, crowding windows, also observed the morbid affair. Curious spectators covered all the buildings around the prison, anxious to catch a glimpse of the gallows, even though the Government had signed only about 100 passes.

The completed scaffold, made of heavy lumber, was 21 feet high (including the crossbeam from which the ropes were hung). The condemned reached the platform by the traditional 13 steps. Two trapdoors attached with heavy iron hinges extended across the front of the platform. Four thick ropes, about eight feet long, dangled from the crossbeam, each ending with a hangman's noose. The scaffold stood about 40 feet from the south wall of the prison. Soldiers had dug four shallow graves close to the gallows and placed four plain coffins nearby.

Carpenters still worked on the gallows even at that late hour. Two men on a tall ladder adjusted the ropes. In spite of efforts to control them, relic hunters hampered the preparations by trying to chip off pieces of the scaffold or secure a piece of rope, even before the hangings took place.

At 11:25, soldiers tested the drops by placing two large cannon balls where the condemned were to stand. When they knocked the props from beneath the trapdoors, one failed to open. After repeated testing, they eventually corrected the problem. Each time soldiers opened the traps, they made a loud crashing sound. Each test jarred the apprehensive prisoners languishing inside.[10]

Shortly before noon, Herold partook of the Sacrament offered by Dr. Olds. Payne, ready to die, continued to talk freely of his past to Dr. Gillette and Doster.

Gillette, still grieving for his own son lost fighting for the Union, persisted in his effort to comfort the young soldier who battled for the South. The condemned youth, preparing for his short trip to the hangman, was the son of a slaveholding Southern Baptist preacher. Dr. Gillette, a Northern Baptist minister who opposed slavery, substituted for the Confederate's absent father. Payne had already given his pocketknife to Major Eckert after Doster refused it. The only possessions he had left were a Bible and his death warrant, both of which he presented to the minister.[11]

Guards brought Mrs. Surratt from her cell and placed her in a chair near the doorway to the prison yard. There she declared again to Father Walter that she was innocent.[12] All the conspirators, with the exception of Payne, proclaimed their innocence to the end.

Spectators, waiting in hushed expectation, were startled at noon by the sound of banging in the upper floors of an adjacent building. They thought it was the signal for starting the gruesome process. As curious eyes turned toward the sound, they saw the well-known photographer Alexander Gardner adjusting his camera, which protruded from the window.

The only woman in the crowd around the gallows was Maj. Mary Edwards Walker, an army surgeon, the first woman to hold such a position. One reporter at the Arsenal noted that she rode a horse like a man. After the war she became a strong supporter of women's rights, wearing the bloomer costume and eventually men's clothes.

Through barred windows, reporters could see Atzerodt. His lady friend from Port Tobacco had left him shortly before, weeping openly. Atzerodt conversed freely about his part in the crime with anyone who would listen, but at noon he was left alone reading a Bible.

As soon as General Hancock arrived at the penitentiary, he hurriedly took Hartranft aside and whispered a few words. Following this brief conversation, Hancock called out in a loud voice, "Get ready General, I want to have everything put in readiness as soon as possible."[13] This signaled friends and relatives to leave and the doomed to prepare for death. About 12:15 guards on the prison walls took their assigned places.

Anna, arriving at the Arsenal, realized there was no hope. Seeking to break the news gently, she asked her mother if she was resigned to her fate. Mrs. Surratt replied that she was. Anna broke down again. Father Walter

Atzerodt watching Herold being prepared for death.

suggested that the prison area was no place for the emotional young woman. She said a tearful good-bye at 12:30, and a guard led her, sobbing, to an upstairs room in the penitentiary. Others throughout the prison could hear her lamentations as she was led away. By 12:45, all visitors not directly concerned with the execution had left. Soldiers removed chairs from the cells and placed them on the scaffold. Finally, guards opened the door leading from the prison to the waiting gallows—a signal that the dreaded moment was near.

At nearly one o'clock, soldiers took their places under the scaffold. Even at this late hour, rumors passed around the prison of an imminent reprieve. At 1:15, General Hancock emerged through the prison door and ordered soldiers to assume the position of dress parade. Then General Hartranft appeared, followed by his associates. Next Mrs. Surratt started the short walk through the prison door to the scaffold. She was half carried by two soldiers and moved very slowly as if to delay the inevitable. Payne, who next stepped into the walled courtyard, was obliged to stop occasionally so as not to hurry her. He seemed determined to maintain the image of an unrepentant Confederate caught doing his duty. Payne stared at the crowd, as he had in the courtroom, with the same calm, defiant attitude.[14] Atzerodt and Herold slowly followed. Dr. Butler helped Atzerodt up the scaffold steps and seated him on the south end. The clergyman then held an umbrella over the bare head of the nervous immigrant.[15]

Mrs. Surratt almost collapsed in her chair. A soldier also shielded her from the blistering July sun with an umbrella. She was dressed, as she had been during the trial, in black with a black bonnet.

Payne took his seat next to Mrs. Surratt, aided by Dr. Gillette. An observer noted that he took his place on the scaffold as though he were sitting down to dinner. He wore the same blue woolen undershirt he had worn for weeks, but he added a straw sailor hat with a ribbon, worn at a jaunty angle. Payne whispered something to Dr. Gillette and then gazed straight ahead into the bright blue sky with no apparent sense of remorse or concern.

Herold hobbled up the steps last with the aid of Dr. Olds and was seated between Payne and Atzerodt. He wore dirty, rumpled clothes and an old slouch hat. He seemed to be repeating prayers whispered to him by the clergyman.

Hartranft read the death warrants in his strong clear voice. Fathers Wigget and Walter then led Mrs. Surratt in her final prayers after which they placed a cross to her lips. Dr. Gillette stepped forward to express gratitude in behalf of Payne—a strange procedure. Payne wanted to thank General Hartranft and others in charge of the prison for their kindness. As Gillette spoke, Payne remained expressionless, his blue eyes gazing dreamily at the few puffy clouds in the summer sky. When the pastor concluded with a prayer, Payne quietly responded, "Amen."

Doctors Butler and Olds followed Dr. Gillette's example. No words came from Mrs. Surratt's spiritual counselors. After the prayer, Dr. Olds turned to Atzerodt and reminded him that while the wages of sin are death, whosoever placed his hope in the Lord Jesus Christ would be forgiven. He concluded with a benediction, "May the Lord God have mercy on you and grant you His peace."[16]

With the ceremonies concluded, a soft command was given, and the prisoners stepped forward toward the dangling nooses. During these proceedings, the priests read portions of the Catholic ritual to Mrs. Surratt. Atzerodt continued to shake uncontrollably as his arms and legs were tied with white cloths.

Sixteen minutes had elapsed since the prisoners entered the yard. As Mrs. Surratt's arms were being bound, she turned her head and spoke to one of the officers. Apparently she complained that it was too tight, because they began to slacken the binding.

Payne bent over to accommodate the hangman's noose, "as if he were assuming a crown."[17] As Captain Rath fitted the noose around his massive neck, he had to make some adjustments. He explained to Payne it would make his death easier. The condemned youth replied accommodatingly, "You know best, Captain"—his last words.[18]

The most solemn moment, according to Doster, watching from a second floor window, was when soldiers removed Mrs. Surratt's bonnet to place the rope around her neck. At that instant, Anna, who had been lying on the floor

Contemporary sketch of the moment soldiers knocked the posts out from under the trapdoors (Library of Congress – USZ62-940).

crying, got up to look out of the window. As the noose fell around her mother's neck, she fell again to the floor in a faint.

Finally soldiers covered the head of each prisoner with a white cloth. This intensified Atzerodt's fears. He mumbled something that sounded like "Shtelmen's take ware" as the ministers drew back from the trapdoors.[19] Atzerodt, who seemed to think that the four would be pushed off the end of the platform, backed away from the edge. Mrs. Surratt pleaded, "Please, don't let me fall."[20]

Atzerodt's muffled voice, barely audible through the cloth hood, seemed to say, "Goodbye, gentlemen who are before me now. May we meet in the other world. God help me now! Oh! Oh! Oh!"[21] As he uttered these last sounds, Captain Rath gave the signal by a wave of his hand. Soldiers knocked away the wooden beams supporting the trapdoors. Four bodies fell abruptly about six feet and jerked up again momentarily. It was 1:26.

For a few minutes Atzerodt's body continued to shake. Payne slowly drew his huge form up until he appeared to be sitting in an imaginary chair. Then he straightened out again. Six minutes later, Payne's swinging body still

Top: Officials on the gallows converse, as four bodies swing below them. Bottom: Curious spectators linger near the gallows as soldiers prepare to bury the four lifeless bodies.

quivered spasmodically. The others hung straight and motionless in the bright sunlight. After a few minutes of stunned silence, soldiers began to move around as usual.

After examining the corpses, surgeons Woodward and George Porter pronounced them dead. About ten minutes later, an officious guard placed a ladder against the scaffold, climbed up and cut down one of the cadavers. It struck the ground with a thud. Authorities quickly reprimanded the overzealous soldier and ordered him down. Guards removed the other bodies with more care, placed them immediately in crude boxes and lowered them into the prepared graves.

Outside the prison walls, venders were busy selling cake and lemonade as if it were a holiday. Spectators lingered around the scaffold until nearly five o'clock, when officers gave orders to clear the courtyard.

Before soldiers cut down the body of Mary Surratt, her lawyers requested permission to give her a Christian burial and had an ambulance waiting. General Hancock said that he did not have authority to allow the body to be taken away and suggested they see Secretary Stanton. The attorneys hurried to Stanton's office but were not allowed to see him. He did send them a note suggesting they consult Judge Holt. Holt insinuated that the request might be considered at the proper time but not at the present.[22] That bit of runaround ended the attorneys' unsuccessful quest.

Alfred C. Gibson, one of the soldiers on duty, stood immediately in front of the scaffold during the executions. When guards removed the bodies, Gibson had the task of preparing four sealed glass containers with the names of each cadaver.[23] Later when the Government allowed the bodies to be exhumed for reburial, these containers identified them.

Shortly before the executions, a vague picture of the man known as Payne emerged, but only after his death did the details become known. He was born in 1844 (his lawyer said 1845) in Alabama, one of nine children of the Reverend and Mrs. George C. Powell. His father, born in Virginia, was descended from the prominent Powell family of that state. The George Powells lived for a while in southwest Georgia before moving to Live Oak, Florida, halfway between Jacksonville and Tallahassee. Payne's preacher-father also worked at farming with a few slaves. Payne, as a young boy, was partly responsible for taking care of the farm. His childhood was typical of the rural South of that time. He obtained only a rudimentary education but was neither ignorant nor stupid.

His father, considered a good preacher, unfortunately was "addicted to whiskey."[24] Eight years after the Civil War, in which he lost his three sons, the Reverend Mr. Powell was dismissed from his church.

At the outbreak of war, Payne's two older brothers enlisted in the Confederate army. Lewis himself enlisted on May 8, 1862, in Jasper, Florida, although only 17 years old. He was assigned to Company I, Second Florida Regiment, under Captain Stewart, and soon ordered to Richmond. Payne fought in the Peninsula Campaign and the Battle of Antietam. During the latter battle, he heard that his two older brothers had been killed in Nathan Bedford Forrest's first raid on Murfreesboro, Tennessee. This catastrophic news undoubtedly influenced Payne's transformation into an impulsive, reckless soldier.

Payne participated in the Confederacy's farthest penetration into Northern territory. On July 3, 1863, in the memorable effort to break through Federal lines at Gettysburg, Union forces took him prisoner and detailed him a nurse in a hospital there. He met Margaret Branson in the Gettysburg hospital. Later he was transferred to West Building Hospital in Baltimore where he visited the Branson boardinghouse. He stayed in Baltimore about six weeks before escaping south again in October 1863.[25]

In Winchester, Virginia, he joined a cavalry regiment. In this group, which fought in the Shenandoah Valley area, Payne gained a reputation for bold deeds. Soon he joined Gen. John S. Mosby's raiders and later used "Mosby" as one of his aliases because of his admiration for the famous leader. As one of Mosby's Raiders, Payne was known as a silent, daring night rider. In a history of Mosby's Batallion there is a reference to "the terrible Lewis Powell" (his real name).[26] He became familiar with the backroads and shortcuts in the area from Warrenton to Winchester and would penetrate Union lines for plunder and prisoners.

Payne participated in Mosby's harassment of Gen. David Hunter's troops in June 1864 after Hunter had given orders for the indiscriminate burning of civilian houses. During this campaign, some of the war's bloodiest atrocities occurred. Rebel forces took few prisoners. Dead Union soldiers were strewn along the roads with notes attached to their bodies proclaiming "shot for house burning." Payne made several wild raids on Hunter's forces, often barely escaping with his life.

These vicious clashes with Hunter's men less than a year before the trial could have been a factor in Payne's efforts to keep his background a mystery. In the first few days of the trial, he still harbored some hope of escaping the gallows. Had his part in Mosby's gruesome raids been uncovered, it might have influenced Gen. David Hunter, president of the Military Commission.

During one of Payne's escapades, he was wounded and taken to a farmhouse in Fauquier County, Virginia, to recuperate. An occupant of the house was Lily Bowie, who had been struck by a fragment from an exploding shell during the battle. A romance developed between these young Southerners. Although Payne did not mention the encounter, Bowie saved an improvised notebook belonging to him which contained some of his poems.

About January 1, 1865, the restless Payne left Fauquier County. The episode of his having saved the lives of two Union soldiers, brought out in the testimony of John Grant, occurred at this time. He exchanged his uniform for civilian clothes and headed north, walking along the railroad tracks.

Near Alexandria, Virginia, Union pickets stopped him. Payne pretended to be a refugee and was taken on to Alexandria. There he took the oath of allegiance, assuming the name Lewis Payne. The real Lewis Payne, who lived in Fauquier County, was formerly United States attorney for the Wyoming Territory.[27]

Payne traveled back to Baltimore to visit the Branson girls again. Although he expected to remain there until the return of peace, he got involved in another daring conspiracy similar—so he thought—to his raids with Mosby.

Exactly how Payne became associated with Booth is not known. The story that Booth saw him destitute on a Baltimore street and remembered him from an inconsequential meeting a few years earlier is not convincing.

In spite of uncomplimentary descriptions of the conspirators by contemporaries, they might have been acceptable citizens under different circumstances. Mrs. Surratt was in many respects a good mother, and Dr. Mudd was a man of genteel reputation. Booth would have been remembered as a gifted actor. After the assassination, he was pictured as an unbalanced madman, but few held that opinion before this treacherous act. Friends generally described him as a fun-loving ladies' man and considered him generous and kind. Observers described Payne as an inhuman brute at the trial, yet he had been known as a serious church leader back home in Florida. Had there been no slavery and no war, he might have become a devoted husband and generous father.

Atzerodt, the most abused because of his "criminal look," was in fact handicapped on account of language difficulties and problems of adjusting to a new land and culture. Yet Atzerodt was not by nature a vicious criminal. His modest work as a painter of carriages in an isolated little village would not ordinarily lead to criminal operations.

John Surratt had been a much-respected student among those preparing for the priesthood. Whatever his weaknesses, he was not a born murderer. The same was true of both O'Laughlin and Arnold, who were average citizens caught up in a violent civil conflict.

Herold, the petted only son among six sisters, was loved and cared for by his widowed mother. Although not a strong character, he was not a killer by nature.

Spangler, while poor and illiterate, was an honest, hardworking stagehand. None of the conspirators had a prison record nor had any been arrested previously.

Some of the Lincoln conspirators were idealists motivated by intense devotion to a cause—an unholy defense of Southern slavery. In the paper Booth left to be published, he wrote that he was fighting to defend the Constitution— one that, according to him, guaranteed slavery. Mrs. Surratt and Dr. Mudd grew bitterly opposed to the Government that deprived them of their property—their slaves. John Surratt left school to fight for a cause espoused by his dead father and his widowed mother. Both Arnold and O'Laughlin had served, like Payne, as Confederate soldiers killing for a cause.

Whatever else may be said to excuse the Rebellion, the primary purpose among Confederate supporters in Maryland was the defense of slavery. More than anything else, this cause transformed, among others, a Sunday school boy, a famous actor, a devoted Christian mother, a candidate for the priesthood and a respected doctor into members of a murderous conspiracy.

Interested observers have raised questions as to what course Lincoln would have taken regarding the hangings. A few months earlier, he was faced with a much less serious case. Friends of John Y. Beall besieged Lincoln with fervent but unsuccessful appeals to stay his execution.

Beall, a young Southerner, dressed as a civilian, had boarded the steamer *Philo Parsons* on Lake Erie in September 1864. He seized the boat, sank another vessel and presumably tried to wreck a train near Buffalo, New York. Federals arrested Beall and tried him by a Military Commission as a spy carrying on irregular warfare against the United States. Beall's defense counsel pleaded that Beall, in the Confederate navy, was just following orders. Jefferson Davis issued a proclamation in December 1864 supporting Beall's contention. The Government proved that Beall was within the jurisdiction of the United States and was not wearing any sign of military service at the time.

Other than granting Beall a six-day reprieve, President Lincoln did nothing. The young Confederate guerrilla was hanged February 24, 1865. Just 49 days later, Booth shot Lincoln. In refusing to repeal the sentence, Lincoln acted in accordance with accepted laws of civilized nations. The penalty for such acts was death.

XLV
Dry Tortugas

If the Nation's newspaper editors accurately reflected public sentiment, the hangings were widely approved. The *New York Times* said that the justice of the verdict would be supported by the whole country.[1] The moral effect of the executions would "extend throughout Christendom," noted the *Boston Post*.[2] The *Boston Evening Transcript* speculated that "nobody will be grieved or shocked at the punishment. . . ."[3] The *Baltimore Sun*, while reporting that the short interval between the sentencing and the execution was unexpected by the public, offered no criticism. Even small isolated papers commented on the hangings. The *Miners Journal* of Pottsville, Pennsylvania, declared the punishment to be just.

Many editorialists singled out Mrs. Surratt for special comment. The *New York Methodist* stated that, in spite of her efforts to make a favorable impression on the Judges by her dress and decorum, she was clearly immersed in the crime. The *Cincinnati Commercial* observed that "strong religious influence" seemed to be pressuring the President in behalf of Mrs. Surratt, but the paper supported the Court's verdict.[4] The Baltimore *Advertizer* editorialized that Mrs. Surratt's efforts to show that her piety was incompatible with the crime were absurd. "The idea of 'virtuous' guise for infernal purposes is one of the stage tricks," commented the paper.[5]

Most Southern-sympathizing papers were noticeably noncommittal in their reports. The *Detroit Free Press* criticized Stanton but carried a detailed account of the execution without adverse comment. The *Atlanta Daily Intelligencer* printed short accounts of the trial and execution, apparently copied from other papers, without explanation, as did the *Natchez Courier*. The *Courier*, however, copied a report from the Rebel-oriented *Chicago Times* about Atzerodt supporting the conspiracy because he heard a sermon on God's curse on slaves. The *New Orleans Times*, one of the few Southern papers linked by telegraph line to Washington, published an account of the execution almost as soon as the *New York Times*. The *New Orleans* editor stressed the rejection of the habeas corpus plea but did not criticize the Court's verdict.

The *Huntsville Advocate* (Alabama) ignored the conspirators but carried a story of a black man's outrage on a white girl. The father of the girl pursued the attacker and, overtaking another black man, questioned him. On receiving an unsatisfactory answer, the irate father shot him. The paper reported that "it was subsequently ascertained that he was not the one who committed the outrage. Mr. C. had shot the wrong man. It is not known whether the culprit has yet been caught."[6] Apparently, the only "culprit" in the case was considered to have been the black man. Clearly the war and the hangings had not solved the Nation's problems.

Evidently the publications did correctly reflect public opinion, as most letters received by the President were congratulatory. Edwin Comer, of Columbus, Ohio, commended the President for the firm and prompt execution of the conspirators "and not even faltering in the case of Mrs. Surratt, for whom much entreaty had been made."[7] He suggested that Jefferson Davis should have been among the condemned.

Benjamin Harris of Philadelphia wrote, "I wish to say that your action in the case of Mrs. Surratt meets with approval. With a few sympathizers of secession it is called cruelty to a woman. Your action will teach bad women that government and men are not at their cruel mercy."[8]

A letter to the President from a Mrs. D. Dickinson expressed "high gratifications and satisfaction at the President's action in regard to the conspiracy trial and execution . . . any yielding to sickly sentimentality . . . would degrade the Nation."[9]

E. W. Eastman, Lieutenant Governor of Iowa, wrote that the "people of Iowa do not thirst for blood, but [are] glad the President refused to commute the sentences of the murderers of President Lincoln."[10]

A writer from West Roxbury, Massachusetts, also rejoiced "that misguided evil doers of the other sex have been taught that womanhood is no excuse for crime."[11]

All traitors should be punished, declared a soldier's widow from Chicago. No letters, however, were received from the deep South.

National opinion, almost unanimously, backed the President's decision although John Brophy and Father Walter continued to criticize the Government. On July 7, Brophy repeated his 16 points against Weichmann before notary public John Callan. They were the same half-truths that Brophy had circulated for weeks. Some, such as the 13th point about Weichmann wanting to go to Richmond, were true. Some, such as his 14th point, that Weichmann summoned Brophy to be a character witness for him and later changed his mind, were misleading. Other points, like the 2nd, that Weichmann confessed only because he was threatened with death by Burnett, were contrary to all known facts.

After both the President and the Secretary of War had examined and rejected Brophy's assertions, he began a campaign that lasted more than 40 years to propagate his bogus views. He tried, unsuccessfully, to get his attacks against Weichmann published in major Washington papers. Then on July 11, four days after the execution, the insignificant *Constitutional Union* printed his article. The paper bragged that although it published extra copies, they quickly sold out. Two days later the *Union* printed the article again because of what it called public demand. Father Walter later joined in the attack against Government officials, especially Stanton.

On July 17, Weichmann answered Brophy's statements again, this time publicly, in the *Washington Chronicle* and for a few days had a hot argument going. He agreed that he had called Brophy as a witness, but Brophy refused to take the stand because "it would bring pain to his mother."[12] This exposure of Brophy seemed to calm the young crusader for a while.

Northern papers published the discovery that Payne's father was a minister living in Florida. Assuming that the Reverend Mr. Powell was unaware of his son's perilous position as the trial began, he must have known in time to have made some response before the execution.

Although William Doster tried repeatedly to get in touch with Payne's parents, more than two months lapsed after the hanging before the minister responded. He claimed that the counsel's first letter did not arrive until the day before the execution and that he got out of his sickbed and started to Washington. In Jacksonville, Florida, he received news of his son's execution. The minister's excuse sounded like John Surratt's—he did not know in time.[13]

The explanation was weak. Doster had sent several urgent requests to Powell a month before the execution. If he was sick, as he claimed, he could have telegraphed authorities. The telegraph lines were open, at least to Jacksonville. Rather than turn back when he heard of the execution, he could have traveled on to Washington to claim his son's body. Relatives made requests for the remains of others, including Booth, but none were made for the body of the young soldier known as Lewis Payne.

The minister belatedly revealed a few more details about his son. His full name was Lewis Thornton Powell. Up to the time of his leaving home, the young man took part enthusiastically in church activities, including the Young Men's Prayer Meeting. Pastor Powell remembered his son's favorite hymn which included the words "Farewell, farewell to all below, My Savior calls, and I must go."[14]

Dr. Gillette wrote to the preacher concerning the few articles his son left. Several months later, Powell answered, requesting that the things be sent to him, although he still showed no interest in retrieving his son's body. When Gillette was slow in dispatching Payne's meager possessions, Powell wrote him again, this time asking about the possibility of moving his son's body. Powell probably never secured his son's few belongings. About all he had left was his death warrant, and that was found among Gillette's papers. It is known, however, that he never claimed his son's body.

Gen. Thomas Ewing wrote his father that he was pleased he had saved his clients from the gallows. Ewing could not bring himself to declare Mary Surratt innocent, but he said he was not certain of her guilt and blamed General Hancock for her execution. Similar sentiments resurfaced later and damaged Hancock's campaign for the presidency of the United States.

While the graves were still fresh, Ewing was thinking about money and his reputation. He wrote that his father's help had not only benefited his clients, but had also "added to the reputation of the firm."[15] Money seemed to be his chief concern, however. John Ford had agreed to pay at least $500 of Spangler's fees. Spangler, relieved that he had escaped hanging, sent a note to Ford indicating that his father could help pay part of the legal fees. Ford did not compensate the lawyer immediately and neither did Spangler's father, causing Ewing growing concern.

Not only was Ford slow in paying, Dr. Mudd still owed the lawyer $200. Mudd wrote that Ewing might have to wait some time to get his money, as "everything on the farm was destroyed."[16] Doster charged Atzerodt's family $375 for his defense. They paid $75 in June 1865. It is not known if he was ever paid in full.

In time, Ewing became more interested in politics than in cash. He continued to practice law in Washington for a while, then returned to Ohio where he was elected to Congress. He lost his bid to become governor of Ohio in 1879. Nothing indicates that his defense of the Lincoln conspirators influenced the election or had any lasting effect on his career.

John Ford asked Orville Browning, who called the executions "murder," to aid him in reopening his theater. Browning accompanied Ford to Stanton's office and interceded for him unsuccessfully.[17]

Less than 48 hours after the hangings, Secretary of Navy Welles visited President Johnson and found him pale and languid. Welles proposed that he seek diversion in a boat trip down the Potomac. Attorney General Speed also suggested a trip for the President, adding that Stanton was not well, and it would be good for the President to take Stanton along. Speed explained that a beautiful boat, the *River Queen*, had been designated for the use of Presidents by the Secretary of War. Lincoln had used the boat on several excursions, the last being his trip to Richmond. Strangely, neither the President nor Secretary Welles had ever heard of such a ship.

Johnson responded that he would think about it and let Welles know. Later that day, he replied that he would like the trip but refused to set foot on the *River Queen*. He wanted a naval vessel. The implication of Johnson's adamant refusal to use the vessel designated by the Secretary of War can only be guessed. But when he took his little excursion, he did so without Stanton.[18]

Several involved in the trial began taking cover, either by making themselves inaccessible or by pretending they had favored less severe punishment or even a civil trial. A rumor spread that the Secretary of War had not approved of the military court. It was not Stanton's nature to back down under such circumstances. When James White wrote him, hinting that the War Secretary probably did not approve of the Commission, Stanton wasted no time or words answering, "I did and do approve . . . [of the] trial, sentences and execution."[19] Nothing could have expressed more clearly his feelings. Stanton remained unequivocal on the subject regardless of opposition.

Newspapers, particularly the *New York Tribune*, were quick to accept almost any accusation against Stanton. One of the most persistent, spread by Father Walter, was that Stanton refused to allow him to provide spiritual assistance to Mrs. Surratt until he promised not to make any statement on the scaffold. The *Washington Evening Star*, a paper generally favorable to the Government, wrote to Stanton, enclosing the accusation of the *Tribune*. C. S. Noyes, who wrote for the *Star*, wanted the Secretary's reaction. Stanton made no reply. General Hartranft had previously stated that the report was false. The newspaper accepted Hartranft's opinion.[20]

Gen. Levi A. Dodd visited Arnold's cell and informed him that four of his companions had just been hanged. Arnold and the three others were still uncertain of their own fates.

They resumed their daily two-hour exercise in the prison yard, but the area was grotesquely changed. The threatening scaffold remained, and four recently covered graves were in plain sight. Day after day Arnold, Mudd, O'Laughlin and Spangler exercised near these awesome reminders.

A visiting reporter noted that the prisoners had little to say about the trial and that "since the execution they have not divulged anything new."[21] He described Dr. Mudd as being in good spirits over his escape from death, adding that the doctor "acknowledges that the testimony of the witness Weichmann in reference to himself is correct."[22] This confession, while remarkable, was not totally surprising. Mudd was by far the most guilty of those given lesser sentences. Having eluded the hangman's noose and facing the certainty of a long prison sentence, he had nothing to lose in confessing his often-denied meeting with Booth, since it compromised no one else.

On July 17, General Hartranft called the four aside separately to inform them of their punishment. That night, at the customary midnight hour, guards marched them silently in double irons to a wharf on the Potomac where a steamboat lay at anchor. Soldiers lined the short distance from the Arsenal to the boat.

With the prisoners aboard, the vessel steamed down the river to Fortress Monroe. There soldiers transferred them by tug, under heavy guard, to a waiting warship, *The Florida*.

In their final weeks at the Arsenal, the inmates were free of the heavy irons, but once aboard the *Florida*, Capt. William Dutton commanded that the irons be replaced on the men's wrists. However, Captain Budd ordered them taken off again. Nevertheless, their feet remained shackled, and in that condition, guards forced them down onto a lower deck in the stifling July heat.

On the voyage to Fortress Monroe, soldiers constantly guarded the prisoners and prohibited them from talking with ship personnel. But on the first day at sea, they were allowed topside for fresh air. There, for the first time, the four determined, by the position of the sun, that the ship was headed south. They had expected to go north to a prison in New York state. The next two days the vessel kept its southerly course. Gradually, they concluded their destination might be in the infamous Dry Tortugas. This group of small islands at the tip of the Florida Keys was the site of Fort Jefferson.

The heat became so oppressive the conspirators were eventually permitted to sleep on the upper deck. When the boat docked at Hilton Head, South Carolina, General Dodd informed them that, even though they traveled under sealed orders, he would reveal their destination as soon as they left port. About noon their fears were confirmed; they were headed for Dry Tortugas.

**"Key West, Florida, 1861, Fort Jefferson, Dry Tortugas." (From a sketch by a
member of the garrison. Wood engraving in "Harper's," Feb. 23, 1861. Library of
Congress — USZ62-360.)**

During the voyage, Sam Mudd again revealed to an officer that
Weichmann's testimony concerning him had been correct. This statement,
published in several newspapers, brought an immediate response. (Mudd's first
confession, while still in the Arsenal, was generally unknown to the public.)
Critics of the Government, astonished by the admission, reasoned that it
could not have come from Dr. Mudd. Others in contact with the imprisoned
doctor confirmed the officer's report. Skeptics, however, continued to brand
such confessions forgeries.[23]

The Florida was not the only ship to transport conspirators away from
home. Five weeks after the prisoners arrived at Fort Jefferson, a Canadian
priest, Father LaPierre, approached Dr. Lewis McMillan, a surgeon working
with the Montreal Ocean Steamship Company. The priest told him of a friend
who planned to travel by ship to Quebec on September 15 and would appreciate the doctor's assistance. On the specified day, Father LaPierre introduced his friend, John Surratt, to McMillan in a secret meeting. Surratt's dyed
hair and glasses had changed his appearance. LaPierre said his friend's name
was McCarty. In Quebec the passenger was transferred to the steamer *The
Peruvian* for the trip overseas. On the journey, "McCarty" bragged to the doctor
about his daring escapades in behalf of the Confederacy. He boasted that
Rebel Secretary of State Benjamin had given him a total of $100,000, although
he did not say what the money was used for.[24]

At Fort Jefferson, Dr. Mudd wrote that conditions on the island were so
pleasant that, if it were not for his family, he "could pass the balance of [his]
days here perfectly content or satisfied." He described the prison as very
healthy. The doctor was supposed to be working in the prison hospital but
confessed that he had "little or no labor to perform...."[25]

Bridge over moat—only entrance to Fort Jefferson. Mudd's cell was on the second tier to left of doorway.

On August 28, 1865, he wrote his wife criticizing the Military Commission and denied that he recognized Booth when he treated him. But again, he admitted that Weichmann's testimony about his meeting with Surratt and Booth was true. Weichmann was wrong about the date, however, which the doctor said was December 23.[26]

This belated confession may have been more significant than the doctor realized. In the trial, Mudd's lawyer emphatically denied the meeting which proved Mudd's early dealings with both Surratt and Booth. Weichmann was frequently mixed up on dates, although most of his statements were substantiated by other witnesses. But his account of Dr. Mudd's pivotal Washington meeting could not be otherwise confirmed, because Booth was dead and Surratt was in hiding. Thus, the doctor's belated confirmation added to Weichmann's overall credibility.

Mudd's confession not only agreed with Weichmann's account in general, but also in particulars, although it differed in interpretation. Mudd claimed that this encounter with Booth was accidental. But he conceded that Booth wanted an introduction to Surratt. He admitted that he talked to Surratt in private but insisted it was only to apologize for introducing him to Booth, whom he did not know well. Mudd's explanation raised more questions than it answered because it proved the doctor had more than casual contact with Booth even before this December meeting, making him among Booth's first contacts.

At the time Sam Mudd made this confession, he was trying desperately to get out of prison. And being certain that he could not deny Weichmann's facts, he hoped his interpretation might refresh Weichmann's memory so that he would "do me the justice, though late, to correct this erroneous testimony."[27]

What the physician could not know was that John Surratt would later be arrested, tried and acquitted. This enabled Surratt to go on a lecture circuit in which he unwittingly destroyed Mudd's "interpretation." In Surratt's famous Rockville lecture, he admitted that he had known Booth before the pretended introduction by Dr. Mudd. Therefore, the supposed "introduction" was clearly a cover for more clandestine matters. Surratt's lecture showed that Mudd's explanation of their private conversation in the hall could not have been correct.

The meeting was obviously not accidental. Even without Surratt's revelations, Mudd had a problem explaining why Booth wanted a person who lived 30 miles from Washington, and whom he supposedly knew only slightly, to introduce him to Surratt, a known Confederate agent living in Washington. Mudd would have been the least likely person to make such an introduction. Making the pretended introduction even more unbelievable, the doctor wrote that Booth wanted to talk with Surratt about helping him "select a good locality for a country residence."[28] Samuel Chester had intimated that Booth used the pretense of buying land in Lower Maryland as a cover for his activities in the kidnap conspiracy.

The doctor's explanation confirmed Weichmann's testimony about Surratt, Mudd and Booth talking together and drawing on a piece of paper. But Mudd declared it was not a secret conversation—that Weichmann could have heard it if he wanted to. Mudd also admitted that after spending some time in Booth's room, he invited the men to his room at the Pennsylvania House where they continued their discussion.

The physician wrote that he did not want to waste time with Booth and suspected him of being a Government agent. Yet, in every known meeting with the actor, he seemed eager to spend more time with Booth than was necessary for normal business. Sam Mudd never claimed Weichmann was involved with Booth, but he stated that Weichmann appeared to be a "Southern man." He concluded his long letter acknowledging that Weichmann had tried to "give what he believed a truthful statement"—a remarkable admission.[29]

Mudd's statement was widely publicized, and neither he nor his family ever denied it. In fact, his daughter included the letter in her biography of her father. In the trial of John Surratt, when defense lawyers were badgering Weichmann over his faulty recollection of dates, they brought up his testimony against Mudd. He admitted he might have been wrong in the dates, but he reminded lawyers that Dr. Mudd himself had confessed that the substance of his statement was correct. The defense let the matter rest.

Reverdy Johnson's concern for his clients appeared to lessen after the trial. John Ford hired him in an effort to obtain Spangler's release after the 1866 Supreme Court decision in the *Ex parte Milligan* case. Mudd's family also engaged Johnson, but the Senator was unsuccessful in his weak attempts to gain their freedom.[30]

Ninety years later, Otto Eisenschiml accused Reverdy Johnson of not trying, asserting that with any real effort, he would have been triumphant. According to Eisenschiml, the lawyer was able to get almost anything he wanted from President Johnson. For instance, in 1867, after voting against the President's program, the Senator had the audacity and the influence to ask for a special appointment for his son-in-law, and obtained it. In 1868 the President appointed Johnson minister to England, one of the most prestigious positions in Government. Eisenschiml saw in all this a Government plot to reward Reverdy Johnson for his withdrawal as defense counsel for Mrs. Surratt.[31] Actually, Senator Johnson's masterful attack on the legality of the military court was the best defense Mary Surratt had.

Even before Sam Mudd arrived at Fort Jefferson, plans were under way to secure his pardon. His cousin, Sister Mary Rose, wrote from Frederick, Maryland, on July 19, 1865, expressing her concern for him and his family. In his cousin's eyes, the doctor was being persecuted "for an act of charity" and was suffering for the cause of Christ. Without asserting his innocence, she expressed satisfaction that the Government had been unable to prove anything against him.[32]

Her closing lines were subject to several interpretations, but the nun seemed to be assuring the family of an organized movement to free the doctor. She implied that the effort could not be discussed in the letter. Sister Mary Rose expressed concern that the military court would be harsh but nevertheless she wrote, "we will have everthing prepared to obtain his speedy release and return to his interesting and lovely family, etc. Alice Burch said she would tell you the rest."[33] Dr. Mudd's wife considered the letter important and sent it to General Ewing.

Richard T. Merrick, member of a distinguished legal family and a prominent Washington lawyer, had served privately as advisory counsel for Dr. Mudd. He also actively sought Mudd's release. (Three years later he served as President Johnson's counsel in the impeachment trial.) Merrick suggested that the family not publish anything in the newspapers, but rather let the affair rest for a while. The attorney promised, "It will wake with greater vigor when the time comes to arouse it. When the time does come, I will let Mrs. Mudd know."[34]

Mudd's family and his defense counsel added their efforts to secure his freedom. Mrs. Mudd sent General Ewing several affidavits, mostly from the doctor's relatives, vouching for his character. Ewing showed the letters to President Johnson, but the President said he would do nothing at that time.

Ewing did not believe Mudd would serve a life sentence. He promised Mrs. Mudd, "He will be returned to you before many months."[35] He tried to encourage the poor woman by picturing the climate in Dry Tortugas as excellent for the doctor's health.

In a further effort to free her husband, Mrs. Mudd also talked to President Johnson. He referred the petitioner to Judge Holt, but he added a note of hope. The President promised to sign release papers if Holt would—a safe promise. Holt stated he could not help. Mrs. Mudd's simple and earnest plea impressed Holt, however. A short time later, Ewing wrote her that the Judge spoke highly of her.

Ewing also sought Orville Browning's support for the prisoner. Browning had gained a reputation for aiding imprisoned Southerners, but he could do nothing for Dr. Mudd.

Suddenly, toward the end of August, the lawyers became very optimistic. Ewing wrote Mrs. Mudd that her husband would soon be out of prison and they would "yet have a long and happy life together." Merrick also wrote her encouragingly the following day, referring to the "coming of a better day."[36]

Two days later the commanding officer at Fort Jefferson received the following notice:

> Sir: Official information has been received at these Headquarters from Washington that a plot exists to release the prisoners at Fort Jefferson. You will take the proper precautions to prevent any uprising of the prisoners, and in case you find this information to be correct take measures to ferret out the leaders and place them in irons,
>
> By command of Brig. Gen. Newton,
> A. C. Pretz
> 1st Lt. and A.A.A.G.[37]

LaFayette Baker had uncovered the plot two weeks earlier.

A couple of days later Dr. Mudd wrote his wife from the Fort:

> A transport has just arrived and will take off at least a hundred prisoners, thereby thinning our ranks considerably. I am so credulous or hopeful as to expect my release upon the arrival of every steamer, and, not receiving, feel disapppointed.[38]

The prisoner mentioned there had been several opportunities for escape, but he thought it might "show guilt." He speculated that if he did escape, he would not be able to return to the United States. He requested newspaper clippings about his imprisonment and wanted "to know the public opinion." Sam Mudd expressed disappointment that neither Stone nor Ewing seemed to be making progress in his behalf and was anxious to hear of new developments. He asked revealingly "whether any more arrests have been made." Dr. Mudd added that he had lost confidence in the people of the North and was thinking seriously about leaving "the country for a foreign land, I believe our condition would be bettered."[39]

Prison officials noticed that when Mudd arrived at Fort Jefferson he brought several good suits. But he never wore them, even though he was given permission, since he worked in the prison hospital.

On September 25, 1865, after two months on Dry Tortugas, Dr. Mudd dressed up in his best clothes and walked out of the Fort onto a United States transport. Apparently Mudd had made an arrangement with Henry Kelly, one of the crew, to help him. Kelly hid the doctor under some planks in the lower hold. Within ten minutes, officials missed the doctor and searched the steamer. After his capture, he implicated Kelly, confessing that the crew member had promised to assist him in his escape but had not kept his promise. Officers arrested Kelly and put him in prison.

Authorities were so relieved at apprehending the doctor, they failed to find four other prisoners who escaped on the boat.

Security at Fort Jefferson was lax and prisoners escaped frequently. Since the conspirators had been confined there, thirty or forty inmates escaped or tried to. Therefore, the officer in charge of Mudd's reconfinement was ordered to:

> see that Dr. Sam'l A. Mudd is placed at "hard labor." Let him be detailed in the Engineer Dept. to wheel sand. And hereafter, when any boat arrives, he will be put in the dungeon and kept there until it departs, and in the future no favors of any kind will be shown him.[40]

The doctor actually got off with a slap on the wrist. Soon after his escape attempt, he wrote his brother-in-law, Jere Dyer, that he had been put in the guardhouse for two days with chains on his hands and feet. As for "hard labor," officers ordered him to clean old bricks. "I worked hard all day," the doctor wrote sarcastically, "and came very near finishing one brick."[41] All Mudd had to do was sleep and answer roll call.

He complained chiefly that "this place is now wholly guarded by Negro troops. . . ." The presence of black soldiers as his guards constantly irritated the doctor. He wrote his wife it was "bad enough to be a prisoner in the hands of white men, your equals under the Constitution," but to be lorded over by blacks was too much.[42] He lamented that this was more than he could submit to and was a major reason he wanted to escape. Throughout his imprisonment, Mudd denounced the "detested and abominable Negro regiment."[43]

Actually the inmates performed little real work. Occasionally when ships visited the island, guards marched prisoners to headquarters and made them clean bricks. Mudd thought this nothing more than a demonstration of the Major's power. Brutality occasionally occurred, but the conspirators were not noticeably mistreated. Usually they performed little hard labor and passed the time making little boxes and picture frames out of shells and colored wood which they sold to visitors and soldiers. In spite of plots, escape attempts, complaints and constant appeals for pardons, the prisoners remained confined, but in relatively pleasant conditions.

This situation changed drastically when officials discovered several cases of yellow fever in August 1867. They moved the first victims to another island, but the disease continued to spread. By the middle of September, the prison hospital was full and the medical staff had to arrange makeshift facilities. When Dr. Smith, the chief physician, died of the fever, officials placed Dr. Mudd in temporary management until another physician could be called.

Dr. Mudd worked incessantly, sacrificially caring for the sick and dying. Yellow fever struck both Arnold and O'Laughlin, along with two-thirds of the prisoners and guards. Arnold survived, but, although Mudd cared for O'Laughlin in his cell, he died. The doctor, understandably proud of his work during the crisis, solicited a promise from Major Stone, commander of the Fort, to make known his services to the authorities at Washington.[44]

Sam Mudd used every effort, legal or otherwise, to secure his release even before the yellow fever epidemic. In 1866, when the Supreme Court decided in the *Milligan* case that the military could not legally try civilians, Mudd saw an opportunity for pardon. But the *Milligan* case was radically different from the Lincoln conspiracy. The President's assassination and the attack on Seward

This revealing photograph, taken in the infamous Fort Jefferson, shows Dr. Mudd dressed as a businessman in tie, vest and highly polished shoes. He is whittling curios to sell sightseers (Nettie Mudd, "The Life of Dr. Samuel A. Mudd").

were bloody crimes committed by Confederate spies and sympathizers to overthrow the United States Government, not simply a dispute over constitutional rights as in the Milligan case.

Later Mudd based his request for freedom on President Johnson's declaration of September 7, 1867, extending full pardon to everyone involved in the Rebellion. But Johnson specifically excluded those engaged directly or indirectly in the assassination of the President "or in any plot or conspiracy in any manner therewith connected."[45]

In September 1868, Judge Boynton of the District Court of the Southern District of Florida responded to Mudd's petitions. He declared that in the Milligan decision, "The crime of murdering the President of the United States, in time of civil war is triable by a Military Commission." And in regard to the amnesty proclamation, he declared that "the crime of being accessory to the murder of the President" was not included in the President's pardon.[46] Thus, in spite of Dr. Mudd's unceasing efforts and the work of his lawyers, the courts were unwavering in their support of the findings of the military court. Boynton requested special consideration, however, on behalf of the doctor because of his medical service during the yellow fever epidemic.

Anxious to publish the first "official" version of the trial, Benn Pitman wasted no time getting his material together. He wrote to defense counselor Ewing asking if he wanted "any alteration made" in his argument for Spangler — and to please let him have any correction.[47] Ewing had already sent Pitman a revised copy of his plea in behalf of Sam Mudd which had been altered to satisfy the lawyer. Some corrections Ewing wanted did not reach Pitman in time, however, as his trial account was already in print. But Pitman wrote back that, for the sake of the lawyer's reputation, he would try to get the printed copy corrected. Pitman's "official" version was not a word-by-word transcription, but a heavily edited account of what leading participants wished they had said.

Pitman had several drawings and photographs of Dr. Mudd taken in connection with the trial, but they were "vile caricatures." Rather than use these pictures, he intended to omit all representations of the doctor "mainly from consideration to his family."[48] Pitman, nevertheless, asked Ewing to try to obtain a good likeness of the doctor. Mudd's picture never reached Pitman, and he included no drawing of the doctor in his publication. The only picture of Mary Surratt in Pitman's book was a personal photograph supplied by her family, not drawings or police pictures as were used for other conspirators. The doctor's and the widow's privileged treatment continued.

Stanton refused to rescind his order closing Ford's Theatre. Ford, naturally, complained about this unconstitutional action without success. Stanton opposed the theater's ever being reopened as a place of amusement. He was particularly distrustful of John Ford, whom he thought wanted to profit financially from the tragedy. In addition, a strong feeling existed that reopening the theater might agitate mob reaction. Most Cabinet members supported Stanton, but Secretary Welles believed that the action arbitrarily deprived Ford of his property. Stanton explained that he had often been compelled to sieze private property. Ford's Theatre remained closed.[49]

Noah Brooks, a Washington writer, noted that "a painful and depressing feature of this tragical business" was the ease with which many well-meaning citizens appeared to forget the awfulness of the crime.[50] Immediately after the hanging, small groups began to manufacture myths defending those executed. Judge Bingham was accused in bitter terms, as were Holt and Stanton.

Forty years later, fables associated with the execution still circulated. One pictured Mrs. Surratt as dead before guards dragged her body to the scaffold. Another affirmed that after President Johnson signed the warrant, he drank himself into alcoholic stupification so that no one could reach him. Investigators disproved both rumors.

The Government had offered thousands of dollars in rewards for apprehension of the conspirators. The largest sum, eventually set at $75,000, was to be paid for Booth's capture. Claimants requested the reward money immediately after the executions. Some who had directed search operations, such as LaFayette Baker, claimed a major share. But numerous noncommissioned soldiers, who had actually carried out the search—particularly those who found Booth—also wanted their part. Stanton appointed a commission, composed of Judge Holt and Gen. E. D. Townsend, to whom all claims were to be submitted. They set January 1, 1866, as the final date for accepting claims. The commission gave most of the credit for Booth's capture to LaFayette Baker but granted him only a small portion of the reward. Baker, among others, complained. Authorities then referred the question to the Congressional Committee on Claims.

Finally, in July 1866, a year after the trial, the Committee on Claims made its report for the distribution of reward money. LaFayette Baker and Everton Conger were to receive the largest shares, $17,500 each. The remainder was to be divided as follows:

Luther B. Baker	$5,000
James R. O'Beirne	2,000
H. H. Wells	1,500
George Cottingham	1,500
Alexander Lovett	1,000
Samuel H. Beckwith	500
Edward P. Doherty	2,500

Twenty-six soldiers of the Sixteenth New York Cavalry, including Sgt. Boston Corbett, were each to be given $1,000 rewards.

So many people objected to this division that Congress refused to accept the report and subsequently reduced Colonel Baker's portion drastically. In the final distribution, Detective Conger received the biggest share, $15,000. Edward Doherty, in command of troops that found Booth and Herold, received the next largest amount, $5,250. Then came LaFayette Baker with $3,500, and his cousin, Luther Baker, with $3,000. James O'Beirne received $2,000, and George Cottingham, who manipulated John Lloyd into his confession, received $1,000, as did H. H. Wells and Alexander Lovett. Soldiers under the command of Doherty, who had surrounded Garrett's barn, divided the bulk of the reward money, $43,000. Each soldier's share came to $1,653.85. Boston Corbett received the same share as the others.

The Government had offered a reward of $25,000 for Atzerodt's capture. Sgt. L. W. Gemmill was given $3,598.59 and Maj. E. R. Artman, who sent his men out from Monocacy Junction, Maryland, to capture Atzerodt, received $1,250. Each of his men, members of the 1st Delaware Cavalry, divided the remaining $20,151.41.

For Payne's capture, Major Smith received $1,000. His men, Richard Morgan, Eli Devore, Charles Rosch, Thomas Sampson and W. M. Wermerskirch, were awarded $500 each. Susan Jackson and Mary Ann Griffin, two black women, received $250 each. Miss Jackson was Mrs. Surratt's servant who told Mrs. Griffin of seeing three mysterious men in the house. Mrs. Griffin passed the information on to her employer, Mr. Kimball, who, along with P. H. Clark, whom he happened to meet on the way to General Augur's office, informed military authorities of this misleading clue. At a time when blacks and women had no champion, these two men each received $500, double the black women's reward.[52]

On September 27, 1865, Mr. Wilding, vice-consul in Liverpool, England, wired Secretary Seward that John Surratt was expected to arrive in a day or two. Three days later, another telegram reported that Surratt was hiding in the oratory of the Catholic Church of the Holy Cross in Liverpool. The vice-consul declared he could do nothing to apprehend Surratt without instructions from the State Department.[53]

William Hunter, Acting Secretary of State, received the telegram but, not knowing what to do, sent his chief clerk, Robert S. Chew, to see Holt. As usual, Holt passed the matter on to Stanton. Ordinarily a question of this nature would have been referred to President Johnson, but Stanton continued to exercise exceptional power. Johnson was busy with Reconstruction. Hunter wired the vice-consul in Liverpool that "upon a consultation with the Secretary of War and the Judge Advocate, it is thought advisable that no action be taken. . . ."[54] Later, before a House Committee investigating the delay in Surratt's arrest, Stanton gave a lame excuse. He claimed the identification of Surratt was not sufficient to warrant his arrest.

On October 25, a Mr. Potter, the consul general at Montreal, wired the State Department that Surratt was still in Liverpool waiting for money to be sent from Canada to enable him to go on to Rome. Then, finally, on November 11, 1865, a dispatch informed the consul general that the Secretary of State of the United States requested a warrant for Surratt's arrest. No extradition request was ever made to the British Government, however.

Four more months passed and nothing was done to apprehend Surratt. On April 23, 1866, more than a year after the assassination, the United States Minister in Rome, Mr. King, sent a dispatch informing the State Department that Surratt, under an assumed name, had joined the Papal Zuoaves and was located in the Italian town of Lezze. Still the United States did nothing. Several months later, on August 8, the Vatican informed the State Department that it would put no obstacle in the way of surrendering Surratt if the United States wanted him. Another two months passed without action, apparently because Secretary of State Seward was sick and absent from his office. On October 16, the Secretary of State belatedly asked if there would be any problem in extradition proceedings, considering the United States had no extradition treaty with the Vatican. The United States minister in Rome replied on November 3, 1866, that there would be no problem, and three days later, officials arrested Surratt in Alexandria, Egypt, after he had made a dramatic escape from Italy.

XLVI
"An Absurdity Unsurpassed"

Leaders in the trial began to bicker with one another after the hangings. A battle was shaping up between Stanton and President Johnson which eventually led to the President's impeachment trial and the resignation of the Secretary of War. Tensions were also building between Holt and Stanton. Furthermore, Johnson's alienation of Radical Republicans caused him to break with John Bingham. The latter eventually became the President's judge in the impeachment trial. Differences between the President and Atty. Gen. James Speed led to Speed's resignation. In addition, Johnson was losing confidence in Judge Advocate Holt, and Speed and Holt were soon to have a falling out.

Attorney General Speed, who had declared the military trial legal, and fellow–Kentuckian Holt had been on opposite sides of political issues for years. Early in the war, when Kentucky was wavering between remaining in the Union or joining the Confederacy, Holt strongly advised President Lincoln not to release prisoners who sought to move Kentucky into the Southern camp. Speed, on the contrary, advised the President to free the prisoners. President Lincoln took his friend Speed's advice. The two powerful Kentuckians managed to get along, after a fashion, until after the trial.

A conflict also developed between President Johnson and Col. LaFayette Baker. The break between them grew gradually and may have been intensified by Baker's small share of the reward. The outward incident that started the rift involved an attractive pardon broker, Mrs. Cobb, who visited the White House constantly, seeking pardons for her clients. The Colonel, determined to put a stop to her sleazy business, set up a fictitious case to trap her. The unwary lady agreed in writing to obtain a pardon for a Captain Hine for $300. After President Johnson signed the pardon, Baker revealed there was no Captain Hine. Furious, Johnson dismissed Baker.[1] The Colonel never forgave the President. In his book *History of the United States Secret Service*, Baker severely criticized both Johnson and Stanton.

Prosecution of Confederate leaders implicated in the assassination remained unresolved. Government officials still believed Holt's assertion that Jefferson Davis had a part in the assassination plans, but they could find no positive proof. Seward wanted the Government to finish sifting through Rebel archives before trying Davis in a military court. Stanton was so fearful of continued

Confederate plots that he maintained a guard around his house and seldom left without a bodyguard. He repeated Conover's wild tales and urged caution on other Cabinet members and particularly on President Johnson.

Although Jacob Thompson had escaped to England, Stanton knew the whereabouts of Tucker, Sanders and Cleary in Canada. He had even received offers of aid in their arrest but made no effort to apprehend them.

Stanton now seemed reluctant to include Davis among the conspirators or even to bring him to Washington. "I do not mean that he shall come here.... His trial and punishment, if there be any, shall be in Virginia," he wrote to Gen. Henry W. Halleck.[2] Clement C. Clay had voluntarily surrendered to Federal authorities. Stanton curiously directed that both Davis and Clay be sent to Fortress Monroe and kept there in solitary confinement without being charged and without having bail either set or denied.

The direct involvement of Confederate leaders in the assassination appeared less certain as time passed. Several denied they had known anything about the plot. Enraged by the accusations, Beverly Tucker defended himself in the *Montreal Gazette*, viciously denouncing President Johnson. He wrote that whoever charged him with such a crime would be dealt with as a common individual, not as the "chief magistrate of a once great and Christian country.... I fearlessly denounce him in all his mighty panoply of power in the plentitude of my own conscious innocence, a wicked and wilful libeler."[3]

The Virginia-born Tucker was nearly 45 years old when Lincoln died. As a young man, Tucker manufactured shot and shell for the army. Afterward he moved to Washington where, as editor of the *Washington Sentinel*, he took an active part in politics. In 1857 President Buchanan appointed him consul in Liverpool.

As the threat of civil war increased, Tucker joined other Virginians in supporting the Confederacy. After brief service in the Confederate army and an unsuccessful mission to Europe, Davis requested him, in 1864, to serve in Canada. Tucker's Canadian mission apparently was to exchange Southern cotton for Northern bacon.[4] Of the various Confederate agents in Canada, Tucker seems to have been the least involved in plots against the Union. He insisted his purpose in Canada was peaceful and wanted to remain ignorant of other Rebel activities. But this admission indicated the other Confederates in Canada were involved in less-than-friendly plots. The Government withdrew reward money for Tucker's arrest in November 1865. but he did not return to the United States until two years later, after wandering through England, Mexico and Canada.[5]

Tucker was the first prominent person to openly accuse President Johnson of involvement in the crime. He calculated that the only man to benefit from the assassination was Andrew Johnson. Tucker referred to Booth's card left for Johnson and the fact that Booth was killed rather than being taken alive, because dead men tell no tales. George S. Bryan, who made a study of American myth making, later asserted that this "is the stuff of which myth is formed."[6] The myth continues to crop up.

George N. Sanders, another member of the Confederate Canadian Cabinet, accused Stanton of complicity in the murder, another tale that will not die. James M. Mason, while abroad, told Englishmen that John Wilkes Booth was actually a Northern Radical who wanted to get rid of Lincoln in order that Radicals might have their way in the Reconstruction.[7] This myth, that Radical Republicans were behind the plot, originated with Confederate leaders, but it continues to find adherents.

William Cleary, clerk to Clement C. Clay, and closely associated with Jacob Thompson, answered accusations against him and other Rebels in a long letter to President Johnson dated November 1865. He accused secret witnesses, including Sanford Conover, of lying. Cleary presented convincing facts to support his accusation. He showed that Confederate leaders had not been in Montreal when the meetings with Conover supposedly took place. He included numerous affidavits to prove his case.

Cleary wrote that the only Confederate agents in Canada were Thompson, Clay and J. P. Holcombe and that "illegitimate" raids and plots were beneath their dignity.[8] Rebel agents apparently were not above "legitimate" raids, which in fact they carried out. Cleary indicated that their chief purpose was to sell cotton, a cover used by other Rebel agents.

Jacob Thompson also declared that he knew nothing of the assassination or of Booth.[9] He did not deny knowing Surratt or having knowledge of the plot to kidnap the President. It is very unlikely that Rebel officials knew of plans to murder Lincoln, which, from most accounts, were born in Booth's twisted mind a few days or hours before the crime. But the evidence linking Confederate leaders to the kidnap plot is undeniable.

L. Q. Washington, chief clerk of the Confederate State Department, revealed that John Surratt came to Richmond on his last trip because a blockade-runner from New York City carrying cipher dispatches had expected to meet a male escort (Gus Howell), who had just been arrested. John Surratt substituted for Howell. Mr. Washington questioned Surratt in Richmond and sent him back to Canada with a letter to Jacob Thompson. He said that Surratt had no idea what the letter contained. This admission by one of the Confederate inner circle tied one chief conspirator directly to Confederate leaders.[10]

Lewis Payne constantly affirmed that he was working under orders of Confederate authorities. He repeated this fact on the day of his execution.[11] The confession was consistent with Payne's attitude. He was a soldier fighting for the South whether at Gettysburg or in Washington. The evidence linking the Confederacy to Booth and the kidnap conspiracy is overwhelming, but there is no evidence associating Jefferson Davis with the murder.

Davis and his friends pressed for a trial. President Johnson was also anxious to punish the supposed culprits. Radical Republicans apparently wanted to try Davis in order to fan the flames of sectional hatred and thus maintain their political grip. This put Stanton and Holt in a dilemma. Stanton seemed to have sensed early in the trial that evidence against Confederate authorities was thin. Holt, even though plagued by lack of concrete facts, remained convinced that Rebel chiefs were guilty and waited uneasily for the evidence.[12]

Both men had convinced President Johnson of the guilt of Davis and his Canadian Cabinet. The reputations of both Stanton and Holt, if not their positions, depended on avoiding scandal that might emerge if Davis were put on trial and proved innocent. Stanton tried to ignore the problem and stand above it while making sure the Government kept Davis in Fortress Monroe.

Sanford Conover was their only hope. Holt held desperately to his wavering trust in Conover. Conover obligingly assured Holt that he had discovered more evidence against Davis. He sent Holt letters offering his further services—for expense money, of course. Early in August 1865, Holt consulted with Stanton about using Conover again, in spite of accumulated evidence of his duplicity. After a personal interview with Conover, Judge Holt hired him to dig up the urgently needed evidence against Davis, to which Stanton agreed.

Conover began to round up friends to join him in duping Holt. He assured his cohorts that Davis would never be brought to trial and that their lies would not really hurt anyone. But it was far from the innocent-sounding game Conover pictured. Ultimately Conover's deceptions came perilously close to convicting the President on impeachment charges.

In addition to false testimony Conover produced for the trial, he now found eight new perjurers for Holt; six men and two women, including his wife. The credulous Holt neglected to check their background and, in his eagerness to save his reputation, did not go beyond a perfunctory interrogation. He sought not truth, but rather material to convict. For the rest of his long life Holt suffered for this mistake.

Conover carefully wrote out spurious statements for his fellow perjurers. He took the additional precaution of being present when Holt questioned each individual. Conover could thus signal the witness when his or her answers were taking the wrong direction.

On August 17, Conover brought forth his first witness, John McGill, a peddler from New York City whose real name was Neally. After hearing Stanton read McGill's testimony before the Cabinet the next day, Gideon Welles observed that the story was "chiefly humbug."[13]

Although Stanton did not reveal what he thought of the information gathered by Holt, he seems to have tolerated the process rather than to have encouraged it. Holt's maneuver did not greatly threaten Stanton. If by chance Jefferson Davis could be connected to the assassination, then Stanton was clear. If the witnesses should be proved false, he could blame it all on Holt. Thus began a brazen attempt to hoodwink American justice.

Authorities took the evidence against Davis in his absence. Furthermore, witnesses testified behind closed doors without opportunity for cross-examination. Even Attorney General Speed recognized the illegality of the Government's position. He wrote that the evidence against Confederate leaders was taken without notifying the accused even though they were available. When Holt decided to publish the "evidence," Speed opposed it, writing that publication "might wrong the Government."[14] Congressman Andrew Rogers noted sarcastically that the Nation's chief attorney seemed to be more concerned that the illegal investigation might harm the Government than that it might hurt the accused. Secretary Stanton agreed with Speed and advised President Johnson not to publish Holt's investigation.

Ugly stories continued to circulate that President Johnson, in some vague way, had been involved in the assassination. His growing differences with Radical Republicans were driving a wedge between him and Congress. Some Radicals viewed the assassination as a possible means of embarrassing Johnson.

The President brought on many of his problems by attempting to handle the perplexing problem of Reconstruction without congressional advice. Congress was not in session when Johnson was sworn in and did not reconvene until December. Thus, for eight months Johnson was left alone with overwhelming decisions. He could have called an extra session of the Thirty-ninth Congress to meet this emergency, but preferred his own program.

Proceeding to work without Congress, the President issued his amnesty proclamation on May 29, 1865, which granted pardon to participants in the Rebellion with certain exceptions. He endeavored to bring rebellious states back into the Union, and he removed restrictions on Southern commerce. However, in many reconstructed states, disguised oppression still flourished even though slavery itself had been outlawed. Radical Republicans, therefore, believed the President was perpetuating the hated system the Union had fought to abolish.

Southern states which were not reconstructed and which refused to establish favorable conditions for freed slaves produced some of Johnson's dilemma. When Congress reconvened, much of the President's work had to be undone. The circumstances of his assuming office added to his difficulties. Johnson was a Democrat, elected by Republicans to the Vice-Presidency, who accidentally became President.

Congress felt resentful that it had been denied its rightful role in the Reconstruction process. Powerful abolitionist Sen. Charles Sumner was among the first to suggest impeachment. Stanton gradually drifted into the Radical camp. By early 1866, the Secretary of War was keeping a close eye on the President and ordered detectives from the War Department to infiltrate the White House. Welles noted that although the Radicals had not yet opened war on the President, Johnson would soon have to face them squarely.[15]

Congress, through its Reconstruction Committee, began to unravel the President's program. They condemned him particularly for refusing to grant voting rights to blacks. Sen. John Sherman supported the President by reminding Congress that in only six Northern states could blacks vote—while in the Territories, over which Congress had complete jurisdiction, blacks had never been given the right to vote.

The battle heated up when Johnson vetoed the Freedman's Bureau Bill. Congress revamped the bill and passed it over the President's veto. Then they passed a series of acts in spite of his vetos.

Johnson worsened his deteriorating position by showing extreme lack of judgment. He could not back away from a challenge and began intemperate diatribes against Congress. He called the secretary of the Senate "a dead duck." Hotheads among the Congressmen entered the fray. Thaddeus Stevens even insinuated that Johnson should be executed. The President responded that the blood of Lincoln should be enough to appease the wrath of those who opposed the Government. He declared boldly (and somewhat prophetically) that he was not afraid of assassins but feared those who strike cowardly.[16]

In addition to Stevens, his most extreme opponents were Charles Sumner, George S. Boutwell and James M. Ashley. The latter two were, indeed, planning cowardly strikes.

On April 9, 1866, Massachusetts Congressman Boutwell submitted a resolution to the United States House of Representatives that the Committee of the Judiciary investigate President Johnson's charges of May 1865 linking Jefferson Davis and Jacob Thompson with Lincoln's assassination. A similar resolution, presented the same day by New York Congressman Henry J. Raymond, requested that President Johnson "take steps for the speedy trial of Jefferson Davis and others for their part in the assassination."[17] The Congressmen believed the investigation would embarrass the President, if not implicate him.

Congress empowered the Committee to inquire into the evidence implicating Jefferson Davis and other Confederates. It called many celebrated witnesses including Attorney General Speed, Secretary of State Seward and Secretary of War Stanton, as well as Judge Advocate Holt. The Committee also had at its disposal tons of Confederate documents.

These documents were so numerous that sorting and careful examination had been impossible in time for the conspiracy trial. As the months passed, the Government examined the archives more thoroughly. But after a year's work, experts still had not completed their task, although they discovered enough to reveal Confederate policy.

Francis Lieber directed the cataloguing and the preserving of Confederate archives in Washington. Lieber, of German birth, and frequently in trouble as a youth for his liberal associations, became a noted author after immigrating to the United States. By 1856 he taught history and political economy at Columbia College in New York. He had held a similar position previously at the University of South Carolina. An ardent Unionist, he had urged South Carolina against secession.

The Committee of the Judiciary called Lieber to testify. Asked if he found papers in the vast file relating to the assassination, he responded, "So far, we have not discovered offers of assassination except of a general character." The archivist added, confidently, that "no doubt some eivdence will appear."[18] The documents proved particularly valuable as records of the operation of Confederate prisons, but they revealed nothing new about Jefferson Davis. The Committee, nevertheless, reported to Congress that there was "probable cause" to link Davis indirectly to the assassination.[19]

Holt's secret interrogation of Conover's witnesses revealed what appeared

As Congressman, George S. Boutwell worked on a bizarre scheme to associate Andrew Johnson with Lincoln's assassins. Later, he became a leader in the President's impeachment. President Grant appointed him Secretary of the Treasury in 1869.

to be astonishing new facts. The Committee lost no time investigating Holt's information. On April 14, 1866, exactly one year after Lincoln's assassination and just five days after Congress established the Committee, they called Judge Holt to testify. He was expected to provide conclusive evidence against Davis.

To the Committee's surprise, Holt began to make excuses. He confessed that he had only verbal testimony and that he had passed it on to the President. Actually, he had given no proof to Johnson. Seeking desperately for someone to share his blame, Holt claimed that Stanton approved his continuing investigation. Holt then asserted inaccurately that the conspiracy trial itself proved Davis' guilt. He referred to various witnesses he had recently examined including F. B. Wright, William Campbell, Joseph Sneivel (or Snevil), Mary Knapp and others. Holt admitted he gave the witnesses money but declared it was only to keep them accessible to the Government. The Committee then asked for an unqualified appraisal. "Should Davis be tried by a Military Commission?" Holt replied, "Davis is clearly guilty," but avoided answering the question.[20]

The Congressmen made a determined effort to associate President Johnson in some way with the assassination, but Holt repeatedly affirmed that he had dealt principally with the Secretary of War. It should have been obvious to the Committee that the President had been left out of previous investigations. The Committee's effort to embarrass Johnson backfired and humiliated Holt instead and, to a lesser degree, reflected unfavorably on Stanton.

After Holt concluded his testimony he was given a stenographer's copy to sign. Before he approved the document, however, he revised his testimony, modifying answers with additions: "as I was informed," "stated to have been," "said to be" and "seemed to be."[21] He now sensed that his "facts" were at least questionable. Before Holt left, the Committee instructed him to produce Conover and also to summon other witnesses he had interviewed.

Congressmen then questioned Sanford Conover and cross-examined him in public for the first time. The results were astounding. The Judiciary Committee read to Conover the testimony he gave in secret during the conspiracy trial, which he affirmed to be correct. The Congressmen then rehashed his sworn testimony that his name was not Sanford Conover, but James Wilson Wallace, and then his later repudiation of this statement. Now Conover confessed that he and Wallace were really the same person.

Hearing Conover's ridiculous explanations, Rep. Andrew Rogers concluded that Holt had mishandled the conspiracy trial. According to military justice, when the accused is not provided with counsel, the Judge Advocate is expected to defend him as well as prosecute the case. This responsibility was difficult to perform fairly. All the accused in the conspiracy trial had counsel. Even so, Rogers contended that Holt made no effort to defend the accused against the abuses of secret testimony and was guilty of accepting evidence that could have easily been disproved by simple cross-examination.

The Congressmen found other problems involving Holt when the Committee questioned Atty. Gen. James Speed on April 25. Speed stated that all the evidence he had against Davis had been supplied by Holt. When asked specifically if he had any papers implicating Davis and Thompson, Speed replied emphatically, "I have not and never had."[22]

The Committee examined Richard Montgomery, another witness provided by Conover. Montgomery assured the Congressmen that his previous testimony was all correct. A week later Conover again testified that his information was accurate. But the Committee made no progress linking Confederate leaders with the assassination. It did find, however, unmistakable signs that Holt and his questionable witnesses supplied the basic testimony against the Rebels.

Then a dramatic and unexpected admission startled the complacent Committee on May 24. Another of Conover's witnesses, Joseph Sneivel (later found to be William H. Roberts), admitted that all of his previous testimony against Davis was absolutely false and had been prepared for him by Conover. Conover had promised Sneivel that he could make easy money simply by telling Holt what he wanted to hear. Conover then prepared Sneivel to be interviewed by Holt on November 4, 1865, four months after the conspiracy trial. This false testimony, along with those of nearly a dozen other perjured witnesses, all gathered by Conover, had satisfied the gullible, if not incompetent, Judge. Even after Sneivel's confession, the bewildered Congressmen supported Holt.

The Committee of the Judiciary, despite its inability to embarrass the President, did come across a little additional proof against the convicted conspirators. One witness, not provided by Conover, James H. Fowle, had served in the Confederate Secret Service. Fowle's testimony, untainted with the falsehoods of Conover's witnesses, provided interesting and hitherto-unknown details of Confederate spy activity involving the Surratts.

Fowle confessed that he took dispatches from Richmond to officials in the United States Government in Washington. He did not identify these Government leaders, but he did name William Prescott Smith, Superintendent of the Baltimore and Ohio Railroad, as one man in high position with whom the Rebels were in contact. The Committee apprehended Smith and interrogated him three days later, but he revealed little.

Fowle provided additional information on the elusive Mrs. Slater, also known as Olivia Floyd. He confirmed the suspicion that she carried dispatches from Richmond to Canada along with her accomplice Augustus Howell. Fowle further revealed that Atzerodt kept three or four boats hidden to transport blockade-runners.[23]

In his first appearance, Fowle refused to identify stations on the Rebel mail line. But when the Committee called him back a few days later, they pressured him into describing a tree stump in St. Mary's County, Maryland, where he left Confederate dispatches.

He confirmed that John Surratt had served as a Rebel spy since May 16, 1863. Surratt later substantiated Fowle's testimony, boasting that he began carrying Confederate mail as soon as he left school. Fowle testified that he had been introduced to Surratt by Howell and had visited with the former in Surrattsville about two months before Lincoln's murder. Fowle's revelations not only corroborated what had been known of John Surratt, Mrs. Slater, Howell and Atzerodt, but also supplied additional evidence which was later confirmed. Fowle explained that the Confederate Government kept each agent ignorant of his peers' activities. Many agents, however, worked in pairs and naturally knew something of their partners' assignments.

The Committee wanted to know the names of other agents. The witness at first refused but later revealed the names of William Woods, William Lomax and the Reverend John Stewarts. Lomax was already well known to authorities, but this was the first mention of Stewarts, also known as "Crazy" Stewarts. He remains another shadowy figure lurking somewhere on the fringes of the Confederate spy network, if not part of the conspiracy itself.

Fowle seemed to know more about Confederate activities in Lower Maryland than previous witnesses, or at least he was willing to reveal more. The Committee pressed him to divulge the Rebel connections with suspects in the assassination plot. He claimed he did not know Booth and did not think Booth received any help from the Confederate Government. When asked about John Lloyd, he replied, "He was trusted by the Confederates." He confessed he knew of Dr. Mudd, declaring, "He was fishy."[24]

In hundreds of interviews, Weichmann's name was never linked directly to the conspiracy; it was associated, however, with the conspirators. Persistent rumors, spread particularly by Mrs. Surratt's supporters, intimated that Weichmann was hiding something. The Committee, therefore, sent for him in Philadelphia where he was residing. In a long interrogation, they asked if his testimony as recorded in Pitman's official account was correct. Weichmann admitted that he made an error in testifying that he had met McCullough on April 2. The date was actually March 26. He also corrected the date he saw John Surratt leave on the aborted kidnapping mission; the date should have been March 16 rather than March 21. He claimed the rest of his testimony was accurate.

Considering the scores of names, places, dates and events he swore to, it was remarkable he could stick by them. The young man had been examined by Government detectives, the Military Commission, and now by the United States Committee of the Judiciary. Later the District of Columbia civil court put him on the witness stand.

Asked if he had any other statements, Weichmann added some points which would "prove conclusively the guilt of Mrs. Surratt."[25] He revealed that a detective in Baker's office named Hubbard informed him that Augustus Howell knew all about the contemplated capture of President Lincoln. Weichmann was careful, as always, to mention names that could be checked. Baker, Hubbard and, presumably, Howell were still available and could have been called by the Congressmen.

The Committee had one last question: When was the last time he saw John Surratt? He had answered that question repeatedly and his response was always the same—he last saw Surratt on April 3, 1865. Until his death, Weichmann had lingering doubts as to Surratt's whereabouts on the night of the murder. Many witnesses swore that they had seen him in Washington that night, but Weichmann never wavered; he never tried to place his former friend at the scene of the crime. Other than these insignificant facts, he revealed little that was not already known.

As the Committee's work dragged on, other witnesses supplied by Conover confessed they had lied to Holt and to the Military Commission. Holt was, therefore, called back to testify on June 18, 1866. This time the Congressmen were less gentle; they probed more thoroughly into Holt's relationship with Conover. In his defense, Holt produced a letter from Conover, dated July 26, 1865, in which Conover claimed he could produce more evidence against Davis. Holt maintained that only after conferring with Stanton did he negotiate with Conover. Stanton backed Holt and placed money at his disposal for expenses. Holt told of Conover's promises and of the witnesses he produced, including two women calling themselves Sarah Douglas and Mary Knapp.

The Judge testified that the first indication he had that the witnesses had lied was when he sent Colonel Turner to New York to find William Campbell. While returning to Washington, Campbell confessed to Turner that his previous testimony was false. He also admitted the other witnesses had lied.

After Holt's startling testimony, Congressman Wilson, chairman of the Committee, telegraphed Conover to return to Washington again so the questionable witnesses might confront him. Conover hurried to the capital and was present when Campbell testified before the Committee. The Congressmen asked him if his previous testimony before the Military Commission had been true. He said it was all false. When asked why he had sworn deceitfully, he explained that Conover informed him that Holt was in a bind to get proof against Davis. Campbell then went over every point of his testimony, denying each part he had sworn to. Conover prepared all of his testimony, he claimed. By this time, the Committee did not know what to believe.

Campbell went even further; he swore that Conover contrived the testimonies of the other witnesses. Joseph Sneivel's real name was Roberts; F. B. Wright was really John Waters; John H. Paterson (or Patten) was Smith. Sarah Douglas was actually Mrs. Dunham, which was also Conover's real name. Subsequent evidence showed that Conover had used his wife, brother-in-law and sister-in-law to deceive the Government.

Conover sat quietly listening to Campbell's amazing confession and said nothing until the witness left the room. The bewildered Holt claimed that he was "utterly astounded."[26] Conover pretended he was also flabbergasted and explained to the confused Congressmen that somebody had corrupted Campbell. The slippery Conover then offered to accompany a member of the Committee to New York and assist in locating other witnesses who would get at the truth. He had used this tactic several times with the naive Holt. The Committee, no less gullible, agreed to Conover's request but, to ensure his return, sent an officer with him. As soon as they got to New York City, Conover eluded the officer and escaped.

When the Congressmen presented their report to the United States House of Representatives, they still had not located Conover. Next they sent Joseph Wilkerson, sergeant of arms of the House of Representatives, to search for Campbell. He was also unsuccessful, as Campbell had left a false address.

Other witnesses paraded before the Committee and filled in details of Conover's fantastic perjury scheme. Sneivel confessed that money was the motive; he received $625 for his part. According to Sneivel, when Holt looked for witnesses, Conover supplied them—always for a fee. He revealed that when authorities began to suspect Conover, he brought in other informants to cover up for him until about a dozen false witnesses were swearing lies for one another. The congressional Committee was now totally baffled.

More details of Conover's methods were soon revealed. He would write out evidence he thought Holt was looking for, and his associates would memorize it. After the witness had learned his part, Conover would accompany him to Holt's office, having previously rehearsed the questions Holt would likely ask. If, however, a question came up that the witness answered incorrectly, Conover would unobtrusively shake his head or make some gesture which alerted his cohort to correct his statement as best he could.

Holt paid Conover for his expenses in finding perjurers, for their travel to Washington and for their time. When a monthly wage was barely $30, the false witnesses were receiving between $300 and $800 for a few hours' work. Conover sought to keep his puppets in line by severely threatening them if they revealed his deception.

Holt's eyes were opened—at least a little. He admitted that the confessions left him with "a strong impression that Conover had been guilty of a most atrocious crime."[27] But he began to defend himself, asserting that he had only given Conover expense money and that, furthermore, only two witnesses confessed they had sworn falsely. He added, pitifully, that the witnesses seemed truthful and their evidence had "not been successfully controverted."[28] Holt was clearly in a bind, but his chief concern was to save his own reputation. He seemed to care little for the reputations of others damaged by the false testimony.

Judge Holt suggested that the testimony of eight witnesses be withdrawn, including the damaging statements concerning Holt's questionable actions given by Campbell and Sneivel. In other words, he wanted the Congressmen to ignore the fact he had given large sums of money to men who lied in secret sessions at the conspiracy trial.

Holt then signed documents relating to his most recent testimony and reluctantly admitted that an enormous hoax had been perpetrated on the Government which he now called a "shameless fraud."[29] Equally shameless were Holt's prolonged efforts to ignore it. The Committee of the Judiciary, except for one member, wanted to conceal the whole episode. Stanton apparently concurred in the cover-up attempt.

Congressman Andrew J. Rogers of New Jersey was the only member of the House Committee wanting the affair brought out in the open. He began to probe more deeply into the fraud.[30]

The investigation continued with the calling of Dr. James Merritt. He had previously testified that he heard the conspiracy discussed and was asked why he made no effort to stop the assassination. Merritt replied that he mentioned the plot to a justice of the peace in Canada named Squire Davidson. The Committee located the only justice of the peace in Canada named Davidson, who denied the story. Furthermore, Merritt had testified at the conspiracy trial that he received no money for his cooperation. Under cross-examination by Rogers, he admitted the War Department had paid him.

At this point other members began to react against Rogers' aggressive examination. They refused to allow Merritt's statement, admitting the deception, included in the final report. The investigation was becoming an embarrassment to Radical Republicans rather than to the President.

Rogers' concern was further heightened when Judge Holt sent a copy of Conover's original trial testimony to the Committee. Along with Conover's evident perjuries, Holt added his own explanation, as if trying to influence the Committee's interpretation. As Congress had ordered the Committee to make its own investigation, Rogers felt Holt's explanations were not only unethical, but revealed ulterior motives.

By this time, President Johnson had released the accused Confederate leader Clement Clay from prison. Congressman Rogers pointed out that the

Andrew J. Rogers, Democratic Congressman from New Jersey. Rogers helped uncover a vast deception against the Government, but Radical Republicans tried to
thwart his efforts (Library of Congress – BH82-4906).

President apparently did not believe the testimony of Merritt either. Rogers
then began a personal investigation into the background and character of each
witness against Confederate leaders and found that all were "either convicted
perjurers or men of infamous life."[31]

He predicted the whole confused pack of lies and wild perjuries "would
simply pass down to posterity as an absurdity unsurpassed in the history of the
Nation."[32] Nevertheless, other Committee members refused to cooperate with
him in exposing the mess. Rogers was finally ostracized and forced to carry on
the investigation without help from the Committee.

The difficulty was partly political. The split between Radical Republicans
and Johnson daily grew more irreconcilable. Some Radicals even seemed disappointed the assassins had been unsuccessful in killing the Vice-President.
Several intimated openly that Johnson had a part in the conspiracy. Johnson's

sympathizers, aware that as Vice-President he had been a target of the assassins, accused the Radicals of suggesting that he plotted his own death.

Johnson, now believing the charges against Confederate authorities were probably false, blamed Judge Holt and, to some degree, Secretary Stanton for the unfounded accusations. Radicals, however, continued their support of Holt and of the War Department. The Judiciary Committee's desire to hide its findings was an essential part of this effort.

Rogers thought the Nation's honor required punishment of the confessed perjurers, but other members voted against him. The majority refused to allow Rogers even to see the paper concerning the testimony. Exasperated, the Congressman from New Jersey brought the attempted cover-up to the attention of the House of Representatives. But the Speaker ruled that Rogers was not entitled to see the official papers until all other members had examined them. He finally got to inspect them at noon, the day before Congress recessed. By that time Rogers had little time to prepare his minority report. The Committee's majority account practically ignored the fantastic ring of perjurers paid by the Government.

Congressman Rogers nevertheless insisted on revealing the hoax, and his minority report created a sensation. It denounced Holt, accusing him of trying to stifle the Committee's investigation. Rogers stated:

> I believe this was done to hide the disgraceful fact that the assassination of Mr. Lincoln was seized upon as a pretext to hatch charges against a number of historical personages, to blacken their private character, and afford excuse for their trial through the useless forms of a Military Commission, and through the ductile instrument of vengeance in the hands of power, murder them.[33]

The report did not accuse Holt of originating the "plot of perjurers," but it criticized the Judge for either using the perjurers or being used by them:

> [The] fact that Mr. Holt did himself pay moneys to more than one of them, to those who ackowledge they swore for money, may awaken suspicion that there was bribery as well as perjury—perhaps not conscious bribery, but the payment for false testimony was committed; though it may have been done innocently, it produced the usual effect of subornation of perjury.[34]

Rogers' revelation hit Holt where it hurt most. It accused him of poor judgment, if not of corruption and bribery. This, Holt could not endure. In several previous disputes, Holt had taken his case to the public in the form of printed "vindications." Rogers forced him to vindicate himself once more. However, before Holt could get his side of the story out, the *New York Herald* began to publish his correspondence with Conover. These letters, seen from Holt's point of view, may have seemed logical, but, as arranged by the *Herald*, they made Holt appear guilty of bribery.

The Judge indignantly demanded a court of inquiry to clear his name. Stanton brought up the subject with President Johnson, who was weary of both Holt and the Secretary of War. Johnson left Holt waiting for more than two months before deciding that a court of inquiry would not be necessary. Stanton, in relating the President's belated decision, added a few conciliatory words. "In communicating the President's decision, it is proper for me to express my own conviction that all charges and imputations against your official conduct are, in my judgment groundless."[35]

Ignoring both the President and Stanton, Holt insisted on justifying himself. His supporters felt that any explanation would be misunderstood and cause him even greater embarrassment. W. W. Winthrop, one of Holt's closest friends, advised him that his friends "need from you no defense to a contemptible slander from such a source."[36] Undeterred, Holt published his vindication in November 1866 in the sympathetic *Washington Chronicle*. Radical Republican newspapers praised Holt's explanation; his enemies thought it was an absurd cover-up.

Evidently the Rogers Report opened President Johnson's eyes. Stanton wrote Holt on December 8 that the President wanted to review testimony referred to in Holt's accusations against Confederate officials.

The Judge Advocate delayed a week in replying, although he had taken only a few hours to name the culprits in the first place. This time, when pressed for confirmation of his charges, he realized he never had concrete evidence. Holt replied to Stanton that the evidence was based on the testimony of Richard Montgomery and Dr. James B. Merritt, but because these men did not want their names known, the testimony was not officially "on file," but was based on "repeated interviews."[37]

XLVII
Impeaching the Impeachers

Radical Republicans long felt President Johnson had misrepresented his position and betrayed them. Actually Johnson had not changed; he remained essentially what he had always been—a rough, hardheaded politician. Republicans had simply misjudged his views. On one occasion, Johnson defied "anyone to point to any of my public acts at variance with the fixed principles which have guided me through life."[1] He fought hard, spoke intemperately, and stubbornly maintained his opinions, before and after becoming President.

His "fixed principles" included a strong dependence on the Constitution, which he believed did not permit secession, but which supported slavery. Johnson constantly denounced secessionists but felt slavery could only be abolished by a Consitutional amendment. He was also a strong advocate of States' rights and vetoed the Freedman's Bureau Bill on grounds that Congress passed it without allowing Southern states representation in the voting. Johnson despised the slaveholding Southern aristocracy and always identified himself with the poor Southerner. He had no wish to see the whole Southern population suffer. Radical leaders apparently could not understand these distinctions.

Republicans made their first effort to impeach the President in 1866 but failed. They continued, however, to fight Johnson, hoping to find some serious charge against him. Later investigations of the Lincoln conspiracy were aimed primarily at Johnson.

The battle did not always follow strict party lines. Republicans as well as Democrats were often divided in their allegiances. However, Republicans generally supported results of the military trial and grew critical of the President. Democrats, for the most part, criticized the trial and were more favorable toward Johnson. These divisions influenced future investigations.

While debating Reconstruction policies before the United States Congress on March 21, 1867, Benjamin Butler accused John Bingham of opposing the President's proposals. Bingham retaliated by referring to Butler's voting record and poor military leadership. Butler admitted that before the war he had "voted fifty-seven times for Jefferson Davis for President." He explained that he thought this would avoid breaking up the Nation, but after the schism, he fought against Davis.

He then turned on Bingham. "The gentleman has had the bad taste to attack me for the reason that I could not do any more injury to the enemies of my country. I agree to that. I did all I could, the best I could." Butler acknowledged that he was chagrined, but, he added, the only victim of Bingham's powers "was an innocent woman hung upon the scaffold, one Mrs. Surratt." He argued that he could bear the memory of Fort Fisher if Bingham "and his present associates can sustain him in shedding the blood of a woman tried by a Military Commission and convicted without sufficient evidence in my judgment."[2]

Bingham prided himself on his ability to cut his opponents down with a burst of ruthless rhetoric, but he was not prepared for Butler's scathing assault and lost his usual composure. We do not know exactly what he replied, because he revised his remarks in the official record, but there is no doubt about his rage.

The dispute between Butler and Bingham continued to disrupt Congress for nearly a week. On March 26, Butler brought up the subject of Booth's diary, which had recently been discussed in one of the Congressional committees. Congressman Butler accused special Judge Advocate Bingham of hiding this vital document from the military court. When soldiers captured Booth, explained Butler, "there was taken from his pocket a diary like the one I now hold in my hand. In this diary Booth had set down day by day his plans, thoughts, motives and the execution of his plans."[3]

Butler was mistaken. Booth did not "set down day by day his plans." Rather, he wrote only during two or three days—April 14, 15 and maybe 16, 1865—and even then Booth was careless with facts. Butler asserted that although the Judges presented Booth's pipe and compass as evidence, they did not mention the diary. He claimed he had examined the diary and that "as now produced, has eighteen pages cut out, the pages prior to the time when Abraham Lincoln was massacred, although the edges as yet show they had all been written over."

The Congressman inquired indignantly if the diary was "whole when it came into the hands of the Government." Also questioned Butler, if it was "good judgment on the part of the gentleman prosecuting the assassins of the President to put in evidence the tobacco pipe which was found in Booth's pocket, why was not the diary, in his own handwriting put in evidence...?"[4]

Butler finally got around to the dark suspicion lingering in the minds of Radicals. He speculated that the diary could have proved "who it was that changed Booth's purpose from capture to assassination." Butler, moving ever closer to accusing the President, raised the question of who would "profit by assassination who could not profit by capture and abduction of the President." He further indicated that the suppressed diary might have revealed Booth's expectations regarding the presidency. But that was impossible now, Butler inferred, because it could not be ascertained what was in the book. The Congressman admitted casually that although the diary might not have been legal evidence, it was morally valid.[5]

Butler used up his allotted time; it was Bingham's turn to address the House. He blasted his opponent with all his considerable ability. After declaring that the diary was absolutely not admissible evidence, he thundered:

I treat with contempt and scorn any intimation from any quarter that I or my associate counsel were under obligations to admit any such evidence. The law does not require it; the common law, the growth of centuries, the gathered wisdom of a thousand years excludes it. But perhaps that great monument of wisdom and learning is not equal to the incomparable genius of the incomparable hero of Fort Fisher.[6]

Democrats burst into laughter at this sarcasm, but it did not please Butler, who requested permission to reply.

Bingham, in no mood to listen to Butler anymore, declined to yield the floor. "No, sir; the gentleman has no right to ask favors at my hands." Bingham then denied that he had ever seen any written plans of the conspiracy. He had previously asked to see the little book Butler waved at the Committee and accused Butler of withholding evidence. "I am not surprised that this gentleman would not let me see the book that he put into his pocket."[7]

Again Butler clamored to speak and again Bingham cut him off sharply. At this point, the Speaker of the House interrupted. "The gentleman from Ohio declines to yield, and must be allowed to proceed without interruption."

Bingham shouted, "I do not care, if having refused to let me inspect the book, he imitated the example given in the vision in the Apocalypse and 'eats it.'"[8]

Congressmen again roared in laughter. Bingham was just warming up:

One word more. The gentleman talks about the spoliated book. Who spoliated the book? That is about as interesting a cry as that to which I referred the other day, "Who killed Cock Robin?" Who knows that it was spoliated or mutilated if that is the gentleman's meaning? If John Wilkes Booth tore pages out of it, was that spoliation or mutilation? The gentleman's words are as impossible as they are unwarranted.

"Let the galled jade wince; our withers are unwrung."

I challenge the gentleman, I dare him here or anywhere in this tribunal, or in any tribunal, to assert that I spoliated or mutilated any book. Why, sir, such a charge, without one tittle of evidence, is only fit to come from a man who lives in a bottle and is fed with a spoon.[9]

At this extemporaneous oratorical exhibition the Democrats, almost delirious, again laughed and burst into spontaneous applause. Only repeated appeals from the Speaker brought the ecstatic House under control. Bingham had more to say, but he had said enough.

The so-called diary that agitated Butler and continued to arouse enemies of the President was brought to public attention by LaFayette Baker. While testifying before the Impeachment Committee a short time earlier, Baker referred to a diary taken from Booth's body, stating that he had given it to Stanton. Ordinarily, the diary would not have created much commotion. but in the highly charged political atmosphere of 1867, it was made to appear mysterious, especially the 18 missing pages. As pictured by critics of the Government, officials kept the diary secret because it contained information incriminating National leaders. The missing pages, according to this theory, were cut out by someone in order to hide evidence.

Actually, the Government did not hide the diary. Holt had mentioned it during the trial and several reporters commented on it. Mr. Wachusett, reporter for the *Boston Advertiser*, wrote about the diary early in the conspiracy trial. He referred to it again on May 31, 1865, along with other documents he thought should have been presented as evidence. The diary was no more "secret" than scores of documents which could not be used. More important than the diary was the other paper mentioned by Wachusett – the paper Booth left to be published in the *Washington Intelligencer*.

The most important documents relating to the conspiracy were the confessions of Atzerodt and Arnold. These vital documents, although referred to, were never permitted as evidence. The rules of court-martial would not even permit the accused to testify, rules which also guided most civil courts at that time. Agents had found evidence against Anna Surratt which some officials sought unsuccessfully to have presented in court. The diary was just one of numerous documents possessed by the Government that presented Booth's distorted account of his actions, but it would have added little to the conspiracy case. Nevertheless, the public was unaware of the document, which gave rise to wild accusations.

Booth did not keep a diary in the usual sense. He used an outdated 1864 diary mostly as scratch paper. It served as combination wallet and notebook. Booth kept pictures of his girl friends in pockets of the so-called diary. The few notes he recorded were scrawled randomly across pages intended for the previous year. The missing pages were not purposely destroyed but seemed to have been taken out by Booth. Dr. Stewart had one of the pages. Booth had written a short note on it and folded it up with the money he paid the doctor.

Butler's ominous intimations concerning Booth's diary animated the House of Representatives to appoint yet another special committee to investigate the assassination. It was to examine any evidence that might implicate persons holding high positions. Early in 1867, the Committee on the Assassination, chaired by Ben Butler, got under way. The Committee was slow getting started and did not function long. When it was formed, the trial of John Surratt was already in progress. The trial served to show the Committee what areas needed further investigation. After the Surratt trial terminated, the Committee on the Assassination had another opportunity to interrogate individuals it felt might be hiding something.

In proposing another investigation, Butler criticized the previous trials as being too restricted by legalities. If the House investigation were to uncover the real truth, he felt, it would have to offer immunity to encourage witnesses to testify freely. He wanted his investigation unhampered by legalistic restrictions.

Butler's Committee, however, could find little new ground to cover. Two trials and several committees had already thoroughly examined the crime. Of the few people it questioned, only one, Henry H. Hine, had not been interrogated previously, and he had nothing to add. Colonel Baker had sent Hine to Canada to uncover Rebel activity. He testified that he found the Sons of Liberty in Canada were planning to release Confederate prisoners in Chicago. The Government had already fully investigated this plot.

Benjamin F. Butler. This Congressman accused Bingham of withholding Booth's diary. Later, as chairman of the Committee on the Assassination, he sought to link Johnson with Lincoln's murder (Library of Congress – USZ62-79314).

The Committee on the Assassination also questioned 27-year-old John P. Brophy, who had been constantly criticizing the conduct of the conspiracy trial for two years. Brophy had boasted that if he only had a chance, he could prove Weichmann a liar and Mrs. Surratt innocent. The Committee gave him a chance. He testified that Weichmann had told him he (Weichmann) had to declare all he knew because if he did not they would hang him like a dog – a story repeatedly told by Brophy and repeatedly denied by Weichmann.

The Government tried successfully to avoid arguments about religion during the trials. But Brophy seemed determined to interject a religious angle. He repeated a thirdhand story that he said Weichmann passed on to him – that Burnett had supposedly told Weichmann – "You know this is a Catholic conspiracy gotten up by the priests and nuns for the purpose of destroying the Government."[10] If Burnett did make such a ridiculous statement, Weichmann never hinted at it, even vaguely.

In the meantime, the Judiciary Committee indicted Sanford Conover for lying. He was tried in February 1867, found guilty and sentenced to ten years'

James M. Ashley. While a Republican Congressman from Ohio, Ashley became involved in an unscrupulous scheme to associate Andrew Johnson with his predecessor's murder (Library of Congress – BH824-5303).

imprisonment. The Government confined him in a Washington jail for the next six months before sending him to the penitentiary. During this time, just as Butler's Committee was getting under way, Conover became involved in another bizarre deception involving National officials.

Conover had no real loyalties to the North, the South, the President, the Congress or any other group. His only concern was his own welfare. Even before his imprisonment, he initiated steps to gain a presidential pardon. A man with so few scruples and with such unmitigated dexterity as a professional perjurer was as dangerous to his enemies as he was profitable to those willing to pay.

Benjamin Butler's Committee created the kind of environment Conover thrived in, and he soon made contact with Butler and James Ashley. These men were among leaders seeking to impeach the President. Ashley, a 42-year-old Republican Congressman from Ohio, was chairman of the Committee on Territories but was otherwise undistinguished. The 50-year-old Butler, however, was a man of notoriety and determination. The South hated him for his arbitrary rule as military commander of New Orleans and for hanging William Mumford for pulling down the United States flag. Butler had just been elected to the House of Representatives and had quickly assumed leadership of the Radicals. In some unknown way, Conover, Butler and Ashley entered into a secret agreement to use the Assassination Committee to discredit the President.

Butler and Ashley planned to use Conover's witnesses to link Johnson with Lincoln's murder. In return for Conover's cooperation, the Republicans promised to maneuver the President into granting him a pardon. It was a tricky subterfuge; timing was crucial. Johnson, of course, was expected to issue his pardon before Conover testified against him. As fantastic as this unscrupulous plot appeared, it came close to succeeding.

While Conover was held in the Washington jail, he managed to round up prospective witnesses. These individuals presented themselves to Butler and Ashley, but Conover was careful not to allow them to actually give their depositions before he secured his pardon.[11] Ashley was to supply the so-called facts needed against the President and Conover was to get his friends to memorize and repeat them—but not under oath. That was the trick. The perjured testimony had to be given in secret meetings in which the witnesses were not put under oath or cross-examined. President Johnson's enemies found a minister named Matchett who was to certify the good character of the witnesses.

Congressman Ashley organized the intrigue. He genuinely believed Johnson had been involved in the Lincoln conspiracy but thought Johnson's friends so controlled the evidence that it was difficult to prove. Thus, in Ashley's mind, providing witnesses who would swear falsely that the President was guilty was simply arriving at the truth by an indirect route.[12]

Ashley explained to Conover the type of evidence he wanted. The Congressman thought it would be possible to prove four points: (1) that Booth had visited President Johnson several times in the Kirkwood Hotel, (2) that Booth had corresponded with Johnson (on this point Conover was to provide individuals who would testify they had carried notes from Booth to Johnson), (3) that evidence had been planted in Atzerodt's room to make it look like Johnson was a target of the conspirators (perjurers were to be produced who would say they had played a small part in the plot and knew that this was part of the plan. Conover would assure his cohorts that Butler's Committee could provide immunity for them), and (4) that Booth, after the inauguration on March 4, had told friends that he had been working with Johnson on a plot to kill the President at the inauguration but that the attempt failed (this was to explain Johnson's strange behavior at the inauguration).[13]

Since Conover's incarceration prevented him from directing all the details, Congressman Ashley agreed to organize and coach the witnesses. Ashley devised the statements the perjurers were to give and promised them rewards.

After Ashley prepared the false witnesses, he presented them to Butler. Upon Butler's approval, they were introduced to other Radical Republicans, who questioned them informally. Butler wanted the witnesses to make formal statements to the Committee on the Assassination before he gained Conover's release from jail. Conover refused, saying he had been promised his freedom, and he would not allow the perjured witnesses to make official statements to the Committee until he received his pardon.

Just how much of this dastardly deception Conover promoted and what part originated with Ashley is difficult to determine, but Ashley tried to get

Conover released. On July 22, 1867, he addressed letters to both Judge Holt and the Hon. A. G. Riddle urging them to sign a request for Conover's pardon. The next day the obliging Holt wrote the President in behalf of Conover. Riddle, former United States Representative from Ohio and, at this time, a member of the Washington Bar, also contacted Johnson, praising Conover for his service to the Government and recommending that he be granted an appropriate reward. Holt apparently read Riddle's recommendation and added a similar note to the bottom of it. In addition to these pleas, Conover sent his own appeal stating that the trial convicting him was irregular.[14]

Four days later, the courts refused Conover's petition for a suspended sentence. On the same day, recommendations secured by Butler and Ashley from influential individuals urging Conover's pardon were presented to the President. By this time, Conover, growing impatient, suddenly turned against Butler and Ashley. He wrote a long, detailed letter to the President, exposing the Radicals' plot against him.[15] In addition to Conover's disappointment in failing to gain his release, he apparently worried that his deceptions were beginning to unravel.

It is not known exactly what happened, but when Conover's witnesses were presented to John Bingham, some of them became fearful. Bingham, well acquainted with details of the assassination, could not easily be fooled by perjured testimony. The Reverend Mr. Matchett, in particular, became apprehensive and did not complete his part.

In Conover's remarkable letter revealing Ashley's scheme, he had the audacity to again ask the President for a pardon. He explained that it would have been easy for him to provide witnesses to prove that Johnson was in correspondence with Booth. But, he said, if the President would pardon him, he would testify against Ashley and Butler and thus impeach the impeachers. Conover added that he was not making these revelations in order to obtain a pardon, but for the sake of justice. He ended his lengthy epistle describing the plot in convincing details and asserting that his wife could verify the facts.

The shrewd Conover had saved Ashley's correspondence, which he included with his letter to the President. He also enclosed messages from Matchett, who was in Toledo, Ohio, at the time. In addition, he sent several articles that had been prepared to prove Johnson's collaboration with Booth. One document involved an elaborate story about a man called Allen, who had supposedly carried letters across the lines from Johnson to authorities in Richmond.[16]

Events during the next few days supported Conover's revelations. His wife visited Matchett on August 2 and told him that she thought Holt's letter to the President should help her husband. But, she added, if not, she would get him out of prison "under a change of office."[17] Apparently she was referring to impeachment efforts. The next day, Matchett wrote the most mysterious letter of the incredible episode and sent it to Holt. Matchett used vague terms about "getting the letters" and mentioned the visit of Conover's wife.

In one strange line, Matchett wrote, "I believe it will be all for the best that he had gone up for a while—she knows not *how* long, I *do; if she will bring me the letters* [italics in the original]."[18] This letter, torn in bits and pasted back together, had somehow come to President Johnson's attention and was preserved among his papers.

Two days later the acting Attorney General sent the President an application for Conover's pardon.

Johnson had been aware of efforts to link him with the assassination but did not know the source of the recent rumors. The President was astonished at the extent to which Butler, Ashley and their associates had gone. Soon after receiving Conover's evidence, the President published most of the incriminating documents in leading newspapers.

Within weeks, authorities moved Conover from Washington to the Federal penitentiary in Albany, New York. President Johnson pardoned him before he left office more than a year later. Johnson had withstood this assault with Conover's belated help, but attacks against him were just beginning.

On August 5, 1867, the day Johnson received Conover's pardon request, he asked Secretary of War Stanton to resign. The President stated that "grave public considerations" made it necessary for him to request the Secretary's resignation. Stanton replied that "grave public considerations" made it imperative for him to remain in his position until the next session of Congress.[19] Johnson dismissed him anyway and ordered General Grant to assume the position. The stage was thus set for impeachment proceedings against the President.

XLVIII
"The Son Is Here Before You"

Federal authorities brought John Surratt back to Washington shortly before Butler's Committee was formed. In February 1867, the Government imprisoned Surratt until his trial could begin in June. At one time in 1867, three separate groups in Washington were investigating the assassination—the Judicial Committee of the Impeachment Investigation, the Congressional Committee on the Assassination, and the trial of John Surratt.

While waiting for his trial, Surratt had opportunity to secure counsel and prepare his defense. Anna—ever faithful to her brother—sold pictures of him dressed in his Papal Zouave uniform to help pay his expenses.

Dist. Atty. Edward C. Carrington and Edwards Pierrepont directed the Government's case. Surratt secured lawyers Joseph H. Bradley, Sr., Joseph H. Bradley, Jr. and Richard T. Merrick. George P. Fisher of the District of Columbia Supreme Court sat as Judge.

Joseph Bradley, Sr., had previously refused to serve as counsel for David Herold in the conspiracy trial. Merrick had been asked to accept Dr. Mudd's defense but refused to serve openly, although he did give advice privately.

The trial of John Surratt rehashed the conspiracy trial, but with some notable differences. For one, it was a civil trial, under the rules of civil law, with a 12-man jury. Although both sides constantly referred to the official records of the conspiracy trial, the evidence was supposed to concern only John Surratt.

Because of strong antagonism between Northerners and Southerners, jury selection became a long and tedious process. They considered only white male citizens. The trial finally got under way on June 17, 1867. The prosecution called 85 witnesses and the defense interrogated 97 in an extremely bitter contest. Many of the same individuals who had taken the stand before the Military Commission were called. They repeated practically the same testimony given previously. For two years Mrs. Surratt's supporters had talked of important new evidence which would prove her innocence. Now they had their chance. The trial of her son became another effort to prove the mother guiltless.

In spite of expectations of great revelations, none emerged. Both Weichmann and Lloyd reiterated their damaging testimony. The basic facts remained the same. Weichmann remained on the stand for three grueling days under the elder Bradley's badgering. He corrected his testimony about dates and brought out a few new facts.

Anna sold copies of this picture of her brother John in his Papal Zouave uniform to help pay his trial expenses (Library of Congress—BH83-917).

Prosecuting attorney Pierrepont, resentful of repeated efforts to bring up the military trial, explained that he had not "come here for the purpose of proving that Mrs. Surratt was guilty, or that she was innocent; and I do not understand why that subject was lugged into this case in the mode that it has been." He accused the counsel of indirectly censuring President Johnson.

His protest had no effect; the defense of John's dead mother remained a major thrust of the proceedings.

At the time of Surratt's trial, President Johnson had practically returned to the Democratic party. Supporters of John Surratt were mostly Democrats, while the Republicans generally favored the Government. Friends of the Surratts began circulating a rumor exonerating President Johnson for his part in the execution of Mrs. Surratt. They claimed the President never saw the plea for clemency because it was attached at the end of the Court's findings in such a way that the President would not see it. It was a flimsy excuse, but it gained momentum.

Edwards Pierrepont, a highly experienced New York lawyer who served as one
of the Government's prosecuting attorneys in its case against John Surratt
(Library of Congress—BH832-770).

Prosecution lawyer Pierrepont wanted to settle the dispute early. He
argued that the Court record and the clemency recommendation had been
presented to the President clearly. Furthermore, he stated that Cabinet
members had discussed the plea, and there was nothing secret about it. "The
President, with his own hand, wrote his confirmation of it, and with his own
hand signed the warrant," claimed Pierrepont.[1] Holding up the document, he
concluded dramatically, "I hold in my hand the original record, and no other
man, as it appears from that record, ordered it."

This did not satisfy the defense. Later, Merrick complained that the
documents were withdrawn from the Court's view too soon. He continued to
assert the President had not seen the plea. The question is still disputed.

The chronology of Mrs. Surratt's trip on the day of the murder had been
scrutinized in the two years since her execution. Defense Attorney Joseph
Bradley, Sr., questioned Weichmann about the timing of the trip, but the
witness gave more details than the lawyer wanted.

Describing Mrs. Surratt's preparations for the journey to Surrattsville,
Weichmann testified that she gave him a ten-dollar note and asked him to hire

a horse and buggy. As he left the parlor, he noticed John Wilkes Booth come in. Weichmann said he went to Howard's Stables and there saw Atzerodt trying unsuccessfully to rent a horse. When he asked Atzerodt's purpose, Atzerodt replied that he wanted "to send off Payne." After getting the buggy he returned to the Surratt house. There he observed that she was still conversing with Booth. He testified, "Booth was standing with his back against the mantel-piece with his arm resting on it, and Mrs. Surratt had her back towards him."

He then went to the buggy and in a few minutes Mrs. Surratt came out. As she started to get in the carriage she said, "Wait, Mr. Weichmann, I must get those things of Booth's." When she came back she had a package about five or six inches, wrapped in brown paper, but he did not see the contents.

Bradley asked, "Did you see what was done with it?"

He responded that she put it in the bottom of the buggy. Mrs. Surratt told him it was brittle and she was afraid it would get wet. "I then helped her into the buggy, and we drove off."[2]

Bradley, apparently unaware of the details, inquired if anything of note occurred on the trip. This gave the witness an opportunity to mention some otherwise unknown evidence. "Yes, sir," he swore. "The buggy was halted once near a blacksmith's shop, about three miles from Washington, on the road to Surrattsville." He explained there were some pickets on the side of the road and soldiers lying on the grass. "Mrs. Surratt had the buggy halted," he testified, "and wanted to know how long those pickets would remain there. She was informed that they were withdrawn about 8 o'clock." According to Weichmann's account she said, "I am glad to know of it" and then drove off.

As Weichmann was testifying, Dr. Mudd, Arnold and Spangler were confined on the island of Dry Tortugas. Mudd was making every effort to gain his release. Thus if Weichmann's testimony could be shaken, it would also help Dr. Mudd's cause. Weichmann had already admitted to the Judiciary Committee his errors in dates. The defense, nevertheless, brought up these mistakes again. Their chief target was the date of Dr. Mudd's meeting with Booth in the National Hotel. Bradley questioned the witness about his testimony at the military trial. "Are you aware that proof was given on that trial that Dr. Mudd was not here at the time you named?"[3]

Weichmann answered confidently that Mudd had admitted openly that he met Booth at the hotel. Bradley, unhappy with the answer, retorted harshly, "I am not asking you what Dr. Mudd admitted. Are you aware that on that trial proof was given that Dr. Mudd was not here at the time you fixed him here?"

"I have read Mr. Bingham's argument."

Still dissatisfied, the lawyer barked, "I am not asking you as to whether you have read Mr. Bingham's argument or not. I repeat my question: Are you aware that on that trial proof was given that Dr. Mudd was not here at the time you fixed him here?"

"I am."

The defense repeated its question about the date. Bradley asked again about the date fixed by the evidence in the military trial. Weichmann admitted that the evidence showed Dr. Mudd was in Washington on December 22, 1865.

"Yet," responded the lawyer, "you on that trial swore that he was here about the 15th of January?"

"To the best of my recollection," answered the witness. Weichmann added, "Another circumstance which comes to my mind as fixing the introduction in the latter part of December, 1864, is that Surratt went to Port Tobacco in the early part of January, 1865."

"Hadn't you thought over all these circumstances before you were examined here yesterday?"

"I have thought over them for the last two years."

"That will do for the present."[4]

The Judge asked the lawyer if he was through with his cross-examination. Bradley replied emphatically he was not. The next day Bradley subjected Weichmann to several more hours of intense interrogation, eventually coming back again to his incorrect date involving Dr. Mudd. "On your examination before the Military Commission, did you not state that you made your first acquaintance with Dr. Mudd about the 15th of January, 1865?"

Weichmann responded for the third time that to the best of his recollection that was the date. Then he issued his repeated offer, "If the Government had permitted me to see the register of the National Hotel to identify the room I could have fixed it positively."

"Did you not state that you were sure it was after the 1st of January?"

"As far as my recollection went at that time, I did."

The elder Bradley continued to hound the witness about the mistaken day, asking why he had now changed his mind about the time.

"What has passed that enables you to fix it with greater certainty?" he inquired.

Weichmann replied that he made it his "business to go to that room to find out positively about what I was testifying."

"Have you found out by the date at which Booth registered himself at the National Hotel?"

"I looked for Booth's name and found it had been cut out."

"My question is, did you find out by looking at the National Hotel register when that room was occupied by Booth?"

The witness answered that he looked at the National Hotel register of December 22, and Booth was not there. He then stated, "I went to the room before I looked at the register."

"I am not asking you about the room. You will please answer my question."

"I knew that room was assigned to him on the 22nd of December before the trial of the assassins, because the date is in the book there."

"The 15th of January?"

"No, sir. The 22nd of December, 1864."

"Have you ascertained from the National Hotel register, or otherwise, when Booth left or gave up room 84?"

Joseph H. Bradley, Sr., defense lawyer in the Surratt trial. Bradley, while a great lawyer, was combative and intemperate (Library of Congress, Handy Studios, Washington, D.C.).

"No, sir."

"You have not ascertained from that book how long he occupied it?"

"No, sir; because Booth's name does not appear on the National Hotel register at all."[5]

The investigation was plagued with names cut out of hotel registers.

The defense failed in its strenuous attempt to discredit Weichmann. The defense, in harrowing Weichmann, apparently intended to frighten him. As usual, Weichmann appeared nervous and uncertain when he first took the stand. To add to his discomfort, John Surratt stared at him throughout the exhausting examination. But gradually Weichmann gained confidence, answering slowly and deliberately. He confirmed his prior testimony with more incriminating details. Weichmann spoke for the first time of Mrs. Surratt's desire on the night of the murder to get home by nine o'clock as she planned to meet a gentleman there. When he asked her if the gentleman was Booth, she made no reply.

With his former friend's gaze fixed on him, Weichmann unhesitatingly brought out increasingly damaging facts. Mrs. Surratt liked Booth, he said, and called him her "pet."[6] On one occasion, he stayed with her in the parlor until 1:00 A.M. He gave additional details of Anna's frantic actions when detectives first visited the boardinghouse. Although Weichmann had said very little about her before the Military Commission, this time he did not hold back.

In the crowded District of Columbia courtroom, he told of a conversation at breakfast on the morning after the murder. "I remember a remark that was made at the table, that 'the death of Abraham Lincoln was nothing more than the death of a nigger in the army.'"

"Who said that?" probed the lawyer.

"Anna Surratt."

"Did you tell that at the assassination trial?"

"I did not."

"Why did you not?"

Weichmann declared it was because he had so much "sympathy for the poor girl."

"Why do you tell it now?"

"Because you drew it out of me and because I have been hunted down and persecuted for the last two years on account of these people."[7]

Surratt's lawyers attempted to picture Weichmann as a conspirator and produced witnesses to cast doubt on his testimony. Weichmann steadfastly maintained that he was used by the conspirators but was not one of them. The defense could find nothing to contradict this contention. Weichmann's only admission was that he may have told Howell his sympathies were with the South. But this was just "Secesh" talk, he maintained.

The question of Booth's diary would not die. Thomas Eckert, who had recently testified before the Judiciary Committee, was put on the stand. The defense asked him to examine Booth's diary. After a brief discussion about a piece of paper on which Booth had penciled a note to Dr. Stewart, Pierrepont cross-examined Eckert.

"Have you seen the paper that you speak of?"

"Yes, sir."

"The one you think is the original?"

"Yes, sir."

Pierrepont held up Booth's diary and asked if it "was part of this book, or a blank left from it."

"I believe it to be a blank leaf from that book."

"Can you find the paper?"

"I do not know. It is my impression you have it. I last saw it in your possession."

The lawyer said he remembered seeing the paper and wanted to know if Eckert thought it was the original. "Yes, sir," he replied.

"Where did you get it?"

"Either from General Baker or his brother [cousin]. It is my impression that I got it from General Baker."[8]

If anyone was holding back evidence, it seemed to be LaFayette Baker.

The only thing the diary proved was that the man killed at Garrett's barn

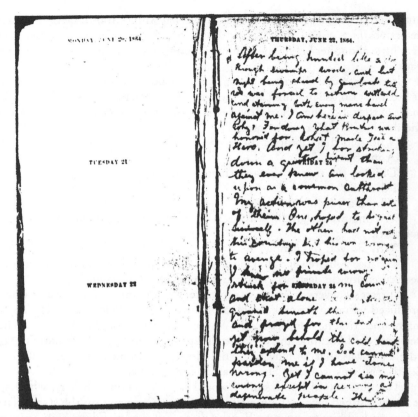

Page from Booth's diary. He probably wrote this about April 22, because he refers to "being hunted like a dog through swamps, woods and last night being chased by gunboats till we were forced to return. . . ." (National Park Service.)

was John Wilkes Booth. Nevertheless, the gullible public listened to stories spread, especially by Baker, implying that after he gave the diary to Stanton, the Secretary of War destroyed some pages and concealed the little book.

Differences between the Surratt trial and the conspiracy trial slowly became evident. Defense lawyers Merrick and Bradley were not only superior to the counsel of the eight conspirators, they were more convinced of their cause. In addition, they had more latitude in which to work. They employed brilliant arguments in behalf of John Surratt.

The defense was further aided by inept handling of the Government's case. For some unaccountable reason, the Government based much of its case on its weakest point—that John Surratt was in Washington on the night of the murder. Surratt's lawyers made a determined and successful effort to show that their client was not in the Nation's capital on April 14, 1865. The defense caught the prosecution in several weak efforts to prove he was.

Both sides brought forth individuals to prove Surratt's whereabouts on April 15. Several defense witnesses placed him in Elmira, New York. The

Government provided 13 witnesses who testified they had seen him in Washington. But some prosecution witnesses were not certain in their identification and some were obviously mistaken.

The strongest statement in behalf of Surratt came from Confederate General E. G. Lee. He gave strong, clear evidence that Surratt arrived in Montreal on April 6 with a dispatch for Jacob Thompson from Confederate Secretary of State Benjamin. The dispatch related to the distribution of Confederate funds. Lee testified that he sent Surratt to Elmira on April 12, where he stayed until the 15th. Surratt returned to Montreal on the 18th. Lee claimed he had the dispatch Surratt had carried, but the Court ruled that it was not admissible evidence.

Several hotel registers provided other strong evidence in favor of Surratt's contention that he was not in Washington on the tragic night. Surratt told his lawyers that he had stayed at the Brainard House in Elmira on April 13 and 14. But when the lawyers searched for the crucial register, it could not be found. Their exhaustive efforts lasted several weeks. They questioned everyone connected with the hotel, but no one could find the register. Every other guest book before and after the missing one was available. Surratt and his lawyers became convinced that the Government had taken it.

Almost as important was the register of the hotel in Canandiagua, New York. The Government was not aware that after leaving Elmira, Surratt was apparently forced to stay over in this little town because Sabbath laws prohibited trains' running on Sunday. Surratt's lawyers located the Webster hotel register with Surratt's assumed name, John Harrison, clearly registered on April 15. But the Government refused to allow the register as evidence. The prosecution objected on grounds the name could have been written by anybody, or Surratt himself could have placed it there later. The guest book could only be presented if someone could testify he saw Surratt write his name. However, the name was signed in Surratt's handwriting in the middle of the page — six names above it and six below.

Critics of the military trial had complained that a major general, shouting out questions to a lowly sergeant, could get just about any answer he wanted. Sergeant Dye testified before both the Military Commission and the Surratt civil trial, and he responded the same way even without generals intimidating him. In the Surratt trial, Dye swore that he had seen John Surratt in Washington on April 15. This puzzled Weichmann, who was uncertain of John's whereabouts on that date. After the trial, he asked Dye if he was positive he had seen Surratt. Dye stated he had absolutely no doubt.

The defense conducted extremely heated interrogations. At one point, Bradley asserted that all the witnesses for the prosecution should be put in the penitentiary. Considering that popular General Grant was a witness, the charge angered the prosecution. Judge Fisher eventually reprimanded Bradley for his bitter cross-examinations, thus creating a running feud between the Judge and the lawyer.

Tempers erupted as the trial labored on through the hot summer months. After court adjourned on July 16, Weichmann and Dr. McMillan were talking

at the corner of 5th and D streets when Mr. Merrick's young clerk, Hall Colgate, passed them. Weichmann asked if he was connected with the counsel for
the defense. Colgate snorted, "What is that to you?" and putting up his fists,
struck at Weichmann. The latter quickly took off his glasses, then on second
thought, chided Colgate that he "was too small," and walked away.[9]

Political and religious bias seemed to have been deliberately introduced.
Passions became so pronounced that some witnesses felt threatened by visitors.
To control the potentially explosive conditions, Stanton provided a group of
blacks to occupy the first three rows in the courtroom to keep order.
Weichmann acknowledged that their presence helped avoid an outbreak of
violence.

Religious tensions appeared early, even in jury selection. Bradley complained that the prosecution had refused to allow Catholics on the jury. On
one occasion the jurors asked if they would be permitted to attend church as
a body. Bradley replied sarcastically that he thought they could go to any
church except the Catholic. Pierrepont declared that the jurors could worship
at any church.[10]

More subtle and effective for the defense was the open display of Catholic
support for Surratt. One day, about twenty students from St. Charles College,
where Surratt and Weichmann had studied, were present. They made a show
of shaking Surratt's hand. One professor, Father John B. Menir, sat next to
Surratt during the proceedings. They all pointedly ignored Weichmann.

The defense introduced several priests to reflect negatively on
Weichmann's character. One young pastor, Father L. Roccofort, who had
been Weichmann's Father Confessor, gave the impression that Weichmann
had admitted he sent secret information to the Confederates. The priest was
not permitted to discuss the issue, but he seemed to impress the jury.

The defense successfully showed that John Surratt was not in Washington
the week before the assassination and that the plot to kill was first considered
only a few days before the crime. Surratt's lawyers contended, therefore, that
he was in no way involved with the assassination. This, of course, placed the
final arrangements for the murder more directly on Mrs. Surratt.

Samuel Arnold, at the time imprisoned in the Dry Tortugas, had a much
better alibi. He had written proof of his disassociation from the conspiracy
even while John Surratt continued to work actively as a leader in the plot.

The defense closed its case with an obvious appeal to sentimentality.
"Three years ago," Merrick soliloquized, "there was in this city a happy
household sitting beside a bright household fire." He described the cheerful innocent family and the drastic changes that engulfed them. "The bright fire is
extinguished; the mother sleeps in a nameless felon's grave," he recited sadly,
adding, "the daugher, burdened and broken-hearted, drags out a wretched life,
and the son is here before you, on trial for his life."

He challenged the jury to let Almighty God guide them so that their "verdict may hereafter and forever be a sweet and pleasant recollection."[11]

On August 10, 1867, after deliberating 72 hours, the jury marched into the
crowded courtroom. The clerk inquired solemnly, "Gentleman of the jury,

George P. Fisher, the presiding judge at the trial of John Surratt (Meserve Collection).

have you agreed upon your verdict?" W. B. Todd, the 57-year-old spokesman, replied, "We have been unable to agree."[12]

Judge George P. Fisher declared that in the case of *The United States v. John H. Surratt,* he would have to dismiss the jury because it was hopelessly deadlocked. The jury was composed of seven Southern-born men, all of whom voted for acquittal, and five Northern- or foreign-born men, all but one of whom voted for conviction.

The Judge then announced that he had "a very unpleasant duty to discharge." Joseph Bradley, Sr., had threatened him during the trial, he revealed. Fisher explained that "no court can administer justice, or live, if its judges are to be threatened with personal violence." He ordered Bradley's name "be stricken from the rolls of attorneys practicing in this court."[13]

This pronouncement motivated a bitter exchange. While Bradley was still raging, the Judge adjourned court and left the room, followed by a large group. Bradley followed close behind, continuing his tirade. Soon an excited crowd

Richard T. Merrick, one of the attorneys defending John Surratt. Merrick was an able lawyer but vindictive and exceedingly harsh toward witnesses (L.C., Handy Studios, Washington, D.C.).

gathered. Bradley handed Judge Fisher a note suggesting that they meet outside the District of Columbia, where they could settle the dispute. He seemed to be challenging the Judge to a duel. In the meantime, guards returned Surratt to jail. Although there was talk of trying him again, the Government allowed him to go free.

Among other things, the extremely acrimonious trial indicated that justice was less likely to be handed down by a highly partisan jury than by a military court. Early in the proceeding, prosecuting attorney Pierrepont stated optimistically that a jury of 12 men in Washington would render a fair verdict but admitted he might be wrong. He declared that a country could not long remain free if it "fails to administer justice on those who commit great crimes." He warned that society must have protection, and "if it cannot come through the civil tribunal, then every good man will hail the military."

The decision to allow one of the chief perpetrators of the conspiracy to go free while the men he recruited were hanged or imprisoned, led many citizens to "hail the military."[14]

The War Department, in justifying the Military Commission, pleaded that the factions in Washington were so impassioned that an impartial judge and jury would be impossible to find. John Surratt's case proved their point.

Booth had written in his diary that he wanted to return to Washington and clear himself. In Washington, he had many Southern friends. What Booth may have counted on to redeem his honor was the system of justice in civil courts. Had he escaped, as Surratt did for two years, and been tried in a Washington civil court, he, too, might have escaped the death sentence. If the Military Commission was guilty of abuses, at least it handed down decisions which most citizens considered justice for the monstrous crime.

In the meantime Ben Butler's Committee on the Assassination, making no progress, decided to send Major Gleason to Fort Jefferson to question the conspirators. Samuel Arnold, always anxious to blame the Government, was eager to go before the Committee. On December 3, 1867, with Gleason acting as notary public, Arnold went over the same ground that had been often covered. Arnold, then 33, repeated the story that Booth called him and O'Laughlin to a meeting in August or September 1864 to consider abducting President Lincoln. He presented the clearest picture yet of the actual plans, revealing that Herold served mostly as Booth's errand boy; that around the middle of March, Payne and Booth were to seize the President in the theater; O'Laughlin and Herold were to put out the gaslights; and Arnold was to jump onto the stage to help carry Lincoln out. Surratt and Atzerodt were to wait across the river to guide the party through Lower Maryland and across into Virginia. Arnold mentioned all but three of the people put on trial—Dr. Mudd, Mrs. Surratt and Spangler. When he made this statement, he was still confined with Mudd and Spangler; his friend O'Laughlin had already died.

Although Arnold had little to fear, he was not completely candid. When asked if he knew the person to whom O'Laughlin had given the guns that were eventually sent to Surrattsville, he said no. Considering his closeness to O'Laughlin, his answer seemed deceptive. He also stated that Booth never mentioned others in the plot and that Booth required an oath of secrecy from everyone involved. Arnold, quick to make excuses for himself, vowed that crucial meetings involving him were accidental.

Officers asked Arnold specifically if he had heard of Dr. Samuel Mudd before the assassination. He replied, surprisingly, that he had known of the doctor. Arnold revealed that he heard Booth mention Mudd's name in a conversation in January 1865 and that Mudd later told him he had a letter of introduction from Booth. These were astonishing disclosures under the circumstances. But he also repeated a fictitious story about Booth's purchase of Mudd's horse.

When questioned about Weichmann, Arnold declared that Weichmann told Booth how many prisoners of war both sides held. But he did not try to implicate Weichmann in the conspiracy.

"Did you know how many horses Booth had when his brother came to see him?" Gleason quizzed.[15] Arnold replied that he did not know. Just what the strange question implied is not known.

The Committee wanted to know how the President was "decoyed into an upper box," implying that the box used by the President that night was not the place Lincoln usually sat. Arnold swore he did not know and that he had absolutely no knowledge that Lincoln was to be assassinated, although he freely admitted his part in the abduction plans. By this time, the Government had released John Surratt, and Arnold was unlikely to face further punishment.

The Committee on the Assassination also examined Spangler, who added nothing. He signed his statement "Edman Spangler."[16] Dr. Mudd faced the interrogator reluctantly.

Ben Butler uncovered no vital information. What little he did discover only confirmed the accuracy of the sentences handed down in the military trial. After a few more weeks' work, the Committee faded away. As the new year, 1868, approached, Butler had more important work. He became one of the leaders impeaching President Johnson, which had been the Committee's purpose all along.

XLIX
Memories of the Terrible Spring

Three years after his trial, when John Surratt felt certain he would not be tried again, he decided to capitalize on popular interest by lecturing on the conspiracy. He planned his first lecture for Rockville, Maryland, on December 6, 1870. Admission was 50 cents (children, half price) to hear the Surratt story. He seemed to attract the entire population. The Rockville Cornet Band opened the program with spirited music. Surratt, now 26 years old, was more mature and a little heavier. In a casual, even humorous style, he assured his audience it was not self-glory, but rather "pecuniary necessity" which led to his lecture tour.

The unconvicted and unrepentant conspirator told how he left St. Charles College in July 1861 (Weichmann said 1862) and became a Confederate spy. His first assignment involved "sending information regarding the movements of the United States Army stationed in Washington ... and carrying dispatches."[1] He spoke of the mail route maintained by the Confederacy. After his family's move to Washington, he became even more active. He met Booth in the fall of 1864. When Surratt told his audience that he finally agreed to cooperate with Booth because he wanted to help the South gain her independence, the crowd broke into applause.

Surratt said the conspirators feared that the Government knew of their activities. While capture of the President was the only plan openly considered at first, Surratt gave an astonishing hint that possibly more drastic action had been discussed. At an early meeting, a member of the conspiracy declared, "If I understand you to intimate anything more than the capture of Mr. Lincoln, I for one, will bid you good-bye."[2] A discussion of the plot lasted all night, according to Surratt.

The attempt in March to capture Lincoln while he visited a hospital on 7th Street, rather than on his trip to the Soldiers' Home, was organized at the last minute. The attempt was unsuccessful because, instead of the President, the conspirators found another man in the carriage. Surratt said he thought it was Salmon Chase, adding, "We did not disturb him as we wanted bigger chase."[3] This play on words brought another laugh from the sympathetic audience. The story, however, was worth more than a laugh; it confirmed Weichmann's testimony of what had happened. Surratt claimed he abandoned the conspiracy after this, but the facts do not support his assertion. But, if he did leave the conspiracy in March, Booth's constant visits to the boardinghouse further implicated his mother.

John Surratt as he appeared about the time of the trial (National Archives photo no. 6185, Brady Collection).

His last trip to Canada more than a week before the assassination was made at the request of Confederate Secretary of State Benjamin. For this trip, which was unrelated to the kidnap attempt, the Confederacy gave Surratt $200 in gold—the only money, he claimed, the Rebels ever paid him. He vowed the Confederate Government was not connected with the conspiracy. Surratt declared the conspirators needed money and, for financial reasons, wanted to acquaint Rebel leaders with the plot. But they never did—they wanted to do it all themselves.

Surratt carried his last dispatch from Benjamin to Canada hidden in a book entitled *The Life of John Brown*. He said he read part of it and was amazed to learn the martyr was seated next to God in heaven. The crowd laughed.

Surratt's narrative was convincing on some points. Weichmann had sworn that when Surratt returned from his last trip to Richmond, he did not spend the night at home, but went to a hotel. Surratt confirmed this fact, claiming that a detective had visited his house and he felt it was safer to stay in a hotel. His reasoning seemed faulty, because he failed to mention that he spent several hours at home exchanging gold for paper money with Holohan.

He revealed that the conspirators seldom used their real names when sending letters to one another. A device Booth used, according to Surratt, was to send letters to him addressed to Louis Weichmann. This confirmed Weichmann's statement about letters meant for Surratt being sent to him. It also shows that Weichmann was not considered one of the conspirators, otherwise Booth would not have written to him in his own name. Surratt, however, affirmed that Weichmann knew about the plan—that "he had been told all about it." According to Surratt, Weichmann wanted to become an active member, but Booth would not allow it because "he could neither ride a horse nor shoot a pistol."[4]

Surratt stated that Weichmann furnished information to the Confederate Government and allowed him to search Government records after office hours. Howell and Arnold said practically the same thing. There were too many accusations against Weichmann on this point to doubt Surratt's assertion.

He received several bursts of applause when he denounced Weichmann in vicious terms. The only time he came close to referring to his mother's innocence was in a statement denouncing Weichmann. "Give me a man who can strike his victim dead," he proclaimed grandly, "but save me from a man who, through perjury, will cause the death of an innocent person."[5] He stopped short of declaring his mother innocent, but he whipped his audience into a frenzy with his imaginary example. He continued to denounce Weichmann, "Away with such a character. I leave him in the pit of infamy which he had dug for himself, a prey to the lights of his guilty conscience."[6] This statement, which received loud applause, better described John Surratt than Louis Weichmann.

The most complete and convincing part of Surratt's lecture concerned his stay in Elmira, New York. He detailed his activities and accused the Government of destroying evidence which proved that he lodged there on the night of the murder. Surratt's strongest evidence proving that he was not in Washington on April 14 was a telegram he sent from Elmira to ascertain Booth's whereabouts. The original telegram was missing, although the telegraph office had a copy.

From Elmira he fled north to Canandaigua, New York, and expected to continue on to New York City. He repeated the trial testimony about staying at the Webster House. Although his name on the register was not admitted as evidence, the cashbook which proved that he had paid for the room (and presumably stayed in the hotel) was found—but not until after his trial. The next morning (Sunday) Surratt saw his name in the papers as the man who attacked Seward. He described how he made his way to Canada and found refuge in a Catholic monastery. Surratt excused his failure to come to his mother's aid by explaining that he was not fully aware of her plight. He claimed that he inquired about her and was assured she was in no danger.

Actually, newspapers repeatedly pictured Mrs. Surratt as among the most guilty and in grave danger. He failed to mention that he had volunteered to give himself up if he were guaranteed immunity. The Government declined his

ODD-FELLOWS' HALL!

7th, above D Street.

FRIDAY EVENING, December 30th.

J. H. SURRATT

WILL MOST POSITIVELY DELIVER HIS

LECTURE!

In WASHINGTON,

On the above date—All Regrets to the country notwithstanding. In which he will give a full and truthful account of his

THRILLING ADVENTURES DURING THE REBELLION

HIS INTRODUCTION TO

J. WILKES BOOTH,

AND THE PLAY ARRANGED TO

Kidnap, not Murder President Lincoln,

The Attempted ABDUCTION and its DEFEAT, together with the ABANDONMENT OF THE PLOT, the

ARREST! TRIAL! ACQUITTAL!

Description of Judge Pierce, Judge Fisher &c., Bingham, M. Barnes and Louis Weichmann. The Lecture will include

SURRATT'S ACCOUNT OF HIMSELF!

From the time of his leaving College; his acute actions during the War; the many perilous journeys from Richmond to Washington.

His Introduction to J. Wilkes Booth

And what ensured as to aid and subsequent interviews; his doubts as to the sanity of that class of conspirators; his own candid
One Side of the Story will make it the other. Attend the Place, the attempt and failure; how it
finally broke through.

INTERVIEW WITH GEN'L LEE,

DELIVERED TO SLIDELL, what was then done!

A PLAN TO RELEASE CONFEDERATE PRISONERS,

The Sharp Shooting. First act of the Death of Lincoln; how J. Wilkinson's party in the conference; he could neither offer
nor forbear; TREASON TO SLIDELL. A full broad in former stage. Loss of the Great Express;
Booth and crippled Telegraph.

WHO STOLE THEM?

With the Counted of Small Sessions

$20,000!

offered by the United States Authorities to A POOR MAN WITH A FAMILY, &c. &c. Narrative of Harper; a Miser; the Postal part
of PRICE of STEEL. Escape and Seizure; long interviews and differences; arrival at Quebec; departure to Europe

Life among the Papal Zouaves in Rome!

ARREST AND RETURN TO THE UNITED STATES!

A CAPTIVE IN IRONS

Trial, Continuing Sixty-two Days

AND

HONORABLE ACQUITTAL.

ADMISSION, - - - - - 50 Cents

Doors open at 7. Lecture to commence at 8 o'clock precisely.
Reserved Seats can be Procured at Ellis' Music Store.

offer. Stanton constantly refused to allow the prime suspects to escape punishment by turning states' evidence.

Surratt, however, admitted that he received copies of the *National Intelligencer*, which carried a full account of the trial. In an extremely revealing statement, he admitted, "I could not have taken any action resulting in good."[7] In fact, he could not have saved his mother and would almost certainly have taken his place at her side on the scaffold. John was preparing for a hunting trip in Canada as his mother walked to the gallows.

When he finished his lecture, the band played "Dixie." Surratt seemed delighted to be alive and mingled with the ladies "till a late hour."

His first lecture was such a success that he and his advisers decided to go on an extended lecture tour. The next stop was New York City where he repeated his speech to an audience of about 300 people at the Cooper Institute. Then on December 29, he lectured at Concordia Hall in Baltimore to approximately 200.

The real test came when he sought to repeat his story in Washington. Sentiment in the city of Lincoln's murder was not the same as that of Rockville or New York City. Surratt's agent was able to secure Lincoln Hall for the speech. But after further consideration, managers of the building decided it would not be an appropriate place for Surratt's tales. He then obtained use of Odd Fellows' Hall at 7th and D streets, only three or four blocks from Ford's Theatre, and about the same distance from his mother's old boardinghouse.

Surratt distributed posters announcing the lecture for Friday evening, December 30, 1870. Along with the admission price of 50 cents, the placards proclaimed, "J. H. Surratt will most positively deliver his lecture in Washington on the above date, all reports contrary notwithstanding." The audacious former Confederate spy promised a "denunciation of Judge Fisher, Judge Pierrepont, Edwin Stanton and Louis Weichmann." He denounced Weichmann, even in the advertisement, as having been "a party to the abduction." The posters declared, "You have heard one side of the story—now listen to the other."[8]

This brazen challenge was too much. On the day before the scheduled speech, the building committee of the Odd Fellows withdrew permission. His friends hurriedly tried to rent the Masonic Hall but were turned down again.

Surratt's agent then sought support from a Catholic priest, who advised Surratt to do nothing to cause trouble. When John first decided to go on the lecture circuit, his religious advisers had declined to express an opinion, but the uproar in Washington changed their minds.

The night before the scheduled Washington lecture police arrested Surratt in Baltimore on the charge of selling tobacco for two years without a license.

Opposite: Announcement of Surratt's lecture in Washington for December 30, 1870. Although he stated that he would "most positively deliver his lecture," enraged citizens forced its cancellation (Lincoln Memorial University Museum).

took place at his (Mudd's) house in the month of Nov 1864 He (Mudd) told Booth that he would have no trouble to effect a crossing of the river at any time as parties were constantly coming and going. He (Mudd) said that in December 1864 he met Booth in the City of Washington near the National Hotel and that Booth took a card from his pocket that appeared to have some address written on it and ask-ed him (Mudd) if he would take him (Booth) to Mrs Surratts house and introduce him to John H. Surratt. He (Mudd) said he made some ex-cuses as he did not wish to introduce Booth to Surratt. Booth appeared very anxious and insisted on an introduction. While we (Booth + Mudd) were con-versing on the sidewalk,

After his release his colleagues secured another hall in Washington, but this time the mayor stepped in. The mayor told Surratt's supporters that more than 300 citizens had signed a petition to cancel the lecture. Still unmoved, Surratt's agent placed an ad in the *Washington Star* announcing the lecture would take place in Carusi's Saloon.

Surratt did not arrive in Washington until the afternoon of the scheduled event. At the appointed hour, a small group gathered around the saloon waiting to hear the conspirator, but they were careful not to reveal their identities. Surratt never appeared, but a newsman later traced him to Seaton Hall. There, in Room 29, the reporter found Surratt, his agent, a Mr. Crobyn and Anna's husband, William Tonry, gathered. Surratt, calm as ever, explained that he had accepted the mayor's suggestion to cancel the lecture. The reporter asked why he did not make a tour through the South. Surratt responded that it was too dangerous as there was no law or order in the South. However, he might speak in Fredericksburg, Virginia, the next night, he suggested. He never did—that ended Surratt's lecture tour.[9]

Nearly three decades elapsed before Surratt ventured into the public eye again, this time even more brazenly defending himself. In the 33 years since the crime, John had come to think of himself in even bolder terms. No longer did he mention his failure to defend his mother. Apparently, he felt the public had forgotten that cowardly act. He rather impressed upon his interviewer, Hanson Hiss of the *Washington Post*, his heroic actions.

Hiss described Surratt as a "refined, highly educated and ... brilliant talker."[10] Surratt maintained his slim form and his mustache, though his sandy brown hair had turned gray. He was 55 but looked more like 70, according to Hiss. Surratt bragged of his ability as a Confederate spy to outwit Union officers. He devoted most of the interview to his daring escapes to Canada, England, Italy and Egypt.

His story had changed in regard to Booth. In the Rockville lecture, he had encouraged wild applause by frequent references to his efforts in behalf of the South and had related in detail his conspiracy with Booth to capture Lincoln. Now that the years had tempered war memories, these rebellious sentiments were less popular. Surratt tailored his account to suit the times. He now declared that he had spurned Booth's kidnap plot from the beginning. He pictured himself as telling Booth the plan was ridiculous. Surratt assured the reporter that he never had anything to do with any conspiracy.

Surratt repeated his account of having met Booth before he was "introduced" to him by Mudd, adding that "Booth came to me with a letter of introduction." He complained that after his capture and trial, his "nervous system was a wreck. I have never gotten over it."[11]

Hanson Hiss was completely taken in. He could easily have checked the

Opposite: Interview of Dr. Mudd for the Assassination Committee. Mudd admitted meeting Booth in November and December 1864. His motive for the crucial December meeting was contradicted later by John Surratt (Benjamin Butler Papers, Library of Congress).

story from numerous sources, including Surratt's Rockville lecture, which the competing *Washington Star* had published. But making no effort to check the facts, Hiss blithely assumed that he had induced Surratt "to tell his story freely; unreservedly and fully" for the first time. The reporter informed his readers that "prior to the three interviews granted me for the *Sunday Post* in which he told me every detail of his life . . . he has refused all the thousands of efforts to urge him to tell the story [because] . . . the wound was too deep."[12]

In fact, the former spy had told his story repeatedly to anyone who would listen, although he changed it gradually from a boast to Dr. McMillan that he had been in Washington on the night of the assassination to his most recent account disclaiming any conspiratorial association at all. Furthermore, the wounds had not been "too deep" to keep Surratt from charging 50 cents to hear his lecture a generation earlier.

After more than three decades of changing his testimony—each time making himself less cowardly and picturing Weichmann as more contemptible—he still had nothing to say about his mother. Not only did John fail to produce the long-promised evidence to prove his mother guiltless, but even his sister Anna remained silent. Perhaps at some point, Anna put it all together, either in conversations with John or through her own experience.

In August 1867, the Government gave John Clampitt a position with the Post Office Department in the Western Territory. It was an innocent appointment, but the mystery makers saw some sinister Government motive in the move. They were not sure whether it was a reward for his having kept quiet about Mary Surratt or an effort to move him so far away that he could not make any comment about the just-concluded Surratt trial.

The Government also appointed Frederick Aiken, Clampitt's co-defender in behalf of the widow, auditor for the Treasury Department. Sensationalists imagined this move to be a reward given for some mysterious service.

A fire destroyed John Clampitt's house in 1897 and, with it, many of his notes regarding the conspiracy trial. Clampitt was apparently working on a book to prove his former client's innocence, which was also destroyed. One writer thought the fire was part of a Government plot to destroy evidence favorable to Mrs. Surratt.[13]

Twentieth-century author Otto Eisenschiml saw a pattern in these events. According to him Mrs. Surratt was promised, and expected, clemency—a theory contrary to all known facts. The Government betrayed her at the last minute, and she was not given an opportunity to proclaim her innocence, according to Eisenschiml. Actually, she was given every opportunity to present any witness or any evidence in her favor before, during and after the trial as the records show. According to Eisenschiml's novel theory, officials did not allow lawyers to converse with her in private, and the lawyers were rewarded by the Government after the trial. He believed Reverdy Johnson was rewarded because he refused to defend her, and his junior partners were rewarded for not telling all they knew. Exactly "what they knew," however, Eisenschiml failed to state clearly.

President Johnson barely won his impeachment battle with Congress but was denied the nomination for another term. In November 1868, the Nation elected General Grant as President, leaving Johnson several months to serve as a lame duck leader. On February 8, 1869, less than a month before he was to leave office, Johnson pardoned Dr. Mudd and later released Arnold and Spangler. Thus the remaining convicted conspirators, unable to win freedom by escape attempts or pleas of innocence, gained the same end as a result of the President's fight with Congress.

Edwin Booth made repeated requests for the remains of his brother, John Wilkes. On February 15, 1869, Johnson gave orders to release the body, as well as those of the four hanged conspirators. Booth's cadaver was found under the flagstone floor of the Arsenal warehouse where it had remained, unknown even to employees, for almost four years. A few hours later undertakers drove a little one-horse wagon into the Arsenal grounds. The body was taken through the streets of Washington without the slightest notice. In contrast to his victim's burial, only a few family members gathered to observe the reinterment at the side of his father in Greenmount cemetery in Baltimore. A simple Episcopal service was read as Booth's mother, Junius Brutus, Edwin and Asia listened with heartfelt grief.[14]

After Andrew Johnson left the White House, he was defeated in his bid for the United States Senate. In 1872 he became a candidate for the House of Representatives. While campaigning in the mountains of East Tennessee, a reporter asked why he had not pardoned Mrs. Surratt and why he had refused to see her daughter on the day of the execution. The former president replied that when Anna came to the White House, he did not know who she was. According to Johnson, Gen. Reuben Mussey, who was in charge of receiving White House guests, told him a crazy woman was downstairs and wanted to see him. Mussey said that she refused to give her name but was crying, tearing her hair and exhibiting signs of insanity. The newsman pressed the issue, asking if he would have pardoned Mrs. Surratt had he known the visitor was Anna.

"I don't think I would," he responded. "She didn't do the shooting but she was an accessory to it which is all the same."[15]

Stanton resumed his law practice after efforts to remove Johnson failed. When Grant became President, he appointed Stanton a Supreme Court Justice. He was immediately confirmed by the Senate, but four days later, Stanton died. After his death on Christmas Eve, 1869, Mary Surratt's friends circulated a rumor that he had committed suicide. The story was easy to disprove as Surgeon General Barnes attended Stanton in his last months. Barnes gave a detailed account of Stanton's illness and natural death.

Nothing reveals Stanton's character or sacrificial efforts more clearly than the meager estate he left. He held high governmental positions for decades and labored in the Cabinets of three Presidents. The war period was noted for scandal and corruption, yet the powerful Stanton died a poor man.

During his last years when he was in debt, several friends who had lent him money wanted to treat the loans as gifts for his service to the country;

Stanton refused. He vowed to pay the debts before he died, and if not, his estate was to pay them. His house was his only property.

Edwards Pierrepont, a close friend, tried to raise $100,000 for Stanton's relief. Before Stanton died, he forced Pierrepont to abandon the project and died in debt, a remarkable fact considering his opportunities for wealth. After his death, friends contributed $60,000 to his family. Stanton surprisingly left nothing to his lawyer son Edwin, not even his law books.

After his release, Edward Spangler spent the remaining 18 months of his life in Dr. Mudd's house. According to Mudd's daughter, Spangler was a good, kind man. After his death, a manuscript was found in his tool chest. The document seemed to have been written by someone else, as dictated by Spangler. The paper provided no startling revelations but bore marks of being genuine as it gave details which could have been known only to Spangler. The former stagehand said he was born in York County, Pennsylvania. Although not sure about his exact age, he thought he was about 43. He had known Booth since boyhood, having worked for Booth's father as a carpenter.

According to the manuscript, Booth asked Spangler to sell his horses, harness and buggy on Monday, April 10, 1865, if he could get $260. The next day Spangler tried unsuccessfully to sell them. The attempted sale was indicative of a definite change in Booth's plans—the buggy had been purchased for use in kidnapping the President.

Spangler's manuscript was significant for what he left out. He denied he knew anything about the hole in the door to the President's box or that he closed the stage door behind Booth. But he did not deny the charge, that he struck Ritterspaugh and ordered him to say nothing about the direction of Booth's flight, nor did he claim to be totally innocent.[16]

Sixteen years after the trial, Johnny Bouquet, a New York columnist, traveled through Lower Maryland in search of material for an article on John Wilkes Booth. There he met a man living near the Surratt house who talked freely about events well known in the area. Apparently much had been kept from the Government by closemouthed Maryland Confederates.

According to the columnist, Mrs. Surratt's neighbors admitted that, while there was considerable pity for the condemned woman, her dignity had been exaggerated. There had been a rumor in the neighborhood that while Mrs. Surratt's husband was yet living "an Italian priest who ministered in that part of the country got in such a flirtation with her that it raised a commotion, and he had to be sent to Boston to get him out of scandal."[17] The story may have been totally false, yet it was published in the New York Tribune, May 8, 1889, during the lifetime of many who would have known of the episode. No one denied the report. Whether true or not, it gave insight into the attitude of Mrs. Surratt's acquaintances. This same reluctance of her neighbors to testify as to her good character had dismayed her lawyers.

Gen. Winfield Scott Hancock was stationed in the Shenandoah Valley when Lincoln died. Authorities summoned him to Washington and made him military Commander of the District of Columbia. In this position he exercised authority over nearly 100,000 men. Hancock became prominent in Democratic

Gen. Winfield S. Hancock. Under President Johnson's orders, he denied a writ of habeas corpus for Mrs. Surratt. Accusations blaming him for her execution were an issue when he ran for President in 1880 (National Archives photo no. 1615, Brady Collection).

party politics after the trial. When he was nominated for President in 1868, Montgomery Blair opposed him on grounds that the General had armed Negros to hunt down President Lincoln's assassins. Years later, the General's wife justified her husband's actions, stating that the order arming blacks had been written by Holt and Stanton, and that Hancock only signed the proclamation.[18]

When Democrats mentioned his possible candidacy again in 1871, a leading St. Louis newspaper brought up the conspiracy trial. The paper denounced Hancock for not saving Mrs. Surratt, declaring that he became "the veritable executioner of that innocent woman and made himself party to one of the most inhuman crimes ever perpetrated in the name of justice."[19] This sort of criticism and abuse embittered the rest of his life.

Hancock preferred not to discuss the charges. He thought that any fair-minded person could see how ridiculous it was to accuse him of an act he sought to prevent. He had repeatedly urged the President to grant her a pardon. As the attacks continued through the years, Hancock changed his mind and began to defend himself. He wrote to Burnett in 1873, stating, "The only true plan is to meet and *crush* [italics his] out this Surratt [thing], not to 'dally it.'"[20]

His first serious opportunity to become president was in the election of 1880. In preparation, Hancock tried to settle accounts with Catholic voters, some of whom continued to blame him for hanging an "innocent woman." Father Walter, who had kept the controversy alive, wrote to Hancock on November 14, 1879, exonerating the presidential aspirant of fault in Mrs. Surratt's death.[21]

On July 17, 1880, Hancock's managers wrote Mrs. Surratt's former lawyer, John W. Clampitt, then a judge in Illinois, in an effort to counter continued criticism. Clampitt responded that the General was a good, kind man and in no way responsible for Mrs. Surratt's supposed ill treatment. He blamed the Republicans, stating that "the trial and execution . . . were demanded at the time by the whole Republican party. . . ."[22]

Hancock lost a close election to Republican candidate James Garfield. Out of nearly 9,000,000 popular votes, Hancock polled only 7,000 less than the winner. It was one of the closest popular elections in American history. As the Catholic vote was crucial in several states, Republican accusations blaming Hancock for Mrs. Surratt's death could have made a difference. The hanging, 15 years earlier, still clouded the lives of many involved.

Some still believed that Weichmann knew more than he revealed. One official recorder at the trial said that Weichmann was "aware of the conspiracy to abduct. . . ." Henri Sainte Marie, a devious friend of both Weichmann and Surratt, wrote in 1866 that Weichmann was as guilty as Surratt. He claimed that in his first meeting with Surratt and Weichmann, they both expressed strong secessionist feelings. Sainte Marie accused Weichmann of stealing copies of army dispatches and giving them to Surratt, who took them to Richmond.[23]

In his Rockville lecture, Surratt declared that Weichmann knew of the kidnap plot; he had been told about it but was not allowed to participate. Booth, he said, was suspicious of Weichmann, but he assured Booth that Weichmann was a "Southern man."

Weichmann wanted to go to Richmond and wrote to the bishop to that end. Augustus Howell also testified that Weichmann was helpful to the Southern cause. Surratt corroborated this, saying that Weichmann was a Southern man who had furnished information to the Confederate Government and had allowed Surratt after-hours access to the office where information on war prisoners was kept. Col. William Wood also accused Weichmann of betraying his trust by giving information to the Confederates.[24] Finding the Confederate cipher among Weichmann's possessions seems to support these suspicions. It also fits Weichmann's character and helps explain the extreme hatred later directed toward him by John and Anna Surratt.

Weichmann was not expected to be a threat. Mrs. Surratt felt confident asking him to drive her to Surrattsville—a foolish move unless he seemed supportive. Yet, even Mary Surratt tried to keep Weichmann ignorant of the real plot. She kept from him the nature of a suspicious visit to the Herndon house.

Weichmann's report of Payne and her son harboring guns and knives in the attic room she casually disregarded. She said little about Mrs. Slater's visits. In one clandestine episode, Mrs. Surratt intervened to get her son off work from the Adams Express Company. She kept Weichmann ignorant of this activity. And she deceived Weichmann about the purpose of her last trip to Surrattsville. In no way could Weichmann be counted among the conspirators, and all attempts in that direction failed. But that he was accepted by the conspirators as a sympathetic Southern supporter is undeniable.

During the conspiracy investigation, Weichmann's father read in Philadelphia papers that his son had been arrested. He took the next train to Washington and talked with his son and police officers. They assured the elder Weichmann that Louis was not part of the conspiracy, but rather was helping solve the crime.

After the trial Weichmann returned to Philadelphia to live with his parents. He secured a job as reporter for the *Globe* newspaper. Weichmann's sisters, even though young girls, could not escape the pressure put on the family by friends of the Surratts. On one occasion a lady frightened the girls, accusing them of belonging to a family responsible for hanging a woman.

Louis suffered more severe treatment. He received numerous letters attacking him, and he was fired upon, escaping death only because of a timely warning from a neighbor. Later, someone shot at him while he was reading by a second-story window of his home. After this, the Government assigned detectives to protect him, and Stanton found him a job in the Philadelphia customshouse, where guards could better shelter him.

The Surratts' hatred never seemed to abate. Weichmann's sisters told how someone claiming to be Anna requested Weichmann to meet her at a certain house in Philadelphia to help translate some foreign letters. Weichmann's father refused to let him go until detectives advised him to keep the appointment, promising to protect him. Someone seemed to be in the house, but when detectives searched it, they could find no one.[25] Ten years after the assassination, cranks continued to pester Weichmann. His sisters blamed the problems on John Surratt's efforts to keep trouble stirred up.

Weichmann kept his customshouse job for 17 years, but when Democrats gained control of the presidency, he lost the position. In February 1889, nearly 24 years after the conspiracy trial, Weichmann still depended on Government officials for help. He wrote Bingham, then back in Ohio, for assistance in finding a job. Seven years later, in 1896, he appealed to Bingham again. Referring to the sacrifices he had made for his country, Weichmann asked the lawyer for some expression in writing "as to what you think of the manner in which I performed my duty to the country and of the reward to which I am entitled. . . ."[26]

Later he moved to Anderson, Indiana, where his brother, Father Fred C. Weichmann, a Catholic priest, and two of his sisters, Mrs. C. O'Crowley and Miss Tillie Weichmann, lived. There he founded the Anderson Business School, the first school of that kind in the city.

His feelings toward Mrs. Surratt changed little through the years. He

continued to remember her as a pious, but guilty, woman who had been influenced by Booth. However, Weichmann slowly came to the conclusion that
Mrs. Surratt had purposely tried to fix the evidence so it would implicate him
and provide alibis for herself and John. She nearly succeeded.

While he gradually clarified the crime in his own mind, he never wavered
in his conclusion of Mrs. Surratt's guilt. "From that first night when the detectives poked that cravat with Lincoln's blood on it right into his face, Lou was
sure she was guilty," his sister said, adding that "he never suspected her before
it happened and he never doubted her guilt after it happened."[27] The day
before he died he nervously told his sisters, "I don't see why she should get into
that trouble, a good-hearted woman like she was."[28]

Weichmann believed the harassment he suffered for 35 years came basically
from members of the Catholic Church. He especially resented Father Walter's
repeated misleading stories. Bordering on the superstitious, the priest had
ceaselessly spread falsehoods about members of the Military Commission. The
pastor pictured them as having died early and violent deaths or of having been
driven to suicide. These myths did not cease even after the seven living
members of the Commission declared to reporters in 1892 that they remained
convinced of the correctness of the sentences. Far from suffering divine punishment, they were enjoying happy, comfortable lives. The two absent members
had died of old age.

The pressure became so intolerable that Weichmann finally left the
Catholic Church. He never attended its services again, even though his
brother, a much-loved priest, was serving a parish close to Anderson.

John Ford harbored resentment against Stanton and Holt for the rest of
his life and continued to denounce the military trial until his death in 1894.
His repeated articles, attesting to Mrs. Surratt's innocence, would have been
more effective if they had not been severely distorted. Ford gave accounts he
must have known to be false, particularly when he wrote of Booth's visit to
Ford's Theatre on the day of the murder. John Ford's brothers, who were there,
had testified that Booth visited the theater about 10:00 A.M. John, who was
in Richmond at the time, asserted that Booth did not even get out of bed until
after 10:00 that morning.[29] Most damaging to the veracity of Ford's criticism
was his account of Reverdy Johnson's speeches before the Military Commission, which he claimed he heard as an eyewitness. Actually, Ford was in prison
during the only time Johnson spoke before the Court. When he wrote of this
event, he was 60 years old, and the event he described had occurred nearly
a quarter of a century earlier.

L
The Stretch of Darkening Folds

Catholic priests and laymen continued to agitate against the Government for decades after the hangings. Stanton, Holt, Weichmann and, occasionally, Andrew Johnson bore the brunt of these attacks. But the Government continued to avoid religious controversies. Father Jacob Walter and John P. Brophy were the most persistent in keeping the conflict alive. With the passage of time, their stories departed farther from the facts. Yet, they dealt with sentiment rather than facts. Twenty-six years following the executions, Father Walter persisted in using every opportunity to discredit leaders in the trial.

Mary Surratt's trip to Surrattsville on the afternoon of the murder strongly implicated her. Facts brought out left no reasonable doubt that her purpose was to aid Booth's escape. Crucial to that fateful trip was the timing, as the trial of John Surratt had emphasized. Father Walter, after years of reflection, must have come to the same conclusion. The priest rearranged the timing in a paper read before the United States Catholic Historical Society in 1891. His other minor mistakes in dates and value judgments could be excused. But the errors related to the time sequence of the April 14 trip are harder to explain.

Father Walter repeated John T. Ford's story that no one had known before noon that the President planned to attend the theater and that Mrs. Surratt had ordered a carriage two hours earlier. If this had been true, it would have been a strong point in Mrs. Surratt's favor during the conspiracy trial. But all the sworn testimony proved the opposite. Mrs. Surratt's defense counsel could not deny the evidence of numerous witnesses. She ordered her carriage soon after Booth first heard that the President would definitely attend the theater. The years had apparently clouded Father Walter's memory.

Trial testimony proved that Booth was in the theater before 11:00 A.M. when workers were busily decorating the presidential box. Directors of the theater indicated that after Booth learned conclusively of Lincoln's proposed visit, he left the theater. After 11:00 he engaged in his final feverish preparations: contacting his fellow conspirators, locating horses and arranging other last-minute details for the getaway. Weichmann, who had Good Friday afternoon off, got to the boardinghouse after 12:00. It was nearly 2:00 P.M. when Mrs. Surratt asked him to rent horses and a buggy at Howard's Stable.

This important point was corroborated by several witnesses. Employees at Howard's Stable knew what hour the carriage was ordered. Some of Mrs. Surratt's other boarders were also aware. Customers at Lloyd's tavern in

Surrattsville knew the hour she arrived. The defense at the conspiracy trial was conscious of the crucial timing but could not deny the obvious point. At John Surratt's trial, lawyers attempted unsuccessfully to question the vital chronology. But nearly a generation later, it was easier to distort the picture—even in a meeting of eminent historians.

Weichmann later directed his most severe criticism at Father Walter, particularly his statements before the Catholic Historical Society. Weichmann wanted to know how the priest knew Mrs. Surratt was innocent when he first talked to the messenger from General Hardie. He had not met her and said he had not paid attention to the trial. According to Weichmann, the priest made his pronouncement on the basis of religious bias rather than on facts.

The night before the executions Father Walter visited the prisoner, heard her confession and prepared her for Holy Communion the next morning. Referring to these activities, Weichmann asked bitterly:

> Ah, Father Walter, why did you not proclaim the innocence of your penitent on the very evening you heard her confession? With her consent, you could have caused it to have been published to the world through the Associated Press, and it would have been read in every prominent newspaper in the United States the next day. Why did you not do it? Through you she could have, if innocent, explained away all the evidence against her, but you permitted her to do nothing of the kind, and suffered her to go down to her grave, without one word in explanation of all that had been testified against her. Had you insisted on a public confession, you might have saved her from a disgraceful death. The theological teachings of the Catholic Church gave you the right to interrupt your penitent just as soon as she told you she was not guilty, and in order to save her life, you should have insisted on her making a public confession.[1]

Three years after Father Walter presented his paper, he died at 66. He was buried close to Mrs. Surratt in Mt. Olivet Cemetery outside Washington.

Fifteen years after the priest's death John Brophy was still busy perpetuating his distorted version of the events. Few remembered the details 43 years after the crime, and most of the participants were dead when he gave an address before the Friendly Sons of St. Patrick. Brophy repeated his story that Stanton hated Catholics. He claimed that both Stanton and Holt were so bigoted that they wanted to convict any suspicious Catholic. He failed to mention that of four Catholics tried (counting John Surratt), only one was hanged, while of the four Protestant conspirators (Booth, Payne, Herold and Atzerodt), three were hanged and one was shot. Spangler and Arnold showed no clear religious preference.

Most participants in the prosecution were relatively free of religious bigotry. Andrew Johnson, Jr., the President's son, was sent to a Catholic school in Georgetown. John Bingham, five years after the trial, was involved in a debate over the establishment of an American minister to the newly created Vatican state. Bingham supported a bill to provide for a consul at Rome but opposed an amendment to it which called for a representative of higher rank. He described the document promulgated in 1864 by Pope Pius IX, known as the Syllabus of Errors, as an attempt to fetter "freedom of conscience." But

Bingham made a strong avowal of his support of all humanity, "whether it be clothed in the faith of the Catholic, or in the faith of the Protestant."[2] The only member of the military court to criticize Catholic leaders was Thomas Harris, who later wrote a book titled *Rome's Responsibility in the Assassination of A. Lincoln*. Harris accused the Roman Catholic Church of morally aiding the conspirators.

Even though Weichmann claimed he left the Catholic Church because he felt he had been unduly persecuted by its members, he adamantly denied that the Church was involved in the crime. Twenty-five years after the assassination and a year before his death, Weichmann wrote to Dr. Porter:

> Father Clinquy [Chiniquy], a converted Catholic priest, some years ago wrote a book in which he distinctly charged the Catholic church with the Assassination. I have read this book and there is not a word of truth in what he says. I agree with you in your remarks in this respect. The priests of Washington for many years after the punishment of Mrs. Surratt made themselves very offensive by saying that she was an innocent woman and that the Government had punished her wrongfully, but all of this has now died out. . . .[3]

Father Charles Chiniquy, to whom Weichmann referred, was among the most radical of several Catholics and former Catholics who brought up the religious element in the crime. Chiniquy left Roman Catholicism after five decades of service to his Church. He claimed that the assassination was inspired by Jesuits because the Church wanted to get rid of President Lincoln.

Nine years before his death, Lincoln, while an attorney in Illinois, had served as Chiniquy's lawyer in a dispute between the priest and Bishop O'Regan of Chicago. Lincoln won the case but refused to accept pay. He did, however, at Father Chiniquy's insistence, finally accept an IOU. According to the priest, Lincoln's defiance of the Church's hierarchy, as well as the Pope's support of Jefferson Davis, were factors that led to the assassination. The former priest used, as an example of the Church's involvement, the hiding of John Surratt in the house of a Canadian priest and Catholics' aid in Surratt's escape to England. Chiniquy's generalities abounded with half-truths and inferences.[4]

Father Chiniquy was not the first or last to stress a religious motive behind the plot. One of the first to accuse his Church was Henri Sainte Marie. He wrote to the State Department on July 10, 1866, that he thought Surratt was being protected by the clergy and that the Lincoln murder was the result of "a deep-laid plot." Sainte Marie added, "We are aware that the priesthood and royalty are and always have been opposed to liberty."[5]

In his study of American myths, George S. Bryan observed that in the mythmaking process "Catholics or ex-Catholics have been foremost in ascribing Lincoln's murder to the Roman Catholic hierarchy."[6]

Another former Catholic, Burke McCarty, repeated these charges against the Church in her exposé *The Suppressed Truth About the Assassins of Abraham Lincoln*. McCarty's book was full of errors such as the report that Atzerodt was known as a Catholic prior to the assassination. Assigning Booth to the same faith, she used the testimony of Rear Adm. George W. Blair that he had seen Booth coming out of St. Aloysius Church just three weeks before the murder. (Actually Atzerodt was Lutheran; Booth, an Episcopalian.) She wrote that when identifying Booth's body aboard the *Montauk*, Blair had seen a Catholic medallion aroung the assassin's neck.[7] These unsubstantiated and insignificant facts indicate how little evidence the author possessed.

McCarty strongly criticized Father Walter. The priest had told of hearing Mrs. Surratt's last confession, which, he implied, showed her innocence. McCarty repeated Weichmann's argument that Father Walter should have made the confession public, asking, "Will the Father deny that under the teachings of the Roman Catholic Church he had an absolute right, with her consent, to make her confession public on this point?"[8]

Years later, still another former Catholic, the well-known "Peoples Padre," Emmett McLaughlin, took up the subject of Rome's involvement. His book, *An Inquiry into the Assassination of Abraham Lincoln*, was a somewhat less-extreme indictment of the Church. He argued that "the Roman Catholic Church was deliberately and culpably involved in the assassination of President Lincoln."[9] But McLaughlin's use of the term "involvement" would include Protestant churches in the South as well.

McLaughlin listed about 17 points which, according to him, implicated the Catholic Church. Some were repetitions of the accusations of Chiniquy and McCarty such as the Vatican's sympathy for the South and the high percentage of Catholics among the conspirators. But McLaughlin developed some new theories such as the desire of some Catholics to support Maximilian's efforts to set up a Catholic empire in Mexico with Confederate help.[10]

These critics showed how individual Catholics were involved in the plot. But none produced evidence that the hierarchy had in any way taken part in the conspiracy. Actually the Catholic hierarchy cooperated with the investigation.

One of several lingering tragedies growing out of the conspiracy was the suspicion it cast on Judge Advocate Holt. The Judge approached life with a somber, no-nonsense demeanor. He was humorless, pompous and vindictive, but he was scrupulously honest and always alert to attacks on his reputation.

More than 20 years after the assassination, Holt continued his feud with his former friend Jacob Thompson. The latter, in an interview in 1883, told how he had befriended Holt. In return, he said, Holt bribed witnesses to implicate him in the assassination. Holt responded by publishing a long pamphlet titled "Reply of Joseph Holt to Certain Calumnies of Jacob Thompson." The old Judge disproved some of his opponent's minor points but hardly touched the main argument.

A much longer and more bitter dispute involved Holt and James Speed. The disagreement developed over President Johnson's belated denial that he had seen the clemency plea for Mrs. Surratt, which implied that Holt had deceived him.

It was completely out of character for Holt to have withheld the clemency recommendation. The plea was not a secret document. Members of the

Cabinet and the Commission knew of it as did some reporters. There was no way to hide it permanently from the President. Holt would have had nothing to gain and much to lose in withholding the plea. By giving the clemency recommendation to the President, Holt and the Commissioners made the President responsible for the decision.

President Johnson, however, had everything to gain by denying that he had seen the document. He was aware that others knew about the clemency plea, but he and Holt were alone when he reviewed the Court's decision. It was the President's word against that of a subordinate. The subordinate, however, prized his reputation immensely. Johnson's reputation for integrity was already somewhat tarnished. He was not an evil man, but he was not above meanness.

Whether or not he had seen the clemency plea was relatively unimportant. The President had the right to pardon Mrs. Surratt without any recommendation. Furthermore, in a trial as notable as the conspiracy trial, the President should have made his own inquiries into the proceedings and the final sentences.

To say he had not seen the clemency recommendation was, in itself, a weak argument for hanging a woman if he had not intended to hang her. The President's refusal to hear pleas in behalf of the condemned showed that his mind was made up—probably before the Military Commission made its decision.

Why Johnson made an issue of the petition is puzzling. He was in favor of hanging Mary Surratt and said so. But to deny two years later, when he was fighting for his political life, that he had ever seen it gave Mrs. Surratt's supporters ammunition to blame Holt. Of all of the conflicts and bitterness growing out of the trial to plague Government leaders, the dispute over the clemency petition was the most lasting and bitter. Holt spent the rest of his life trying to prove he had presented the mercy recommendation to the President.

Partisans have concocted elaborate explanations to show how Holt supposedly deceived the President. One of Johnson's biographers, Robert W. Winston, told of his personal examination of the trial documents in 1926 but admitted all he could discover was that the papers indicated "rough treatment." However, he believed, as some others, that the petition was placed at the back of the Court findings in such a way that the President did not see it—perhaps, purposely.[11]

Holt's supporters asserted that the clemency plea was not only seen by Johnson but discussed openly in a Cabinet meeting. Others claimed that the Cabinet could not have considered the clemency petition because there was no meeting of the Cabinet between the time it was written and the hanging. There was no scheduled meeting, but it was stated publicly that every member of the Cabinet had considered the petition, and each one rejected it. When this statement was made in August 1867, all the Cabinet members were alive. Although they were prohibited from discussing details of Cabinet meetings, they were free to deny the statement, yet none did. Members who commented at all, directly or indirectly, admitted that both the Cabinet and the President knew about the mercy petition.

James O. Harrison of Lexington, Kentucky, always supported Holt, and Holt's correspondence with Harrison over the years provided comfort to the Judge. Harrison's consolation became more valuable as Holt grew older and his friends decreased. The Judge published a defense in a September 1873 issue of the *New York Tribune*. At the same time he wrote Harrison that the defenders of Mrs. Surratt seemed to "breed lies as does a Mississippi swamp, mosquitos."[12] He was not concerned about his conduct at the trial, but with the continuing dispute over the clemency plea.

Early in the quarrel, former Atty. Gen. James Speed partially supported Holt. In a letter dated March 30, 1873, Speed wrote:

> After the finding of the Military Commission that tried the assassins of Mr. Lincoln, and before their execution, I saw the record of the case in the President's office, and attached to it was a paper, signed by some of the members of the Commission, recommending that the sentence against Mrs. Surratt be commuted to imprisonment for life....[13]

Speed mentioned nothing about discussing the clemency plea in the Cabinet meeting. James Harlan, Secretary of the Interior, made it clear, however, that such a discussion did take place. He wrote, "I remember distinctly the discussion of the question of the commutation of the sentence of death pronounced on her by the Court to imprisonment for life, had by members of the Cabinet, in the presence of President Johnson."[14]

Harlan indicated this was not a formal Cabinet meeting, but rather a private discussion by several Cabinet members.

James M. Wright, chief clerk in the Adjutant General's office, through which the documents passed, stated that the mercy recommendation was in plain sight when the papers were brought to President Johnson. The President's private secretary, Gen. R. D. Mussey, noted that after Holt and Johnson had spent two or three hours going over the Court's findings, the President told him that he had reached a decision on the executions. Mussey added that he was "very confident, though not absolutely sure, that it was at this interview Mr. Johnson told me the Court had recommended Mrs. Surratt to mercy." According to the President's secretary, Johnson argued that "if she was guilty at all, her sex did not make her any less guilty...."[15]

Even Judge Bingham added his testimony in behalf of Holt, stating:

> After the execution I called upon Secretaries Stanton and Seward and asked if this petition had been presented to the President before the death sentence was by him approved, and was answered by each of those gentlemen that the petition was presented to the President and was duly considered by him and his advisors before the death sentence upon Mrs. Surratt was approved....[16]

Gen. James A. Ekin, one of the Commissioners signing the mercy plea, asked Holt about it after the trial. The General remembered that Holt told him the President had carefully examined the sentences, including the clemency plea, "but that he could not accede to or grant the petition, for the reason that there was no [one] in the South more violent in the expression and practice of treasonable sentiments than the Rebel women...."[17]

These conclusive statements should have been enough to satisfy the Judge.

He was "vindicated," but it was not enough for the proud old man. He wanted complete vindication. He wanted Speed to state what happened in the Cabinet session and declare that former President Johnson was a "base liar."

While most participants were anxious to let the subject drop, the sensitive Holt kept it up. He wrote Harrison in 1873 that no one could know how "humiliating this controversy" had been for him, but it was necessary, he added, that he defend his "official and personal honor." Holt continued, "I trust this is the last appeal I shall ever have to make to a public from which I have never received favor and but rarely justice."[18] He was wrong on both counts. The public had held him in great honor in the early years of the war. He was wrong also about this being his last appeal to the public; it proved to be among the first.

Harrison was inclined to support both of his fellow-Kentuckians, Speed as well as Holt, in the growing rift. Holt, therefore, felt he needed to enlighten Harrison. In a letter to Harrison he started by praising Speed as a "man of honor" and a longtime personal friend but added that Speed was suppressing truth which was destroying Holt's character. Holt's "complete vindication" required only that Speed tell what happened in the Cabinet meeting.[19] This quest for "complete vindication" made Holt an increasingly lonely, bitter old man.

Ten years later, Holt was still seeking vindication, but his tone had changed. It was pitiful. He was still bitter, but there was less expression of hope. The aging Judge seemed resigned to his fate.

Eighteen years had passed since the hanging, but there was little letup in the abuse hurled at the Government and against Holt. Holt complained that he had been pursued for years by hatred and vituperation and had no idea why he should be described as a "hard and cruel man." "I have ceased to expect any change in my favor. Having published repeated and elaborate vindications of myself and produced the fullest measure of proof of my innocence . . . I have rested my case," he wrote Harrison.[20]

This pledge was premature. Holt had not rested his case. He was to fight until his death for "complete vindication." But in 1883, after years of fighting, he was tired—he promised to trust his soul to that "mightier tribunal where there will be no cloud to obscure the searchlight of truth."[21] His one consolation was that he had "no family, no wife or children over whose innocent lives the cloud enveloping myself could stretch its darkening folds."[22] This picture of self-pity and resignation did not characterize the earlier Holt. This correspondence, written in the shaky penmanship of an old man, was deceiving. Holt had not given up; his harshest attacks were yet to come.

Earlier in 1883 Holt wrote to the declining former Attorney General. He enclosed several pamphlets supporting his case, stating that "nothing but your own testimony is needed to render my vindication so complete as to silence the most malignant of my traducers. This testimony I asked of you in 1873, and now solicit it again, but not wholly as a personal matter."[23]

A question raised by Holt and brought up often since is whether the President of the United States can use his high office as "a craven refuge from accountability for official action." This was not a private question, Holt wrote, but a public one which concerned the whole country, and one on which the Nation expected Speed to speak. He continued, "Your unwillingness, thus to speak to it in 1873, seemed to have arisen from an exaggerated estimate of a rule which once prevailed in regard to the inviolability of Cabinet counsels and secrets."[24]

He indicated that in 1883 the rule was practically dead and that, even if it were binding, it would have had no application to this case because no rule could bind a man to conceal a criminal act. "In a word the rule never has been, and never should be so constructed as to become a shelter for perfidy or crime," he admonished.[25]

In closing, the Judge made a pitiful appeal:

> Allow me to add, that we are now, each of us, far advanced in years, so that whatever is to be done for my relief should be done quickly. While, however, it is sadly apparent that I can remain here but a little while longer, I have not been able to bring myself to the belief, that you will suffer the closing hours of my life to be darkened by a consciousness that this cloud, or even a shred of it, is still hanging over me—a cloud which can be dissipated at once and forever, by a single word spoken by yourself....[26]

Holt had addressed Speed as the Honorable James Speed, but Speed replied, on April 25, addressing Holt as General. He wrote that he had not answered sooner because he had lost his spectacles and was busy on two law cases. But he promised to look over the papers, "and after carefully reading them will write to you."[27]

Considering Holt's earnest, almost agonizing plea for promptness, Speed's failure to reply seemed calculated. After waiting two months, Holt again wrote the former Attorney General. The old Judge Advocate could not disguise his feelings. "It would be needless to express, as I feel it, the bitterness of the disappointment which this treatment of my appeal to you has occasioned me."[28]

This communication got results. Speed replied quickly, noting Holt's sharp rebuke. He detailed the various matters which had kept him too busy to reply, then repeated his promise to do "all that my sense of right and honor will permit."[29]

Four more months followed without a word. Again Holt wrote his fellow–Kentuckian, "This prolonged silence on your part declares, as emphatically as words could do, that it is not your purpose to give me the information which I asked of you...."[30]

Speed answered immediately, returning the papers Holt had sent him. "After very mature and deliberate consideration, I have come to the conclusion that I cannot say more than I have said."[31]

Disappointed, Holt waited nearly two months to write Speed again, this time, a long, blistering letter. Holt stated that he was made to appear dishonest by Johnson's false statements and he wanted to regain his respect. He asserted that Speed possessed information that was a crime to withhold. "You hold it simply as a sacred trust for whom it most concerns, and you can no more rightfully deprive me of it than you could rightfully deprive me of any other treasure of mine which might by accident fall into your hands."[32] He condemned Speed in extremely harsh terms.

Although Speed was in his seventies, he was young enough to be stung by Holt's reasoning. He replied in a short, cold note.

> Dear Sir:
> I had hoped that my letter of October 25, 1883 would be regarded by you as a finality; and put an end to all correspondence between us on the subject thereof.[33]

A few sentences of justification ended the communication.

Holt passed his 80th birthday before he received indirect satisfaction from Speed. Two months before Speed died in 1887, he was asked to deliver a speech at the annual meeting of the Ohio Commandery of the Loyal Legion, at Cincinnati. Speed's friends, realizing the old gentleman would not live much longer, and knowing that he was the only person who could satisfy Holt's obsessive quest for "complete vindication," begged the former Attorney General to allude to Holt and if possible clear his name.[34] Complying, Speed incorporated into his speech words intended to nullify President Johnson's accusation against Holt. Toward the end, referring to the conspiracy trial, he noted that the trial had cast blame on his "distinguished friend" Judge Holt. "In every particular he was just and fair," declared Speed. Holt did not need any vindication from him, he noted, but he was speaking "because I know reflections have been made, and because my position enabled me to know the facts, and because I know the perfect purity and uprightness of his conduct."[35]

A small audience of about 300 heard the speech. It did not immediately reach the person most affected. Holt had to wait another year to learn of Speed's declaration. Still trying to clear his name, he wrote to John Mason Brown, asking if the former Attorney General had told him anything about the clemency plea before he died. Brown alluded to Speed's Cincinnati speech, stating that Speed died with the conviction he had exonerated Holt.[36]

Holt thought the speech was too little, too late. Some months later he gave his revealing correspondence with Speed to the *North American Review* for publication.

He lived another six years lonely, bitter and almost forgotten in a darkened room close to Capitol Hill. Only a few old friends paid him any attention. Horatio King, who had served on Buchanan's Cabinet a few months while Holt was Secretary of War, occasionally looked in on the old Judge. King reported that Holt suffered excruciating pain in his last years.[37]

Another friend of many years, Thomas Harris, tried to keep in touch with his old comrade. He wrote King two years before Holt's death that Holt had been the victim of party spirit and warped judgment—the evidence was overwhelming that "Andy Johnson was not only mean and cowardly but fake."

Holt could take some satisfaction from the efforts of both King and Harris. King had praised Holt in an article which appeared in the *Century Magazine*, April 1890. The old man appreciated King's efforts and told him so. Harris also wrote an article about the trial which presented Holt in a favorable light. Harris concluded that Holt's character had been fully vindicated and that "he will have an honorable mention in history."[38] This prediction was too optimistic. What little mention Holt has received in history has not been altogether honorable.

Before the conspiracy trial when the Government was praising Holt for his loyalty to the Union, *Vanity Fair Magazine* printed the following verse in his honor:

> There is a golden moment in the life of every Ruler when he may by an honest and fearless act, imperishably bind himself to posterity.

These words proved prophetic. They referred to Holt's glorious support of the Union, but the "honest and fearless act" that bound him to posterity was his association with the military trial, which was remembered long after his political exploits were forgotten.

More than 20 years after his death, the *Louisville Courier-Journal* ran a full-page illustrated feature on "Kentuckians Who Made History." Included with James Speed and former United States Vice-President Richard Johnson was Joseph Holt.[39] Not surprisingly, the writer claimed that Holt's place in history was secured because of his leadership in the assassination trial. Forgotten were his achievements in several presidential campaigns; his work as Commissioner of Patents, Postmaster-General, Secretary of War, Judge Advocate General of the army and head of the Bureau of Military Justice. Holt, a man of outstanding qualities and achievements, was best-remembered for an "honest and fearless act" that caused him prolonged anguish.

Weichmann was not quite 60 when he died, lonely and broken by endless hounding. As he lay dying on June 2, 1902, his concern was the same as it had been for 37 years—to certify the truthfulness of his trial testimony. He called for pen and paper, which his sisters brought, and dictated this statement:

> This is to certify that every word I gave in evidence at the assassination trial was absolutely true; and now I am about to die and with love I recommend myself to all truth-loving people.[40]

He died soon after signing the statement. The doctor certified the cause of death "Cardiac Asthma."

Even his death created false rumors. Some said he was denied the last rites of the Catholic Church. Actually, a priest gave him extreme unction and his brother conducted a requiem mass for him in St. Mary's Church.

With the beginning of a new century, memories of the terrible spring night in 1865 were fading. Yet, a younger generation renewed interest in the subject and stirred the recollections of still-living participants. David Miller DeWitt, researching his book on the assassination, wrote to Sam Arnold. Arnold responded from Johns Hopkins Hospital on October 13, 1904, revealing a few facts not generally known. His first contact with Booth concerning the kidnap plot occurred in August 1864. This was earlier than the generally accepted origin of the conspiracy. According to Arnold, the Baltimore and Washington conspirators were unknown to one another before March 17, 1865, although both groups knew Booth and Surratt. He declared he had never heard of Weichmann or seen him before the trial, thus exonerating the much-maligned prosecution witness. It was too late; Weichmann had died two years earlier.

<u>The Plan of Escape.</u>

was to place Mr. Lincoln in the buggy purchased for that purpose, and cross Eastern Branch Bridge. Surratt and Atzerodt, alias Port Tobacco, were to follow them to where they had a boat concealed; turn the horse loose, place the President in the boat, and cross the Potomac to the Virgina shore, and thence to ~~walk~~ make our way to Richmond. Surratt knew the route and was to act as pilot.

Samuel B. Arnold.

A box painted black, like unto a sword-box, was sent by Booth from the Hotel, by the porter there, in our room. The next day it was transferred in a wagon, O'Laughlin acting as pilot, to some place. I was not present. After giving the box to the driver, went to Georgetown and O'Laughlin had the full charge of it. M. O'Laughlin said he took it to Mr. ~~Head's~~ Herold's, and from thence the unknown* carried it home. Took the guns out and carried them to Pedee.2) This latter ~~chance~~ clause Booth told me.

Samuel B. Arnold.

<u>Witness. V. Randall, E. G. Horner, Baltdmore, April 18, 1865.</u>

Note: Beside this written statement of Arnold's, he verbally communicated the facts that Booth was the correspondent of Doctors Mudd, Garland and Queen. This fact was told the Secretary when I presented him Arnold's statement.

J. L. McPhail.

* Herold; was
2. [illegible] such place as Pedee, It was probably
J. B. [illegible]
[illegible]

Arnold's confession. Last page of a typewritten statement prepared for John Surratt's trial, never used. Officer McPhail noted that Arnold "verbally communicated that fact that Booth was the correspondent of Doctors Mudd, Garland and Queen." Notes were probably added by Judge Fisher (George P. Fisher Papers, Library of Congress).

Arnold admitted he knew Mrs. Surratt but refrained from saying anymore about her. He also stated that, while at Dry Tortugas, Dr. Mudd and Spangler told him they had no connection with Booth. But this contradicted the men's own statements. Arnold expressed his belief that Spangler "would never have been taken into his [Booth's] confidence," but he said nothing about his view of Mudd's innocence.[41] The gist of Arnold's letter, written more than 39 years after the crime, was that he believed Spangler to have been innocent.

In the Washington area in 1908, hundreds of people still remembered the assassination; many older citizens had played some part in it. Clara E. Laughlin, in preparation for a book on the murder, visited the capital city to interview these participants. Ellen Spencer Mussey, widow of General Mussey, stated that the President had seen the clemency petition and had given strict orders that no one be allowed to see him in behalf of the prisoners. General Mussey sympathized with Anna and had his own personal buggy brought to the White House portico in case there might be a last-minute reprieve. He kept the buggy there until he heard the tolling of the church bells announcing the execution.[42]

Anna never fully recovered from the traumatic events. Unable to bear living in the house on H Street, she stayed for a short time with John Brophy and his wife and then lived with the Holohans. After passing through a period of ostracism, she married a government clerk, William P. Tonry. Some believed Federal authorities dismissed him for marrying Anna. For a while the couple lived in poverty. But Tonry eventually became a professor and a highly respected chemist in Baltimore.

Their improving financial and social position relieved some strain in Anna's life, but she continued to suffer emotionally and physically. Her hair turned white in her early thirties. She remained subject to fits of extreme nervousness, bordering on insanity. Living in Baltimore, close to the Tonrys, were Anna's brother John and his family. Isaac Surratt returned to the United States from Monterrey, Mexico, in 1866. He also moved to Baltimore, where he lived quietly. With the passage of years, John and Anna gradually let the conspiracy issue rest.

After serving as professor at Gonzaga College, John Brophy became a clerk in the Supreme Court. He remained active in the early 1900s. In an address in 1908, he repeated his old accusation that Stanton caused Mrs. Surratt's death because of his hatred of Catholics. Although Weichmann and Stanton were dead, Brophy continued perpetuating his long-disproved falsehoods.

After the Government permitted the removal of the conspirators' bodies from the Old Arsenal grounds, Mrs. Surratt's relatives moved her remains to the consecrated grounds of Mount Olivet, a Catholic cemetery in the Washington area. Forty years after her frantic efforts to save her mother, Anna Surratt Tonry was buried next to her in a plot donated by the cemetery. The body of Mrs. Surratt's son Isaac lies on the other side of his mother. His family buried John Surratt in Baltimore. Ironically, John Lloyd was interred about 100 yards from Mrs. Surratt's grave. Mount Olivet also contains the graves of Thomas Harbin, Anna Ward, John and Eliza Holohan and Father Jacob A. Walter.

Others involved in the tragedy lie in marked graves throughout the country except for Lewis Powell (Payne), whose body was unclaimed.

Long after the headstone marking Mrs. Surratt's grave had been broken and her name almost obscured, some unknown admirer continued to leave flowers. About 1970, the old stone was replaced by a new grave marker with a bronze plaque stating that she was

> swept by events and emotions surrounding the assassination of Lincoln from obscurity to the limelight of a military trial and inglorious death on a scaffold and whose guilt in the conspiracy is still questioned.[43]

When the last accused conspirator died in 1916, the world worried about another war. Things had changed. The reunited Nation had developed into an industrial power. Billy Sunday was holding a revival meeting in Baltimore as John Surratt lay on his deathbed with pneumonia. The United States had not yet entered World War I when he died at 9:00 P.M. on April 21. The 72-year-old Surratt had been ill for nearly two months. His wife and two of his four children stood by his bedside. In his last years, Surratt refused to talk about the assassination, and discussion of the subject was forbidden in his home. Shortly before his death, he burned all his papers relating to the conspiracy. The month his family buried him, *The Birth of a Nation* opened at Ford's Theatre.

The Surratts could not get the facts straight, even in the death notice, which stated that "he was in Elmira, New York, when Lincoln was assassinated." This part, often disputed, was probably true. But the obituary added incorrectly that he fled to Canada, England, Ireland, Egypt and South America. Surratt never made it to South America, but, after all, he could not resist embellishing the story.[44]

Epilogue

Occasionally some event in the twentieth century still excites memories of the violent scenes of Good Friday, 1865. However, after the 1920s, only a few smoldering cinders of the former inferno remained to be rekindled.

The high-backed rocking chair in which Lincoln sat when shot became an object of interest after most of the participants were forgotten. The rocker, which was not usually placed in the presidential box, was part of a suite of furniture purchased for the reception room at Ford's Theatre. When ushers began to use the area for lounging and loitering, Henry Clay Ford put the piece in his sleeping room at the theater. While decorating the presidential box, Ford asked one of the stagehands to bring the chair to the box. A few days after the crime, *Frank Leslie's Illustrated Newspaper* sent an artist to make a drawing of the high-backed rocker. The rocker remained in the box even after authorities closed the theater.

The War Department bought the furnishings of the presidential box in 1902 and exhibited some of the pieces in the Smithsonian Museum. But the chair, for some reason, was not put on exhibit. The Government kept it for years in the basement of the Smithsonian.

In the early 1920s the 73-year-old widow of Henry Clay Ford appealed to then–Secretary of War Davis to return the chair to her. Someone had offered her a large sum for the rocker, which she claimed, incorrectly, had been taken out of her home for Lincoln's use. She said she was destitute and by selling the rocking chair, she would have money to live comfortably for the rest of her life. The Government denied her request. Some later accounts indicate the chair was eventually returned to her and she sold it.

The celebrated high-backed rocker next surfaced in the 1930s, when a writer for the *Saturday Review of Literature* noticed it in an auction catalogue.[1] Another famous Henry Ford, founder of the Ford Motor Company, eventually bought it and moved it to Dearborn, Michigan. He first placed it in the courthouse where Lincoln had practiced law, which had been moved from Illinois to Dearborn. Now it is housed in the Henry Ford Museum in Dearborn. In 1934 U.S. Rep. George A. Dondero tried to have the chair returned to Ford's Theatre, but the automobile magnate refused.

Heirs of Dr. Samuel Mudd also seemed interested in profiting financially from the treatment of their relative. In April 1934, one of Dr. Mudd's descendants, Samuel Mudd of St. Paul, Minnesota, requested Sen. Millard Tydings

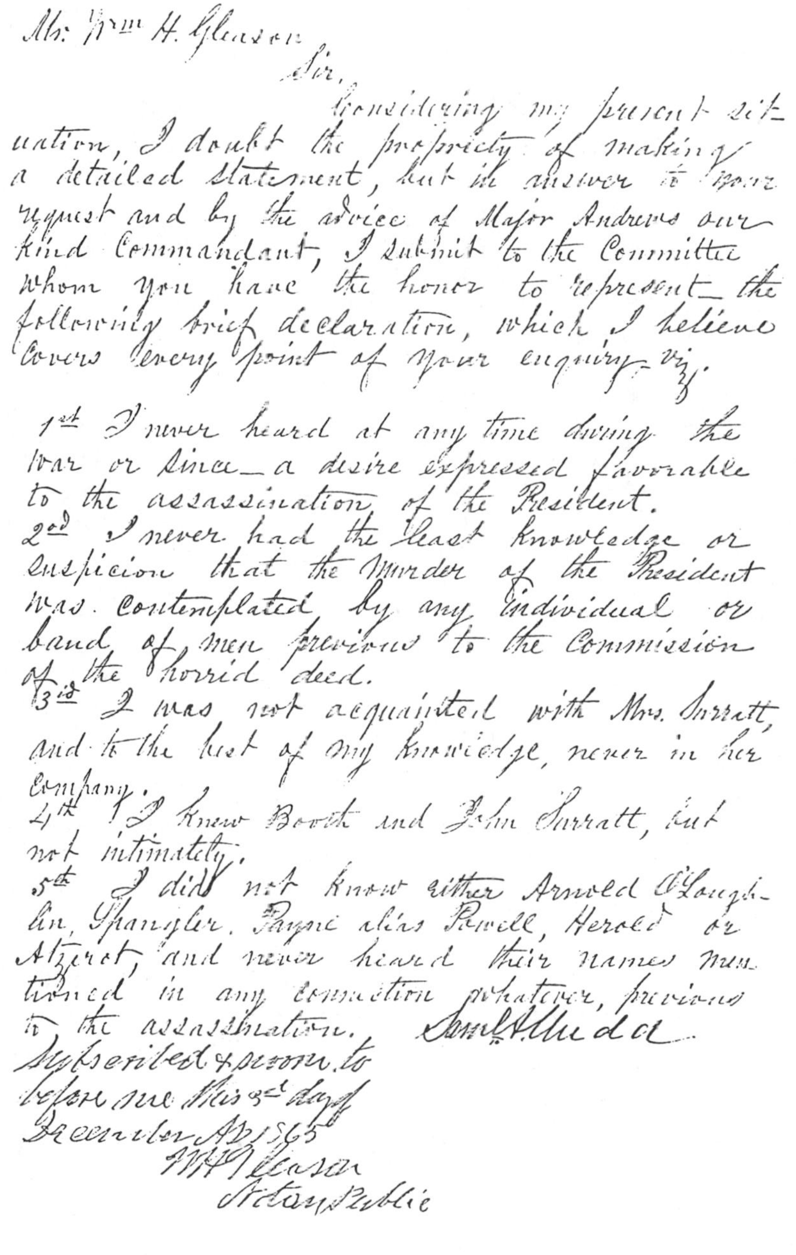

Mr: Wm H. Gleason,
                    Sir,
                            Considering my present sit-
uation, I doubt the propriety of making
a detailed statement, but in answer to your
request and by the advice of Major Andrews our
kind Commandant, I submit to the Committee
whom you have the honor to represent the
following brief declaration, which I believe
Covers every point of your enquiry viz.

1st I never heard at any time during the
War or Since a desire expressed favorable
to the assassination of the President.
2nd I never had the least knowledge or
suspicion that the Murder of the President
was contemplated by any individual or
band of men previous to the Commission
of the horrid deed.
3rd I was not acquainted with Mrs. Surratt,
and to the best of my knowledge, never in her
Company.
4th I knew Booth and John Surratt, but
not intimately.
5th I did not know either Arnold O'Laughlin, Spangler, Payne alias Powell, Herold or
Atzerot, and never heard their names mentioned in any connection whatever, previous
to the assassination.   Saml A Mudd

Subscribed & sworn to
before me this 3d day
December AD 1865
            WH Gleason
            Notary Public

Dr. Mudd's statement. While at first refusing to answer questions, Mudd made this signed statement at Fort Jefferson. He pleaded ignorance of the murder plot but admitted her "knew Booth and John Surratt." The date is incorrect; it should be 1867 (Benjamin F. Butler Papers, Library of Congress).

of Maryland to ask Congress to grant $200,000 for the relief of the heirs. The request alleged, incorrectly, that soldiers looking for Booth burned Dr. Mudd's house. It also declared that Mudd was innocent.[2]

Nearly two years later, Congressman Randolph, Democrat of West Virginia, introduced another resolution concerning the doctor. He proposed that a tablet be placed in the ruins of Fort Jefferson in recognition of Dr. Mudd's "innocence of a crime for which he was held prisoner for four years."[3]

In the same year, 1936, Twentieth Century–Fox released a film titled *Prisoner of Shark Island*, which dealt with the convicted conspirator's imprisonment. Nettie Mudd Monroe of Baltimore, Dr. Samuel Mudd's daughter, was paid $2,000 by the film company for motion picture rights. The contract provided that Monroe see and edit the film before it was shown. She later claimed the company violated the contract.

Prospects of the availability of the Lincoln Papers created a flurry of interest in 1947–48. Robert Todd Lincoln had most of his father's papers put in vaults in the Manuscript Division of the Library of Congress, where they were kept from public view. His will directed that the documents not be opened until 21 years after his death. Robert Lincoln died July 26, 1926.

A year before the papers were made public, a rash of speculation concerning them appeared in newspapers. Bob Considine wrote in the *Washington Post* that the items might clear up the "mysterious circumstances surrounding the assassination...."[4] Of special concern was the popular theory that men in high places, particularly Stanton, were involved in the plot.

As the time approached, speculation increased. On July 20, 1947, just a week before the material was to be released, E. B. Long predicted that the papers would probably not be sensational. Paul Angle, director of the Chicago Historical Society, also speculated that the Lincoln documents would reveal nothing startling. Dr. Otto Eisenschiml, who had implicated Stanton in his book *Why Was Lincoln Shot?* also believed that the collection would be a flop as far as revealing anything sensational. Lloyd Lewis, author of *Myths After Lincoln*, said he did not expect Robert Lincoln to have preserved anything "that would alter the accepted portrait of Lincoln." As it turned out, these predictions were accurate. The long-awaited revelations proved unexciting. They threw little new light on the assassination plot.

In October 1959, Pres. Dwight Eisenhower authorized the placing of a bronze plaque at Fort Jefferson commemorating Dr. Mudd's efforts in combating yellow fever. In July 1973, the Michigan Legislature adopted a resolution stating that Dr. Mudd "was innocent of any complicity in the assassination of President Abraham Lincoln" and that he was unjustly convicted.[5] Pres. Jimmy Carter in 1979 declared his personal belief in Dr. Mudd's innocence.

Several National and local committees cooperated in remodeling Mary Surratt's country house, and on May 1, 1976, it was opened as a tourist attraction. Her boardinghouse on H Street still stands in the 1980s, housing a Chinese restaurant. Citizens interested in the Surratts formed a Mary Surratt Club, and a high school near Clinton, Maryland (formerly Surrattsville), was named Surratt High School in her honor.

Chapter Notes

I. "Blood, Blood, All Around"

1. *Trial of the Assassins and Conspirators for the Murder of Abraham Lincoln* (Philadelphia: Barclay and Co., 1865), p. 33 [this version of the trial is based primarily on the Associated Press report and will be cited hereafter as "Associated Press Account"]; and *Trial of the Assassins and Conspirators at Washington City, D.C., May and June 1865* (Philadelphia: T. B. Peterson and Brothers, 1865), pp. 72–75 [this version of the trial is based on the *Philadelphia Inquirer* report and hereafter will be cited as "*Philadelphia Inquirer* Account"].

2. *Ibid.*

3. *Ibid.*

4. *Philadelphia Inquirer* Account, p. 72; Associated Press Account, p. 33; *New York Press*, 4 September 1891.

5. *Ibid.*

6. *New York Commercial Advertiser*, 22 April 1865.

7. *Ibid.*

8. Horace Porter, "Campaigning with Grant," *The Century Magazine*, October 1897, p. 892.

9. Associated Press Account, pp. 29–30.

10. *New York Post*, 8 July 1884.

11. *Washington Star*, 29 March 1918.

12. William F. Ferguson, *I Saw Booth Shoot Lincoln* (Cambridge: Houghton Mifflin, The Riverside Press, 1930), pp. 28–29.

13. Eleanor Ruggles, *Prince of Players, Edwin Booth* (New York: W. W. Norton and Co., Inc., 1953), p. 180.

14. James Horan, *Mathew Brady. Historian with a Camera* (New York: Bonanza Books, 1955), photograph No. 313 and *Washington Star*, 14 April 1894.

15. *Washington Star*, 29 March 1918.

16. *Washington Star*, 14 April 1894.

17. *Washington Star*, 14 April 1918.

18. *Philadelphia Inquirer* Account, p. 128.

19. *Ibid.*, p. 82.

20. Dr. John K. Lattimer argues that there was no protective collar to save Seward. See John K. Lattimer, *Kennedy and Lincoln Medical and Ballistic Comparisons of Their Assassinations* (New York: Harcourt Brace Jovanovich, 1980), p. 102.

21. Associated Press Account, p. 30.

22. *Washington Star*, 14 April 1894; and Metro Police Department, District of Columbia, Day Book, 8th Precinct, 14 April 1865.

23. *The Magazine of History*, February 1911, Vol. XIII.

24. John C. Nicolay and John Hay, *Abraham Lincoln, A History*, 10 vols. (New York: The Century Co., 1886), IV: 301.

25. Records of the District of Columbia Police Blotter, 14 April 1865.

26. Richards to Weichmann, 7 May 1898. Lewis Weichmann, *A True History of the*

Assassination of Abraham Lincoln and the Conspiracy of 1865, ed. Floyd E. Risvold (New York: Alfred A. Knopf, 1975), p. 412.

27. Richards to Weichmann, 29 April 1898. Weichmann, *A True History of the Assassination*, p. 411; and James Tanner, *While Lincoln Lay Dying* (Philadelphia: Union League of Philadelphia, 1868), p. 4.

28. Police Blotter, 17 April 1865.

29. Unidentified newspaper article, no date, Washingtonia Collection, Martin Luther King Library, Washington, D.C.

30. Police Blotter, 14 April 1865.

31. Metro Police, Day Book, 14 April 1865.

II. Two Horsemen Riding Very Fast

1. James Tanner, *While Lincoln Lay Dying* (Philadelphia: Union League of Philadelphia, 1868), p. 5.

2. Ruggles, pp. 19–20.

3. *Ibid.*, pp. 60–61.

4. Asia Booth Clarke, *The Unlocked Book: A Memoir of John Wilkes Booth by His Sister*, ed. Eleanor Farjeon (London: Faber and Faber Limited, 1938), p. 148.

5. Ruggles, p. 124.

6. *Philadelphia Inquirer* Account, p. 17.

7. *Ibid.*, p. 68.

8. Charles A. Dana, *Recollections of the Civil War, With the Leaders at Washington and in the Field in the Sixties* (New York: D. Appleton and Co., 1902), p. 281.

9. Associated Press Account, pp. 29–30; *Philadelphia Inquirer* Account, p. 60.

10. Richards to Weichmann, 24 May 1897. Weichmann, *A True History of the Assassination*, p. 415.

11. Sterling Edwards, "I Remember Lincoln's Funeral," *American Motorist*, February 1932.

III. While the President Still Breathes

1. Thirty-three years later when Richards recalled the events, he said he was sure that he went to the house with the other detectives, but in his report to Stanton on May 12, 1865, he made no reference to his visit. Considering the pressure connected with the investigation and his faulty recall of several events, it is likely that Richards was mistaken about his visit to the Surratt house after the murder. Richards to Weichmann, 24 May 1898, Weichmann, pp. 414–415.

2. Frank A. Flower, *Edwin McMasters Stanton* (Akron, Ohio: The Sadfield Publishing Co., 1905), p. 281.

3. Abott A. Abott, *The Assassination and Death of Abraham Lincoln, President of the United States of America* (New York: American News Co., 1865), p. 10. Otto Eisenschiml indicates that the dispatch was not actually telegraphed at 3:00 in the morning, but some time later, and thus assumed Stanton was hiding something. The facts show that, far from obstructing the search, the Secretary of War did more than anyone else to promote a thorough and complete investigation, although he was cautious in identifying Booth absolutely. Otto Eisenschiml, *In the Shadow of Lincoln's Death* (New York: Wilfred Funk, Inc., 1940).

4. *Philadelphia Inquirer* Account, p. 66.

5. *Washington Post*, 16 April 1905.

6. AGO, Roll 6, No. 258; Metro Police Day Book, 15 April 1865.

7. AGO, Roll 6, Nos. 131–142.

8. Weichmann's name does not appear on the Police Blotter as having been arrested at this time, although he was closely watched.

9. AGO, Roll 6, No. 145.

10. Metro Police Day Book, 15 April 1865.

11. *Ibid.*

IV. Someone to Fill the Vacuum

1. Tanner, *While Lincoln Lay Dying*, p. 6; also, Noah Brooks, *The Century Magazine*, May 1895, pp. 17–26.

2. Orville H. Browning, *The Diary of Orville Hickman Browning*, ed. James G. Randall (Springfield: Illinois State Historical Library, 1933), p. 20.

3. L. E. Chittenden, *Personal Reminiscences by L. E. Chittenden* (New York: Richmond, Croscup and Co., 1893), pp. 238–240.

4. *Ibid.*, pp. 238–240.

5. Gideon Welles, *Lincoln on Reconstruction*, cited by Bruce Catton, *Never Call Retreat*, Vol. III of *The Centennial History of the Civil War* (Garden City, N.Y.: Doubleday and Co., Inc., 1965), p. 457.

6. "Abraham Lincoln," *Appleton's Cyclopaedia of American Biography*, 6 vols., ed. James Grant Wilson and John Fiske (New York: D. Appleton and Co., 1898), III: 725.

7. Charles A. Dana, *Recollections of the Civil War, With Leaders at Washington and in the Field in the Sixties* (New York: D. Appleton and Co., 1902), pp. 274–276.

8. *Philadelphia Inquirer* Account, p. 87.

9. Quoted in *The Miners Journal*, Pottsville, Pa., 27 April 1865.

10. *Ibid.*, 29 April 1865.

11. Ruggles, *Prince of Players*, p. 184.

12. Clarke, *The Unlocked Book*, p. 126.

13. Police Blotter, 15 April 1865.

14. *Washington Star*, 29 March 1918. Atzerodt later said that he threw his knife away in this general vicinity.

15. Salmon P. Chase, *Diary*, pp. 268–269. Some sources say the oath was taken in Johnson's hotel room.

16. James Blaine, *Twenty Years in Congress*, 2 vols. (n.p., n.d.), II: 9.

17. *Ibid.*, p. 10. In his original speech, Johnson had assured the citizens of Illinois that he would follow Lincoln's policies, but at the suggestion of his devoted friend Preston King, this avowal was omitted from the published version.

18. Albert Dagget, "Tragic Memories," *Washington Star*, 14 April 1894.

19. Police Blotter, 15 April 1865.

V. The Man Called Mars

1. Flower, *Edwin McMasters Stanton*, p. 22.

2. *Ibid.*, p. 39.

3. David Miller DeWitt, *The Impeachment and Trial of Andrew Johnson: Seventeenth President of the United States, A History* (n.p., 1903; reprint ed., New York: Russell and Russell, 1967), p. 252.

4. Horatio King, "King and Stanton," *The New England Magazine*, December 1893.

5. Evan R. Jones, *Lincoln and Stanton, Historical Sketches* (London: Frederick Warne and Co., 1875), p. 106.

6. Brooks, *Washington, D.C. in Lincoln's Time*, p. 36.

7. Edward Bates, *Diary* (n.p.: American Historical Association, n.d.), p. 485.

8. Ulysses S. Grant, *Personal Memoirs of U. S. Grant*, 2 vols. (London: Sampson Low, Marston, Searle and Rivington, 1886), 1: 104.

9. *Ibid.*, p. 536.

10. Gideon Welles, *Diary of Gideon Welles*, 2 vols. (Boston: Houghton Mifflin, 1911), 2: 19 April 1865.

11. King, "King and Stanton," *New England Magazine*, December 1893.

12. Jones, *Lincoln and Stanton*, p. 118. Italics in the original.

13. David Homer Bates, *Lincoln and the Telegraph Office* (New York: The Century Co., 1907), p. 390.

14. *Ibid.*, p. 391.

15. Flowers, *Edwin McMasters Stanton*, p. 369.

16. Almira Russell Hancock, *Reminiscences of Winfield Hancock by His Wife* (New York: Charles L. Webster and Co., 1887), p. 88.

17. John Cottrell, *Anatomy of an Assassination* (New York: Funk and Wagnalls, 1966), p. 231.

18. Dana, *Recollections of the Civil War*, p. 158.

19. James Blaine, *Twenty Years in Congress*, 2 vols. (n.p., n.p.), 1: 563.

20. Browning, *The Diary of Orville Hickman Browning*, p. 17.

21. Dana, *Recollections of the Civil War*, pp. 236–238.

22. *Eulogies Delivered on the Occasion of the Announcement of the Death of Hon. Edwin M. Stanton, by Members of the Bar, D.C. Supreme Court* (Washington, D.C: Parks and History Association, 1970), p. 52.

VI. ". . . Find the Murderer"

1. Dana, *Recollections of the Civil War*, pp. 276–279.

2. *Ibid.*, p. 277. At the conspiracy trial it was thought that the letter was written to Booth, who was using the name of Louis, but by the time of the Surratt trial, this theory had changed. The new theory was that Booth had written the letter to Louis, who was identified as Louis Payne. David Miller DeWitt, *The Assassination of Abraham Lincoln and Its Expiation* (n.p., 1909; reprint ed., Newport, N.Y.: Books for Libraries, 1970), p. 262.

3. *Ibid.*, pp. 277–278.

4. *Trial of John H. Surratt*, 2 vols. (Washington, D.C.: Government Printing Office, 1867), pp. 396–398; *Washington Chronicle*, 21 May 1867.

5. *The Magazine of History*, February 1911, p. 64; AGO, Roll 5, No. 153.

6. *Trial of John H. Surratt*, pp. 396–398.

7. *Philadelphia Inquirer* Account, pp. 130–131.

8. *The Century Magazine*, April 1896. Italics in the original.

9. *Ibid.* Italics in the original.

10. AGO, Roll 3, No. 625.

11. *Philadelphia Inquirer* Account, p. 118.

12. AGO, Roll 6, No. 201.

13. AGO, Roll 6, No. 005.

14. AGO, Roll 1, No. 43.

15. AGO, Roll 7, No. 37.

16. AGO, Roll 3, Nos. 634–638.

17. LaFayette C. Baker, *History of the United States Secret Service* (Philadelphia: King and Baird, 1868; reprint ed., New York: AMS Press, Inc., 1973), p. 525.

VII. Easter Sunday, 1865

1. William E. Doster, *Lincoln and the Episodes of the Civil War* (New York and London: G. P. Putnam's Sons, The Knickerbocker Press, 1915), p. 94.

2. Constance Green, *Washington Village and Capital, 1800–1878* (Princeton, N.J.: Princeton University Press, 1962), pp. 248–287.

3. Browning, *The Diary of Orville Hickman Browning*, p. 21.

4. Adolphe de Chambrun, *Impressions of Lincoln and the Civil War: A Foreigner's Account*, trans., Aldebert de Chambrun (New York: Random House, 1962), pp. 98–106.

5. *Washington Star*, 17 April 1865.

6. Carl Sandburg, *Abraham Lincoln: The War Years*, 4 vols. (New York: Harcourt, Brace and Co., 1939), 4: 347.

7. *Ibid.*, pp. 348–349.

8. *Washington Star*, 17 April 1865.

9. *Washington Star*, 18 April 1865.

10. *Philadelphia Inquirer Account*, p. 67.

11. LaFayette Baker to Stanton, July 7, 1866. LaFayette Charles Baker, *History of the United States Secret Service* (Philadelphia: King and Baird, 1868; reprint ed., New York: AMS Press, Inc., 1973), p. 526.

12. George Alfred Townsend, *The Life, Crime and Capture of John Wilkes Booth* (New York: Dick and Fitzgerald Publishers, 1865), p. 42.

13. Baker, *History of the United States Secret Service*, p. 530.

14. *Trial of John Surratt*, 1: 396–398; Metro Police Day Book, 16 April 1865.

15. Quoted in Sandburg, *Abraham Lincoln*, 4: 341.

16. Quoted in Sandburg, *Ibid.*, 4: 346.

VIII. First Confessions

1. Townsend, *The Life, Crime and Capture*, p. 12.

2. *Philadelphia Inquirer Account*, p. 106.

3. *Washington Star*, 17 April 1865.

4. George S. Bryan, *The Great American Myth* (New York: D. Appleton and Co., 1940), p. 238; also AGO, Roll 5, Nos. 346 and 490.

5. AGO, Roll 6, No. 541.

6. *Baltimore American*, 9 December 1902. (His confession was first made public by the *Baltimore American*, 19 January 1869.)

7. George P. Fisher Papers, Box 2, Manuscript Division, Library of Congress; also Weichmann, *A True History of the Assassination*, p. 385.

8. Unidentified newspaper clipping, Lincoln Collection, *Lincoln Relics in Washington*, Martin L. King Public Library, Washington, D.C.

9. Walter Lowenfels, *Walt Whitman's Civil War* (New York: Alfred A. Knopf, 1960), p. 257.

10. George Alfred Townsend, *Cincinnati Enquirer*, 14–19 April 1892, cited by Weichmann, *A True History of Assassination*, p. 48.

11. *Philadelphia Inquirer Account*, pp. 93–94.

12. AGO, Roll 7, No. 598; also *Trial of John H. Surratt*, 1: 396–398.

13. AGO, Roll 1, no number.

14. *Trial of John H. Surratt*, 1: 396–398.

15. Weichmann, *A True History of the Assassination*, pp. 224–225.

16. Helen Jones Campbell, *Confederate Courier* (New York: St. Martin's Press, 1964), p. 31.

17. Weichmann, *A True History of the Assassination*, p. 13.

18. *Ibid.*, pp. 12–13.

IX. The Honor of a Lady

1. AGO, Roll 2, No. 300.

2. AGO, Roll 2, No. 1091; also *Philadelphia Inquirer* Account, pp. 74–75. Documents in the National Archives indicate that it was Officer Devoe who asked for the door to be opened, but in the conspiracy trial, Major Smith was credited with the conversation.

3. *New York Times*, 18 April 1865; also *Philadelphia Inquirer* Account, pp. 74–75.

4. *Philadelphia Inquirer* Account, pp. 74–75.

5. AGO, Roll 6, Nos. 235–237. Most of this interrogation is from the National Archives collection.

6. AGO, Roll 6, No. 235.

7. Mary W. Porter, *The Surgeon in Charge* (Concord, N.J.: Rumford Press, 1949), pp. 13–14.

8. AGO, Roll 6, No. 247.

9. *Ibid.*, Nos. 246–247.

10. *Ibid.*

11. Cited by Theodore Roscoe, *The Web of Conspiracy: The Complete Story of the Men Who Murdered Abraham Lincoln* (Englewood Cliffs, N.J.: Prentice Hall, 1959), p. 247; also AGO, Roll 6, Nos. 247–249.

12. AGO, Roll 6, Nos. 242–246. An omission occurs in the transcript of the interview here. A blank space was left where the name of the priest should have been written.

13. *Ibid.*, No. 250.

14. *Ibid.*, also Roscoe, *The Web of Conspiracy*, p. 249.

X. A View of Swampoodle

1. *Philadelphia Inquirer* Account, p. 73.

2. Marshall, *American Bastille*, pp. 321–346; also Virginia Lomax, *The Old Capitol and Its Inmates by a Lady* (New York: E. J. Hale and Co., 1867), p. 83 and Jacob Mogelever, *Death to Traitors: The Story of General LaFayette C. Baker, Lincoln's Forgotten Secret Service Chief* (Garden City, N.Y.: Doubleday and Co., Inc., 1960), pp. 117–118.

3. Rose O'Neal Greenhow, *My Imprisonment* (London: Richard Bently, Publisher, 1863), p. 208.

4. Stanton to Phillips, 21 February 1861, Philip Phillips Papers, Manuscript Divison, Library of Congress.

5. Journal of Mrs. Eugenia Phillips, 11 September 1861, Phillips Papers, Box 1.

6. Phillips to Stanton, 23 September 1861, Phillips Papers, Box 2.

7. Marshall, *American Bastille*, pp. 328–329.

8. *Ibid.*, pp. 337–339.

9. *Ibid.*, p. 335.

10. Lomax, *The Old Capitol and Its Inmates*, pp. 66–71.

XI. "Communication with Jeff Davis"

1. George Alfred Townsend, *Frank Leslie's Illustrated Newspaper*, date illegible.

2. *Ibid.*

3. *Ibid.* The house today is painted a reddish hue, which some authorities determined to be the original color; however, writers in the 1860s described it as white.

4. *Washington Chronicle*, 21 May 1867.

5. Campbell, *Confederate Courier*, p. 14.

6. *Washington Post*, 3 April 1898.

7. *Washington Chronicle*, 21 May 1867.

8. Baker, *History of the United States Secret Service*, pp. 102–112.

9. *Ibid.*, pp. 479–480.

10. John Surratt to his cousin, Belle Seaman, 16 December 1863 (Italics in the original), cited in *Ibid.*, p. 560.

11. AGO, Roll 4, No. 278.

XII. Unanswered Questions

1. AGO, Roll 6, No. 317.

2. AGO, Roll 1, no number.

3. *Ibid.*, Nos. 515–538.

4. AGO, Roll 2, No. 32; AGO, Roll 6, No. 113.

5. *Washington Star*, 7 December 1881.

6. John F. Coyle, undated newspaper clipping, Lincoln Collection, Martin Luther King Public Library, Washington, D.C.

7. Vaughn Shelton, *Mask for Treason — The Lincoln Murder Trial* (Harrisburg, Penn.: Stackpole Books, 1965), p. 412.

8. AGO, Roll 2, No. 398.

9. AGO, Roll 2, Nos. 223–225.

10. AGO, Roll 1, No. 28 (old number).

11. AGO, Roll 3, Nos. 1098–1100.

12. AGO, Roll 4, No. 412.

13. AGO, Roll 3, No. 758.

14. Baker, *History of the United States Secret Service*, p. 529.

15. *Philadelphia Inquirer Account*, pp. 52–53, 56.

16. Baker, *History of the United States Secret Service*, p. 483.

17. Townsend, *The Life, Crime and Capture*, p. 42.

18. Baker, *History of the United States Secret Service*, p. 491.

19. *Magazine of History*, 2 February 1911, pp. 60–61.

20. *Ibid.*, p. 62.

21. *Ibid.*, pp. 62–63.

22. AGO, Roll 4, No. 375.

23. *Ibid.*, No. 379.

24. *Tyler's Quarterly Historical and Genealogical Magazine*, July 1940, p. 9; also *The Assassination of President Lincoln and the Trial of the Conspirators*, comp. Benn Pitman (New York: Moore, Wiltstach and Baldwin, 1865).[This latter source was referred to as the official version of the trial and hereafter will be cited as "Official Trial Version."]

25. Ford Papers, Maryland Historical Society, Baltimore, Maryland.

26. *Ibid.*

27. *Ibid.*

28. *Washington Star*, reprinted in the *New York Post*, 3 July 1884.

XIII. Lamentations for a Modern Moses

1. Charles Sabin Taft, M.D., unidentified article.

2. Noah Brooks, *The Century Magazine*, May 1985, pp. 17–26. Also Townsend, *The Life, Crime and Capture*, p. 13.

3. *Washington Star*, 20 April 1865.

4. Sandburg, *Abraham Lincoln: The War Years*, 4: 390.

5. *Ibid.*

6. de Chambrun, *Impressions of Lincoln and the Civil War*, p. 114.

7. Sandburg, *Abraham Lincoln: The War Years*, 4: 391.

8. *New York Post*, 8 July 1884.

9. *Washington Star*, 20 April 1865.

10. Sterling Edwards, "I Remember Lincoln's Funeral."

XIV. ". . . To Get Him Across"

1. AGO, Roll 2, No. 537.

2. *Ibid.*, No. 427.

3. AGO, Roll 5, No. 153.

4. Official Trial Version, p. 124.

5. George Alfred Townsend, "How Wilkes Booth Crossed the Potomac," *The Century Magazine*, April 1884, pp. 822–832.

6. *Ibid.*, p. 828.

7. J. E. Buckingham, Sr., *Reminiscences and Souvenirs of the Assassination of Abraham Lincoln* (Washington: Press of Rufus H. Darby, 1894), pp. 69–71.

8. Townsend, "How Wilkes Booth Crossed the Potomac," p. 830.

9. Buckingham, *Reminiscences and Souvenirs*, p. 67.

10. *Philadelphia Inquirer* Account, p. 57.

XV. The Conspiracy Puzzle

1. AGO, Roll 5, No. 150.
2. *Ibid.*
3. AGO, Roll 5, No. 153.
4. *Philadelphia Inquirer* Account, p. 53.
5. Flower, *Edwin McMasters Stanton*, pp. 62–64.
6. AGO, Roll 5, No. 160.
7. AGO, Roll 5, No. 161.
8. AGO, Roll 6, No. 305.
9. AGO, Roll 2, No. 427.
10. *Ibid.*
11. AGO, Roll 7, Nos. 557–581.
12. AGO, Roll 6, Nos. 227–229.
13. AGO, Roll 6, No. 205.
14. AGO, Roll 6, No. 287.
15. AGO, Roll 6, No. 19.
16. AGO, Roll 7, No. 221.
17. AGO, Roll 5, Nos. 437–439.
18. AGO, Roll 5, Nos. 266–272.
19. AGO, Roll 4, No. 111.
20. AGO, Roll 6, No. 495.
21. AGO, Roll 4, No. 412.
22. *The Century Magazine*, April 1884, p. 826.
23. *Ibid.*, p. 823.
24. *Ibid.*, p. 826.
25. Buckingham.
26. AGO, Roll 5, No. 332.

XVI. Conflicting Evidence

1. Cited in *Washington Star*, 20 April 1865.
2. *Ibid.*
3. AGO, Roll 5, No. 487.
4. AGO, Roll 4, Nos. 402–404.
5. *Ibid.*
6. AGO, Roll 3, No. 1282.
7. AGO, Roll 3, No. 692.
8. AGO, Roll 3, Nos. 747–751.
9. *Ibid.*
10. AGO, Roll 7, No. 370.
11. AGO, Roll 7, No. 373.
12. AGO, Roll 7, Nos. 368–369.
13. *Washington Star*, 15 April 1890.

14. *Ibid.*
15. AGO, Roll 2, Nos. 22–47.
16. AGO, Roll 2, Nos. 45–47.
17. Browning, *Diary of Orville Hickman Browning*, p. 25.
18. AGO, Roll 2, italics in original.
19. LaFayette Baker to Stanton. Baker, *History of the United States Secret Service*, p. 526.
20. Undated clipping from the *Washington Star*, Lincoln Collection, Martin Luther King Public Library, Washington, D.C.
21. LaFayette Baker, *History of the United States Secret Service*, p. 531.
22. Lomax, *The Old Capitol and Its Inmates*, pp. 85–86.

XVII. "Tell My Mother I Died for My Country"

1. John G. Nicolay to his fiancée, 24 April 1865, John G. Nicolay Manuscripts, Manuscript Division, Library of Congress
2. AGO, Roll 3, No. 663.
3. AGO, Roll 3, No. 598.
4. AGO, Roll 3, No. 601.
5. AGO, Roll 3, No. 602.
6. *Philadelphia Inquirer* Account, pp. 57–58.
7. *The Century Illustrated Monthly Magazine*, April 1896, pp. 910–911.
8. *Philadelphia Inquirer* Account, pp. 57–58.
9. *Ibid.*
10. *Ibid.*, p. 81.
11. *Ibid.*, pp. 57–58.
12. *Harper's Weekly*, 13 May 1865.
13. LaFayette Baker, *History of the United States Secret Service*, p. 540.
14. Hibben, Henry B., *Official History of the Washington Navy Yard* (1890, cited by the *Washington Star*, 15 April 1890).
15. Undated newspaper clipping, *The Dearborn Independent*, Lincoln Collection, Martin Luther King Public Library, Washington, D.C.
16. Hibben, *The Official History of the Washington Navy Yard*, cited in the *Washington Star*, 15 April 1890.

XVIII. Filling in the Gaps

1. AGO, Roll 2, Nos. 462–465.
2. AGO, Roll 2, No. 55.
3. AGO, Roll 1.
4. AGO, Roll 3, No. 186.
5. AGO, Roll 3, No. 189.
6. AGO, Roll 3, Nos. 274–275.
7. AGO, Roll 3, No. 196.
8. AGO, Roll 3, No. 200.
9. District of Columbia Recorder of Deeds, Books No 56, 195 and 245 (new numbering system).
10. AGO, Roll 6, No. 213.
11. AGO, Roll 7, No. 376. The words "runs the gauntlet" are uncertain because in the original manuscript they are not legible.
12. AGO, Roll 3, No. 69.
13. Union Provost Marshal's File, Microfilm M345, Roll 261, Item 81.
14. Lomax, *The Old Capitol and Its Inmates*, p. 155.
15. *Ibid.*, pp. 151–152.

16. AGO, Roll 4, No. 457.
17. AGO, Roll 4, No. 471.
18. AGO, Roll 4, No. 481.
19. AGO, Roll 4, No. 472.
20. Affidavit of Augustus Howell, John Ford Papers, Maryland Historical Society.
21. *Ibid.*
22. AGO, Roll 6, Nos. 101, 105.
23. AGO, Roll 4, No. 307.

XIX. "I Do Not Know, Sir — I Declare I Do Not Know"

1. AGO, Roll 5, Nos. 492–493.
2. AGO, Roll 5, No. 493.
3. AGO, Roll 5, No. 497.
4. AGO, Roll 5, Nos. 400–412.
5. AGO, Roll 5, Nos. 409–410.
6. AGO, Roll 5, No. 408.
7. AGO, Roll 3, Nos. 1046–1050.
8. *Ibid.*
9. AGO, Roll 6, No. 213.
10. AGO, Roll 6, Nos. 217–218.
11. AGO, Roll 6, Nos. 220–221.
12. AGO, Roll 6, No. 225.
13. AGO, Roll 6, No. 226.
14. AGO, Roll 5, No. 169.
15. *Ibid.*

XX. "Any Statement You Make Will Be Used"

1. AGO, Roll 6, No. 171.
2. AGO, Roll 6, No. 172.
3. AGO, Roll 6, Nos. 173–175.
4. AGO, Roll 6, Nos. 175–176.
5. AGO, Roll 6, Nos. 177–178.
6. AGO, Roll 6, No. 180.
7. AGO, Roll 6, Nos. 180–181.
8. AGO, Roll 6, No. 181.
9. AGO, Roll 6, Nos. 181–191.
10. AGO, Roll 6, Nos. 192–194.

XXI. The Final List

1. AGO, Roll 5, No. 495.
2. *Ibid.*, No. 500.
3. *Ibid.*, Roll 6, Nos. 462, 466.
4. *Ibid.*, Roll 4, No. 200.
5. *Ibid.*, Roll 6, No. 472.
6. *Ibid.*, Nos. 499–500.
7. *Ibid.*
8. AGO, Roll 6, No. 507, and Roll 2, No. 1076.
9. *Ibid.*, Roll 5, No. 495.
10. *Ibid.*, Roll 6, Nos. 447–449.

11. Bates, *Lincoln in the Telegraph Office*, pp. 379–380.

12. Stanton to Hancock, 29 April 1865, Edwin Stanton Papers, Vol. 26, Manuscript Division, Library of Congress.

XXII. Care That They Not Escape

1. Stanton to Hancock, 29 April 1865, Edwin Stanton Papers, Vol. 29, Manuscript Division, Library of Congress.

2. Union Provost Marshal's File, Microfilm Roll No. 261.

3. Bates, *Lincoln in the Telegraph Office*, p. 382.

4. Samuel B. Arnold, *Defense and Prison Experiences of a Lincoln Conspirator, Statements and Autobiographical Notes* (Hattiesburg, Miss.: Book Farm, 1943), p. 17.

5. Lomax, *The Old Capitol and Its Inmates*, pp. 171–176.

6. *Ibid.*, p. 176.

7. *Baltimore Advertizer*, 8 May 1865.

8. AGO, Roll 2, No. 1047.

9. AGO, Roll 2, Nos. 766–784.

10. Mary Porter, *The Surgeon in Charge* (Concord, N.H.: Rumford Press, 1948), p. 8.

11. *Ibid.*, pp. 8–9.

12. *Ibid.*, pp. 9–10.

13. AGO, Roll 2, No. 28.

14. AGO, Roll 2, Nos. 906–909.

15. *Washington Chronicle*, 21 May 1867.

16. AGO, Roll 2, Nos. 1194–1200.

17. AGO, Roll 3, Nos. 249–251. Also, AGO, Roll 2, Nos. 796 and 882; AGO, Roll 2, Nos. 533–534.

18. AGO, Roll 2, Nos. 791–844.

XXIII. ". . . And Others Unknown"

1. Reverdy Johnson Papers, No. 15, Manuscript Division, Library of Congress.

2. *New York Tribune*, 17 October 1864.

3. *Ibid.*

4. Andrew Johnson Papers, No. 14.

5. Joseph Holt, Pamphlet, *Reply of Joseph Holt to Certain Calumnies of Jacob Thompson* (n.p. 1833[?]).

6. Judge Joseph Holt Papers, Box 93, Nos. 11, 12, Manuscript Division, Library of Congress.

7. *The Conspiracy Trial for the Murder of the President. And the Attempt to Overthrow the Government by the Assassination of Its Principal Officers*, ed. Benjamin Perley Poore [this account will hereafter be referred to as the B. P. Poore Account], based primarily on the *Washington National Intelligencer* report (Boston: J. E. Tilton and Co., 1865). In this version of the trial testimony, Poore used the spelling "Saunders" instead of "Sanders."

8. Beverly Tucker, *Address to the People of the United States, 1865*, ed. James Harvey Young (Emory University, Ga.: Emory University Publications, Sources and Reprints, Series V, 1948).

9. *New York Times*, 6 May 1865, p. 8.

10. *Ibid.*, 7 May 1865.

11. *New York Tribune*, 5 and 6 May 1865.

12. *Montreal Gazette*, cited in *Washington Star*, 9 May 1865.

13. *Ibid.*

14. Buckingham, *Reminiscences and Souvenirs*, pp. 53–57.

15. *Ibid.*

16. *Ibid.*
17. *Ibid.*

XXIV. "A Horrid Sight"

1. Edward Bates, *Diary*, pp. 482–483.
2. Henry L. Burnett, "Some Incidents in the Trial of President Lincoln's Assassins, A Paper Read by General Henry L. Burnett at a Meeting of the Commandery, State of New York, Military Order, Loyal Legion, December 5, 1888" (printed for the Commandery of New York, New York: Appleton and Co., 1891).
3. Welles, *Diary of Gideon Welles*, 2: 9 May 1865.
4. Bates, *Diary*, p. 483.
5. Chase to President Johnson, John Russell Young Papers, Container No. 2, Manuscript Division, Library of Congress.
6. William de Hart, "Military and Martial Law," *North American Review*, April 1866, pp. 335–345.
7. *Ibid.*
8. In the 1930s, the question still agitated legal minds. In Cooley's 1931 edition of *Constitutional Law*, he suggested that a Military Commission would probably have authority over civilians prosecuted for giving aid to the enemy if the acts were committed during a time of war or in the theater of war. Constitutional law expert John Curran of the De Paul University College of Law, however, believed that such acts were unconstitutional if civil courts were open. *Cooley on Constitutional Law*, 4th ed., 1931, cited by John Curran, "Lincoln Conspiracy Trial and Military Jurisdiction Over Civilians," *Notre Dame Lawyer*, November 1933, pp. 26–49.
9. de Hart, "Military and Martial Law," p. 342.
10. Andrew Johnson to Stanton, 1 May 1865, Edwin Stanton Papers, Vol. 26, Manuscript Division, Library of Congress.
11. Official Trial Version, p. 17.
12. August V. Kautz Papers, Daily Journal 1865, Manuscript Division, Library of Congress.
13. Official Trial Version, pp. 18–19.
14. *Ibid.*, p. 20.
15. *Washington Star*, 10 May 1865.
16. Paul H. Giddens, "Benn Pitman on the Trial of Lincoln's Assassins," *Tyler's Quarterly Historical and Genealogical Magazine*, July 1940, p. 12.
17. Cyrus B. Comstock Papers, diary entry, 8 May 1865, Manuscript Division, Library of Congress.
18. Horace Porter, "Campaigning with Grant," *The Century Magazine*, October 1897, pp. 879–890.
19. Kautz Papers, Daily Journal, 9 May 1865.
20. *New York Times*, 12 May 1865.
21. AGO, Roll 2, No. 919.
22. *New York Tribune*, 10 May 1865; Nettie Mudd, *The Life of Dr. Samuel A. Mudd* (New York and Washington: the Neale Publishing Co., 1906), p. 113 and *New York Tribune*, 10 June 1883 (notice of Merrick's death).
23. Comstock Papers, Box 8.
24. *Ibid.*
25. *Ibid.*
26. *Ibid.*
27. Official Trial Version, p. 18.
28. B. P. Poore Account, p. 10.
29. Kautz Papers, Daily Journal, 10 May 1865.
30. AGO, Roll 3, Nos. 372–377.

31. Brooks, *Washington, D.C. in Lincoln's Time*, p. 22
32. John Sherman, *John Sherman's Recollections of Forty Years*, 2 vols. (New York: Greenwood Press, 1968), 1: 355.
33. William Tecumseh Sherman, *Memoirs of General William T. Sherman*, 2 vols. (New York: D. Appleton and Co., 1875), 2: 365.
34. AGO, Roll 4, No. 208.

XXV. Abhorrence of All Things Secret

1. *Constitutional Union*, 10 May 1865.
2. *Philadelphia Inquirer*, 12 May 1865.
3. *Washington Star*, 10 May 1865.
4. Alfred H. Guernsey and Henry M. Alden, *Harper's Pictorial History of the Great Rebellion in the United States* (New York: Harper Brothers, 1866, reprinted in facsimile reproduction by the Fairfax Press, n.d., under the title *Harper's Pictorial History of the Civil War*), p. 778.
5. *Ibid.*
6. Eaton, Clement, *Jefferson Davis* (New York: Macmillan Publishing Co., Inc., The Free Press, 1977), p. 260.
7. Bruce Catton, *Never Call Retreat*. Vol. 3 of *The Centennial History of the Civil War* (Garden City, N.Y.: Doubleday and Co., Inc., 1965), p. 463.
8. Guernsey and Alden, *Harper's Pictorial History of the Civil War*, p. 780.
9. AGO, Roll 3, Nos. 367–368.
10. Mary Bernard Allen, "Joseph Holt," Ph.D. Dissertation, University of Chicago, 1927, p. 56.
11. Lawrence A. Gobright, *Recollections of Men and Things at Washington During the Third of a Century* (Philadelphia: Claxton, Remsen and Haffelfinger, 1869).
12. Allen, "Joseph Holt," p. 90.
13. *New York Times*, 11 May 1865.
14. *Ibid.*
15. George F. Milton, *The Age of Hate* (Hamden, Ct.: Anchor Books, 1965), p. 197.
16. *New York Tribune*, 6 May 1865.
17. *New York Times*, 12 May 1865.
18. *New York World*, 3 May 1865.
19. *Boston Journal*, 9 May 1865.
20. Doster, *Lincoln and the Episodes of the Civil War*, p. 257.
21. *Ibid.*, p. 32.
22. Ruggles, *Prince of Players*, pp. 164–165.
23. B. P. Poore Account, p. 46.

XXVI. Justice in Epaulets

1. *Washington Star*, 15 May 1865.
2. *Boston Advertiser*, 18 May 1865.
3. Reverdy Johnson, *A Reply to the Review of the Judge Advocate General Holt of the Proceedings, Findings and Sentences of The Court-Martial in the Case of Major General Fitz-John Porter and a Vindication of That Officer* (Baltimore: John Murphy and Co., 1863).
4. Marshall, *American Bastille*, p. 727.
5. Bernard C. Steiner, *Life of Reverdy Johnson* (New York: Russell and Russell, 1970), p. 54.
6. *Ibid.*, footnote.
7. *Ibid.*, p. 103, footnote.

8. B. P. Poore Account, p. 51. Official Trial Version indicates incorrectly that this conversation took place on 12 May.
9. Official Trial Version, p. 22.
10. B. P. Poore Account, p. 52.
11. *Ibid.*, p. 54.
12. *Philadelphia Inquirer* Account, pp. 22–23.
13. *Ibid.*, p. 23.
14. *Ibid.*
15. Associated Press Account, pp. 23–24.

XXVII. On Trial but Not in Chains

1. Official Trial Version, pp. 113–118, Associated Press Account, pp. 22–26 and *Philadelphia Inquirer* Account, pp. 24–28. Various reports have been used in reconstructing the interrogation, but the principal chronicle used in this chapter is the B.P. Poore Account.
2. B.P. Poore Account, p. 70.
3. *Philadelphia Inquirer* Account, p. 24.
4. *Ibid.*, pp. 24–25.
5. B.P. Poore Account, p. 75. This chronicle of the trial includes the emotions and actions of the witnesses.
6. *Ibid.*
7. *Ibid.*, p. 78.
8. *Ibid.*, p. 79.
9. *Ibid.*, p. 81.
10. *Ibid.*, p. 83.
11. *Ibid.*, p. 84.
12. *Ibid.*, p. 86.
13. *Ibid.*, p. 87.
14. *Ibid.*, p. 89.
15. *Ibid.*, p. 91.
16. *Ibid.*, p. 94.
17. *Ibid.*
18. *Ibid.*
19. *Ibid.*, pp. 95–96.
20. *Ibid.*, p. 97.
21. *Ibid.*, pp. 97–100.

XXVIII. A Large Boot, Slit Down the Side

1. The best descriptions of the courtroom and the prisoners come from newspaper reporters. Much of this was found in the *Washington Star*, 15–17 May 1865.
2. *Boston Advertiser*, 17 May 1865.
3. *Philadelphia Inquirer* Account, p. 35.
4. *Ibid.*, p. 36.
5. *Ibid.*, p. 37.
6. *Ibid.*, p. 38.
7. Kautz Papers, Daily Journal.
8. Bates, *Lincoln in the Telegraph Office*, pp. 382–383.
9. *Washington Star*, 16 May 1865.
10. *Ibid.*
11. Associated Press Account, 16 May 1865.
12. *Ibid.*

13. *Philadelphia Inquirer* Account, p. 52.
14. *Ibid.*, pp. 52–53.
15. *Ibid.*, p. 53.
16. *Ibid.*
17. *Ibid.*
18. *Ibid.*
19. *Ibid.*, pp. 53–54.
20. *Ibid.*, p. 54.
21. *Ibid.*, p. 55.
22. *Ibid.*
23. *Ibid.*
24. *Ibid.*
25. AGO, Roll 2, No. 1188.

XXIX. "We Are the Assassins of the President"

1. Associated Press Account, p. 30.
2. Descriptions of the prisoners and the courtroom were given in many leading newspapers. For 17 May 1865, see especially *Boston Daily Advertiser, New York Times* and *New York Tribune.*
3. *Philadelphia Inquirer* Account, p. 56.
4. *Ibid.*, p. 57.
5. *Ibid.*
6. *Ibid.*
7. *Ibid.*, p. 58.
8. *Boston Advertiser*, 18 May 1865.
9. *Philadelphia Inquirer* Account, p. 59.
10. *New York Times*, 18 May 1865.
11. *Harper's Weekly*, 13 May 1865.
12. *Philadelphia Inquirer* Account, p. 59.
13. *Ibid.*
14. Unidentified newspaper clipping, Lincoln Collection, Martin Luther King Public Library, Washington, D.C.
15. *Philadelphia Inquirer* Account, p. 61.
16. *Ibid.*, p. 62.
17. *Ibid.*
18. de Chambrun, *Impressions of Lincoln and the Civil War*, pp. 135–141.

XXX. Confessions, Blockade-Runners and Secret Ciphers

1. *Boston Daily Advertiser*, 19 May 1865 and *New York World*, 18 May 1865.
2. *Boston Evening Journal*, 18 May 1865.
3. Brooks, *Washington, D.C. in Lincoln's Time*, p. 240.
4. *New York Tribune*, 18 May 1865.
5. *Detroit Free Press*, 17 May 1865.
6. B. P. Poore Account, p. 307.
7. *Philadelphia Inquirer* Account, pp. 20–21.
8. *Ibid.*, p. 63. In the testimony as recorded by the *Philadelphia Inquirer*, Weichmann answered, "She drove *us* to the door in a buggy...." It seems that a typographical error was made—in this context it should have read, "She drove *up* to the door..."
9. *Ibid.*
10. *Ibid.*
11. *Ibid.*, p. 64.

12. *Ibid.*
13. *Ibid.*
14. *Ibid.*, pp. 64–65.
15. *Ibid.*, p. 64.
16. *Ibid.*, pp. 64–65.
17. *Ibid.*, p. 65.
18. *Ibid.*
19. *Ibid.*
20. *Ibid.*, p. 68.
21. Eisenschiml, *In the Shadow of Lincoln's Death*, pp. 171–174.

XXXI. "Yes, That's the Man"

1. *Washington Star*, 20 May 1865.
2. *Boston Advertiser*, 20 May 1865; *Washington Star*, 8 and 20 May 1865.
3. *Philadelphia Inquirer* Account, p. 72.
4. *Ibid.*, p. 73.
5. *Ibid.*, p. 75.
6. *Ibid.*
7. *Ibid.*, p. 76 and Associated Press Account, p. 34.
8. *Philadelphia Inquirer* Account, p. 72.
9. *Ibid.*
10. *Ibid.*
11. *Ibid.*
12. *Ibid.*
13. *Boston Transcript*, 20 May 1865.
14. Associated Press Account, pp. 35–36 and *Philadelphia Inquirer* Account, pp. 78–79.
15. *Philadelphia Inquirer* Account, p. 79.
16. *Ibid.*, p. 80.
17. *Ibid.*, pp. 80–81.

XXXII. Empty Sleeves Dangling in the Spring Air

1. *Boston Transcript*, 22 May 1865.
2. *Boston Journal*, 22 May 1865.
3. *Philadelphia Inquirer*, reprinted in the *New York Tribune*, 23 May 1865.
4. Bancroft to Alex Bliss, 12 May 1865, George Bancroft Papers, Box 2, Manuscript Division, Library of Congress.
5. *New York Tribune*, 24 May 1865.
6. *Philadelphia Inquirer* Account, p. 82.
7. *Ibid.*, p. 83.
8. *Ibid.*
9. Welles, *Diary of Gideon Welles*, 2: 297.
10. *Ibid.*, p. 296.
11. *Ibid.*, p. 297.
12. Ulysses Simpson Grant, *Personal Memoirs of U. S. Grant*, 2 vols. (London: Sampson Low, Marston, Searle and Rivington, 1886), p. 105.
13. William T. Sherman, *Memoirs of General William T. Sherman*, 2: 366.
14. *Ibid.*, p. 377.
15. Dana, *Recollections of the Civil War*, p. 290.
16. *Boston Daily Advertiser*, 26 May 1865.
17. *Philadelphia Inquirer* Account, p. 86.
18. *Ibid.*

19. *Ibid.*, p. 87.
20. *Ibid.*
21. *Ibid.*
22. *Ibid.*
23. *Ibid.*, p. 88.
24. *Ibid.*
25. *Ibid.*
26. Associated Press Account, p. 38.

XXXIII. In Defense of Mary Surratt

1. *Philadelphia Inquirer* Account, p. 88.
2. *Ibid.*
3. *Ibid.*, pp. 88–89.
4. *Ibid.*, p. 89.
5. *Ibid.*
6. AGO, Roll 3, Nos. 1001–1002, 592–594 and Roll 1, No. 28.
7. Cited by Roscoe, *The Web of Conspiracy*, pp. 229–230.
8. *Philadelphia Inquirer* Account, p. 89.
9. *Ibid.*
10. *Ibid.*, pp. 89–90.
11. *Ibid.*, p. 90.
12. *Boston Advertiser*, 26 May 1865.
13. *Philadelphia Inquirer* Account, p. 90.
14. *Ibid.*
15. *Ibid.*, p. 92.
16. *Boston Advertiser*, 26 May 1865.
17. *New York Times*, 26 May 1865.
18. *Boston Journal*, 27 May 1865.
19. *New York Times*, 26 May 1865.
20. *New York World*, 26 May 1865.
21. *Philadelphia Inquirer* Account, p. 93.
22. *Ibid.*
23. *Ibid.*
24. *Ibid.*

XXXIV. A Loyal Citizen?

1. *Washington Star*, 29 May 1865.
2. *Philadelphia Inquirer* Account, p. 99.
3. *Ibid.*
4. *American and Commercial Advertizer* (Baltimore), 29 May 1865.
5. *Philadelphia Inquirer* Account, p. 100.
6. *Ibid.*
7. *Ibid.*
8. *Ibid.*, p. 101.
9. *Ibid.*, p. 102.
10. *Ibid.*, p. 103.
11. *Washington Star*, 29 May 1865.
12. *Philadelphia Inquirer* Account, p. 103.
13. *Ibid.*
14. *Ibid.*
15. AGO, Roll 3, No. 105.

16. AGO, Roll 3, No. 108.
17. AGO, Roll 3, No. 109.

XXXV. A Growing Weariness

1. *New York World*, 26 May 1865.
2. *North American Review*, September 1880, p. 232.
3. *Philadelphia Inquirer* Account, p. 104.
4. *Ibid.*
5. *Ibid.*
6. The *Washington Intelligencer* did print an account of this episode, 31 May 1865.
7. *Philadelphia Inquirer* Account, p. 105.
8. *Ibid.*, p. 106.
9. *Ibid.*
10. *Ibid.*, p. 107.
11. Nettie Mudd, ed., *The Life of Dr. Samuel A. Mudd* (New York and Washington: The Neale Publishing Co., 1906), pp. 36–39.
12. *Philadelphia Inquirer* Account, p. 110.
13. Brooks, *Washington, D.C. in Lincoln's Time*, pp. 240–241.
14. *Philadelphia Inquirer* Account, p. 111.
15. *Ibid.*, p. 112.
16. *Ibid.*

XXXVI. "Where Is Ma?"

1. Official Trial Version, p. 64.
2. *Philadelphia Inquirer* Account, p. 11.
3. Official Trial Version, p. 65.
4. *Ibid.*
5. *Philadelphia Inquirer*, 31 May 1865.
6. *Philadelphia Inquirer* Account, p. 113.
7. *Ibid.*, p. 114.
8. *Ibid.*; and Official Trial Version, p. 65.
9. *Boston Daily Advertiser*, 31 May 1865.
10. *Philadelphia Inquirer*, 31 May 1865.
11. *Philadelphia Inquirer* Account, p. 114.
12. *Ibid.*
13. *Ibid.*, p. 115.
14. *Ibid.*, p. 116.
15. *New York Times*, 31 May 1865.
16. *Philadelphia Inquirer* Account, p. 116.
17. *Boston Daily Advertiser*, 31 May 1865.
18. *New York Times*, 31 May 1865.
19. AGO, Roll 3, No. 136.
20. AGO, Roll 2, Nos. 136–137.
21. *Boston Herald*, Feature Section, 1 December 1929.
22. *Washington Chronicle*, 21 May 1867.
23. *Philadelphia Inquirer* Account, p. 116.
24. *Ibid.*
25. Douglas, *I Rode with Stonewall*, p. 346.
26. *Philadelphia Inquirer* Account, p. 116.
27. *New York Tribune*, 31 May 1875.
28. Douglas, *I Rode with Stonewall*, p. 346.

29. *Philadelphia Inquirer* Account, p. 116.
30. Union Provost Marshal's File, Roll 261.
31. *Philadelphia Inquirer* Account, p. 117.
32. Thomas Ewing Family Papers, Box 251, Manuscript Division, Library of Congress.
33. *Ibid.*
34. *Philadelphia Inquirer*, 31 May 1865.
35. *Boston Daily Advertiser*, 31 May 1865.
36. *Philadelphia Inquirer* Account, p. 120.

XXXVII. Guilt and Insanity

1. AGO, Roll 1, No. 730.
2. *Boston Advertiser*, 31 May 1865.
3. AGO, Roll 7, Nos. 66–79.
4. AGO, Roll 2, No. 866 and Eisenschiml, *In the Shadow of Lincoln's Death*, p. 171.
5. Doster, *Lincoln and the Episodes of the Civil War*, p. 277.
6. *New York Tribune*, 17 June 1883.
7. *New York World*, 2 June 1865.
8. *Ibid.*
9. *Ibid.*
10. *Cincinnati Commercial*, 2 June 1865.
11. W. W. Cleary, *The Protest of W. W. Cleary* (Toronto: Lovell and Gibson, 1865), p. 28.
12. Seymour J. Frank, "The Conspiracy to Implicate the Confederate Leaders in Lincon's Assassination," *Mississippi Valley Historical Review*, March 1954, pp. 529–656.
13. *Ibid.*, p. 637.
14. *New York World*, 2 June 1865.
15. *New York Times*, 3 June 1865.
16. *Philadelphia Inquirer* Account, p. 124.
17. *Ibid.*
18. *Ibid.*, pp. 124–125.
19. *Ibid.*, p. 125.
20. *Ibid.*
21. *Ibid.*
22. *Ibid.*, p. 126.
23. *Ibid.*, p. 127.

XXXVIII. Rebel Complicity?

1. *Washington Star*, 3 June 1865.
2. *Philadelphia Inquirer*, 3 June 1865.
3. *Philadelphia Inquirer* Account, p. 129.
4. *Ibid.*
5. *Ibid.*, p. 131.
6. *Ibid.*
7. *Ibid.*
8. *Ibid.*, p. 132.
9. *Washington Star*, 5 June 1865 and article by C. Rath, *New York Press*, 4 September 1898.
10. *Washington Star*, 2 June 1865.
11. *Ibid.*, 5 June 1865.
12. *New York World*, 19 June 1865.
13. Official Trial Version, p. 143.

14. *Ibid.*
15. *Philadelphia Inquirer* Account, p. 143.
16. *Ibid.*, p. 144.
17. AGO, Roll 1, No. 32.
18. *Ibid.*
19. J. B. Jones, *A Rebel War Clerk's Diary*, 2 vols. (n.p.: J. B. Lippincott and Co., 1866), 2: 175.
20. Bates, *Lincoln in the Telegraph Office*, pp. 80–81.
21. *Ibid.*, p. 291.
22. Jones, *A Rebel War Clerk's Diary*, 2: 260.
23. *Boston Daily Advertiser*, 31 May 1865.
24. AGO, Roll 3, No. 650.
25. *Atlantic Monthly*, July 1865.
26. *Chicago Tribune*, 8 November 1865.
27. George A. Townsend, *The Life, Crime and Capture of John Wilkes Booth: With a Full Sketch of the Conspiracy of Which He was the Leader, and the Pursuit, Trial and Execution of His Accomplices* (New York: Dick and Fitzgerald, 1865), p. 64.

XXXIX. What He Knew and When

1. AGO, Roll 3, No. 397.
2. *Philadelphia Inquirer* Account, p. 146.
3. *Ibid.*, p. 147.
4. *Ibid.*
5. *Ibid.*
6. *Ibid.*, pp. 147–148.
7. *Ibid.*, p. 148.
8. *Ibid.*
9. *Ibid.*
10. *Ibid.*, p. 149.
11. *Ibid.*
12. *Ibid.*, p. 151.
13. Mudd, *The Life of Dr. Samuel A. Mudd*, p. 28.
14. *Ibid.*
15. *Ibid.*, p. 29.
16. Kautz Papers, Daily Journal, 27–30 May 1865, Manuscript Division, Library of Congress.
17. *Ibid.*, 9 June 1865.
18. Edwin Stanton Papers, vol. 27, unsigned letter 12 June 1865, Manuscript Division, Library of Congress.
19. *Ibid.*, vol. 27.
20. Browning, *The Diary of Orville Hickman Browning*, pp. 30–33.
21. Stanton to Hancock, 19 June 1865, Stanton Papers, vol. 27.
22. Gray to Stanton, 20 June 1865, Stanton Papers, vol. 27.
23. Horace Porter Papers, Box 5, typescript, "Tragedy of a Nation," Manuscript Division, Library of Congress.
24. *Ibid.*
25. *Philadelphia Inquirer* Account, p. 153.

XL. ". . . What a Phenomenon He Was"

1. *Washington Star*, 8 February 1928; quoits are flat rings of rope which are thrown at a stake in a game also called quoits.

2. Noah Brooks, *Washington, D.C. in Lincoln's Time*, p. 240.

3. *New York Times*, 2 June 1865.

4. *Philadelphia Inquirer* Account, p. 155.

5. *Ibid.*, pp. 155–156.

6. Doster, *Lincoln and the Episodes of the Civil War*, p. 266.

7. *Ibid.*

8. *Ibid.*, p. 167.

9. *Ibid.*

10. *Ibid.*, p. 268.

11. *Washington Star*, 12 June 1865.

12. Kautz Papers, Daily Journal, 15 June 1865.

13. *Philadelphia Inquirer* Account, p. 156.

14. *Ibid.*

15. *Ibid.*

16. Associated Press Account, pp. 57–58.

17. *Ibid.*

18. *Constitutional Union* (Washington, D.C), 16 June 1865.

XLI. Education for Murder

1. AGO, Roll 4, Nos. 422–426.

2. AGO, Roll 4, No. 424.

3, AGO, Roll 3, No. 108.

4. AGO, Roll 3, Nos. 1154–1155.

5. *Ibid.*

6. AGO, Roll 3, No. 109.

7. AGO, Roll 7, Nos. 361–363.

8. John Dix to Stanton, 24 June 1865, Stanton Papers, vol. 2.

9. Margaret Leech, *Reveille in Washington, 1860–1865* (New York: Grosset and Dunlap, 1941), p. 307.

10. Browning, *The Diary of Orville Hickman Browning*, p. 15.

11. *Ibid.*, pp. 15–19.

12. *Philadelphia Inquirer* Account, p. 168.

13. *Ibid.*, pp. 168–171.

14. Associated Press Account, p. 75.

15. *New York Tribune*, 17 June 1883.

XLII. After Mature Consideration

1. Holt Papers, Container 92.

2. Official Trial Version, pp. 247–248.

3. *Ibid.*, p. 248.

4. B. P. Poore Account, p. 16.

5. *Ibid.*, pp. 18–19.

6. *Ibid.*

7. *New York Tribune*, 17 June 1883.

8. George A. Townsend, "How Wilkes Booth Crossed the Potomac," *The Century Magazine*, April 1884, p. 826.

9. *Ibid.*, p. 227.

10. *New York Tribune*, 17 June 1883.

11. Holt Papers, Container 92.

12. Burnett, "Some Incidents in the Trial of President Lincoln's Assassins. . "

13. Andrew Johnson Papers, Microfilm 16, Manuscript Division, Library of Congress.

14. Welles, *Diary of Gideon Welles*, 2: 6, July 1865.

15. Andrew Johnson Papers, Microfilm 16.

16. *Ibid.*

17. Paper delivered by General Henry L. Burnett, George Townsend Papers, scrapbook of newspaper clippings, no date, Manuscript Division, Library of Congress.

18. *New York Times*, 7 July 1865.

19. *Washington Star*, 7 July 1865, *New York Times*, 7 July 1865 and *Philadelphia Inquirer*, 7 July 1865.

20. Doster, *Lincoln and the Episodes of the Civil War*, p. 271.

21. *New York Tribune*, 7 July 1865.

XLIII. Death Cells

1. Seaton to Hardie, November 1865, General James A. Hardie Papers, Manuscript Division, Library of Congress.

2. *Ibid.*, Bishop Purcell to Hardie, 28 November 1865.

3. *Ibid.*, Farrea to Hardie, 2 August 1865.

4. *Ibid.*, printed memorandum.

5. *Ibid.*

6. *Ibid.*

7. Rev. J. A. Walter, "The Surratt Case—A True Statement of Facts Concerning this Notable Case," paper read before the United States Catholic Historical Society, 25 May 1891, and published in *The Church News*, 16 August 1891.

8. *New York Tribune*, 17 July 1865.

9. Spaulding to Hardie, 23 July 1865, Hardie Papers.

10. *The Church News*, 16 August 1891.

11. *Ibid.*

12. John W. Clampitt, "The Trial of Mrs. Surratt," *North American Review*, September 1880, pp. 223–233.

13. *North American Review*, April 1889.

14. *Ibid.*

15. Andrew Johnson Papers, Microfilm 16.

16. *Ibid.*

17. Unidentified newspaper article, Lincoln Collection, Martin Luther King Library.

18. *Washington Chronicle*, 8 July 1865.

19. *Ibid.*

20. *Ibid.*

21. *Ibid.*

22. *Ibid.*

23. Clampitt, *North American Review*, p. 235.

24. *Ibid.*

25. Mary Allen, "Joseph Holt," Ph.D. Dissertation (University of Chicago, 1927).

26. Marshall, *American Bastille*, p. 721.

27. George C. Gorham, *Life and Public Services of Edwin M. Stanton*, 2 vols. (London: Sampson Low, Marston, Searle and Rivington, 1886), 1: 117.

28. Records of the Columbia Historical Society, vol. XXII, pp. 10–11.

29. AGO, Roll 5, No. 207.

30. *New York Press*, 4 September 1898.

XLIV. Thirteen Steps

1. *Washington Chronicle*, 10 July 1865.

2. Thomas Ewing Family Papers, Box 251, Manuscript Division, Library of Congress.

3. *Philadelphia Inquirer* Account, p. 208.

4. Ewing Family Papers, Box 251.

5. *Ibid.*

6. *Philadelphia Inquirer*, 8 July 1865.

7. Ewing Family Papers, Box 251.

8. John Surratt, Rockville Lecture.

9. *Trial of John Surratt*, I: 75.

10. *Washington Star*, 7 July 1865, and *Washington Constitutional Union*, 7 July 1865.

11. Amy Bassett, *Red Cross Reveries on the Home Front and Overseas* (Harrisburg, Penn. The Stackpole Co., 1961), p. 37.

12. Walter, "The Surratt Case," *The Church News*, 16 August 1891.

13. *Philadelphia Inquirer*, 8 July 1865.

14. Doster, *Lincoln and the Episodes of the Civil War*, p. 271.

15. L. L. Stevens, *Life, Crimes and Confessions of the Assassins* (Troy, NY: n.p. 1865).

16. *Philadelphia Inquirer*, 8 July 1865.

17. Stevens, *Life, Crimes*, p. 56.

18. *New York Press*, 4 September 1898 and Ralph Borrenson, *When Lincoln Died* (New York: Appleton-Century, 1965).

19. Alfred C. Gibson, *Washington Star*, 8 February 1928.

20. *Washington Star*, 7 July 1865.

21. *Ibid.*

22. *Washington Evening Star*, reprinted in the *New York Times*, 17 July 1865.

23. Gibson, *Washington Star*, 8 February 1928.

24. E. H. Gore, *History of Orlando Baptists*, cited by Vaughn Shelton, *Mask for Treason: The Lincoln Murder Trial* (Harrisburg, Penn.: Stackpole Books, 1965), p. 390.

25. Shelton, *Mask for Treason*, p. 393.

26. Weichmann, *A True History of the Assassination*, p. 80.

27. *Philadelphia Weekly Times*, 6 June 1882, cited by Weichmann.

XLV. Dry Tortugas

1. *New York Times*, 7 July 1865.

2. *The Boston Post*, 7 July 1865.

3. *The Boston Transcript*, 7 July 1865.

4. *Cincinnati Daily Commercial*, 6 July 1865.

5. *Baltimore Advertizer*, 1 July 1865.

6. *Huntsville Advocate* (Alabama), 2 July 1865.

7. Comer to Johnson, 8 July 1865, Andrew Johnson Papers, Microfilm 16, Manuscript Division, Library of Congress.

8. Harris to Johnson, 7 July 1865, *Ibid.*

9. Dickinson to Johnson, 8 July 1865, *Ibid.*

10. Eastman to Johnson, 8 July 1865, *Ibid.*

11. Roxbury, Mass. (signature illegible) to Johnson, 8 July 1865, *Ibid.*

12. *Washington Constitutional Union*, 19 July 1865.

13. Doster, *Lincoln and the Episodes of the Civil War*, p. 272.

14. Rev. George Powell to Gillette, 7 November 1865, Lewis Thornton Powell Papers, Manuscript Division, Library of Congress.

15. Thomas Ewing, Jr., to Thomas Ewing, Sr., 7 July 1865, Thomas Ewing Family Papers, Box 251, Manuscript Division, Library of Congress.

16. Mudd to Thomas Ewing, Jr., 17 November 1865, *Ibid.*

17. Browning, *The Diary of Orville Hickman Browning*, p. 37.

18. Welles, *Diary of Gideon Welles*, 9 July 1865.

19. White to Stanton, 12 July 1865, Stanton Papers, vol. 28.

20. *Ibid.*

21. *New York Tribune*, 17 July 1865.
22. *Ibid.*
23. Mudd, *The Life of Dr. Samuel A. Mudd*, p. 42.
24. Weichmann, *A True History of the Assassination*, pp. 332–334.
25. Mudd, p. 115.
26. *Ibid.*, p. 42.
27. *Ibid.*, p. 45.
28. *Ibid.*, p. 43.
29. *Ibid.*, p. 45.
30. Otto Eisenschiml, *In the Shadow of Lincoln's Death*, p. 144.
31. *Ibid.*, p. 145.
32. Mudd, *The Life of Dr. Samuel A. Mudd*, p. 110.
33. *Ibid.*
34. *Ibid.*, p. 113.
35. *Ibid.*, p. 122.
36. *Ibid.*, p. 117.
37. *Ibid.*, p. 118.
38. *Ibid.*
39. *Ibid.*, p. 119.
40. *Ibid.*
41. *Ibid.*, p. 124.
42. *Ibid.*, p. 123.
43. *Ibid.*, pp. 131–132.
44. *Ibid.*, p. 265.
45. Gary R. Planck, "Lincoln's Assassination: More 'Forgotten' Litigation—ex parte Mudd," *Lincoln Herald*, Summer 1974, p. 89.
46. *Ibid.*
47. Pitman to Thomas Ewing, Jr., 11 July 1865, Thomas Ewing Family Papers, Box 251.
48. Pitman to Thomas Ewing, Jr., 24 August 1865, *Ibid.*
49. Welles, *Diary of Gideon Welles*, p. 331.
50. Brooks, *Washington, D.C. in Lincoln's Time*, p. 242.
51. Baker, *History of the United States Secret Services*, pp. 563–565.
52. Clara E. Laughlin, *The Death of Lincoln: The Story of Booth's Plot, His Deed and the Penalty* (New York: Doubleday and Company, 1909), Appendix XXVI.
53. *The Congressional Globe*, 39th Congress, 2nd Session, Report No. 33.
54. *Ibid.*

XLVI. "An Absurdity Unsurpassed"

1. Benjamin Perley Poore, *Reminiscences of Sixty Years in the National Metropolis*, vol. 2 (Tecumseh, Michigan: A. W. Mills, Publishers, 1886), pp. 200–201.
2. Official Records, Series I, vol. XLIX, Pt. II 759, cited by Horace Greeley, *The American Conflict*, 2 vols. (New York: Negro Universities Press, Reprint, 1969), 2: 655.
3. Beverly Tucker, *Address to the People of the United States, 1865*, edited by James Harvey Young (Emory University, Georgia: Emory University Publications, Sources and Reprints, Series V. 1948), p. 15.
4. *Ibid.*, p. 10.
5. *Ibid.*, p. 11.
6. George S. Bryan, *The Great American Myth* (New York: Carrick and Evans, 1940), p. 386.
7. *Ibid.*, pp. 386–387.
8. William W. Cleary, *The Protest of W. W. Cleary* (Toronto: Lovell and Gibson, 1865), p. 7.
9. *Philadelphia Inquirer*, 23 May 1865.

10. George A. Townsend, *Frank Leslie's Illustrated Newspaper*, date not clear.

11. *New York Times*, 8 July 1865.

12. Greeley, *The American Conflict*, 2: 631–642.

13. Welles, *Diary*, 18 August 1865, cited by *Ibid.*, p. 642.

14. U.S. Congress, House, Report No. 104, 39th Congress, 1st Session, p. 31.

15. Welles, *Diary*, 2: 395–404.

16. Guernsey and Alden, *Harper's Pictorial History*, p. 819.

17. *The Congressional Globe*, 39th Congress, 1st Session, pp. 1854–1855.

18. Testimony of Francis Lieber, Benjamin F. Butler Papers, Box 175, Manuscript Division, Library of Congress.

19. U.S. Congress, House, Report No. 104, 39th Congress, 1st Session.

20. Butler Papers, Box 175.

21. *Ibid.*

22. *Ibid.*

23. *Ibid.*

24. *Ibid.*

25. *Ibid.*

26. *Ibid.*

27. *Ibid.*

28. *Ibid.*

29. *Ibid.*

30. U.S. Congress, House, Report No. 104, 39th Congress, 1st Session.

31. *Ibid.*, p. 37.

32. *Ibid.*, p. 39.

33. Mary Bernard Allen, "Joseph Holt," Ph.D. Dissertation, University of Chicago, 1927, p. 154.

34. *Ibid.*

35. *The Century Illustrated Monthly Magazine* April 1890.

36. W. W. Winthrop to Holt, 6 August 1866, Holt Papers, cited by Allen, "Joseph Holt," pp. 157–158.

37. Andrew Johnson Papers, Microfilm Roll 25, Manuscript Division, Library of Congress.

XLVII. Impeaching the Impeachers

1. *Appleton's Cyclopaedia of American Biography*, ed., James Grant Wilson and John Fiske, 1898 ed., s.v. "Johnson, Andrew."

2. DeWitt, *Impeachment and Trial of Andrew Johnson*, p. 214.

3. U.S. Congress, House. *The Congressional Globe*, debate between Benjamin Butler and John Bingham, 39th Congress, 2nd Session, 2 March 1867, p. 363.

4. *Ibid.*

5. *Ibid.*

6. *Ibid.*, p. 364.

7. *Ibid.*

8. *Ibid.*

9. *Ibid.*

10. Benjamin F. Butler Papers, Box 175, Manuscript Division, Library of Congress.

11. Seymour J. Frank, "The Conspiracy to Implicate Confederate Leaders in Lincoln's Assassination," *The Mississippi Valley Historical Review*, March 1954, pp. 629–656.

12. Andrew Johnson Papers, Box 25, Manuscript Division, Library of Congress; and *Washington Star*, 10 August 1867.

13. *Ibid.*

14. *Ibid.*

15. *Ibid.*

16. *Ibid.*
17. Andrew Johnson Papers, Box 25, Library of Congress.
18. *Ibid.*
19. Guernsey and Alden, *Harper's Pictorial History.*

XLVIII. "The Son Is Here Before You"

1. *Ibid.*
2. *Trial of John H. Surratt in the Criminal Court for the District of Columbia*, 2 vols. (Washington, D.C.: Government Printing Office, 1878), 1: 391.
3. *Ibid.*, 1: 415.
4. *Ibid.*
5. *Ibid.*, 1: 425.
6. John Surratt, *Life and Trial and Adventures of John Surratt, the Conspirator: A Correct Account and Highly Interesting Narrative of His Doings and Adventures from Childhood to the Present Time* (Philadelphia: Barclay, 1867), p. 71.
7. *Ibid.*, p. 72.
8. *Trial of John H. Surratt*, 2: 829.
9. *Washington National Intelligencer*, 17 July 1867.
10. Surratt, *Life and Trial*, p. 59.
11. *Ibid.*, p. 108.
12. *Ibid.*, p. 134.
13. *Ibid.*
14. Edwards Pierrepont, *Argument of Hon. Edwards Pierrepont to the Jury on the Trial of John H. Surratt for the Murder of President Lincoln* (Washington, D.C.: Government Printing Office, 1867), p. 15.
15. *The Baltimore American*, 9 December 1902.
16. Butler Papers, Box 175.

XLIX. Memories of the Terrible Spring

1. *Washington Evening Star*, 9 December 1870.
2. *Ibid.*
3. *Ibid.*
4. *Ibid.*
5. *Ibid.*
6. *Ibid.*
7. *Ibid.*
8. Poster, Library of Congress Collection, Rare Book Division.
9. *Washington Evening Star*, 31 December 1870.
10. *Washington Post*, 3 April 1898.
11. *Ibid.*
12. *Ibid.*
13. Eisenschiml, *In the Shadow of Lincoln's Death*, pp. 145–156.
14. Clarke, *The Unlocked Book*, pp. 176–177.
15. George Alfred Townsend Papers (Notebook, clipping of article from *The Boston Traveler*, no date), Manuscript Division, Library of Congress.
16. Laughlin, *The Death of Lincoln*, Appendix XXVIII, p. 317.
17. "Johnny Bouquet's Walks," *New York Tribune*, 8 May 1881.
18. Hancock, *Reminiscences of Winfield Scott Hancock by His Wife*, p. 109.
19. Burnett, "Some Incidents in the Trial of President Lincoln's Assassins," p. 24.
20. *Ibid.*
21. Frederick E. Goodrich, *The Life and Public Services of Winfield Scott Hancock, Major-General, U.S.A.* (Boston: Lee and Shepard, 1880), p. 223.

22. *Ibid.*

23. Eisenschiml, *In the Shadow of Lincoln's Death,* p. 180.

24. *Ibid.*, p. 186.

25. Lloyd Lewis, *Myths After Lincoln* (New York: Harcourt, Brace and Co., 1929), p. 260.

26. Eisenschiml, *In the Shadow of Lincoln's Death,* p. 179.

27. Lewis, *Myths After Lincoln,* p. 262.

28. *Ibid.*

29. John Ford, *The North American Review,* April 1389, pp. 485–493.

L. The Stretch of Darkening Folds

1. Weichmann, *A True History of the Assassination,* p. 323.

2. John A. Bingham, *Argument of John A. Bingham* (Washington: Government Printing Office, 1865), p. 4.

3. Porter, *The Surgeon in Charge,* p. 17.

4. Charles Chiniquy, *Fifty Years in the Church of Rome* (Grand Rapids, Michigan: Baker Book House, 1958), p. 471.

5. George S. Bryan, *The Great American Myth* (New York: Carrick and Evans, Inc., 1940), p. 387.

6. *Ibid.*

7. Burke McCarty, *The Suppressed Truth About the Assassination of Abraham Lincoln* (Philadelphia: Burke McCarty, publisher, 1924), p. 95.

8. *Ibid.*, p. 221.

9. Emmett McLaughlin, *An Inquiry into the Assassination of Abraham Lincoln* (New York: Lyle Stuart, Inc., 1963), p. 17.

10. *Ibid.*, p. 161.

11. Robert W. Winston, *Andrew Johnson, Plebian and Patriot* (New York: Henry Holt and Co., 1928), p. 288.

12. Holt to Harrison, 11 September 1873, James O. Harrison Papers, Box 11, Manuscript Division, Library of Congress.

13. Horatio King, "Open Letter," *The Century Illustrated Magazine,* April 1890, p. 956.

14. *Ibid.*

15. *Ibid.*

16. *Ibid.*

17. *Ibid.*

18. Holt to Harrison, 20 December 1873, James O. Harrison Papers, Manuscript Division, Library of Congress.

19. *Ibid.*

20. Holt to Harrison, 11 November 1883, Harrison Papers.

21. *Ibid.*

22. *Ibid.*

23. Joseph Holt and James Speed, with introduction by Allen Rice, "New Facts About Mrs. Surratt: Correspondence of Judge Holt and Hon. James Speed," *North American Review,* July 1888, p. 84.

24. *Ibid.*

25. *Ibid.*, pp. 84–85.

26. *Ibid.*, p. 85.

27. *Ibid.*, p. 86.

28. *Ibid.*

29. *Ibid.*, p. 87.

30. *Ibid.*

31. *Ibid.*, p. 88.

32. *Ibid.*, p. 91.

33. *Ibid.*, p. 93.

34. John Mason Brown to Holt, 29 April 1889, Judge Joseph Holt Papers, Manuscript Division, Library of Congress.

35. *The North American Review*, September 1888, p. 314.

36. Brown to Holt, 29 April 1889, Judge Joseph Holt Papers, Manuscript Division, Library of Congress.

37. Horatio King to Thomas Harris, 27 October 1892, Horatio King Papers, Box 13, Manuscript Division, Library of Congress.

38. *Ibid.*, Harris to King, 3 April 1893.

39. *Louisville Courier-Journal*, 15 July 1917.

40. Weichmann, *A True History of the Assassination*, Appendices, Obituary of Louis J. Weichmann, p. 405.

41. DeWitt, *The Assassination*, Appendix, Note III, p. 263.

42. *Washington Evening Star*, 24 January 1909.

43. Mary Surratt's grave marker, Mount Olivet Cemetery, Archdiocese of Washington, Washington, D.C.

44. *Baltimore Sun*, 22 April 1916.

Epilogue

1. *Saturday Review of Literature*, 17 February 1934.

2. *Washington Herald*, 23 April 1934.

3. *Washington Evening Star*, 24 February 1936.

4. *Washington Post*, 21 April 1946.

5. Mudd, *The Life of Dr. Samuel A. Mudd* (Linden, Tenn.: Continental Book Co., 1975, Reprint of the Neale Publishing Co., 1906 edition), foldout, back cover.

Selected Bibliography

Books

Abott, Abott A. *The Assassination and Death of Abraham Lincoln, President of the United States of America.* New York: American News Co., 1865.

Arnold, Samuel Bland. *Defense and Prison Experiences of a Lincoln Conspirator, Statements and Autobiographical Notes.* Hattiesburg, Miss.: Printed for the Bock Farm, 1943.

Baker, LaFayette Charles. *History of the United States Secret Service.* Philadelphia: King and Baird, 1868; reprint ed., New York: AMS Press, Inc., 1973.

_____. *Spies, Traitors and Conspirators of the Late Civil War.* Philadelphia: John E. Potter and Co., 1894.

Bassett, Amy. *Red Cross Reveries on the Home Front and Overseas.* Harrisburg, Penn.: The Stackpole Co., 1961.

Bates, David Homer. *Lincoln in the Telegraph Office.* New York: The Century Company, 1907.

Bates, Edward. *Diary.* American Historical Association, n.d.

Bingham, John A. *Argument of John A. Bingham.* Washington: Government Printing Office, 1865.

_____. *The Enforcement of the Constitution,* n.p., 1871.

Bishop, James A. *The Day Lincoln Was Shot.* New York: Harper and Brothers, 1955.

Blaine, James. *Twenty Years in Congress.* 2 vols., n.p., n.d.

Borrenson, Ralph. *When Lincoln Died.* New York: Appleton-Century, 1965.

Brooks, Noah. *Washington, D.C. in Lincoln's Time.* n.p., 1895.

Browning, Orville Hickman. *The Diary of Orville Hickman Browning.* Edited by James G. Randall. Springfield: Illinois State Historical Library, 1933.

Bryan, George S. *The Great American Myth.* New York: Carrick and Evans, 1940.

Buchanan, James. *Mr. Buchanan's Administration.* New York: D. Appleton and Co., 1866.

Buckingham, J. E., Sr. *Reminiscences and Souvenirs of the Assassination of Abraham Lincoln.* Washington: Press of Rufus H Darby, 1894.

Busch, Francis S. *Enemies of the State, Notable American Trials Series.* Indianapolis: The Bobbs-Merrill Co., Inc., 1954.

Campbell, Helen Jones. *The Case for Mrs. Surratt.* New York: G. P. Putnam's Sons, 1943.

_____. *Confederate Courier.* New York: St. Martin's Press, 1964.

Carter, Samuel, III. *The Riddle of Dr. Mudd.* New York: G. P. Putnam's Sons, 1974.

Catton, Bruce. *The Centennial History of the Civil War,* 3 vols. Garden City, N.Y.: Doubleday and Co., Inc., 1965. Vol. 3: *Never Call Retreat.*

Chase, Salmon P. *Inside Lincoln's Cabinet,* Edited by David Donald. New York: Longmans, Green and Co., 1954.

Chiniquy, Charles. *Fifty Years in the Church of Rome.* Grand Rapids, Mich.: Baker Book House, 1958.

Chittenden, L. E. *Personal Reminiscences by L. E. Chittenden.* New York: Richmond, Croscup and Co., 1893.

Clarke, Asia Booth. *A Memoir of John Wilkes Booth by His Sister, The Unlocked Book.* Edited by Eleanor Farjeon. London: Faber and Faber, Ltd., 1938.

Cleary, W. W. *The Protest of W. W. Cleary.* Toronto: Lovell and Gibson, 1865.

Cottrell, John. *Anatomy of an Assassination.* New York: Funk and Wagnalls, 1966.

Crenson, Gus A. *Andrew Johnson and Edwin Stanton.* n.p., 1949.

Dana, Charles A. *Recollections of the Civil War, With the Leaders at Washington and in the Field in the Sixties.* New York: D. Appleton and Co., 1902.

de Chambrun, Adolphe. *Impressions of Lincoln and the Civil War: A Foreigner's Account.* Translated by Aldebert de Chambrun. New York: Random House, 1962.

DeWitt, David Miller. *The Assassination of Abraham Lincoln and Its Expiation.* New York: Macmillan, 1909; reprint ed., Freeport, N.Y.: Books for Libraries, 1970.

_____. *The Impeachment and Trial of Andrew Johnson: Seventeenth President of the United States, A History.* 1903; reprint ed., 1967. New York: Russell and Russell.

_____. *The Judicial Murder of Mary E. Surratt.* Baltimore: John Murphy and Co., 1895; reprint ed., St. Clair Shores, Michigan: Scholarly Press, 1970.

Doster, William E. *Lincoln and the Episodes of the Civil War.* New York and London: G. P. Putnam's Sons, The Knickerbocker Press, 1915.

Douglas, Henry Kyd. *I Rode with Stonewall.* Chapel Hill: The University of North Carolina Press, 1940.

Eaton, Clement. *Jefferson Davis.* New York: Macmillan Publishing Co., Inc., The Free Press, 1977.

Eisenschiml, Otto. *In the Shadow of Lincoln's Death.* New York: Wilfred Funk, Inc., 1940.

_____. *Why Was Lincoln Murdered?* Boston: Little, Brown and Co., 1937.

Flower, Frank A. *Edwin McMasters Stanton.* Akron, Ohio: The Sadfield Publishing Co., 1905.

Forrester, Izola. *This One Mad Act.* Boston: Hale, Cushman and Flynt, 1937.

Gobright, Lawrence A. *Recollections of Men and Things at Washington During the Third of a Century.* Philadelphia: Claxton, Remsen and Haffelfinger, 1869.

Goodrich, Frederick E. *The Life and Public Services of Winfield Scott Hancock, Major-General, U.S.A.* Boston: Lee and Shepard, 1880.

Gorham, George C. *Life and Public Services of Edwin M. Stanton,* 2 vols. Boston: Houghton, Mifflin and Co., 1899.

Grant, Ulysses Simpson. *Personal Memoirs of U. S. Grant,* 2 vols. London: Marston, Searle and Rivington, 1886.

Gray, Wood. *The Hidden Civil War.* New York: The Viking Press, 1942.

Greeley, Horace. *The American Conflict,* 2 vols. New York: Negro Universities Press, reprint, 1969.

Green, Constance. *Washington Village and Capital, 1800–1878.* Princeton, N.J.: Princeton University Press, 1962.

Greenhow, Rose O'Neal. *My Imprisonment.* London: Richard Bently, Publishers, 1863.

Hancock, Mrs. Winfield Scott (Almira Russell). *Reminiscences of Winfield Scott Hancock by His Wife.* New York: Charles L. Webster and Co., 1887.

Harris, Thomas Mealey. *The Assassination of Lincoln, A History of the Great Conspiracy: Trial of the Conspirators by a Military Commission and a Review of the Trial of John H. Surratt.* Boston: American Citizens Co., 1892.

_____. *Rome's Responsibility for the Assassination of Abraham Lincoln.* Pittsburgh, Penn.: Williams Publishing Co., 1897.

Hayman, LeRoy. *O Captain! The Death of Abraham Lincoln.* New York: Four Winds Press, 1968.

Headley, John W. *Confederate Operations in Canada and New York.* New York: Neal Publishing Co., 1906.

Hibben, Henry B. *Official History of the Washington Navy Yard*. n.p., 1890.

Higdon, Hal. *The Union vs Dr. Mudd*. Chicago: Follett Publishing Company, 1964.

Horan, James D. *Confederate Agent, A Discovery in History*. New York: The Fairfax Press, 1954.

_____. *Mathew Brady, Historian with a Camera*. New York: Bonanza Books, 1955.

Horner, Harlan Hoyt. *Lincoln and Greeley*. Champaign, Illinois: University of Illinois Press, 1953.

Hunter, David. *Report of the Military Service of General David Hunter, U.S.A.* New York: D. Van Nostrand Co., 1892.

Hyman, Harold M. *Era of the Oath*. Philadelphia: Univ. of Pennsylvania Press, 1954.

Johannsen, Robert W. *Stephen A. Douglas*. New York: Oxford University Press, 1973.

Johnson, Reverdy. *A Reply to the Review of the Judge Advocate General Holt of the Proceedings, Findings and Sentences of the Court-Martial in the Case of Major General Fitz-John Porter and a Vindication of that Officer*. Baltimore: John Murphy and Co., 1863.

Jones, Evan R. *Lincoln and Stanton, Historical Sketches*. London: Frederick Warne and Co., 1875.

Lattimer, John K. *Kennedy and Lincoln: Medical and Ballistic Comparisons of Their Assassinations*. New York: Harcourt Brace Jovanovich, 1980.

Laughlin, Clara E. *The Death of Lincoln: The Story of Booth's Plot, His Deed and the Penalty*. New York: Doubleday and Company, 1909.

Leech, Margaret. *Reveille in Washington, 1860-1865*. New York: Grosset and Dunlap, 1941.

Lewis, Lloyd. *Myths After Lincoln*. New York: Harcourt, Brace and Company, 1929; reprinted, 1940.

Lomax, Virginia. *The Old Capitol and Its Inmates by a Lady*. New York: E. J. Hale and Co., 1867.

Lowenfels, Walter. *Walt Whitman's Civil War*. New York: Alfred A. Knopf, 1960.

McCabe, _____. *Behind the Scenes in Washington*. n.p., n.d.

McCarty, Burke. *The Suppressed Truth About the Assassination of Abraham Lincoln*. Philadelphia: By the Author, 1924.

McCulloch, Hugh. *Men and Measures of Half a Century*. New York: Da Capo Press, 1970.

McKee, Irving. *"Ben-Hur" Wallace, The Life of General Lew Wallace*. Berkeley and Los Angeles, University of California Press, 1947.

McLaughlin, Emmett. *An Inquiry Into the Assassination of Abraham Lincoln*. New York: Lyle Stuart, Inc., 1963.

Marshall, John A. *American Bastille*. n.p., n.d.

Martin, Edward W. *Behind the Scenes in Washington*. n.p.: Continental, 1873.

Maury, William M. *Washington, D.C., Past and Present: The Guide to the Nation's Capital*. New York: CBS Publications in cooperation with the United States Capitol Historical Society, 1975.

Milton, George Fort. *The Age of Hate*. Hamden, Conn.: Anchor Books, 1930; reprint ed., 1965.

Mogelever, Jacob. *Death to Traitors: The Story of General LaFayette C. Baker, Lincoln's Forgotten Secret Service Chief*. Garden City, N.Y.: Doubleday and Co., Inc., 1960.

Moore, Guy W. *The Case of Mrs. Surratt*. Norman. Ok.: Univ. of Oklahoma Press, 1954.

Mudd, Nettie, ed., *The Life of Dr. Samuel A. Mudd*. New York and Washington: The Neale Publishing Co., 1906.

Nicolay, John G. and John Hay. *Abraham Lincoln, A History*, 10 vols. New York: The Century Co., 1886; reprint ed., 1914.

Oldroyd, Osborn H. *The Assassination of Abraham Lincoln, Flight, Pursuit, Capture, and Punishment of the Conspirators*. Washington, D.C.: By the Author, 1901.

Piatt, Donn. *Memories of Men Who Saved the Union*. n.p., 1887.

Pierrepont, Edwards. *Argument of Hon. Edwards Pierrepont to the Jury on the Trial of John H. Surratt for the Murder of President Lincoln.* Washington: Government Printing Office, 1867.

Pitman, Benn and Jerome B. Howard. *In Reporting Style of Phonography.* Cincinnati: The Phonographic Institute Company, 1910.

Pittenger, William. *Oratory, Sacred and Secular.* n.p., 1868.

Poore, Benjamin Perley. *Reminiscences of Sixty Years in the National Metropolis,* 2 vols. Tecumseh, Michigan: A. W. Mills, Publishers, 1886.

Porter, Mary W. *The Surgeon in Charge.* Concord, N.H.: Rumford Press, 1949.

Pratt, Fletcher. *Stanton, Lincoln's Secretary of War.* Westport, Conn: Greenwood Press, 1970.

Roscoe, Theodore. *The Web of Conspiracy: The Complete Story of the Men Who Murdered Abraham Lincoln.* Englewood Cliffs, N.J.: Prentice-Hall, 1959.

Ross, Ishbel. *Rebel Rose.* New York: Harper Bros., 1954.

Ruggles, Eleanor. *Prince of Players, Edwin Booth.* New York: W. W. Norton and Co., Inc., 1953.

Sandburg, Carl. *Abraham Lincoln: The War Years,* 4 vols. New York: Harcourt, Brace and Co., 1939.

Seward, Frederick W. *The Life of W. H. Seward.* n.p., n.d.

Shelton, Vaughan. *Mask for Treason: The Lincoln Murder Trial.* Harrisburg, Penn.: Stackpole Books, 1965.

Sherman, John. *John Sherman's Recollections of Forty Years,* 2 vols. New York: Greewood Press, 1968.

Sherman, William Tecumseh. *Memoirs of General William T. Sherman,* 2 vols. New York: D. Appleton and Co., 1875.

Speed, James. *James Speed — A Personality by James Speed, His Grandson.* Louisville, Ky.: Press of John P. Morton and Co., 1914.

Starkey, Larry. *Wilkes Booth Came to Washington.* New York: Random House, 1976.

Steiner, Bernard C. *Life of Reverdy Johnson.* New York: Russell and Russell, 1914; reprint ed., 1970.

Stern, Philip Van Doren. *The Man Who Killed Lincoln.* New York: Random House, 1939.

Stevens, L. L. *Lives, Crimes and Confessions of the Assassins.* Troy, N.Y.: 1865.

Surratt, John H. *Life, Trial and Adventures of John H. Surratt, The Conspirator: A Correct Account and Highly Interesting Narrative of His Doings and Adventures from Childhood to the Present Time.* Philadelphia: Barclay, 1867.

Swisshelm, Jane Grey. *Crusader and Feminist.* St. Paul, Minn.: The Minnesota Historical Society, 1934.

Tanner, James. *While Lincoln Lay Dying: A Facsimile Reproduction of the First Testimony Taken in Connection with the Assassination of Abraham Lincoln as Recorded by Corporal James Tanner* Philadelphia: The Union League of Philadelphia, 1968.

Tindall, William. *Standard History of the City of Washington.* n.p., n.d.

Townsend, George Alfred. *Katy of Catoctin: Or the Chain-Breakers, A National Romance.* New York: D. Appleton and Co., 1866.

_____. *The Life, Crime, and Capture of John Wilkes Booth: With a Full Sketch of the Conspiracy of Which He Was the Leader, and the Pursuit, Trial and Execution of His Accomplices.* New York: Dick and Fitzgerald, Publishers, 1865.

Tucker, Beverly. *Address to the People of the United States, 1865.* Edited by James Harvey Young. Emory University, Georgia: Emory University Publications, Sources and Reprints, Series V, 1948.

Turner, Thomas Reed. *Beware the People Weeping: Public Opinion and the Assassination of Abraham Lincoln.* Baton Rouge and London: Louisiana State University Press, 1982.

Weichmann, Louis J. *A True History of the Assassination of Abraham Lincoln and the Conspiracy of 1865*. Edited by Floyd E. Risvold. New York: Alfred A. Knopf, 1975.
Welles, Gideon. *Diary of Gideon Welles*, 3 vols. Boston: Hougton Mifflin, 1911.
Whitman, Walt. *Walt Whitman's Diary*. n.p., n.d.
Winston, Robert W. *Andrew Johnson, Plebian and Patriot*. New York: Henry Holt and Co., 1928.

Pamphlets and Miscellaneous Papers

Barnard, Job. "Early Days of the Supreme Court of the District of Columbia," Records of the Columbia Historical Society, vol. 22, 1919, pp. 1–35. Read before the Society, January 15, 1918.
Bingham, Hon. John A., et al. "The Mission to Rome, Remarks before the House of Representatives, May 9, 1870." Washington, D.C.: Cunningham and McIntosh, 1870.
Burnett, General Henry L. "Some Incidents in the Trial of President Lincoln's Assassins: A Paper Read by General Henry L. Burnett at a Meeting of the Commandery, State of New York, Military Order, Loyal Legion, Decemer 5, 1888." New York: D. Appleton and Co., 1891 (printed for the Commandery of New York).
Eisenschiml, Otto. "Reviewers Reviewed." A paper read at the University of Michigan. Ann Arbor: The William L. Clements Library, 1940.
"Eulogies Delivered on the Occasion of the Announcement of the Death of Hon. Edwin M. Stanton, by Members of the Bar, D.C. Supreme Court." Washington: Judd and Detweiler, 1870.
Holt, Joseph. "Reply of Joseph Holt to Certain Calumnies of Jacob Thompson," n.p., 1883 (?).
_____. "Review of the Judge Advocate of the Proceedings, Findings and Sentence of General Court Martial, Held in the City of Washington for the Trial of Major General Fitz-John Porter of the United States Volunteers." Washington: Washington Daily Chronicle Press, 1863.
_____. "Treason and Its Treatment. Remarks of Hon. Joseph Holt at a Dinner in Charleston, S.C. on the Evening of the 14th of April, 1865. After the Flag Raising at Fort Sumter." New York: New York Young Men's Republican Union, 1865.
"Jefferson Davis and His Complicity in the Assassination of Abraham Lincoln, President of the United States and Where the Traitor Shall Be Tried for Treason." Philadelphia: Sherman and Co., Printers, 1866.
"Lincoln in Washington," vol. 1 and "Lincoln Relics in Washington," vol. 4. Martin Luther King Public Library, Washington, D.C. Washingtonia Division, Abraham Lincoln Collection, 4 vols. (clippings from newspapers and magazines compiled by the Library).
Pierrepont, Edwards, "Argument of Hon. Edwards Pierrepont to the Jury on the Trial of John H. Surratt for the Murder of President Lincoln." Washington: Government Printing Office, 1867.
Rogers, James Webb. "Madame Surratt, A Drama in Five Acts." Washington: Judd and Detweiler, 1879; reprint ed., 1926. (Poem, not based on historical facts.)
"The Surratt House and the Saga of Mary Surratt," Pamphlet of the Maryland-National Capital Park and Planning Commission, Committee for the Restoration of the Mary Surratt House.

Government Documents and Archival Material

Case Files of Investigation by Levi C. Turner and LaFayette C. Baker, 1861–66. Case File 4119, Microfilm No. 797. National Archives.

District of Columbia Record of Deeds, Liber 56. Washington, D.C.

Metro Police Department, District of Columbia, Day Book, 8th Precinct, April 14–19, 1865. National Archives.

Office of the Provost Marshal, Microfilm 345, Box 261, National Archives.

Records of the Columbia Historical Society, Vol. 22.

Records of the District of Columbia, Police Blotter, Detective Corps., Friday, April 14–19, 1865. National Archives.

Records of the Office of the Judge Advocate General, Investigation and Trial Papers Relating to the Assassination of President Lincoln. Microfilm No. 599 (16 Rolls), National Archives.

U.S. Congress. House. *Alleged Hostile Organization Against the Government Within the District of Columbia.* H. R. 79 36th Congress, 2nd Session, February 4, 1861.

U.S. Congress. House. *Assassination of Lincoln.* Submitted to the Committee on the Judiciary by A. J. Rogers on July 28. H. R. 104, 39th Congress, 2nd Session, 1866.

U.S. Congress. House. Debate between Benjamin Butler and John Bingham, 39th Congress, 2nd session. *The Congressional Globe,* 2 March 1878.

U.S. Congress. House. "John H. Surratt," Submitted to the Committee on the Judiciary by F. E. Woodbridge on March 2. H. R. 33, 39th Congress, 2nd Session, 1867.

Records of the Trials

The Assassination of President Lincoln and the Trial of the Conspirators. Compiled by Benn Pitman [Official Version]. New York: Moore, Wilstach and Baldwin, 1865.

The Conspiracy Trial for the Murder of the President: And the Attempt to Overthrow the Government by the Assassination of Its Principal Officers. Edited by Benjamin Perley Poore [based primarily on the *Washington Intelligencer* report]. Boston: J. E. Tilton and Co., 1865.

Trial of John H. Surratt in the Criminal Court for the District of Columbia, 2 vols. Washington, D.C.: Government Printing Office, 1867.

Trial of the Assassins and Conspirators at Washington City, D.C., May and June 1865 [complete and unabridged – prepared on the spot by special correspondents and reporters of the *Philadelphia Inquirer*]. Philadelphia: T. B. Peterson and Brothers, 1865.

Trial of the Assassins and Conspirators for the Murder of Abraham Lincoln [based primarily on the Associated Press reports]. Philadelphia: Barclay and Co., 1865.

Reference Works

Appleton's Cyclopedia of American Biography, 6 vols. Edited by James Grant Wilson and John Fiske. New York: D. Appleton and Co., 1898.

Boatner, Mark Mayo, III. *The Civil War Dictionary.* New York: Davis McKay Company, Inc., 1959.

Guernsey, Alfred H. and Henry M. Alden. *Harper's Pictorial History of the Civil War.* New York: Harper Brothers, n.d.; reprint ed., facsimile of the original *Harper's Pictorial History of the Great Rebellion in the United States,* 2 vols. n.p.: The Fairfax Press of the Barre Publishing Co., Inc., vol. 1, 1866 and vol. 2, 1868.

The War of the Rebellion, A Compilation of the Official Records of the Union and Confederate Armies. 130 vols., Washington: Government Printing Office, 1880–1901.

Manuscript Collections Consulted

Manuscript Division, Library of Congress

George Bancroft – Alex Bliss Papers
Edward Bates Collection
Benjamin F. Butler Papers
Cyrus B. Comstock Papers
Charles Dana Papers
Thomas Ewing Family Papers
George P. Fisher Papers
John Wien Forney Papers
James H. Hardie Papers
James O. Harrison Papers
Judge Joseph Holt Papers
Andrew Johnson Papers
Reverdy Johnson Papers
August V. Kautz Papers
Laura Keene Papers
Horatio King Papers
James S. Knox Papers

Mrs. Hugh Lee (Mary Greenhow) Diary
Lincoln Papers
John George Nicolay Papers
Philip Phillips Papers and Eugenia Phillips Collection
Horace Porter Papers
Lewis Thornton Powell Papers
William Anderson Scott Papers
Edwin Stanton Papers
Philip Van Doren Stern Papers
Thaddeus Stevens Papers
George Alfred Townsend Papers
Gideon Welles Papers
John Russell Young Papers

Maryland Historical Society, Baltimore

John T. Ford Papers

Dissertations and Unpublished Papers

Allen, Mary Bernard. "Joseph Holt." Ph.D. dissertation, University of Chicago, 1927.

Bogarad, Allen B. "A Rhetorical Analysis of the Speaking of John A. Bingham with Emphasis on His Role in the Trial of the Lincoln Conspirators." Ph.D. Dissertation, Ohio State University, 1963.

Grenson, Gus A. "Andrew Johnson and Edwin M. Stanton: A Study in Personalities, 1866–68." Master's Thesis, Georgetown University, 1949.

Porter, Horace. "Tragedy of the Nation." Typescript account of the assassination. n.d.

Periodicals

"The Assassins of Lincoln," North American Review, September 1888.

"The Chicago Conspiracy," Atlantic Monthly, July 1865, pp. 108–120.

Civil War Times Illustrated, Album: Illustrating the Assassination of Abraham Lincoln. Washington, D.C.: Parks and History Association, 1970.

Clampitt, John W. "The Trial of Mrs. Surratt," North American Review, September 1880, pp. 223–233.

"The Close of Lincoln's Career," The Century Magazine, May 1895, pp. 23–26.

Curran, John W. "Lincoln Conspiracy Trial and Military Jurisdiction Over Civilians," Notre Dame Lawyer, 9 (November 1933): 26–49.

———. "Lincoln Conspiracy Trial – Mysterious Phases," Notre Dame Lawyer 11 (March 1935): 259–276.

DeHart, William. "Observations on Military Law, and the Constitution and Practice of Courts Martial," North American Review 211 (April 1866): 334–345.

Ford, John T. "Behind the Curtain of a Conspiracy," North American Review 148 (April 1889): 485–493.

Frank Leslie's Illustrated Newspaper, (20 May, 27 May, 22 July 1865).

Giddens, Paul H. "Benn Pitman of the Trial of Lincoln's Assassins," *Tyler's Quarterly Historical and Genealogical Magazine* 22 (July 1940): 6–21.

Gleason, D. H. L. "Conspiracy Against Lincoln," *The Magazine of History* 13 (February 1911): 59–65.

Gray, John A. "The Fate of the Lincoln Conspirators." *McClures Magazine* October 1911).

King, Horatio. "The Assassination of President Lincoln," *New England Magazine* (December 1893), pp. 430–431.

————. "Open Letter," *The Century Illustrated Magazine* 39 (April 1890): 955–957.

Mason, Victor Lewis. "Four Lincoln Conspiracies," *The Century Magazine* 51 (April 1896) 51: 889–911.

Miers, Earl Schenck. "Epilogue to Ford's Theatre," *Saturday Review* (July 3, 1954), p. 16.

"New Facts About Mrs. Surratt: Correspondence of Judge Holt and Hon. James Speed," introduced by Allen Thorndike Rice, *North American Review* 147 (July 1888): 83–94.

Planck, Gary R. "Lincoln's Assassination: More 'Forgotten' Litigation—ex parte Mudd," *Lincoln Herald* (Summer 1974), pp. 86–89.

Porter, Horace. "Campaigning with Grant, *The Century Magazine* 104 (October 1897): 879–898.

Seymour, Frank J. "The Conspiracy to Implicate Confederate Leaders in Lincoln's Assassination," *The Mississippi Valley Historical Review* 90 (March 1954): 629–656.

Taft, Charles Sabin. "Abraham Lincoln's Last Hours" *The Century Magazine* 45 (1893).

Townsend, George Alfred. "How Wilkes Booth Crossed the Potomac," *The Century Magazine* (April 1884), pp. 822–832.

Walter, J. A. "The Surratt Case—A True Statement of Facts Concerning this Notable Case." (Read before the United States Catholic Historical Society, 25 May 1891.) *The Church News,* (16 August 1891).

Weik, Jesse W. "A New Story of Lincoln's Assassination, An Unpublished Record of an Eye-Witness," *The Century Magazine,* 135 (February 1913): 499–561.

Newspaper Articles

"Alleged Impeachment Conspiracy; Statements of Sandford Conover, Alias Dunham." *Washington Star,* 10 August 1867.

Barbee, David Rankin. Letter to Editor, *Washington Star,* 12 February 1949.

"Broadway Notebook" column. *New York Tribune,* 10 June 1883.

Brown, Paul. "Booth in Maryland." *Washington Post,* 12 February 1939.

"The Case of Mrs. Surratt, Another View." "Letters from the People" column. *New York Tribune,* 2 September 1873.

"Doctor Set Booth's Leg, Heirs Ask $200,000 Relief." *Washington Herald,* 23 April 1934.

Evans, Jessie Fant. "Lincoln's Blood Stains Cuff Owned by Mrs. S. P. Thompson." Unidentified newspaper clipping from "Lincoln Relics in Washington," vol. 4 of Abraham Lincoln Collection, Washingtonia Division, 4 vols., Martin Luther King Public Library, Washington, D.C.

"Experts Doubt Lincoln Vault Hides Sensation." *Washington Post,* 20 July 1947.

"Ford Widow Asks for Lincoln Chair." *Washington Star,* 23 December 1928.

Forney, D.D. *Washington Star,* 27 June 1891.

"General Hancock and the Surratt Case." *New York World*, 5 August 1880.

George Townsend's interview with Judge Holt concerning Mrs. Surratt. *Washington National Republican*, 17 December 1883.

"Hancock and the Civil Law." *New York Tribune*, 4 August 1880, p. 4.

"He Almost Saved Lincoln." *The Boston Sunday Globe*, 12 December 1897.

"His [Arnold's] Answers Under Fire, Daring the Conspirators Shown in His Examination." *Boston American*, 9 December 1902.

Hiss, Hanson. "John H. Surratt's Story." *Washington Post*, 3 April 1898.

"Identification of J. Wilkes Booth." *The Dearborn Independent*, n.d.

"John Ford's Recollections." *Washington Star*, 7 December 1881.

"John H. Surratt Dead." *Baltimore Sun*, 22 April 1916.

"Johnny Bouquets' Walks," *New York Tribune*, 8 May 1881.

"Letters from the People; The Case of Mrs. Surratt, Another View." *New York Tribune*, 2 September 1873.

"Lincoln Check Stirs Memories of 2 D.C. Men." *Washington Post*, 10 November 1944.

"The Lincoln Relics." *Sunday Star* (Washington, D.C.), 3 January 1909.

"Mrs. Surratt Again." *Washington Chronicle*, 19 September 1873.

Murphy, Edward V. "Edward V. Murphy Convinced that Mrs. Mary E. Surratt Was Not Guilty of Complicity in the President's Murder." *New York Times Magazine*, 19 April 1916.

New York Tribune, July 1865.

"Pleaded for Pardon, Episode of the Execution of Mrs. Surratt." *Washington Post*, 21 July 1901.

Pope, Virginia. "Lincoln Devote Ends Long Years of Labor," *New York Times*, 19 September 1926.

"President Believed Seeking Chair Once Used by Lincoln." *Washington Star*, 17 October 1929.

Proctor, John Clagett. "When Lincoln Lived in Washington." *Sunday Star* (Washington, D.C.), 13 February 1944.

"Review of the Judge Advocate General of the Proceedings, Findings and Sentence of a General Court Martial Held in the City of Washington for the Trial of major General Fitz-John Porter of the United States Volunteers," *Washington Daily Chronicle Press*, 1863.

Richards, A. C. "Detective Defends Weichmann." *Washington Post*, 18 April 1891.

"Shall We Mark the Spot of Mrs. Surratt's Execution?" *Washington Post*, 10 October 1909.

Stanley, Kimmel. *Washington Star*, 9 February 1936. (Article concerning Officer John F. Parker.)

"The Surratt Case Once More." Letter to the editor. *New York Tribune*, 11 September 1873.

"Surratt Relics Lost, Fire Destroys Home of the Man Who Served Warrant." *Washington Post*, 25 November 1912.

Surratt's Rockville Lecture. *Washington Star*, 7 December 1870.

"Tanner Also Present, Was in the Group Around the Death Bed of Lincoln." *Washington Post*, 16 April 1905.

"Tragic Memories, Some Interesting Reminiscences of a Thrilling Night, Why Booth Was Not Soon Captured." *Washington Star*, 14 April 1894.

"Was Mrs. Surratt Manacled?" *New York Tribune*, 16 September 1873.

Washington Morning Chronicle, 21 May 1867.

Weichmann, Louis J. "Pursued by his Foes; Mr. Weichmann Submits Testimonials of Character." *Washington Post*, 18 April 1891.

"Will Lincoln's Papers Cause Furor in 1947?" *Washington Post*, 26 April 1946.

Newspapers Consulted

American and Commercial Advertizer
(Baltimore)
Atlanta Daily Intelligencer
Baltimore American
Baltimore Sun
Boston Daily Advertiser
Boston Evening Journal
Boston Evening Transcript
Boston Free Press
Boston Herald
Boston Post
Boston Sunday Globe
Chicago Times
Cincinnati Daily Commercial
The Colored Tennessean (Nashville)
Constitutional Union (Washington,
D.C.)
Dearborn Independent
Detroit Free Press
Huntsville Advocate (Alabama)
Louisville Courier-Journal
Miners Journal (Pottsville, Penn.)
Natchez Courier
National Spectator

New Orleans Times
New York Evening Post (semiweekly)
New York Herald
New York News
New York Press
New York Times and New York
Magazine
New York Tribune
New York World
Philadelphia Inquirer
Philadelphia Public Ledger
Port Tobacco Times (weekly)
Richmond Inquirer
Times (London)
Washington Constitutional Union
Washington Daily Morning Chronicle
Washington Daily News
Washington Evening Star and the Sunday
Star
Washington Herald
Washington National Intelligencer
Washington National Republican
Washington Post
Washington Times

Index

A

M

N